T0351799

Fiscal Policy and Management in East Asia

NBER—East Asia Seminar on Economics
Volume 16

Fiscal Policy and Management in East Asia

Edited by **Takatoshi Ito and Andrew K. Rose**

The University of Chicago Press

Chicago and London

TAKATOSHI ITO is professor of economics at the University of Tokyo
and a research associate of the National Bureau of Economic Research
and the Tokyo Center for Economic Research. ANDREW K. ROSE is
the Bernard T. Rocca Jr. Professor of International Trade and director
of the Clausen Center for International Business and Policy at the Haas
School of Business, University of California, Berkeley, and a research
associate of the National Bureau of Economic Research.

The University of Chicago Press, Chicago 60637
The University of Chicago Press, Ltd., London
© 2007 by the National Bureau of Economic Research
All rights reserved. Published 2007
Printed in the United States of America

16 15 14 13 12 11 10 09 08 07   1 2 3 4 5
ISBN-13: 978-0-226-38681-2 (cloth)
ISBN-10: 0-226-38681-3 (cloth)

Library of Congress Cataloging-in-Publication Data

NBER-East Asia Seminar on Economics (16th : 2005 : Manila,
Philippines)
    Fiscal policy and management in East Asia / edited by Takatoshi
Ito and Andrew K. Rose.
        p. cm.—(National Bureau of Economic Research conference
report)
    "This volume contains a selection of papers presented at the
sixteenth annual East Asia Seminar on Economics . . . held in
Manila, the Philippines on June 23–25, 2005"—Intro.
    Includes index.
    ISBN-13: 978-0-226-38681-2 (cloth : alk. paper)
    ISBN-10: 0-226-38681-3 (cloth : alk. paper)
    1. Fiscal policy—East Asia—Congresses. 2. East Asia—
Economic policy—Congresses. I. Ito, Takatoshi, 1950–   II. Rose,
Andrew K., 1959–   III. National Bureau of Economic Research.
IV. Title.
HJ1390.5.N34 2005
339.5'2095—dc22

                                               2006038399

Relation of the Directors to the
Work and Publications of the
National Bureau of Economic Research

1. The object of the NBER is to ascertain and present to the economics profession, and to the public more generally, important economic facts and their interpretation in a scientific manner without policy recommendations. The Board of Directors is charged with the responsibility of ensuring that the work of the NBER is carried on in strict conformity with this object.

2. The President shall establish an internal review process to ensure that book manuscripts proposed for publication DO NOT contain policy recommendations. This shall apply both to the proceedings of conferences and to manuscripts by a single author or by one or more co-authors but shall not apply to authors of comments at NBER conferences who are not NBER affiliates.

3. No book manuscript reporting research shall be published by the NBER until the President has sent to each member of the Board a notice that a manuscript is recommended for publication and that in the President's opinion it is suitable for publication in accordance with the above principles of the NBER. Such notification will include a table of contents and an abstract or summary of the manuscript's content, a list of contributors if applicable, and a response form for use by Directors who desire a copy of the manuscript for review. Each manuscript shall contain a summary drawing attention to the nature and treatment of the problem studied and the main conclusions reached.

4. No volume shall be published until forty-five days have elapsed from the above notification of intention to publish it. During this period a copy shall be sent to any Director requesting it, and if any Director objects to publication on the grounds that the manuscript contains policy recommendations, the objection will be presented to the author(s) or editor(s). In case of dispute, all members of the Board shall be notified, and the President shall appoint an ad hoc committee of the Board to decide the matter; thirty days additional shall be granted for this purpose.

5. The President shall present annually to the Board a report describing the internal manuscript review process, any objections made by Directors before publication or by anyone after publication, any disputes about such matters, and how they were handled.

6. Publications of the NBER issued for informational purposes concerning the work of the Bureau, or issued to inform the public of the activities at the Bureau, including but not limited to the NBER Digest and Reporter, shall be consistent with the object stated in paragraph 1. They shall contain a specific disclaimer noting that they have not passed through the review procedures required in this resolution. The Executive Committee of the Board is charged with the review of all such publications from time to time.

7. NBER working papers and manuscripts distributed on the Bureau's web site are not deemed to be publications for the purpose of this resolution, but they shall be consistent with the object stated in paragraph 1. Working papers shall contain a specific disclaimer noting that they have not passed through the review procedures required in this resolution. The NBER's web site shall contain a similar disclaimer. The President shall establish an internal review process to ensure that the working papers and the web site do not contain policy recommendations, and shall report annually to the Board on this process and any concerns raised in connection with it.

8. Unless otherwise determined by the Board or exempted by the terms of paragraphs 6 and 7, a copy of this resolution shall be printed in each NBER publication as described in paragraph 2 above.

Contents

Acknowledgments

This volume contains a selection of papers presented at the sixteenth annual *East Asia Seminar on Economics.* EASE 16 was held in Manila, the Philippines, on June 23–25, 2005. The local sponsor was the Philippine Institute for Development Studies (PIDS).

EASE is co-organized by: the National Bureau of Economic Research (NBER) in Cambridge, MA; the Productivity Commission of Australia; the Hong Kong University of Science and Technology; the Korea Development Institute in Seoul; Singapore Management University; the Chung-Hua Institution for Economic Research in Taipei; the Tokyo Center for Economic Research; and the Chinese Center for Economic Research in Beijing. We thank all our sponsors—especially the NBER and PIDS—for making EASE 16 possible. The conference department of NBER, in particular Carl Beck and Brett Maranjian and the publication department led by Helena Fitz-Patrick, as usual, made the organization and publication process easier and smoother.

The local organization was superb, and we gratefully acknowledge their support and help in organizing the conference. Special thanks go to Dr. Joseph T. Yap, president of PIDS, and Dr. Mario Lamberte, former president of PIDS.

Introduction

Takatoshi Ito and Andrew K. Rose

This volume contains a selection of papers presented at the sixteenth annual East Asia Seminar on Economics. EASE 16 was held in Manila, the Philippines, on June 23–25, 2005. The local sponsor was the Philippine Institute for Development Studies (PIDS), and we gratefully acknowledge their support and help in organizing the conference.

EASE-16 was organized around the topic of "Fiscal Policy and Management." This is a topic of perennial interest to economists since fiscal institutions and outcome are both intrinsically important and vary widely across countries. This volume highlights the problems and challenges that East Asian developing countries face, as well as the United States and Japan.

Rich countries are plagued by regulation and taxation that seem excessive, resulting in avoidable inefficiencies that still do not provide enough revenue to cover government spending. Still, policy outcomes do not seem to have been particularly egregious in rich countries, especially at the macroeconomic level. By way of contrast, some poor countries do have consistently poor policy outcomes. For instance, inflation and trade taxes among developing countries are consistently higher in developing countries than in the OECD average. Why do developing countries tend to rely so much on inefficient tax systems? Tackling this important topic head on, Gordon and Li present a pair of models that might account for the differences be-

Takatoshi Ito is professor of economics at the University of Tokyo and a research associate of the National Bureau of Economic Research and the Tokyo Center for Economic Research. Andrew K. Rose is the Bernard T. Rocca Jr. Professor of International Trade, director of the Clausen Center for International Business and Policy at the Haas School of Business, University of California, Berkeley, and a research associate of the National Bureau of Economic Research.

tween fiscal outcomes in rich and poor countries. One political-economy theory for the poor performance of developing countries rests on the idea that vested interests that represent only a small part of the economy capture the policy apparatus and use it to distort outcomes to their benefit. Another idea rests on the hypothesis that information on taxable activities is simply more difficult both to obtain and use in developing countries because of the difficulty of monitoring financial transactions. After developing these alternatives, Gordon and Li perform the important task of taking their predictions to the data to compare and contrast the actual performance of their theories. They find serious problems with the traditional political economy model, while there is considerable (but not definitive) support for the financial transactions theory. We think this pair of hypotheses set the stage for the subject matter of the book and points the direction for an important and interest future research program.

The relationship between public and private sector economic behavior is one of the largest issues in the broad area of fiscal policy. Understanding the interplay between public and private activity is critical to formulating good policy. If public-sector activity stimulates private-sector activity by providing complements like social and physical infrastructure, then there is a strong case to be made for government intervention. But if private and public spending are actually substitutes so that the latter crowds out the former, then the case for public intervention is diminished accordingly. Thus it is appropriate that the next three papers of this volume address the relationship between activity of the public and private sectors. Kwan takes a direct and empirical approach using macroeconomic data for a number of East Asian countries. Using time-series techniques he finds that considerable heterogeneity in the degree of complementarity between private and public spending in the nine countries he considers. That said, the elasticities are typically small and indicate that for most countries, the two types of spending are substitutes rather than complements; Indonesia and Singapore provide the only evidence of public sector complementarity, and Thailand and Malaysia are countries with strong substitutes between public and private sector spending. A similar approach is taken by Hur, who focuses on Korea. Hur's paper is typical of a large literature that analyzes the efficacy of fiscal policy at the individual country member. Hur measures the effects of different types of fiscal policy using a structural time-series technique. In essence, he regresses the behavior of detrended GDP on detrended current and past government expenditures and revenues. Hur finds that most fiscal multipliers are strikingly small and only have transient real effects. Keynesian-style stabilization policy via the fiscal channel is accordingly difficult for Korean policymakers.

One need not examine this issue using aggregated data. Chetty and Looney address the same problem while taking advantage of a pair of microeconomic panel datasets that follow people in a rich large country (the

United States) and a poor large country (Indonesia). They are interested in a fundamental economic activity, in particular the consumption of food. Their results are striking in that they find a similar economic shock—unemployment—is followed by similar responses of food consumption in these very different countries. Still, there is also a striking difference between the countries; unemployment in Indonesia is associated with considerable economic dislocation, in stark contrast to the American experience. One particularly troubling issue is the fact that Indonesian spending on education drops significantly during a spell of household unemployment. This converts a transitory shock into an economic cost with a long-run consequence, and provides a compelling argument for a more effective social safety net.

Man is different from most other species of animals in that an abundance of resources tends to reduce rather than increase fertility. The enormous increase in the standard of living experienced in East Asia and the OECD since the Second World War has led to a dramatic reduction in birth rates. This fact, combined with increased longevity, has led to potentially explosive fiscal problems. In particular, the future obligations that governments have undertaken to provide pensions and health care for their citizens look far more costly than the revenues governments will have with which to provide these expenditures, given that the dependency ratio (the ratio of the retired to the working age population) is expected to rise. This problem of fiscal sustainability is a widespread phenomena that includes aging countries from Europe (e.g., Italy, Spain, and Germany), North America (the United States and Canada), and East Asia. All this is made worse by the fact that governments have run large fiscal debts during recent decades with more favorable demographic patterns. How then can governments cover their future spending? Research that investigates this issue is of the highest importance; the figures involved are simply astronomical. The next two chapters address the international aspects of the coming problem of double fiscal crunch.

Fehr, Jokisch, and Kotlikoff investigate long-run issues of fiscal sustainability and are particularly interested in the relationship between rich Northern and poor Southern countries. They use a complex simulation model that includes models for large aging Western economies (Europe, the United States, and Japan). The innovation here is to include China, a country that is also aging quickly but is large, poor, and growing quickly. Fehr, Jokisch, and Kotlikoff still find the standard set of depressing findings; future governments of the three advanced countries will only be able to find the funds to pay for their promised spending if taxes are raised dramatically. Still, the news is not all bad, since Chinese savings and labor enable not only dramatic growth in China but also continued growth in the rest of the world. In a sense China is expected to become the saver for the world, provided that future generations continue to save.

Villanueva and Mariano also use a model that focuses on external debts, while providing an explicit set of economics dynamics that links borrowing to growth, capital accumulation, and productivity. They apply their model to Philippine data. Their key findings are eminently reasonable; they imply that increased saving by both the public and private sectors is the only way to escape future disaster. If this seems like common sense, it is; the depressing realization is that increasing savings is still a task beyond the ability of most governments.

Clearly, international movements of factors, goods, and prices will have substantial effects on the long-run sustainability of fiscal burdens. Still, the most important effects and policies are likely to be domestic in nature. Accordingly, the next six chapters in this volume deal with different aspects of the problem of fiscal sustainability from an essentially national perspective. Au-Yeung, McDonald, and Sayegh look at how Australia should deal with risks to funds it saves for pensions provided to the public sector (referred to as *superannuation* by those down under). Using a model that optimizes the weights of the government's portfolio from a mixture of domestic and foreign stocks and bonds, they find, as expected, that the portfolios depend on the nature of shocks that are striking the economy. But, they provide some evidence that the Australian economy has been subject to more demand shocks than supply shocks, which supports purchasing domestic national bonds. They also show that to reduce overall risk, foreign equities are an appropriate investment. Llanto is also interested in future government liabilities but is particularly concerned with their implicit nature in the Philippines. He proposes a number of ways for the government to measure and handle its contingent liabilities, such as guarantees of private infrastructure projects.

Two chapters are particularly concerned with fiscal sustainability in Korea, a rich but rapidly aging society. Koh provides a lucid overview of fiscal developments and institutions in Korea over the last thirty years. He shows that government policy has generally been restrained, aside from an appropriate fiscal stimulus that results from automatic stabilizers that kicked in during the crisis of 1997–1998. Nevertheless, the legacy of the financial crisis is a nontrivial government debt, and this burden along with unfunded pension liabilities has resulted in a potentially unsustainable path for the Korean public sector. Chun corroborates this finding by employing a generational accounting framework so as to be able to disentangle the impact of flows and policies across different generations. He uses a standard model of behavior over the life cycle to predict savings rates, and forecasts a dramatic reduction in Korean savings as the population continues to age.

The final pair of chapters are also devoted to fiscal sustainability but are focused on Japan. The world's second largest economy has considerable liabilities as well as another rapidly aging population. As a critical part of both the regional and global economy, Japanese fiscal trends are thus highly worthy of careful scrutiny. Doi, Ihori, and Mitsui focus on the financial management of the public debt, and are particularly interested in the problem of maturity structure. Japanese long-term interest rates are quite low, despite the fact that government obligations appear to be quite high relative to both GDP and comparable levels in other developed countries. Doi, Ihori, and Mitsui accordingly analyze the sustainability of a set of Japanese fiscal policies and recommend a set of policies to alleviate the fiscal burden while enhancing confidence in the government's ability to service its debt. Fukui and Iwamoto are also interested in fiscal sustainability, but with particular reference to the burden of providing health- and long-term care to Japan. They propose a method and assumptions different from the government projection to forecast required funding in the future, in particular with regard to the labor participation rate, per capita health, and long-term care costs. Economists will be reassured to note that the well-understood generational transfers of a pay-as-you-go system are greatly alleviated by an alternative strategy of self-funded payments. On the other hand, the magnitude of the payments required to finance future health care is frightening; Fukui and Iwamoto find that an increase by at least one third is required, and conduct extensive sensitivity analysis on their simulation model to check the insensitivity of this result.

I

Fiscal Systems in Developing and Developed Countries

1

Puzzling Tax Structures in Developing Countries: A Comparison of Two Alternative Explanations

Roger Gordon and Wei Li

Economic policies in developing countries often differ sharply from those commonly advocated by economists, generating advice to adopt policies more consistent with both the successful practices in richer countries and/or those that appear best based on existing economic theories.

For example, economists advocate a stable currency and low tariff rates. Yet inflation rates in developing countries are often high, as are tariff rates.

Economists advocate setting up procedures to protect property rights, and establishing a rule of law in particular to aid in the legal enforcement of contracts and in dispute resolution. Yet, complaints by firms in developing countries about costly and time-consuming procedures, under-the-table fees, and arbitrary outcomes are common.

Economists strongly discourage state ownership of firms.[1] Yet in developing countries state ownership of firms is common. State ownership of banks is even more common.

Taxes certainly require some interference with market transactions, so the advice would be to enact taxes with a broad base and low rates so as to lessen the efficiency costs resulting from the distortions created by the tax structure. Broad-based taxes, such as a value-added tax, certainly do play an important role in poorer as well as richer countries. However, a much larger share of revenue in developing than in developed countries comes

Roger Gordon is a professor of economics at the University of California, San Diego, and a research associate of the National Bureau of Economic Research. Wei Li is an associate professor of business administration at the Darden School of Business, University of Virginia.

We would like to thank participants at EASE-16, and especially Andrew Rose, Firouz Gahvari, Francis Liu, and Michael Alba for comments on an earlier draft. We would also like to thank the World Bank for financial support for this project.

1. Where monopoly power is present, exceptions might be made, though even here government regulatory oversight is typically preferred to government ownership.

from taxes with a narrow base. Even when broad-based taxes are used, the evidence suggests that in practice revenue is collected from only a fraction of the activity that by statute should be covered.

In each case, economists normally advocate a shift toward policies that reduce interference in the functioning of markets.

If existing policies in poorer countries are so costly, though, why are such policies adopted to begin with? The deviation from conventionally recommended policies is systematic among poorer countries, and has existed for many years, making it hard to dismiss this evidence as being a result of some officials misunderstanding the implications of the policies they choose. Why would developing countries choose to impose such costs on themselves?

A common explanation for such seemingly perverse policies in developing economies falls under the general category of *political economy* problems. Here, the presumption is that these policies are designed to benefit select groups within a country who have unusually strong political influence. In particular, a government can favor these groups by designing the tax system to transfer resources to them, and perhaps by interfering with market allocations so as to alter equilibrium market prices in ways that benefit particular favored industries. But these policies may still impose large costs on the rest of the population, justifying altruistic intervention from outside.

Gordon and Li (2005) develop an alternative hypothesis for such policies. Here, the key assumption is that poorer countries face much more severe enforcement problems with their tax systems. Enforcement depends heavily on the availability of information from outside a firm about the scale of any firm's economic activities. Such information, largely coming from the firm's recorded transactions through the financial sector, is essential to double-check the information reported by the firm. When firms use the financial sector, they leave a paper trail, facilitating tax enforcement. In contrast, cash transactions are virtually impossible to monitor and tax, to the point that the informal economy and the cash economy are often used as synonyms. When countries have both a financial sector that provides little value-added to firms, and firms that receive very heterogeneous benefits from using the financial sector, then the forecasted outcome is high tax rates in practice paid only by those firms strongly dependent on the financial sector, so a narrow tax base, with other firms avoiding tax through relying entirely on cash transactions. The result can be large intersectoral distortions favoring the informal economy.

Gordon and Li (2005) then argue that the government can lessen these intersectoral distortions through tariff protection of firms facing high effective tax rates, through inflation as a tax on firms that rely on cash to avoid tax, through controls on lending so as to redirect credit to heavily taxed sectors, and through red tape and fees that impose nontax costs on businesses that in practice pay little or no taxes.

Section 1.1 provides a derivation of the forecasted tax policy coming from a Grossman-Helpman (1994) style political economy model, and a comparison of these forecasts with those derived in Gordon-Li (2005). The forecasts from the two models differ in many respects. The political economy model certainly forecasts favorable tax treatment of sectors that can lobby the government effectively. However, while the model forecasts lower or even negative tax rates on income earned in the favored sector, as long as such means are available to aid these industries it does not forecast tariff protection for these sectors, inflation, or other forms of interference with market transactions.[2] The theory would not forecast an informal (untaxed) sector, at least beyond the sectors that are effective in lobbying the government. Unlike in the Gordon-Li model, tariff protection and subsidized credit should be for sectors that face relatively low tax rates, rather than relatively high tax rates. The two models also have contrasting forecasts for the size of government and the progressivity of the tax structure in poor versus rich countries.

In section 1.2, we look at the empirical evidence more closely to compare the evidence with the forecasts from these two models. Some forecasts are shared by the models and some contrast. This evidence is almost entirely consistent with the forecasts from the Gordon-Li model, and almost entirely inconsistent with the forecasts from the political economy model. Section 1.3 then contains a brief set of concluding remarks.

1.1   Alternative Forecasts for Economic Policies

1.1.1   Conventional Model

In this section, we develop the implications of a political economy model, and summarize the implications of the Gordon-Li model in a simple setting. To set the context, though, we first develop a model of policy in a more conventional setting.

Assume that the country is small and open, so is a price taker in the international market for the two consumption goods. These international prices are denoted by p_1 and p_2. Both goods are produced in the domestic economy, and the domestic wage rate, w, and domestic interest rate, r, adjust to clear factor markets. Assume that good 2 is imported and good 1 is exported.[3]

The government is considering the choice of tax rates on the domestic output of the two goods, denoted by s_1 and s_2, along with a tariff at rate τ_2

---

2. If tax rates cannot vary by industry to the extent desired, however, then the model does forecast tariff protection and subsidized credit to favored firms.

3. Here we assume that workers and capital can move without cost between the two domestic industries, so that there is one set of factor prices characterizing the economy as a whole.

on imports of good 2, and a tax at rate t_K on domestic capital.[4] Consumer prices are then equal to $p_i(1 + \tau_i)$. The net-of-tax prices domestic firms face for output of the two goods are $p_i(1 + \tau_i)(1 - s_i)$, while the user cost of capital to a firm is $r + t_K$.

The indirect utility function for individual i is denoted by $V_i(p_i[1 + \tau_1]$, $p_2[1 + \tau_2], r, w) + W_i(G)$, where G measures expenditures on public services. A conventional model for optimal tax policy assumes that the government chooses Pareto efficient policies, so maximizes a weighted sum of the welfare of individuals and the utility of government officials, who consume what tax revenue is left net of the cost of public services:[5]

$$(1) \quad \max_{\tau_2, s_1, s_2, t_K, G} \sum_i \{V_i[p_1(1 + \tau_1), p_2(1 + \tau_2), r, w] + W_i[G]\}$$
$$+ U(R - G),$$

Using the aggregate economy's budget constraint, tax revenue R equals gross domestic output minus domestic consumption, all evaluated at world prices: $R = \sum_j p_j(f_j - C_j)$.

By maximizing over the size of government services, G, trading off benefits to residents with foregone consumption of government officials, we can rewrite the government's objective function as:

$$(1a) \quad \max_{\tau_2, s_1, s_2, t_K} \sum_i \{V_i[p_1(1 + \tau_1), p_2(1 + \tau_2), r, w]\} + S\left[\sum_j p_j(f_j - C_j)\right]$$

for some function $S(\cdot)$ that captures the overall benefits from extra tax revenue.

This model is the basic framework used in deriving optimal tax rates. To replicate a tax rate on labor income, there would need to be a uniform sales tax rate ($s_1 = s_2$) along with implicit expensing for capital investments ($rt_K = -s_1$). Taxes on capital income may well arise in such a derivation, and would appear through a tax rate on capital above this figure. Distortions to relative consumer prices could be implemented through a tariff along with an offsetting tax on domestic production of that good, as happens with a VAT. Such distortions could arise, for example, if those with a low marginal utility of income have high relative demand for one of the two goods. To preserve productive efficiency, however, as forecast by Diamond and Mirrlees (1971), the model would require that

$$\frac{p_1(1 - s_1)}{p_2(1 + \tau_2)(1 - s_2)} = \frac{p_1}{p_2}$$

4. We also include in the notation a placeholder tariff on good 1, denoted τ_1, just to simplify some of the notation, even though we normalize the tariffs by setting $\tau_1 = 0$.

5. This model simultaneously captures the behavior of both *benevolent* and *malevolent* governments, by allowing officials to extract private benefits from unspent tax revenue, but also having them care about individual utilities.

so that sales tax rates adjust to compensate for any tariffs, so as to leave the net-of-tax price faced by producers unchanged by the introduction of the tariff.

In such a setting, there are no grounds for interfering further with market allocations: as forecast by Diamond-Mirrlees, production should remain efficient. As a result, the model cannot help explain state ownership of firms or banks, or any government regulations interfering with market allocations. As set up here, the model does not include a role for *money,* so does not allow an analysis of the optimal inflation rate. One simplified way to introduce money into the model is by including real cash balances as a third consumer good. To replicate a proportional tax on labor income, the sales tax rates should again be equal across goods, implying an equal proportional mark-up over the real costs of each good. The real cost of money, as noted by Friedman (1969), is virtually zero, implying a price of money so a nominal interest rate of virtually zero.

1.1.2   Gordon-Li Model

Gordon and Li (2005) add one new issue into the previous model: tax enforcement. They assume that firms can be monitored and taxed only if they make use of the financial sector, thereby leaving a paper trail.[6] The real benefits of using the financial sector, per se, for a firm in industry j is assumed to equal $a_j p_j (1 + \tau_j) f_j$, so is proportional to the value of the firm's output. The cost of using the financial sector is that the firm becomes subject to tax.[7] Since pretax output from a firm using the financial sector is $(1 + a_j)(1 + \tau_j) p_j f_j$, sales tax and capital tax payments would together equal $s_j p_j (1 + \tau_j)(1 + a_j) f_j + t_K K_j$. Firms then make use of the financial sector only if benefits exceed costs, or if

$$(2) \qquad a_j(1 + \tau_j) p_j f_j > s_j(1 + \tau_j) p_j(1 + a_j) f_j + t_K K_j.$$

This adds to the conventional analysis a set of constraints on the feasible tax rates imposed on each industry. Any tax rates violating equation (2) will induce disintermediation and collect no revenue from that industry.

In richer countries, use of the financial sector may be valuable enough that none of these constraints are binding. In poorer countries, though, the financial sector may operate much less well (the a_j are smaller), so that these constraints become an important consideration in any discussion of tax policy. The lower are the a_j within a country, the lower are feasible tax rates and as a result the lower would be government revenue. As seen in the following, government revenue as a fraction of GDP is in fact much lower in poorer than in richer countries. The conventional model, in contrast,

---

6. The paper also explores more briefly the implications for tax policy if the government can only observe physical inputs to production (e.g., capital, the number of workers). Policy implications are largely the same, except for those specifically linked to the banking sector.

7. Tariffs are collected regardless.

does not help explain this unless government revenue is less valued in poorer countries.

The presumption in Gordon and Li is that capital-intensive industries will value much more the use of the financial sector, and so have a higher a_j.[8] To begin with, this will imply a higher s_j in capital-intensive industries when some of the constraints in equation (2) become binding.

When firms *within* an industry are heterogeneous, though, then a higher s_j will collect more revenue from some firms while inducing others to shift into the cash economy. Depending on the distribution of the a_j within an industry, tax rates can potentially be quite high, with some firms paying this high tax rate and others avoiding it through disintermediation. The conventional model does not include any structure sufficient to explain the presence of an informal economy.

Given differences in the optimal s_j across industries, Gordon and Li then explore the role of various other policies to lessen the misallocations resulting from differences in the optimal s_j across industries in response to the constraints in equation (2). Tariffs may now be used even if they would not be used otherwise. Not only can tariffs help collect additional revenue, but they can also lessen the distortions created by the differential sales tax rates by industry by shifting domestic production into the heavily taxed industries. If the heavily taxed good is imported, then these two potential benefits reinforce and trade will be discouraged. In contrast, if the heavily taxed good is exported, then these two potential benefits conflict and trade may even be encouraged.

Given the efficiency costs arising from a shift of activity out of the most highly taxed (capital-intensive) sectors, one mechanism to reduce this shift is state ownership of the most capital-intensive firms. Through state ownership, the government can in principle ensure that the sector has the efficient scale and capital intensity. This potential efficiency gain can quickly become large as tax rates increase, and with high enough tax rates can dominate the efficiency loss that occurs due to state ownership per se.

An alternative mechanism to increase the scale of activity in the heavily taxed sectors is to provide them cheap credit. This can be done through state ownership of the banking sector. While providing cheap credit to heavily taxed firms results in losses for the state-owned banks, the government can in principle cover these losses through the resulting tax revenue collected from the extra capital invested in these heavily taxed sectors.

8. This could occur because capital-intensive firms are larger and so have more customers who are physically distant, making use of financial intermediaries to handle payments of more value. Capital-intensive firms will also face lumpy expenditures to purchase capital, making bank loans of more value. To convince banks of their credit worthiness, maintaining an active account with the bank may be essential. Larger firms may also not be able to effectively monitor all of the employees who handle cash, and prefer instead to shift to noncash payments through use of the banking sector.

When firms *within* each industry are homogeneous and the government can set a separate sales tax rate for each industry, then tax rates would be set so that all firms satisfy the constraints in equation (2). Any sales tax rate in an industry high enough to violate equation (2) would create a Pareto loss, since the government would lose its tax base in that industry while firms are left indifferent, relative to a rate that just satisfies equation (2).

Money is now demanded in particular by firms that avoid taxes by joining the cash economy, so that inflation becomes a targeted tax on firms otherwise avoiding tax.[9]

The larger the informal sector the higher the benefits relative to the costs of inflation.

Capital taxes can help focus tax liabilities on capital-intensive firms, who are the most tied to using the financial sector and so the least likely to shift into the informal sector in response.

Government red tape and regulatory controls on firm entry can be another mechanism to hinder activity in lightly taxed if not entirely untaxed sectors. Even if no revenue is collected directly through such intervention, to the extent domestic production shifts as a result into more heavily taxed sectors, there can still be a net efficiency benefit from such policies.

To see this more formally, consider an individual's choice between being an employee in the formal sector versus working in the informal sector. We assume that the individual makes this choice to maximize indirect utility of $V(w)$.[10] Within the formal sector, the effective wage rate for individual j is $w_j = (1 - s_j)p_j f_{Lj}$, where f_{Lj} measures the marginal product of labor in the industry. Let the effective wage rate in the informal sector be $(1 + n_j)p_j f_{Lj}$. Here, n_j is a parameter that varies by individual, reflecting that individual's best available informal jobs and the value of a_j (positive or negative) in that sector, so can be either positive or negative. There is some joint density function $g(w_j, n_j)$ for w_j and n_j. Without government intervention, the individual shifts to the informal sector whenever $n_j > -s_j$.

The government is affected by this choice, though, given that output in the formal sector is taxable whereas output in the informal sector is not. If output in the formal sector is subject to a sales tax at rate s, then tax revenue drops by $sw_j L_j/(1 - s)$ if the individual leaves the formal sector. Individual choices are then inefficient, since they ignore this fiscal externality.

What if at some cost, F, the government can hire tax inspectors to locate and identify businesses operating in the informal sector? We assume that these inspectors cannot observe $(1 + n_j)p_j f_{Lj}$, nor hours of work, but only the fact that the individual is working in the informal sector. Many of the people working in the informal sector presumably are extremely poor,

9. The feasible *inflation* tax would itself be constrained, though, by the option firms have to use a foreign rather than a domestic currency for transactions.
10. The other arguments of V are suppressed, to economize on notation.

making it unattractive on distributional grounds to impose a fixed monetary fee for working in the informal sector.[11] Instead, consider the imposition of nontax (time) costs on firms in the informal sector, generated through red tape. Assume in particular that the government can impose a time cost of H on each individual in the informal sector.[12] Then the individual shifts into the informal sector if and only if $(1 + n_j)p_j f_{Lj}(L - H) > (1 - s_j)p_j f_{Lj}L$ or equivalently if $n_j > (H - s_j L)/(L - H)$.

Even though red tape imposes costs on those in the informal sector while collecting no revenue directly, still the government may well choose to create red tape. The key gain is the resulting shift of higher skilled individuals into the formal sector, with the resulting increase in tax revenue.

Stated formally, start from $H = 0$ and consider the change in the government's objective function from a marginal increase in H:

$$(3) \quad -\int_0^\infty \int_{-s}^\infty V_I (1 + n)wg(w, n)dndw + S' \int_0^\infty \left(\frac{s}{1 - s} \right) wL \frac{\partial n^*}{\partial H} g(w, -s)dw,$$

where $n^* = (H - sL)/(L - H)$ represents the skill level just indifferent between being in the formal or the informal sectors, so that $\partial n^*/\partial H = (1 - s)/L$, evaluated at $H = 0$. Expression (3) can easily be positive, in which case red tape is a useful means of expanding the formal sector. This is more likely to occur to the extent that $S' \gg V_I$ and $s \gg 0$, implying in addition that the average value of n among those in the informal sector will be small or negative.

The Gordon-Li model took the range of values of the a_j, measuring the value to each firm j of making use of the financial sector, as exogenous. While the state of skills and technology within the financial sector are largely outside of the direct control of the government, the government does control the regulatory environment under which the financial sector operates. Changes such as providing deposit insurance, or speeding the clearing of interbank payments, presumably will shift up the distribution of the a_j. Surprisingly, the government does not necessarily have an incentive to adopt such policies, even given the objective function we have assumed. Consider the welfare effects of an increase in the values of a_j in industries at the bottom end of the distribution, sufficient to pull firms in these industries into the formal sector. They now pay at least some taxes,

---

11. One possible explanation for this poverty is that capital and skilled labor are complementary in production, so that the capital-intensive firms in the formal sector employ very few unskilled workers.

12. What if tax inspectors can learn each individual's productivity? They would then have an incentive to charge a firm an amount just sufficient to leave them indifferent to remaining in the informal sector, given H, enforced by the threat of revealing their income to the tax authorities. The only substantive change is a redistribution from informal firms to tax inspectors, leading in equilibrium to a fall in the amount F they require in wages from the government. Given such a fall in the expense of imposing the costs H on informal firms, the government may encourage such corruption.

which is in itself a welfare gain.[13] By documenting their activity with a bank, firms entering the formal sector should also now qualify for bank credit that they would not previously have had access to. This credit comes at the expense of loans to firms in industries already in the formal sector, who in this example face higher tax rates. On net, tax revenue could well fall, with the drop in payments from high-taxed sectors perhaps more than offsetting the taxes paid by firms newly entering the formal sector.

When the behavioral responses lead to a fall in tax revenue, efficiency falls as well, so that such an improvement in the performance of the financial sector may not be an attractive option to the government.

Of course, large enough improvements in the a_i will necessarily be a welfare gain, since the constraints in equation (2) all become less binding and eventually nonbinding. Policy will change continuously with the relaxation of these constraints. In particular, as the financial sector improves, to begin with we expect to see a drop in the size of the informal sector, and with the broader tax base less extreme tax rates on the most capital-intensive firms. With smaller intersectoral distortions, the needs for distorting tariffs, inflation, state ownership of firms or banks, and use of capital taxes all drop.

One example of such a transition in policy, an example that led us to develop this model, is the case of China during the 1990s, as described in Gordon and Li (2005). At the beginning of this decade, the national government was unable to collect much of any revenue from small- and medium-sized firms, so that its tax revenue came almost entirely from taxes on larger state-owned firms.[14] Its observed policies were very much consistent with those forecast previously, with tax rates that varied strongly by sector, controls over the allocation of credit, and high tariff rates.[15] In 1994, there was a series of reforms that led to a sharp increase in the national government's ability to collect taxes from small- and medium-sized firms.[16] With this successful attempt to broaden its tax base, the national government shifted policy generally away from the policies forecast previously toward a set of more conventional policies, agreeing to cut tariffs through joining the World Trade Organization (WTO), eliminating government control over lending practices at the banks, shifting heavily away from re-

13. When firms just become willing to shift into the formal sector, by construction they are just indifferent. But the government receives extra revenue, so that there is a gain in overall welfare, and in efficiency.

14. In particular, local governments were responsible for monitoring and assessing taxes on small- and medium-sized firms, and were effective in hiding taxable activity from the national government.

15. There was little use of inflation, however.

16. An important part of this tax reform had the national government take over responsibility from local governments for monitoring and assessing taxes on smaller firms. In China, the role of the financial sector in tax enforcement was much more limited than in other developing countries, since each firm had a party representative whose job in part was to monitor the taxable activity of the firm. The level of government to which this party representative was responsible changed as of 1994.

liance on sector-specific excise taxes and taxes on capital (corporate income taxes) toward a broad-based value-added tax (VAT), and beginning the process of downsizing the size of the state-owned enterprises (SOE) sector, and the role of the government in this sector.

Even when increasing the value provided by the financial sector does raise welfare, however, it does not follow that subsidies to the financial sector, artificially raising the values of the a_i, raise welfare. Intuitively, a competitive banking sector will in equilibrium pass along the value of any subsidies to its customers, so that the maximum tax these customers will be willing to pay to make use of the banking sector goes up by just the size of the subsidy. The extra tax payments are then just sufficient to cover the cost of the subsidy.

More formally, assume that the costs to the bank of supplying services to firms in industry j, per dollar of sales that must be intermediated, is x_j, implying total costs of $x_j p_j (1 + \tau_j) f_j$. Similarly, assume the gross benefits to firms in industry j from using the banks are $b_j p_j (1 + \tau_j) f_j$. With a competitive banking sector, the price firms pay for banking services equals the cost of provision of these services, so that the net benefits to firms equal $(b_j - x_j) p_j (1 + \tau_j) f_j \equiv a_j p_j (1 + \tau_j) f_j$. What if the government now provides a subsidy to the provision of financial services to this industry, paying some amount $\sigma_j p_j (1 + \tau_j) f_j$ to the banks? With a competitive banking sector, this subsidy will be passed along to the customers in the form of a lower price, so that the net benefits to a firm from using the financial sector rise to $(a_j + \sigma_j) p_j (1 + \tau_j) f_j$. Following the logic of equation (2), this figure now equals the maximum taxes that can be collected from this industry. Subtracting off the costs of the subsidy, however, the maximum *net* revenue from this industry remains equal to $a_j p_j (1 + \tau_j) f_j$. As long as all tax rates can adjust, the same revenue on net is collected with the subsidy as without.

The same argument also implies that taxes on the financial sector crowd out other sources of revenue one for one. Since it would be very difficult to design the tax structure on the financial sector to replicate the flexibility the government has in choosing each of the sales tax rates and the capital-income tax rate, taxes on the financial sector will normally end up being less effective than taxes on each of the industries making use of the financial sector.

1.1.3   Political Economy Model

There are a variety of modeling approaches taken within the political economy literature to characterize the nature of the implicit objectives faced by the government when choosing policies. The approach we take is inspired by the work of Grossman and Helpman (1994), who assume that special interests that have solved their internal free-rider problem can provide *contributions* to a party in power linked at the margin to the degree to which the party aids that interest group. The result is that the government puts more weight on the utility of that interest group than it otherwise would.

To explain more perverse policies in developing countries, the presumption is then that these contributions distort policy more severely in developing than in developed countries. Distortions are least costly in the Grossman-Helpman framework when either no industries or all industries contribute, since in either case the weights remain undistorted across industries. If we assume that most all industries in developed countries actively lobby the government, then developing countries end up with worse policies if a smaller fraction of industries are able to lobby effectively.

Solving the free-rider problem within an industry is easier when there are fewer firms in the industry. We presume that capital-intensive industries have larger individual firms and fewer firms in the industry as a whole, so that the subset of industries able to lobby the government will largely represent the most capital-intensive sectors.

One issue, though, is how to capture the benefits going to an industry from any given government policies, since in the previous model the income of any individual simply depends on the amounts of labor and capital they provide to the market, and not on which industry they work for or invest in. In order to capture this, we instead assume that at the date that policy is being set factors cannot change industries, even if the supply of factors to their current industry can adjust in response to policy changes. In addition, for simplicity we assume that individuals work and invest in the same industry.

As shown in Bernheim and Winston (1986), the equilibrium bribes in such a setting are equivalent to those in which lobbying industries pay monetary bribes to officials equivalent to the benefits they receive due to the policies adopted by the government, relative to a given fallback position. The equilibrium bribe by industry j, denoted by B_j, then satisfies: $V_j(p_1(1 + \tau_1), p_2(1 + \tau_2), r_j, w_j; -B_j) + W_j(G) = U_j^*$. The default utility level, U_j^*, is determined from the constraint that the bribe must be sufficient to allow the government and the other bribing industries to do as well as they could have done collectively had this one industry not actively bribed the government—if not, the bribe would not be accepted.

For simplicity, we assume that bribes are as valuable to officials as explicit but unspent tax revenue. Certainly, both are cash that officials can use to finance perks if not private consumption. The only difference is that oversight and possible punishment for accepting under-the-table payments may be different than for using tax revenue for personal advantage.[17] To the extent bribes are less valuable to officials than extra tax revenue, then equi-

---

17. Grossman-Helpman (1994), in contrast, assume that bribes can only be spent on political campaigns, reflecting current institutional constraints in the United States. There are no similar constraints to our knowledge in any developing country.

librium tax rates in lobbying industries will be higher than we find in the following, and conversely.

If $j \in L$ is the set of industries that actively lobby the government, then the resulting objective function for the government is:

$$\max_{\tau_2, s_1, s_2, t_K, G} \left\{ \sum_{j \notin L}(V_j + W_j) + \sum_{j \in L}(U_j^*) + S\left[\sum_j p_j(f_j - C_j) - G \right] \right\},$$

where we assume a composite individual working for each industry. Here, bribes show up implicitly in government revenue through their effects on equilibrium consumption among members of lobbying industries.

The resulting first-order conditions for s_k equals

(4) $$S'\left[\sum_j p_j\left(\frac{\partial f_j}{\partial s_k} - \frac{\partial C_j}{\partial s_k} \right) \right] = V_{kl}[p_k(1 + \tau_k)f_k] \text{ for } k \notin L,$$

and

$$\sum_j p_j\left(\frac{\partial f_j}{\partial s_k} - \frac{\partial C_j}{\partial s_k} \right) = 0 \text{ for } k \in L,$$

where V_{kl} denotes the marginal utility of income for the kth individual. For nonbribing industries, the government trades off the revenue it gets with the welfare loss to individuals. Since we assume that $S' > V_{kl}$, in equilibrium the efficiency costs of the tax must at the margin just offset the welfare gain from shifting a given amount of resources to the government. Note that an increase in the sales tax rate on lobbying industries matters only to the extent that it affects government revenue. No individual utilities change, since consumer prices are unaffected, while the effects on utility of any changes in factor prices in lobbying industries are fully offset through changes in the bribes.

The individuals' collective budget constraint equals

(5) $$\sum_j p_j(1 + \tau_j)C_j + \sum_{j \in L} B_j = \sum_j p_j(1 - s_j)(1 + \tau_j)f_j - t_K K, \text{ implying that}$$

$$\sum_j p_j\left(\frac{\partial f_j}{\partial s_k} - \frac{\partial C_j}{\partial s_k} \right) = \delta_k p_k(1 + \tau_k)f_k + \sum_j p_j \tau_j \frac{\partial C_{jk}}{\partial s_k} + t_K \frac{\partial K_k}{\partial s_k}$$

$$+ p_k[s_k(1 + \tau_k) - \tau_k]\frac{\partial k_k}{\partial s_k},$$

where $\delta_k = 1$ for $k \notin L$ and $\delta_k = 0$ otherwise.

Substituting into equation (4), it is straightforward to show that

(6) $$\delta_k\left(1 - \frac{V_{kl}}{S'} \right) - \sum_j p_j \tau_j \varepsilon_I^{C_{jk}} \frac{C_{jk}}{I_k} - t_K \varepsilon_{p_k^*}^{K_k} \frac{K_k}{p_k^* f_k} = \frac{s_k(1 + \tau_k) - \tau_k}{(1 - s_k)(1 + \tau_k)} \varepsilon_{p_k^*}^{f_k},$$

where, ε_Y^X represents the elasticity of X with respect to Y, where $p_k^* \equiv p_k(1 + \tau_k)(1 - s_k)$ and where $I_k = p_k^* f_k - t_K K_k$. All three elasticities are positive under any reasonable assumptions.

To begin with, equation (6) suggests that the optimal effective tax rate $s_k(1 + \tau_k) - \tau_k$ will be negative for industries actively bribing the government to the extent $\tau_2 > 0$ and $t_K > 0$. At the optimum, a marginal increase in the subsidy to production in a lobbying industry should have no net effect on government revenue. While a marginal increase in the subsidy is in itself a net revenue cost, since more output needs to be subsidized, the extra production also generates extra revenue to the extent that the resulting increases in investment and consumption are taxable. At the optimal tax rates, these effects should exactly offset each other.

For firms not actively bribing the government, for whom $\delta_k = 1$, optimal tax rates presumably will be positive. If the three elasticities in equation (6) are the same among these industries, if there are no differences in the marginal utility of income across these industries, and if consumption patterns are the same for people in all industries, then the effective tax rate will be lower in more capital-intensive industries if $t_K > 0$, in effect to compensate for this other source of revenue from these industries.

The key forecasted difference in sales tax rates is then between industries that actively bribe officials and other industries. The forecast of a lower (or negative) tax rate on capital-intensive industries is one clear difference between the political economy model and the Gordon-Li model.

What about the optimal tariff rate? Consider the welfare effects of an increase in τ_m on imports of goods produced by bribing industries, with a compensating increase in s_m so as to leave $s_m(1 + \tau_m) - \tau_m$ consistent with equation (6). This combined change in tax rates has no effects on the factor incomes of any individual, so does not help per se to redistribute to individuals in bribing industries. It does raise the consumer price for good m faced by all individuals, and so helps aid those in lobbying industries to the extent that individuals in these industries tend *not* to consume the output from their own industries. As discussed in Saez (2002), such a tariff may also be justified on efficiency grounds if a drop in consumption of good m leads to increases in factor supplies beyond what happens simply due to income effects.

Neither of these justifications for a tariff would exist if the utility function is weakly separable between consumption and factor supplies (e.g., $U[L, K, h\{C_1, C_2\}]$), and if the utility function is the same for individuals in different industries. Even if these assumptions are violated, there is no reason to expect that individuals working in favored industries tend *not* to consume output from these industries, or that factor supplies are more responsive to the prices of goods produced by capital-intensive industries. The model does not then help to explain the existence of tariffs protecting favored industries.

To what degree would subsidies to capital ($t_K < 0$) be used to aid bribing (capital-intensive) industries? Even better targeted would be a subsidy to capital invested in bribing industries, implemented for example through subsidized loans restricted to these industries.[18] Note that a reduction in the output tax rate, s_k, affecting bribing industries is equivalent to a proportional subsidy to both capital and labor employed within this industry. When could a further subsidy just to capital in the industry be chosen?

If all the individuals working in the industry collude together in bribing the government, then the government receives the benefits accruing to both groups, so a capital subsidy per se makes sense only if it has favorable efficiency effects. This could occur if the supply elasticity of capital is less than that for labor. As noted by Judd (1987), while the very short-run supply of capital is extremely inelastic, the long-run supply in contrast should be extremely elastic, suggesting if anything attempts to restrict taxes/subsidies to labor whenever the government has a longer time perspective.

If only the capital owners in an industry bribe the government, then the government does have an incentive to manipulate the returns to labor versus capital in the industry. Natural policies suggested by such an objective are subsidized loans to the industry or a tax structure within the industry favoring capital over labor income.

If capital but not labor is highly mobile across industries, the model would instead forecast a low uniform tax (or subsidy) rate on capital, a high tax rate on labor in the disfavored industries, and no tariffs. Following equation (6), the labor income tax rate in favored industries would have the opposite sign of the tax/subsidy rate on capital.

Whether capital is mobile or not, these results contrast sharply with the forecasts from the Gordon-Li model, which forecasts capital taxes as a way to focus the tax burden on firms that are most dependent on the financial sector, and heavier tax payments by capital-intensive than by labor-intensive firms.

If the government for some reason could not provide the desired differential sales or labor income tax rates in favored versus disfavored industries, then tariffs can be a second-best way of favoring certain industries. A tariff is second best since not only does it raise the returns earned within that industry but it also distorts consumer choices in ways that in general are not desired. In contrast to the Gordon-Li model, tariff protection would be given to sectors facing the lowest rather than the highest tax rates.

Grossman and Helpman (1994) fully recognized that their model would imply output subsidies for lobbying industries and no tariffs as long as the government can freely make use of this full range of policy tools. They as-

---

18. To induce banks to provide subsidized credit to particular customers, explicit subsidies to such loans, or loan guarantees, would be one approach. State ownership of the banking sector, with the government covering losses incurred on subsidized loans, is another.

sumed, though, that output subsidies were not available as an option to the government. The complication they note to justify this assumption arises from implications for the default utility levels U_j^*. Each industry must pay enough in bribes to ensure that the government plus other bribing industries together are at least as well off as they would be if they refuse the bribe. If these groups are in a position to aggressively exploit any given industry, then this industry will need to pay them a lot in exchange for changing policies. Their opportunity to exploit any given industry is less if policies are restricted to tariffs. They argue that this consideration dominates if there are few other industries that are not lobbying, since benefits to a newly lobbying industry then must come almost entirely from those who must be bribed. If the group of other industries that are not lobbying is large, however, then this issue will be second order relative to the gains from use of a more effective policy tool.

Among richer countries, where we presume that most industries actively lobby the government, their argument suggests that policies will be restricted to tariffs.[19] If the fraction of industries that actively lobby the government is small in developing countries, then even by their argument we would not expect to see any such restrictions on policy. In fact, excise taxes are an important component of the tax systems in developing countries. According to the political economy model, this should not be surprising. But given this, tariffs should not be used.

In the Grossman-Helpman model, the more industries that lobby the government, the lower is overall tax revenue. (Bribes of course do not show up in the reported revenue figures.) If fewer industries actively bribe the government in developing countries, then the size of government should be larger in developing countries, a forecast sharply contrary to the forecast from the Gordon-Li model.

Another implication of the political economy model is that as more industries actively bribe the government, concern with redistribution shrinks. In particular, the government has no ability left to affect the utility levels within bribing industries, since they are implicitly set at the default levels U_j^* Any redistribution is restricted to individuals in nonbribing industries, yet the offsetting efficiency costs remain fully relevant. The larger the number of individuals working in bribing industries, therefore, the less is concern with redistribution. If fewer industries are actively involved in bribery in developing countries, then these countries should focus more on redistributive effects of the tax structure, and so should place more weight on taxes, such as the personal income tax, that are particularly effective at

19. Lobbying industries would need to make this decision collectively, however, and in an enforceable way, since each industry on its own would prefer to be aided through output subsidies rather than tariff protection. While we know of no such explicit restrictions on policy, it is true that excise taxes/subsidies play much less of a role in richer countries than in poorer countries.

shifting the tax burden from rich to poor. This forecast is strongly contrary to that coming out of the Gordon-Li model, in which taxes on labor income should play little role in poorer countries.

Does the model help explain the greater prevalence of state ownership of firms among developing countries? One potential role for state ownership is to ensure that promised bribes are in fact paid, making it easier for the government to change policy as promised. Would we expect more pressure toward state ownership as a result in developing countries? We think not. State ownership presumably has high efficiency costs. Another potentially more effective mechanism for enforcing payments, assuming the government officials remain in power, is to ignore the industry's interests in future policy setting if it reneges on a promised payment now—a tit-for-tat strategy. This threat is more effective the longer the current government expects to remain in power. Our presumption is that tenure of government officials is longer in developing countries, making state ownership of less value as an enforcement mechanism there than in developed countries. State ownership would also plausibly be more prevalent when equilibrium bribes are larger. Equilibrium bribes should be larger in countries where more industries lobby the government, and so need to be compensated if chosen policies are not in their interests. Again, the model seems to suggest, if anything, more use of state ownership in developed countries.

Within this political economy model, there are no incentives per se to use inflation—there is no motivation for use of cash beyond those in the standard model. Similarly, there are no grounds for introducing red tape and other nontax forms of harassment. If activity in unfavored sectors is to be penalized, better to do it through the tax structure and collect revenue in the process.

1.2   Data on Behavior of Poorer Versus Richer Countries

We turn next to an analysis of available data on tax and related policies among a group of 125 countries for which we could obtain adequate data.[20] In the appendix, we list our data sources and the definition of the variables used in this paper. In reporting data, we have grouped these countries into four quartiles based on their GDP per capita in 1990 measured in constant 2000 U.S. dollars. Quartile 1 represents the richest countries, and quartile 4 the poorest.

We focus first on the evidence regarding forecasts from the Gordon-Li and the *political economy* models when they are the same, and then turn to forecasts that conflict between the two models.

20. We would very much like to thank Andrei Shleifer for making available to us the data used in La Porta, Lopez de Silanes, and Shleifer (2002), and Friedrich Schneider for making available to us his estimates of the size of informal economy.

Throughout we treat skill/technology differences across countries as exogenous, driving not only differences in GDP per capita but also the quality of the financial sector and the ease with which firms within an industry can coordinate on lobbying. Certainly, the types of policy differences we focus on can affect a country's long-run growth rate, and the utility provided from employing existing factor inputs, but these policy differences should have little direct effect on factor supplies or on overall output.

1.2.1   Similar Forecasts in the Two Models

Table 1.1 provides information regarding several forecasts that are comparable in the two models, even if the rationales are very different.

One forecast in common is that the tax structure in poorer countries will make more use of taxes with differential rates by industry. In the Gordon-Li model, tax rates will be higher on the capital-intensive industries, since they cannot so easily shift into the informal sector. In the political economy model, tax rates will be lower for capital-intensive industries, responding to their active lobbying efforts. So both models forecast rate differences by industry, though the direction of the forecasted rate differences are opposite.

The key tax whose rate easily varies by industry is nongeneral taxes on production and sales, primarily consisting of excise taxes. Column (2) of table 1.1 reports the fraction of tax revenue coming from nongeneral production taxes. The data show little variation in the use of excise taxes by income level, possibly because sin taxes and environmental (e.g., gasoline) taxes play a more important role in richer countries, offsetting the role of excise taxes both models focus on.

Unfortunately, at this point we have no data sufficient to test the conflicting forecasts between the two theories regarding which industries face lower versus higher tax rates. While our understanding is that poorer countries rely heavily on revenue from capital-intensive industries—particularly oil, mining, and other extractive industries, where tax collection is particularly easy—we have not at this point found data to confirm this impression.

Table 1.1   Tests when forecasts are similar

	GDP per capita in 1990 (2000 $)	Excise taxes (% of revenue)	Corporate taxes (% of revenue, 1990–2001 average)	Percent government ownership of banks, 1995
Quartile 1	20,768	19.6	9.5	24.2
Quartile 2	3,834	16.2	17.9	40.5
Quartile 3	1,451	19.5	14.2	47.0
Quartile 4	436	20.3	14.2	67.2

Notes: Countries are classified by GDP per capita in 1990 into four quartiles, with quartile 1 the richest and quartile 4 the poorest. The number in each cell is the average of each listed variable among countries in each income quartile.

Both models plausibly forecast more use of taxes on capital income among poorer countries. In the Gordon-Li model, this occurs in order to shift the tax burden onto the firms that are least likely to shift into the informal sector in response. If capital is mobile across sectors, then the political economy model trades off the desire to tax capital in nonlobbying industries and to subsidize capital in lobbying industries. If the aggregate size of the lobbying sectors is smaller in poorer countries, then capital-income taxes should be higher in these countries. We presume that the corporate income tax represents the main tax on income from capital and report the share of revenue coming from the corporate income tax in column (3) of table 1.1. This share shows a weak pattern of being higher in poorer countries, but the evidence is not dramatic.

Both models also suggest that poorer countries could well use state-owned banks as a mechanism to provide cheap credit to capital-intensive firms. In the Gordon-Li model, this is done to redirect credit to sectors paying high tax rates. In the political economy model, this is done if capital owners in particular lobby the government. As seen in column 4 in table 1.1, the fraction of the ten largest banks owned by the government is substantially higher in poorer than in richer countries, though state ownership of banks is still nontrivial even in rich countries. No data are available on whether firms receiving subsidized loans pay unusually low or unusually high tax rates.

1.2.2   Contrasting Forecasts in the Two Models

One clear difference in the forecasts from the two models regards the size of tax revenue relative to GDP. In the Gordon-Li (GL) model, enforcement is more difficult in poorer countries, due to a poorer quality financial sector, so that revenue is lower. In contrast, in the political economy (PE) model, tax revenue is higher in poorer countries given the assumption that fewer industries actively lobby the government. The evidence is reported in column 1 of table 1.2. Here, we find that revenue as a fraction of GDP in the richest quartile is double that in the poorest quartile, and a strongly increasing function of per capita GDP, consistent with the GL but not the PE model.

The two models also have conflicting forecasts regarding the use of tariffs. In the Gordon-Li model, tariffs would clearly be attractive if the country is a net importer of capital-intensive goods.[21] In the political economy model, tariffs would not be used unless lobbying industries collectively manage to restrict any aid they receive to take the form of tariff protection. The model forecasts that this restriction could well be imposed in richer countries, where most industries lobby the government, but not in

---

21. In standard trade models, poor countries specialize in labor-intensive industries, and so should be importers of capital-intensive goods.

Table 1.2   Tests when forecasts differ

	Tax revenue (% of GDP, 1990–2001 average)	Tariff revenue (% of revenue) 1990–2001 average	Personal income plus sales taxes (% of tax revenue, 1990–2001 average)	Seigniorage (% of GDP, 1990–2001 average)	SOE output (% of GDP)	Cost to register a business (% of GNI per capita, 2001–02 average)	Informal economy (% of GDP, 1990–91)
Quartile 1	26.6	6.0	50.0	0.5	0.1	0.11	13.5
Quartile 2	21.4	17.7	37.0	1.7	1.8	0.21	26.9
Quartile 3	17.5	22.3	32.7	2.1	1.5	0.50	34.2
Quartile 4	13.3	28.8	30.2	2.3	8.4	1.97	28.8

Note: See table 1.1 notes.

poorer countries. The evidence on tariffs is reported in column 2 of table 1.2. Tariffs are used far more heavily in poorer countries, consistent with the GL but not the PE model.

Another forecast that differs across the two models regards the use of the personal income tax or broad-based taxes on consumption. In the GL model, such taxes on labor income (when earned or spent) should play little role, since this shifts the tax burden onto the firms least tied to the financial sector. In contrast, in the PE model, redistribution should matter more in poorer countries, where a smaller fraction of the economy is actively involved in lobbying. The data on the fraction of tax revenue collected by the personal income tax and general taxes on goods and services is reported in column 3 of table 1.2, and shows much more of a role for broad-based taxes in richer countries, consistent with GL.

Another difference between the two models regards inflation. The GL model forecasts inflation as a way to tax the informal sector, representing the only sector that relies heavily on cash transactions. The PE model follows the conventional optimal tax model in forecasting no use of an inflation tax. The size of seigniorage as a fraction of GDP is reported in column 4 of table 1.2. Here we do find that poorer countries rely far more heavily on inflation taxes than do richer countries, consistent with GL.

The models also differ in their forecasts regarding the prevalence of state ownership of firms. In the GL model, state ownership is used to offset the distortions created by the high tax rates on these firms. In the PE model, state ownership is one mechanism to ensure that bribes are in fact paid in response to favorable policies. Since equilibrium bribes should be larger in developed countries, where more industries must be compensated if the chosen policies are contrary to their interests, the model suggests greater pressure toward state ownership among developed countries. Column 5 of table 1.2 documents that the output of SOEs as a share of GDP is much larger in poorer countries, consistent with the GL model.

A further difference regards the use of red tape to hinder activity in labor-intensive sectors, and in the informal sector. Such policies fall out naturally in the GL model as a way to hinder activity in sectors that pay little or no taxes. In the PE model, regular income and sales taxes dominate use of red tape. In column 6 of table 1.2 we report data on one possible indicator of red tape: the cost to register a new business.[22] These costs are clearly higher in poorer countries, consistent with GL.

The two models focus on very different attributes of an economy in making forecasts for policy. In the GL model, the driving force is a poorly functioning financial sector, making it all too easy for firms to shift into the cash economy in order to avoid taxes. We should then see poorer countries

---

22. Results are qualitatively the same using another possible indicator: the time required to start a business legally.

having much larger informal sectors, because of their more poorly functioning financial sectors. In the PE model, rather than having the small firms that constitute the informal sector being de facto tax exempt, taxes should fall primarily on these firms. Data on the size of the informal sector are reported in column 7 of table 1.2. The size of the informal sector as a fraction of GDP in the poorest quartile is more than double that in the richest quartile, consistent with GL.

To test for evidence that the informal sector tends to be large when the financial sector functions poorly, we ran a regression forecasting the size of the informal sector as a function of one or another indicator of the quality of the financial sector, along with log (per capita GDP), average literacy, and population density as control variables.[23]

Results are reported in table 1.3. Columns 1 and 2 report results for unweighted regressions. As robustness checks, in columns 3 and 4 we weight observations by GDP (in U.S. dollars) while in columns 5 and 6 we weight by population. In all of these specifications, a poorly functioning financial sector strongly predicts a large informal sector, whereas the other control variables play little role.

In the PE model, the key driving force of course is political lobbying pressure that leads governments to favor one sector over another. If politics is playing such a dominant role in the choice of tax policy, we would expect to see very different tax policies chosen by governments that are classified as left wing versus right wing. To provide some evidence on this, we recalculate the figures on tax policy reported in table 1.1, instead classifying countries into four quartiles based on their ideological orientation, with quartile 1 being the most right wing and quartile 4 being the most left wing. Results appear in table 1.4. Here, we find that ideology has no obvious connection to tax policy, except perhaps for a higher reliance on tariffs by the most left-wing governments.

1.3   Conclusions

Tax policies in practice differ dramatically between poorer and richer countries. Richer countries rely primarily on broad-based income and consumption taxes, and make little use of tariffs or seigniorage as sources of revenue. Poorer countries, in contrast, make much less use of broad-based taxes, relying instead on excise taxes, tariffs, and seigniorage. In the process, though, they collect much less revenue as a fraction of GDP than is collected in richer countries. Corruption and red tape are also far more common in poorer countries.

---

23. One indicator is overhead costs in the financial sector, relative to its total assets. The other is the interest rate spread, measured by net interest revenue divided by the stock of interest-bearing assets.

Table 1.3   Factors affecting size of informal economy

	(1)	(2)	(3)	(4)	(5)	(6)
Overhead costs	1.752	1.081	1.772	1.571	2.028	1.430
	(0.584)***	(0.53)**	(0.494)***	(0.388)***	(0.624)***	(0.550)**
Interest rate spread						0.007
						(0.016)
Log(GDP per capita)	-0.031	-0.030	-0.010	-0.011	0.002	-0.166
	(0.016)*	(0.017)*	(0.013)	(0.013)	(0.016)	(0.094)*
Adult literacy rate	-0.060	-0.026	-0.065	-0.028	-0.176	-0.023
	(0.097)	(0.101)	(0.108)	(0.102)	(0.090)*	(0.013)*
Log(population density)	-0.003	-0.005	-0.012	-0.008	-0.027	
	(0.010)	(0.010)	(0.010)	(0.010)	(0.012)**	
No. of observations	60	60	60	60	60	60
Adjusted R^2	0.23	0.16	0.41	0.44	0.35	0.31

Notes: In all the regressions, the dependent variable is the size of informal economy in 2001. An intercept term is included in all regressions, but its estimates are not reported in the table. Columns (1) and (2) show estimates of coefficients and their standard errors resulting from ordinary least squares regressions on the cross-section of countries. Columns (3) and (4) report results from weighted least squares regressions using the 1999 GDP in current U.S. dollars as the weighting variable. Columns (5) and (6) report results from weighted least squares regressions using the 1999 population as the weighting variable. Numbers in parentheses are standard errors.

***Significant at the 1 percent level.
**Significant at the 5 percent level.
*Significant at the 10 percent level.

Table 1.4   Tests for role of ideology in tax policy

	GDP per capital, 1990 (2000 $)	Tax revenue (% of GDP)	Tariff revenue (% of GDP)	Income taxes (% of revenue)	Income taxes + VAT (% of revenue)
Quartile 1	6,956	20.0	15.8	31.9	45.6
Quartile 2	10,778	22.3	13.6	36.2	48.9
Quartile 3	8,465	23.9	11.3	31.7	48.3
Quartile 4	2,556	17.7	26.3	30.5	46.1

Notes: Countries are classified into four quartiles by the average ideological orientation of the chief executive's party in the period 1980 to 1989, with quartile 1 the most right wing and quartile 4 the most left wing. The number in each cell is the average of each listed variable among countries in each income quartile.

The question this paper focuses on is why these policy differences arise. We develop the implications of two alternative models for such policy differences. One, a model initially developed in Gordon-Li (2005), focuses on the tax enforcement problems that arise when firms find it easy to shift into the cash economy, thereby avoiding leaving any paper trail and making tax enforcement extremely difficult. The government is then left relying for revenue on the remaining industries that cannot so easily shift into the cash economy to evade tax. With such large differential tax rates, a wide range of other policies may make sense as second-best means to lessen the resulting misallocations. Within this model, the policies forecast are *third* best, handling as well as is feasible the informational problems faced in collecting revenue.

The second model assumes that the political pressures faced in poorer countries are very different than in richer countries, leading to a very different set of policy choices. If particular industries in poorer countries have been able to lobby the government effectively for protection, then the chosen policies can be very different than when political support for the government is more broad based, at least across industries. If such political pressures explain the perverse policies chosen in poorer countries, then there are clear grounds for using international agencies to help induce countries to shift to policies more in the interests of their population as a whole.

In this paper, we explore the implications of such a political economy model in detail, building on the framework developed in Grossman-Helpman (1994). While such a model easily forecasts more favorable sales tax rates or income tax rates on factors employed in favored industries, it does not so easily explain tariffs, seigniorage, or red tape. Only if sales or income tax rates cannot vary by industry to the extent desired might tariffs make sense.

The paper then reexamines the data to see to what degree each model is consistent with the data. Some forecasts are naturally in common, while others are very different. As discussed in the paper, the forecasts from the two models differ sharply with regard to the relative use of tariffs, seigniorage, capital-income taxes, personal-income taxes, and the overall size of tax revenue in poorer versus richer countries. In each case, the forecasts from the Gordon-Li model are very much consistent with the data, while those from the political economy model are not.

The paper in addition examines data related to the key underpinnings of each model. In the Gordon-Li model, a weak financial sector implies that little is lost by a firm from shifting to the cash economy as a means of evading taxes. Countries with a poorly functioning financial sector should then as a result have a large informal economy, and with a large informal economy choose a *perverse* tax structure to deal with the resulting pressures. We document both such relationships.

In the political economy model, tax policy should depend heavily on the nature of the political pressures faced by the government. Left-wing governments represent ones that face very different pressures than right-wing governments, and so should choose very different tax policies. We examine to what degree this is true, and find little difference in tax policies across governments of different ideologies.

Unfortunately, some of the key differences are not at this point testable; for example, the Gordon-Li model forecasts that the highest tax rates will be paid by capital-intensive industries (that find it hardest to shift to the cash economy), whereas in the political economy model these industries should face the lowest tax rates (since they can most easily solve the internal free-rider problems and lobby the government for support).

The data at this point are limited, so no tests are definitive. That the implications of the two models for policy are so different implies that much is at stake in such tests. Within the political economy model, the key problem is differences in the political pressures faced in poorer than in richer countries, and in particular the smaller fraction of industries in poorer countries that are organized enough to lobby the government. Outside pressure to adopt more conventional tax policies can potentially compensate as a way to aid the population as a whole. In the Gordon-Li model, in contrast, the key problem is a weak financial sector, making tax evasion easy. Reform efforts then need to focus on improving the quality of the financial sector. Outside pressure to shift to more conventional tax policies, without simultaneously improving the financial sector, will likely cause more harm than good.

There certainly is a large body of empirical work at this point suggesting the importance of financial sector reforms in economic growth. The Gordon-Li model provides a different underpinning for the role financial reform plays, arguing that financial reform improves not only the allocation of credit across firms but also induces a shift in government policies more broadly to ones that create fewer distortions to market allocations.

Appendix

Table 1A.1   **Description of the variables**

Variable name	Description and source
	Taxation
Tax revenue (% of GDP)	Tax revenue (GFS line 11) as a proportion of GDP, average for the period 1990 to 2001. *Source:* Authors' calculations based on IMF (2004).
Tariff revenue (% of GDP)	Taxes on international trade and transactions (GFS line 115) as a proportion of GDP, average for the period 1990 to 2001. *Source:* Authors' calculations based on IMF (2004).
Income taxes (% of revenue)	Sum of personal and corporate income taxes (GFS line 1111 and 1112) as a proportion of tax revenue (GFS line 11), average for the period 1990 to 2001. *Source:* Authors' calculations based on IMF (2004).
VAT (% of revenue)	Value-added taxes (GFS line 11411) as a proportion of tax revenue (line 11), average for the period 1990 to 2001.
Corporate income taxes (% of revenue)	Corporate income taxes (GFS line 1112) as a proportion of tax revenue (GFS line 11), average for the period 1990 to 2001. *Source:* Authors' calculations based on IMF (2004).
Seigniorage (% of revenue)	Seigniorage is measured as the increase in reserve money (IFS line 14). *Source:* Authors' calculations based on IFS (2005).
	Regulation of entry
Cost to Register a Business (% of GNI per capita)	The cost of obtaining legal status to operate a firm as a share of per capita GNI, average for 2001 and 2002. It includes all identifiable official expenses. *Source:* World Bank (2005). For data methodology, see Djankov, La Porta, Lopez de Silanes, and Shleifer (2002).
Time to Start a Business (days)	The time it takes to obtain legal status to operate a firm, in business days, average for 2001 and 2002. *Source:* World Bank (2005). For data methodology, see Djankov, La Porta, Lopez de Silanes, and Shleifer (2002).
	Informal economy
Size of informal economy (% of GDP)	Measured as the size of shadow economy estimated by Schneider (2004), using methodology documented in Schneider and Enste (2000). Estimates for 1990–91 and 2001–02 are used in this paper.
	Government ownership
Government ownership of banks in 1995	Share of the assets of the top 10 banks in a given country owned by the government of that country in 1995. *Source:* La Porta, Lopez de Silanes, and Shleifer (2002).
SOE output (% of GDP)	SOE value added of all nonfinancial SOEs as a proportion of GDP of the economy at market prices, average for the period 1978 to 1981. *Source:* La Porta, Lopez de Silanes, and Shleifer (2002).
	Quality of the financial sector
Overhead costs, 1980–89	Accounting value of a bank's overhead costs as a share of its total assets, average for the period 1980 to 1989. *Source:* Beck, Demirgüç-Kunt, and Levine (2000), updated data published March 14, 2005.

(*continued*)

Table 1A.1   (continued)

Variable name	Description and source
Interest rate spread, 1980–89	Accounting value of bank's net interest revenue as a share of its interest-bearing (total earning) assets, average for the period 1980 to 1989. *Source:* Beck, Demirgüç-Kunt, and Levine (2000), updated data published March 14, 2005.
	Ideology
Right-wing ideology, 1980–89	Average of the ideological orientation of the chief executive's party for the period 1980 to 1989. The ideological orientation is coded as 1 for right, 0 for center, and –1 for left.
	Other variables
GDP per capita, 1990	GDP per capita in 2000 constant dollar, converted using market or official exchange rate. *Source:* World Bank (2005).
Adult literacy rate, 1980–89	Percent of people ages 15 and above who are literate, average for the period 1980 to 1989. *Source:* World Bank (2005).
Population density, 1980–89	Number of people per square kilometer, average for the period 1980 to 1989.

Source: World Bank (2005).

References

Beck, Thorsten, Asli Demirgüç-Kunt, and Ross Levine. 2000. A new database on the structure and development of the financial sector. *World Bank Economic Review* 14:597–605.

Bernheim, D., and M. Whinston. 1986. Menu auctions, resource allocation, and economic influence. *Quarterly Journal of Economics* 101:1–31.

Diamond, Peter, and James Mirrlees. 1971. Optimal taxation and public production. *American Economic Review* 61:8–27.

Djankov, Simeon, Rafael La Porta, Florencio Lopez de Silanes, and Andrei Shleifer. 2002. The regulation of entry. *Quarterly Journal of Economics* 117 (1): 1–37.

Friedman, Milton. 1969. The optimal quantity of money. In *The optimal quantity of money and other essays.* Chicago: Aldine.

Gordon, Roger, and Wei Li. 2005. Tax structure in developing countries: Many puzzles and a possible explanation. NBER Working Paper no. 11267. Cambridge, MA: National Bureau of Economic Research.

Grossman, Gene, and Elhanan Helpman. 1994. Protection for sale. *American Economic Review* 84:833–50.

International Monetary Fund. 2004. *Government financial statistics,* CD-ROM (May).

———. 2005. *International Finance Statistics.* IFS Online, accessed between February and April 2005.

Judd, Kenneth. 1987. The welfare cost of factor taxation in a perfect-foresight model. *Journal of Political Economy* 95:675–709.

La Porta, Rafael, Florencio Lopez de Silanes, and Andrei Shleifer. 2002. Government ownership of banks. *Journal of Finance* 57 (1): 265–301.

Saez, Emmanuel. 2002. The desirability of commodity taxation under non-linear income taxation and heterogeneous tastes. *Journal of Public Economics* 83:217–30.

Schneider, Friedrich G. 2004. The size of the shadow economies of 145 countries all over the world: First results over the period 1999 to 2003. Bonn, Germany: IZA Discussion Paper no. 1431.

Schneider, Friedrich, and Dominik Enste. 2000. Shadow economies: Size, causes, and consequences. *Journal of Economic Literature* 38 (1): 77–114.

World Bank. 2005. *World Development Indicators,* WDI Online, accessed March and April, 2005.

Comment   Francis T. Lui

The Gordon-Li paper provides a stimulating and insightful analysis on why certain *perverse* economic policies are adopted in developing countries. For instance, why do they adopt possibly harmful inflationary policy, set up high tariffs, pursue state ownership of firms and banks, and tolerate resource-wasting red tapes? In the literature, the rent-seeking approach, or its variants, such as the political economy model advanced by Grossman and Helpman (1994), can be used to address some of these issues. Interest groups, who have different degrees of political influences, can lobby the government to choose policies in their favor. The outcomes are often undesirable from the perspective of efficient allocation of resources.

The Gordon-Li paper proposes a competing hypothesis to the political economy approach. It highlights the difficulties of tax collection in many developing countries. The significant transaction costs involved could induce them to adopt various kinds of second or third best policies for making tax collection more effective.

According to Gordon and Li, their model can generate some outcomes that are similar to those of Helpman and Grossman, but there are also sharply different implications. The more important ones are as follows. First, companies in capital-intensive industries are more likely to pay lower taxes in the Grossman-Helpman model because they are lobbyists that are more powerful. On the other hand, in the Gordon-Li model, they are viewed as those that cannot escape from the tax agencies and therefore are forced to pay more. Second, Gordon and Li believe that the Grossman-Helpman model is not able to explain why governments, especially those in developing countries, adopt inflationary policies. But in the Gordon-Li model, this is taken as a convenient means for governments that lack effective tax agencies to collect revenues. Third, Gordon and Li believe that the Grossman-Helpman model cannot explain why red tape exists. The former

Francis T. Lui is a professor of economics and director of the Center for Economic Development at the Hong Kong University of Science and Technology.

regard red tape as a means for the government to deter otherwise tax-paying firms to escape into an informal sector, where firms can avoid tax payments more easily.

It is not clear that the two approaches are fundamentally inconsistent. Once we generalize the Grossman-Helpman model by treating branches of the government as interest groups themselves, the phenomena outlined previously can also be accounted for.

Take the example of red tape. Can its existence not be derived from a political economy model? In the literature on corruption, red tape is often treated as an instrument through which corrupt government officials can make profits. Bureaucrats themselves can be powerful lobbyists within the government who want to protect their own interests. This can be done by creating and maintaining red tape that strengthens and justifies the authorities it possesses.

In the Gordon-Li model, red tape is targeted on firms that want to go into the informal sector. This may not always be the case. If a firm wants to hide itself in the informal sector, possibly illegally, why should it bother with the red tape?

I do not see why inflationary policy is incompatible with the political economy approach. Government branches need revenue. If they saw that inflationary tax is effective in protecting their interests, they would support the policy. For instance, in the 1980s, many state-owned enterprises in China tried hard to expand their sizes, but that would require more expenditure. This eventually induced them to force the government to print more money. Thus, inflation could also be the result of a political economy model.

The paper has ranked tax revenue as share of GDP according to the ideological inclination of the country, and has found no obvious relationship between the two. This is regarded as a refutation of the political economy model because countries with different ideologies may face different political pressures. However, one can legitimately ask how ideology is to be measured. For instance, if we define left-wing government as one that favors larger government spending, there will necessarily be a relationship between revenue collected and the *ideology* of the government.

The paper argues that improvement in the financial sector may attract low-quality firms to reenter the formal sector. They could be new competitors for loans and credits. High-quality firms would find it less attractive to stay in the formal sector. These firms might leave, resulting in lower tax revenue for the government. It would be strange if this happened. If low efficiency firms find it profitable to stay, why would good firms be forced to leave?

In short, the Gordon-Li and Grossman-Helpman models are not substitutes for each other. It makes more sense if we regard them as complementary.

Reference

Grossman, Gene, and Elhanan Helpman. 1994. Protection for sale. *American Economic Review* 84:833–50.

Comment   Michael M. Alba

Summary

Why are economic conditions—obviously beside the definitional divide in incomes and living standards—so different between rich and poor countries? In developing economies, why are inflation and tariff rates higher, property rights and the rule of law not well established, red tape rife, and corruption endemic? Why are government-owned or controlled firms—particularly banks—so ubiquitous, tax evasion so pervasive, and the tax base so narrow? In contrast to the political economy literature, which points to government capture by politically powerful groups as the source of these perverse outcomes, Gordon and Li (2005a, 2005b) hypothesize that the culprit is a developing-country government's limited capability to enforce tax laws, due, on the one hand, to informational and monitoring constraints when firms transact business on a cash basis, thus leaving no record, and, on the other hand, to the low and variable productivity gains that firms obtain when using the financial sector, thus providing them little incentive to switch from the tax-evading informal sector to the tax-paying formal sector. Accordingly, firms that cannot do without the financial sector, such as the large or capital-intensive ones, are those that are most highly taxed and that constitute the narrow tax base. In a second-order response, the government then acts to reduce the burden on these firms by providing tariff protection, rationing credit, and subsidizing loans (thus explaining government ownership of banks); at the same time, it can increase the costs of informal sector firms by using inflation as a tax on cash holdings and by imposing red tape, regulatory barriers to entry, and other non-tax costs. As an extreme measure, the government may even opt for control of capital-intensive firms to ensure that, although heavily taxed, these firms continue to operate at the appropriate scale and capital intensity.

Michael M. Alba is an associate professor of economics at De La Salle University in Manila, Philippines.

I wish to thank the organizers of the NBER EASE 16, particularly Andrew Rose and Takatoshi Ito of NBER, and Josef Yap of PIDS, for the opportunity to critique Gordon and Li (2005a) and the authors, Roger Gordon and Wei Li, for the thoroughness of the analyses that was especially instructive. Not having studied public economics, I learned much from the exercise, including certain "tricks of the trade," such as those involved in the formulations of the social welfare function (i.e., equations [1a] and [1b]), the use of different taxes to achieve the same outcome, and the derivation of equations (3) and (6).

To provide a point of comparison, Gordon and Li (2005a) also develop a political economy model based on Grossman and Helpman (1994). In this alternate paradigm, the perverse policies derive from the bargaining process between (free of the free-rider problem) industries that bribe the party in power and a government that maximizes a social welfare function that is specified as a sum of the industry utilities and the overall benefits of government revenue net of spending. The equilibrium outcome is that the degree of protection given to a particular industry depends on the value of its bribe to the government relative to the harm favoring it has on general welfare, including that of the other bribing industries. More specifically, the model predicts that the optimal effective tax rate for a bribing industry will be negative, as long as the industry is subject to a capital tax or import tariffs are levied on some industries, whereas that of a nonbribing industry may be positive. Moreover, under certain conditions, the optimal effective tax rate will be lower in more capital-intensive industries if it is already subject to—and precisely to compensate for—a capital tax. On the other hand, no plausible reason will be seen for using tariffs to protect bribing industries, unless differential sales tax rates cannot be imposed. Neither will there be reasonable grounds, in general, for imposing a capital tax (or providing a capital subsidy) against levying an output tax (or reducing the sales tax rate). But if the need exists, the superior policy, because it is more sharply targeted, will be to subsidize loans for capital investments in these industries, which may require government guarantees or state ownership of banks.

Two key elements of this political economy model are (a) the constraint on the social welfare function that a bribe by any industry will be acceptable only if it allows the government and the other bribing industries to be as well off as when the industry in question does not bribe and (b) the proportion of the bribing industries. The constraint has the effect, in equilibrium, of setting the utilities of the bribing industries to their default levels, that is, the level of welfare that each industry would attain, had all the other bribing industries submitted acceptable bribes. The proportion of bribing industries, for its part, circumscribes the extent to which the government can trade off the value of the bribe received with the harm favoring the industry does to the welfare of the society as a whole. Thus, because the bribing industries are assured of their default utility levels, the higher the fraction of the bribing industries, the less leeway the government has for making tradeoffs.

Assuming that fewer industries have the resources to bribe the government in developing countries, one may then draw out the following predictions from the political economy model: For poor countries, (a) overall tax revenue (as a proportion of output) and the size of the government will be higher, and (b) there will be greater flexibility to implement redistributive tax measures, such as a progressive income tax structure.

Finally, state ownership of firms can be explained as a way for the government to ensure that bribes are paid, which implies the poorest countries will have more state-owned firms, since proportionately they will have the fewest industries with a capacity to bribe. On the other hand, there are no grounds for using inflation and red tape as policy measures.

To test the predictions of the two models against the empirical evidence, Gordon and Li (2005a) put together a cross-section data set consisting of 125 countries. They find that the empirical evidence is consistent with three of the four forecasts that are similar between the two models, but only with those of the Gordon-Li model among the forecasts that are dissimilar. Specifically, they find that poor countries apparently have higher capital taxes as well as higher proportions of government-owned banks and other enterprises,[1] although in each case the data are not sufficiently detailed to distinguish the deeper, divergent motives of the two models. On the other hand, the data show that poor countries have lower tax revenues (as a proportion of GDP), higher tariff revenues (as a proportion of government revenues), lower income and sales tax revenues (as a percentage of tax revenues), a higher inflation tax, more red tape, and larger informal sectors.

Critique

What can one make of these models and the empirical evidence? The easy conclusion to draw is that the evidence is still quite tentative, because the data are not detailed enough to allow more than general and suggestive tests. Indeed, for this reason, some of the tests have a contrived feel. For instance, the prediction that capital-income taxes will be levied in the political economy model seems a bit forced, given that, under the framework, the superior policy is to levy an output tax. A second example is in the appropriation of the bribing industries as the informal sector, simply because they have tax exempt status. Yet another example is in the use of the cost to register a new business and the time required to start a business legally as indicators not just of red tape per se, but of red tape intended for the informal sector. Arguably, the majority of informal sector firms do not register their businesses as this would only leave a paper trail for government inspectors to track. Indeed, either the respondents of the World Bank survey from which the data were generated are unlikely to belong to the shadow economy or the informal sector respondents are likely to be undersampled. Perhaps more to the point, formal sector firms are just as likely to be affected by these time and financial costs, unless there are fast lanes for firms that are able to show tax payment certificates. On the other hand, in

---

1. In the political economy model, a higher capital-income tax can be levied on the many nonbribing industries to offset capital subsidies to the fewer capital owners who bribe the government.

the regression of the size of the informal economy, the log of per capita GDP may have an error-in-variable problem, inasmuch as the measurement of GDP does not cover the output of the informal sector, which is likely to be proportionally more significant in poorer countries. In other words, the economic output is likely to be more undercounted in poor countries, which tend to have proportionally larger informal sectors.

As for the models, a problem is that the political economy model that is developed is not a good benchmark, because under no set of conditions can it replicate certain stylized facts in developing economies, such as the existence of an informal sector (unless it is made artificially equivalent to the bribing industries that, as a consequence, pay no taxes) and red tape and the use of inflation as a policy measure. A better alternative model is one that can replicate all the perverse outcomes in developing countries but under different assumptions, for example, an economy mired in a low-level equilibrium trap because either the political power of certain groups is threatened by economic growth or a predatory state preys on, that is, extorts and threatens—and is not just bribed by—the productive sector (see, e.g., Hoff and Stiglitz [2001]).

Another problem is that, in the two models, the extent of corruption is circumscribed by the tradeoff at the margin between the benefits of government expenditures to the people and the benefits of unspent revenue to the government in the case of the Gordon-Li model and the value the government assigns to a bribe and the harm that policies favoring the bribing industries can have on the general welfare in the case of the political economy model. Alas, in the developing countries, extortion rather than bribery can be the order of the day, and predators or rivals are not always so well meaning or morally squeamish. Indeed, the game can be played for keeps, as in the following example from McCoy (1994, 429):

> In June 1972, Eugenio Lopez, Sr., stood at the summit of Philippine public life. Starting as a provincial bus operator, he had risen in only sixteen years to become chairman of the country's largest media conglomerate and president of its leading utility, the Manila Electric Company. His brother was finishing a [second] term as vice-president of the Philippines. . . . Using his formidable media assets, he had recently defeated the country's president, Ferdinand Marcos, in a bitter battle over the spoils of power. . . .
>
> Only three months later, President Marcos declared martial law and destroyed Eugenio Lopez. After imprisoning his eldest son on capital charges, Marcos forced Lopez to sign over his shares in the Manila Electric Company and had to watch silently while a presidential crony plundered his media conglomerate. Forced into exile, stripped of his wealth, and tortured by the threat of his son's execution, Lopez died of cancer in 1975 in a San Francisco hospital.

It is difficult to get at the ultimate reasons for taxation and inflation policies. But as far as government ownership of firms is concerned, the Philippines is a counterexample to the Gordon-Li model. In the late 1980s, the country privatized the Philippine National Bank (PNB), then the largest government-owned bank, and, in the late 1990s, it auctioned off Metro Manila's water distribution utility to two concessionaires. In the first case, it was because the bank's financial position had become unsustainable, in large part due to its portfolio of bad loans mostly to Marcos cronies— which is a dangerous possibility for the government in the Gordon-Li model, if the highly taxed, capital-intensive firms become chummy with government-owned banks. In the second case, it was because the Metropolitan Waterworks and Sewerage System, a government-owned corporation, could not afford the capital investments necessary to maintain the quality of water distribution services. Since then the PNB's financial position has improved, as has the quality of water distribution in Metro Manila.

In any case, if the Gordon-Li model is an accurate account of the perverse economic policies in developing countries, then the policy implication is to speed up the implementation of financial sector reforms to raise the marginal benefits that firms gain from financial intermediation. The real danger, however, is that the model will be used by some rent-seeking government to stop anticorruption initiatives on the argument that corruption will vanish anyway once the benefits from using the financial sector are obtained.

References

Gordon, Roger H., and Wei Li. 2005a. Puzzling tax structures in developing countries: A comparison of two alternative explanations. NBER Working Paper no. 11661. Cambridge, MA: National Bureau of Economic Research.
———. 2005b. Tax structure in developing countries: Many puzzles and a possible explanation. NBER Working Paper no. 11267. Cambridge, MA: National Bureau of Economic Research.
Grossman, Gene M., and Elhanan Helpman. 1994. Protection for sale. *American Economic Review* 84 (4): 833–850.
Hoff, Karla, and Joseph E. Stiglitz. 2001. Modern economic theory and development. In *Frontiers of development economics: The future in perspective,* ed. Gerald M. Meier and Joseph E. Stiglitz, 389–459. Oxford: Oxford University Press.
McCoy, Alfred W. 1994. Rent-seeking families and the Philippine State: A history of the Lopez family. In *An anarchy of families: State and family in the Philippines,* ed. Alfred W. McCoy, 429–536. Quezon City, Philippines: Ateneo de Manila University Press.

II

The Impact of Government Policy on Private Behavior

2

The Direct Substitution between Government and Private Consumption in East Asia

Yum K. Kwan

2.1 Introduction

An important issue in the design of fiscal policy is the substitutability between government and private consumption. If the private sector derives utility from government-provided goods and services and regards private and government consumption as close substitutes, an increase in government consumption will be offset by a corresponding decrease in private consumption, rendering the size of the fiscal multiplier relatively small and even potentially negative. On the other hand, if private and government consumption are complements, an expansionary fiscal policy will be relatively effective in stimulating aggregate demand as private consumption will reinforce the initial fiscal impulse. While it is easy to give examples of *individual* private and government goods that are substitutes or complements, it is an empirical question whether *aggregate* private and government consumption are substitutes or complements for a particular economy during a certain period. The purpose of this chapter is to empirically study the substitutability issue for nine East Asian countries—the four northeast countries: China, Hong Kong, Japan, and Korea, and the five southeast countries: Indonesia, Malaysia, Philippines, Singapore, and Thailand.

Traditional macroeconomic models assume that government consumption works through its impact on private consumption through wealth

Yum K. Kwan is associate professor of economics at the City University of Hong Kong.

The author gratefully acknowledges useful comments from Gregory Chow, Takatoshi Ito, Mario Lamberte, Charles Leung, Kiyoshi Mitsui, Andrew Rose, and seminar participants, and financial support from the Research Center for International Economics, City University of Hong Kong, and the Center for Economic Development, Hong Kong University of Science and Technology.

effect or interest rate effect. Private consumption is crowded out either because the consumers may feel poorer as a result of negative wealth effect or they may be induced to postpone consumption in response to deficit-financed government spending. Bailey (1971) and Barro (1981) first suggest incorporating government consumption into the representative agent decision problem, making the public sector part of the general equilibrium system. The idea is that many government goods are to some extent substitutes for private consumption goods. Moreover, government purchases may also serve as useful inputs to the private production function so that government consumption can be productive. This is in contrast to the traditional models in which government consumption are regarded as purely wasteful or unrelated to private consumption or production. In recent theoretical literature, the interaction between government and private consumption has been assigned a central role in the study of fiscal policy, in both the neoclassical real business cycle fashion (e.g., Aiyagari, Christiano, and Eichenbaum 1992 and Baxter and King 1993) and the new Keynesian fashion with monopolistic competition, increasing returns, and nominal rigidities (e.g., Devereux, Head, and Lapham 1996 and Ganelli 2003). However, depending on their assumptions about market structure and technology, these models can predict totally different reactions of private consumption in response to government spending shocks.

On the empirical front, a large literature has been developed to estimate the relationship between government and private consumption. Kormendi (1983) and Aschauer (1985) are representative of the earlier approach that relies on estimating a consumption function. Karras (1994), Ni (1995), Evans and Karras (1996), and Fiorito and Kollintzas (2004) are some of the more recent contributions along this approach. Ni's paper also provides a useful survey of the literature. The empirical analysis in this paper follows Amano and Wirjanto (1997, 1998), who make use of the cointegration approach of Ogaki (1992) and Ogaki and Park (1997) to estimate the preference parameter that governs the relationship between government and private consumption. The idea is to exploit the long-run restriction imposed by the intraperiod first-order condition that characterizes the optimal choice of private and government consumption. Ho (2001), Chiu (2001), and Okubo (2003) are some recent contributions along the same line.

The rest of the chapter is organized as follows. Section 2.2 presents the empirical model in detail. We provide a structural interpretation to the cointegrating regression model by deriving it as an equilibrium condition. Section 2.3 provides a brief description of government expenditures in East Asia. The data and empirical results are presented in section 2.4. Section 2.5 concludes.

2.2   The Empirical Model

The empirical work in this paper centers around a cointegrating regression that relates the logarithm of private and government consumption ratio, C_t/G_t, to the logarithm of their relative price P_t^g/P_t^c:

(1) $$\ln(C_t/G_t) = \alpha + \beta \ln(P_t^g/P_t^c) + u_t$$

where $\ln(C_t/G_t)$ and $\ln(P_t^g/P_t^c)$ are both difference-stationary I(1) processes, and u_t is a stationary I(0) process. Formal statistical evidence for the cointegration property will be provided in the following. The slope parameter β is the elasticity of substitution between private and government consumption. A positive (negative) β means that the two goods are substitutes (complements). One attractive feature of cointegrating regression is that the slope parameters can be estimated consistently without the assumption that the regressors are econometrically exogenous. In equation (1), for example, β can still be estimated consistently even though there may be stationary omitted variables or measurement errors.

So far equation (1) is treated as a pure statistical relationship between the consumption ratio of private and government goods and their relative prices. It is possible to provide the equation a structural interpretation by deriving it as an equilibrium condition, following the ideas of Ogaki (1992), Ogaki and Park (1997), and Ogaki and Reinhart (1998). Assume that the representative consumer values two goods, private and government, according to an expected lifetime utility function subject to stationary preference shocks:

(2) $$U = E_t\left[\sum_{j=0}^{\infty} \delta^j u(C^*_{t+j})\right]$$

where

(3) $$C^*_i = [\phi\varepsilon_t C_t^{1-(1/\sigma)} + (1 - \phi)v_t G_t^{1-(1/\sigma)}]^{1/[1-(1/\sigma)]}$$

(ε_t, v_t) are random preference shocks that are assumed to be strictly stationary, have unit means, and finite variances. The stationarity assumption amounts to say preferences are stable in the long run. The period utility function is assumed to possess the usual properties $u' > 0$ and $u'' < 0$. (ϕ, σ) are preference parameters that characterize the representative agent's utility function: ϕ is the relative weight assigned to private goods and σ is the substitution parameter that measures the curvature of the indifference curves. Given time separability of the utility function, the optimal consumption bundle will have to satisfy the equality between marginal rate of substitution and relative price:

(4) $$\frac{\partial U/\partial G_t}{\partial U/\partial C_t} \equiv \frac{v_t(1 - \phi)G_t^{-1/\sigma}}{\varepsilon_t\phi C_t^{-1/\sigma}} = \frac{P_t^g}{P_t^c}.$$

Taking logarithm and rearranging yields

$$(5) \qquad \ln\left(\frac{C_t}{G_t}\right) = -\sigma \ln\left[\frac{(1-\phi)}{\phi}\right] + \sigma \ln\left(\frac{P_t^g}{P_t^c}\right) - \sigma \ln\left(\frac{v_t}{\varepsilon_t}\right)$$

Stable preferences implies that the residual term, $-\sigma \ln(v_t/\varepsilon_t)$, is stationary and hence equation (5) should be a cointegrating regression, provided that log consumption ratio, $\ln(C_t/G_t)$, and log price ratio, $\ln(P_t^g/P_t^c)$, are both I(1) processes. In other words, the stable preferences assumption, together with the consumer optimality condition in equation (4), imposes a cointegration restriction on the movements of the log consumption ratio and the log price ratio series. Equation (5) provides a structural interpretation to equation (1), which can be regarded as the reduced-form equation with parameters and residuals related to their structural counterpart via the relationships

$$(6) \qquad \alpha = -\sigma \ln\left[\frac{(1-\phi)}{\phi}\right], \beta = \sigma, u_t = -\sigma \ln\left(\frac{v_t}{\varepsilon_t}\right).$$

Notice that equation (5) is a theoretical demand equation, whereas equation (1) is an empirical equation describing the equilibrium quantities and prices. Just like the classical supply-and-demand simultaneous equation model, interpreting equation (1) as the demand equation requires identification assumption. In general, to identify the demand equation, we need variability from the supply side and the demand side should be relatively stable. Since the supply side has to do with production, which is subject to technological improvement, it is reasonable to expect the quantity-supplied series should be highly persistent, which can be modeled as a stochastic trend. The demand side, on the other hand, has to do with taste and it is reasonable to expect preference shocks are relatively stable in comparison with technological shocks. In the context of demand analysis, Ogaki (1992) has shown formally that the assumptions of stable preferences and a stochastic trend in the quantity supplied are sufficient to ensure identification of a cointegrating demand equation like equation (1).

In the theoretical analyses of Bailey (1971) and Barro (1981), followed by the empirical work of Kormendi (1983), Aschauer (1985), and Evans and Karras (1996), among many others, the effective consumption is specified as a weighted average of private and government consumption:

$$(7) \qquad C_t^* = C_t + \theta G_t.$$

In this setup each unit of government goods is equivalent to θ units of private goods, irrespective of the current consumption level of the two goods. In other words, the indifference curves for the two goods are linear, which corresponds to the extreme case of $\sigma = +\infty$ in the CES aggregator function in equation (3). Clearly this is an empirically restrictive assumption, albeit a convenient one for analytical tractability.

2.3   Government Expenditures in East Asia

Table 2.1 reports a summary of the government expenditures by economic type (in percentage of GDP) for the Asian countries studied in this paper, together with the corresponding figures for the United States for comparison. The data source is World Bank (2004), which in turn is based on the primitive data in the *IMF Government Financial Statistics Yearbook.* Total government outlays are comprised of government purchase of goods and services, wages and salaries for government employees, public capital investment, transfer payments, and interest payments of outstanding government debts. In terms of total outlays, the governments of the Asian countries are comparable in size to that of the United States, except for the Malaysia government, which stands out as the outlier of the group. The pattern of government expenditures among the Asian countries is more heterogeneous. Japan and Korea seem to differ from the rest of the Asian countries and their government expenditure patterns are broadly comparable to that of the United States. The governments of Hong Kong and the five ASEAN countries, on the other hand, spend relatively more on goods and services and on government employee payroll. Table 2.1 also reveals that the Asian governments devote a considerable amount of resources on capital investments, presumably most are on public infrastructure and, for the five ASEAN countries, also on national enterprises. This is in sharp contrast to the United States in which public investment is only 1 percent of GDP. Among the heavy public investors, the Indonesian government

Table 2.1   Government expenditure by economic type 1991–2000 (% of GDP)

	Goods and services	Wages and salaries	Interest payments	Subsidies and other current transfers	Capital expenditure	Total
Northeast Asia						
Hong Kong	7.2	4.4	0.0	4.7	4.2	20.5
Japan[a]		2.3[b]	3.1	9.0	2.5	16.9
Korea[a]	5.1	2.2	0.5	8.2	2.9	18.9
Southeast Asia						
Indonesia	4.1	2.3	2.1	3.9	6.9	19.3
Malaysia[a]	10.6	6.5	3.7	5.0	4.8	30.6
The Philippines	9.2	5.6	4.4	2.8	2.5	24.5
Singapore	9.8	5.0	1.3	2.4	5.0	23.4
Thailand	9.4	5.4	0.7	1.3	6.5	23.4
United States	5.0	1.9	3.1	12.3	1.0	23.3

Source: World Bank (2004) for countries other than Hong Kong. Hong Kong figures are compiled from the *Hong Kong Annual Digest of Statistics,* various years.

[a]Figures are annual average of 1991–2000, except for Japan (1981–90), Korea (1991–97) and Malaysia (1991–97).

[b]For Japan, the figure for goods and services and wages and salaries is the sum of the two components.

stands out as the largest by devoting 6.9 percent of GDP to public investment, followed by Thailand (6.5 percent), Singapore (5.0 percent), and Malaysia (4.8 percent). Another noteworthy component is transfer payments. The transfer payments of the Asian governments are all relatively low compared with the corresponding U.S. figure of 12.3 percent, with Japan and Korea registering the highest government transfers in the 8 to 9 percent range, and Thailand reporting the lowest transfers of only 1.3 percent of GDP. Clearly the low transfers in the ASEAN countries and Hong Kong reflect the relatively underdeveloped social security system and other formal welfare schemes.

2.4 Empirical Results

We use annual data for 1960 to 2002 from the *World Development Indicators* (World Bank 2004) whenever possible to ensure crosscountry compatibility. Missing or erroneous entries are reconstructed from local sources. Private and government consumption are taken to be the relevant expenditure series from the National Income and Product Accounts (NIPA). The consumption ratio, C_t/G_t, is calculated from the constant price private and government consumption series. The two price series, P_t^g and P_t^c, are simply the respective implicit price deflators constructed by dividing the nominal series by the constant price counterpart.

We begin by examining the time series properties of the log consumption ratio series, $\ln(C_t/G_t)$, and the log price ratio series, $\ln(P_t^g/P_t^c)$. Figure 2.1 depicts the two series for all nine Asian countries. The strong persistency and comovements of the two series are clearly discernable from the plots, giving an initial impression that they are likely to be I(1) and cointegrated. Table 2.2 reports formal panel unit root test results. It is well known that unit root tests have low power and the problem may be even worse for our application as we have short time series. To better utilize sample information, we pool the nine countries' data to perform panel unit root tests, which have been shown to be more powerful than the individual time series version. All three panel unit root tests draw the same conclusion: the unit root null hypothesis is not rejected for the level series but is strongly rejected for the first differenced series. This shows that the log consumption ratio and the log price ratio series are indeed I(1). Moreover, the asymmetry of the p-values for the level series in the IPS test and the ADF-Fisher chi-square test suggest that log consumption ratio is the less integrated series—in the sense that it has a weaker random walk component—than the log price ratio. This has important implications to the specification of the cointegrating regression. It is well known that cointegrating regression is not invariant to normalization choice—deciding which variable to put on the left-hand side as the regressand—and different choices may imply dif-

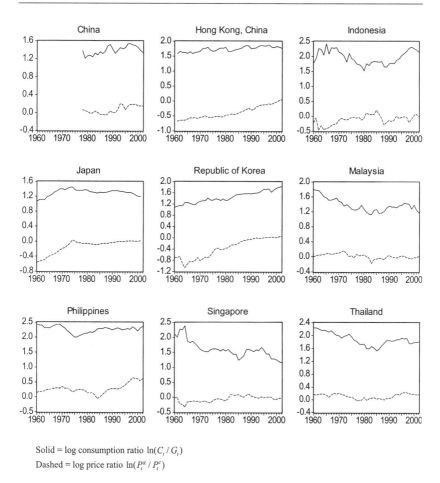

Solid = log consumption ratio $\ln(C_t / G_t)$

Dashed = log price ratio $\ln(P_t^g / P_t^c)$

Fig. 2.1   Private and government consumption ratio and relative price
Notes: Solid = log consumption ratio $\ln(C_t/G_t)$; dashed = log price ratio $\ln(P_t^g/P_t^c)$.

ferent estimates for the same parameter. For example, instead of running regression equation (1), we could have run the reverse regression with the log price ratio normalized as the regressand to obtain an estimate of $(1/\beta)$. In finite sample the estimates from the direct and reverse regressions may be far from being reciprocal to each other and they can also have drastically different statistical properties. According to Ng and Perron (1997), in the context of cointegrating regression, it is preferable to put the less integrated series as the regressand and the more integrated series as the regressor. Applying the Ng-Perron rule, this means that designating the log consumption ratio series as the regressand as in equation (1) is indeed the right choice.

Table 2.2   **Panel unit root tests**

	$\ln(C/G)$	$\Delta \ln(C/G)$	$\ln(P_g/P_c)$	$\Delta \ln(P_g/P_c)$
IPS W-statistic	0.6551	15.2985	0.6002	14.0852
	(0.2562)	(0.0000)	(0.7258)	(0.0000)
ADF-Fisher Chi-square	20.3887	196.183	15.7766	178.734
	(0.3114)	(0.0000)	(0.6081)	(0.0000)
PP-Fisher Chi-square	18.0178	262.871	18.6922	270.737
	(0.4545)	(0.0000)	(0.4110)	(0.0000)

Notes: P-values are in parentheses. H_0: Each country follows an individual unit root process. H_1: At least one country's process is trend stationary. Exogenous variables: individual effects, individual linear trends. Cross-sectional units: China, Hong Kong, Indonesia, Japan, Korea, Malaysia, The Philippines, Singapore, and Thailand. Time period: China 1978–2002; other countries 1960–2002. IPS = IM, Pesaran, and Shin (2003). ADF-Fisher and PP-Fisher are Maddala and Wu (1999) Fisher-type tests constructed by combining the *p*-values from individual augmented Dickey-Fuller (ADF) and Phillips-Perron (PP) unit-root tests.

Table 2.3 reports panel estimation results for equation (1) with country-specific fixed effects. The cointegration property of equation (1) is confirmed by the two panel cointegration tests: the null hypothesis of no cointegration is decisively rejected by Kao's (1999) ADF test, but the null of cointegration cannot be rejected according to the McCoskey and Kao (1998) LM test. Turning to the elasticity of substitution between private and government consumption—the coefficient of $\ln(P_t^g/P_t^c)$—it can be seen that the estimates are all significantly positive, ranging between 0.57 and 1.05 with small standard errors, and varying across different estimation methods and sample periods. The empirical results suggest that on average private and government consumption in East Asia are substitutes with an elasticity of substitution midway between 0.5 and 1.

We also estimate an unrestricted version of equation (1) as a simple specification check:

$$(8) \qquad \ln\left(\frac{C_t}{G_t}\right) = \alpha + \beta_1 \ln(P_t^g) + \beta_2 \ln(P_t^c) + u_t$$

Equation (1) is a restricted version of equation (8) with $\beta_1 + \beta_2 = 0$. Estimates of β_1 and β_2 that are similar in magnitude but opposite in sign provide evidence in favor of the restriction and hence equation (1). As can be seen from table 2.3, the pattern of the parameter estimates is in general supportive of equation (1); and the evidence is especially strong when all nine Asian countries are included in the sample for the period 1978 to 2002 (panel B). According to the fully efficient DOLS estimates, government and private consumption in East Asia from 1978 to 2002 have a substantial degree of substitutability with an elasticity of substitution around 1, implying a Cobb-Douglas aggregator function for equation (3).

From a policy perspective, the panel estimate may not be of much prac-

Table 2.3   **Panel cointegrating regressions**

	Regressors			Cointegration test	
	$\ln(P_t^g/P_t^c)$	$\ln(P_t^g)$	$\ln(P_t^c)$	ADF	LM
A. 8 Asian countries (excluding China), 1960–2002					
OLS	0.5722			−5.5516	0.6516
	(0.0614)			[0.0000]	[0.2573]
OLS		0.7975	−0.8847	−4.3753	2.4090
		(0.0639)	(0.0698)	[0.0000]	[0.0080]
DOLS	0.7555				
	(0.0651)				
DOLS		1.0132	−1.1132		
		(0.0607)	(0.0646)		
B. 9 Asian countries (including China), 1978–2002					
OLS	0.6373			−6.8337	0.5369
	(0.1064)			[0.0000]	[0.2957]
OLS		0.5958	−0.5718	−6.7290	0.4498
		(0.1361)	(0.1709)	[0.0000]	[0.3264]
DOLS	1.0589				
	(0.0999)				
DOLS		0.9740	−0.9073		
		(0.1250)	(0.1591)		

Notes: Regressand = $\ln(C_i/G_i)$. *P*-values are in square brackets. All regressions include country-specific fixed effect (unreported). DOLS = Kao and Chiang (2000) panel dynamic OLS. The regression is augmented with one lead and one lag of the first difference of the regressors (unreported). ADF = Kao (1999) panel ADF test for the null hypothesis of no cointegration. The lag length in the test regression is chosen by the Schwarz criterion. LM = McCoskey and Kao (1998) panel LM test for the null hypothesis of cointegration.

tical relevance, as it tells us little about any individual country. Table 2.4 therefore reports cointegrating regression results for the nine Asian countries individually. We also report the corresponding results for the United States for comparison. To check robustness, we try three different estimation methods that are all asymptotically efficient procedures for estimating cointegration regressions. The three methods are Phillips and Hansen's (1990) fully modified ordinary least square (FM-OLS), Park's (1992) canonical cointegrating regression (CCR), and Stock and Watson's (1993) dynamic ordinary least squares (DOLS). In general the parameter estimates are stable across the three estimation methods. Comparing the DOLS estimates of the elasticity of substitution across countries, Malaysia and Thailand come up with the highest values of 1.66 and 1.51, respectively, which are comparable to the value of 1.5 of the United States. On the other extreme are Indonesia and Singapore for which the negative elasticities of substitution of −0.92 and −1.76, respectively, imply that private and government consumption are strong complements. The four northeast Asian countries, China, Hong Kong, Japan, and Korea, share a moderate elas-

Table 2.4   Individual cointegrating regressions

	FM-OLS		CCR		DOLS	
	Intercept	$\ln(P_t^g/P_t^c)$	Intercept	$\ln(P^g/P_t^c)$	Intercept	$\ln(P_t^g/P_t^c)$
Northeast Asia						
China	1.3334	0.6699	1.3335	0.6691	1.3526	0.6524
	(0.0161)	(0.1452)	(0.0161)	(0.1513)	(0.0216)	(0.2136)
Hong Kong	1.8645	0.3242	1.8656	0.3269	1.8772	0.3424
	(0.0245)	(0.0556)	(0.0259)	(0.0575)	(0.0260)	(0.0468)
Japan	1.3063	0.2962	1.3064	0.2986	1.3329	0.4149
	(0.0204)	(0.1026)	(0.0192)	(0.0758)	(0.0119)	(0.0780)
Korea	1.6748	0.5770	1.6755	0.5778	1.6468	0.5233
	(0.0297)	(0.0594)	(0.0300)	(0.0591)	(0.0177)	(0.0331)
Southeast Asia						
Indonesia	1.8534	−0.9809	1.8574	−0.9273	1.8613	−0.9243
	(0.1038)	(0.5449)	(0.1030)	(0.5090)	(0.0449)	(0.2614)
Malaysia	1.3427	1.6028	1.3421	1.6218	1.3420	1.6601
	(0.0255)	(0.3979)	(0.0257)	(0.4106)	(0.0193)	(0.3488)
The Philippines	2.2307	0.0458	2.2334	0.0328	2.2179	0.0707
	(0.0423)	(0.1288)	(0.0421)	(0.1333)	(0.0361)	(0.1207)
Singapore	1.4852	−1.9452	1.4836	−1.9716	1.4933	−1.7679
	(0.0556)	(0.4855)	(0.0563)	(0.5069)	(0.0371)	(0.3586)
Thailand	1.7239	1.3858	1.7241	1.3841	1.7057	1.5149
	(0.0684)	(0.5139)	(0.0646)	(0.4778)	(0.0440)	(0.3447)
United States	1.4284	1.5373	1.4298	1.5155	1.3818	1.5078
	(0.0291)	(0.2304)	(0.0292)	(0.1677)	(0.0184)	(0.1642)

Notes: Standard errors in parentheses. Time period: China 1978–2002; other countries 1960–2002. FM-OLS = Fully modified OLS; CCR = Canonical cointegrating regression; DOLS = Dynamic OLS. FM-OLS and CCR use Andrews' automatic bandwidth selection method in computing the long-run variance matrix. DOLS includes one lead and one lag of the first difference of the regressors in the augmented regression.

ticity of substitution ranging from 0.41 in Hong Kong to 0.65 in China. The Philippines, on the other hand, has a numerically small and statistically insignificant elasticity of substitution of 0.07, indicating little substitution in private and government consumption.

Indonesia and Thailand provide an interesting case of contrast. The estimated elasticity of substitution between private and government consumption is –0.92 for Indonesia and 1.51 for Thailand. Government consumption is a strong substitute to private consumption in Thailand, implying that a fiscal contraction that makes government goods relatively more expensive will induce substantial expansion in private consumption, thereby offsetting or even outweighing the negative impact of the fiscal contraction on aggregate demand. The Indonesian government consumption, in contrast, is a strong complement to private consumption, implying that a fiscal contraction that makes government goods relatively more expensive will generate a large negative income effect that outweighs the substitution effect, leading to a concomitant contraction in private consumption expenditure that further depresses aggregate demand. These predictions about the two economies' reaction to fiscal austerity seem to be consistent with what have been observed during the 1997 Asian financial crisis. What explains the cross-country diversity in the substitution between private and government consumption? In their international study, Evans and Karras (1996) find a statistically significant negative relationship between the share of government expenditure that goes to national defense and the degree of substitutability between private and government consumption. The idea is that the higher is the defense share, the higher is the public goods component in government consumption, which reduces its ability to substitute for private consumption. In table 2.5 we collect together for the nine East Asian countries their national defense expenditure shares, education expenditure shares, and estimated elasticities of substitution between private and government consumption. The entries are sorted by the substitution elasticities for ease of comparison. Apparently neither the education share nor the defense share can explain the empirical pattern of the substitution elasticities for all nine countries. However, the correlation between the defense shares and substitution elasticities is –0.24, confirming the empirical findings of Evans and Karras (1996). The strong complementarity between private and government consumption in Singapore seems to be testimonial to the Evans-Karras story, in view of the favorable international ratings of the Singaporean education system and other infrastructure, and the government's well-documented role in the country's economic success (e.g., Low 1998 and Krause, Tee, and Yuan 1987). The case of Indonesia may appear to be defiant of the Evans-Karras

Table 2.5   **Government expenditures and substitutability**

	Education (% of expenditure) (1)	Defense (% of expenditure) (2)	(1) + (2)	Elasticity of substitution (DOLS estimate) (4)
Singapore	21.0	26.5	47.5	–1.76
Indonesia	9.8	6.6	16.4	–0.92
The Philippines	15.7	10.5	26.2	0.07
Hong Kong	14.5	0.0	14.5	0.34
Japan	6.2	4.4	10.6	0.41
Korea	18.8	20.0	38.8	0.52
China	2.4	16.3	18.7	0.65
Thailand	21.3	15.6	36.9	1.51
Malaysia	20.4	11.7	32.1	1.66
Correlation with (4)	0.07	–0.24	–0.12	

Notes: The reported expenditure figures are annual average of 1991–95.
Source: World Bank (2004) for countries other than Hong Kong. Hong Kong figures are compiled from the *Hong Kong Annual Digest of Statistics,* various years.

explanation: the expenditures on education and defense are only moderate and yet private and government consumption appear to be complements, according to the negative sign of the substitution elasticity. One potential explanation is the well-known fact that the Indonesian government heavily subsidizes the private sector, including fuel, electricity, fertilizer, and other basic goods, and these subsidies are complementary to other goods in the private-consumption bundle; see for example Hill (1996, 1999) and World Bank (2006). When the Indonesian government adjusts these subsidies in tandem with the overall government spending, this will generate the observed comovements of private and government consumption that gives rise to the estimated negative elasticity of substitution.

2.5 Conclusion

In this chapter we have estimated the degree of substitution between private and government consumption in nine East Asian countries. On average there is substantial substitutability between private and government consumption, implying there will be direct crowding out of private consumption by government consumption. Such direct crowding-out effect will reinforce the conventional interest rate and wealth effect crowding-out channels to make fiscal policy relatively ineffective in East Asia. We also find that the substitutability between private and government consumption varies among the Asian countries. Government and private consumption turn out to be complements in Indonesia and Singapore, but they are substitutes in other Asian countries with different degrees of substitutability. There is no obvious quantitative variable that can explain each country's empirical estimates, although the share of government expenditure that goes to education and national defense seems to be negatively correlated with substitutability. Future study on this issue will need a more careful examination of each country's institutional details—one will have to understand what sort of government services those public-consumption figures represent—before further conclusion can be drawn.

References

Aiyagari, Rao, Lawrence Christiano, and Martin Eichenbaum. 1992. The output, employment and interest effect of government consumption. *Journal of Monetary Economics* 30:73–86.
Amano, Robert A., and Tony S. Wirjanto. 1997. Intratemporal substitution and government spending. *Review of Economics and Statistics* 79:605–9.
———. 1998. Government expenditures and the permanent-income model. *Review of Economic Dynamics* 1:719–30.
Aschauer, David. 1985. Fiscal policy and aggregate demand. *American Economic Review* 75 (1): 117–27.

Bailey, Martin J. 1971. *National income and the price level: A study in macroeconomic theory.* 2nd Edition. New York: McGraw-Hill.

Barro, Robert J. 1981. Output effects of government purchases. *Journal of Political Economy* 89 (6): 1086–121.

Baxter, M., and Robert G. King. 1993. Fiscal policy in general equilibrium. *American Economic Review* 83:343–50.

Chiang, Min-Hsien, and Chihwa Kao. 2002. Nonstationary panel time series using NPT 1.3—A user guide. Center for Policy Research, Syracuse University.

Chiu, Ru-Lin. 2001. The intratemporal substitution between government spending and private consumption: Empirical evidence from Taiwan. *Asian Economic Journal* 15 (3): 313–23.

Devereux, Michael, Allen Head, and Beverly Lapham. 1996. Monopolistic competition, increasing returns, and the effects of government spending. *Journal of Money, Credit, and Banking* 28:233–54.

Evans, Paul, and Georgios Karras. 1996. Private and government consumption with liquidity constraints. *Journal of International Money and Finance* 15 (2): 255–66.

Fiorito, Riccardo, and Tryphon Kollintzas. 2004. Public goods, merit goods, and the relation between private and government consumption. *European Economic Review* 48:1367–98.

Ganelli, Giovanni. 2003. Useful government spending, direct crowding-out and fiscal policy interdependence. *Journal of International Money and Finance* 22: 87–103.

Hill, Hal. 1996. *The Indonesian economy.* Cambridge, UK: Cambridge University Press.

———. 1999. *The Indonesian economy in crisis: Causes, consequences and lessons.* Singapore: Institute of Southeast Asian Studies.

Ho, Tsung-wu. 2001. The government spending and private consumption: A panel cointegration analysis. *International Review of Economics and Finance* 10: 95–108.

Im, Kyung So, M. Hashem Pesaran, and Yongcheol Shin. 2003. Testing for unit roots in heterogeneous panels. *Journal of Econometrics* 115 (1): 53–74.

Kao, Chihwa. 1999. Spurious regression and residual-based tests for cointegration in panel data. *Journal of Econometrics* 90 (1): 1–44.

Kao, Chihwa, and Min-Hsien Chiang. 2000. On the estimation and inference of a cointegrated regression in panel data. *Advances in Econometrics* 15:179–222.

Karras, Georgios. 1994. Government spending and private consumption: Some international evidence. *Journal of Money, Credit, and Banking* 26 (1): 9–22.

Kormendi, Roger. 1983. Government debt, government spending, and private sector behavior. *American Economic Review* 73 (5): 994–1010.

Krause, Lawrence, Koh Ai Tee, and Lee (Tsao) Yuan. 1987. *The Singapore economy reconsidered.* Singapore: Institute of Southeast Asian Studies.

Low, Linda. 1998. *The political economy of a city-state: Government-made Singapore.* Singapore: Oxford University Press.

Maddala, G. S., and S. Wu. 1999. A comparative study of unit root tests with panel data and a new simple test. *Oxford Bulletin of Economics and.5 Statistics* 61: 631–52.

McCoskey, S., and Chihwa Kao. 1998. A residual-based test of the null of cointegration in panel data. *Econometric Review* 17:57–84.

Ng, Serena, and Pierre Perron. 1997. Estimation and inference in nearly unbalanced nearly cointegrated systems. *Journal of Econometrics* 79 (1): 53–81.

Ni, Shawn. 1995. An empirical analysis on the substitutability between private consumption and government purchases. *Journal of Monetary Economics* 36: 593–605.

Ogaki, Masao. 1992. Engle's law and cointegration. *Journal of Political Economy* 100 (5): 1027–46.

Ogaki, Masao, and Joon Y. Park. 1997. A cointegration approach to estimating preference parameters. *Journal of Econometrics* 82 (1): 107–34.

Ogaki, Masao, and Carmen M. Reinhart. 1998. Measuring intertemporal substitution: The role of durable goods. *Journal of Political Economy* 106 (5): 1078–98.

Okubo, Masakatsu. 2003. Intratemporal substitution between private and government consumption: The case of Japan. *Economic Letters* 79:75–81.

Park, Joon Y. 1992. Canonical cointegrating regression. *Econometrica* 60:119–43.

Phillips, Peter C. B., and Bruce Hansen. 1990. Statistical inference in instrumental variables regression with I(1) processes. *Review of Economic Studies* 57:99–125.

Stock, James, and Mark Watson. 1993. A simple estimator of cointegrating vectors in higher order integrated systems. *Econometrica* 61 (4): 783–820.

World Bank. 1997. *World Development Report 1997—The state in a changing world.* New York: Oxford University Press.

———. 2004. *World development indicators 2004 CD-ROM.* Washington, DC: World Bank.

———. 2006. *Investing for growth and recovery: The World Bank brief for the consultative group on Indonesia.* Washington, DC: World Bank.

Comment   Kiyoshi Mitsui

In most macroeconomic models, evaluation of the effects of fiscal policies requires an understanding of the relationship between government spending and private consumption. This relationship crucially depends on whether private and government consumption are substitutes or complements (in an Edgeworth-Pareto sense). As Amano and Wirjanto (1998) show, when the intertemporal elasticity of substitution for consumption of the composite good is more (less) than the intratemporal elasticity of substitution between private and government consumption, the private and government consumption are Edgeworth-Pareto complements (substitutes). The issue of the intratemporal elasticity of substitution that this study deals with, therefore, has an important policy implication.

Before commenting on this study, I would like to place it in the context of the literature on this issue. The literature can be grouped into two strands from the standpoint of government behavior. In one strand of literature, it is assumed that government consumption is given exogenously. In the other, the government is assumed to behave optimally so that the level of government consumption is determined as the first-best solution.

Studies in the former strand of literature utilize the intertemporal first-order conditions (or Euler equations) of an optimal consumption model. It is often assumed that utility is a function of the effective consumption, which is the linear combination of private and government consumption.

Kiyoshi Mitsui is a professor of economics at Gakushuin University.

This linearity assumption gives the impression that it entails the linearity of indifference curves for private and government consumption. Under the assumption of exogeneity, however, this is not the case. As Karras (1994) points out, a function of government consumption can be added, without any revision of the basic argument, to the utility function in order to make the indifferent curve nonlinear. As Ni (1995) shows, however, the estimates of substitutability are affected by the specification of the utility function.

Studies in the latter strand make use of the intraperiod first-order condition in addition. The intraperiod first-order condition requires that the marginal rate of substitution between private and government consumption is equated to the relative purchase price of government consumption to the price of private consumption. Assuming that effective consumption is a linear combination of private and government consumption implies the linearity of the indifference curve in this case, since the government consumption is obtained by government's optimization. The linearity of effective consumption is, therefore, a very restrictive assumption in this context.

The latter group of literature can be grouped into two subgroups depending on whether intertemporal optimization condition is taken into account in addition to the intraperiod optimization condition. Amano and Wirjanto (1998), Okubo (2003), and Esteve and Sanchis-Llopis (2005) estimate both the intraperiod and intertemporal first-order conditions, because it is important for their analysis to examine whether private and government consumption are Edgeworth-Pareto complements or substitutes. Intertemporal elasticity of substitution, therefore, has to be assumed to be constant in order to estimate the intertemporal first-order condition.

In contrast, Chiu (2001) and this study both restrict their attention on the intratemporal elasticity of substitution between private and government consumption (or the intraperiod first-order condition) so that it is possible for them to use a more general utility function. Though Karras (1994) and Ho (2001) empirically test the substitutability for a number of countries in the former strand of literature, there are few cross-country empirical studies in the latter strand of literature. An important contribution of this paper, therefore, is to bring some empirical evidences from East Asian countries under a less restrictive utility function. One of the main empirical findings is that the estimates of the elasticity of substitution between private and government consumption are ranging between 0.57 and 1.05.

The first issue I would like to comment on is the estimation of the intertemporal elasticity of substitution. Though it requires the additional assumption on the constancy of the intertemporal elasticity, it is worth estimating the intertemporal elasticity in order to assess the Edgeworth-Pareto substitutability.

The second comment is concerned with the assumption about the optimality of the government behavior. This underlying assumption might be

difficult to hold in some countries in East Asia. The validity of this optimality assumption itself is, therefore, a very important issue to be tested in
these countries.

My third comment has to do with a liquidity constraint. This paper assumes that all private agents do not face a liquidity constraint so that the
level of their consumptions depends only on the relative price of government consumption with respect to private consumption. With regard to
East Asian countries, however, it is worth investigating the possibility that
a sizable fraction of consumers are subject to liquidity constraints. When a
part of private agents is subject to a binding liquidity constraint, their consumption can be assumed to depend on current or transitory disposable
income.

In concluding, this paper gives us important insights on the substitutability issue for East Asian countries. I would appreciate Professor Kwan's
paper to work in this interesting area of research.

References

Amano, Robert A., and Tony S. Wirjanto. 1998. Government expenditures and the
    permanent-income model. *Review of Economic Dynamics* 1:719–30.
Chiu, Ru-Lin. 2001. The intratemporal substitution between government spending
    and private consumption: Empirical evidence from Taiwan. *Asian Economic
    Journal* 15 (3): 313-23.
Esteve, Vicente, and Juan Sanchis-Llopis. 2005. Estimating the substitutability be-
    tween private and public consumption: The case of Spain, 1960–2003. *Applied
    Economics* 37:2327–34.
Ho, Tsung-wu. 2001. The government spending and private consumption: A panel
    cointegration analysis. *International Review of Economics and Finance* 10:95–
    108.
Karras, Georgios. 1994. Government spending and private consumption: Some in-
    ternational evidence. *Journal of Money, Credit, and Banking* 26 (1): 9–22.
Ni, Shawn. 1995. An empirical analysis on the substitutability between private con-
    sumption and government consumption. *Journal of Monetary Economics* 36:
    593–605.
Okubo, Masakatsu. 2003. Intratemporal substitution between private and govern-
    ment consumption: The case of Japan. *Economic Letters* 79:75–81.

Comment   Mario B. Lamberte

The paper empirically verifies the extent of direct substitution between
government and private consumption in nine East Asian countries. A pos-

Mario B. Lamberte was formerly the president of the Philippine Institute for Development
Studies (PIDS) and is currently a microfinance manager of EMERGE, a Philippine government project supported by USAID.

itive sign of the elasticity of substitution indicates substitutability between government and private consumption, thereby making fiscal policy relatively ineffective. The reverse holds true when a negative sign of elasticity of substitution obtains.

The author finds that there is substantial substitutability for the nine East Asian countries as a whole using pooled data. However, looking at individual countries, he finds varying results: Thailand and Malaysia show substantial substitutability between government and private consumption; Singapore and Indonesia show complementarity; the North East Asian economies including Hong Kong show moderate elasticity of substitution; and the Philippines show statistically insignificant elasticity of substitution.

The questions are:

1. Why are the results so different, especially in the case of Southeast Asia where cases of substitutability and complementarity between government and private consumption exist?

2. While the author mentions the contrasting result between Indonesia and Thailand, what about similarity in results for Singapore and Indonesia?

Let me offer some factors that could help explain some of the results.

For Thailand, the government had been running government surpluses except in the years after the 1997 financial crisis.

For Indonesia, the result may have been driven by the large government subsidies.

For Singapore, the public sector is quite large and the retirement fund has been an important source of funds until recently when the Singapore government encouraged large state-owned enterprises to issue bonds to develop the bond market.

The Philippine case is quite interesting because the analyses show statistically insignificant results. There are three factors that may help explain those results. First, growth in private consumption has been relatively stable over the years despite swings in the economy. A large part of it could have been fueled by remittances that in recent years have reached about U.S. $8 billion dollars, which could easily be about a quarter of gross merchandise exports. Second, government debt service has been very high, accounting for 20 percent of total government expenditure. Moreover, there are rigidities in government expenditure. Roughly 70 percent of annual government budget is earmarked for personal services, thus leaving only about 10 percent for capital expenditures. Third, national government expenditure does not include expenditures undertaken by large state-owned corporations.

Measuring the Effectiveness
of Fiscal Policy in Korea

Seok-Kyun Hur

3.1 Introduction

The purpose of this paper is to empirically test whether fiscal adjustments can contribute to smoothing economic fluctuations. It is well known that there have been two competing views on this issue, one of which—known as Keynesian—emphasizes the effectiveness of fiscal policy, and the other of which—the so-called new classical school—refutes it on the grounds of the crowding-out effect and Ricardian equivalence. Considering that these two conflicting arguments stem from the emphasis on the different perceptions of reality (such as the bounded rationality and finite lives of economic agents), it would be more appropriate to do an empirical analysis rather than continue theoretical debates.

This research mainly concerns a trajectory of GDP induced by variations in fiscal expenditure and taxation policy.[1] We estimate three variable vector autoregression (VAR) models or structural VAR models with Korean fiscal data in order to measure the magnitudes of fiscal multipliers dynamically following changes in fiscal expenditure and taxation. However, the quarterly Korean fiscal and GDP data (covering from 1979 Q1 to

Seok-Kyun Hur is a fellow at the Korea Development Institute.

The author acknowledges valuable comments from Wei Li, Fred Yum, Youngsun Koh, and other participants at the 16th NBER-EASE in Manila. He is also grateful to Hyun-Ah Kim for research assistance. All remaining errors are his own.

1. In discussing the validity of fiscal policy in reigning business cycles, the importance of timeliness matters as much as the directions of policy effects due to the presence of policy time lags. To rephrase, the effectiveness of fiscal policy would not be achieved unless it is well synchronized with the changes in the economic environments. However, it would constitute another paper beyond the scope of this one to evaluate the stabilizing function of fiscal policy.

2000 Q4) reveal that expansive fiscal policy has no significant or substantial effect on boosting the economy.

In order to check the robustness of our results, we assign different combinations of identifying restrictions on the disturbances of the tested SVAR systems and measure the corresponding fiscal multipliers. Shock identification strategies are elected based on the institutional aspect of fiscal activities (i.e., how the government reacts to business cycles by means of controlling the size of tax revenues and expenditures). Observing how the estimated values of fiscal multipliers vary with respect to the restrictions, we find that the estimated fiscal multipliers of Korea decay very fast in addition to their small size and low statistical significance.

Then, considering the dependency of Korean economy on the foreign sector, we extend the three variable SVARs to four variable ones by adding a variable reflecting external shocks. Results from the four variable SVARs confirm those from the three variable models while the significance of the effectiveness of fiscal policy is generally enhanced.

The contents of the paper are organized as follows. Section 3.2 surveys the relevant literature (from both Korean and foreign sources) on the issue. Section 3.3 introduces an analytical tool of the paper, basically a SVAR system. Started from the usual Cholesky decomposition, we extend the setup to include other strategies of identification borrowed from Blanchard and Perotti (2002) and Koh (2002). Section 3.4 provides empirical results from applying the methodologies defined in section 3.3 to the case of Korea. Finally, section 3.5 concludes.

3.2   Literature

Currently available literature on the effectiveness of fiscal policy is easily classified into two groups by methodologies. The first group of papers calibrates a general equilibrium model and provides either comparative statics or a transitional path in response to variations in fiscal stance of the government. The use of the general equilibrium setup is desirable for its internal consistency. However, it cannot provide an exact closed-form solution. Thus, inevitably it resorts to diverse numerical techniques to get a solution.

On the other hand, the second group of papers estimate a reduced equation or a system of reduced equations liking fiscal variables with GDP or a component of income identity (for example, aggregate consumption).[2] In return for its relatively easy application, such econometric approaches are criticized for the absence of economics. Hence, their proper implementation should be based on theoretical reasoning.

Our paper positions itself in the second category. This is because the re-

---

2. Some literature focuses on price variables (such as interest, GDP deflator, and exchange rates) rather than these quantity variables.

sults from a general equilibrium setup are likely to be predetermined by the parametric assumptions. In other words, the parametric structure of the setup may exaggerate the relation between any pair of target variables in a certain direction, which is either presumed or unknown for most cases. In contrast, the econometric approach is relatively free from such an issue of predetermination. Of course, the econometric approach is not perfectly exempt from the contamination of biases. For example, a single-equation approach (Feldstein 1982, Kormendi 1983, and Lee and Sung 2005) should come up with a proper strategy for eliminating the potential biases. Accordingly, our paper adopts a structural VAR setup, which is known to avoid the endogeneity or simultaneity among the variables involved.

In this section, rather than display all the spectrum of the relevant literature aforementioned, we narrow down the scope to cover ones using a VAR setup.[3]

3.2.1 Korean Literature

Several selections from the Korean literature, all of which disseminate Korean fiscal and macro data with a VAR setup to evaluate the effectiveness of fiscal policy on the aggregate economy, are summarized in table 3.1. Clearly, we can see that their results diverge in regard to the effectiveness of fiscal policy depending on the data sets and the choice of key variables.

Another notable point is that most of Korean literature using a VAR setup rely only on the Cholesky decomposition for a shock-identifying strategy. Admittedly, Cholesky decomposition is one of the most basic shock-identification schemes in VAR, and so it cannot represent all the possible contemporaneous relations among the disturbances. In this context, we need to search for other shock-identifying strategies from the foreign literature on this issue and apply them to the available Korean fiscal data.

3.2.2 Foreign Literature

Most of the research on the effectiveness of fiscal policy adopts a structural VAR setup. According to De Castro and Hernandez de Cos (2006), the literature using SVAR are categorized into four groups, as shown in table 3.2, by differences in the fiscal shock-identifying strategies.[4]

Such popularity of SVAR lies in the fact that it is less dependent on the existing economic theory and is less susceptible to the symptoms of endogeneity and cointegration among the variables of our interest.[5] However,

---

3. For the literature of other approaches, see Hemming, Kell, and Mahfouz (2002).

4. Perotti (2004) classifies the SVAR literature into three groups. De Castro and Hernandez de Cos (2006) add an additional group of the literature, which includes Blanchard and Perotti (2002) and Perotti (2004).

5. Even when cointegrated relations exist among the key variables, the use of plain vanilla VAR can still be advocated on the grounds that the parameters are estimated consistently and the estimates have the same asymptotic distribution as those of differenced data (Hamilton 1994).

Table 3.1 The effectiveness of fiscal policy measured by VAR approach (in Korean literature)

	Methodology	Results
Park, J. (1995)	Single equation approaches (Feldstein 1982 and Kormendi 1983. VAR (Cholesky decomposition).	Ricardian Equivalence Hypothesis is not sustained by either of the single-equation approaches. An impulse response of private consumption to the government expenditure reveals the positive effect over a long time horizon.
Kim, S. (1997)	VAR (Cholesky decomposition). The government expenditures are classified into six subgroups and their impacts on consumption, investment, and income are separately estimated.	The impact of government expenditures differs significantly item by item. The government investment tends to boost private economic activities whereas the government consumption is likely to crowd them out.
Park, H., and J. Choi (1997)	VAR with seven variables (Cholesky decomposition). The seven variables are government expenditure, bonds, money stock, interest rate, exchange rate, consumption, and current account balance.	Not able to reject Ricardian equivalence theorem. Insignificant impact of fiscal deficit, government debt, and spending increase on consumption, interest rate, exchange rate, and current account balance.
Choi, J. (2002)	Estimation of asset demand functions with the inclusion of the government bond. Causality analysis of a VAR system.	The government debt doesn't seem to be perceived as net wealth by consumers. Insignificant impact of government debt and money stock (not hi-powered money) on real GDP, nominal GDP, and GDP deflator.
Kim, S. (2003)	Structural VAR of all the components of national income identity (private consumption, investment, net export, and the remaining sectors) with dummy variables identifying a structural break (Cholesky decomposition). Fiscal variables, such as government consumption, investment, and tax revenues, are given exogenously in the VAR system.	After the currency crisis, the impact of government expenditure on GDP changed signs from $(-)$ to $(+)$. During the same period, the impact of the government investment on the private investment as well as the government consumption on the private consumption changed signs from $(-)$ to $(+)$.
Kim, S. (2005)	Structural VAR of GDP, price (P) and money stock (M) with dummy variables considering a structural break (before and after the currency crisis). Fiscal variables, such as government consumption, investment, and tax revenues, are given exogenously in the VAR system.	Before the currency crisis, an exogenous shock from the government expenditures had negative influence on price and money stock while it has positive influence on GDP. After the currency crisis, the exogenous government expenditure shock had negative influence on price and GDP, while it has positive influence on the money stock.

Table 3.2   ˙   **Various shock identification strategies adopted in measuring the effectiveness of fiscal policy**

	Shock identification strategy
Ramey and Shapiro (1998) and Edelberg, Eichenbaum, and Fisher (1999)	VAR models with dummy variables specifying certain episodes (such as wars and drastic changes in fiscal stance).
Mountford and Uhlig (2002)	VAR with sign restrictions on the impulse response functions.
Fatas and Mihov (2000), Favero (2002), and De Castro (2004)	SVAR (Cholesky decomposition).
Blanchard and Perotti (2002), Perotti (1999), and Hoppner (2002)[a]	SVAR using institutional information and quarter dependence.

[a]Hoppner (2002), following the shock representation by Blanchard and Perotti (2002), concentrates on distinguishing the direct effect of fiscal shock from the indirect effect of the Automatic Stabilization Mechanism (ASM).

the use of SVAR is more challenging in analyzing the fiscal policy than in analyzing the monetary policy for several reasons, such as the existence of uncertain or unidentifiable policy lags and the automatic stabilization mechanism. These factors, combined with the low frequency of fiscal data (mostly quarterly), cause technical difficulties in identifying sources of correlations or causalities among the disturbances of the VAR system and disentangling the contributions of the built-in stabilization mechanism. Thus, the recent development in analyzing the fiscal policy using the VAR setup naturally has been concentrated on handling those problems.

3.3   Methodology

Our model adopts a SVAR system based on Blanchard and Perotti (2002) and De Castro (2004). Accordingly, it emphasizes the design of a shock-identification scheme so that it can allow more realistic contemporaneous relations among key variables in the SVAR equations.

Here we choose three key variables—real GDP (Y_t), government expenditure (G_t), and tax revenue (T_t). All of them are logarized after being divided by population size. A vector consisting of these three variables, X_t, is assumed to follow a VAR system:

$$(1) \qquad X_t = A(L)X_{t-1} + D_t + U_t, \; X_t \equiv \begin{pmatrix} T_t \\ G_t \\ Y_t \end{pmatrix}, \; U_t \equiv \begin{pmatrix} t_t \\ g_t \\ y_t \end{pmatrix}$$

In the previous equation, each element of the vector D_t represents the long-term trend of the corresponding variable, which is, in turn, assumed to have no influence on the long-term trends of the other variables. Such long-run independence among the variables indicates our implicit assumption that there is no long-run effect of fiscal measures on GDP. Thus, our model is focused on evaluating the effectiveness of fiscal policy not in terms of raising the long-run economic growth but in terms of controlling the short-term fluctuations.

Before discussing further the detrending procedure, we have to consider that all the components in X_t tend to have seasonality. Blanchard and Perotti (2002) introduce quarterly dependency to the estimation of $A(L)$ in a form of $A(L, q)$ instead of using seasonally adjusted data. Depending on the number of observations available, the use of the quarterly dependent version of equation (1) could be considered. Otherwise, a usual method of eliminating the seasonality, such as X-12, could be applied.

So far the VAR system in equation (1) has not been fully specified. Detailed assumptions on the disturbance term U_t as well as the long-term trend D_t are added as follows. To begin with, two types of detrending procedures are taken in the paper. One is linearly detrending with respect to time (X^{LD}) and the other is detrending by Hodrick-Prescott filtered data (X^{DHP}).

$$X_t^{LD} \equiv X_t - Dt, \; X_t^{DHP} \equiv X_t - X_t^{HP}$$

By plugging X^{LD} or X^{DHP}, we represent the VAR system of equation (1) in a neat way.

$$(2) \qquad X_t^{DHP} = A(L)X_{t-1}^{DHP} + U_t$$

$$X_t^{LD} = A(L)X_{t-1}^{LD} + U_t$$

The long-term time trend D_t disappears in equation (2) because the vectors X^{LD} and X^{DHP} are consisting of detrended variables.

Second, our paper tries three different specifications on the disturbance term U_t. A general form of U_t could be represented as follows ($[e_t^t, e_t^g, e_t^y]$ are orthogonal to each other):

$$(3) \qquad \begin{pmatrix} t_t \\ g_t \\ y_t \end{pmatrix} \equiv \begin{pmatrix} 0 & \alpha_2 & \alpha_3 \\ \beta_1 & 0 & \beta_3 \\ \gamma_1 & \gamma_2 & 0 \end{pmatrix} \begin{pmatrix} t_t \\ g_t \\ y_t \end{pmatrix} + \begin{pmatrix} 1 & a_2 & a_3 \\ b_1 & 1 & b_3 \\ c_1 & c_2 & 1 \end{pmatrix} \begin{pmatrix} e_t^t \\ e_t^g \\ e_t^y \end{pmatrix}$$

Due to identifiability, equation (3) requires additional restrictions on the coefficients. As special cases of the previous equation, we consider Cholesky decomposition (in various combinations of ordering variables) and two identification strategies exploiting institutional information.

First, the Cholesky decomposition restricts the coefficients of equation (3) in the following way (for example, in the order of tax revenue, expenditure, and GDP):

$$(4) \qquad \begin{pmatrix} t_t \\ g_t \\ y_t \end{pmatrix} \equiv \begin{pmatrix} 0 & 0 & 0 \\ 0 & 0 & 0 \\ 0 & 0 & 0 \end{pmatrix} \begin{pmatrix} t_t \\ g_t \\ y_t \end{pmatrix} + \begin{pmatrix} 1 & 0 & 0 \\ b_1 & 1 & 0 \\ c_1 & c_2 & 1 \end{pmatrix} \begin{pmatrix} e_t^t \\ e_t^g \\ e_t^y \end{pmatrix}$$

Identification of shocks by Cholesky decomposition, though easy to use, is vulnerable to change in the order of decomposition, which is usually arbitrarily set.[6] Therefore, in the case of using the Cholesky decomposition without any prior information about the structure of shocks, all the probable combinations of shock orderings should be tested and compared for robustness check.[7]

Another problematic feature of Cholesky decomposition lies in that it defines the contemporaneous relation among the disturbance term U_t only in a recursive way. Accordingly, nonrecursively structured contemporaneous relations could not be identified by the Cholesky decomposition. Furthermore, the misspecification of the contemporaneous relation results in an imprecise estimation of impulse responses both in terms of sign and magnitude.

Second, as a typical example of institutional identification strategies, we adopt Blanchard and Perotti (B-P; 2002), whose shock identification is represented as

$$(5) \qquad \begin{pmatrix} t_t \\ g_t \\ y_t \end{pmatrix} = \begin{pmatrix} 0 & 0 & \alpha_3 \\ 0 & 0 & \beta^3 \\ \gamma_1 & \gamma_2 & 0 \end{pmatrix} \begin{pmatrix} t_t \\ g_t \\ y_t \end{pmatrix} + \begin{pmatrix} 1 & a_2 & 0 \\ b_1 & 1 & 0 \\ 0 & 0 & 1 \end{pmatrix} \begin{pmatrix} e_t^t \\ e_t^g \\ e_t^y \end{pmatrix}$$

Equation (5) reduces the number of parameters to estimate by borrowing the information on the GDP (or tax base) elasticities of tax revenue (α_3) from external sources. In addition, B-P assume the GDP shock has no contemporaneous impact on the government spending ($\beta_3 = 0$). Then, they divide equation (5) into two cases by setting $a_2 = 0$, or $b_1 = 0$, alternatively.

The third identification strategy, which also depends on the institutional information, borrows the restrictions on β_1 and β_3 ($= 0$) from the budget data in addition to α_3, based on the almost common perception that the government of Korea has kept the principle of "Expenditure within Revenue" since the 1980s (Koh 2002 and Lee and Kim 2004).[8] Due to the long

6. In most cases shock ordering is determined by the Granger causality test. However, the test itself is very vulnerable to permitted number of lags. Furthermore, it cannot put shocks in order when the causality holds in both directions between any pair of the variables.

7. De Castro (2004) analyzes a five-variable VAR model with varying orders of Cholesky decomposition. The five variables include price and interest rate in addition to GDP, government spending, and tax revenue. Due to the inclusion of the price variables, the five-variable setup could examine the crowding-out effect revealed on them.

8. Quoted from Koh (2002): "One important principle in fiscal management was established in this period. It was the principle of 'Expenditure within Revenue,' or the balanced

tradition of balanced budget, the level of expenditure still tends to be determined within the revenue forecasts. Exploiting such fiscal conservatism, we assign a restriction on β_1 by running a regression of expenditure increment on tax revenue increase and borrowing the coefficient thereof. Compared with previous identification strategies, the third one highlights the contemporaneous relation in the disturbance term U_t.

$$
(6) \qquad \begin{pmatrix} t_t \\ g_t \\ y_t \end{pmatrix} \equiv \begin{pmatrix} 0 & \alpha_2 & \alpha_3 \\ \beta_1 & 0 & \beta_3 \\ \gamma_1 & \gamma_2 & 0 \end{pmatrix} \begin{pmatrix} t_t \\ g_t \\ y_t \end{pmatrix} + \begin{pmatrix} 1 & 0 & 0 \\ 0 & 1 & 0 \\ 0 & 0 & 1 \end{pmatrix} \begin{pmatrix} e_t^t \\ e_t^g \\ e_t^y \end{pmatrix}
$$

In the next section we report the results from applying equations (4) through (6) to equation (2) sequentially. Impulse-response functions are estimated with their 95 percent confidence intervals.[9] By comparing the results derived from different contemporaneous relations among the shocks, we could check the robustness of the SVAR models.

3.4   Empirical Results

3.4.1   Data

Our empirical works are based on the data in *Monthly Statistical Bulletin,* published by Bank of Korea. The data set includes the period from 1979Q1 to 2000Q4. However, its time coverage cannot be extended beyond year 2000 because, as of 2001, the Korean government introduced a new fiscal information system based on the consolidated budget, which is not compatible with the old data. Furthermore, the new data set of consolidated budget is not back-dated prior to 1994. Though the concept of consolidated budget seems more appropriate for the purpose of our research, we choose the Bank of Korea data for their relatively long span of time series.

Figure 3.1 draws the past trends of the government expenditure, tax revenue, and GDP, all of which are measured in logarized per capita real terms. It shows all the three variables tend to follow certain time trends. In addition, though not apparent in the figure, we observe that strong seasonality is present in all of the three variables. Thus, we process the data by eliminating seasonality (X-12) and the long-term time trend (linear time trend or H-P filtered) sequentially.

In order to check the presence of nonstationarity, Augmented Dickey Fuller (ADF) unit root tests are done for the variables, which are already seasonally adjusted and detrended (X^{LD}, X^{DHP}). The tests report that only

---

budget principle. While not formalized in a law or a regulation, it acted as self-discipline imposed on the budget authorities against imprudent management of the budget."

9. The confidence level of 95 percent is used because it is a sort of academic norm. However, when the results are reflected on policy making, the level of 95 percent may not be taken as a golden rule.

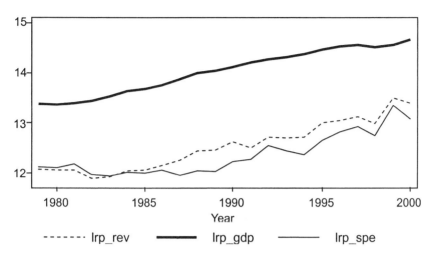

Fig. 3.1   Trends of government expenditure, tax revenue, and GDP (quarterly data from 1979Q1–2000Q4)

the linearly detrended Y_t (the logarized per capita real GDP) seems to follow $I(1)$.[10]

3.4.2   Results

Tested models have in common that all the variables used are logarized and their differences denote change rates of the corresponding variables. Accordingly, the values of impulse responses denote the GDP growth rates over a certain period following an innovation (of a certain magnitude) in the growth rate of tax revenue, or expenditure, or GDP itself.

In addition, the size of innovation to be applied in calculating an impulse response function is set to be 1 standard deviation of each error term in (e_t^t, e_t^g, e_t^y). Hence, the elasticity of per capita GDP with respect to either of the fiscal stimuli is defined to be the ratio of log GDP change (GDP growth rate) to the sample standard deviation of the corresponding innovation term (the change rate of the relevant fiscal variable).

Considering that the current government expenditure and tax revenue in Korea is roughly 25 to 30 percent of GDP in size, we can convert the elasticity of per capita GDP to fiscal stimulus into a usual fiscal multiplier by multiplying 3 or 4 to the elasticity.

Lag orders used in the VAR estimations are set to four, as is selected by Akaike's Information Criteria (AIC). The lag order of 4 is quite common in other literature using quarterly data, such as Blanchard and Perotti (2002) and De Castro (2004).

10. Rothenberg and Stock (1997) show that the coefficients of a VAR system estimated by OLS are consistent even though some level variables follow I(1).

Table 3.3   Impulse-response functions of key variables (linearly detrended) by
                         Cholesky ordering (in the order of tax revenue, expenditures, GDP)

Quarter	OIRF(1)	Lower(1)	Upper(1)	OIRF(2)	Lower(2)	Upper(2)
0	0.0034	–0.0001	0.0068	0.0042	0.0009	0.0076
1	0.0011	–0.0037	0.0058	0.0054	0.0008	0.0101
2	–0.0013	–0.0073	0.0047	0.0067	0.0011	0.0123
3	–0.0033	–0.0102	0.0037	0.0075	0.0010	0.0141
4	–0.0049	–0.0121	0.0023	0.0042	–0.0027	0.0112
5	–0.0064	–0.0139	0.0010	0.0038	–0.0036	0.0113
6	–0.0084	–0.0160	–0.0008	0.0031	–0.0046	0.0108
7	–0.0089	–0.0167	–0.0011	0.0021	–0.0059	0.0100
8	–0.0087	–0.0166	–0.0008	0.0016	–0.0065	0.0096
9	–0.0088	–0.0168	–0.0008	0.0011	–0.0071	0.0093
10	–0.0088	–0.0169	–0.0008	0.0003	–0.0080	0.0087

Notes: 95 percent lower and upper bounds reported. (1) impulse = tax revenue, and
response = GDP. (2) impulse = expenditures, and response = GDP.

Cholesky Decomposition

Table 3.3 summarizes the estimation results of equation (4) in the order
of tax revenue, government expenditure, and real GDP with the linearly
detrended data. Dividing the responses of GDP to the impulses of tax revenue and the government spending in table 3.3 by the estimated sample
standard deviations of innovation terms $(e_t^t, e_t^g, e_t^y) = (0.085, 0.058, 0.016)$,
we can obtain the elasticities of GDP with respect to fiscal stimuli, which
can be in turn converted into series of fiscal multipliers. Figure 3.2 draws
impulse-response functions for all the three variables.

According to table 3.3, impulse responses of GDP have significantly
negative values for the sixth to tenth quarters after a shock in tax revenue.
On the other hand, impulse responses to an expenditure shock hold significantly negative signs up to the third quarter. By dividing them first by $(e_t^t,$
$e_t^g) = (0.085, 0.058)$ each and multiply them by 3 to 4 next, we can convert
these significant estimates of impulse responses to fiscal multipliers.[11] The
accumulated fiscal multipliers of tax revenue and government spending
(up to 10 quarters) are about –2 ~ –1.5 and 1.2 ~ 1.6.[12] Though these numbers seem plausible in terms of signs and magnitudes, they are based on the
estimates for c_1 and c_2, which interpret the contemporaneous relations between t_t, g_t and y_t imprecisely.[13] Therefore, the results in table 3.3 should not
be heavily relied on.

11. An accumulated fiscal multiplier is the sum of fiscal multipliers up to the current period.
12. Here an accumulated fiscal multiplier is defined to be the sum of impulse responses,
which reject a null hypothesis of zero value with 5 percent significance.
13. Especially the estimate for c_1 holds a positive sign, which implies that tax revenue increase has positive contemporaneous impact on GDP. However, it would be more appropriate to assume that GDP increase has positive contemporaneous impact on tax revenue,
whereas tax increase has negative contemporaneous impact on GDP.

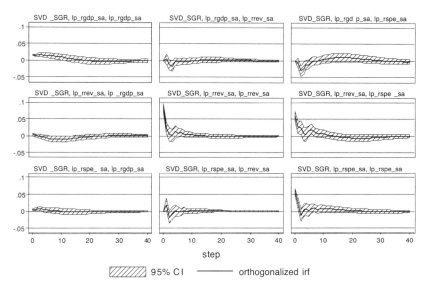

Fig. 3.2   Impulse-response functions of key variables (linearly detrended) by Cholesky ordering (in the order of tax revenue, expenditures, GDP)

Table 3.4 summarizes the estimation results of equation (4) with the data detrended by H-P filter. In this case, the responses of GDP to the impulses of tax revenue and the government spending are either very small or statistically insignificant.[14] Figure 3.3 draws impulse-response functions for all the three variables.

In table 3.4 impulse responses of GDP have significantly positive signs for the first two quarters following a shock in tax revenue, while impulse responses to an expenditure shock hold significantly positive signs up to the second quarter and significantly negative signs for the sixth and seventh quarters. The positive effects of tax revenue increase as well as the negative effects of government expenditure increase on GDP are contrary to our general notion of Keynesianism. The accumulated fiscal multipliers of tax revenue and government expenditure range in $0.3 \sim 0.5$ and $0.03 \sim 0.05$ respectively. However, as in the previous case, these numbers are based on the imprecise estimates for c_1 and c_2. Therefore, the results in table 3.4 should not be heavily relied on, either.

The previous two cases of Cholesky decomposition are done in the order of tax revenue, government expenditure, and GDP. As for other possible combinations of shock ordering, we find the impulse-response functions diverging not only in their sign and size but also in their timing of effects and statistical significance.

14. For this case, the estimated sample standard deviations of innovation terms are $(e_t^t, e_t^g, e_t^y) = (0.077, 0.056, 0.013)$.

Table 3.4   Impulse-response functions of interest variables (detrended by H-P filter) by Cholesky ordering (in the order of tax revenue, expenditure, GDP)

Quarter	OIRF(1)	Lower(1)	Upper(1)	OIRF(2)	Lower(2)	Upper(2)
0	0.0053	0.0023	0.0082	0.0039	0.0011	0.0067
1	0.0042	0.0005	0.0080	0.0038	0.0002	0.0074
2	0.0033	−0.0010	0.0077	0.0025	−0.0017	0.0067
3	0.0027	−0.0019	0.0072	0.0020	−0.0024	0.0065
4	0.0022	−0.0024	0.0067	−0.0023	−0.0068	0.0022
5	0.0002	−0.0031	0.0035	−0.0025	−0.0064	0.0013
6	−0.0013	−0.0039	0.0014	−0.0034	−0.0068	−0.0001
7	−0.0019	−0.0044	0.0006	−0.0036	−0.0067	−0.0006
8	−0.0017	−0.0043	0.0009	−0.0025	−0.0051	0.0001
9	−0.0014	−0.0039	0.0011	−0.0016	−0.0040	0.0009
10	−0.0009	−0.0032	0.0013	−0.0006	−0.0030	0.0018

Note: See table 3.3 notes.

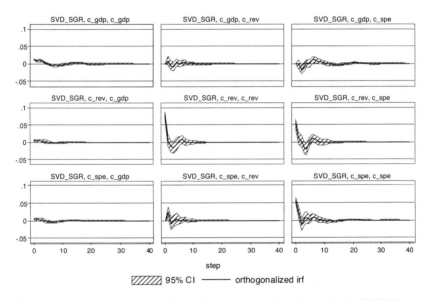

Fig. 3.3   Impulse-response functions of interest variables (detrended by H-P filter) by Cholesky ordering (in the order of tax revenue, expenditure, GDP)

Identification by Using Institutional Information (B-P [2002])

B-P (2002), based on equation (5), borrow institutional information on α_3 from the calculation of GDP or tax bases elasticities of tax revenues. The additional restrictions, such as $\beta_3 = a_2 = 0$ or $\beta_3 = b_1 = 0$, seem rather arbitrary. While repeating the same procedure as in B-P (2002), we adopt the

Table 3.5   **Estimation of contemporaneous effect ($\alpha_3 = 1.09$ and $\beta_3 = 0$)**

	γ_1	γ_2	$a_2(b_1 = 0)$	$b_1(a_2 = 0)$
	A Linearly detrended			
Estimate	−0.086***	0.129***	0.659***	0.656***
t-value	−2.73	4.03	7.90	7.90
	B. Detrended by H-P filter			
Estimate	−0.037***	0.110***	0.603***	0.655***
t-value	−1.37	4.1	7.32	7.32

***Significance level of less than 1 percent.

elasticities of tax revenues in Korea from Park and Park (2002) and assign $\alpha_3 = 1.09$.[15]

Table 3.5 shows the estimation results of the contemporaneous effects using the residuals of the VAR systems in equation (2). The signs of contemporaneous effects of innovations in tax revenues and spending on the disturbance of GDP (γ_1 and γ_2) are consistent with our anticipation that tax increase reduces GDP while spending spurs it.

Table 3.6 compares the indirect contemporaneous effect of the automatic stabilization mechanism (ASM) and the direct contemporaneous effect of discretionary fiscal policy. The direct contemporaneous effects of fiscal innovations are measured by the estimates of γ_1 and γ_2. However, the changes in GDP influences back the tax revenue and the government spending in the form of t_t and/or g_t, from which the ASM takes over. Summing up the direct and the indirect contemporaneous effects, we obtain the value of total contemporaneous effect following an innovation in the fiscal sector.

From table 3.6, we see that the positive indirect contemporaneous effects of the ASM dominates the negative direct impact of discretionary fiscal impulse in the case of tax shocks and $a_2 = 0$, while the direct effect of a spending shock is always greater than the indirect effect of the ASM followed.

In times of nonintervention, it is known that the built-in ASM smoothes out the fluctuation of a business cycle and reduces the need for government intervention. But in times of government intervention, the presence of the ASM works as friction against a policy maker, who intends to resize his or her fiscal programs for the purpose of controlling the business cycle. The results from table 3.6 indicate that the adjustment in tax has more to lose than to win, at least contemporaneously, once it is used, whereas that in the government spending still maintains its validity as intended.

15. Park and Park use the consolidated budget data from 1991 to 2002 (annual). They classify the current tax revenues in Korea in four groups (income tax, corporate tax, indirect tax, and social security contribution) and calculate the elasticity of tax revenue with respect to tax base for each group. $\alpha_3 = 1.09$ is the weighted average of the four tax elasticities by the proportion of tax revenues to GDP.

Table 3.6   Decomposition of contemporaneous effects as a sum of the direct effect from discretionary policy and the indirect effect from automatic stabilization mechanism (ASM; $\alpha_3 = 1.09$ and $\beta_3 = 0$)

	$a_2 = 0$		$b_1 = 0$	
	Tax	Spending	Tax	Spending
A. Linearly detrended				
Discretionary policy	–0.086	0.129	–0.086	0.129
ASM	0.087	–0.016	0.012	–0.064
Contemporaneous effects	0.001	0.113	–0.074	0.065
B. Detrended by H-P filter				
Discretionary policy	–0.037	0.110	–0.037	0.110
ASM	0.081	–0.014	0.018	–0.025
Contemporaneous effects	0.044	0.096	–0.019	0.085

Figures 3.4–3.9 display the impulse-response functions of GDP with respect to tax revenue, government expenditure, and GDP, using the linearly detrended data, while figures 3.10–3.15 display the impulse-response functions using the data detrended by H-P filter. Comparing these two groups of figures, we infer that the linear time trend may detect (or exaggerate) the persistence of the fiscal shocks on GDP treatment of long-term trends, whereas H-P filter detrending may miss (or underestimate) the persistence. Especially, the persistence of tax revenue on GDP varies drastically depending on the treatment of long-term trends.[16]

Whichever detrending method may be taken, the figures of impulse responses show that the positive effect of expenditure policy is statistically significant only in the very short run (no longer than three quarters). On the other hand, the effect of tax increase is not significant in any case. Converted into fiscal multipliers, even the significant impulse responses have very small magnitudes less than 0.4. Hence, the effectiveness of fiscal policy is not confirmed under B-P identification strategy.[17]

Identification by Using "Expenditure within Revenue" Principle

The third identification strategy (6) borrows the restrictions on β_1 ($= 0.598$) from the government budget data in addition to α_3, based on the perception of the "Expenditure within Revenue (EWR)" rule prevalent in the 1980s and 1990s in Korea. This identification strategy differs from B-P (2002) in that it allows contemporaneous duplex relation between x_t and g_t.

16. Tax policy seems to have more persistent effect on GDP than revenue policy under the linear time trend, which tends to leave the nonlinear long-term trend. Accordingly, it remains a question whether the tax policy influences the long-term GDP growth or the nonlinear long-term trends of tax and GDP incidentally commove in a linear way.

17. Disregarding the 95 percent confidence interval and focusing on the fitted line of the impulse responses, we could have obtained the high value of accumulated fiscal multipliers in figure 3.4, figure 3.7, and figure 3.8.

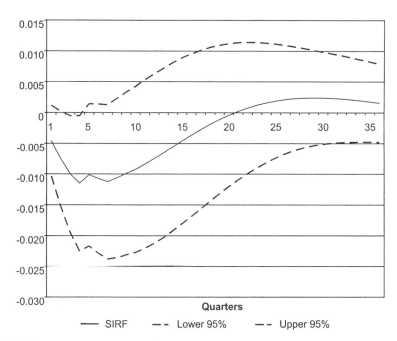

Fig. 3.4   Impulse responses of GDP to tax revenue estimated by B-P (2002; linearly detrended and setting $b_1 = 0$)

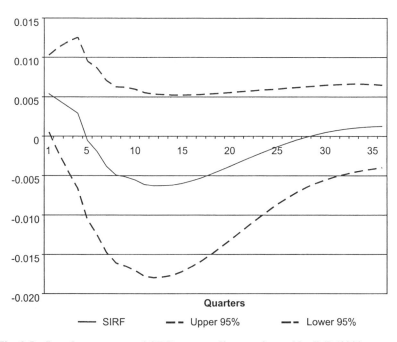

Fig. 3.5   Impulse responses of GDP to expenditure estimated by B-P (2002; linearly detrended and setting $b_1 = 0$)

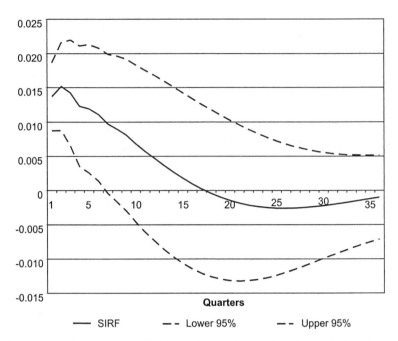

Fig. 3.6 Impulse responses of GDP on GDP estimated by B-P (2002; linearly detrended and setting $b_1 = 0$)

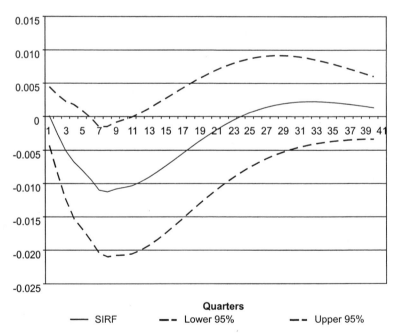

Fig. 3.7 Impulse responses of GDP to tax revenue estimated by B-P (2002; linearly detrended and setting $a_2 = 0$)

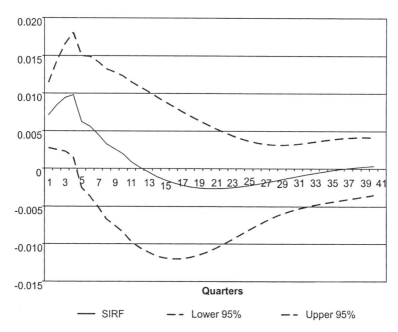

Fig. 3.8   Impulse responses of GDP to expenditure estimated by B-P (2002; linearly detrended and setting $a_2 = 0$)

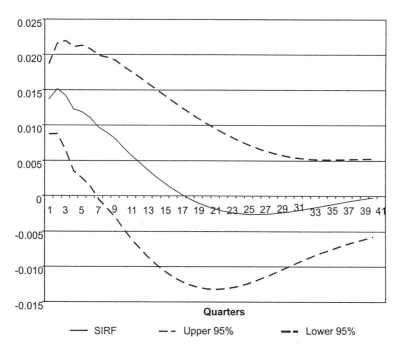

Fig. 3.9   Impulse responses of GDP on GDP estimated by B-P (2002; linearly detrended and setting $a_2 = 0$)

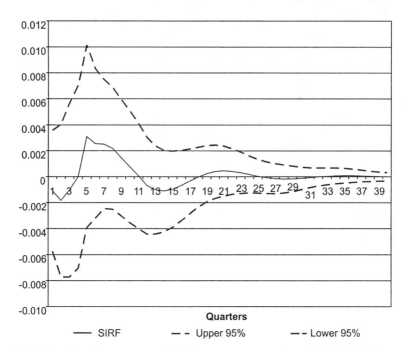

Fig. 3.10   Impulse responses of GDP to tax revenue estimated by B-P (2002; detrended by H-P filter and setting $b_1 = 0$)

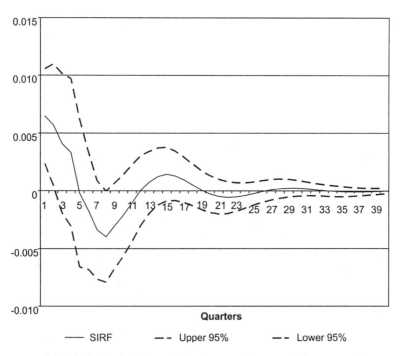

Fig. 3.11   Impulse responses of GDP to expenditure estimated by B-P (2002; detrended by H-P filter and setting $b_1 = 0$)

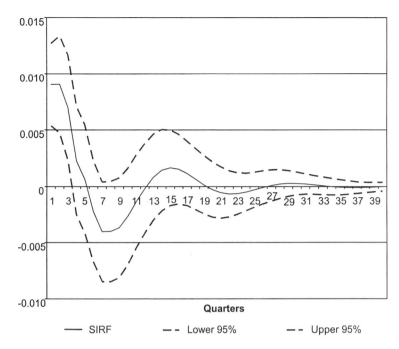

Fig. 3.12   Impulse responses of GDP on GDP estimated by B-P (2002; detrended by H-P filter and setting $b_1 = 0$)

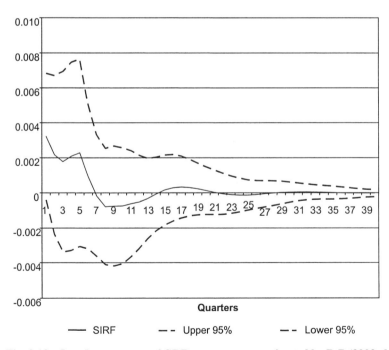

Fig. 3.13   Impulse responses of GDP to tax revenue estimated by B-P (2002; detrended by H-P filter and setting $a_2 = 0$)

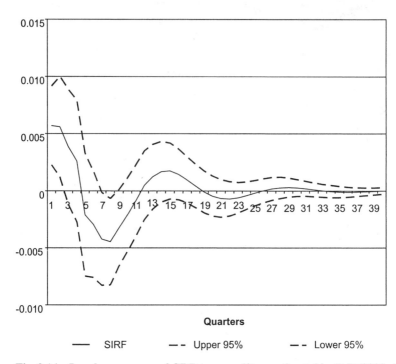

Fig. 3.14   Impulse responses of GDP to expenditure estimated by B-P (2002; de-trended by H-P filter and setting $a_2 = 0$)

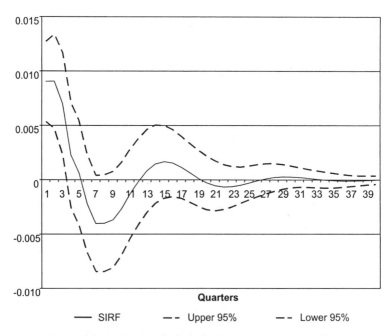

Fig. 3.15   Impulse responses of GDP on GDP estimated by B-P (2002; detrended by H-P filter and setting $a_2 = 0$)

Instead it restricts that the errors of the disturbances, (e_t^t, e_t^g, e_t^y), should be orthogonal to each other.

Table 3.7 reports the estimated contemporaneous effects of fiscal disturbances on GDP. The signs of the direct contemporaneous effects (γ_1 and γ_2) are consistent with those in table 3.5. For both detrending methods, the contemporaneous effects from the ASM are much greater than those of the discretionary tax shocks (table 3.8), which is opposite to the case of spending shocks. Such prevailing effect of the ASM, which works against the intended direction of discretionary revenue policy, is consistent with Keynesian wisdom that tax multiplier is smaller than that of spending.

Figures 3.16–3.18 draw the impulse responses of GDP to tax revenue, expenditure, and GDP with the linearly detrended data, and figures 3.19–3.21 draw the impulse responses with the data detrended by H-P filter. Some notable points from the figures are as follows. First, increasing spending has a significantly positive effect on GDP for the first 3 to 5 quarters regardless of a detrending method (though their magnitudes are also negligible when converted into fiscal multipliers). Second, tax increase has

Table 3.7   Estimation of contemporaneous effect ($\alpha_3 = 1.09$, $\alpha_2 = 0$, $\beta_1 = 0.598$, $\beta_2 = 0$)

	γ_1	γ_2
A. Linearly detrended		
Estimate	–0.056*	0.082***
t-value	–1.84	2.67
B. Detrended by H-P filter		
Estimate	–0.014	0.075**
t-value	–0.55	2.86

***Significance level of less than 1 percent.
**Significance level of less than 5 percent.
*Significance level of less than 10 percent.

Table 3.8   Decomposition of contemporaneous effects as a sum of the direct effect from discretionary policy and the indirect effect from automatic stabilization mechanism (ASM; $\alpha_3 = 1.09$, $\alpha_2 = 0$, $\beta_1 = 0.598$, $\beta_2 = 0$)

	Tax	Spending
A. Linearly detrended		
Discretionary policy	–0.056	0.082
ASM	0.062	–0.076
Contemporaneous effects	0.006	0.006
B. Detrended by H-P filter		
Discretionary policy	–0.014	0.075
ASM	0.022	–0.070
Contemporaneous effects	0.008	0.005

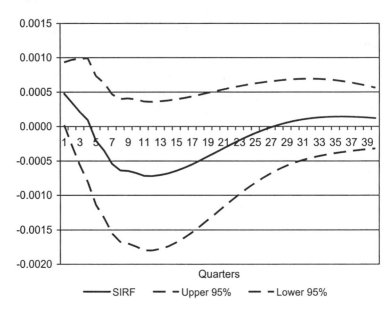

Fig. 3.16   Impulse responses of GDP to tax revenue estimated by alternative institutional identifying restrictions (linearly detrended)

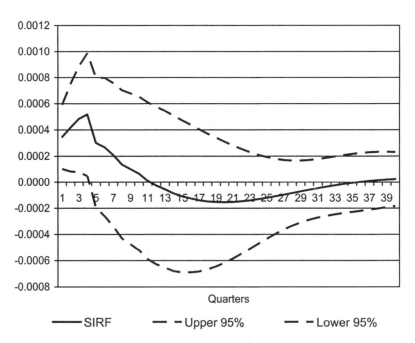

Fig. 3.17   Impulse responses of GDP to expenditure estimated by alternative institutional identifying restrictions (linearly detrended)

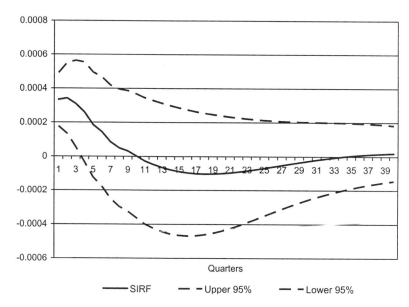

Fig. 3.18   Impulse responses of GDP on GDP estimated by alternative institutional identifying restrictions (linearly detrended)

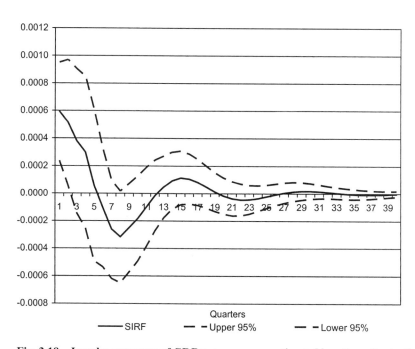

Fig. 3.19   Impulse responses of GDP to tax revenue estimated by alternative institutional identifying restrictions (detrended by H-P filter)

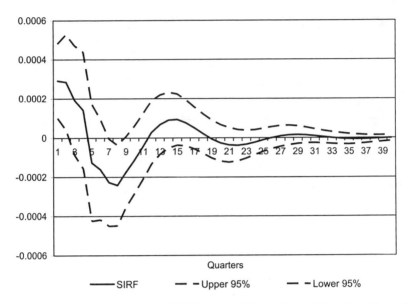

Fig. 3.20 Impulse responses of GDP to expenditure estimated by alternative institutional identifying restrictions (detrended by H-P filter)

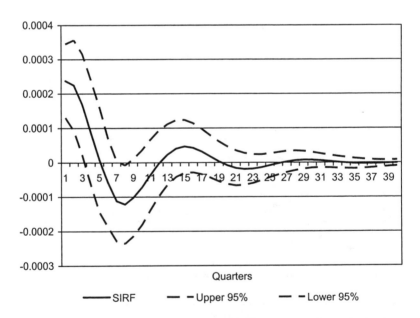

Fig. 3.21 Impulse responses of GDP on GDP estimated by alternative institutional identifying restrictions (detrended by H-P filter)

a positive effect (very short lived), which is opposite to our anticipation. As previously mentioned, it can be attributed to the dominant contemporaneous effect of the ASM. Furthermore, it seems that the persistence of the counteractive effect from the ASM dilutes the negative effect of tax increase on GDP over a long horizon, leading to insignificant fiscal impulses.

So far we have considered various identification strategies starting from usual Cholesky decomposition in this section. Their results show different predictions on the effects from discretionary fiscal policy not only in terms of magnitudes but also in terms of signs. Though most of them confirm that the expansionary fiscal stance (whether it is tax cut or spending spree) has expansionary effect on the economy, we cannot believe that this demonstrates the effectiveness of the fiscal policy considering most of the 95 percent significance intervals cover both negative and positive ranges.

3.4.3 Results from 4 Variable VARs Allowing Outside Shocks

In this section we check whether there exist omitted variables and if their inclusion would determine the signs of effects between fiscal variables and business cycle.

Considering the trade dependence of the Korean economy, we infer that shocks of foreign origination may have critical impacts on the Korean economy, which will result in different estimations of impulse-response functions. Hence, we select the per capita real GDP of US(Y_t^{US} in logarithms) and the real effective exchange rate of Korean currency (logarized REER) for the most critical omitted variables and we add these two variables to the estimation of (2) one by one.[18] The importance of the U.S. economy in determining the growth path of the Korean economy is needless to say. REER is included because its time path has been very responsive to the past economic turmoils including the recent currency crisis.[19]

Shock-identification strategies for the new set of four-variable VAR systems take a dual approach, which maintains (4) through (6) among the existing three variables and requires Cholesky decomposition between a newly introduced variable for external shocks and the vector of the existing variables.

Table 3.9 summarizes the estimation results of the four-variable VAR systems in terms of elasticities (both one period and accumulated).[20] The elas-

---

18. In addition to them, we try the Terms Of Trade (TOT) as an exogenous variable to equation (2). However, the previous results stay unchanged.

19. Following Ramey and Shapiro (1998), the VAR literature treats certain economic episodes with dummies. However, this way of identifying structural breaks is not appropriate for our analysis because the end point of the data set (2000 Q4) is not far enough from the starting point of the Korean currency crisis (1997 Q4). In this situation, REER can be substituted for a dummy of the currency crisis.

20. Divided by the proportion of government expenditure or revenue to GDP, these elasticities are easily converted into the fiscal multipliers (in the unit of Korean currency). Though it varies year by year, the proportion of government expenditure or revenue to GDP is approximately 25 to 30 percent. Thus, the fiscal multipliers will be approximately three to four times of the elasticities in table 3.9.

Table 3.9   The elasticities of real GDP to the shocks from various sources

Group	Shock identification	Elasticity	External shock	Revenue (tax) shock	Expenditure shock
I	Cholesky	One period	n.a.	n.a.	0.086(0)
	decomposition	Accumulated	n.a.	n.a.	0.153(0~1)
	BP(2002):	One period	n.a.	0.043(1)	0.137(2)
	$a_2 = 0$	Accumulated	n.a.	0.081(0~1)	**0.3840(0~2)**
	BP(2002):	One period	n.a.	−0.170(3)	n.a.
	$b_1 = 0$	Accumulated	n.a.	**−1.745(0~13)**	n.a.
	EWR	One period	n.a.	−0.131(7)	0.094(1)
		Accumulated	n.a.	**−1.492(0~17)**	0.171(0~1)
II	Cholesky	One period	n.a.	n.a.	0.069(0)
	decomposition	Accumulated	n.a.	n.a.	0.135(0~1)
	BP(2002):	One period	n.a.	0.042(0)	0.107(0)
	$a_2 = 0$	Accumulated	n.a.	0.042(0)	0.199(0~1)
	BP(2002):	One period	n.a.	−0.044(0)	0.079(0)
	$b_1 = 0$	Accumulated	n.a.	−0.078(0~1)	0.151(0~1)
	EWR	One period	n.a.	n.a.	0.078(0)
		Accumulated	n.a.	n.a.	0.152(0~1)
III	Cholesky	One period	−0.283(2)	n.a.	0.068(0)
	decomposition	Accumulated	−1.316(0~5)	n.a.	0.068(0)
	BP(2002):	One period	−0.283(2)	0.053(0)	0.097(0)
	$a_2 = 0$	Accumulated	−1.316(0~5)	0.249(0~3)	0.097(0)
	BP(2002):	One period	−0.283(2)	−0.125(2)	n.a.
	$b_1 = 0$	Accumulated	−1.317(0~5)	**−1.848(0~24)**	n.a.
	EWR	One period	−0.277(2)	n.a.	0.070(0)
		Accumulated	−1.102(0~4)	n.a.	0.070(0)
IV	Cholesky	One period	−0.203(1)	0.043(0)	0.071(0)
	decomposition	Accumulated	−0.659(0~3)	0.043(0)	0.071(0)
	BP(2002):	One period	−0.203(1)	0.060(0)	0.095(0)
	$a_2 = 0$	Accumulated	−0.659(0~3)	0.116(0~1)	0.095(0)
	BP(2002):	One period	−0.203(1)	−0.048(1)	0.072(0)
	$b_1 = 0$	Accumulated	−0.659(0~3)	−0.142(0~3)	0.072(0)
	EWR	One period	−0.198(1)	n.a.	0.072(0)
		Accumulated	−0.638(0~3)	n.a.	0.072(0)

Note: All numbers in parentheses denote the corresponding quarter(s) to the elasticities on the left.

ticities are calculated by dividing the impulse-response functions by the standard deviations of the corresponding orthogonalized disturbance terms e_t^x, e_t^t, e_t^g, and e_t^y. Then the elasticities are recorded only when their signs are statistically significant in 95 percent confidence intervals. Groups (I) and (III) describe the results from running the VAR model with the linearly detrended data while groups (II) and (IV) deal with the data detrended by H-P filter. In the meantime, groups (I) and (II) include the real per capita GDP of US in log scale as a measure for the exogenous shock whereas groups (III) and (IV) use the logarized REER instead. In each group, the four-identification strategies, which are defined in the previous section, are dealt with.

Compared with the previous three-variable VAR setup, the following points are notable in the results from the four-variable VAR. First, the significance of fiscal stimulus in boosting the economy has been enhanced overall regardless of the origination of the shock (either from the revenue or expenditure of the government). The increased significance of the fiscal impact can be attributed to the inclusion of the new variables (real per capita GDP of the United States and REER), which eliminate noises in the real per capita GDP of Korea.

Second, however, the magnitudes of the fiscal multipliers (which will be approximately 3 to 4 times of the elasticities) still remain small. Out of the 16 cases in table 3.7, only three cases report the accumulated fiscal multipliers greater than 1 for a revenue shock and one case for an expenditure shock.[21] Since these four exceptions deal with the linearly detrended data in common, it is inferred that the linear detrending may not be satisfactory to catch the nonlinear time trend of the real GDP. Combined with the linear detrending, it seems that the B-P (2002) identification strategy of setting $b_1 = 0$ emphasizes or exaggerates the transmission channels of a revenue shock.

Third, the persistence of fiscal stimuli is very short lived and cannot last longer than three quarters, except the three cases, all of which respond to a revenue shock. This persistence issue also seems to be linked to the selection of a detrending method.

Summing up, we see that the effectiveness of fiscal policy is significantly enhanced by introducing external shocks. However, in most cases the magnitudes of the fiscal multipliers and the duration of effectiveness are small or short lived, which are violated only when the linear detrending is adopted.

3.4.4   Robustness of the Results to Other Variations in Specification

The previous tested models are based on several restrictions, which are, we may suspect, possible causes of driving fiscal policy ineffectiveness. Among the restrictions, we are particularly interested in comprehending whether the selection of different lag orders, sample periods and filters as well as differencing some nonstationary variables, would confirm the effectiveness of fiscal policies.

First, we elect other criteria of lag orders. Previously, lag orders were selected by Akaike's Information Criteria (AIC). According to Lutkepohl (1993), the Bayesian Information Criteria (BIC) provides consistent estimates of the true lag order, whereas minimizing the AIC tends to overestimate the true lag order. The use of BIC to the Korean data suggests the lag

---

21. The arbitrarily set criterion for the accumulated fiscal multiplier is 1. To maintain the budget balance after a fiscal expansion, the accumulated fiscal multiplier should exceed $1/\tau$ (τ = Tax_revenue/GDP), so called a balanced budget fiscal multiplier. Considering that $\tau \approx 0.25$ in Korea, the balanced budget fiscal multipliers should be about four. In table 3.4, only three cases of revenue shocks report fiscal multipliers greater than four. For the rest of the cases fiscal expansion will aggravate the fiscal consolidation.

of one, which is much smaller than the lag of four prescribed by AIC. Thus, we run the previously defined VAR setup with the reduced lag of one. However, these results also fail in confirming the effectiveness of fiscal policy.

Second, we introduce a dummy variable, which discerns the sample periods in two parts—before and after a currency crisis in late 1997. Even with the currency crisis dummy included, the effectiveness of fiscal policies cannot be significantly identified.[22]

Third, we adopt the Baxter and King's (1995) band pass filter instead of the H-P filter. The replacement of the detrending filter does not change the results of policy ineffectiveness.[23]

Fourth, in order to handle the nonstationarity of some variables, we take a routine measure of differencing all the variables or the real GDP only. Another option we choose is to investigate possible cointegration among the series and take a vector error correction form accordingly (Hamilton 1994). However, in either of them expansionary effects of fiscal stimuli are not confirmed.

3.5   Concluding Remarks

Summing up, our paper has shown that the effectiveness of fiscal policy is not significantly identified in Korea regardless of policy measures, tax reduction, or spending increase, or of methods of identifying shocks.[24] Though significantly identified in some cases, the effect from the fiscal policy is either very small in magnitude or it phases out very quickly or it is caused by linear detrending.[25] Such a low contribution of fiscal policy in economic stabilization provides many points to ponder in steering the future research on this issue.[26]

There are various ways of explaining the low performance of fiscal policy as a vehicle of boosting Korean economy. The first and easiest guess would be to accept the new classical argument. However, the question of

22. The BOK data set ends in the fourth quarter of 2000 and the number of observations after the currency crisis is very small. Accordingly, we compare the results from the consolidated budget data, which cover the period from 1994 to 2005 Q2 for cross-check.

23. In this case the confidence intervals are not shrinking along the passage of time.

24. Lee and Sung (2005) compare the estimators for the fiscal responsiveness of Korea to GDP shocks from OLS and IV estimation, and they report that both estimators are almost identical. Their results, mainly intended to eliminate the estimation bias for the fiscal responsiveness, can be interpreted to imply indirectly that fiscal expansion has no substantial effect on GDP.

25. In applying Cholesky decomposition, there are some cases in which the substantial effects of fiscal stimuli are significantly identified. Even in those cases, the estimates for the fiscal multipliers are based on the imprecise identification of contemporaneous relations among the shocks. Remember that in the estimation of the four variable SVARs, all the four cases, which have fiscal multipliers greater than one, use the linearly detrended data.

26. The use of consolidated budget data instead of the BOK data cannot support the effectiveness of fiscal policy, either.

why the effectiveness of fiscal policy that is confirmed in other countries is refuted in the case of Korea still remains unsolved.[27]

The second guess is that there may not exist one-to-one correspondence between fiscal stance and the transition of a business cycle, such as matching fiscal expansion with booming or fiscal tightening with landing. In other words, there may be nonlinearity between fiscal measures and business cycles. Or there may exist an omitted and unobservable variable, the value of which changes the relationship between the fiscal variables and GDP. In such circumstances, the VAR models would not be able to detect the effectiveness of fiscal policy even if it is effective.[28]

Anyway, our paper comes to the findings, which are exactly opposite to the generally accepted Keynesian theory. Even so, it is still too early to replace it with the new classical theory. For example, Ricardian equivalence is an example of fiscal policy ineffectiveness. It does not cover all the transmission channels of fiscal policies, which our VAR setup evaluates in sum. In contrast, our setup does not identify exactly how the Ricardian equivalence argument works in an economy. Therefore, based on the achievements made by this paper, it is more desirable to continue our research in both of the following directions: verifying other possible transmission mechanisms of fiscal policies theoretically and comparing jointly their magnitudes of influence on the macro economy empirically.

References

Agenor, P-R., C. J. McDermott, and E. S. Prasad. 1999. Macroeconomic fluctuations in developing countries: Some stylized facts. IMF Working Paper 99/35. Washington, DC: International Monetary Fund.

Baxter, M., and King, R. 1995. *Measuring business cycles: Approximate band-pass filters for economic time series*. NBER Working Paper no. 5022. Cambridge, MA: National Bureau of Economic Research.

Becker, T. 1997. An investigation of Ricardian equivalence in a common trends model. *Journal of Monetary Economics* 39 (3): 405–31.

27. For one of pretests, we have done cross-country cross-sectional comparisons using World Development Indicators (by World Bank) as a measure to detect the effectiveness of fiscal policy. The result shows that the higher the government sector takes the portion in the aggregate economy the more stable the economy will be. In contrast, it also shows that the fluctuation of fiscal size doesn't have much to do with economic stabilization. Intuition behind this seemingly contradictory phenomenon is that the size of the government sector contributes to economic stability not because it can control business cycles but because it crowds out the private sector, which is more volatile than the government sector.

28. As another pretest, we ran a VAR model consisting of the estimated conditional volatilities of the growth rates in fiscal expenditures, tax revenues, and per capita real GDP in order to verify the stabilization effect of fiscal policies. The results showed that the increased volatility of fiscal expenditure growth alleviates the volatility of the GDP growth rate, which even partially supports this conjecture.

Blanchard, O. J., and R. Perotti. 2002. An empirical characterization of the dynamic effects of changes in government spending and taxes on output. *Quarterly Journal of Economics* 117:1329–68.

Choi, Jong-Soo. 2002. An empirical analysis on the Barro-Ricardo equivalence hypothesis. *Korean Journal of Public Economics* 7 (1)

De Castro, F. 2004. The macroeconomic effects of fiscal policy in Spain. *Applied Economics* 38 (May): 913–24.

De Castro, F., and P. Hernandez de Cos. 2006. *The economic effects of exogenous fiscal shocks in Spain: A SVAR approach.* European Central Bank Working Paper no. 647.

Edelberg, W., M. Eichenbaum, and J. Fisher. 1999. Understanding the effects of shocks to government purchases. *Review of Economic Studies:* 166–206.

Fatas, A., and I. Mihov. 2000. *The effects of fiscal policy on consumption and employment: Theory and evidence.* INSEAD, mimeo.

Favero, C. 2002. *How do European monetary and fiscal authorities behave?* CEPR Working Paper no. 3426.

Feldstein, M. 1982. Government deficits and aggregate demand. *Journal of Monetary Economics* 9:1329–68.

Hamilton, J. 1994. *Time series analysis.* Princeton, NJ: Princeton University Press.

Hemming, R., M. Kell, and S. Mahfouz. 2002. The effectiveness of fiscal policy in stimulating economic activity—A review of the literature. IMF Working Paper. 02/208. Washington, DC: International Monetary Fund.

Hoppner, F. 2002. *Fiscal policy and automatic stabilizers: A SVAR perspective.* Institute for International Economics, University of Bonn Lennestr.

Kim, Seong-Suhn. 1997. Relative economic effects of sectoral government expenditures on consumption, investment and income. *The Korean Journal of Public Finance* 12 (1).

———. 2003. A study on the structural change of fiscal policy after Korean currency crisis. *Quarterly Economic Analysis* 9 (4).

———. 2005. A comparison study on the fiscal spending effects to income, price money between pre- and post-currency crisis periods in Korea. *The Korean Journal of Public Finance* 20 (1).

Koh, Y. 2002. *Public expenditure management in Korea.* Mimeo.

Kormendi, R. 1983. Government debt, government spending and private sector behavior. *American Economic Review* 73 (5): 994–1010.

Lee, I., and G. Kim. 2004. Economic effects of fiscal policy and tasks toward sound public finance. *Korean Journal of Public Economics* 9:253–94.

Lee, Y., and T. Sung. 2005. *Fiscal policy, business cycles, and economic stabilization: Evidence from industrial and developing countries.* Mimeo.

Lutkepohl, H. 1993. *Introduction to multiple time series analysis,* 2nd ed. New York: Springer.

Mountford, A., and H. Uhlig. 2002. *What are the effects of fiscal policy shocks.* CEPR Working Paper no. 3338.

Park, Ha-Seob, and Choi, Jong-Soo. 1997. Some empirical tests on the Ricardian neutrality hypothesis in Korea. *The Korean Journal of Public Finance* 12 (2).

Park, Jong-Koo. 1995. Government spending and private consumption. *The Korean Journal of Public Finance* 9.

Park, Ki-baeg, and Park, Hyung-soo. 2002. *Fiscal role in economic stabilization.* Korea Institute of Public Finance.

Perotti, R. 1999. Fiscal policy in good times and bad. *Quarterly Journal of Economics* 114:1399–1436.

———. 2004. *Estimating the effects of fiscal policy in OECD countries.* Innocenzo

Gasparini Institute for Economic Research (IGIER) Working Paper no. 276. Milan, Italy: IGIER.

Ramey, V., and M. Shapiro. 1998. Costly capital reallocation and the effects of government spending. *Carnegie-Rochester Conference Series on Public Policy* 48:145–94.

Rothenberg, T., and J. Stock. 1997. Inference in a nearly integrated autoregressive model with non-normal innovations. *Journal of Econometrics:* 269–86.

Comment   Wei Li

The objective of Dr. Hur's paper is to estimate the impact of fiscal policy in Korea. To achieve this goal, Dr. Hur uses quarterly GDP, government revenue, and spending data between 1979:Q1 and 2000:Q4 and estimates structural VAR models. The paper's methodology follows those in Blanchard and Perotti (2002) and Perotti (2004), among others. In one of the SVAR models, it utilizes Korean institutional features—namely, the fiscal principle of expenditure within revenue—to impose identification restrictions. The author finds that estimated fiscal multipliers are in general small using a three variable—GDP, revenue, and spending—SVAR model, but they are larger when a fourth exogenous variable—U.S. GDP or the Real Effective Exchange Rate—is added. One note on presentation: It would be more informative if the impulse responses were transformed to report the Korean won response of each variable to a won shock to one of the fiscal variables—the conventional measure of a fiscal multiplier.

Before discussing the models and the data, let me first review the general economic environment in Korea during the sample period. Between 1979 and 2000, Korea underwent rapid economic transformation. In 1979, the first year in the sample, per capita GDP was $3,322 in constant 2000 U.S. dollars and agriculture contributed to 21 percent of GDP (World Bank 2006). By 2000, the end year in the sample, per capita GDP more than tripled to $10,884, and the contribution of agriculture to GDP fell to only 5 percent. The country's tax system also underwent structural changes. Based on data from the University of Michigan World Tax Database (2006) revenue collected from taxes on international trade and transfers fell from 19 percent of total revenue in 1979 to 7 percent in 1997, while tax revenue as a proportion of GDP increased only marginally from 15 percent to 16 percent. The data also show that the top personal income tax rate was cut from 89.25 percent in 1979 to 40 percent in 1997, during which personal income tax comprised 14.6 percent of total tax revenue in 1979 and 19.0 per-

Wei Li is an associate professor of business administration at the Darden School of Business, University of Virginia.

cent in 1997. However, like other newly industrialized economies, Korea still had a relatively larger informal economy than the richest economies in the world in 2000: based on Schneider's (2004) estimates, the informal economy in Korea stood at 27.5 percent in 2000, compared to 8.6 percent in the United States.

The rapid growth in Korea during the sample period may complicate the SVAR approach to estimating the size of fiscal multipliers. An observed change in tax revenue may be the result of a tax reform that altered the tax structure. The change in tax structure may have implications on the size of the informal sector and hence the tax base, as discussed in Gordon and Li (2006). Take for example a cut in the personal income tax rate. If this cut in tax rate reduces the informal economy by inducing people to switch their employment from the informal economy to the formal economy, it will increase the tax base and observed GDP, even if we assume that those already employed in the formal economy do not change their labor supply. Tax reforms in the presence of a significant informal economy may therefore offset, at least partially, the effect of the standard Keynesian tax multiplier. Consider another example in which we assume that there is an increase in government spending. In the presence of a significant informal economy, some of the government spending will inevitably be leaked into the informal economy, thereby reducing the measured response observed in the formal economy. The presence of a sizable informal economy may thus reduce the observed size of the spending multiplier. The discussion so far offers perhaps another alternative interpretation of the author's findings that the measured fiscal multipliers are small.

For an earlier draft of the paper, I suggested that the author incorporate the terms of trade variables as exogenous variables in the SVAR model. The author reported that adding the terms of trade variables to the SVAR did not change the results much. However, adding either U.S. GDP or the Real Effective Exchange Rate (REER) increased the estimates of the fiscal multipliers markedly. These findings are consistent with my suggestion, which is based on the Gordon and Li (2006) model of taxation in developing countries.

Let me explain the story still using the terms of trade variables. Gordon and Li (2006) show that in the context of a developing country with a sizable informal economy and hence an untaxed sector, if goods produced by the taxed sector are imported, the government would have an incentive to levy a tariff on imports in that sector in order to protect its tax base. Assume that the country is small, and so takes the terms of trade that it faces as given. While the trade distortions change the incentive that firms face, they do not change the terms of trade that the country faces.

Suppose that there is an increase in import prices in the world market (hence a fall in the terms of trade). This would shift domestic production toward the taxed sector, raising the domestic tax base and tax revenue. This conjecture is indeed observed in the data. Table 3C.1 shows the regression results. The dependent variable is the annual logarithmic change in the effective tax rate, measured as the ratio of revenue to GDP. The two dependent variables are annual logarithmic changes in import prices and export prices. The regression also includes lagged dependent variables on the right hand side. The data are obtained from the International Financial Statistics published by the IMF in 2005. The sample covers countries in the IFS database with available annual data from 1950 to 2004.

Since changes in export prices and import prices are exogenous for a small country, this specification is in fact an autoregressive model with exogenous terms of trade shocks. For large developed economies in the sample, this autoregressive model is likely misspecified. So in estimation, I divide the countries into four income quartiles based on GDP per capita in 1990. Quartiles 1 and 2 are countries with above-median incomes and quartiles 3 and 4 are countries with below-median incomes. The regression was run for each of the four subsamples of countries. Table 3C.1 shows that for countries with below-median income, an increase in import prices

Table 3C.1

	Income quartile			
	1	2	3	4
Intercept	0.013	0.015	0	0.007
	(0.004)	(0.01)	(0.008)	(0.007)
Δ ln(unit value of imports)	0.08	0.001	0.239	0.122
	(0.067)	(0.096)	(0.078)***	(0.06)**
Δ ln(unit value of exports)	–0.095	–0.1	0.004	0.039
	(0.071)	(0.065)	(0.069)	(0.033)
Δ ln(tax revenue/GDP_1)	–0.005	–0.322	–0.266	–0.175
	(0.046)	(0.075)***	(0.084)***	(0.078)**
Δ ln(tax revenue/GDP_2)	–0.036	–0.046	0.059	–0.091
	(0.047)	(0.07)	(0.082)	(0.072)
No. of observations	786	185	153	178
Adjusted R^2	–0.002	0.08	0.116	0.041

Notes: Dependent variable = Δ ln(tax revenue/GDP). The dependent variable is the annual logarithmic change in the effective tax rate, measured as the ratio of revenue to GDP. The two dependent variables are annual logarithmic changes in import prices and export prices. The regression also includes lagged dependent variables on the right-hand side. The data are obtained from the International Financial Statistics published by the IMF in 2005. The sample covers countries in the IFS database with available annual data from 1950 to 2004. The sample countries are divided into four income quartiles based on GDP per capita in 1990. Quartiles 1 and 2 are countries with above-median incomes and quartiles 3 and 4 are countries with below-median incomes. The regression was run for each of the four subsamples of countries. The numbers in parentheses are standard errors.
***Significant at the 1 percent level.
**Significant at the 5 percent level.

would increase the effective tax rate. But changes in export prices do not have statistically significant effects on the effective tax rate. How do changes in the terms of trade affect a developing country's income? Stylized facts show that among developing countries, there is a strong positive correlation between GDP and the terms of trade (Agenor, McDermott, and Prasad, 1999).

So the Gordon and Li (2006) model would forecast a negative relationship between tax revenue and GDP. Based on this line of logic, I suggested that the terms of trade be included as exogenous variables in the SVAR model.

It is a bit surprising that the inclusion of terms of trade variables does not change the size of the fiscal multipliers much but the inclusion of either the U.S. GDP or the REER does. This is because an increase in U.S. GDP or an appreciation in the REER can, in general, improve a small country's terms of trade. It is likely that data on import prices or export prices are measured with errors. For example, the data may not adequately differentiate between quality improvements and pure price changes. For Korea this may be particularly problematic as the country moved up in the quality chain quickly during the sample period.

Let me turn next to the data. Figure 3.1 in the paper shows that, since 1985, tax revenues have exceeded spending. This is inconsistent with consolidated central government budget data from the Ministry of Finance and Economy, which show that the Korean government experienced budget deficits in the early 1990s and in the late 1990s. Is it possible that the revenue and spending are not *matching pairs?* To the extent that revenue consistently exceeded spending during the sample period, when in fact there were two episodes of budget deficits, is β_1, the elasticity of spending with respect to revenue, in the paper underestimated? If so, how does it affect the estimated fiscal multipliers?

In sum, the paper does not find strong fiscal multipliers in the Korean context. The author points out two hypotheses: the new classical hypothesis and the nonlinearity hypothesis (model misspecification). My remarks give two more speculative hypotheses: the informal economy hypothesis and the terms of trade hypothesis. Both are based on Gordon and Li (2006). None of these hypotheses have been tested directly using Korean data, although one could interpret the estimation using U.S. GDP and REER as included exogenous variables as an indirect test of the terms of trade hypothesis.

References

Agenor, P-R., C. J. McDermott, and E. S. Prasad. 1999. Macroeconomic fluctuations in developing countries: Some stylized facts. IMF Working Paper. 99/35. Washington, DC: International Monetary Fund.
Blanchard, O. J., and R. Perotti. 2002. An empirical characterization of the dy-

namic effects of changes in government spending and taxes on output. *Quarterly Journal of Economics* 117:1329–68.

Gordon, R. H., and W. Li. 2006. Tax structures in developing countries: Many puzzles and a possible explanation. NBER Working Paper no. 11267. Cambridge, MA: National Bureau of Economic Research.

International Monetary Fund. 2005. *International financial statistics.* Washington, DC: IMF.

Schneider, F. 2004. The size of shadow economies in 145 countries from 1999 to 2003. Linz, Austria: Johannes Kepler University.

University of Michigan. n.d. *World Tax Database.* http://www.bus.umich.edu/OTPR/otpr/introduction.htm, accessed August 2006.

World Bank. 2006. *World development indicators.*

Comment   Yum K. Kwan

How would Korean GDP react to shocks initiated from taxation and government spending? This is essentially the question the author would like to answer using the methodology of structural VAR analysis. As the entire paper is empirical and the findings inevitably depend on the adopted statistical models, the author has also conducted an extensive sensitivity analysis to ensure that the key conclusion is robust against various technical assumptions, an exercise that no doubt lends more credibility to the empirical findings. The paper also includes a summary of the relevant literature on the issue—particularly those written in Korean and unlikely to be accessible to international readers—which should be useful to anyone interested in the fiscal policy effectiveness issue and the Korean economy.

The author focuses on evaluating the effectiveness of fiscal policy in the business cycle frequency and therefore uses detrended data series in the VAR analysis. Two time-trend models are considered—deterministic linear time trend and the Hodrick-Prescott (HP) filter—and all results in the paper are reported in parallel with respect to these two detrending schemes. I am not sure whether the deterministic time trend case is of interest at all. First, the deterministic linear time trend model is not supported by the data—formal statistical tests usually suggest stochastic time trend (i.e., the presence of unit root) rather than deterministic time trend—as the author himself acknowledges this is indeed the case for the Korean output series. The presence of unit root in the VAR system will render the impulse-response function (IRF) difficult to interpret, as the IRF depends on the moving average representation of the system, which itself may not even exist at all. Second, deterministic linear detrending is seldom used in the business cycle literature because deviations from linear time trend are usually too persistent

Yum K. Kwan is associate professor of economics at the City University of Hong Kong.

to be regarded as cyclical fluctuations over the business cycle. Third, even if we ignore the technical issue of unit root and nonexistence of moving average representation, the linear time trend case suggests incredibly long-lasting fiscal impact on detrended output. For example, the impulse response in figure 3.4 suggests that a tax shock can move output off trend for as long as ten years, which is just incredible to me.

One interesting finding of the paper is the predominant role of the automatic stabilization mechanism (ASM), which to a large extent neutralizes the contemporaneous effect of discretionary fiscal policy. Unfortunately, the paper says very little about how those numbers in tables 3.4 and 3.6 are derived. Table 3.4 is based on the Blanchard and Perotti model reported in (5) with the parameter β_3 set to zero. The model therefore rules out any feedback effect on government spending from either output or tax, implying that the government spending component of the ASM should be zero, which is inconsistent with what is reported in table 3.4.

The key finding of the paper is that fiscal policy in Korea has a weak impact on output, both in size and in persistency. We can question whether the fiscal data used in the analysis really contains any discretionary component at all, if the Korean government had really followed the rule of "Expenditure within Revenue" during the sample period, which is essentially a balanced budget principle. If tax and spending are really determined by the fiscal authority, who pays no attention to output fluctuations, we should expect the two fiscal series and the output series to run on separate courses and therefore there should not be any intricate lead and lag relationship between them. This perhaps can explain why the VAR analysis in the paper uncovers no significant causal relationship from the two fiscal series to the output series.

4

Income Risk and the Benefits of Social Insurance
Evidence from Indonesia and the United States

Raj Chetty and Adam Looney

4.1 Introduction

Social safety nets in developing countries are far smaller than in developed economies. In 1996, the average expenditure on social insurance as a fraction of GDP in countries with below-median per capita income was 6.8 percent; the corresponding figure in above-median countries was 18.5 percent (International Labour Organization 2000).[1] In the rapidly growing developing economies of South and East Asia, social insurance may be viewed as an unnecessary precaution that could potentially hamper growth without yielding substantial welfare gains. However, income shocks are prevalent in these economies. For example, at least 15 percent of households in the Indonesian Family Life Survey report some type of income shock in a given year. Recent large-scale shocks in this region such as the financial crises and the Asian tsunami further underscore the point that rapidly growing economies are not immune to large fluctuations. Hence, studying the welfare consequences of social insurance in developing economies is an important issue from a public finance perspective.

This paper takes a step in this direction by comparing the effects of shocks on consumption and other behaviors in developing and developed

Raj Chetty is an assistant professor of economics at the University of California, Berkeley, and a faculty research fellow of the National Bureau of Economic Research. Adam Looney is an economist in the Division of Research and Statistics of the Board of Governors of the Federal Reserve System.

We have benefited from comments by Pranab Bardhan, Roger Gordon, Mario Lamberte, Ted Miguel, anonymous referees, and conference participants. James Sly and Bhuvan Jain provided excellent research assistance. The analysis and conclusions set forth are those of the authors and do not indicate concurrence by other members of the research staff or the Board of Governors of the Federal Reserve.

1. See section 4.2 for further details on this data.

countries. The goal of this analysis is to provide empirical estimates of elasticities that are relevant in assessing the welfare consequences of social insurance in low-income economies.

Social insurance can only be beneficial if private insurance markets are inadequate. A straightforward and intuitive method of testing for full private market insurance frequently implemented in the development literature is to examine consumption fluctuations associated with shocks (Townsend 1994). We begin our analysis by comparing the effects of unemployment on consumption in the United States and Indonesia. We use two large-panel datasets that contain consumption and labor force data for each of these countries—the Panel Study of Income Dynamics (PSID) and the Indonesian Family Life Survey (IFLS). We compare the growth rate of food consumption for agents who remain employed and agents who report job loss in the two panels. The mean and median consumption drop associated with unemployment in both economies is roughly 10 percent. The similarity in the consumption drop is remarkable given that Indonesia has no formal UI system whereas the United States insures nearly 50 percent of the pre-unemployment wage for most individuals. It follows that the introduction of a social safety net in Indonesia would have a relatively small effect in terms of smoothing consumption, since consumption fluctuations are not very large to begin with.

While this finding might suggest that unemployment insurance cannot have large benefits in developing economies, it is important to examine the efficiency costs of the behaviors used by households to smooth consumption before drawing normative conclusions. If individuals mitigate consumption falls by resorting to costly measures (e.g., removing children from school) publicly provided insurance could increase welfare by obviating the need for such measures (Morduch 1999; Holzmann and Jørgensen 2001; Dercon 2002). It is plausible that low-income households resort to very costly measures to maintain consumption because their pre-unemployment consumption appears close to subsistence levels. In the Indonesian sample, the average household devotes nearly 70 percent of its budget to food, compared to 20 percent in the United States. Moreover, many households consume significantly fewer staples (such as rice) when the household head becomes unemployed, suggesting that subsistence constraints are likely to be a concern.

We make inferences about the cost of income smoothing in Indonesia by examining the methods households use to mitigate the income loss associated with unemployment. Strikingly, parents appear to sharply reduce expenditures on children's education substantially during idiosyncratic unemployment spells (see also Thomas et al. 2004, who document similar patterns during the Asian financial crisis). To the extent that these reductions permanently diminish children's educational attainment, the welfare costs of transitory unemployment shocks could be particularly large and long lived. In addition, more than 30 percent of households report raising labor supply to maintain their income stream. This high degree of responsiveness is further evidence that consumption-smoothing requires substantial changes in economic behavior for many Indonesian households. In contrast, households in the United States typically accomplish consumption smoothing by much less costly methods: depleting buffer stocks, borrowing, and using social insurance benefits (Dynarski and Gruber 1997).

In summary, the empirical evidence suggests that social insurance against transitory shocks in developing countries could have substantial welfare benefits by reducing the use of inefficient smoothing techniques even though consumption volatility may not fall much. In a companion paper (Chetty and Looney 2006), we establish this point formally in a simple model of risk and insurance by showing that the marginal benefit of insurance can be large when consumption drops are small because a high level of risk aversion leads to use of costly smoothing methods.

Of course, since we focus only on the benefits of social insurance in this paper, one cannot conclude from the results here that introducing a large safety net will raise aggregate welfare. The efficiency costs of social safety nets (e.g., reduced employment or opportunity costs such as forgone infrastructure or health investments) may also be large. On the other hand, the provision of unemployment insurance could also have efficiency-enhancing effects such as improved job matches and increased productivity (Acemoglu and Shimer 1999). Hence, the most important lesson of this study is perhaps that further research on social insurance programs in developing economies would be useful given their potential benefits.

The remainder of the paper proceeds as follows. The next section briefly describes existing social safety nets around the world. Section 4.3 compares the effects of unemployment on consumption in the United States and Indonesia empirically. Section 4.4 presents evidence on the cost of consumption smoothing methods used in Indonesia. Section 4.5 offers concluding remarks.

4.2 Social Safety Nets in Developing Countries

The size of the formal government-provided social safety net is substantially smaller in developing countries than in developed economies. According to statistics collected by the International Labour Organization (2000) for 91 countries in 1996, the average GDP share of social insurance—defined as total expenditures on social security, disability insurance, unemployment insurance, insurance against work-related injuries, and government provided health insurance—was 12.5 percent, with a range spanning 0.7 percent to 34.7 percent. Panel A of figure 4.1 plots the fraction of GDP devoted to social insurance programs against PPP-adjusted GDP per capita for these countries (with log scales). There is a

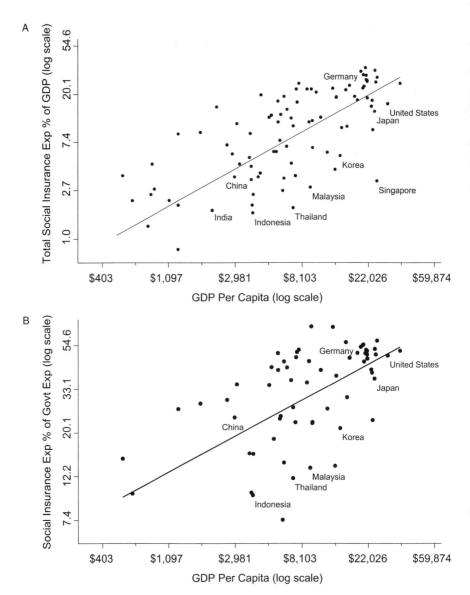

Fig. 4.1 *A,* **Social insurance versus GDP per capita in 1996;** *B,* **government budget share of social insurance versus GDP per capita**

Sources: Social Insurance statistics are from ILO (2000); GDP statistics are from the Penn World tables.

Notes: GDP is measured in 1996 U.S. dollars. Panel *A* shows relationship between social insurance share of GDP and GDP per capita. Panel *B* shows relationship between social insurance share of government budget and GDP per capita.

striking positive correlation between these two variables. As shown in specification 1 of table 4.1, a 1 percent increase in GDP per capita is associated with a 0.7 percent increase in the GDP share of social insurance in this cross-section. Perhaps more interestingly, the share of social insurance in government expenditure is also significantly higher in richer countries (panel B of figure 4.1 and specification 2 in table 4.1). Wealthier countries not only have higher government expenditures, but they also devote a larger fraction of those expenditures to social insurance.

Notably, the rapidly growing East Asian economies are on average 1.3 log units below the trend line plotted in figure 4.1. In other words, they devote about 10 percentage points less of GDP to social insurance than other countries of similar income. East Asian economies devote on average 4.9 percent of their GDP to social insurance, compared with 16.5 percent in the United States and 22 percent in Europe. The positive relationship between GDP per capita and social safety nets is evident even among the small subsample of East Asian economies, with Indonesia having the lowest income and expenditure on social insurance and Japan having the highest of both.

These statistics understate the size of the social safety net in developing countries because they ignore other forms of in-kind and charity assistance, such as minimum food grants and non-governmental (NGO) aid.

Table 4.1   **Relationship between social insurance and per capita GDP**

	SI as % of GDP vs. GDP (log SI % of GDP) (1)	SI as % of government expenditure vs. GDP (log SI % of government expenditure) (2)	Continent dummies (log SI % of GDP) (3)	East Asian countries (log SI % of GDP) (4)
Log GDP per capita	0.630	0.351	0.357	0.674
	(0.070)**	(0.064)**	(0.069)**	(0.062)**
Constant	–3.376	0.267		–3.673
	(0.626)**	(0.589)		(0.550)**
East Asia indicator				–1.318
				(0.250)**
Continent dummies	No	No	Yes	No
No. of observations	89	64	89	89

Sources: Social insurance statistics are from ILO (2000); GDP statistics are from the Penn World tables.
Notes: Social insurance is defined as sum of expenditures on social security, disability insurance, unemployment insurance, insurance against work-related injuries, and government-provided health insurance. East Asian countries in the sample are Indonesia, Japan, Korea, Malaysia, Thailand, and Singapore. GDP is measured in 1996 U.S. dollars. For columns (1), (3), and (4), dependent variable is log SI % of GDP. For column (2), dependent variable is log SI % of government expenditure.

However, these types of programs are generally quite limited in size (Gough et al. 2004) and have two features that considerably limit their scope relative to western social safety nets. First, they are often means-tested and so may not provide consumption-smoothing benefits to a majority of the population. Second, aid tends to flow toward large-scale catastrophes (such as the recent tsunami), with significantly fewer funds available for the smaller but more numerous idiosyncratic shocks like unemployment or disability.

There are many reasons that developing countries might choose not to implement such social safety nets. The most plausible reason is that financing such systems is infeasible given limitations on the government's ability to raise revenue (Gordon and Li 2005). While it is important to understand the political economy of social insurance in developing countries, the purpose of this study is to assess the normative value of such a program if it could be implemented. As illustrated by the recent introduction of a formal unemployment insurance system in Korea, some of these countries are reaching a point where such systems are feasible, making this normative question of practical relevance.

4.3   Consumption Fluctuations in Indonesia and the United States

The first step in determining whether there is a role for social insurance is to determine whether private insurance markets are adequate for agents to smooth consumption over shocks. The standard method of testing for full consumption insurance, originally implemented by Cochrane (1991) using U.S. data and Townsend (1994) using data on Indian farmers, is to directly examine the effect of idiosyncratic shocks such as job loss, health changes, or weather shocks on consumption. Under the assumption that utility is additively separable over consumption and leisure, a drop in consumption associated with these shocks is evidence that insurance markets are incomplete. More recently, in the public finance literature, Gruber (1997) and Browning and Crossley (2001) have implemented tests of full insurance that do not rely on additive separability by examining whether the size of consumption drops during unemployment spells is related to the amount of government-provided unemployment insurance. Their estimates show that with full unemployment insurance, consumption would not fall at all during job loss, implying that most or all of the consumption fluctuations identified in prior studies are indeed attributable to incomplete insurance rather than complementarity between consumption and leisure.

Following this literature, we begin our comparison of the welfare gains of social insurance in developing versus developed economies by examining consumption fluctuations. We first establish consistent measures of consumption drops for a specific shock in two economies. The shock we focus on is unemployment, since it is a well-defined and common event in both types of economies. We focus on the United States as the developed economy, primarily because of our familiarity with the institutions and the availability of the longitudinal Panel Study of Income Dynamics (PSID) data there. We focus on Indonesia as the developing economy because it has high-quality panel data with a design very similar to the PSID. Indonesia also has minimal social insurance, making it an ideal laboratory in which to investigate the response of families to idiosyncratic shocks in a low-income economy without any social safety net. In this paper, we report results on the effects of unemployment on food consumption; as we discuss in the following, other analysis using broader measures of consumption from different datasets yields results similar to those we report here for food.

Our methods and empirical results are borrowed from and consistent with a large body of prior work. Most relevant are studies that examine responses of Indonesian households to shocks. The general consensus of these papers on Indonesia and of the literature on developing countries more generally is that transitory shocks seldom translate into significant fluctuations in consumption. This is because households have developed a variety of coping mechanisms, such as depleting household wealth and assets or borrowing (Frankenberg, Smith, and Thomas 2003), increasing family labor supply (Beegle, Frankenberg, and Thomas 2000; Cameron and Worswick 2003), and reducing investments in children's health and education (Frankenberg, Thomas, and Beegle 1999; Thomas et al. 2004). The smoothness of consumption has been taken to imply that economic shocks are not costly and that the scope for publicly provided social insurance for transitory shocks is small (Morduch 1995; Cameron and Worswick 2003).[2] Our goal here is to examine the validity of this normative conclusion by comparing behavioral responses to risk in Indonesia and the United States.

4.3.1   Data

We use two household-level panel datasets in this study. The first is the Panel Study of Income Dynamics (PSID), which tracks approximately 8,000 households and their children over more than 30 years in the United States. We use an extract of the PSID that contains consistently defined annual data between 1980 and 1993. The second is the Indonesian Family Life Survey (IFLS), which follows roughly 7,500 households over a span of seven years, with interviews in 1993, 1997, and 2000.

To examine the impact of unemployment shocks, we focus on households for which longitudinal data exist and with household heads who were employed at the time of the immediately preceding interview. Hence, we include only households in which the head was employed one year before the

2. Studies that examine large, persistent health shocks in Indonesia (Gertler and Gruber 2002, Gertler, Levine, and Moretti 2001) do find large consumption drops. However, Gertler and Gruber observe that their results offer "little insight into consumption smoothing of more likely and less costly risks" that are our primary focus here.

current interview in the PSID, and three or four years before in the IFLS.[3] We discuss in the following how the lack of annual data in the IFLS could affect the comparison between the datasets.

Table 4.2 provides summary statistics on these households. Inflation in Indonesia was high over this time period, largely due to the 1998 financial crisis. The price level rose an average of 91 percent in the three- to four-year periods between interviews. In comparison, average annual inflation in the United States was 5 percent over our sample. The IFLS statistics reported in table 4.2 are deflated using an aggregate CPI series from the Asian Development Bank and are converted to year 2000 dollars using the US/Rupiah exchange rate as of January 2000. The PSID statistics are deflated using the standard CPI series from the BLS. Note that real food consumption growth rates are small in both samples. In our empirical analysis, we use nominal growth rates for transparency, since inflation rates are thought to differ significantly across goods and regions in Indonesia around the financial crisis. Not surprisingly, nominal growth rates are much higher in the IFLS sample than in the PSID.

The most striking differences between the samples are in economic characteristics. PSID household heads earn on average $31,828 per year and PSID households consume $7,255 of food per year ($2,687 per person). In contrast, IFLS households report average total incomes of $1,484, and consume approximately $926 in food each year ($162 per person). Note that this figure includes food purchased and food produced (important given the large number of farmers in the data). Unemployment shocks appear more frequently in the IFLS data: approximately 8 percent of heads of household become unemployed between interview waves while 4 percent become unemployed between years in the PSID.

An important summary statistic in assessing a household's ability to smooth consumption is asset holdings. In Indonesia, the median household holds total assets of $2,692, which is substantially larger than annual income for many households. However, most of this wealth is held in farm and housing. Median liquid wealth (savings, stocks, and jewelry) is only $21, indicating that consumption smoothing using liquid assets would be infeasible for many households. Frankenberg, Smith, and Thomas (2003) report that few households move when they face shocks, suggesting that homes and farms are not directly used to smooth consumption, either. Individuals could in principle take secured loans against their farm and housing collateral when shocks occur. Studying the extent to which individuals are able to use such secured loans to smooth consumption is an interesting direction for further research.

Because of data constraints, we define unemployment spells slightly dif-

3. We include all unemployed PSID households, and not just those who report receiving unemployment benefits.

Table 4.2   **Summary statistics for IFLS and PSID**

	Mean	Median	Standard deviation
IFLS (Indonesia)			
Currently unemployed	8%	0	27%
Age of head	48	46	25
Married	83%	1	37%
College	6%	0	24%
Number of people in household	5.7	5.0	2.5
Food consumption	$926	$703	$1,065
Read food consumption growth rate	4%	3%	61%
Inflation rate	91%	132%	42%
Staples consumption	$191	$144	$247
Total consumption	$1,604	$1,073	$2,047
Wage income of head	$580	$308	$1,056
Other family members earn income	58%	1	49%
Total household income	$1,484	$811	$3,569
Total household assets	$7,525	$2,692	$17,189
Home and land	$5,625	$1,999	$12,054
Equipment, livestock, vehicles, and other	$1,587	$352	$8,057
Liquid assets (cash, stock, jewelry)	$313	$21	$2,295
No household member is a farmer	58%	1	49%
Education expenditure	$144	$49	$344
Positive education expenditure	77%	1	42%
PSID (United States)			
Currently unemployed	4%	0	21%
Age of head	38	36	12
Married	65%	1	48%
College	40%	0	49%
Number of people in household	2.7	3.0	1.4
Food consumption	$7,255	$6,303	$4,646
Real food consumption growth rate	2%	3%	56%
Inflation rate	5%	4%	2%
Wage income of head	$31,828	$27,285	$30,267

Notes: All monetary values are annual figures in real 2000 U.S. dollars. Education expenditure data are for households with children under 24 years old. For Indonesia, number of observations = 12,236; number of households = 7,197. For the United States, number of observations = 70,889; number of households = 11,685.

ferently in the two samples. In the PSID, a household head is defined to be unemployed if he or she is not working and searching for a job at the time of the interview. Replicating this measure in the IFLS is not always possible because weekly employment data (module TK) for the 1997 interview has not yet been publicly released. Instead, we use a question corresponding to employment status during the last 12 months. In 1993 and 2000, when both weekly and annual employment statistics are available, these measures are highly correlated and we find that the effects of unemployment on consumption are very similar regardless of which variable is used. We use the annual employment variable to maximize the sample size and to avoid focusing only on changes in outcomes over seven years, as required if we dropped 1997 interview information.

A concern with our definition of unemployment in the IFLS data is that the IFLS annual employment variable provides little detail on employment status, so that we cannot always differentiate involuntary unemployment from endogenous transitions out of the labor force such as retirement. The work by Frankenberg, Thomas, and Beegle (1999) addresses this issue better by using additional unpublished data. The results we report in the following are very similar to their results. In addition, when we restrict the sample to cases for which we do know whether the individual is still in the labor force, we obtain similar point estimates. These findings suggest that this limitation of our data is not a significant source of bias.

4.3.2   Results

We begin our analysis with a simple comparison of growth rates of food consumption in the United States and Indonesia. Define the growth rate of food consumption for household i from year t to year t' as

$$g_{it} = \log c_{it} - \log c_{it'}$$

where c_{it} denotes household i's food consumption in period t. Ideally, the gap between t and t' would be small, but in Indonesia data are available only every three to four years, while in the United States data are annual. In the baseline analysis, we attempt to get as close a measure to the true drop as possible in each dataset, by examining the growth rate from t to $t + 1$ in the United States and t to $t + 3$ or $t + 4$ (as data permit) in Indonesia.

Our basic identification strategy is to divide our sample of employed heads-of-household in the preperiod year t' into two groups: Job losers, who reported being unemployed at the time of the survey in year t, and job keepers, who reported still having a job. We then compare the distribution of growth rates for these two groups to estimate the effect of unemployment on consumption. The key identification assumption that must hold for this method to give a consistent estimate of the causal effect of unemployment on consumption growth is that the *treatment* group of job losers and the *control* group of job keepers have identical consumption growth rates absent the shock. This identification assumption may be questionable given that individuals prone to job loss are generally lower skill types, and therefore may have relatively lower rates of trend wage and consumption growth in a society with increasing income inequality. In this case, the simple differences in the following will overstate the true consumption drop caused by unemployment. We implement some tests to address this concern in the following.

We first demonstrate the effect of unemployment on food consumption using the long-time series available in the PSID data with an *event study* in figure 4.2. This figure is constructed by redefining as year 0 the year of job loss for the set of household heads who lost their jobs once during the PSID sample. We then plot real average annual consumption growth rates (more precisely, change in real log household consumption) against year relative to year of job loss (e.g., –3 is three years before job loss). The figure shows that food consumption grows at a real rate of roughly 2 to 4 percent per year before time 0, and then drops by nearly 10 percent in the year of job loss. Consumption then recovers gradually over the next few years back to its original level. This graph confirms that unemployment causes a sharp, temporary decline in consumption for the typical household in the United States, consistent with the results of Cochrane (1991) and Gruber (1997). Unfortunately, a similar graph showing a long pre-event and postevent period cannot be drawn for Indonesia because there are at most three observations per household in the IFLS. We are therefore forced to compare single observations on growth rates in consumption from time –1 to time 0 across job losers and job keepers to identify the effect of unemployment in the IFLS. We adopt a similar strategy in the PSID for purposes of comparability.

We begin our comparison of Indonesia and the United States with a nonparametric, graphical analysis of the effect of job loss on food con-

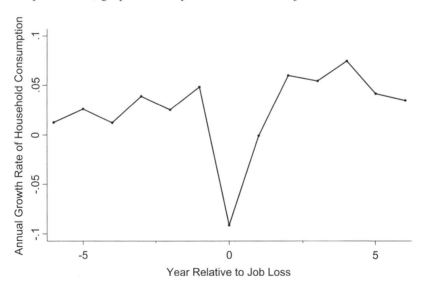

Fig. 4.2   Effect of unemployment on consumption growth in the United States
Source: PSID 1980–93.
Notes: Sample consists of all household heads who experienced exactly one unemployment spell between 1980 and 1993 in the PSID. Annual growth rates of food consumption are computed as change in log of real (CPI deflated) food consumption from year $t-1$ to year t. Year of job loss is normalized at 0 and all other years are defined as difference relative to that year.

sumption. We estimate kernel densities for the distribution of nominal growth rates by employment status in each country. Following the convention in the consumption growth literature (see, e.g., Zeldes 1989 or Gruber 1997), we trim outliers (the lower and upper 2 percent of the reported distribution), though our results are insensitive to this restriction. The kernel densities are estimated using an *optimal* bandwidth chosen to minimize the asymptotic mean squared error of the fitted distribution. Panel A of figure 4.3 plots the density of growth rates for job losers (red) and keepers (blue) in Indonesia. It is clear that unemployment leads to a left-shift in the distribution, indicating that households are unable to fully smooth consumption over this transitory shock. The medians of each distribution are depicted by vertical lines of corresponding color. The median nominal growth rate of food consumption for job keepers in the sample is 67 percent (due to the high rate of inflation in Indonesia over this period), in comparison with a growth rate of 56 percent for job losers. Hence, at the median, unemployment appears to reduce food consumption by approximately 11 percent.

Panel B of figure 4.3 plots analogous densities for the United States. Again, it is clear that agents are not fully insured, consistent with the results of Gruber (1997). Of greater interest here is the comparison of these distributions to their analogs in Indonesia. The distribution of growth rates reported by Indonesian households has variance twice as high as that in the United States, which could be either because of measurement error or because outcomes in developing countries tend to be more stochastic. Despite this general difference in the distributions, the within-sample difference between job losers and job keepers is strikingly similar. In the United States, the median nominal growth rate for job keepers is approximately 8.5 percent, compared to –1.5 percent for job losers. Hence, job loss appears to reduce food consumption by approximately 10 percent in the United States, only 1 percent different from the Indonesian value. Other quantiles of the distribution shifts are also quite similar across the two economies.[4]

We now examine the robustness of this conclusion to controls using a more structured regression analysis. We estimate specifications of the following form:

(1) $$g_i = \alpha + \beta \text{unemp}_i + \theta X_i + \varepsilon_i$$

where $\text{unemp}_i = 1$ if the agent reports unemployment at time t', $\text{unemp}_i = 0$ if the agent is employed at time t', and X_i denotes a vector of covariates.

---

4. The estimated consumption drops become *larger* in the PSID if we use changes from t to $t + 3$ (as in the IFLS). Hence, using a comparable strategy across the two data sets only further reinforces the point that consumption is as smooth during shocks in Indonesia as it is in the United States.

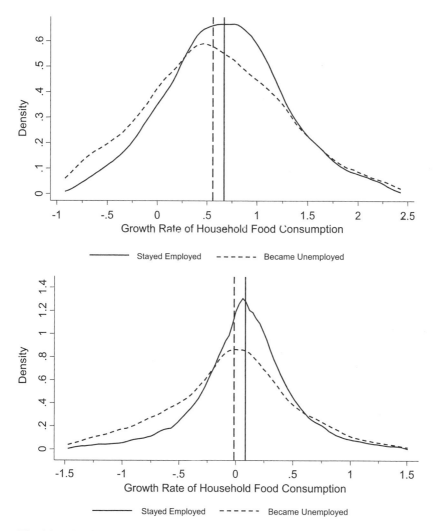

Fig. 4.3 *A,* **Effect of unemployment on food consumption in Indonesia;** *B,* **Effect of unemployment on food consumption in the United States.**

Sources: For panel *A,* IFLS (1993–2000). For panel *B,* PSID (1980–93).

Notes: In each panel, vertical lines denote median for density of corresponding color. Sample consists of all household heads in IFLS or PSID who reported being employed at the time of previous interview. *Stayed Employed* group includes household heads who remain employed in interview *t. Became Unemployed* group includes household heads who are not working at time of interview *t.* Growth rate of household food consumption is defined as nominal difference in log food consumption in interview *t* and interview *t* − 1. Gap between interviews is one year in PSID and three or four years in IFLS. Observations with growth rates in top 2 percent or bottom 2 percent of unconditional food growth distribution in each dataset are discarded to trim outliers. Kernel densities are estimated using an optimal bandwidth procedure.

The key coefficient β equals the effect of job loss on the consumption growth rate.

Table 4.3 reports several estimates of equation (1) for Indonesia and the United States. The first specification is estimated with OLS using no controls except year dummies. Consistent with the graphical results, unemployment is estimated to reduce consumption by about 9 percent in the United States and 10 percent in Indonesia. The second specification introduces several controls: age, gender, marital status, education, and region dummies (to control for differential inflation patterns). The coefficient estimates on the unemployment dummy are essentially unchanged. These results show that after controlling for observable heterogeneity in trend growth rates across job losers and job keepers, consumption drops remain quite similar in the two countries.

Table 4.3   **Effect of unemployment insurance on food consumption in Indonesia and the United States**

	(1) No controls		(2) With controls		(3) Only those unemployed exactly once	
	U.S.	Indonesia	U.S.	Indonesia	U.S.	Indonesia
Unemployed dummy	−0.087	−0.097	−0.106	−0.078	−0.095	−0.098
	(0.006)***	(0.027)***	(0.010)***	(0.022)***	(0.017)***	(0.038)**
People in household			0.01	−0.005	0.012	−0.004
			(0.002)***	(0.002)**	(0.005)**	(0.007)
Age			−0.001	0.000	0.000	0.001
			(0.000)***	(0.000)	(0.001)	(0.000)
Married			0.033	0.057	0.032	0.02
			(0.007)***	(0.027)**	(0.018)*	(0.06)
Sex			−0.012	−0.007	0.006	−0.035
			(0.007)*	(0.014)	(0.017)	(0.03)
School			0.000	−0.005	0.000	0.005
			(0.000)	(0.008)	(0.001)	(0.025)
Year dummies	Yes	Yes	Yes	Yes	Yes	Yes
Province/state dummies	No	No	Yes	Yes	Yes	Yes
No. of observations	50,769	11,284	50,763	11,284	7,894	1,231

Notes: Dependent variable = food consumption growth rate (change in log household food consumption). Sample includes all households who remain in panel for two or more years in which head is employed in previous observation. Observations with nominal food consumption growth rates in bottom 2 percent and top 2 percent of distribution are discarded to trim outliers. Dependent variable in all specifications is $\log(c_t) - \log(c_{t-1})$, where $t - 1$ refers to the previous observation (one year lag in PSID, three or four years in IFLS). Unemployed dummy is 1 if head of household is not working at time of interview; else 0.

***Significant at the 1 percent level.

**Significant at the 5 percent level.

*Significant at the 10 percent level.

The third specification tests the *common trends* identification assumption more directly by restricting the sample to individuals who lost jobs at some point within the panel. In this specification, the counterfactual for the job losers in year t' are individuals who lost their jobs at some other point in the dataset. The advantage of this specification in terms of identification is that growth rates in consumption for job losers are compared to what is arguably a better *control* group. The problem of unobservable differences between job losers and keepers is mitigated in the restricted sample by identifying purely from variation in the date of job loss rather than whether or not job loss occurred. As shown in the last two columns of the table, this smaller sample yields estimates that are generally similar to the original results, supporting the claim that the causal effect of the unemployment shock on consumption is being identified.

One concern with these results is that unemployment shocks induce changes in consumption because of changes in expectations about permanent income rather than a transitory shock. To test this alternative hypothesis, we compared consumption growth rates from period t to $t + 1$ for individuals who became unemployed in period t versus those who kept their jobs in period t. We find that consumption grows 8 to 10 percent *more* from t to $t + 1$ for the job losers, indicating that food consumption recovers to pre-unemployment levels within three years after the shock for the average household. This result supports the view that unemployment is a transitory shock that affects consumption because of inability to smooth.

We also conducted a series of other robustness checks and sensitivity analyses that are not reported in the table. Quantile regressions generally yield estimates very similar to the OLS results. Different trimming criteria for outliers, such as 1 percent or 5 percent, also yield similar results. Broader measures of consumption also follow a similar pattern. Gruber (1998) augments the results from the PSID with broader measures of consumption from the Consumer Expenditure Survey and finds that the decline in total consumption mirrors that of food consumption. We find a similar decline in total consumption in the IFLS sample as well (not reported).

An additional concern specific to the Indonesian sample is that all households, including job keepers, may have reduced consumption during the Asian Financial Crisis in 1997 to 1998. This could bias our estimates of the consumption drop associated with unemployment downward in this sample. To address this concern, we split the sample in two and repeated the analysis using the job losers/keepers in 2000 and job losers/keepers in 1997 separately. The estimates of the consumption drop associated with unemployment are similar in both subsamples. This suggests that the financial crisis does not create significant bias: If consumption was unusually low throughout the economy in 1997, job keepers should have experienced excess growth in consumption between 1997 and 2000, biasing the estimate of the consumption drop *upward* in the 2000 sample.

To summarize, the evidence from the IFLS and the PSID suggests that idiosyncratic unemployment shocks lead to temporary consumption fluctuations of similar magnitude in the United States and Indonesia. This similarity is surprising given that the United States has a large UI system that replaces approximately 50 percent of preunemployment wages for most individuals, whereas Indonesia has very little formal social insurance (figure 4.1).

These results may appear to suggest that families in Indonesia (and perhaps other developing economies) have *adequate* insurance because they are able to maintain a reasonably smooth consumption path when faced with shocks, as originally suggested by Townsend's (1994) classic study of Indian farmers. In this case, social insurance would offer relatively modest welfare gains in these economies. However, the smoothness of household consumption may belie significant costs of income risk if households resort to costly smoothing methods. Intuitively, social insurance may provide welfare gains if it crowds out the use of more costly smoothing techniques. The next section explores how households maintain consumption while unemployed in Indonesia.

4.4   The Costs of Consumption Smoothing

Households would resort to costly consumption smoothing techniques only if the welfare costs of reductions in consumption are large. We therefore first evaluate the nature of consumption reductions in Indonesia to determine whether such reductions are likely to have large welfare costs.

The average household in the IFLS devotes nearly 70 percent of its total expenditure to food (in contrast with 20 percent in the PSID). This suggests that Indonesians may have to reduce consumption of basic necessities much more than households in the United States when shocks occur. To provide direct evidence on this hypothesis, we study the effect of unemployment shocks on the consumption of staple foods (including rice, corn, cassava, and flour) in Indonesia. Consumption of these goods would presumably fall only in the most dire circumstances, when agents are unable to reduce consumption on *luxuries,* which have lower marginal utility. We implement empirical specifications analogous to equation (1) to test whether staples consumption falls in households experiencing unemployment shocks relative to households that do not experience such shocks. The sample specifications and trimming procedures are analogous to those described previously for total food consumption.

We begin with an OLS regression on the full sample. The estimate in column (1) of table 4.4 indicates that mean consumption of staple foods falls by 6 percent during unemployment spells; however, the estimate is not statistically significant. As one might expect, the magnitude of this decline is smaller than the drop in total food consumption (see table 4.3) and total

Table 4.4   **Effect of unemployment on consumption of staples**

	OLS (1)	Median reg. (2)	OLS, no farmers (3)
Unemployed dummy	−0.060	−0.100	−0.119
	(0.039)	(0.035)***	(0.048)**
People in household	−0.009	−0.005	−0.013
	(0.004)**	−0.004	(0.006)**
Age	0.000	0.000	0.001
	(0.000)	(0.000)	(0.001)
Married	0.129	0.147	0.060
	(0.047)***	(0.043)***	(0.068)
Sex	0.042	0.048	0.037
	(0.024)*	(0.022)**	(0.033)
School	0.052	0.042	0.080
	(0.014)***	(0.013)***	(0 020)***
Year dummies	Yes	Yes	Yes
Province dummies	Yes	Yes	Yes
No. of observations	9,466	9,466	5,205

Notes: Dependent variable = staples consumption growth rate (change in log staples consumption). Sample includes all IFLS households who remain in panel for two or more years and in which head is employed in previous observation. Observations with nominal staples consumption growth rates in bottom 2 percent and top 2 percent of distribution are discarded to trim outliers. Dependent variable in all specifications is $\log(c_t) - \log(c_{t-1})$, where $t - 1$ refers to the previous observations. Unemployed dummy is 1 if head of household is not working at time of interview; 0 otherwise. Median regression is a quantile regression at the 50th percentile. No farmers specification excludes all households with one or more individual working on a farm.
***Significant at the 1 percent level.
**Significant at the 5 percent level.
*Significant at the 10 percent level.

consumption (not shown) because households are presumably more willing to cut back on *luxuries* than *necessities*. A kernel density plot (not shown) for growth in staples consumption by job status analogous to panel A of figure 4.3 reveals a clear downward shift in consumption of staples for job losers who experience the most negative growth rates, but little shift for those who fared better. This is consistent with the claim that only the worst off reduce consumption of staples. This suggests that even though the change in the mean growth rate may not be statistically significant, other moments could reveal a more robust response. Column (2) of table 4.4 confirms this point by showing that median staples growth rate is 10 percent lower for job losers relative to keepers. This estimate is highly statistically significant. Column (3) shows that the mean drop in staple consumption is 12 percent among households without any farmers, who might have less capacity to store crops. In sum, these results indicate that many households reduce consumption of the most basic and important sources of nutrition when the household head loses his job. These findings are consistent with those of Beegle, Frankenberg, and Thomas (2000) and Frankenberg, Smith, and Thomas (2003), who study the effects of the 1998 Asian Financial Crisis on consumption using an augmented IFLS sample.

The fact that income shocks force households to reduce consumption of basic necessities makes it plausible that they would use very costly methods to smooth consumption. We now document some of these methods directly.[5] One particularly costly method is reducing educational expenditures on children. The first three specifications in table 4.5 report the effect of unemployment shocks on educational investment. In these regressions, we restrict the sample to households with children under 24 years of age who reported educational expenses at the time of the previous interview. Specifications (1) and (2) examine extensive-margin (participation) effects by using a dummy for positive household educational expenditure as the dependent variable. The results reported in column (1) imply that families experiencing unemployment were 13 percentage points more likely to stop spending on education entirely (presumably by withdrawing their children from school). This is a large reduction relative to the sample mean of 77 percent participation in education in this group. Controlling for household characteristics reduces the estimated magnitude of this response slightly, but does not alter the conclusion that unemployment shocks significantly reduce the likelihood a household will spend on education. Column (3) examines the intensive margin by changing the dependent variable to the log change in education expenditures (with 2 percent trimming as previous). Median educational expenditure falls by 12 percent in households experiencing unemployment. Average educational spending (not shown) falls by less than 12 percent, largely because richer households do not appear to reduce expenditures as much as poorer households, for reasons similar to the staples results. Figure 4.4 shows the distributional shift on the intensive margin, confirming the regression results visually.

These results indicate that many households reduce spending on education to mitigate the income loss during an unemployment shock. A concern with the interpretation of these results is reverse causality. One might worry that families with children who finish school are those in which the parent stops working, generating the observed correlation. However, Frankenberg, Thomas, and Beegle (1999) and Thomas et al. (2004) have documented similar patterns in educational expenditure among households affected by the Asian Financial Crisis. These studies take advantage of this large exogenous shock to address the identification concerns more carefully, suggesting that shocks do indeed cause reductions in education.

A second behavioral response, which perhaps has a lower cost than reducing human capital accumulation but is nonetheless more costly than

---

5. The behavioral responses examined here are only two examples among many possibilities. Examining the costs of other consumption smoothing methods used by households would be very useful.

Table 4.5 **Other responses to unemployment: Evidence of risk aversion**

	Educational expenditures			Other family members' labor supply		
	Extensive margin (education dummy)		Intensive margin (log Δ ed exp)	Extensive margin (participation dummy)		Intensive margin (log Δ other fam inc)
	No controls (1)	With controls (2)	Median reg. (3)	No controls (4)	With controls (5)	Median reg. (6)
Unemployed dummy	-0.13	-0.09	-0.12	0.17	0.15	0.11
	(0.02)***	(0.02)***	(0.07)	(0.02)***	(0.02)***	(0.07)*
People per household		0.01	-0.03		0.06	0.02
		(0.00)***	(0.01)***		(0.00)***	(0.01)***
Age		0.00	-0.01		0.00	0.00
		(0.00)***	(0.00)***		(0.00)***	(0.00)
Married		0.13	-0.03		0.07	0.28
		(0.02)***	(0.09)		(0.03)***	(0.09)***
Sex		0.01	-0.05		0.04	0.21
		(0.01)	(0.04)		(0.01)***	(0.04)***
School		0.06	0.05		0.00	-0.04
		(0.01)***	(0.02)**		(0.01)	(0.02)*
Year dummies	Yes	Yes	Yes	Yes	Yes	Yes
Province dummies	No	Yes	Yes	No	Yes	Yes
No. of observations	7,700	7,457	6,156	6,778	6,407	3,478

Notes: Sample includes all IFLS households who remain in panel for two or more years and in which head is employed in previous observation. Dependent variable in columns (1) and (2) is an indicator for whether household reported positive education expenditures. Only households with positive education expenditures in previous year are included in columns (1) and (2). Dependent variable in column (3) is log change in education expenditures in both previous year and current year. In column (3), outliers are trimmed at upper and lower 2 percent, as in table 4.3. Dependent variable in columns (4) and (5) is an indicator for whether any household member besides the head is earning income in current year. Only households in which no other member besides head was working in prior year included in columns (4) and (5). Dependent variable in column (6) is log change in other family members' income, with 2 percent trimming analogous to that in table 4.3. Sample in column (6) includes households reporting positive nonhead income in both previous year and current year. Unemployed dummy is 1 if head of household is not working at time of interview; 0 otherwise. Median regression is a quantile regression at the 50th percentile.

***Significant at the 1 percent level.

**Significant at the 5 percent level.

*Significant at the 10 percent level.

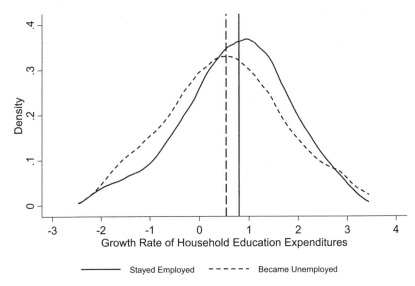

Fig. 4.4   Effect of unemployment on education (intensive margin)
Source: IFLS 1993–2000.
Note: Vertical lines denote median for density of corresponding color. Sample consists of all household heads in IFLS who reported being employed at the time of previous interview and who report positive educational expenditures in both previous interview and current interview. *Stayed Employed* group includes household heads who are not working at time of interview *t*. Growth rate of is defined as nominal difference in log educational expenditure in interview *t* and interview *t* – 1. Gap between interviews is three or four years in IFLS. Observations with growth rates in top 2 percent or bottom 2 percent of unconditional educational expenditure growth distribution are discarded to trim outliers. Kernel densities are estimated using an optimal bandwidth procedure. See table 4.5 for corresponding results on extensive margin.

depleting savings, is augmenting labor supply by other members of the household. Columns (4) through (6) of table 4.5 examine labor supply responses. On the extensive margin, Column (4) shows that other household members are 17 percentage points more likely to work for wages when the head of household becomes unemployed. Controlling for other household characteristics does not significantly affect this conclusion. Column (6) examines the income earned by other family members on the intensive margin with a specification analogous to (3) for educational expenditures. The point estimate suggests that income earned by other household members increases by 11 percent in households in which the head becomes unemployed. Figure 4.5 corroborates this result visually. These results suggest that unemployment shocks increase the labor supply of other family members along a variety of margins. Part of these effects may again be due to reverse causality. But other studies (e.g., Beegle, Frankenberg, Thomas 2000, Cameron and Worswick 2003, Frankenberg, Smith, and Thomas 2003) report similar responses in terms of labor market participation, second jobs,

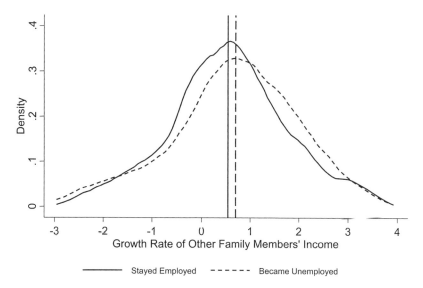

Fig. 4.5   Effect of unemployment on others' labor supply (intensive margin)
Source: IFLS 1993–2000.
Note: Vertical lines denote median for density of corresponding color. Sample consists of all household heads in IFLS who reported being employed at the time of previous interview and who report positive income from other family members in both previous interview and current interview. *Stayed Employed* group includes household heads who remain employed in interview *t*. *Became Unemployed* group includes household heads who are not working at time of interview *t*. Growth rate of is defined as nominal difference in log of other family members' income in interview *t* and interview *t* – 1. Gap between interviews is three or four years in IFLS. Observations with growth rates in top 2 percent or bottom 2 percent of unconditional other-income growth distribution are discarded to trim outliers. Kernel densities are estimated using an optimal bandwidth procedure. See table 4.5 for corresponding results on extensive margin.

and additional hours of work among household members using better identification of exogenous shocks.

The methods used to smooth consumption in Indonesia contrast sharply with corresponding patterns in the United States. Dynarski and Gruber (1997) examine how households smooth variable earnings in the United States. They find that (a) transfer income (e.g., unemployment insurance) replaces 15 cents of every dollar of lost income, (b) changes in tax burdens replace 26 to 35 cents per dollar lost, and (c) savings are used to replace the remaining 25 to 40 cents. In addition, Cullen and Gruber (2000) observe that there is no change in labor supply of secondary earners at the mean when household heads lose their jobs in the United States. On the human capital margin, there is some anecdotal evidence that investment in human capital (e.g., graduate school applications) *rises* during recessions in the United States, as people substitute timing of education intertemporally to periods when the opportunity cost of going to school is low. These points suggest that households in lower-income countries use much more costly smoothing mechanisms than those in developed economies.

4.5 Conclusion

Unemployment shocks induce remarkably similar reductions in food consumption in the United States and Indonesia. However, households in Indonesia use much more costly methods to smooth consumption than households in the United States. Even though they may have little effect on consumption volatility, social insurance programs could yield substantial welfare gains in developing economies by reducing the need for these costly behaviors. These gains would arise because households would not be forced to pull children out of school or send additional members into the workforce to maintain consumption in the short run.

The results of this paper indicate that programs such as unemployment insurance *could* be beneficial in certain domains. Additional empirical work is required to determine whether increases in social insurance benefits actually do reduce inefficient behavior in developing economies. Another important caveat is that we have not examined the types of social insurance programs that would be feasible in developing countries. If these programs were to offer only limited or unequal coverage (e.g., to public-sector employees), then they could induce additional behavioral distortions (such as a preference for public-sector work) that could exacerbate economic inefficiency. Further research is required to determine whether the constraints imposed by the political economy of developing countries would permit welfare-enhancing social insurance programs. This research agenda is especially relevant for South and East Asian economies as they reach a phase of development in which implementation of a formal social safety net is feasible.

References

Acemoglu, Daron, and Robert Shimer. 1999. Efficient unemployment insurance. *Journal of Political Economy* 107:893–928.
Beegle, Kathleen, Elizabeth Frankenberg, and Duncan Thomas. 2000. *Labor market transitions of men and women during an economic crisis: Evidence from Indonesia.* RAND Labor and Population Working Paper 00-11. Santa Monica, CA: RAND.
Browning, Martin, and Thomas Crossley. 2001. Unemployment insurance levels and consumption changes. *Journal of Public Economics* 80:1–23.
Cameron, Lisa, and Christopher Worswick. 2003. The labor market as a smoothing device: Labor supply responses to crop loss. *Review of Development Economics* 7 (2): 327–41.

Chetty, Raj, and Adam Looney. 2006. Consumption smoothing and the welfare consequences of social insurance in developing economies. *Journal of Public Economics* 90:2351–56.

Cochrane, John H. 1991. A simple test of consumption insurance. *Journal of Political Economy* 99:957–76.

Cullen, Julie, and Jonathan Gruber. 2000. Does unemployment insurance crowd out spousal labor supply? *Journal of Labor Economics* 18:546–72.

Dercon, S. 2002. Income risk, coping strategies, and safety nets. *The World Bank Research Observer,* 17 (2): 141–66.

Dynarski, Susan, and Jonathan Gruber. 1997. *Can families smooth variable earnings?* Brookings Papers on Economic Activity. 1:229–305.

Frankenberg, Elizabeth, James Smith, and Duncan Thomas. 2003. Economic shocks, wealth and welfare. *Journal of Human Resources* 38 (2): 280–321.

Frankenberg, Elizabeth, Duncan Thomas, and Kathleen Beegle. 1999. *The real costs of Indonesia's economic crisis: Preliminary findings from the Indonesia family life surveys, DRU-2064-NIA/NICHD.* Santa Monica, CA: RAND.

Gertler, Paul, and Jonathan Gruber. 2002. Insuring consumption against illness. *American Economic Review* 92 (1): 51–70.

Gertler, Paul, David Levine, and Enrico Moretti. 2001. *Do microfinance programs help families insure consumption against illness?* Mimeo.

Gordon, Roger, and Wei Li. 2005. *Tax structures in developing countries: Many puzzles and a possible explanation.* NBER Working Paper no. 11267. Cambridge, MA: National Bureau of Economic Research.

Gough, Ian, Geof Wood, Armando Barrientos, Phillipa Bevan, Peter Davis, and Graham Room. 2004. *Insecurity and welfare regimes in Asia, Africa and Latin America: Social policy in development contexts.* Cambridge: Cambridge University Press.

Gruber, Jonathan. 1997. The consumption smoothing benefits of unemployment insurance. *American Economic Review* 87:192–205.

———. 1998. Unemployment insurance, consumption smoothing, and private insurance: Evidence from the PSID and CEX. *Research in Employment Policy* 1:3–31.

Holzmann, Robert, and Steen Jørgensen. 2001. Social risk management: A new conceptual framework for social protection, and beyond. *International Tax and Public Finance* 8 (4): 529–56.

International Labour Organization. 2000. *World labour report 2000: Income security and social protection in a changing world.* Geneva: International Labour Office.

Morduch, Jonathan. 1995. Income smoothing and consumption smoothing. *Journal of Economic Perspectives* 9 (3): 103–14.

———. 1999. Between the market and the state: Can informal insurance patch the safety net? *World Bank Research Observer* 14 (2): 187–207.

Thomas, Duncan, Kathleen Beegle, Elizabeth Frankenberg, Bondan Sikoki, John Strauss, and Graciela Teruel. 2004. Education in a crisis. *Journal of Development Economics* 74 (1): 53–85.

Townsend, Robert. 1994. Risk and insurance in Village India. *Econometrica* 62 (3): 539–91.

Zeldes, Stephen. 1989. Consumption and liquidity constraints: An empirical investigation. *Journal of Political Economy* 97 (2): 305–46.

Comment   Roger Gordon

Government policies differ systematically between poorer and richer countries. One striking difference is the much smaller weight given to social insurance programs among poorer countries, particularly those in East Asia.

Past work on this topic has provided one possible explanation for this lack of social insurance. Evidence from household surveys among various developing countries suggests that transitory shocks to household income lead to remarkably little variation in household consumption. But if household consumption does not vary much, the presumption naturally has been that there is little potential welfare gain from smoothing consumption further through unemployment insurance or other safety net programs. Given the many distortions to incentives that these programs create, if potential benefits are low, then it should not be at all surprising that these programs are not used much among developing countries.

Raj Chetty and Adam Looney, in this paper, provide confirming evidence from a household survey in Indonesia that household consumption does not vary much in response to unemployment of the household head. They compare the response of consumption to unemployment in the United States and Indonesia, and remarkably find about the same drop in consumption in the two countries, in each case a relatively modest 10 percent.

Nonetheless, they question the inference others have drawn from such data that there is little room for insurance gains through the introduction of unemployment insurance programs. In particular, they argue that the fall in consumption may have been so small just because any fall is particularly costly to the household. Rather than suffering a loss in consumption, the household instead may seek out other sources of funds, potentially at great cost to the household. For example, Chetty and Looney document that household expenditures on the education of their children drop substantially in response to an unemployment spell, potentially leading to a large long-run fall in the earnings potential of these children. In addition, there is a clear increase in the labor supply of other household members, suggesting a major disruption to the household. Even given these responses, household consumption of rice and other staples still drops noticeably, particularly among nonfarm households, suggesting the substantial financial stress unemployed households are experiencing.

Given the high cost these households apparently accept to alleviate any fall in consumption, the welfare cost of even the observed 10 percent fall in consumption could well be large. This in turn suggests that the welfare benefit from introduction of unemployment insurance could potentially be large.

Roger Gordon is a professor of economics at the University of California, San Diego, and a research associate of the National Bureau of Economic Research.

I very much agree with these arguments, and with Chetty and Looney's judgment in interpreting the empirical evidence. Nonetheless, my role as a discussant is to point out places where the evidence is less than compelling. I will focus in turn on three issues. First, is it so clear that the costs borne by the Indonesian household in coping with unemployment are so dramatic? Second, how confident can we be in the consistency of the point estimates suggesting a very modest fall in consumption in response to unemployment? Third, even if this drop is costly, how confident can we be that unemployment insurance would help alleviate this fall?

How Big Are the Costs of Coping?

Chetty and Looney very appropriately suggest based on the reported empirical evidence on coping strategies followed by Indonesian households that their coping responses may be very costly. How costly in fact are these coping mechanisms?

The most costly would appear to be the drop in expenditures on education. One possible interpretation of this drop, however, is that the schools are providing a short-term loan to the parents, with little or no change in the education of the children. Within a closely knit community, such sharing of short-term financial risks could well develop and be sustainable. Direct evidence on the schooling patterns of the children, both during the unemployment spell and thereafter, would strengthen this claim.

How costly is it for other household members to enter the labor force? A married couple faces time demands within the household, and financial pressure to earn money outside the household. Given the fixed costs of going to work, it may make sense for only one member of the couple to work. On economic grounds, the choice of which member works should depend on comparative advantage: relative wage rates in the labor force versus relative productivities within the household. If there were little difference in comparative advantage between husband and wife, then they might easily be able to shift roles in response to one having been laid off. While there could well be clear differences in comparative advantage, or fixed costs of finding a job, these have not been documented. The fact that consumption falls so little suggests little cost.

To the extent that households have accumulated assets, any reduction in standard of living would be spread across all future dates, and not entirely absorbed through a drop in current consumption. According to the data reported in the paper, Indonesian households have remarkably high assets relative to income. As reported in table 4.2, mean household assets are $7,525 while mean total family income is only $1,484 and mean labor income of the head a mere $580. With assets equal to five times total family income and thirteen times the labor income of the potentially unemployed head, households have huge reserves to draw on to help cover short-run expenses if the head becomes unemployed. Chetty and Looney point out that many of these assets may be illiquid. Even so, they should provide good collateral for loans, particularly in response to an event that is likely to reflect only a short-run drop in household income.

If households can make use of these assets to smooth consumption, then the change in consumption should largely reflect the change in permanent income. If so, the 10 percent fall in consumption would reflect a 10 percent fall in permanent income.

For the foregone income while unemployed to lead to a 10 percent fall in permanent income, the expected spell length would need to be several years (e.g., 10 percent of the remaining time in the labor force), rather than the more typical several months, so seems implausible. However, it would be entirely plausible that the expected earnings in future employment will have dropped by 10 percent due to becoming unemployed.

Assets are presumably so large to protect against just such shocks to future income. That people feel compelled to build up such large reserves, implying postponing consumption until much later in the lifecycle, is itself a reflection of the lack of insurance, and also the potentially higher risks faced by Indonesian households compared with those in the United States. Again, according to the data in table 4.2, the coefficient of variation (the standard deviation divided by the mean) of total household income in Indonesia is 2.4, compared with only 0.95 in the United States, suggesting that Indonesian households face far more risk than do U.S. households. The coefficient of variation in their food consumption is also higher than in the United States: 1.15 versus 0.64. However, the degree of smoothing of income shocks in Indonesia is a bit higher than in the United States. In particular, the ratio of the coefficient of variation in food consumption compared with the coefficient of variation in total household income is 0.47 in Indonesia compared with 0.67 in the United States, suggesting that Indonesian household are able to smooth a larger fraction of their income fluctuations. This is true even without being able to rely on unemployment insurance and even given the much larger fraction of their income spent on food.

Size of Fall in Consumption Caused by Unemployment

The paper compares the changes in consumption over time for those who become unemployed to the change in consumption for those who remain at work, with various controls, and finds that consumption of the unemployed falls by 10 percent relative to the consumption of those who remain employed. How confident can we be that this estimate reflects the causal effect of unemployment?

Keep in mind that this estimate measures the fall in consumption *relative* to what happened for those who did not become unemployed. Yet, this time period (spanning the financial crisis in Asia) involved particularly large shocks for all households, and not just for those who became unemployed. As a reflection of this, average household consumption as reported in table 4.2 is 108 percent of total household income, something that is clearly not sustainable. This suggests that households as a group are receiving unusually low income at the moment relative to the standard of living they feel is sustainable.

Even employed households then seem to be experiencing a downturn in income, and presumably compensate through some drop in consumption. The estimates reflect the additional drop in consumption for those who become unemployed.

Chetty and Looney do provide one robustness check for the role of the Asian financial crisis, by splitting the samples into data for 1997 and 2000. They find similar results for the two years, and infer that their results are not strongly affected by the financial crisis. The timing of their data, unfortunately, is not ideal for such a test, since the financial crisis affected Indonesia only for the last few months of 1997, and some residual effect of the crisis would still have been present in 2000.

That current income falls *more* for the unemployed than for the employed seems clear, though no attempt has been made to estimate the differential fall in income. Regardless, the size of the drop in permanent income for those who remain employed compared with those who become unemployed is not so clear. The unemployed, for example, could represent those who quit because they were more optimistic of finding better employment elsewhere.

Probably the longest spells of unemployment arise when households move to a new location in search of a better job. The greater the potential improvement in earnings, the longer the spell of unemployment they would be willing to endure in exchange. In equilibrium, expected permanent income may not change due to this move. It may even go up if only those households able to accumulate sufficient reserves to carry them through this spell of unemployment move to these better locations, limiting the supply of migrants.

Effects of Unemployment Insurance on the Drop in Consumption

Chetty and Looney argue that a small fall in consumption in response to unemployment does *not* necessarily imply that the potential welfare benefit from provision of unemployment insurance is also small. Individuals could well be sufficiently risk averse that alleviating even this small fall in consumption could have substantial welfare benefits. That the fall in consumption is so small could in fact be indirect evidence that individuals are very risk averse.

How much of an effect, though, would provision of unemployment insurance in Indonesia have in lessening the fall in consumption following unemployment, and thereby raising welfare? That the fall in consumption is virtually identical to that estimated in the United States raises questions about the size of any potential benefits from UI. The United States has a sizeable UI program while Indonesia provides little or no government assistance to the unemployed. Seeing an equal fall in consumption in the two countries suggests in itself that the provision of unemployment insurance provides no net smoothing of consumption. Given its distortions to layoff decisions and to spell lengths, this comparison raises serious questions about the value of the program.

Cross-country comparisons, of course, require great caution. *Unemployment* could reflect very different circumstances in Indonesia than in the United States. The unemployed, for example, may have much better access to informal jobs in Indonesia than in the United States, offsetting much of the fall in earnings in Indonesia. If the percent fall in current income is much greater in the United States than in Indonesia, and households in both countries are credit constrained, yet the fall in consumption is the same in both countries, then there is indirect evidence that unemployment insurance does help. Unemployment insurance can be very effective at relaxing credit constraints, and so can be effective at smoothing consumption to the degree that households are credit constrained.

The potential role of unemployment insurance in smoothing consumption would be very different, though, if the unemployed are not credit constrained. For the credit constrained, unemployment benefits should raise consumption dollar for dollar. In contrast, if individuals are able to smooth consumption over time by drawing on their assets, or through borrowing against future earnings, then consumption fluctuates only due to fluctuations in expectations about permanent income.

Unemployment insurance makes no attempt to insure uncertainty about the earnings in one's future job. At best, unemployment insurance covers some fraction of the foregone income while unemployed. Yet the lost earnings while unemployed may be small relative to the loss in the present value of lifetime earnings resulting from an unemployment spell. For example, if an unemployment spell on average lasts for f percent of a year, and subsequent jobs pay on average a percent less than one's current job, then the net percent loss in lifetime income due to unemployment equals approximately $f(r - g) + a(1 - f[r - g])$, where r is the real interest rate and g is the growth rate in earnings. If $f \approx .5$ (more typical in the United States would be around .2), $a \approx .1$ implying a 10 percent fall in earnings, and $r - g \approx .04$, then the loss in future earnings is five times as large in present value as the lost wages while unemployed. Yet UI at best offsets only a fraction of these lost wages, and so a very small fraction of the drop in lifetime income. Unemployment insurance will therefore be largely ineffective at smoothing consumption to the extent that fluctuations in consumption reflect fluctuations in lifetime income.

To what extent are observed fluctuations in consumption in Indonesia due to credit constraints rather than fluctuations in lifetime income? To the extent that individuals have sufficient assets (or sufficient borrowing capacity) to finance their consumption until they are reemployed, then the current fall in consumption should reflect the size of the fall in lifetime earnings, and not the fall in current income while unemployed. The sizeable assets available to Indonesian households certainly suggest that they are in a position to smooth consumption.

To what degree are Indonesian households credit constrained, in spite of their substantial assets? More concretely, to what degree is the fall in their consumption larger than would be expected based on the change in their lifetime income caused by becoming unemployed, suggesting the presence of credit constraints?

To judge this, it would be helpful to see evidence on the effects of unemployment on lifetime incomes in Indonesia. With the survey data, what is feasible is to measure the effects of unemployment on expected earnings three years later. To what degree are expected earnings lower in year $t + 2$ for those unemployed in year t, relative to earnings in year $t - 2$, compared with the outcomes for those who do not become unemployed? How does the 10 percent drop in their relative consumptions compare with the relative percent drop in their future earnings? To begin with, any excess drop in consumption provides an estimate of the degree to which credit constraints are binding. Of course, the answer here may depend strongly on the stage in the lifecycle, with the young presumably more credit constrained than the middle-aged.

One other complication, though, is that the variance of future income could be greater for the unemployed than for those who are employed in year t. Facing greater uncertainty, the unemployed may reduce their current consumption as a form of precautionary savings, even without any liquidity constraints. Unemployment insurance plays little role in alleviating this future uncertainty, and so would have little effect on current consumption if precautionary savings rather than liquidity constraints explain the current fall in consumption.

In sum, the observed fall in consumption in Indonesia following unemployment can reflect a fall in permanent income, increased precautionary savings, and/or the presence of liquidity constraints. Unemployment insurance would be effective at smoothing consumption largely to the degree to which liquidity constraints explain the observed fall.

Summary

In sum, Chetty and Looney argue that there could be large potential welfare gains from the introduction of unemployment insurance in Indonesia, to help alleviate costly coping mechanisms in response to unemployment, particularly the drop in spending on education. Whether unemployment insurance would plausibly be effective at alleviating such costs, though, is a separate question that merits further investigation.

Comment   Mario B. Lamberte

The paper empirically shows that idiosyncratic unemployment shocks lead to consumption fluctuation of similar magnitude in the United States and Indonesia. One may conclude from these results that developing economies like Indonesia have adequate social insurance because they can smooth consumption paths in the face of shocks despite the absence of formal social insurance similar to those that can be found in developed economies. If so, the implication is that formal social insurance for developing economies offers small marginal welfare gains. However, this may not necessarily be the case. By developing a normative framework, Chetty was able to demonstrate that a small drop in consumption after a shock can be attributed to either of the two: (a) agents are able to easily and inexpensively smooth consumption by borrowing or through informal insurance mechanisms, or (b) agents are risk averse to fluctuations and are inclined to undertake costly consumption-smoothing actions. In the first case, formal social insurance will yield small marginal welfare gains, while in the second case the same will generate large marginal welfare gains. He then went on to provide three sets of evidence for the presence of high risk aversion in Indonesia. This being the case, formal social insurance can therefore yield large marginal welfare gains.

One of the interesting proofs offered by Chetty that point out the possibility of having high risk aversion in Indonesia is that households undertook costly consumption-smoothing methods by reducing educational expenditures on children to deal with temporary idiosyncratic shock. As is well known, the Philippines was also adversely affected by the recent Asian financial crisis, and there were pieces of evidence that households attempted to fend off a decline in consumption by making some adjustments. Reyes et al. (2001, 168), for instance, made the following conclusion from their analysis:

> Even if figures from different data sources did not match, still it was clear that the crisis had the following effects: (1) enrollment in both elementary and secondary school levels had increased but at a lower rate than the usual rate; (2) households had allowed their older children already in school to continue, but postponed the enrollment of new entrants both

Mario B. Lamberte was formerly the president of the Philippine Institute for Development Studies (PIDS), and is currently a microfinance manager of EMERGE, a Philippine government project supported by USAID.

at the elementary and secondary levels; (3) dropout rate of those already in school was not affected in the elementary and private secondary school but increased in public secondary schools;[1] and (4) children had smaller food and transportation allowances.[2]

Given the previous, the Philippines could be in the same league as Indonesia as far as this paper is concerned.

The inverse relationship between the drop in consumption and risk aversion is key to the paper's argument that formal social insurance can have large marginal welfare gains. Since the drop in consumption in the face of idiosyncratic shock has been observed to be small in Indonesia, empirically proving the existence of high risk aversion becomes crucial. While I agree with the author that a la Binswanger method of inferring risk aversion can lead to misleading results, however, I still feel uncomfortable with the author's method of inferring risk aversion. Take for example the first indicator of risk aversion that is based on average household income cited by the author. One can imagine a situation wherein two groups of households have the same average household income, yet one may show greater risk aversion than the other. That is, when faced with two investments with the same expected return but two different risks, one prefers the one with the lower risk. Another is labor supply response. When some members of the family are involuntarily unemployed, looking for a menial job while the household head is temporarily unemployed may not be a costly labor response. Unfortunately, I could not offer an alternative method for empirically verifying degrees of risk aversion of households.

Assuming that high risk aversion is present in developing economies, an important issue that must be addressed, which the paper has intentionally not covered, is how to finance such a formal social insurance system. Most developing economies are usually confronted with a tax structure and tax administration system that is inefficient, resulting in low tax effort. This cannot be easily fixed in a reasonably short period of time, and institutions to run a social insurance scheme are either absent or inefficient, thereby exposing such scheme to a greater moral hazard problem. That is why the role of an informal insurance system and informal credit market as consumption-smoothing mechanisms cannot be underemphasized in developing economies. Unfortunately, the author has not examined in detail the importance of these mechanisms relative to risk aversion in Indonesia. In the Philippines, for instance, 63 percent of households surveyed availed from

---

1. This may mean that poor households who normally send their children to free public high school education were more adversely affected by the crisis and asked older children to leave school to save money (i.e., food and transportation allowance) and probably to put them in the labor market.

2. It could be that parents force their children to consume cheaply priced, but low quality food and to walk to school instead of taking a bus, jeepney, or tricycle. So, while children continue to go to school, their school performance suffers.

credit during the crisis period mainly from informal money lenders (Reyes et al. 2001). Of the amount borrowed, 27 percent went to support school expenses of children; 21 percent to pay for medical expenses of sick household members; 19 percent for house repair; and another 16 percent to support household activities. Borrowing from the informal credit market could be a less costly response than reducing human capital accumulation. While I agree that NGOs are not a reliable source of social insurance, relatives and neighbors are known to fill that gap to a certain extent.

Reference

Reyes, Celia M., Rosario G. Manasan, Aniceto C. Orbeta, Jr., and Generoso de Guzman. 2001. Impact of the East Asian crisis on households. In *Economic crisis. . . once more,* ed. M. Lamberte, 145–98. Makati: Philippine Institute for Development Studies.

III

International Long-Run
Sustainability Issues

Will China Eat Our Lunch or Take Us to Dinner? Simulating the Transition Paths of the United States, the European Union, Japan, and China

Hans Fehr, Sabine Jokisch, and Laurence J. Kotlikoff

5.1 Introduction

This paper develops a dynamic, life-cycle, general equilibrium model to study the interdependent demographic, fiscal, and economic transition paths of China, Japan, the United States, and the European Union. Each of these countries/regions is entering a period of rapid and significant aging that will require major fiscal adjustments. Understanding how national aging and the fiscal reaction to national aging will affect the macroeconomies of these regions is important. If the macroeconomic response is favorable, governments can do less and take more time to deal with what's coming. If the opposite is true, governments must do more and do it more quickly.

Our past research (Fehr, Jokisch, and Kotlikoff 2004a, 2004b, 2005) suggested an unfavorable macroeconomic response to national aging arising from a growing shortage of physical capital relative to human capital. This long-term capital shortage sufficed to reduce the model's real wage per unit of human capital by 20 percent over the course of the century. The model's predicted major decline in capital per unit of human capital connects to the model's predicted major rise in payroll and income tax rates. These tax

Hans Fehr is a professor of economics at the Julius-Maximilians-Universität Würzburg. Sabine Jokisch is a researcher in the department of environmental and resource economics, environmental management at the Centre for European Economic Research. Laurence J. Kotlikoff is a professor of economics at Boston University and a research associate of the National Bureau of Economic Research.

We thank Charles Horioka, Bernd Raffelhüschen, and Reinhold Schnabel for providing key data. Research support by the U.S. Social Security Administration, Boston University, the Deutsche Forschungsgemeinschaft, and the Universitätsbund Würzburg is gratefully acknowledged.

hikes, in turn, reflect the need to pay pension and health care benefits to increasingly older populations. As originally stressed by Feldstein (1974), raising taxes on workers to make transfers to the elderly reduces the amount of capital workers individually and collectively can and will accumulate.

But our earlier studies, with their dismal forecasts that the interaction of aging and huge fiscal commitments to the elderly will undermine the macroeconomies of the developed world, omitted two issues. Both of these issues are taken up here, and both militate against a severe capital shortage.

The first is government investment. In our prior studies we treated all government purchases as current consumption. There is some logic for doing so, since many so-called government investment goods (e.g., tanks, office buildings to house bureaucrats, space vehicles) may make little or no contribution to the nation's output and productivity and, indeed, may do the opposite. On the other hand, the lion's share of government investment, be it in constructing roads, erecting schools, building research labs, does seem to be productive.

Treating what governments call *investment* as investment in the model doesn't entirely eliminate the predicted long-term capital shortage, but it does significantly mitigate it. Compared with its 2004 value, the model's real wage per unit of human capital in 2100 is reduced by only 4 percent rather than by 20 percent.

The second omission is China. As everyone knows, China is already a major producer of world output. Its GDP now equals roughly one ninth of U.S. output. China is also absorbing Western and Japanese technology at a rapid clip. This acquisition of technology, in combination with improved education, holds the prospect for ongoing real income growth in China. But, given China's exceptionally high saving rate, more income growth in China means more Chinese saving that can be invested in the developed world as well as in China.

The potential for China and other developing countries to bail out the developed world, at least in terms of its capital needs, has recently been advanced by Jeremy Siegel (2005). But China has a long way to go if it is to play such a role. China's per capita income and wealth levels are currently only a small fraction—probably less than 15 percent—of the developed world's levels. Of course, China has lots of capitas—its population is 2.6 times the combined populations of the United States, Japan, and the European Union. Still, China's current total holdings of wealth appear to be less than one quarter and could easily be less than one tenth of total wealth holdings across the four regions.

Moreover, Chinese saving behavior may change. It's certainly far from what one would expect to see. One would think that having low current income, but the prospect of much higher future income, would lead the Chinese to spend most of what they now produce. But, if official statistics are to be believed, nothing could be further from the truth. According to OECD

(2002) data, the Chinese private sector appears to be saving 40.0 percent of private available output, defined as net national income minus government purchases of goods and services. This extraordinarily high Chinese private-sector saving rate explains why the Chinese are currently exporting more capital to the rest of the world than they are importing. Based on European Commission (2005) data, the comparable private-sector saving rates in the United States, Japan, and the European Union are only 4.0 percent, 11.5 percent, and 11.1 percent, respectively.

China is also remarkable when it comes to aging. Like the developed world, China is getting older. But it's projected over the next half century to age much more rapidly than the United States, Japan, or the European Union. This doesn't mean that China will end up older than these regions. It just means it will make the transformation from a relatively young to a very old society much more rapidly than its trading partners in the developed world.

As table 5.1 details, only 6.8 percent of today's Chinese are 65 and older compared with 17.2 percent in Japan, 16.4 percent in the European Union, and 12.3 percent in the United States. In 2050, 23.6 percent of the Chinese population will be 65 plus. This is larger than the 20.6 percent elderly share projected for the United States, but smaller than the 28.6 and 35.9 percent shares projected in the European Union and Japan, respectively. So the rapidity of China's aging doesn't reflect where it will end up, but where it is starting.

The fact that China, like Japan and the West, is aging and faces significant fiscal obligations associated with that process suggests that China's inclusion in our model would make little difference to the model's unpleasant prediction of a looming capital shortage. But because of China's much higher rates of growth and saving, and because its population is so large, adding China can, as documented in the following, transform a capital shortage into a capital glut. Whether or not this occurs depends on how China's fiscal policy and saving behavior evolve. If, over the course of the next 50 years, China adopts fiscal arrangements and saving propensities that are similar to those of developing nations, China will make only a modest contribution to the world's supply of capital, leaving real wages per unit of human capital at the end of this century only about 4 percent higher than they are today. If, on the other hand, China limits growth in public expenditures and the Chinese people continue to eschew consumption, China will save enough for its own capital needs as well as those of the developed world, leaving real wages per unit of human capital at the end of this century roughly 60 percent above the current level.

The usefulness of these findings depends, of course, on the realism of our model. Our life-cycle model's features are a mouthful. The model includes age-, region-, and year-specific fertility and mortality rates; lifespan uncertainty; age-, region-, and year-specific pension; disability, health care,

Table 5.1   **Comparing actual and simulated population projections**

Year	2000	2010	2020	2030	2040	2050	2100
Population projection—United States							
Fertility rate							
Model	2.11	2.05	2.00	1.95	1.90	1.85	1.77
Official[a]	2.11	2.08	2.03	1.95	1.89	1.85	
Life expectancy at birth							
Model	81.7	82.1	82.5	83.0	83.4	83.8	83.8
Official[a]	77.1	78.3	79.1	79.9	81.0	81.6	
Total population[b]							
Model	276.2	307.3	340.0	366.4	385.8	400.3	442.0
Official[a]	285.0	314.9	344.3	370.4	391.4	408.7	
Age structure[c]							
<15							
Model	21.6	20.1	19.7	18.5	18.2	17.8	15.9
Official[a]	21.8	20.5	20.0	19.3	18.5	17.9	
15–64							
Model	66.2	67.2	64.0	61.4	61.7	62.1	60.7
Official[a]	65.9	66.6	64.1	61.5	61.7	62.1	
65–90							
Model	12.2	12.7	16.3	20.1	20.2	20.1	23.3
Official[a]	12.3	12.8	15.9	19.2	19.8	20.0	
Population projection—European Union							
Fertility rate							
Model	1.46	1.53	1.60	1.67	1.74	1.82	1.82
Official[d]	1.58	1.61	1.68	1.77	1.84	1.85	
Life expectancy at birth							
Model	82.2	82.7	83.2	83.6	84.1	84.6	84.6
Official[d]	78.6	80.0	81.1	82.0	83.0	83.6	
Total population[b]							
Model	376.4	385.8	390.9	391.1	384.1	372.1	340.6
Official[a]	377.3	383.2	384.4	382.8	377.8	369.8	
Age structure[c]							
<15							
Model	16.9	15.3	14.5	14.3	14.3	14.8	16.5
Official[a]	16.7	15.3	14.4	14.4	14.7	15.0	
15–64							
Model	66.9	66.9	64.7	60.8	57.7	57.2	59.7
Official[a]	66.9	66.5	64.7	60.8	57.5	56.7	
65–90							
Model	16.2	17.8	20.8	24.9	28.0	28.0	23.9
Official[a]	16.3	18.2	21.0	24.7	27.8	28.3	
Population projection—Japan							
Fertility rate							
Model	1.28	1.37	1.47	1.56	1.66	1.75	1.91
Official[a]	1.32	1.37	1.49	1.68	1.81	1.85	
Life expectancy at birth							
Model	83.8	84.6	85.4	86.2	87.0	87.8	87.8
Official[a]	81.6	83.5	85.1	86.6	87.7	88.1	

Table 5.1   (continued)

Year	2000	2010	2020	2030	2040	2050	2100
Total population[b]							
Model	126.7	128.9	127.1	121.8	114.2	108.8	84.8
Official[a]	127.0	128.0	125.6	121.0	115.7	109.7	
Age structure[c]							
<15							
Model	14.6	13.4	12.5	11.9	12.5	12.9	16.0
Official[a]	14.6	13.6	12.4	11.8	12.6	13.0	
15–64							
Model	68.2	64.1	59.2	58.1	55.0	52.1	56.3
Official[a]	68.2	64.0	59.5	57.8	53.0	50.4	
65–90							
Model	17.2	22.5	28.2	30.0	32.5	35.0	27.7
Official[a]	17.2	22.4	28.1	30.4	34.4	36.5	
Population projection—China							
Fertility rate							
Model	1.62	1.67	1.71	1.76	1.80	1.85	2.01
Official[e]	1.32	1.37	1.49	1.68	1.81	1.85	
Life expectancy at birth							
Model	75.8	76.7	77.5	78.4	79.3	80.2	80.2
Official[e]	71.5	72.6	73.8	75.3	77.1	78.7	
Total population[b]							
Model	1273.1	1360.7	1455.0	1490.7	1481.3	1430.8	1181.8
Official[e]	1274.0	1354.5	1423.9	1446.5	1433.4	1392.3	
Age structure[c]							
<15							
Model	24.6	19.5	18.3	16.5	15.6	16.3	18.5
Official[e]	24.8	19.5	18.4	16.9	15.6	15.7	
15–64							
Model	68.6	73.3	70.6	67.8	63.1	61.6	61.7
Official[e]	68.4	72.2	69.7	66.8	62.1	60.7	
65–90							
Model	6.8	7.2	11.1	15.7	21.3	22.0	19.8
Official[e]	6.8	8.3	11.9	16.3	22.3	23.6	

[a]UNPD (2003), medium variant projections.
[b]In millions.
[c]In percent of total population.
[d]UNPD (2003), medium variant projections, Western Europe.
[e]UNPD (2005), medium variant projections.

and other government-transfer policies; region- and year-specific government purchases of goods and services; region-specific levels of debt; high, middle, and low earners within each cohort in each region; region-specific personal wage income, capital income, corporate income, and payroll taxes; international capital mobility; technological change; quadratic costs of adjusting each region's capital stock; age-specific inheritances; age-specific and unintended bequests; intertemporally separable CES utility functions in consumption and leisure; region-specific Cobb-Douglas production functions; the presence of children's utility in parents' utility functions when the children are young; exogenously specified age-, earnings class-, region-, and year-specific immigration; and region- and cohort-specific time preference rates.

As with our other three regions, to accommodate Chinese saving behavior, we've set the Chinese time preference rate to match the current observed saving rate for China. And we've calibrated the multifactor productivity coefficient in the Chinese production function to match the current observed Chinese relative wage. The big questions with respect to China's calibration, however, are not how to treat current saving preferences and technology, but rather how to model future saving preferences and technology.

Consider first the issue of technology. It seems reasonable to believe that the level of Chinese technology will converge to that of the West. The unknown is the rate of convergence. In this study we assume that the Chinese multifactor productivity coefficient rises gradually, reaching the United States, Japanese, and European Union rates by mid century. But we also consider slower and faster rates of technological convergence.

Now consider modeling future Chinese saving behavior. Here we examine two alternative assumptions. The first is that the Chinese time preference rate remains fixed through time at the very low rate needed to calibrate the current Chinese saving rate. The second is that successive cohorts of Chinese gradually adopt Western saving behavior such that the Chinese born in 2050 and thereafter have the same time preference rate as Americans in 2004.

5.2   Our Model and Its Predecessors

The development of dynamic life-cycle simulation models was stimulated by Feldstein's (1974) article contending that government pension systems lower national saving. Early dynamic analyses of government pension programs and other policies include Kotlikoff (1979), Summers (1981), Auerbach and Kotlikoff (1983, 1987), and Seidman (1986). More recent papers have considered the importance of land, earnings uncertainty, political economy considerations, liquidity constraints, different options for funding Social Security, and human capital decisions. These studies include Hubbard and Judd (1987); Imrohoroglu, Imrohoroglu, and Joines (1995, 1999); Kotlikoff (1996); Huang, Imrohoroglu, and Sargent (1997); Huggett and Ventura (1999); Cooley and Soares (1999a, 1999b); De Nardi, Imrohoroglu, and Sargent (1999); Kotlikoff, Smetters, and Walliser (1998a, 1998b, 1999, and 2002); Raffelhüschen (1989, 1993); Heckman, Lochner, and Taber (1998); Bohn (2001); Smetters and Walliser (2004); Nishiyama and Smetters (2004); and Fehr and Habermann (2005).

This model, like our previous ones, builds on Auerbach-Kotlikoff's (1987) overlapping generation (OLG) model. Auerbach and Kotlikoff also simulated demographic transitions, but their model assumed that all agents gave birth at a fixed age, died and bequeathed at a fixed age, and received inheritances at a fixed age. Kotlikoff, Smetters, and Walliser (2001) advanced the Auerbach-Kotlikoff model by incorporating age-specific fertility and inheritance, lifespan extension, intragenerational earnings heterogeneity, and additional fiscal institutions. Fehr, Jokisch, and Kotlikoff (2004a,b, 2005) included lifespan uncertainty as well as bequests arising from incomplete annuitization. They also introduced multiple regions with international capital mobility and immigration.

As in Kotlikoff, Smetters, and Walliser (2001), our model features monozygotic reproduction with agents in their child-bearing years giving birth each year to fractions of children. This means of finessing marriage and family formation permits us to incorporate changes through time in age-specific fertility rates and to closely line up our model's age-specific population shares to those forecast for the four regions.

We assume that agents care about their children's utility when they are young and, as a consequence, make consumption expenditures on behalf of their children (pay for their consumption), but only when the children are young. We also assume that agents die with realistic mortality probabilities starting at age 68. Agents fully appreciate the uncertainty of their longevities and maximize, at any point in time, their expected remaining lifetime utilities. The inclusion of lifespan uncertainty permits a realistic modeling of bequests and inheritances.

We generate bequests by assuming that agents fail to annuitize their assets in old age. Hence, when they die, they leave undesired bequests to their children. Since agents die at different ages and have children of different ages, their heirs also inherit at different ages. Agents who were born when their parents were young receive inheritances later in their life than do their younger siblings. Finally, uninsurable lifespan uncertainty leads agents to gradually reduce their consumption in old age.

Our model also includes capital adjustment costs. As is well known, these costs can drive temporary wedges between the marginal products of capital in different regions and lead the market values of capital assets to temporarily differ from their replacement costs. Thus inclusion of adjustment costs in the model generates what amounts to regional stock markets and permits us to explore how population aging affects world stock prices through time.

A final, but very important, feature of our framework is its intracohort disaggregation. As in Kotlikoff, Smetters, and Walliser (2001), we consider three income classes within each generation, each with its own earnings ability. Immigrants are also split into these income classes permitting us to simulate the arrival of immigrants with different stocks of human and physical capital.

The following sections present the general structure of our model. A more detailed description of the three-country model is provided in Fehr et al. (2003).

5.2.1   Demographics

Each region is populated by households who live at most to age 90. Consequently, there are 91 generations with surviving members at any point in time. The individual life cycle of a representative agent is described in figure 5.1. Between ages 0 and 20 our agents are children who earn no money and are supported by their parents. At age 21 our agents leave their parents and go to work. Between ages 23 and 45 our agents give birth to fractions of children at the beginning of each year (i.e., the first [fraction of] children are born when the agents are 23 and the last are born when they are age 45). An agent's first-born children (fractions of children) leave home when the parents are age 43, while the last-born leave when the agents are age 66. Our agents die between ages 68 and 90. The probability of death is 1 at age 91. Children always outlive their parents, meaning that parents always outlive grandparents. To see this note that if a parent reaches age 90, his or her oldest children will be 67. These are children who were born when the parent was age 23.

In each year new immigrants in each skill and age group arrive with the same number and age distribution of children and the same level of assets as natives of the identical skill and age. Since the demographic structure has the same general form in all four regions, it suffices to discuss a representative region and omit region indices.

To specify the current and future demographic structure of each region we start with year-2000 age-specific population ($\overline{N}[a, 2000]$) and age-specific net-immigration ($\overline{NM}[a, 2000]$) counts.[1]

In constructing existing as well as future age-population counts, we have to link each initial cohort between the ages of 1 and 68 to those of their parents who are still alive. The reason is that children receive bequests from their parents, and the levels and timing of these inheritances depend on the ages of their parents. This linkage is achieved by applying past fertility rates to each cohort under age 69 in year 2000. If, for example, 15 percent of the parents of newborns in 1980 were 25 years old, then 15 percent of the 20-year-olds in year 2000 are assigned to parents age 45.

In addition, each cohort is split into three income classes, k. Specifically, we assume that 35 percent of each cohort belong to the lowest income class,

---

1. Although the economic model starts in year 2004, we chose year 2000 as the initial year for the population projections due to data availability.

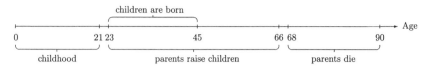

Fig. 5.1   The individual life cycle

10 percent to the top income class, and the remaining 55 percent to the middle income class. We denote the population vector for year t as $N(a, t, s, k)$ where $a = 1, \ldots, s = 23, \ldots, 45, k = 1, 2, 3$. The term s references the age of the parent at the time of birth of agents age a in 2000.

To determine the evolution of the population in each region over time, we applied region-, age-, and year-specific mortality and fertility rates to the cohorts alive in year 2000 as well as to their children as they reach their ages of fertility and mortality. In the baseline path the exogenous current and future mortality and fertility rates follow the medium variant of the United Nations population projection (UNPD, 2003 for the United States, the European Union, and Japan; UNPD, 2005 for China).

According to this projection, mortality rates will decline in all three regions over time. Consider the Japanese, whose 2000 life expectancy equaled 81.6. According to official projections, Japan's life expectancy in 2050 will reach 88.1. The Japanese, who now have a 4.5 year higher life expectancy than Americans and a 3.0 higher life expectancy than European Union citizens, will continue to maintain their longevity lead through time. Indeed, projected 2050 U.S. life expectancy doesn't even exceed current Japanese life expectancy! In China, life expectancy is now a full 10 years lower than life expectancy in Japan. And this 10 year gap is projected to continue for the next half decade.

Table 5.1 shows our agent's life expectancies at birth in the baseline path, which is kept constant after year 2050. The respective numbers are higher than the actual values, since our model's agents don't die prior to age 68. However, the model's life expectancies conditional on reaching age 60 are close to those reported by the UNPD (2005).

Total fertility rates currently equal 2.1, 1.3, 1.6, and 1.5 in the United States, Japan, China, and the European Union, respectively. Nevertheless, the United Nations expects fertility rates in all three regions to converge to 1.85 children by 2050. This path of fertility rates is also shown in table 5.1. In the baseline path, we assume annual net immigration of 1 million per year in the United States, 450,000 in the European Union, and 54,000 in Japan. Net immigration into China is negative. The number of net emigrants is fixed at its current value of 390,000 people per year. Given the population age structure in year 2000 as well as projected future fertility, mortality, and net immigration rates, we compute the population vector $N(a, t, s, k)$ for the years t between 2001 and 2050. After year 2050, fertility rates are endogenously adjusted in order to achieve zero population growth and a stable population age structure. Since net immigration is positive in the United States, the European Union, and Japan, the population-stabilizing post-2050 fertility rates are below 2.0. Equivalently, the fertility rates in China are set above 2.0 after 2050 due to net emigration.

Table 5.1 also shows projected changes over time in total populations and population age structures. Due to high fertility and net immigration rates, the U.S. population is projected to increase from 275 million in 2000 to 442 million in 2100. In Europe, the population falls over the century from 375 to 340 million, and in Japan, the population falls from 126 million to 85 million. The Chinese population decreases by even more—from 1.3 billion to 1.2 billion.

As one would expect, the population share of those 65 and older increases in all four regions. There are, however, big differences in the aging process across the four regions. First, in the United States and China the absolute decrease of the shares of the young population through 2050 are almost the same as for the working-age population. In contrast, the European Union and Japan experience much larger absolute declines in the share of the population that is of working age. Second, the share of elderly increases to a much larger extent in Japan and China compared to the United States and the European Union.

Table 5.1 indicates that our model's demographic machinery does a remarkably good job matching official projections for the four regions both with respect to the absolute number and age compositions of their respective populations. We now describe this machinery in more detail.

The total number of children of an agent age a in income class k in year t is recorded by the following function

$$(1) \quad KID(a, t, k) = \sum_{j=u}^{m} \frac{N(j, t, a - j, k)}{\sum_{s=23}^{45} N(a, t, s, k)} \quad 23 \leq a \leq 65, k = 1, 2, 3,$$

where $u = max(0; a - 45)$ and $m = min(20, a - 23)$. Recall that agents younger than 23 have no children and those over 65 have only adult children (i.e., $KID(a, t, k) = 0$ for $0 \leq a \leq 22$ and $66 \leq a \leq 90$). Agents between these ages have children. Take, for example, a 30-year-old agent. Such an agent has children who were born in the years $(a - j)$ since she or he was 23. In year t, these children are between age $0 \leq j \leq 7$. The KID-function (1) sums the total number of kids of the respective parent-income class generation and divides it by the total number of parents of age a in year t who belong to income class k. This function takes into account that the family's age structure will change over time due to changing fertility. This approach permits the distribution of births by the ages of parents to change over time—an important improvement relative to the birthing process stipulated in Kotlikoff, Smetters, and Walliser (2001).

5.2.2 The Household Sector

As previously mentioned, we do not distinguish between natives and immigrants once the immigrants have joined the native earnings- and age-specific cohorts. The model's preference structure is represented by a time-separable, nested, CES utility function. Remaining lifetime utility $U(j, t, s, k)$ of a generation of age j at time t whose parents were age s at time of birth and who belongs to income class k takes the form

$$(2) \qquad U(j, t, s, k) = V(j, t, s, k) + H(j, t, s, k),$$

where $V(j, t, s, k)$ records the agent's utility from her or his own goods and leisure consumption and $H(j, t, s, k)$ denotes the agent's utility from the consumption of her or his children. The two subutility functions are defined as follows:

$$(3) \quad V(j, t, s, k) = \frac{1}{1 - \frac{1}{\gamma}} \sum_{a=j}^{90} \left(\frac{1}{1 + \theta} \right)^{a-j}$$
$$\cdot P(a, i)[c(a, i, s, k)^{1-(1/\rho)} + \alpha \ell(a, i, s, k)^{1-(1/\rho)}]^{[1-(1/\gamma)]/[1-(1/\rho)]}$$

$$(4) \quad H(j, t, s, k) = \frac{1}{1 - \frac{1}{\gamma}} \sum_{a=j}^{90} \left(\frac{1}{1 + \theta} \right)^{a-j} P(a, i)KID(a, i, k)c_K(a, i, s, k)^{1-(1/\gamma)},$$

where $c(a, i, s, k)$ and $\ell(a, i, s, k)$ denote consumption and leisure, respectively, and i is defined as $i = t + a - j$. The children's consumption of income class k parents who are age a in period i and whose parents were age s at the time of their birth is defined as $c_K(a, i, s, k)$. Note that the number of children is independent of the grandparent's age at the time of the birth of the parents.

Since lifespan is uncertain, the utility of consumption in future periods is weighted by the survival probability of reaching age a in year i

$$(5) \qquad P(a, i) = \prod_{u=j}^{a} [1 - d(u, u - a + i)],$$

which is determined by multiplying the conditional survival probabilities from year t (when the agent's age is j) up to year i. Note that $d(j, t)$ is the mortality probability of an agent age j in year t. The parameters θ, ρ, α and γ represent the *pure* rate of time preference, the intratemporal elasticity of substitution between consumption and leisure at each age a, the leisure preference parameter, and the intertemporal elasticity of substitution between consumption and leisure in different years, respectively.

In maximizing utility, agents choose their demand for leisure subject to the constraint that leisure in each period not exceed 1, which is the time endowment. The determination of the shadow values of these leisure constraints, when these constraints are binding, is included as part of the maximization. To ensure that agents retire by a designated maximum retirement age, we set the net wage at that age and thereafter to zero.

Given the asset endowment $a(j, t, s, k)$ of the agent in year t, maximization of equation (2) is subject to a lifetime budget constraint defined by the sequence:

$$(6) \quad a(j + 1, t + 1, s, k) = [a(j, t, s, k) + I(j, t, s, k)][1 + r(t)]$$
$$+ w(t)E(a, k)[h(a, t) - \ell(a, t, s, k)]$$
$$- T(j, t, s, k) - c(j, t, s, k)$$
$$- \text{KID}(j, t, k)c_K(j, t, s, k),$$

where $r(t)$ is the pretax return on savings and $I(j, t, s, k)$ denotes the inheritance the agent receives in year t. When the parents die between age 68 and 90, their remaining assets are split between their children. Consequently, inheritances of agents who are age j in year t and whose parents were age s at their birth are defined by:

$$(7) \quad I(j, t, s, k) = \frac{d(j + s)\overline{A}(j + s, t, k)}{\sum_{u=23}^{45} N(j + s - u, t, u, k)}.$$

The numerator defines the aggregate assets of income class k parents who die in year t at age $j + s$. The denominator defines these parents' total number of children who are between ages $j + s - 45$ and $j + s - 23$ in year t. The receipt of inheritances requires us to distinguish members of each cohort according to the ages of their parents at birth. The parents' ages at death determine when the children receive their inheritances. While the oldest children (born when their parents are age 23) receive their inheritances between ages 45 and 67, the youngest children (born when their parents are age 45) receive their inheritances earlier in life, between ages 23 and 45.

As in Altig et al. (2001) and Kotlikoff, Smetters, and Walliser (2001), we assume that technical progress causes the time endowment $h(\cdot)$ of each successive generation to grow at the rate λ.

$$(8) \quad h(a, i) = (1 + \lambda)h(a, i - 1).$$

The proposition here is not that time, per se, expands for successive generations, but rather that each successive generation is more effective in using time to either perform work or enjoy leisure. Treating technical change in this manner is essential to ensure that the economy achieves a long-run steady state. The assumption of labor-augmenting technical change would not, for example, be compatible with a long-run steady state given the nature of the model's preferences. And having the economy achieve a long-run steady state provides, in effect, the terminal conditions needed by our algorithm to solve for the model's equilibrium transition path.

Gross labor income of the agent in year t is derived as the product of her or his labor supply and her or his wage rate. The latter is the product of the gross wage rate $w(t)$ in period t and the age- and class-specific earnings ability,

$$(9) \qquad E(a, k) = \xi(k)e^{4.47+0.033(a-20)-0.00067(a-20)^2}(1 + \lambda)^{a-21}$$

with $\xi(1) = 0.2$, $\xi(2) = 1.0$, $\xi(3) = 5.0$.

The middle-income class profile is taken from Auerbach and Kotlikoff (1987). The shift parameters $\xi(k)$ are then applied to derive income class-specific profiles. Moreover, since technological change is an important determinant of secular growth over the life cycle, we multiply the age-specific longitudinal earnings ability profile by the term involving λ. Hence, the longitudinal age-wage profile is steeper the greater is the rate of technological change.

The net taxes $T(j, t, s, k)$ of an agent in year t consist of consumption, capital income, and progressive wage taxes as well as social security contributions net of pension and disability benefits received. Due to our assumed ceiling on payroll tax contributions, pension, disability insurance, and health care average and marginal payroll tax rates differ across agents. Each agent's pension benefits depend on her or his preretirement earnings history, while health care and disability transfers are provided on a per capita basis to all eligible age groups.

Given individual consumption, leisure, and asset levels of all agents, we can compute aggregate variables. For example, the aggregate value of assets $A(t + 1)$ in period t is computed from

$$(10) \qquad A(t + 1) = \sum_{k=1}^{3} \sum_{a=21}^{90} \underbrace{\sum_{s=23}^{45} a(a + 1, t + 1, s, k)N(a, t, s, k)}_{\overline{A}(a + 1, t + 1, k)}.$$

Since households die at the beginning of each period, we have to aggregate across all agents who lived in the previous period in order to compute $\overline{A}(a + 1, t + 1, k)$, which we need for the calculation of bequests; see equation (7). If we aggregate across agents who live in period $t + 1$, that is,

$$(11) \qquad \mathscr{A}(t + 1) = \sum_{k=1}^{3} \sum_{a=21}^{90} \sum_{s=23}^{45} a(a, t + 1, s, k)N(a, t + 1, s, k),$$

assets of the arriving immigrants of period $t + 1$ are included.

Finally, aggregate labor supply of agents in year t, $L(t)$, is computed from the individual labor supplies,

$$(12) \qquad L(t) = \sum_{k=1}^{3} \sum_{a=21}^{90} \sum_{s=23}^{45} E(a, k)[h(a, t) - \ell(a, t, s, k)]N(a, t, s, k).$$

5.2.3   The Production Sector

The economy is populated by a large number of identical firms, the total number of which is normalized to unity. Aggregate output (net of depreciation) is produced using Cobb-Douglas production technology,

$$(13) \qquad F[K(t), L(t)] = \phi K(t)^{\varepsilon} L(t)^{1-\varepsilon}$$

where $K(t)$ is aggregate capital in period t, ε is capital's share in production, and ϕ is a technology parameter. Since we posit convex capital adjustment cost, the firms' marketable output in year t, $Y(t)$, is given by the difference between gross output and adjustment costs,

$$(14) \qquad Y(t) = F[K(t), L(t)] - \frac{0.5\psi\Delta K(t)^2}{K(t)}$$

where $\Delta K(t)$ measures investment in year t. The term ψ is the adjustment cost coefficient. Larger values of ψ imply higher marginal costs of new capital goods for a given rate of investment. The installation technology is linear homogeneous and shows increasing marginal cost of investment (or, symmetrically, disinvestment): faster adjustment requires a greater than proportional rise in adjustment costs.

Corporate taxes, $T^k(t)$, are given by

$$(15) \qquad T^k(t) = \tau^k(t)[Y(t) - w(t)L(t) - \epsilon(t)\Delta K(t)]$$

where $\tau^k(t)$ and $\epsilon(t)$ define the corporate tax rate and the immediate write-off share of investment expenditures, respectively. Since adjustment costs are fully, and investment expenditures are partly, deductible from the tax base, arbitrage between new and existing capital implies that the latter has a price per unit of

$$(16) \qquad q(t + 1) = 1 - \epsilon(t)\tau^k(t) + \frac{[1 - \tau^k(t)]\psi\,\Delta K(t)}{K(t)}.$$

Similarly, the arbitrage condition arising from profit maximization requires identical returns to financial and real investments:

$$(17) \quad r(t)q(t) = [1 - \tau^k(t)]\left\{ F_{K(t)} + 0.5\psi\left[\frac{\Delta K(t)}{K(t)} \right]^2 \right\} + q(t + 1) - q(t).$$

The left side gives the return on a financial investment of amount $q(t)$, while the return on one unit of real capital investment is the net return to capital (which includes the marginal product of capital $F_{K(t)}$ plus the reduction in marginal adjustment costs) and capital gains.

5.2.4   The Government Sector

The consolidated government issues new debt $\Delta B(t)$ and collects corporate taxes and net taxes from households in order to finance general government expenditures $G(t)$ as well as interest payments on its debt:

$$(18) \quad \Delta B(t) + T^k(t) + \sum_{k=1}^{3} \sum_{a=21}^{90} \sum_{s=23}^{45} T(a, t, s, k)N(a, t, s, k) = G(t) + r(t)B(t).$$

With respect to public debt, we assume that the government maintains an exogenously fixed ratio of debt to output. The progressivity of the wage tax system is modeled as in Auerbach and Kotlikoff (1987). Specifically, marginal wage tax rates rise linearly with the tax base.

$PY(t)$ defines the aggregate payroll tax base, which differs from total labor earnings due to the ceiling on taxable wages. This ceiling is fixed at 250, 200, 168, and 300 percent of average income in the United States, the European Union, Japan, and China, respectively. Aggregate average social security payroll tax rates $\hat{\tau}^p$, $\hat{\tau}^h$, and $\hat{\tau}^d$ are computed each period from the relevant budget constraint for the program and region in question,

$$(19) \quad \hat{\tau}^p(t)PY(t) = PB(t) \quad \hat{\tau}^h(t)PY(t) = HB(t) \quad \text{and} \quad \hat{\tau}^d(t)PY(t) = DB(t),$$

where $PB(t)$, $HB(t)$, and $DB(t)$ are total outlays of the pension, health care, and disability systems, respectively. For China we assume that disability insurance is part of the state pension system. Hence, we do not calculate separate disability insurance payroll tax rates for this country.

Due to contribution ceilings, individual pension, disability, and health insurance payroll tax rates can differ from the payroll tax rate. Above the contribution ceiling, marginal social security contributions are zero and average social security contributions fall with the agent's income. To accommodate this nonconvexity of the budget constraint, we assume that the highest earnings class in each region pays pension and, in the European Union, Japan, and China, health insurance payroll taxes, up to the relevant ceilings, but faces no pension and no health care payroll taxes at the margin. The other earnings classes are assumed to face the full statutory tax rate on all earnings. The disability payroll taxes in the United States, the European Union, and Japan are modeled in an equivalent manner. However, since there is no ceiling on U.S. Medicare taxes, all earnings groups are assumed to face the health insurance payroll tax at the margin.

If a k-income class agent, whose parents were s years old at his or her birth, retires in year z at the exogenously set retirement age $\bar{a}(z)$, her or his pension benefits $Pen(a, i, s, k)$ in years $i \geq z$ when he or she is age $a \geq \bar{a}(z)$ depend linearly on her or his average earnings during his or her working time $\overline{W}(z, s, k)$:

$$(20) \qquad Pen(a, i, s, k) = \omega_0 + \omega_1 \times \overline{W}(z, s, k).$$

The region-specific parameters ω_0, ω_1 in the United States, the European Union, and Japan were chosen in order to approximate replacement rates relative to individual lifetime earnings as reported in Whitehouse (2002). In China, we assumed a pension-replacement rate of 50 percent of average preretirement earnings. There is little reliable data to assess the accuracy of this replacement rate assumption. But the assumption seems reasonable given the Chinese government's recent decision to recognize the unfunded liabilities of state-owned enterprise.

General government expenditures $G(t)$ consist of government purchases of goods and services, including educational expenditures and health outlays. Over the transition, general government purchases of goods and services are held fixed as a percent of national income. Age-specific education and disability outlays are held fixed per capita over the transition with an adjustment for technological change. Age-specific health outlays are also held fixed per capita, but are assumed to grow at twice the rate of technological change during the first 25 years of the transition. Afterward, the age-specific levels of these outlays grow at the same rate as technological change. Note that while the outlays of the health care systems are treated as government expenditures, disability benefits are modeled as direct transfers to the households. The government's budget, equation (18), is balanced each year by adjusting the intercept in our linear equation determining the average wage tax rate.

5.2.5 World Equilibrium

Up to now we've described the model for the representative economy. The four regions of the model are, however, connected through the world capital market. A condition of this market is that the value of aggregate world assets equals the market value of the world-wide capital stock plus the value of all outstanding government bonds;

$$(21) \qquad \sum_{x \in W} \mathcal{A}(t, x) = \sum_{x \in W} [q(t, x)K(t, x) + B(t, x)],$$

with $W = \{$U.S., EU, Japan, China$\}$.

5.2.6 Solving the Model

To simulate the model we need, of course, to specify preference, technology, and policy parameters. Table 5.2 reports these values, which, in the case of preference and technology parameters, are mostly taken from Kotlikoff, Smetters, and Walliser (2001).

The multifactor technology coefficient in the U.S. Cobb-Douglas function was set to generate a U.S. marginal product of labor of 1.0 in the initial year 2004. For the European Union and Japan we simply adopted this technology level. For China the technology level was set to achieve a 2004 real wage equal to 15 percent of the U.S. level. During the transition we

Table 5.2   **Parameter values of the model**

	Symbol	U.S.	EU	Japan	China
			Value		
Utility function					
Time preference rate	θ	0.01	0.00	0.01	−0.13
Intertemporal elasticity of substitution	γ		0.25		
Intratemporal elasticity of substitution	ρ		0.4		
Leisure preference parameter	α		1.5		
Production function					
Technology level	ϕ	1.01	1.01	1.01	0.24
Capital share in production	ε		0.25		
Technical progress	λ		0.01		
Policy parameters					
Consumption tax rate (%)	τ^c	10.2	23.6	14.7	20.0
Capital tax rate (%)	τ^r	11.0	14.0	8.0	0.0
Corporate tax rate (%)	τ^k	12.0	18.0	16.0	0.0
Expensing fraction (%)	ϵ	0.0	20.0	40.0	0.0
Debt (% of national income)	B/Y	33.3	38.9	41.4	10.0
Age of retirement		63	60	60	60

gradually adjust China's technology level such that it reaches the developed world level in 2050.

The time-preference rates in the four regions were set to match the model's 2004 ratios of private consumption to national income to the region-specific values reported in European Commission (2005). The United States, the European Union, and Japanese time-preference rates are held fixed through time. But in line with our baseline assumption that the Chinese public will eventually adopt American spending habits, we gradually raise the time-preference rate of successive Chinese cohorts so that the cohorts that reach adulthood (age 21) in 2030 and thereafter have the time-invariant U.S. time-preference rate.

The model's debt levels in the four regions were chosen to accord with real government interest payments reported in European Commission (2005) for the year 2004. The maximum ages of retirement are taken from Blöndal and Scarpetta (1999) for the United States and the European Union, from Whitehouse (2002) for Japan and from OECD (2002) for China. We set the consumption tax rate, personal capital income tax rate, corporate income tax rate, and expensing rate for the United States, the European Union, and Japan in line with the structure of indirect and direct tax revenues reported in European Commission (2005). We use OECD (2002) data to determine China's consumption tax rate, but assume China has no personal capital income or corporate income taxes. It may well be that such taxes exist in China, but we have no reliable information to understand their magnitudes.

Our wage tax systems are assumed to be progressive, with the parameters of these tax systems in each region set so as to generate what seem to be realistic average and marginal tax rates, which are reported in the following.

In calibrating health expenditures in our model, we apply the Japanese age-specific government healthcare expenditure profile for Japan as well as China. In the case of the European Union, we use the German profile. For the United States, the Medicare program applies only to households 65 and older. We assume uniform Medicare expenditures by age. We make the same uniform age-distribution assumption with respect to the disability insurance systems in the United States, the European Union, and Japan, which we assume applies only to those older than 20 and younger than 65.

In the case of the United States, European Union, and Japan, total social insurance outlays for pensions, disability, and health, measured as a share of national income, are set to accord with the values of these totals reported in European Commission (2005). But we determined the composition of these expenditures as between the three types of benefits using data reported in Docteur and Oxley (2003), European Commission (2003), and OECD (2001) and invoking the assumption for the European Union and Japan that their ratios of disability expenditures to pension expenditures is the same as prevails in the United States. Note that our baseline path assumes a gradual 20 percent cut in Japanese pension replacement rates through 2017, which was recently legislated by the Japanese government. For China our division of social insurance outlays is restricted to pensions plus disability payments, on the one hand, and health expenditures, on the other. Calibration here is based on OECD (2002).

We use the German age-specific education profile for all regions in the model and rescale it to get realistic education outlays in year 2004 in each region (see the following). In addition to these parameter values, our model requires an initial distribution of assets by age and income class for each region. These profiles are region specific.[2]

To run our model as an open-world economy, we also need to specify total world assets and how these assets are distributed across regions. The model's level of total world assets was set to generate a capital-output ratio of 3.0 in our model in the absence of China. Our additional assumption that per capita wealth in China equals 10 percent of per capita wealth in the developed countries sufficed to pin down the capital-output ratio in the four-region model, namely 2.3.

In our simulations with adjustment costs, we also need to specify, for 2004, the base year, the shares of wealth in each country owned by citizens

2. The profile of Japanese average net wealth by age was provided by Charles Horioka, while the European age-specific average wealth profiles were adjusted from German data provided by Reinhold Schnabel. We calculated a U.S. age-wealth profile using the 1998 Survey of Consumer Finances. For China, we adopted the Japanese age-net wealth profile.

of each region. The reason is that the endogenous determination of capital prices in each region will differentially affect wealth holdings of each region's nationals depending on where they hold their wealth. The data needed to determine the region-specific allocation of each region's wealth holdings are not available. Consequently, we make the following, admittedly crude, assumption. We assume that each U.S., E.U., Japanese, and Chinese nationals own 70 percent of the capital installed in their region and that the remaining 30 percent is owned equally by foreigners from the other three regions. In the case of the United States, for example, we assume that the Japanese, European Unioners, and Chinese each own 10 percent of the U.S. capital stock, where these holdings include government claims.

The initial (year 2004) world capital stock, the allocation of this capital stock across regions, the regional ratios of government debt to national income, and the international, intergenerational, and intragenerational distributions of assets constitute the initial conditions needed to solve for the perfect foresight general equilibrium transition path of the economy. The algorithm we use to solve the model employs Gauss-Seidel iteration.

Specifically, our algorithm starts with initial guesses for capital stocks and labor supplies in each region for the post-2004 years of the transition. Next we compute from equation (16) the path of the qs—the region-specific market prices of capital. The path for the world interest rate is derived from the arbitrage condition (17) for the United States. Next, region-specific wage rates are computed for each year by setting them equal to their respective marginal products of labor.

The initial region-specific capital values, our working value of q in 2004, and 2004 initial region-specific debt levels suffice to determine total worldwide wealth in 2004 using the world capital market equilibrium condition (21). These aggregate values are then distributed to the agents of each region based on the initial 2004 region-specific wealth shares and region-specific age-asset profiles.

Given these initial individual asset holdings, our initial guesses of tax rates/tax function parameters, as well as the derived time paths of wage and interest rates, we calculate household consumption, saving, and labor supply decisions. The first-order conditions and lifetime budget constraints determining these decisions are fairly complex and certainly do not omit of closed-form solutions. Part of this complexity arises because of the progressive nature of our assumed wage tax structures, which means that marginal tax rates are themselves endogenous and need to be determined jointly with life-cycle consumption, saving, and labor supply decisions. This is done using Gauss-Seidel iteration. We refer to this as *interloop* convergence. As indicated momentarily, we also use Gauss-Seidel iteration to determine the time path of the economy's macroeconomic variables. We refer to this iteration on macrovariables as *outerloop* convergence.

The next step in our overall solution algorithm uses the annual revenues and Social Security benefit payments implied by these household decisions to update annual tax rates/tax parameters. We also update the model's region-specific time paths of government debt. These updates are based on equations (18) and (19).

Aggregating individual labor supplies in each year provides new time paths of aggregate region-specific labor supplies. Determining new time paths of capital stocks in each region is a bit more involved. First, we use year-2004 wealth holdings plus agent-specific saving decisions to determine agent-specific asset holdings in each year during the transition. Second, we aggregate agent-specific assets at each date to determine a time path of aggregate worldwide asset holdings. Third, use equation (17) to substitute out for $\Delta K(t)/K$—the percentage change in capital—in equation (16). Finally, we equate the interest rates in Japan, the European Union, and China to that in the United States using the modified versions of equation (16). Given our working values of the qs, this provides us with three equations in a given year to solve for the four region-specific capital stocks. The fourth equation comes from the worldwide capital market condition, which, given our working values of qs and debt, provides another equation in the four unknown region-specific capital stocks.

The new values for the aggregate supplies of capital and labor in each region in each year are then weighted with the initial guesses of these variables to form new guesses of their time paths. The algorithm then iterates until the region-specific time paths of capital stocks and labor supplies converge to a fixed point.

We give our economy 300 years to reach to a steady state. In fact, our model reaches a steady state to many decimal places decades prior to year 300. It also converges very tightly around the equilibrium transition path. However, when we include capital adjustment costs finding the equilibrium transition path is very time consuming even on today's most powerful desktop PCs. Doing so requires finding the path with no such costs, which can be done relatively quickly, and then using the region-specific capital and labor supply equilibrium paths from that simulation as the initial guesses for a run with very small adjustment costs. We then use the results of the small adjustment costs simulation as initial guesses for a simulation with somewhat higher adjustment costs and proceed in this manner until we've solved the model with our desired level of adjustment costs. Given the time required for these calculations, we assumed no adjustment costs in all but one simulation presented in the following. The simulation with adjustment costs is of the base-case transition. The results indicate that inclusion of reasonable adjustment costs makes little difference to the results.

5.3   Initial Equilibrium and the World Economy's Baseline Transition Path

Table 5.3 reports key macroeconomic variables in 2004 in the four regions. Note that there is a fairly close accordance between actual and computed values of private consumption and government purchases measured as a share of national income. The one exception is E.U. government purchases. The official data seem too low given the reported ratio of tax revenues to national income. In our calibration, we chose to benchmark government purchases based on the ratio of tax revenues to national income.

The reported ratios of educational expenditure to national income are very close to actual levels.[3] In the case of pension, health, and disability expenditures, we closely match the shares of national income received in the form of social contributions in the United States, the European Union, and Japan as reported in European Commission (2005). In China, the level of health expenditures measured as a share of national income was set in accord with WHO (2004, 136). The resulting social security payroll tax rates come close to observed levels. Concerning the overall structure of tax revenues, the assumed tax rates on capital income, corporate income, and consumption as well as the expensing fractions (see table 5.2) yield a realistic pattern.[4]

The baseline simulation ignores adjustment costs. Hence, capital prices do not change during the transition. However, due to the differences in the expensing fractions for the corporate tax, capital prices deviate from one in the European Union and Japan. Thus the capital price is 0.964 in the European Union and 0.936 in Japan throughout the transition, while it is 1.000 in the United States and China. Finally, the model's year-2004 capital-output ratios seem reasonable not only relative to U.S. Commerce Department figures, but also in terms of the year-2004 marginal product of capital, which equals 9.8 percent.

Next we turn to the simulation results for the baseline transition. The transition paths for the four regions are reported in the upper panels of tables 5.4 to 5.7 for the United States, the European Union, Japan, and China. Note that region-specific ratios of national income, the capital stock, the supply of labor, and the pretax wage rate are all expressed relative to the U.S. values in year 2004.

Although the four economies are aging, the baseline path shows a steady increase in effective labor supply in the United States, the European Union, and Japan. This may seem surprising especially for Japan and the European Union, where the population and work force decline over time (see table 5.1). The explanation lies in our assumption that each successive cohort has a higher effective time endowment, which admits greater effective

---

3. See OECD (2003a, 178; 2003b, 71, 77).
4. Actual values are calculated from European Commission (2005) and OECD (2003c).

Table 5.3   The year 2004 of the baseline path

	Model				Official			
	U.S.	EU	Japan	China	U.S.	EU	Japan	China
National income								
Private consumption	79.7	65.1	70.5	52.4	79.3	67.3	69.3	49.5
Government purchases of goods and services	18.7	31.0	21.9	17.9	17.4	24.3	21.7	17.6
General public expenditures	10.9	19.3	12.3	13.8				
Aggregate education outlays	5.9	6.0	4.4	2.1	5.9	6.0	4.3	2.1
Aggregate health benefits	1.9	5.7	5.2	2.0	2.5	6.2	6.8	2.0
Current account	2.8	8.3	13.8	-16.1	-6.1	0.5	4.5	1.9
Government indicators								
Social contributions received	8.1	16.4	13.9	7.7	7.9	16.6	13.4	
Aggregate pension benefits	5.3	9.2	7.6	5.2	5.7	11.6	10.8	3.0
Aggregate health benefits	1.9	5.7	5.2	2.0	2.5	6.2	6.8	2.0
Aggregate disability benefits	0.9	1.5	1.1	0.0	0.9			
Pension contribution rate (%)	7.7	14.2	12.1	8.0	10.6		17.3	11.0
Health-care contribution rate (%)	2.5	8.8	8.2	3.1	2.9		8.5	8.0
Disability-insurance contribution rate (%)	1.4	2.3	1.8	0.0	1.9			
Interest payment on public debt (%)	3.3	3.8	4.1	1.0	3.0	3.5	3.7	0.8
Tax revenues (%)	20.3	30.3	21.9	15.8	20.6	31.0	19.1	14.8
Direct taxes	12.2	14.9	11.5	5.3	12.5	15.1	8.9	2.8
Personal income taxes	9.2	10.5	7.5	5.3	9.5	10.7	4.7	0.7
Wage taxes	5.7	5.9	4.9	5.3				
Capital taxes	3.5	4.6	2.6	0.0				
Corporate income taxes	3.0	4.4	4.0	0.0	3.0	4.4	4.2	2.1
Indirect taxes	8.1	15.4	10.4	10.5	8.1	15.9	10.2	12.0
Wage tax rates (%)								
Average	7.8	8.0	6.6	7.1				
Marginal	14.2	13.9	11.9	8.9				
Capital-output ratio	2.2	2.2	2.3	2.6				
Capital-labor ratio	3.0	2.9	3.1	0.5				
Interest rate (%)	9.8	9.8	9.8	9.8				

Sources: For official path, European Commission (2005) for the United States, the European Union, and Japan; OECD (2002) for China.

Note: All figures are in percent of national income if not stated differently.

Table 5.4 Simulation results for the United States

Year	Index of national income	Index of capital stock	Index of labor supply	Current account/NI	Index of pretax wage	Interest rate	Social security cost rate	Average wage tax
Base case								
2004	1.00	1.00	1.00	.028	1.00	.098	.116	.078
2010	1.13	1.19	1.12	-.039	1.02	.093	.119	.070
2020	1.47	1.92	1.35	-.144	1.09	.075	.138	.069
2030	1.89	3.04	1.62	-.168	1.17	.061	.164	.078
2050	2.63	4.11	2.28	.054	1.16	.063	.171	.093
2075	3.29	4.05	3.08	.037	1.07	.080	.207	.080
2100	4.11	4.67	3.96	.017	1.04	.087	.230	.068
Constant time preference in China								
2004	1.00	1.00	1.00	.024	1.00	.098	.116	.078
2010	1.13	1.20	1.11	-.053	1.02	.093	.119	.070
2020	1.46	1.99	1.33	-.210	1.11	.072	.138	.069
2030	1.90	3.50	1.57	-.323	1.22	.054	.163	.078
2050	3.02	8.39	2.17	-.253	1.40	.036	.151	.087
2075	4.62	18.45	2.95	-.171	1.58	.025	.153	.081
2100	6.09	26.09	3.78	-.084	1.62	.023	.164	.078
Lower technology growth in China								
2004	0.98	0.98	0.99	-.063	1.00	.099	.117	.074
2010	1.17	1.35	1.11	-.115	1.05	.085	.114	.073
2020	1.55	2.28	1.37	-.158	1.14	.067	.130	.077
2030	1.95	3.41	1.63	-.142	1.20	.056	.160	.085
2050	2.67	4.29	2.29	.059	1.17	.061	.171	.096
2075	3.24	3.86	3.07	.044	1.06	.083	.211	.082
2100	4.06	4.50	3.94	.016	1.03	.089	.233	.069

(*continued*)

Table 5.4 (continued)

Year	Index of national income	Index of capital stock	Index of labor supply	Current account/NI	Index of pretax wage	Interest rate	Social security cost rate	Average wage tax
Constant fertility in all regions								
2004	1.00	1.00	1.00	.028	1.00	.098	.116	.078
2010	1.13	1.19	1.12	-.039	1.02	.093	.119	.070
2020	1.47	1.92	1.35	-.147	1.09	.075	.138	.070
2030	1.89	3.06	1.62	-.180	1.17	.061	.164	.080
2050	2.73	4.34	2.35	.033	1.16	.062	.166	.098
2075	3.69	4.67	3.43	.024	1.08	.078	.188	.093
2100	4.81	5.42	4.64	.033	1.04	.087	.209	.079
Higher life expectancy in all regions								
2004	1.00	1.00	1.00	.024	1.00	.098	.116	.077
2010	1.14	1.22	1.12	-.046	1.02	.092	.119	.070
2020	1.49	2.02	1.36	-.152	1.10	.073	.138	.069
2030	1.93	3.29	1.63	-.182	1.19	.058	.168	.077
2050	2.75	4.72	2.31	.043	1.19	.057	.184	.090
2075	3.42	4.46	3.14	.052	1.09	.075	.228	.079
2100	4.23	4.92	4.05	.020	1.05	.085	.254	.065
Doubling immigration in all regions								
2004	1.01	1.00	1.00	.026	1.00	.098	.116	.076
2010	1.17	1.22	1.14	-.044	1.02	.093	.117	.069
2020	1.57	2.04	1.45	-.148	1.09	.076	.131	.069
2030	2.10	3.34	1.80	-.170	1.17	.062	.153	.079
2050	3.13	4.84	2.71	.048	1.16	.064	.160	.091
2075	4.17	5.14	3.90	.035	1.07	.080	.198	.078
2100	5.41	6.22	5.18	.021	1.05	.085	.224	.063
Rise in health expenditures by 3% in all regions								
2004	1.00	1.00	1.00	.028	1.00	.098	.116	.078
2010	1.14	1.20	1.12	-.039	1.02	.093	.120	.070
2020	1.47	1.93	1.35	-.140	1.09	.075	.143	.069
2030	1.89	3.05	1.62	-.166	1.17	.061	.177	.079

2050	2.63	4.06	2.29	.054	1.15	.064	.184	.094
2075	3.28	3.96	3.09	.037	1.06	.081	.224	.082
2100	4.10	4.55	3.97	.017	1.03	.089	.248	.070
Financing benefits by general tax revenues								
2004	1.00	1.00	1.00	.028	1.00	.098	.116	.078
2010	1.13	1.20	1.12	-.039	1.02	.093	.116	.073
2020	1.47	1.92	1.35	-.144	1.09	.075	.116	.090
2030	1.88	3.05	1.61	-.172	1.17	.061	.116	.125
2050	2.63	4.13	2.28	.054	1.16	.063	.116	.146
2075	3.27	4.04	3.07	.037	1.07	.080	.116	.169
2100	4.07	4.59	3.93	.018	1.04	.087	.116	.178
Financing benefits by debt								
2004	1.00	1.00	1.00	.031	1.00	.098	.116	.078
2010	1.13	1.18	1.11	-.039	1.01	.094	.116	.070
2020	1.47	1.88	1.35	-.146	1.09	.077	.116	.069
2030	1.86	2.99	1.60	-.164	1.17	.061	.166	.098
2050	2.61	3.91	2.29	.044	1.14	.066	.173	.116
2075	3.24	3.74	3.10	.035	1.05	.085	.210	.123
2100	4.03	4.21	3.99	.016	1.01	.094	.234	.119
Cut of replacement rates in all regions								
2004	1.00	1.00	1.01	.029	1.00	.098	.116	.078
2010	1.14	1.21	1.12	-.039	1.02	.092	.117	.069
2020	1.48	1.99	1.35	-.143	1.10	.073	.126	.068
2030	1.91	3.19	1.62	-.169	1.18	.059	.144	.076
2050	2.66	4.39	2.26	.054	1.18	.060	.148	.088
2075	3.35	4.46	3.06	.034	1.10	.074	.176	.076
2100	4.21	5.21	3.94	.016	1.07	.079	.194	.065
Privatizing pensions								
2004	1.01	1.00	1.02	.021	0.99	.100	.038	.077
2010	1.17	1.29	1.13	-.047	1.03	.089	.039	.068
2020	1.54	2.26	1.36	-.144	1.13	.067	.044	.065
2030	1.99	3.77	1.62	-.171	1.24	.052	.054	.071
2050	2.81	5.79	2.22	.050	1.27	.048	.052	.076
2075	3.68	7.01	2.99	.018	1.24	.052	.060	.062
2100	4.71	8.76	3.85	.010	1.23	.053	.065	.054

Table 5.5   Simulation results for the European Union

	Year	Index of national income	Index of capital stock	Index of labor supply	Current account/NI	Index of pretax wage	Interest rate	Social security cost rate	Average wage tax
Base case	2004	1.42	1.38	1.45	.083	0.99	.098	.253	.080
	2010	1.53	1.57	1.53	.032	1.01	.093	.265	.060
	2020	1.79	2.27	1.67	−.052	1.08	.075	.286	.051
	2030	2.03	3.17	1.76	−.083	1.16	.061	.327	.058
	2050	2.28	3.44	2.00	.031	1.14	.063	.381	.071
	2075	2.57	3.06	2.44	.014	1.06	.080	.380	.079
	2100	3.19	3.50	3.11	.020	1.03	.087	.367	.074
Constant time preference in China	2004	1.42	1.38	1.45	.081	0.99	.098	.253	.080
	2010	1.53	1.58	1.53	.025	1.01	.093	.265	.060
	2020	1.81	2.38	1.66	−.094	1.09	.072	.286	.053
	2030	2.09	3.71	1.74	−.194	1.21	.054	.321	.066
	2050	2.69	7.21	1.95	−.215	1.39	.036	.329	.101
	2075	3.67	14.11	2.36	−.157	1.56	.025	.273	.123
	2100	4.76	19.68	2.99	−.076	1.60	.023	.261	.120
Lower technology growth in China	2004	1.41	1.36	1.44	.005	0.99	.099	.255	.078
	2010	1.58	1.78	1.53	−.035	1.04	.085	.255	.071
	2020	1.89	2.71	1.69	−.069	1.12	.067	.272	.072
	2030	2.11	3.57	1.79	−.057	1.19	.056	.317	.075
	2050	2.31	3.60	2.01	.037	1.16	.061	.377	.081
	2075	2.54	2.93	2.44	.022	1.05	.083	.385	.082
	2100	3.15	3.38	3.10	.020	1.02	.089	.369	.074
Constant fertility in all regions	2004	1.42	1.38	1.44	.082	0.99	.098	.253	.080
	2010	1.53	1.56	1.53	.030	1.01	.093	.265	.060
	2020	1.78	2.25	1.66	−.054	1.08	.075	.287	.050
	2030	2.01	3.14	1.74	−.083	1.16	.061	.329	.055
	2050	2.17	3.34	1.90	.034	1.15	.062	.394	.062

2075	2.19	2.67	2.06	.017	1.07	.078	.424	.060
2100	2.45	2.67	2.39	.005	1.03	.087	.412	.065
Higher life expectancy in all regions								
2004	1.43	1.38	1.45	.081	0.99	.098	.253	.080
2010	1.55	1.60	1.54	.029	1.01	.092	.264	.061
2020	1.83	2.40	1.69	−.056	1.09	.073	.286	.053
2030	2.09	3.44	1.78	−.090	1.18	.058	.330	.059
2050	2.39	3.98	2.04	.022	1.18	.057	.397	.069
2075	2.68	3.39	2.50	.026	1.08	.075	.402	.079
2100	3.29	3.70	3.18	.023	1.04	.085	.390	.072
Doubling immigration in all regions								
2004	1.43	1.38	1.45	.082	0.99	.098	.253	.080
2010	1.55	1.58	1.55	.030	1.00	.093	.263	.060
2020	1.85	2.32	1.72	−.052	1.08	.076	.281	.052
2030	2.14	3.30	1.86	−.084	1.15	.062	.317	.060
2050	2.53	3.79	2.22	.032	1.14	.064	.360	.075
2075	3.02	3.61	2.86	.016	1.06	.080	.364	.079
2100	3.89	4.33	3.77	.023	1.03	.085	.356	.069
Rise in health expenditures by 3% in all regions								
2004	1.43	1.38	1.45	.084	0.99	.098	.253	.080
2010	1.54	1.58	1.54	.033	1.01	.093	.270	.061
2020	1.80	2.29	1.68	−.050	1.08	.075	.303	.053
2030	2.04	3.18	1.77	−.086	1.16	.061	.359	.061
2050	2.30	3.43	2.02	.026	1.14	.064	.413	.078
2075	2.59	3.03	2.48	.011	1.05	.081	.412	.090
2100	3.22	3.46	3.17	.017	−.02	.089	.399	.087
Financing benefits by general tax revenues								
2004	1.42	1.38	1.45	.084	0.99	.098	.253	.080
2010	1.53	1.57	1.53	.032	1.01	.093	.253	.071
2020	1.79	2.17	1.67	−.051	1.08	.075	.253	.081
2030	2.02	3.17	1.75	−.085	1.16	.061	.253	.124
2050	2.26	3.44	1.98	.028	1.15	.063	.253	.184
2075	2.56	3.06	2.43	.013	1.06	.080	.253	.195
2100	3.17	3.46	3.10	.021	1.03	.087	.253	.178

(continued)

Table 5.5 (continued)

	Year	Index of national income	Index of capital stock	Index of labor supply	Current account/NI	Index of pretax wage	Interest rate	Social security cost rate	Average wage tax
Financing benefits by debt	2004	1.42	1.38	1.44	.080	0.99	.098	.253	.080
	2010	1.52	1.55	1.53	.026	1.00	.094	.253	.060
	2020	1.79	2.23	1.68	-.063	1.07	.077	.253	.051
	2030	1.96	3.04	1.70	-.112	1.16	.061	.340	.112
	2050	2.26	3.28	2.01	.006	1.13	.066	.383	.135
	2075	2.58	2.89	2.50	-.012	1.04	.085	.378	.196
	2100	3.27	3.31	3.28	-.009	1.00	.094	.359	.225
Cut of replacement rates in all regions	2004	1.43	1.39	1.46	.085	0.99	.098	.251	.080
	2010	1.55	1.60	1.54	.036	1.01	.092	.260	.060
	2020	1.82	2.36	1.68	-.044	1.09	.073	.267	.050
	2030	2.06	3.32	1.76	-.074	1.17	.059	.293	.055
	2050	2.29	3.66	1.98	.040	1.17	.060	.332	.061
	2075	2.59	3.33	2.39	.017	1.09	.074	.333	.062
	2100	3.22	3.86	3.05	.022	1.06	.079	.320	.057
Privatizing pensions	2004	1.46	1.40	1.49	.097	0.98	.100	.107	.085
	2010	1.60	1.71	1.57	.055	1.02	.089	.111	.063
	2020	1.90	2.69	1.70	-.015	1.12	.067	.116	.049
	2030	2.15	3.95	1.77	-.044	1.22	.052	.127	.048
	2050	2.41	4.81	1.93	.070	1.26	.048	.137	.035
	2075	2.78	5.12	2.28	.020	1.22	.052	.139	.022
	2100	3.52	6.34	2.92	.024	1.21	.053	.135	.021

Table 5.6   Simulation results for Japan

	Year	Index of national income	Index of capital stock	Index of labor supply	Current account/NI	Index of pretax wage	Interest rate	Social security cost rate	Average wage tax
Base case	2004	0.49	0.50	0.49	.138	1.01	.098	.221	.066
	2010	0.50	0.53	0.49	.082	1.02	.093	.257	.043
	2020	0.54	0.72	0.49	-.050	1.10	.075	.299	.027
	2030	0.60	1.00	0.52	-.070	1.18	.061	.301	.031
	2050	0.60	0.95	0.52	.060	1.17	.063	.359	.022
	2075	0.61	0.77	0.57	.027	1.08	.080	.354	.026
	2100	0.71	0.83	0.69	.028	1.05	.087	.328	.027
Constant time preference in China	2004	0.49	0.50	0.49	.139	1.01	.098	.220	.066
	2010	0.50	0.54	0.49	.081	1.03	.093	.256	.043
	2020	0.55	0.76	0.49	-.085	1.11	.072	.295	.028
	2030	0.63	1.17	0.51	-.172	1.23	.054	.291	.039
	2050	0.72	2.03	0.51	-.180	1.41	.036	.304	.051
	2075	0.89	3.62	0.56	-.127	1.59	.025	.256	.067
	2100	1.10	4.82	0.68	-.050	1.63	.023	.227	.065
Lower technology growth in China	2004	0.48	0.49	0.48	.057	1.00	.099	.224	.067
	2010	0.51	0.61	0.49	0.016	1.06	.085	.248	.050
	2020	0.57	0.86	0.50	-.066	1.14	.067	.283	.040
	2030	0.63	1.12	0.52	-.040	1.21	.056	.290	.041
	2050	0.61	1.00	0.52	.065	1.18	.061	.354	.028
	2075	0.60	0.73	0.57	.034	1.07	.083	.360	.026
	2100	0.71	0.80	0.68	.028	1.04	.089	.332	.025
Constant fertility in all regions	2004	0.49	0.50	0.49	.138	1.01	.098	.222	.066
	2010	0.49	0.53	0.49	.081	1.02	.093	.257	.043
	2020	0.54	0.71	0.49	-.053	1.10	.075	.300	.026

(continued)

Table 5.6 (continued)

	Year	Index of national income	Index of capital stock	Index of labor supply	Current account/NI	Index of pretax wage	Interest rate	Social security cost rate	Average wage tax
	2030	0.60	0.99	0.51	-.068	1.18	.061	.302	.027
	2050	0.56	0.91	0.48	.069	1.17	.062	.378	.009
	2075	0.48	0.62	0.44	.021	1.09	.078	.425	-.004
	2100	0.48	0.55	0.46	-.010	1.05	.087	.400	.007
Higher life expectancy in all regions	2004	0.49	0.50	0.49	.142	1.00	.098	.220	.067
	2010	0.50	0.55	0.49	.087	1.03	.092	.255	.044
	2020	0.55	0.76	0.50	-.047	1.11	.073	.298	.027
	2030	0.62	1.08	0.52	-.072	1.20	.058	.305	.030
	2050	0.63	1.10	0.53	.059	1.20	.057	.367	.019
	2075	0.63	0.85	0.58	.036	1.10	.075	.382	.021
	2100	0.73	0.87	0.70	.033	1.06	.085	.350	.021
Doubling immigration in all regions	2004	0.49	0.50	0.49	.138	1.01	.098	.221	.066
	2010	0.50	0.54	0.49	.083	1.02	.093	.256	.043
	2020	0.54	0.72	0.50	-.048	1.10	.076	.296	.027
	2030	0.62	1.00	0.53	-.068	1.17	.062	.297	.031
	2050	0.63	0.99	0.54	.058	1.16	.064	.349	.024
	2075	0.66	0.83	0.62	.028	1.08	.080	.343	.027
	2100	0.79	0.94	0.76	.030	1.05	.085	.320	.026
Rise in health expenditures by 3% in all regions	2004	0.49	0.50	0.49	.139	1.01	.098	.221	.066
	2010	0.50	0.54	0.49	.085	1.02	.093	.261	.044
	2020	0.54	0.73	0.50	-.049	1.10	.075	.316	.028
	2030	0.61	1.00	0.52	-.075	1.18	.061	.336	.032
	2050	0.60	0.95	0.52	.055	1.16	.064	.399	.027
	2075	0.62	0.76	0.58	.023	1.07	.081	.394	.034
	2100	0.72	0.82	0.70	.027	1.04	.089	.365	.036

Financing benefits by general tax revenues

Year								
2004	0.49	0.50	0.49	.142	1.01	.098	.221	.065
2010	0.49	0.53	0.49	.086	1.02	.093	.221	.072
2020	0.54	0.72	0.49	-.052	1.10	.075	.221	.091
2030	0.60	1.00	0.51	-.074	1.18	.061	.221	.098
2050	0.60	0.96	0.51	.060	1.17	.063	.221	.140
2075	0.61	0.77	0.57	.025	1.08	.080	.221	.142
2100	0.71	0.82	0.68	.030	1.05	.087	.221	.120

Financing benefits by debt

Year								
2004	0.48	0.50	0.48	.125	1.01	.098	.221	.065
2010	0.49	0.53	0.48	.061	1.02	.094	.221	.043
2020	0.54	0.71	0.50	-.076	1.09	.077	.221	.027
2030	0.55	0.91	0.47	-.161	1.18	.061	.328	.170
2050	0.61	0.94	0.53	.004	1.15	.066	.354	.158
2075	0.64	0.76	0.61	-.028	1.05	.085	.339	.265
2100	0.78	0.84	0.77	-.030	1.02	.094	.302	.331

Cut of replacement rates in all regions

Year								
2004	0.49	0.50	0.49	.131	1.00	.098	.222	.066
2010	0.50	0.54	0.49	.072	1.03	.092	.256	.044
2020	0.54	0.75	0.49	-.063	1.11	.073	.295	.029
2030	0.61	1.05	0.52	-.080	1.19	.059	.296	.034
2050	0.61	1.03	0.52	.057	1.19	.060	.352	.026
2075	0.63	0.86	0.57	.018	1.11	.074	.345	.033
2100	0.75	0.94	0.70	.021	1.08	.079	.315	.038

Privatizing pensions

Year								
2004	0.49	0.50	0.49	.134	1.00	.100	.100	.071
2010	0.51	0.58	0.49	.081	1.04	.089	.110	.047
2020	0.57	0.85	0.50	-.042	1.14	.067	.129	.032
2030	0.64	1.24	0.52	-.064	1.24	.052	.138	.033
2050	0.65	1.36	0.51	.068	1.28	.048	.157	.014
2075	0.69	1.33	0.55	.055	1.25	.052	.155	.016
2100	0.83	1.58	0.68	.008	1.24	.053	.143	.024

Table 5.7   Simulation results for China

	Year	Index of national income	Index of capital stock	Index of labor supply	Current account/NI	Index of pretax wage	Interest rate	Social security cost rate	Average wage tax
Base case	2004	1.33	1.52	8.90	-.161	0.98	.111	.071	0.71
	2010	2.29	2.76	9.78	-.020	0.24	.093	.082	.088
	2020	4.23	6.31	10.13	.078	0.42	.075	.085	.076
	2030	5.82	10.71	8.99	.091	0.65	.061	.115	.043
	2050	8.52	15.15	7.87	-.029	1.09	.063	.189	-.015
	2075	9.57	13.44	8.62	-.018	1.12	.080	.269	-.002
	2100	11.31	14.65	10.47	-.014	1.09	.087	.277	.019
Constant time preference in China	2004	1.33	1.52	8.95	-.155	0.15	.098	.111	.073
	2010	2.33	2.82	9.92	-.007	0.24	.093	.082	.092
	2020	4.56	7.06	10.77	.115	0.43	.072	.080	.094
	2030	7.01	14.62	10.38	.161	0.68	.054	.099	.086
	2050	12.12	38.24	9.27	.121	1.32	.036	.149	.063
	2075	14.80	67.12	9.05	.100	1.65	.025	.224	.013
	2100	17.66	86.13	10.54	.053	1.69	.023	.260	-.010
Lower technology growth in China	2004	1.39	1.58	9.36	.020	0.15	.099	.110	.097
	2010	1.90	2.52	10.30	.095	0.19	.085	.096	.089
	2020	2.80	4.71	11.00	.147	0.26	.067	.112	.058
	2030	3.40	6.77	10.31	.124	0.33	.056	.151	.012
	2050	4.48	8.21	9.99	-.063	0.45	.061	.224	-.054
	2075	5.02	6.83	11.54	-.043	0.44	.083	.282	-.016
	2100	6.00	7.57	14.11	-.025	0.43	.089	.283	.016
Constant fertility in all regions	2004	1.33	1.52	8.91	-.160	0.15	.098	.111	.071
	2010	2.29	2.76	9.78	-.018	0.24	.093	.082	.088
	2020	4.23	6.29	10.12	.081	0.42	.075	.085	.076
	2030	5.80	10.68	8.96	.095	0.65	.061	.115	.043
	2050	8.27	14.95	7.60	-.025	1.09	.062	.193	-.018
	2075	8.57	12.35	7.66	-.016	1.13	.078	.293	-.012

2100	9.35	12.03	8.68	.018	1.08	.087	.305	.012
Higher life expectancy in all regions								
2004	1.33	1.52	8.96	-.157	0.15	.098	.111	.073
2010	2.32	2.82	9.85	-.015	0.24	.092	.083	.090
2020	4.33	6.67	10.24	.082	0.43	.073	.086	.079
2030	6.01	11.65	9.13	.097	0.66	.058	.117	.047
2050	8.94	17.48	8.01	-.023	1.12	.057	.202	-.015
2075	10.00	14.88	8.84	-.027	1.14	.075	.303	-.013
2100	11.65	15.44	10.71	-.016	1.10	.085	.318	.017
Doubling immigration in all regions								
2004	1.33	1.52	8.90	-.159	0.15	.098	.111	.071
2010	2.28	2.74	9.75	-.016	0.24	.093	.083	.089
2020	4.20	6.21	10.07	.085	0.42	.076	.085	.076
2030	5.73	10.43	8.89	.101	0.65	.062	.117	.042
2050	8.27	14.61	7.67	-.032	1.09	.064	.192	-.017
2075	9.16	12.91	8.26	-.023	1.12	.080	.273	-.003
2100	10.79	14.19	9.95	-.021	1.09	.085	.278	.021
Rise in health expenditures by 3% in all regions								
2004	1.33	1.51	8.91	-.163	0.15	.098	.111	.071
2010	2.29	2.77	9.78	-.022	0.24	.093	.084	.089
2020	4.25	6.35	10.15	.076	0.42	.075	.090	.077
2030	5.84	10.73	9.02	.092	0.65	.061	.150	.045
2050	8.53	15.00	7.92	-.028	1.08	.064	.238	-.012
2075	9.57	13.17	8.68	-.017	1.1	.081	.303	.001
2100	11.30	14.30	10.54	-.013	1.08	.089	.285	.022
Financing benefits by general tax revenues								
2004	1.32	1.52	8.90	-.164	0.15	.098	.111	.071
2010	2.29	2.76	9.79	-.021	0.24	.093	.111	.063
2020	4.25	6.34	10.16	.078	0.42	.075	.111	.053
2030	5.84	10.78	9.00	.093	0.65	.061	.111	.047
2050	8.47	15.15	7.81	-.029	1.09	.063	.111	.060
2075	9.43	13.27	8.49	-.018	1.12	.080	.111	.149
2100	11.16	14.33	10.36	-.014	1.08	.087	.111	.176

(continued)

Table 5.7 (continued)

Year	Index of national income	Index of capital stock	Index of labor supply	Current account/NI	Index of pretax wage	Interest rate	Social security cost rate	Average wage tax
Financing benefits by debt								
2004	1.33	1.52	8.91	-.154	0.15	.098	.111	.071
2010	2.28	2.73	9.77	-.012	0.23	.094	.083	.088
2020	4.21	6.16	10.12	.087	0.42	.077	.085	.075
2030	5.81	10.62	8.99	.106	0.65	.061	.115	.043
2050	8.40	14.37	7.87	-.016	1.07	.066	.191	-.018
2075	9.27	12.21	8.54	-.007	1.09	.085	.274	-.010
2100	10.79	12.87	10.27	-.001	1.06	.094	.283	.007
Cut of replacement rates in all regions								
2004	1.33	1.51	8.94	-.162	0.15	.098	.111	.072
2010	2.31	2.80	9.82	-.020	0.24	.092	.081	.089
2020	4.29	6.55	10.17	.076	0.42	.073	.077	.077
2030	5.91	11.25	9.02	.088	0.66	.059	.101	.044
2050	8.62	16.20	7.82	-.031	1.11	.060	.162	-.014
2075	9.76	14.82	8.57	-.017	1.15	.074	.225	-.002
2100	11.54	16.29	10.38	-.013	1.12	.079	.231	.017
Privatizing pensions								
2004	1.33	1.50	9.01	-.171	0.15	.100	.031	.077
2010	2.36	2.98	9.91	-.031	0.24	.089	.028	.094
2020	4.49	7.51	10.33	.061	0.44	.067	.030	.083
2030	6.28	13.55	9.19	.076	0.69	.052	.039	.052
2050	9.18	21.55	7.74	-.038	1.19	.048	.052	-.007
2075	10.69	23.20	8.33	-.012	1.29	.052	.055	-.002
2100	12.66	26.84	9.95	-.011	1.28	.053	.053	.010

labor supply by each successive cohort. Thus, the future decrease in the actual labor force is offset in the European Union, Japan, and China and the growth in the actual number of workers in the United States is augmented. However, effective labor supply grows at much different rates in the regions. In Japan it increases over the century by 41 percent. In the European Union it more than doubles over the same period. And in the United States it increases over the century by a factor of almost four.

The evolution of effective labor supply in China is particularly interesting. During the next two decades effective labor supply increases, then it declines until mid century when it begins to increase again. This complex pattern reflects major changes in substitution and income effects over the transition, the demographic changes themselves, as well as the ongoing technological change. By the end of the century, China's effective labor supply is larger, but only 18 percent larger, than it is today.

Due to the dramatic aging of populations, social security tax rates increase through 2050 by 5.5 percentage points in the United States, by 12.8 percentage points in the European Union, by 13.8 percentage points in Japan, and by 7.8 percentage points in China. Over the century the respective increases are 11.4 percentage points in the United States and the European Union, 10.7 percentage points in Japan, and 16.6 percentage points in China. These changes constitute very major percentage payroll tax hikes given the base-year values. In the United States and China, for example, the model is predicting more than a 100 percent rise in payroll tax rates.

Despite the rising payroll tax burden, capital stocks rise dramatically in all regions over the course of the century. The capital stock increases by a factor of 4.7 in the United States, by a factor of 2.5 in the European Union, by a factor of 1.7 in Japan, and by a factor of 9.6 in China. In China this development is due to high investment rates associated with high private saving and the assumed rapid catch-up in the country's level of technology. The other regions also benefit from the economic boom in China. As the development of the current accounts suggests, initially capital mainly flows from the three developed regions to China. However, in subsequent decades the asset holdings of the United States, the European Union, and Japan in China decline and capital starts to flow from China to all three of these regions. After 2050, this is reversed again so that capital flows from the United States, the European Union, and Japan back to China. This reversal is expected; it reflects the repatriation of Chinese foreign capital earnings back to China.

The differences across the four regions in the growth of effective labor supply and capital stock and, in the case of China, in the evolution of the multifactor productivity coefficient materially affects overall economic growth. In the United States, output grows by a factor of 4.1 over the next 100 years. It grows by a factor of 2.2 in the European Union, 1.4 in Japan, and 8.5 in China. The larger increase in capital compared to labor supply leads to an increase in the pretax wage rate in the developed economies of almost 16 percent through the middle of the century. In China wages rise by more than 700 percent thanks, primarily, to the gradual increase in China's technology level. After 2050, however, growth in labor supply exceeds growth in capital stocks in all regions so that the wage rate starts to decline. At the end of the century real wages per unit of human capital in the developed economies are still above 2004 levels, but only 4 percent higher.

As one would expect, the worldwide capital deepening in the first half of the century and capital shallowing in the second half has a major impact on the world interest rate. Between 2004 and 2030 the world interest rate declines by 370 basis points—from .098 to .061. This is followed by an increase to a 2100 level of .087 percent. Wage tax rates follow a similar pattern—declining in the first half of the century and rising in the second half.

This interesting pattern in the evolution of factor prices reflects China's ongoing rapid growth and its assumed gradual change in saving behavior. During the first half of the century, China makes a major contribution to worldwide capital formation. In the second half of the century, more and more of its cohorts have adopted U.S. preferences with respect to spending and the Chinese saving engine starts to sputter and fail.

To understand better the role of China in worldwide capital formation, let's consider what would happen were the developed world forced to evolve without the ability to import capital from China.

5.4   The World Economy's Baseline Transition Path Excluding China

Table 5.8 reports baseline transition paths for the developed economies if we calibrate the model as previously, but simply exclude China. Doing so has dramatic effects. Capital stocks in all three regions in the initial years of the transition are much higher compared to the four-country case since more capital now remains in the developed world. For example, in 2010 the capital stock index in the United States is 1.60 compared with 1.02 in the four-country simulation (see table 5.4). In both simulations, the capital stock is measured relative to the U.S. value in 2004 in the four-country simulation.

Interestingly, even though the developed world has more capital to work with initially, real wages are actually lower in 2010 than in the transition with China. The reason is that labor supply is initially also much higher in the developed world in the no-China simulation. Presumably this reflects the income effect of having lower real wages in the medium term when China is no longer serving as the developed world's saving machine.

With China out of the picture, the developed regions' capital stocks increase much less rapidly over time. This puts a significant damper on output growth. During the first half of the century, capital growth is somewhat larger than labor supply growth. Thus wage rates increase by approximately

Table 5.8   Simulation results for the three-region simulation

	Year	Index of national income	Index of capital stock	Index of labor supply	Current account/NI	Index of pretax wage	Interest rate	Social security cost rate	Average wage tax
U.S.	2004	1.01	1.37	1.01	-.057	1.00	.072	.114	.076
	2010	1.16	1.60	1.17	-.050	1.00	.072	.116	.078
	2020	1.45	2.04	1.43	-.039	1.01	.070	.141	.080
	2030	1.70	2.45	1.68	-.041	1.02	.069	.183	.084
	2050	2.30	3.00	2.34	.008	0.99	.075	.193	.090
	2075	3.07	3.71	3.20	.010	0.96	.081	.214	.082
	2100	3.97	4.78	4.16	-.001	0.96	.082	.231	.077
EU	2004	1.45	1.90	1.47	.014	0.99	.072	.250	.083
	2010	1.57	2.08	1.59	.014	0.99	.072	.259	.077
	2020	1.75	2.40	1.76	.023	1.00	.070	.296	.067
	2030	1.83	2.55	1.83	.025	1.01	.069	.365	.056
	2050	1.99	2.52	2.05	-.013	0.98	.075	.428	.056
	2075	2.40	2.81	2.53	-.012	0.95	.081	.398	.082
	2100	3.08	3.59	3.26	.000	0.95	.082	.374	.093
Japan	2004	0.50	0.68	0.50	.077	1.01	.072	.216	.061
	2010	0.51	0.71	0.51	.072	1.01	.072	.250	.049
	2020	0.53	0.75	0.52	.030	1.02	.070	.307	.034
	2030	0.55	0.79	0.54	.044	1.02	.069	.335	.026
	2050	0.52	0.70	0.53	.014	0.99	.075	.410	.010
	2075	0.57	0.71	0.59	-.004	0.97	.081	.375	.028
	2100	0.70	0.85	0.72	.008	0.97	.082	.339	.041

2 percent and the world interest rate decreases by about 30 basis points. In the second half of the century, however, all three regions experience a capital shortage due to the high tax burden. As a consequence, wage rates decline. Indeed, the 2100 wage per unit of human capital is 4 percent below its 2004 level, and the interest rate is 100 basis points above its base year value. The lower level of real wages in the no-China transition leads to higher average wage and payroll tax rates, both of which limit capital accumulation.

The current accounts show that capital flows primarily to the United States during the coming decades due to its younger population and higher population growth rate. After 2050, capital flows to the European Union and increasingly to Japan as the Europeans and Japanese repatriate their U.S.-earned income.

As indicated in the introduction, the no-China developed world transition path shows a relatively modest capital shortage compared to our previous findings reported in Fehr, Jokisch, and Kotlikoff (2004a, 2004b, 2005). The main reason, again, is that we are now calibrating the model to include government investment. In addition, we've switched to using European Commission (2005) data for our measures of social contributions received. This lowers, somewhat, initial payroll tax rates as well as subsequent payroll tax hikes.

5.5   Adjustment Costs

Table 5.9 repeats the base-case simulation, but includes capital adjustment costs. A comparison of this table with the first panels in tables 5.4 through 5.7 shows that adjustment costs make very little difference to the four-region dynamic equilibrium. The initial levels and times paths of regional stock prices per unit of physical capital (the ratio of market value to replacement cost) are, however, interesting.

In 2004, E.U. stock prices are 5.1 percent lower than U.S. stock prices. Japanese stock prices are 12.6 percent lower, and Chinese stock prices are 16.1 percent higher. The model predicts increases in stock values in all four regions for the next 10 to 20 years, depending on the region, followed by a long-term decline in stock values. The U.S. stock market value is 1.000 in 2004, hits 1.062 in 2020, and falls to .917 in 2100. The European Union's 2004 stock market value is .949. It's .979 in 2020 and then gradually falls to .882 in 2100. Japan's 2004 stock market value is .874. In 2020 it's .938, but then falls to .851 by century's end. And China's stock market value starts at 1.161, reaches 1.196 in 2020, and declines to .914 in 2100.

5.6   Examining China's Saving and Absorption of Technology

This section returns to the four-region model without adjustment costs and examines the importance of our assumptions about the evolution of

Table 5.9 Simulation results for the base case with adjustment costs

	Year	Index of national income	Index of capital stock	Index of labor supply	Current account/NI	Index of pretax wage	Capital price	Interest rate	Social security cost rate	Average wage tax
U.S.	2004	1.02	1.00	1.02	-.015	1.00	1.000	.098	.114	.083
	2010	1.16	1.22	1.13	-.072	1.02	1.038	.088	.116	.075
	2020	1.46	1.87	1.38	-.145	1.08	1.062	.068	.136	.073
	2030	1.86	2.74	1.65	-.114	1.14	1.017	.054	.166	.081
	2050	2.61	3.72	2.32	.040	1.13	0.907	.066	.173	.094
	2075	3.26	3.88	3.07	.039	1.07	0.902	.084	.208	.077
	2100	4.09	4.53	3.95	.017	1.04	0.917	.087	.230	.064
EU	2004	1.48	1.38	1.53	.034	0.98	0.949	.098	.244	.104
	2010	1.61	1.64	1.61	.005	1.01	0.970	.088	.253	.084
	2020	1.85	2.28	1.74	-.042	1.08	0.979	.068	.258	.069
	2030	2.05	3.00	1.82	-.036	1.14	0.933	.054	.326	.069
	2050	2.30	3.33	2.02	.033	1.14	0.843	.066	.378	.072
	2075	2.55	3.01	2.41	.027	1.06	0.368	.084	.382	.062
	2100	3.15	3.39	3.07	.023	1.03	0.882	.087	.370	.052
Japan	2004	0.47	0.50	0.46	.100	1.02	0.874	.098	.229	.049
	2010	0.49	0.55	0.47	.046	1.05	0.909	.088	.261	.030
	2020	0.53	0.72	0.49	-.069	1.11	0.938	.068	.303	.021
	2030	0.60	0.91	0.52	-.057	1.16	0.901	.054	.308	.032
	2050	0.61	0.95	0.52	.045	1.17	0.804	.066	.356	.035
	2075	0.61	0.78	0.56	.036	1.09	0.818	.084	.352	.031
	2100	0.71	0.82	0.68	.026	1.05	0.851	.087	.329	.030
China	2004	1.24	1.52	8.57	-.066	0.15	1.161	.098	.110	.052
	2010	2.04	2.32	9.45	.025	0.23	1.235	.088	.085	.074
	2020	3.78	4.81	9.95	.086	0.39	1.196	.068	.088	.068
	2030	5.42	8.25	9.05	.059	0.61	1.080	.054	.117	.045
	2050	8.36	12.84	8.06	-.025	1.04	0.937	.066	.187	.004
	2075	9.66	13.32	8.69	-.023	1.12	0.885	.084	.264	.018
	2100	11.37	14.48	10.51	-.014	1.09	0.914	.087	.277	.036

Chinese saving behavior and the rate at which China absorbs developed-world technology. Specifically, we first consider keeping the time-preference rate of successive Chinese cohorts at the same level calibrated for all Chinese cohorts for 2004 in the base-case transition. Next we assume the technology coefficient in the Chinese Cobb-Douglas production function rises only to half, rather than 100 percent, of the U.S. level by 2050 and remains at that value thereafter.

5.6.1   Constant Time-Preference Rate in China

The second simulation reported in tables 5.4 through 5.7 permanently maintains the Chinese time-preference rate at its year-2004 level. Doing so has dramatic consequences. In particular, the 2100 world stock of capital is 5.9 times higher than in the base case! China not only becomes the world's saver, it also becomes the world's investor, sending huge flows of capital to the developed world over the course of the century. By 2100, the capital stocks in the United States, the European Union, and Japan are 5.6, 5.6, and 5.8 times their initial values, respectively.

This huge impetus to capital formation has a major impact on economic growth in all four regions, leaving world output roughly 50 percent higher in 2100 than it would otherwise have been. This is true notwithstanding a basically unchanged supply of labor in the four regions. The rough constancy of labor supply reflects competing income and substitution effects arising from roughly 55 percent higher long-run (year 2100) levels of the real wage per unit of human capital. The long-run capital glut also leads to a very major decline in the world real interest rates—from 9.8 percent in 2004 to 2.3 percent in 2100.

The long-run rise in real wages has a major effect on long-run payroll tax rates, although it does very little to payroll tax rates over the next three decades. Year-2100 payroll tax rates are now 16.4 percent instead of 23.0 percent in the United States, 26.1 percent instead of 36.7 percent in the European Union, 22.7 percent instead of 32.8 percent in Japan, and 26.0 percent instead of 27.7 percent in China. Higher output growth immediately translates into increased government expenditures. This explains the higher wage tax rates in the medium and long run.

5.6.2   Slower Technology Growth in China

Our next simulation, reported in the third panels of tables 5.4 through 5.7, assumes that the multifactor technology coefficient in the Chinese production function rises by 2050 to only 50, rather than 100 percent, of the U.S. level and remains fixed at half the U.S. level thereafter. As a comparison with the base case shows, slower Chinese technological growth means much lower capital demand, output, and real wage levels in China. Indeed, in 2100 the Chinese capital stock and output levels are just over half of their base-case values. And the Chinese real wage is only 39 percent of what it otherwise would have been.

In contrast to what happens to China's capital stock, China's labor supply is significantly higher along the entire transition path. This reflects the income effects (relative to the base case) experienced by the Chinese in receiving lower real wages as well as smaller inheritances. These income effects matter to labor supply from the get-go. Indeed, the immediate increase in labor supply explains why Chinese output and capital stock levels are initially higher than they are in the base case.

The rise in China's labor supply doesn't suffice to offset the lower path of wages with respect to determining the Chinese payroll tax base. Consequently, social security payroll tax rates are markedly higher during this transition.

The most interesting thing about this simulation of slower Chinese technological progress is what happens to the economies of the developed world. The answer, surprisingly, is very little. Although China saves much less than in the base case, it also demands significantly less capital. Consequently, the United States, the European Union, and Japan end up with essentially the same capital stocks, wage rates, and tax rates over time that they enjoy in the base case.

The welfare effects of this simulation are given in table 5.10. The numbers show the change in welfare measured as an equivalent variation and expressed as a percentage of remaining lifetime resources for cohorts born between 1920 and 2030. As expected from the macroeconomic development, middle-aged and future cohorts in China experience large welfare losses due to reduced wages and increased payroll tax rates during their lifetimes. The welfare changes for developed world cohorts are, in contrast, quite small.

5.7 Population Policies

In this section we analyze three different population scenarios. The first scenario keeps fertility rates fixed at their initial levels. The second scenario considers increases in life expectancy relative to the base case. The third scenario doubles rates of immigration in all four regions.[5]

5.7.1 Fixed Fertility Rates in All Regions

The fourth panels in tables 5.4 through 5.7 show the impacts of keeping the initial fertility rate of 2.11 births per woman in the United States, 1.46 births in the European Union, 1.28 births in Japan, and 1.62 births in China fixed through 2050.[6]

The higher short-term U.S. fertility rate increases that country's total

---

5. A more extensive analysis of how different population policies affect the future fiscal and economic development in the developed world is presented in Fehr, Jokisch, and Kotlikoff (2004a, 2004b).

6. After 2050 fertility rates gradually adjust again in order to achieve a zero long-run population growth rate.

Table 5.10 Welfare effects of lower technology growth in China

Birth year	U.S. income class			EU income class			Japan income class			China income class		
	(1)	(2)	(3)	(1)	(2)	(3)	(1)	(2)	(3)	(1)	(2)	(3)
1920	-0.73	-0.49	-0.10	-0.68	-0.48	-0.15	-0.70	-0.40	-0.11	1.05	2.24	2.06
1930	-1.58	-0.18	-0.38	-1.25	-1.08	-0.63	-1.57	-1.16	-0.55	0.22	1.33	1.31
1940	-2.34	-1.88	-0.72	-2.01	-1.74	-1.02	-2.40	-1.94	-1.12	-1.06	0.10	0.40
1950	-1.53	-1.43	-1.02	-1.98	-1.76	-1.15	-2.25	-1.98	-1.35	-10.08	-8.07	-4.25
1960	-0.10	-0.66	-0.98	-0.21	-0.79	-1.10	-0.26	-0.85	-1.11	-21.70	-17.12	-7.99
1970	1.61	0.54	-0.50	0.97	0.06	-0.86	1.22	0.24	-0.75	-28.60	-22.17	-9.05
1980	2.35	1.32	0.10	1.12	0.33	-0.65	1.55	0.68	-0.39	-33.45	-24.66	-7.85
1990	2.16	1.35	0.33	1.38	0.80	-0.22	2.10	1.35	0.17	-40.40	-30.67	-12.50
2000	1.38	0.90	0.28	0.71	0.39	-0.20	1.46	0.99	0.18	-45.17	-35.54	-18.92
2010	0.57	0.38	0.14	-0.03	-0.09	-0.20	0.66	0.48	0.10	-48.43	-38.65	-22.54
2020	0.05	0.07	0.07	-0.46	-0.35	-0.14	0.12	0.14	0.08	-51.18	-41.00	-24.34
2030	-0.40	-0.21	0.00	-0.74	-0.52	-0.09	-0.33	-0.16	0.09	-53.03	-42.83	-25.89

population as well as its effective labor supply. The latter variable is first affected in 2026 when the first cohort generated by the higher birth rate enters the labor force. Effective labor supply and national income in 2100 are raised by 17 percent relative to the baseline simulation. Due to the younger population age structure and the increased labor supply, social security contribution rates in the United States decrease. In 2100 the social security payroll tax is 20.9 percent, compared to 23 percent in the base case. However, the average wage tax rate rises. Compared with the base-case results, the average wage tax rate is 1.1 percentage points higher in 2100. This reflects the need to finance additional government expenditures associated with the population increase. The capital stock keeps pretty close track with the higher time path of labor supply. In 2100 the capital stock is 16 percent higher relative to the base case.

In the case of the European Union, Japan, and China, holding fertility rates fixed at their 2004 values for the next 45 years leads to smaller work forces and populations. In the European Union labor supply and national income in 2100 are 23 percent below their baseline values. These are big differences. In China, effective labor supply and national income in 2100 are both 17 percent lower. And in Japan, the maintenance of current fertility patterns through 2050 reduces effective labor supply at the end of the century by 33 percent and national income by 32 percent. Indeed, the absolute size of the Japanese economy, as measured by national income, is smaller in 2100 than in 2004 notwithstanding almost 100 years of technological progress!

Lower fertility rates raise dependency ratios in the three developed regions. This necessitates larger increases in social security tax rates. On the other hand, average wage tax rates are slightly reduced during the transition since government expenditures on education decrease with the reduction in the number of young people and general government expenditures decrease with the reduction in population growth. The higher payroll taxes in China, Japan, and the European Union lead households to save less and export more capital to the United States. Thus, capital stocks in the three regions decline during the second half of the century. Finally, since capital-labor ratios are little affected in the four regions, wage rates and the world interest rate remain almost the same as in the baseline path.

5.7.2   Higher Life Expectancies in All Regions

Now we consider a simultaneous rise in longevity in all regions. To be precise, we gradually raise life expectancy in each region through 2050 by approximately 3 years (i.e., life expectancy in 2050 is 86.8 years in the United States, 87.6 years in the European Union, 91 years in Japan, and 83.3 years in China). These values for the developed regions find support in the projections of Tuljapurkar, Li, and Boe (2000). Simulation results for this scenario are reported in the fifth panels of tables 5.4 through 5.7.

Greater longevity leads to more saving for retirement as well as more labor supply to help generate this saving. Consequently, the labor supply and the capital stock increase in all four regions compared to the base case. The broadening of the tax base implies a slight decline in wage tax rates in the medium and long run. However, at the same time, higher life expectancy leads to a rise in dependency ratios. Hence, the year-2100 social security contribution rates are increased by 2.4 percentage points in the United States, 2.3 percentage points in the European Union, 2.2 percentage points in Japan, and 4.1 percentage points in China. Since the increase in capital exceeds the increase in labor, wage rates rise slightly during the transition. Consequently, the values of the world interest rate are lower than in the baseline path.

5.7.3   Doubling of Immigration in All Regions

The sixth panels in tables 5.4 through 5.7 show the impacts of immediately and permanently doubling immigration in all four regions. This means, for example, that in 2004 2 million immigrants enter the United States, 900,000 enter the European Union, 108,000 enter Japan, and 780,000 exit China.

As is clear from the figures for effective labor supply, doubling immigration makes a material difference to the long-run supply of labor in all four regions. Take the developed regions. Relative to the baseline simulation, this policy raises effective labor supply in 2100 by 31 percent in the United States, by 21 percent in the European Union, and by 10 percent in Japan. The remarkable thing is how long it takes for immigration to alter effective labor supplies. In the United States, for example, the effective supply of labor is only 11 percent larger in 2030 despite a doubling of immigration starting in 2004. The comparable figures for the European Union and Japan are 6 percent and 2 percent.

Given that the developed world's severe fiscal problems associated with aging will begin to appear well before 2030, it would seem that even a doubling of immigration is *too little too late*. This, indeed, is what the other figures in the second panel of results show. Relative to the baseline simulation, doubling immigration makes little difference to any of the three countries in terms of their macroeconomic variables.

Take the United States. In 2030 the payroll tax rate is 15.3 percent with a doubling of immigration—not much lower than the 16.4 percent rate without the extra immigrants. In 2100 the payroll tax rate is 22.4 percent, compared with 23.0 percent under base-case immigration policy. Factor prices are also essentially unchanged by a doubling of immigration. In 2030, the pretax wage is 1.17 in both simulations. And in 2100, the pretax wage is 1.05 compared to 1.04 in the base case. The explanation here is that while the long-run U.S. labor supply rises by 31 percent, the long-run capital stock rises by 33 percent, leaving the long-run capital-labor ratio essentially unchanged.

If the long-run real wage in the United States stays fixed, but labor supply rises by 31 percent, why doesn't the payroll tax rate and, for that matter, the average wage tax rate fall by 31 percent in light of the 31 percent larger long-run supply of effective labor? The answer is that the model provides new immigrants with public goods and social insurance benefits on the same basis as existing natives. And doubling the number of immigrants on an across-the-board basis ends up costing the U.S. government almost as much in additional expenditures as the U.S. government earns in additional revenues. As tables 5.5 and 5.6 indicate, the same can be said of the European Union and Japan.

Of course, the opposite happens in China. Higher emigration reduces China's long-run labor supply by 5 percent and long-run capital stock by 3 percent. More emigrants means a reduction in the taxable wage base and thus an increase in payroll tax rates. However, as the results indicate, the changes in payroll tax rates are quite small.

Table 5.11 reports the welfare effects of doubling immigration. Almost all cohorts in the developed regions experience welfare gains, albeit mostly very small ones. For initially younger and future generations these gains stem from the reduction in payroll taxes. The gains are smaller for members of the high-skilled class because the ceiling on key payroll taxes limits the benefits they can experience from cuts in these taxes. Welfare gains are generally higher in the United States and the European Union. This is particularly true of younger and future cohorts. Indeed, for the low-skilled cohort born in 2030, the welfare gain is 2.07 percent in the European Union and 1.35 percent in the United States, but only 1.03 percent in Japan. Unlike the gains of initial older generations, these gains are substantial. They appear to reflect the reduction in excess burden arising from even the modest reductions in marginal tax rates arising from the immigration reform.

Initially, middle-aged people in China experience small welfare gains that are mainly due to small reductions in the average wage tax. In contrast, younger and future cohorts experience welfare losses. Of course, the reasons are the higher payroll tax rates throughout the transition. As one would expect from the macroeconomic outcomes, welfare effects in China are much smaller than in the developed regions.

5.8   Social Security Policies

This section considers different social insurance policy scenarios. The first is a larger increase in health expenditures than that assumed in the base case. The second and third scenarios analyze the consequences of different financing methods for the social security systems. The fourth scenario considers cuts in state pension systems. The final scenario is a privatization of public pension systems.

Table 5.11   Welfare effects of doubling immigration in all regions

Birth year	U.S. income class			EU income class			Japan income class			China income class		
	(1)	(2)	(3)	(1)	(2)	(3)	(1)	(2)	(3)	(1)	(2)	(3)
1920	0.00	0.00	0.00	0.00	0.00	0.00	0.01	0.00	0.00	0.00	0.00	0.00
1930	0.03	0.02	0.01	0.02	0.02	0.02	0.04	0.03	0.02	0.02	0.02	0.02
1940	0.06	0.05	0.03	0.06	0.05	0.04	0.08	0.07	0.05	0.08	0.08	0.06
1950	0.13	0.09	0.04	0.10	0.08	0.05	0.11	0.10	0.07	0.21	0.18	0.11
1960	0.07	0.06	0.04	0.04	0.06	0.05	0.05	0.07	0.06	0.22	0.18	0.11
1970	-0.03	0.01	0.01	0.02	0.06	0.05	0.00	0.04	0.05	0.11	0.12	0.09
1980	0.69	0.50	0.23	0.21	0.19	0.07	0.03	0.06	0.05	-0.05	0.04	0.06
1990	0.64	0.47	0.19	0.41	0.34	0.02	0.05	0.07	0.01	-0.20	-0.06	0.05
2000	0.89	0.67	0.30	0.79	0.65	0.03	0.18	0.17	-0.01	-0.29	-0.14	0.03
2010	1.04	0.78	0.37	1.28	1.05	0.10	0.39	0.32	0.00	-0.25	-0.12	0.04
2020	1.12	0.83	0.39	1.70	1.40	0.20	0.68	0.53	0.04	-0.18	-0.09	0.01
2030	1.35	0.98	0.44	2.07	1.68	0.30	1.03	0.79	0.10	-0.21	-0.14	-0.03

5.8.1 Increased Health Expenditures

In this simulation, health expenditures increase by 3 percent during the first 25 years of the transition instead of the 2 percent rate assumed in the base case. The simulation results are shown in the seventh panels of tables 5.4 through 5.7.

Of course, higher health expenditures increase social security contributions. The additional increase in payroll taxes depends on the relative sizes of overall health expenditures and populations in each region. Thus, in 2030, payroll tax rates are 1.3 percentage points in the United States, 3.2 percentage points in the European Union, and 3.5 percentage points in Japan and China above their baseline values. In year 2100 the difference is 1.8 percentage points in the United States, 3.2 percentage points in the European Union, 3.7 percentage points in Japan, and 0.8 percentage points in China.

The higher payroll tax burden leads to lower net wages. Consequently, medium-term and long-run capital stocks are below their respective base-case values. The lower capital formation is partly offset by higher capital inflows into the three developed regions from China during the first decades of the century. This explains the slightly increased output growth during this period. In the long run, output in the United States and China is lower compared to the base case, and higher in the European Union and Japan. This is due to the adjustment in effective labor supply in order to offset the income losses. Higher output growth during the first decades and lower wages in the second half of the century lead to an additional increase in wage tax rates.

The welfare effects of this simulation as reported in table 5.12 confirm our macroeconomic findings. Apart from small welfare gains for initially older generations in the European Union and Japan, all cohorts already alive in the initial year and all future cohorts experience welfare losses from increased health expenditures. The explanation is the higher payroll and wage tax rates. Since the additional tax burden increases with time, welfare losses rise with the birth year of the observed generations. Note also the differences in welfare losses between the four regions. Generations in the European Union and Japan are hurt much more than people in the United States and China. This indicates the bigger size in health expenditures in the former two regions and thus the larger rise in tax rates.

5.8.2 Financing Social Security Benefits at the Margin with General Tax Revenues

Next we consider a scenario in which payroll tax rates are fixed at their year-2004 value throughout the transition. The budgets of the social security systems are then financed by general tax revenues. The results are reported in the eighth panels of tables 5.4 through 5.7.

Table 5.12   Welfare effects of a rise in health expenditures by 3 percent in all regions

Birth year	U.S. income class			EU income class			Japan income class			China income class		
	(1)	(2)	(3)	(1)	(2)	(3)	(1)	(2)	(3)	(1)	(2)	(3)
1920	0.00	0.01	0.00	0.07	0.08	−0.01	0.07	0.04	−0.02	−0.02	−0.01	−0.01
1930	−0.03	−0.01	−0.01	0.05	0.07	−0.02	0.04	0.02	−0.03	−0.04	−0.03	−0.03
1940	−0.05	−0.03	−0.02	0.03	0.04	−0.03	0.02	0.00	−0.05	−0.08	−0.07	−0.06
1950	−0.06	−0.04	−0.02	−0.06	−0.03	−0.04	−0.07	−0.05	−0.05	−0.17	−0.14	−0.08
1960	−0.08	−0.06	−0.03	−0.29	−0.19	−0.08	−0.33	−0.22	−0.08	−0.19	−0.15	−0.05
1970	−0.18	−0.13	−0.06	−0.69	−0.50	−0.14	−0.77	−0.55	−0.13	−0.26	−0.19	−0.04
1980	−0.35	−0.25	−0.13	−1.17	−0.88	−0.23	−1.26	−0.92	−0.19	−0.42	−0.25	−0.02
1990	−0.67	−0.49	−0.26	−2.17	−1.73	−0.45	−2.32	−1.79	−0.35	−0.78	−0.48	−0.07
2000	−1.08	−0.79	−0.44	−3.29	−2.68	−0.71	−3.49	−2.72	−0.56	−1.29	−0.88	−0.29
2010	−1.35	−0.98	−0.54	−4.05	−3.36	−0.91	−4.20	−3.29	−0.71	−1.72	−1.22	−0.53
2020	−1.50	−1.08	−0.58	−4.54	−3.81	−1.04	−4.77	−3.79	−0.83	−1.90	−1.34	−0.58
2030	−1.68	−1.22	−0.64	−4.91	−4.15	−1.15	−5.23	−4.20	−0.93	−2.02	−1.42	−0.61

Balancing the future budgets of the social security systems by general tax revenues increases the wage tax rate in all four regions. In year 2100, the average wage tax rate is now 17.8 percent in the United States, instead of 6.8 percent in the base case. In the European Union it is 17.8 percent instead of 7.4 percent, in Japan 12.0 percent instead of 2.7 percent, and in China 17.6 percent instead of 1.9 percent. Note that the wage tax rates do not increase as much as the payroll tax rates would otherwise have risen because there is no ceiling on wages subject to taxation. This differentially reduces the welfare of high-earnings agents. It also reduces their ability to save and their desire to work. Thus capital stocks, labor supply, and national income are lower than in the base case. The course of current accounts, wage rates, and interest rates are, however, little changed.

Table 5.13 records the welfare effects of this policy. Agents in the low- and middle-income classes experience welfare gains since they now face a lower tax burden. Note also the differences in welfare effects between the developed regions, which stem from the different extents of population aging in the three regions. At first glance it might be surprising that initially middle-aged and younger cohorts in the low- and middle-income classes in China experience small welfare losses and those in the high-income class enjoy welfare gains. The reason is that payroll taxes in China decline in the base-case transition during the first few decades. Keeping payroll tax rates fixed at the year-2004 level translates into lower average wage tax rates during these decades than would otherwise be the case. This, of course, hurts people in the low- and middle-income class, while those in the high-income class gain.

5.8.3 Financing Social Security Benefits with Government Debt

This scenario examines the consequences of financing social security benefits through 2029 with government debt. To be precise, we keep payroll tax rates in each region fixed at their year-2004 values through 2029. We also fix the intercept and the progressive terms of our wage tax rate formula at their 2004 values. The government's general budget and the budgets of the social security systems are then balanced with government debt. Starting in year 2030, payroll tax rates and the intercept of the payroll tax rate formula endogenously adjust to balance social security systems and government general budgets, respectively. In the years 2030 and thereafter we keep government debt fixed as a share of national income. The ninth panels in tables 5.4 through 5.7 report results.

In the United States debt increases from 33.3 percent of national income in 2004 to 73.8 percent in 2100, in the European Union from 38.9 percent in 2004 to 134.6 percent in 2100, and in Japan from 41.4 percent in 2004 to 249.5 percent in 2100. In China, payroll tax and wage tax rates decline, with some minor exceptions, in each year during the first few decades of the base-case transition. Consequently, holding these tax rates fixed through

Table 5.13   Welfare effects of financing benefits by general tax revenues in all regions

Birth year	U.S. income class			EU income class			Japan income class			China income class		
	(1)	(2)	(3)	(1)	(2)	(3)	(1)	(2)	(3)	(1)	(2)	(3)
1920	-0.02	-0.01	0.00	-0.05	-0.03	-0.04	-0.08	-0.04	-0.23	0.00	0.02	-0.08
1930	-0.02	-0.01	0.00	-0.05	-0.04	-0.05	-0.08	-0.04	-0.19	0.00	0.01	-0.08
1940	-0.04	-0.02	-0.01	-0.06	-0.05	-0.04	-0.10	-0.06	-0.26	-0.02	-0.01	-0.10
1950	-0.02	-0.02	-0.01	-0.02	-0.02	-0.02	0.05	0.02	-0.14	-0.19	-0.15	0.02
1960	0.00	-0.01	-0.01	0.09	0.04	-0.03	0.37	0.23	-0.12	-0.34	-0.27	0.11
1970	0.05	0.02	-0.02	0.22	0.14	-0.10	0.62	0.43	-0.34	-0.30	-0.24	0.10
1980	0.12	0.07	-0.08	0.39	0.27	-0.20	0.80	0.58	-0.50	-0.20	-0.18	0.04
1990	0.20	0.13	-0.16	0.73	0.56	-0.62	1.19	0.91	-0.94	-0.02	-0.07	-0.03
2000	0.28	0.19	-0.25	1.13	0.89	-1.09	1.47	1.11	-1.17	0.21	0.11	-0.13
2010	0.33	0.23	-0.28	1.48	1.21	-1.53	1.75	1.34	-1.43	0.35	0.23	-0.19
2020	0.34	0.25	-0.35	1.65	1.38	-1.87	2.05	1.62	-1.82	0.38	0.26	-0.30
2030	0.35	0.26	-0.49	1.65	1.40	-2.06	2.18	1.75	-2.09	0.44	0.30	-0.46

2030 in China means running a surplus. Indeed, in 2100 government debt in China is negative 38.8 percent of national income, rather than positive 10 percent—its base-case year 2100 value.

Higher debt ultimately implies higher average tax rates in order to finance higher interest payments. In 2100, average wage tax rates are 11.8 percent in the United States, 21.9 percent in the European Union, and 30.5 percent in Japan. The corresponding 2100 base-case average wage tax rates are 6.8 percent in the United States, 7.4 percent in the European Union, and 2.7 percent in Japan.

These are, obviously, huge increases. Of course, one would expect that capital formation, labor supply, and output growth to be greatly reduced by this policy. But this doesn't happen thanks to China's surplus.

Next consider the welfare effects of this policy shown in table 5.14. Initial middle-aged and younger generations in the United States, the European Union, and Japan gain from this policy reform. This reflects, of course, the fact that they enjoy constant rather than rising tax rates through 2030. The gains are largest in Japan since in the baseline path the increase in social security contributions is the largest. Future cohorts in the developed regions experience remarkably large welfare losses. These stem from the large increase in wage taxes to finance the higher government debt. Take, as an example, members of the 2030 Japanese birth cohort. They experience a 20.25 percent welfare loss. These show the dramatic increase in excess burdens due to the adjustment in the wage taxes. The opposite is observed in China. Here middle-aged people lose from the reform since they now face higher payroll tax burdens. Future cohorts, however, experience welfare gains from the lower and even negative wage taxes.

5.8.4   Cutting Pension-Benefit Replacement Rates

As mentioned, our baseline path includes the legislated cut of the pension replacement rates in Japan of 20 percent that is being phased in between now and 2017. We now assume the same cut in all other regions over the same period. The simulation results are reported in the tenth panels of tables 5.4 through 5.7. In 2100, social security contribution rates are reduced by 3.6 percentage points in the United States, by 4.7 percentage points in the European Union, and by 4.6 percentage points in China compared to the respective baseline values. As one would expect, this policy increases capital formation in the three regions. Thus the long-run capital stock is increased by 11.6 percent in the United States, by 10.3 percent in the European Union, and by 11.2 percent in China relative to the base case. At the same time, labor supply is slightly reduced, and output growth increases. The higher capital-labor ratios lead to higher wages and lower interest rates during the transition. Due to higher wage income, the average wage tax rates in the three regions are lower than in the baseline path.

The pension reform in the United States, the European Union, and

Table 5.14 Welfare effects of financing benefits by debt

Birth year	U.S. income class			EU income class			Japan income class			China income class		
	(1)	(2)	(3)	(1)	(2)	(3)	(1)	(2)	(3)	(1)	(2)	(3)
1920	0.01	-0.02	0.00	-0.09	-0.12	0.02	-0.28	-0.18	0.08	0.07	0.06	0.03
1930	0.09	0.05	0.02	-0.04	-0.07	0.06	-0.19	-0.09	0.10	0.13	0.12	0.08
1940	0.18	0.13	0.06	0.06	0.02	0.11	-0.10	-0.02	0.19	0.29	0.28	0.20
1950	0.26	0.19	0.11	0.35	0.23	0.15	0.62	0.42	0.26	0.56	0.48	0.29
1960	0.43	0.31	0.17	0.83	0.60	0.27	2.27	1.53	0.44	0.46	0.39	0.24
1970	0.53	0.44	0.27	1.53	1.18	0.42	3.50	2.59	0.62	0.21	0.24	0.20
1980	0.23	0.28	0.24	0.90	0.87	0.34	1.75	1.62	0.39	0.23	0.32	0.20
1990	-0.07	0.10	0.18	0.06	0.32	0.07	-0.62	0.00	-0.39	-0.02	0.17	0.22
2000	-1.00	-0.58	-0.14	-2.45	-1.69	-0.69	-6.90	-5.10	-2.30	-0.53	-0.22	0.09
2010	-3.03	-2.16	-1.06	-7.01	-5.74	-2.21	-15.80	-12.97	-5.31	-1.00	-0.60	-0.18
2020	-3.55	-2.52	-1.22	-8.56	-7.11	-2.85	-17.05	-14.03	-5.95	-0.93	-0.49	-0.05
2030	-4.08	-2.89	-1.36	-10.72	-9.06	-3.77	-20.25	-16.94	-7.42	-0.75	-0.30	0.16

China also affects the Japanese economy in the future. Higher capital stocks in the United States, the European Union, and China lead to larger capital imports by Japan. Consequently, Japan's capital stock and national income is also higher compared to the base case. The increase in wages during the transition lowers payroll tax rates slightly since labor supply remains unaffected. However, the average wage tax rate increases due to the higher growth in general government expenditures arising from higher output growth.

As the welfare effects in table 5.15 indicate, initially middle-aged people lose from this policy reform in all four regions. In the United States, the European Union, and China this reflects the cut in pension replacement rates. People now receive lower benefits than under the baseline scenario. In Japan the losses stem from the increases in the average wage tax rate. Initial older cohorts in the four regions are almost unaffected. Initial young and future cohorts, however, gain in all four regions. The reason is mainly the reduction in payroll and wage tax rates in the United States, the European Union, and China and the increased wages that outweigh the benefit losses. In Japan, the welfare gains of the low- and middle-income classes also stem from the reduction in payroll taxes and the higher wages. The highest income classes are adversely affected by the increase in the wage tax rate.

5.8.5   Privatizing Pensions

Our final reform is complete pension privatization, which we model as the elimination of any new public pension benefit accrual coupled with the establishment of individual accounts. The reform entails paying off all accrued benefits to all those retired in 2004 and to all those working in 2004 when they reach retirement. To approximate this payoff of accrued benefits we pay all initial retirees their full benefits over time and pay post-2004 retirees benefits in retirement whose values are linearly phased out over a 45-year period starting in 2004. Thus, the members of the cohort retiring in 2005 receive in public pension benefits 44/45ths of what they would otherwise have received. The members of the cohort retiring in 2006 receive 43/45ths of what they would have received and so on.

We finance the move to individual accounts via consumption taxation. Specifically, we completely eliminate those payroll taxes used to finance state pensions and impose a new consumption tax in each region to pay, over time, all accrued benefits. By 2078 all accrued pension benefits have been paid off, so the new consumption tax rates from that point on are zero.

The key feature of the reform is not *privatization* per se, but rather the intergenerational redistribution associated with moving to private accounts. The redistribution comprises three elements. First, the shift from payroll to consumption taxation reduces the tax burden on current and future workers and shifts it onto current retirees. Second, paying current workers (those working in 2004) when they reach retirement only their accrued

Table 5.15   Welfare effects of a cut of replacement rates in all regions

Birth year	U.S. income class			EU income class			Japan income class			China income class		
	(1)	(2)	(3)	(1)	(2)	(3)	(1)	(2)	(3)	(1)	(2)	(3)
1920	0.21	0.12	0.00	0.34	0.23	-0.04	-0.10	-0.03	0.00	0.04	0.18	0.25
1930	0.10	0.03	-0.03	0.28	0.17	-0.10	-0.20	-0.12	-0.05	-0.05	0.08	0.16
1940	-0.02	-0.08	-0.09	0.13	0.03	-0.17	-0.36	-0.26	-0.15	-0.27	-0.13	0.00
1950	-2.84	-1.59	-0.48	-3.04	-1.75	-0.48	-0.45	-0.36	-0.23	-3.71	-3.14	-1.79
1960	-1.80	-1.11	-0.46	-2.98	-1.84	-0.57	-0.23	-0.27	-0.25	-3.18	-2.55	-1.32
1970	-0.49	-0.34	-0.25	-1.11	-0.70	-0.35	0.06	-0.11	-0.25	-1.71	-1.39	-0.73
1980	0.67	0.46	0.08	0.41	0.35	-0.10	0.23	0.01	-0.23	-0.74	-0.74	-0.43
1990	1.64	1.15	0.38	2.29	1.83	0.36	0.60	0.28	-0.13	0.50	0.07	-0.29
2000	2.84	1.76	0.64	4.21	3.33	0.78	0.83	0.41	-0.12	2.03	1.23	0.19
2010	3.04	2.13	0.79	5.76	4.57	1.11	0.98	0.50	-0.15	3.33	2.22	0.83
2020	3.51	2.42	0.86	6.87	5.48	1.34	1.16	0.62	-0.20	3.84	2.53	0.93
2030	4.02	2.77	0.94	7.58	6.07	1.48	1.31	0.71	-0.31	4.36	2.86	1.00

state pension benefits rather than their projected benefits represents a cut in transfer payments that hurts those workers but benefits future workers who would otherwise have had to help pay for those benefits. Third, factor price changes arising from this policy help later generations at the cost of hurting earlier ones. Specifically, later generations benefit from higher real wages, while earlier generations lose from receiving lower returns on their assets.

There is no need to formally model the private accounts in which agents would be forced to save as part of this privatization reform. The reason is that our agents face no liquidity constraints. Hence, they are free to borrow against their private account balances if they wish to consume more than their disposable income net of contributions to these accounts. Consequently, forcing our agents to save has no impact on their behavior.[7]

In the United States, the additional consumption tax rate needed to pay off accrued pension benefits is initially 6.8 percent and gradually declines thereafter. The U.S. payroll tax rate declines immediately by 7.8 percentage points. Over the transition, the payroll tax rate rises by 2.7 percentage points since expenses for health care and disability insurance grow.

In the European Union, the added consumption tax rate has an initial value of 15.0 percent and then declines. Because of this reform, the payroll tax is reduced by 14.6 percentage points in year 2004 and rises to a maximum of 13.9 percent in 2075. In Japan, the consumption tax rate is initially 11.1 percent. It then rises to a maximum of 12.7 percent in 2016 before declining. The payroll tax is 12.1 percentage points lower in 2004. And the maximum value reached is 15.7 percent in 2050. Finally, the initial rate of the new consumption tax in China is 10.5 percent. The payroll tax rates is initially reduced by 8 percentage points and rises to its maximum value of 5.5 percent in 2075.

Of course, since part of the tax burden is shifted from payroll taxes toward consumption taxes, the burden on younger households falls and that on the elderly rises. The intergenerational redistribution associated with the consumption tax depresses aggregate consumption, which permits an increase in national saving and capital formation. The long-run consequences of this reform are dramatic in all three regions. Relative to the base-case simulations, the year 2100 capital stock increases by 87.6 percent in the United States, by 81.1 percent in the European Union, by 90.4 percent in Japan, and by 83.2 percent in China.

The higher capital stocks increase gross wages, which rise by 2100 by approximately 18 percent in all four regions. The combination of higher gross

---

7. Including liquidity constraints would require solving our agents' utility maximization problems using dynamic programming. Doing so would be much more time consuming. It would also introduce a degree of approximation error into the solution that we avoid with our current formulation in which we find the solutions to the first-order conditions and budget constraints of our agents to a very high degree of precision using Gauss-Seidel iteration.

wages and reduced payroll and wage taxes boosts net wages, which almost double in the four regions. The reductions in labor supplies in the four regions, reported in tables 5.4 to 5.7, are a direct consequence of the positive income effects experienced by younger generations. Finally, capital accumulation leads to lower year-2100 interest rates.

Of course, the advantageous macroeconomic effects of privatization come at a cost, which is shown in table 5.16. The reform entails a major redistribution from older generations in all four economies toward younger and future generations. The intergenerational and intragenerational redistribution is less severe in the United States compared to the European Union, Japan, and China, whose initial consumption tax rates are much higher.

The elderly are hurt because they are now forced to pay for their pension benefits via the consumption tax. Younger and future generations benefit enormously from the policy since they face a much lower payroll tax burden during their working years and experience much higher wages. Consider middle-earning agents in the United States. The oldest such agents included in table 5.16—those born in 1920—experience a 2.9 percent reduction in welfare. In contrast, the youngest such agents included in the table—those born in 2030—enjoy a 12.2 percent rise in welfare. The corresponding welfare losses and gains experienced by the 1920 and 2030 middle classes are 6.1 percent and 23.5 percent in the European Union, 5.3 percent and 15.9 percent in Japan, and 6.3 percent and 13.3 percent in China.

Another key feature of table 5.16 is that the poor initial elderly experience larger welfare losses than the middle class or rich initial elderly. The explanation for this differential welfare loss is that both the poor and rich elderly are constrained with respect to their consumption of leisure because they are both fully retired. However, the rich elderly are consuming a lot more than the poor. Hence, while both the rich and the poor experience roughly the same percentage reduction in consumption from the imposition of the consumption tax, the impact on their utilities are not the same because (a) their initial consumption-leisure ratios differ and (b) utility is not separable with respect to the two arguments.

5.9   Conclusion

The developed world and China all face enormous demographic changes that will greatly challenge their already overly stressed fiscal institutions. Fortunately, our dynamic life-cycle model suggests there may be a macroeconomic silver lining to this very gray demographic cloud. The silver lining is China, whose continued rapid acquisition of technology and human capital and extraordinarily high rate of saving can dramatically raise the world's supply of capital. Assuming the developed world's capital market

Table 5.16   Welfare effects of privatizing pensions in all regions

Birth year	U.S. income class			EU income class			Japan income class			China income class		
	(1)	(2)	(3)	(1)	(2)	(3)	(1)	(2)	(3)	(1)	(2)	(3)
1920	-4.72	-2.88	-1.01	-8.92	-6.14	-3.39	-8.12	-5.31	-2.32	-7.11	-6.34	-4.36
1930	-5.14	-3.19	-1.08	-9.06	-6.39	-3.73	-8.84	-5.78	-2.42	-6.73	-6.01	-4.12
1940	-5.73	-3.82	-1.48	-9.42	-6.67	-3.73	-9.49	-6.60	-3.25	-7.14	-6.43	-4.48
1950	-6.31	-4.17	-2.11	-9.06	-6.22	-3.12	-6.01	-4.37	-2.81	-9.38	-8.07	-5.68
1960	-4.50	-3.17	-2.09	-5.82	-4.05	-3.05	-1.94	-1.62	-2.45	-8.63	-7.02	-4.49
1970	-1.69	-1.19	-1.57	-2.40	-1.29	-2.60	0.35	0.55	-2.10	-7.01	-5.71	-3.47
1980	1.22	1.18	-0.34	0.97	1.51	-1.59	2.20	2.31	-1.29	-5.52	-4.69	-2.50
1990	3.67	2.99	0.73	5.19	5.36	0.22	4.56	4.62	-0.15	-2.17	-2.54	-2.37
2000	7.10	5.28	1.80	11.93	10.22	1.77	8.29	7.09	0.61	5.13	2.71	-0.51
2010	10.84	7.60	2.72	19.36	15.48	3.31	12.78	9.99	1.35	12.82	8.31	2.74
2020	14.59	9.89	3.48	26.20	20.25	4.62	17.83	13.38	2.12	17.11	10.89	3.81
2030	18.27	12.21	4.22	30.92	23.49	5.50	21.54	15.90	2.64	21.21	13.34	4.65

remains open, China will gradually become the developed world's major source of capital.

Indeed, assuming China attains the developed world's living standard by the middle of this century and also maintain its very high propensity to save, it will raise real wages in the developed world by 40 percent. This is over and above real wage increases arising from technological change. Even were China to gradually adopt Western spending habits, real wages at mid century will be 16 percent higher than is currently the case. This again is above and beyond what technological change can be expected to deliver.

Moreover, China's contribution to the developed world's own development is positive in the short as well as long runs. Even though capital initially moves from the developed world to China, there are no major short-run reductions in developed-world real wages. The reason is that the prospect of higher future real wages leads developed-world workers to supply less current labor. This keeps initial developed-world capital-labor ratios and the real wages on which they depend from falling.

Absent China, our model suggests a very gradual decline in the developed world's capital intensivity with real wages per unit of human capital 4 percent lower at the end of the century than they are today. This is much less ominous news than we delivered in previous studies that omitted China. The reason is that we now incorporate government investment, which implies more developed world saving.

In addition to examining China's role in world economic development and incorporating government investment, this study has entertained a variety of demographic and fiscal scenarios. Our demographic scenarios, which we apply to all four regions simultaneously, are (a) maintaining fertility rates at their current generally very low levels for much longer than governments now project, (b) increasing longevity at faster than projected rates, and (c) immediately and permanently doubling rates of immigration.

Each of these demographic changes has very little impact on the overall macroeconomic situation, but each makes a nontrivial difference to where payroll tax rates end up. For example, Japan's payroll tax rate ends up 25 percent higher at the end of the century if its fertility rate fails to rise to the now-projected 2050 level; the European Union's payroll tax rate ends 5 percentage points higher in 2030 if E.U. life expectancy rises by 3 years more by 2050 than now expected; and the U.S. payroll tax rate is reduced by 1 percent in 2050 if it doubles its rate of immigration.

Our policy simulations raised the rate of growth of health expenditures over the next quarter century, switched—at the margin—to income-tax finance of government pension benefits, financed future increases in aggregate pension benefits via increases in income taxes rather than payroll taxes, and privatized state pension systems by paying off accrued pension benefits with a consumption tax. Each of these policies has important impacts on the macroeconomy. But the one with the biggest impact is the privatization of state pensions, which more than doubles long-run ratios of physical capital per unit of human capital and raises long-run real wages by roughly a quarter. The policy delivers major benefits to future generations, both because of the higher wages they earn and the dramatically lower payroll tax rates that they face.

To conclude, there is no reason to believe that China is currently eating our lunch or will do so in the near future. On the contrary, there is good reason to believe that China is in the process of taking us to dinner by slowly but surely becoming the world's biggest saver and the developed world's major supplier of capital.

References

Altig, D., A. J. Auerbach, L. J. Kotlikoff, K. A. Smetters, and J. Walliser. 2001. Simulating fundamental tax reform in the United States. *American Economic Review* 91:574–95.

Auerbach, A. J., and L. J. Kotlikoff. 1983. An examination of empirical tests of social security and savings. In *Social policy evaluation: An economic perspective,* ed. E. Helpman et al., 161–79. San Diego, CA: Academic Press.

———. 1987. *Dynamic fiscal policy.* Cambridge: Cambridge University Press.

Bohn, H. 2001. Social security and demographic uncertainty: The risk sharing properties of alternative policies. In *Risk aspects of investment based social security reform,* ed. John Campbell and Martin Feldstein, 203–41. Chicago: University of Chicago Press.

Blöndal, S., and S. Scarpetta. 1999. The retirement decision in OECD countries. Economics Department Working Paper no. 202, OECD, Paris.

Cooley, T. F., and J. Soares. 1999a. A positive theory of social security based on reputation. *Journal of Political Economy* 107:135–60.

———. 1999b. Privatizing social security. *Review of Economic Dynamics* 2:731–55.

De Nardi, M., S. Imrohoroglu, and T. J. Sargent. 1999. Projected U.S. demographics and social security. *Review of Economic Dynamics* 2:575–615.

Docteur, E., and H. Oxley. 2003. Health-care systems: Lessons from the reform experience. Economics Department Working Paper no. 374, OECD, Paris.

European Commission. 2003. The budgetary challenges posed by ageing populations. European Economy: Reports and Studies no. 4, 2001, Brussels.

———. 2005. Statistical annex to European economy, Spring 2005. Retrieved from http://europa.eu.int/comm/economy_finance/publications/european_economy/statisticalannex_en.htm.

Fehr, H., and C. Habermann. 2005. Risk sharing and efficiency implications of progressive pension arrangements. Mimeo, University of Wuerzburg.

Fehr, H., G. Halder, S. Jokisch, and L. J. Kotlikoff. 2003. A simulation model for the demographic transition in the OECD—Data requirements, model structure and calibration. Wuerzburg Economic Papers no. 45, University of Wuerzburg.

Fehr, H., S. Jokisch, and L. J. Kotlikoff. 2004a. Fertility, mortality, and the developed world's demographic transition. CESifo Working Paper no. 1326, Munich.

———. 2004b. The role of immigration in dealing with developed world's demographic transition. *Finanzarchiv 60:*296–324.

————. 2005. The developed world's demographic transition—The roles of capital flows, immigration, and policy. In *Social security reform—Financial and political issues in international perspective,* ed. R. Brooks and A. Razin, 11–43. Cambridge: Cambridge University Press.

Feldstein, M. S. 1974. Social security, induced retirement, and aggregate capital accumulation. *Journal of Political Economy* 82:905–26.

Heckman, J. J., Lochner, L., and C. Taber. 1998. Tax policy and human capital formation. *American Economic Review* 88:293–97.

Huang, H., S. Imrohoroglu, and T. Sargent. 1997. Two computational experiments to fund social security. *Macroeconomic Dynamics* 1:7–44.

Hubbard, G. R., and K. L. Judd. 1987. Social security and individual welfare: Precautionary saving, borrowing constraints, and the payroll tax. *American Economic Review* 77:630–46.

Huggett, M., and G. Ventura. 1999. On the distributional effects of social security reform. *Review of Economic Dynamics* 2:498–531.

Imrohoroglu, A., S. Imrohoroglu, and D. H. Joines. 1995. A life cycle analysis of social security. *Economic Theory* 6:83–114.

————. 1999. Social security in an overlapping generations economy with land. *Review of Economic Dynamics* 2:638–65.

Kotlikoff, L. J. 1979. Social security and equilibrium capital intensity. *Quarterly Journal of Economics* 93:233–54.

————. 1996. Privatizing social security: How it works and why it matters. In *Tax policy and the economy,* ed. J. M. Poterba , vol. 10, 1–32. Cambridge, MA: MIT Press.

Kotlikoff, L. J., K. Smetters, and J. Walliser. 1998a. The economic impact of privatizing social security. In *Redesigning social security,* ed. H. Siebert, 327–48. Tübingen: J. C. B. Mohr.

————. 1998b. Social security: Privatization and progressivity. *American Economic Review* 88:137–41.

————. 1999. Privatizing social security in the U.S.—Comparing the options. *Review of Economic Dynamics* 2:532–74.

————. 2001. Finding a way out of America's demographic dilemma. NBER Working Paper no. 8258. Cambridge, MA: National Bureau of Economic Research.

————. 2002. Distributional effects in a general equilibrium analysis of social security. In *The distributional effects of social security reform,* ed. M. S. Feldstein and J. Liebman, 327–61. Chicago: University of Chicago Press.

Nishiyama, S., and K. Smetters. 2005. Consumption taxes and economic efficiency with idiosyncratic wage shocks. *Journal of Political Economy* 113:1088–1115.

OECD. 2001. *Ageing and income: Financial resources and retirement in 9 OECD countries.* Paris: OECD.

————. 2002. *China in the world economy: The domestic policy challenges.* Paris: OECD.

————. 2003a. *Education at a glance: OECD indicators 2003.* Paris: OECD.

————. 2003b. *Financing education—Investments and returns: Analysis of the world education indicators, 2002 edition.* Paris: OECD.

————. 2003c. *Revenue statistics 1965–2002.* Paris: OECD.

Raffelhüschen, B. 1989. *Anreizwirkungen des Systems der sozialen Alterssicherung. Eine dynamische Simulationsanalyse.* Frankfurt a.M., Peter Lang.

————. 1993. Funding social security through Pareto optimal conversion policies. In *Public pension economics, Journal of Economics/Zeitschrift für Nationalökonomie,* ed. B. Felderer, 7:105–31.

Siegel, J. 2005. *The future for investors.* New York: Crown Business.

Seidman, L. S. 1986. A phase-down of social security: The transition in a life cycle growth model. *National Tax Journal* March: 97–107.

Smetters, K., and J. Walliser. 2004. Opting out of social security. *Journal of Public Economics* 88:1295–306.

Social Security Advisory Board. 1999. *The 1999 technical panel on assumptions and methods.* Washington, DC: Social Security Advisory Board.

Summers, L. H. 1981. Capital taxation and accumulation in a life cycle growth model. *American Economic Review* 71:533–44.

Tuljapurkar, S., N. Li, and C. Boe. 2000. A universal pattern of mortality decline in the G7 countries. *Nature 405:*789–92.

United Nations Population Division (UNPD). 2003. *World population prospects: The 2002 revision,* http://esa.un.org/unpp/.

———. 2005. *World population prospects: The 2004 revision,* http://esa.un.org/unpp/.

Whitehouse, E. 2002. Pension systems in 15 countries compared: The value of entitlements. Discussion Paper 02/04, Centre for Pensions and Superannuation, Sydney.

WHO. 2004. *The World Health Report 2004.* Geneva: World Health Organization.

Comment   Yasushi Iwamoto

The Chinese National Offshore Oil Company's attempt to buy Unical Corp., a U.S. oil and gas company, has recently provoked a heated debate. Although the political aspects tended to be focused on, Professors Fehr, Jokisch, and Kotlikoff's paper pointed out that Chinese investment into the United States and other developed countries will be a natural consequence of the aging process of the global economy. This kind of phenomenon is not a threat to the developed world, but actually helps to solve the problem caused by population aging, to some extent.

The effect of aging on the economy is an important policy issue in many countries around the world. The economic analysis first treated it as a problem of the national economy, using a closed-economy model. Auerbach et al. (1989) is a seminal work that extends the analytical framework to a multicountry model, in which capital is mobile across the border. Taking account of China, this paper successfully opens up a new horizon and helps to increase our knowledge. At the same time, the authors have achieved many important extensions to behavioral equations of the simulation model: saving, bequests, labor supply, fertility, government investment, and social insurance among others. This paper sets a new standard that other researchers should work hard to reach.

What is changed dramatically by introducing China is a process of cap-

Yasushi Iwamoto is a professor of economics at the University of Tokyo.

ital formation. Introducing China into a simulation model of the global economy, this paper shows that focusing only on the developed countries can be misleading. China helps to improve economic conditions of the developed world through providing capital. To look at this role of China, let us compare simulations without China and with China. In table 5.8, which focuses on the European Union, Japan, and the United States, the interest rate will increase from 7.2 percent in 2004 to 8.2 percent in 2100, while it will first decline until 2030. In the developed world, an aging process will lower the capital-labor ratio. On the other hand, when China is included in the simulation, the interest rate in 2100 will be 8.7 percent, which is lower than the 2004 level (9.8 percent). Therefore, capital deepening will occur in this century. The wage in the developed world will increase along with it. A comparison of the two scenarios indicates that looking at only the developed world misses a very important aspect of global aging, and leads to an incorrect insight into the future of the global economy.

Although various sensitivity analyses provided in the paper seem to assure the reliability of the scenario that China will "take the developed world to dinner," other aspects not considered in the paper may lead to a different scenario. I would like to address a few points.

An important point missing in this paper is a constraint on energy consumption or environmental pollution. If China grows like a setting of the simulation, the energy consumption is very likely to exceed the supply. In this case, the growth of China as well as the rest of the world will be stagnant.

If China will have a great impact on the aging process of the global economy, other big developing countries like Brazil, India, and Russia may have a significant impact, too. Thus, a larger scale simulation model may be called for to capture the impact of global aging. Since an accurate specification of behavioral equations is a difficult task, however, our future faces the uncertainty, which is not easy to be resolved.

The simulation study of the aging hinges on the underlying population projections. This paper follows the U.N. population projection, which assumes that the fertility rate in every country will converge to 1.85 in the long run. Due to this setting, the U.N. projection may diverge from the projection made in each country. For example, the current Japanese official projection assumes that the fertility rate will converge to 1.38 in the long run. The Japanese public pension program is designed so that it is sustainable on this projection. If the Japanese could rely on the U.N. population projection, the policy debate on the public pension reform would have been much easier. From the viewpoint of Japanese citizens, the setting of the United Nations as well as this paper is too optimistic.

The paper provides a variety of policy simulations and derives insightful findings. The authors found that the biggest impact was exerted by privatizing public pensions. On the other hand, increasing immigration is *too little too late* to solve a fiscal problem caused by population aging. Since the paper does not count noneconomic costs of accepting immigrants, an actual merit of immigration may be smaller than illustrated by their simulation. When we look at the impact of these policies on the production factors, a difference is significant. When the immigration in the United States is doubled, the labor input in 2100 will increase by 31 percent from the baseline case. In contrast, when the U.S. public pension is privatized, the capital stock in 2100 will increase by 88 percent from the baseline case. I basically agree with these findings.

Although it seems that promoting capital formation may be easier than increasing the labor force, we should note that this kind of inference should implicitly assume implementation costs of these policies are roughly equal. Actually, the privatization of public pension is a radical change. In their simulation, it is also associated with a radical tax reform; it eliminates the payroll tax that finances the existing public pension, and finances all accrued benefits with a new consumption tax. In the case of the European Union, the necessary increase in consumption tax rate at the start of privatization is 15 percentage points, and the payroll tax rate decreases by 14.6 percentage points. If we consider this kind of radical reform, one may wonder why we do not think about a radical population policy—say, the policy that increases the number of immigrants by a factor of 10 or 20.

What is difficult here is that we do not have an appropriate scientific criterion that makes different kinds of policies comparable. For example, when we compare the distortion effects of taxation, we usually consider tax policies that raise the same revenue. Comparing the promotion of immigration and the privatization of public pension lacks such kind of standardization. This is not a fault of this paper, but it is the problem faced by all researchers. I hope the future research will develop a satisfactory measure of comparing policies discussed here. At this moment the authors present reasonable sets of policies, and I am sympathetic to their choice of policy scenarios.

Finally, I would like to point out that their policy analyses show that some important point is not altered even when we incorporate China. The cut of public pension benefit or the privatization will help to increase the capital stock and private consumption. While it lowers the welfare of existing generations slightly, the welfare of future generations is significantly improved. This fact accords with previous researchers who did not take account of China. Imbalance of burdens among generations should be solved by public policy of each country. Although China partially improves situations of developed countries, it will never solve all problems. What we should note is that each country first has to carry out a wise policy. This paper conveys this message convincingly.

Reference

Auerbach, A. J., R. Hagemann, L. J. Kotlikoff, and G. Nicoletti. 1989. The economics of aging population: The case of four OECD countries. *OECD Economic
Studies* 12:97–130.

Comment   Cielito F. Habito

In its earlier version submitted to the EASE 16 conference for review
("The Developed World's Demographic Transition—The Roles of Capital
Flows, Immigration, and Policy"), the study analyzed the demographic
transitions occurring in the United States, the European Union, and Japan
(i.e., the *developed world*) and their welfare implications, via impacts on
the pension system and on fiscal management. Using an overlapping-
generations model that incorporates most of the state-of-the-art features
employed in such demographic models (more on this follows), simulations
yielded alarming results: (a) in a do-nothing scenario, payroll taxes would
have to at least double to support benefits committed to the elderly; (b)
macroeconomic feedback effects of aging populations lead to a significant
capital shortage that dramatically lowers real wages (by 19 percent) and
raises real interest rates (by over 400 basis points); and (c) even substantial
immigration would do little to mitigate the fiscal squeeze. One way out that
would exact short-term pain (i.e., welfare losses for current generations including the elderly) is to close down at the margin existing government pension systems and use consumption taxes to pay off their accrued liabilities.
This would raise the welfare of future generations enormously, with those
in Europe and Japan benefiting the most.

That analysis of course ignored the fact that there is much else in the
world beyond the United States, Europe, and Japan. The addition of high-
saving China into the picture dramatically changes the results, with China
emerging as the savior that bails out the developed world from impending
major fiscal troubles and real wage declines. Even if China's saving rate
eventually falls to the U.S. levels, it still manages to spare the developed
world from eventual real wage declines, and instead permits substantial
real wage increases. All the more if one further considers India and Southeast Asia, the other dynamic and high-saving economies in Asia. In effect,
the developed world will be saved from potentially debilitating difficulties
by the developing world, with their high saving rates and lower dependency
ratios.

The study is of great interest to those in East Asia for at least three rea-

Cielito F. Habito is a professor of economics at Ateneo de Manila University, and director
of the Ateneo Center for Economic Research and Development.

sons. First, the fiscal situations in the United States, the European Union, and Japan have profound implications on East Asian economies, given the strong trade and investment linkages between the region (outside of Japan) and these three large economies. Macroeconomic management in developing East Asian economies is currently heavily conditioned by the record deficits (external and fiscal) being incurred by the United States, for example. Second, for labor-surplus economies like the Philippines, the study gives reason not to expect any dramatic shifts in immigration policy in the developed world, as there seems to be little incentive for them to loosen up on immigration based on a long-run economic-stability argument. Third, the study provides a useful framework and approach for analyzing the future of pension systems in East Asia, different demographics notwithstanding.

In the Philippines, in particular, it is hard to identify with the study as the demographics are dramatically different, and indeed in the opposite situation of having a much larger younger population due to traditionally high population growth rates. Demographics are in fact among the least of its concerns in plotting the future of its pension system. The country's pension problems trace more to issues on the proper investment of retirement funds, and politicization of the management of benefits and contributions.

In the developed-country case, the analysis leads to an important policy implication: government needs to ease itself out of running public pension systems and move toward privatizing them. This implication is largely conditioned by the baby boom–baby bust phenomenon undergone by the three major developed economies modeled. For the Philippines and many developing countries with different demographics, the policy implication for pension privatization does not necessarily have as compelling an appeal as it would have in the developed countries. Temporary labor migration—an important feature in the labor markets of the Philippines and other similarly situated countries—also presents unique questions on implications for pension policy.

The various features incorporated into the life-cycle model with overlapping generations make the model employed in the study truly state of the art. An important improvement has been the inclusion of government investment in the formulation, the omission of which in the earlier version (i.e., treating government purchases as government consumption) appeared to unduly magnify the negative effects of the demographic trends on real wages and human welfare. Admittedly, the complexity of the system being modeled necessitates a good deal of simplifying assumptions (e.g., immigrants have the same asset endowments and preferences as native counterparts; people die between ages 68 and 90).

It is not clear from the paper whether adequate sensitivity analyses have been undertaken on some of the key assumptions and parameters used in building the analysis, but this would be an important test on the robustness of the model's simulation results. Unfortunately, the dramatic difference made by the inclusion of government investment and the addition of China appears to be an indication of strong sensitivity of simulation results to model parameters and features. It is likewise not clear whether the basic life-cycle assumptions are uniform for the United States, Europe, Japan, and China. The differences explicitly modeled are on demographic variables and immigration rates, but cultural differences certainly lead to differences in life-cycle decisions (e.g., bequest motives, income dependence on parents).

The incorporation of uncertainty in specific key elements of the model, particularly lifespan uncertainty, is useful to better model mortality and bequest behavior using available probabilistic information—and it adds better realism to the model. The inclusion of capital adjustment costs is also a good realistic element.

The modeling framework suffers from the same constraint suffered by CGE models (i.e., validation is only possible for the benchmark data set). Because of this, one cannot really validate the dynamic outcomes of the model, making sensitivity analysis all the more important.

Still, the model is the most comprehensive so far in capturing the various elements in the life-cycle/overlapping-generations system. The interesting extension would be the inclusion of the remaining major economic regions in the world not yet captured so far in the analysis.

6

External Debt, Adjustment, and Growth

Delano P. Villanueva and Roberto S. Mariano

6.1 Introduction

High ratios of external debt to GDP in selected Asian countries have contributed to the initiation, propagation, and severity of the financial and economic crises in recent years, reflecting runaway fiscal deficits and excessive foreign borrowing by the private sector. More importantly, the servicing of large debt stocks has diverted scarce resources from investment and long-term growth. Applying and calibrating the formal framework proposed by Mariano and Villanueva (2005) to Philippine data, we explore the joint dynamics of external debt, capital accumulation, and growth. The relative simplicity of the model makes it convenient to analyze the links between domestic adjustment policies, foreign borrowing, and growth. We estimate the optimal domestic saving rate that is consistent with maximum real consumption per unit of effective labor in the long run. As a by-

Delano P. Villanueva was visiting professor at the School of Economics and Social Sciences, Singapore Management University, when this paper was written; he was former advisor of the International Monetary Fund Institute and research director of the South East Asian Central Banks (SEACEN) Research and Training Centre. Roberto S. Mariano is viceprovost for research and dean of the School of Economics and Social Sciences at Singapore Management University and professor emeritus of Economics at the University of Pennsylvania.

We would like to thank, without implicating, Thorvaldur Gylfason, Partha Sen, Sunil Sharma, and an anonymous referee for useful comments; David Fernandez and Fee Ying Tan of JP Morgan for providing the data on spreads; Bangko Sentral ng Pilipinas' Governor Amando Tetangco, Jr., and members of the Monetary Board for a stimulating discussion; Deputy Governor Diwa Guinigundo and his staff for Philippine macroeconomic data and valuable inputs; discussants at the NBER/EASE 16 Conference in Manila during June 23–25, 2005, particularly Takatoshi Ito and Andrew Rose, for helpful suggestions; and Choon Yann Leow for excellent research assistance.

product, we estimate the steady-state ratio of net external debt to GDP that is associated with this optimal outcome.

The framework is an extension of the standard neoclassical growth model that incorporates endogenous technical change and global capital markets. The steady-state ratio of the stock of net external debt to GDP is derived as a function of the real world interest rate, the spread and its responsiveness to the external debt burden and market perception of country risk, the propensity to save out of gross national disposable income, rates of technical change, and parameters of the production function.

Being concerned primarily with the long-run interaction between external debt, growth, and adjustment, our nonstochastic paper is not about solvency or liquidity per se. However, a continuous increase in the foreign debt to GDP ratio will, sooner or later, lead to liquidity and, ultimately, solvency problems. Steady-state ratios of external debt to GDP belong to the set of indicators proposed by Roubini (2001, 6): ". . . *a non-increasing foreign debt to GDP ratio* is seen as a practical sufficient condition for sustainability: a country is likely to remain solvent as long as the ratio is not growing." Cash-flow problems, inherent in liquidity crises, also emerge from an inordinately large debt ratio that results from an unabated increase over time. In our proposed analytical framework, we allow debt accumulation beyond the economy's steady-state growth rate as long as the expected net marginal product of capital exceeds the effective real interest rate in global capital markets. When the return-cost differential disappears, net external debt grows at the steady-state growth of GDP, and the debt ratio stabilizes at a constant level, a function of structural parameters specific to a particular country. Among all such steady state debt ratios, we estimate an optimal debt ratio that is associated with the value of the domestic saving rate that maximizes consumer welfare.

The main results of the extended model are as follows.

1. The optimal domestic saving rate is a fraction of the income share of capital (the standard result is that the optimal saving rate is equal to capital's income share).

2. Associated with the optimal saving rate and maximum welfare is a unique steady-state net foreign debt to GDP ratio.

3. The major policy implications are that fiscal consolidation and the promotion of private saving are critical, while overreliance on foreign saving (net external borrowing) should be avoided, particularly in an environment of high cost of external borrowing that is positively correlated with rising external debt.

4. For debtor countries facing credit rationing in view of prohibitive risk spreads, even at high-expected marginal product of capital and low risk-free interest rates, increased donor aid targeted at expenditures on education, health, and other labor-productivity enhancing expenditures

would relax the external debt and financing constraints while boosting per capita GDP growth.

The plan of this paper is as follows. Section 6.2 describes the structure of our open-economy growth model with endogenous technical change. We begin with a brief review of the relevant literature and incorporate some refinements to the closed-economy model. First, Gross National Disposable Income (GNDI) instead of GDP is used, since net interest payments on the net external debt use part of GDP, while positive net transfers add to GDP, leaving GNDI as a more relevant variable in determining domestic saving.[1] Second, the marginal real cost of external borrowing is the sum of the risk-free interest rate and a risk premium, which is an increasing function of the ratio of the stock of net external debt to the capital stock. That is to say, inter alia, as the proportion of external debt rises, the risk premium goes up, and so does the effective cost of external borrowing, even with an unchanged risk-free interest rate. Third, via enhanced learning by doing, technical change is made partly endogenous.[2] On the balanced growth path, we then derive the optimal value of the domestic saving rate that maximizes the steady-state level of real consumption per unit of effective labor. Section 6.3 applies the optimal growth framework to the Philippines. Section 6.4 draws some implications for fiscal policy and external debt management. Section 6.5 concludes.

6.2   The Formal Framework

6.2.1   Brief Survey of the Literature

The Solow-Swan (1956) model has been the workhorse of standard neoclassical growth theory. It is a closed-economy growth model in which exclusively domestic saving finances aggregate investment. In addition, the standard model assumes that labor-augmenting technical change is exogenous, which determines the equilibrium growth of per capita output.

There have been two developments in aggregate growth theory since the Solow-Swan (1956) model appeared. First, technical change was made partly endogenous and partly exogenous. Conlisk (1967) was the first to introduce endogenous technical change into a closed-economy neoclassical growth model, in which the saving rate was assumed fixed. This was followed by the recent endogenous growth literature using endogenously and optimally derived saving-rate models (Romer 1986, Lucas 1988, Becker, Murphy, and Tamara 1990, Grossman and Helpman 1990, and Rivera-Batiz and Romer 1991, among others). Among all classes of closed-economy

---

1. In the Philippines, workers' remittances included in private transfers average $7 to $8 billion per year, or some 12 percent of GDP.

2. See Villanueva (1994).

growth models, the steady-state properties of fixed (Villanueva 1994) and optimally derived saving-rate models are the same.[3]

The second development was to open up the Conlisk (1967) model to the global capital markets. An early attempt was made by Otani and Villanueva (1989), followed by Agénor (2000) and Mariano and Villanueva (2005). The fixed saving-rate models of Otani and Villanueva (1989) and Mariano and Villanueva (2005) are variants of Conlisk's (1967) endogenous-technical change model and Arrow's (1962) *learning-by-doing* model, wherein experience (measured in terms of either output or cumulative past investment) plays a critical role in raising productivity over time.

In Mariano and Villanueva (2005), the aggregate capital stock is the accumulated sum of domestic saving and net external borrowing (the current account deficit). At any moment of time, the difference between the expected marginal product of capital, net of depreciation, and the marginal cost of funds[4] in the international capital market determines the proportionate rate of change in the external debt-capital ratio. When the expected net marginal product of capital matches the marginal cost of funds at the equilibrium capital-labor ratio, the proportionate increase in net external debt (net external borrowing) is fixed by the economy's steady-state output growth, and the external debt/output ratio stabilizes at a constant level. Although constant in long-run equilibrium, the steady-state external debt ratio shifts with changes in the economy's propensity to save out of national disposable income, the marginal cost of funds in world capital markets, the depreciation rate, the growth rates of the working population and any exogenous technical change, and the parameters of the risk-premium, production, and technical change functions.

The major shortcoming of the Mariano and Villanueva (2005) model is its inability to pin down the steady-state external debt ratio that is consistent with maximum consumer welfare. We correct this shortcoming in the present paper. On the balanced growth path, if consumption per unit of effective labor (or any monotonically increasing function of it) is taken as a measure of the social welfare of society, we choose the domestic saving rate that maximizes social welfare by maximizing long-run consumption per unit of effective labor. Consistent with this optimal outcome is a steady-state ratio of net external debt to total output. Using parameters for the Philippines to calibrate the extended model, we show that it is locally stable, with a steady-state solution characterized by a constant capital/

---

3. Lucas (1988) specifies the effective labor $L = hN$, where h is human capital per head, and N is working population. His h variable is our variable A in $L = AN$ (the variable is T in Otani and Villanueva [1989] and Villanueva [1994]; see equation (12) of our present paper), interpreted as a labor-augmenting technology or labor productivity multiplier.

4. Risk-free interest rate plus a risk premium. The LIBOR, U.S. Prime Rate, U.S. Federal Funds Rate, or U.S. Treasury, deflated by changes in an appropriate price index in the United Kingdom or United States, typically represents the risk-free interest rate. The risk premium is country specific and a positive function of a country's external debt burden and other exogenous factors capturing market perceptions of country risk.

effective labor ratio, an optimal domestic saving rate, and a unique external debt/capital ratio.[5] The latter interacts with long-run growth and domestic adjustment and is determined jointly with other macroeconomic variables, including a country's set of structural parameters.

6.2.2 The Extended Model

Our model can be summarized as follows:[6]

(1) $Y = Lk^{\alpha}$ (GDP)[7]

(2) $GNDI = Y - NFP + NTR$ (GNDI)

(3) $CAD = S^f = C + I - GNDI$ (Current account deficit)

(4) $C = cGNDI$ (Consumption function)

(5) $NFP = rD$ (Net factor payments)

(6) $NTR = \tau Y$ (Net transfers)

(7) $\dot{D} = CAD$ (Net debt issue)

(8) $d = \dfrac{D}{K}$ (Debt-capital ratio)

(9) $\dfrac{\dot{d}}{d} = \alpha k^{\alpha-1} - \delta - r$ (External borrowing function)

(10) $r^e = r^f + \phi d$ (Effective interest rate)

(11) $\dot{K} = I - \delta K$ (Capital growth)

(12) $L = AN$ (Effective labor)

(13) $\dot{N} = nN$ (Working population growth)

(14) $\dot{A} = \theta\left(\dfrac{K}{N}\right) + \lambda A$ (Technical change function)

---

5. For empirical external debt research using various statistical techniques, see Manasse, Roubini, and Schimmelpfennig (2003); Reinhart, Rogoff, and Savastano (2003); Kraay and Nehru (2004); Patillo, Poirson, and Ricci (2004); and Manasse and Roubini (2005). For a survey, see Kraay and Nehru (2004).

6. The numeraire is the foreign price of the investment good. Thus, P^d/eP^f is multiplied by residents' saving (in constant dollars), where P^d is the price of domestic output, e is the exchange rate in quantity of local currency units per unit of foreign currency, and P^f is the price of the investment good in foreign currency. Foreign saving denominated in foreign currency is deflated by P^f to get the real value. Similarly, the marginal real cost of external borrowing is the sum of the world interest rate and risk premium in foreign currency less the rate of change in P^f. Since model simplicity is our primary concern, we abstract from the effects of movements of these variables by arbitrarily assigning unitary values to these price and exchange rate indices without loss of generality. Incorporation of these variables in the extended model is straightforward and is done in Otani and Villanueva (1989).

7. Any production function will do, as long as it is subject to constant returns to scale. See Inada (1963).

(15) $k = \dfrac{K}{L}$ (Capital/effective labor ratio)

Here, Y is real GDP; K is physical capital stock; L is effective labor (in efficiency units, man-hours or man-days); A is labor-augmenting technology (index number); N is working population; k is the capital/effective labor ratio; GNDI is gross national disposable income; NFP is net factor payments; NTR is net transfers; CAD is external current account deficit; S^f is saving by nonresidents; C is aggregate consumption; I is gross domestic investment; D is net external debt[8]; d is the net external debt/capital ratio; r is the marginal real cost of net external borrowing; r^e is the effective world interest rate; r^f is the risk-free interest rate; τ, δ, ϕ, n, λ, and α are positive constants; and θ is the learning coefficient, as in Villanueva (1994). In a closed economy (when $D = 0$, $S^f = 0$) with technical change partly endogenous ($\theta > 0$), the model reduces to the Villanueva (1994) model; additionally, if technical change is completely exogenous ($\theta = 0$), the model reduces to the standard neoclassical (Solow-Swan) model.

Consumption in the extended model reflects the openness of the economy—consumption is gross national disposable income plus foreign saving less aggregate investment.[9] Here, $s = 1 - c$ is the propensity to save out of gross national disposable income. After we solve for the balanced growth path, we choose a particular value of s that maximizes social welfare (long-run consumption per unit of L).[10]

The transfers/grants parameter τ may be allowed to vary positively with the domestic savings effort s. Donors are likely to step up their aid to countries with strong adjustment efforts. Finally, donor aid τ earmarked for education, health, and other labor-productivity enhancing expenditures is expected to boost the learning coefficient θ.

Foreign saving is equivalent to the external current account deficit, which is equal to the excess of domestic absorption over national income or, equivalently, to net external borrowing (capital plus overall balance in the balance of payments)—noted in equations (3) and (7).

The derivation of the effective cost, r, of net external debt, $D (= D^{gross} - A)$ is as follows: Assume a linear function for the effective interest rate $r^e = r^f + \phi d$, where $0 < \phi < 1$ (equation 10); the second term is the spread that is increasing in d.[11] Net interest payments on net external debt

---

8. D is defined as external liabilities minus external assets; as such, it is positive, zero, or negative as external liabilities exceed, equal, or fall short of, external assets.

9. From the national income identity (3).

10. Thus, the saving ratio $s = 1 - c$ will be chosen endogenously.

11. An increase in d raises the credit risk and thus the spread. The parameter ϕ is likely to be negatively correlated with the domestic saving effort. Countries with high domestic saving rates appear to enjoy low spreads (for given debt ratios) because of the quality of their adjustment policies—good fiscal policy, conservative monetary policy, and the like.

$$= r^e D^{\text{gross}} - r^f A,$$

$$= (r^f + \phi d) D^{\text{gross}} - r^f A$$

$$= r^f (D^{\text{gross}} - A) + \phi d D^{\text{gross}}$$

$$= r^f (D^{\text{gross}} - A) + \phi \left(\frac{D}{K} \right) D^{\text{gross}}$$

$$= r^f D + \phi \left(\frac{D}{K} \right) D^{\text{gross}}$$

Dividing both sides by D,

$$(16) \quad r = r^f + \frac{\phi D^{\text{gross}}}{K} = r^f + \frac{\phi (D + A)}{K} = r^f + \phi d + \phi \left(\frac{A}{Y} \right) k^{(\alpha - 1)}$$

$$r = r^f + \phi [d + \varepsilon k^{(\alpha - 1)}].$$

where D^{gross} is gross external liabilities, A is gross external assets, $D = D^{\text{gross}} - A$, and $A/Y = \varepsilon$. Assume that the gross external assets, A, are a constant (minimum) fraction of GDP: $A = \varepsilon Y$.[12] In the case of the Philippines, $\varepsilon = 0.214$ at present.

The optimal decision rule for net external borrowing is specified in equation (9)—at any moment of time, net external borrowing as percent of the total outstanding net stock of debt is undertaken at a rate equal to the growth rate of the capital stock plus the difference between the expected marginal product, net of depreciation, and the marginal real cost of funds, r.[13] A more general law of motion for external capital is:

$$(9') \quad \frac{\dot{d}}{d} = \beta [\alpha k^{(\alpha - 1)} - \delta - r],$$

where $\beta > 0$ measures the speed of adjustment of external capital to the discrepancy between capital's expected net marginal product and the world real interest rate. In his discussion of the Villanueva (1994) model in the context of open global capital markets, Agénor (2000, 594) obtains the key result that the steady-state values of capital intensity and the debt-to-capital ratio are locally stable if and only if the *adjustment speed of external capital is sufficiently large* (Appendix A of the present paper

---

12. A rule of thumb is that the variable A represents three to four months of imports.

13. Equations (7) and (9) equate net foreign saving with net foreign borrowing, which is not strictly true. Net foreign saving (sum of capital, financial, and overall accounts in the balance of payments) includes debt (bonds and loans) and nondebt-creating flows (equities and foreign direct investment); both flows use up a portion of GDP, with the latter as dividends and profit remittances abroad. Our variables D and r, respectively, should be interpreted broadly to include equities and foreign direct investment, as well as dividends and profit remittances.

demonstrates local stability of long-run equilibrium), that is, $\beta > ([\eta + s\{1 - \eta\}]/[1 - \alpha])d_0$, where η is the ratio of tax revenue to national income, s is the ratio of domestic saving to national income, α is the elasticity of output with respect to the capital stock, and d_0 is the initial debt-to-capital ratio.[14]

When the expected yield-cost differential is zero and k is at its steady-state value k^*[15], the net external debt as ratio to output stabilizes at a constant level.[16] However, this constant debt level may not necessarily be optimal in the sense of being associated with maximum consumer welfare. For it to be so, it has to be associated with a particular value of the domestic saving rate that maximizes long-run consumption per effective labor.

6.2.3 Reduced Model

By successive substitutions, the extended model reduces to a system of two differential equations in k and d.[17]

$$(17) \quad \frac{\dot{k}}{k} = \left\{ \frac{s[(1 + \tau)k^{\alpha-1} - rd]}{(1 - d)} \right\} + \left[\frac{(\alpha k^{\alpha-1} - \delta - r)d}{(1 - d)} \right] - \left[\frac{\delta}{(1 - d)} \right]$$

$$- \theta k - n - \lambda$$

$$= H(k, d)$$

$$(18) \quad \frac{\dot{d}}{d} = \alpha k^{\alpha-1} - \delta - r = J(k, d)$$

where r is a function of k and d—given by equation (16).

Long-run equilibrium is obtained by setting the reduced system (17) and (18) to zero, such that k is constant at k^* and d is constant at d^*. It is characterized by balanced growth: K, L, and D grow at the same rate $\theta k^* + n + \lambda$. It also implies the condition $\alpha k^{*\alpha-1} - \delta - r(d^*, k^*; r^f) = 0$, which is the optimal rule for external net borrowing to cease at the margin.[18]

---

14. In the application of our framework to the Philippines, fully described in section 6.3, using $s = 0.188$, $\eta = 0.186$, $d_0 = 0.13$ (historical averages from 1993 to 1998), and $\alpha = 0.4$, the adjustment speed β should be at least 0.073. Our assumed unitary value is much larger than this minimum.

15. An asterisk denotes steady-state value of any variable.

16. The steady-state current account balance may be positive (deficit), zero (in balance), or negative (surplus). This follows from the steady-state solution $(\dot{D}/Y)^* = g^*d^*/k^{*(\alpha-1)}$, where g^* is the steady-state growth rate of output, d^* is the steady-state debt-capital ratio, and k^* is the steady-state capital-effective labor ratio. As mentioned in footnote 8 and defined by equation (8), the variable d^* is the ratio of net external debt (external liabilities minus external assets) to the capital stock and can be positive, zero, or negative. More precisely, $-1 < d^* < 1$, depending on whether the accumulated sum of domestic savings is less than, equal to, or greater than the aggregate capital stock (accumulated sum of aggregate investments).

17. It can be seen that in a closed economy, $d = \tau = 0$, equation (18) drops out and, thus, equation (17) is identical to the Villanueva (1994) model (equation 9, p. 7). Further, with $\theta = 0$, equation (17) reduces to the Solow-Swan model.

18. When the yield-cost differential is zero, net external borrowing as percent of the outstanding net stock of debt proceeds at the steady-state growth rate of output.

The steady-state solutions for k^*, d^*, and r^* are:

$$(19) \quad \left\{ \frac{s[(1 + \tau)k^{*(\alpha-1)} - r^*d^*]}{(1 - d^*)} \right\} - \frac{\delta}{(1 - d^*)} - \theta k^* - n - \lambda = 0$$

$$(20) \quad d^* = \frac{[(\alpha - \phi\varepsilon)K^{*(\alpha-1)} - \delta - r^f]}{\phi}$$

$$(16') \quad r^* = r^f + \phi d^* + \phi\varepsilon k^{*(\alpha-1)}$$

Long-run equilibrium is defined by point $Q(d^*, k^*)$ in figure 6.1.[19] In regions N and W, the dynamics force d to increase, and in regions S and E, the dynamics force d to decrease. In regions N and E, the dynamics force k to decrease, and, in regions S and W, the dynamics force k to increase. Any initial point, like point A, leads to a movement toward the equilibrium point, Q, with a possible time path indicated by the line AQ.

6.2.4   Restrictions on External Financing

Using the definition of d (equation [8]), the law of motion for external capital as specified in equation (9) can be restated as:

$$(9') \quad \frac{\dot{D}}{D} = \frac{\dot{K}}{K} + ak^{(\alpha-1)} - \delta - r.$$

Using the definition of k (equation [15]) and substituting equations (12) through (14) into equation (17), we obtain $\dot{K}/K = \theta k + n + \lambda + H(k, d)$. Substituting this into equation (9'),

$$(9'') \quad \frac{\dot{D}}{D} = \theta k + n + \lambda + H(k, d) + \alpha k^{(\alpha-1)} - \delta - r, \text{ where } r = r(d, k; r^f).$$

Equation (9'') says that at any moment of time, the amounts of external financing vary with levels of k and d. In long-run equilibrium (i.e., in the steady state), external financing as percent of the debt stock is equal to the GDP growth g^* (noting that $H[k, d] = 0$ and $\alpha k^{[\alpha-1]} - \delta - r = 0$, and that, by the assumption of constant returns, GDP grows at the same rate as capital and effective labor),

$$(9''') \quad \left(\frac{\dot{D}}{D}\right)^* = \left(\frac{\dot{K}}{K}\right)^* = \left(\frac{\dot{Y}}{Y}\right)^* = g^*(k^*, d^*)$$

In other words, in the short run, there are no limits on the absolute level of the debt stock or on its increment. External financing is ruled in the short run by equation (9'') (a function of k and d, given r^f). In the long run, external debt grows at the same rate as GDP, given by equation (9''') (a function of k^* and d^*).

In figure 6.1, the speed of adjustment to long-run equilibrium (charac-

---

19. For the derivation of the slopes of the curves shown in figure 6.1, see appendix A.

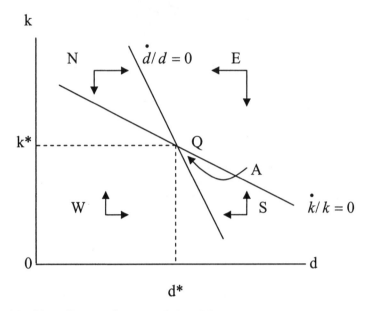

Fig. 6.1   Phase diagram of the extended model

terized by, among other conditions, a zero return-cost differential in global capital markets) varies with the initial values of k and d. In growth modeling, the speed of adjustment of state variables like d and k usually refers to the number of periods (e.g., years) it takes for the variables to adjust to their long-run equilibrium values. In figure 6.1, an adjustment trajectory may be that, if initially, $d < d^*$, but $k > k^*$, d increases at first slowly, then accelerates toward d^*, aided by k falling to k^* and thus raising capital's net marginal product, which in turn induces higher capital inflows. Or, if initially both $d < d^*$ and $k < k^*$, d monotonically increases toward d^* (as does k toward k^*), with more or less the same speed each period. There are other trajectory paths with different adjustment speeds in the north, east, and south quadrants of figure 6.1. Adjustment speeds of our model have been numerically solved by Chen (2006), confirming different adjustment speeds depending on the initial values of output growth (a function of initial values of k and d), and on whether the adjustment starts from above or below g^*. A finite albeit slow adjustment of external capital is what is observed empirically, both domestically and especially for foreign capital.

6.2.5   Optimal Growth

In the steady state, output per unit of effective labor is $y^* = k^{*\alpha}$. If y^* is considered a measure of the standard of living, and since $dy^*/dk^* > 0$, it is possible to raise living standards by increasing k^*. This can be done by adjusting the domestic saving rate s, for example, by raising the public sector saving rate and assuming imperfect Ricardian equivalence.[20] If consumption per unit of effective labor is taken as a measure of the social welfare of the society, the saving rate s that maximizes social welfare by maximizing long-run consumption can be determined. Phelps (1966) refers to this path as the *Golden Rule of Accumulation.*

From equation (3), steady-state consumption per unit of effective labor is

$$\left(\frac{C}{L}\right)^* = \left(\frac{GNDI}{L}\right)^* + \left(\frac{S^f}{L}\right)^* - \left(\frac{I}{L}\right)^* = (1 + \tau)k^{*\alpha} - r^*d^*k^*$$

$$+ \left\{ \left[\frac{(dK/dt)}{K}\right]^* + \alpha k^{*[\alpha-1]} - \delta - r^* \right\} d^*k^*$$

$$- \left\{ \left[\frac{(dK/dt)}{K}\right]^* + \delta \right\} k^*,$$

and since $\alpha k^{*(\alpha-1)} - \delta - r^* = 0$,

$$= (1 + \tau)K^{*\alpha} - r^*d^*k^* - (1 - d^*)k^* \left[\frac{(dK/dt)}{K}\right]^* - \delta k^*$$

where

$$r^* = r^f + \phi[d^* + \varepsilon k^{*(\alpha-1)}].$$

Also in the steady state,

$$\left[\frac{(dK/dt)}{K}\right]^* = \theta k^* + n + \lambda.$$

Thus,

(21) $\left(\dfrac{C}{L}\right)^* = (1 + \tau)k^{*\alpha} - r^*d^*k^* - (1 - d^*)(\theta k^* + n + \lambda)k^* - \delta k^*.$

Maximizing $(C/L)^*$ with respect to s, and noting that

$$d^* = \frac{[(\alpha - \phi\varepsilon)K^{*(\alpha-1)} - \delta - r^f]}{\phi} \text{ and } r^* = r^f + \phi[d^* + \varepsilon k^{*(\alpha-1)}],$$

(22) $\dfrac{\partial\left(\dfrac{C}{L}\right)^*}{\partial s} = \left\{ (1 + \tau)\alpha k^{*(\alpha-1)} - r^*d^* - \delta - \left(\dfrac{1}{\phi}\right) \right.$

$$\cdot [(r^* + \phi d^*)(\alpha - \varepsilon\phi)](\alpha - 1)k^{*(\alpha-1)} - (1 - d)\theta k^*$$

$$- [2(\alpha - \varepsilon\phi) + \varepsilon](\alpha - 1)d^*k^{*(\alpha-1)}$$

$$\left. - \left[1 - d^* - (\alpha - \varepsilon\phi)(\alpha - 1)\left(\dfrac{1}{\phi}\right)k^{*(\alpha-1)} \right]g^* \right\}\dfrac{\partial k^*}{\partial s} = 0$$

20. There is ample empirical evidence that, at least for developing countries, the private sector saving rate does not offset one to one the increase in the public sector saving rate.

Since $\partial k^*/\partial s > 0$, the Golden Rule condition, is[21]

$$(1 + \tau)\alpha k^{*(\alpha-1)} - r^*d^* - \delta = [1 - d^* - (\alpha - \varepsilon\phi)(\alpha - 1)\left(\frac{1}{\phi}\right)k^{*(\alpha-1)}]g^*$$

$$+ [2(\alpha - \varepsilon\phi) + \varepsilon](\alpha - 1)d^*k^{*(\alpha-1)}$$

$$+ \left(\frac{1}{\phi}\right)[(r^* + \phi d^*)(\alpha - \varepsilon\phi)](\alpha - 1)k^{*(\alpha-1)}$$

$$+ (1 - d)\theta k^*$$

or,

$$M = sUZ + V + W + X - \frac{U\delta}{(1 - d^*)},$$

or,

(23)
$$s = \frac{M - V - W - X + \dfrac{U\delta}{1 - d^*}}{UZ}.\text{[22]}$$

where,

$$M = (1 + \tau)\alpha k^{*(\alpha-1)} - r^*d^* - \delta;$$

$$U = [1 - d^* - (\alpha - \varepsilon\phi)(\alpha - 1)\left(\frac{1}{\phi}\right)k^{*(\alpha-1)}];$$

$$V = [2(\alpha - \varepsilon\phi) + \varepsilon](\alpha - 1)d^*k^{*(\alpha-1)};$$

$$W = \left(\frac{1}{\phi}\right)[(r^* + \phi d^*)(\alpha - \varepsilon\phi)](\alpha - 1)k^{*(\alpha-1)};$$

$$X = (1 - d^*)\theta k^*;\text{ and }$$

$$Z = \frac{[(1 + \tau)k^{*(\alpha-1)} - r^*d^*]}{(1 - d^*)}.$$

M is capital's net (of depreciation) marginal product less interest payments on the stock of net external debt. The first-order condition (22) says that for social welfare to be maximized the domestic saving rate should be raised to a point where the net return to capital is a multiple of the long-run growth rate of output. X is nothing more than the open-economy[23]

---

21. The second-order condition for a maximum, $\partial^2(C/L)^*/\partial s^2 < 0$, is a tediously long algebraic expression that, when evaluated at the steady-state values solved for the Philippines, yields a value of -0.01847. See last page of appendix A.

22. This expression for the optimal s uses the relation $g^* = \theta k^* + n + \lambda = \{s[(1 + \tau)k^{*(\alpha-1)} - r^*d^*] - \delta\}/(1 - d^*)$, substituting it for g^* in equation (22).

23. Reduced by a factor $(1 - d^*)$. When $d = 0$, this term becomes θk^* in Villanueva (1994).

version of the endogenous component of labor-augmenting technical change—the component of $(dA/dt)/A$ induced by learning that occurs at a higher level of capital intensity, which, in turn, is caused by a higher domestic saving rate. If there are no learning ($\theta = 0$), no net external debt ($d^* = 0$), and no net transfers ($\tau = 0$), equation (22) reduces to $\alpha k^{*(\alpha-1)} - \delta = \lambda + n$, which is the familiar Golden Rule result from standard neoclassical growth theory (i.e., the optimal net rate of return to capital equals the natural growth rate). If there is learning ($\theta > 0$) and there are no net external debt ($d^* = 0$) and no net transfers ($\tau = 0$), equation (22) reduces to the Villanueva (1994) Golden Rule result, $\alpha k^{*(\alpha-1)} - \delta = g^* + \theta k^*$, where $g^* = \theta k^* + \lambda + n$. The effect of opening up the economy to global capital and labor markets is to raise the optimal net rate of return to capital beyond $\lambda + n$ or even beyond $g^* + \theta k^*$ when $\theta > 0$—when there is learning by doing—because of four factors.

First, when the domestic saving rate s is raised, the equilibrium growth rate g^* will be higher than $\lambda + n$, by the amount of $\theta \partial k^*/\partial s$. Second, capital should be compensated for the effect on equilibrium output growth through the induced learning term θk^*. Third, when the domestic saving rate is raised, the equilibrium debt stock d^* will be lower, releasing resources toward more capital growth; the effective interest rate r^* also will be lower pari passu with a lower spread, further increasing domestic resources for investment and growth. Fourth, the availability of foreign saving to finance capital accumulation enhances long-run growth, up to a point.

An alternative interpretation of the previous Golden Rule can be given. A standard neoclassical result is that the optimal saving rate s should be set equal to the income share of capital, α. To see this, set $d^* = \tau = \theta = 0$, and since $\partial k^*/\partial s > 0$, the Golden Rule condition is the standard relation

$$\alpha k^{*(\alpha-1)} - \delta = n + \lambda,$$

that is, the net (of depreciation) return to capital equals the steady-state natural growth rate. Since $s k^{*(\alpha-1)} - \delta = n + \lambda$,

$$s k^{*(\alpha-1)} - \delta = \alpha k^{*(\alpha-1)} - \delta,$$

or,

$$s = \alpha.$$

If $d^* = \tau = 0$ and technical change is partly endogenous ($\theta > 0$), the modified Golden Rule is

$$\alpha k^{*(\alpha-1)} - \delta = g^* + \theta k^*,$$

which is Villanueva's result (1994).
Since $s k^{*(\alpha-1)} - \delta = g^*$,

$$\alpha k^{*(\alpha-1)} = s k^{*(\alpha-1)} + \theta k^*,$$

or,

$$s = \alpha - \theta k^{*(2-\alpha)}.$$

In general, Villanueva (1994) shows that for any income share of capital $\pi = k^* f'(k^*)/f(k^*)$, where $f(\cdot)$ is the intensive form of the production function, $s = \sigma\pi$, where the fraction $\sigma = (g^* + \delta)/(g^* + \delta + \theta k^*)$.[24] Here, $g^* + \delta + \theta k^* = f'(k^*)$ is the gross social marginal product of capital, inclusive of the positive externalities arising from the learning associated with capital accumulation in an endogenous growth model. Equivalently put, income going to capital as a share of total output should be a multiple of the amount saved and invested in order to compensate capital for the additional output generated by endogenous growth and induced learning. A value of π equal to s, implicit in the standard model, would undercompensate capital and thus be suboptimal from a societal point of view.

The open economy's optimal domestic saving rate, given by equation (23), is higher than $\alpha - \theta k^{*(2-\alpha)}$ given by Villanueva (1994), reflecting the inherent risks involved in foreign borrowing.[25]

In general, the existence, uniqueness, and stability of the steady-state equilibrium are not guaranteed. However, appendix A shows that for a Cobb-Douglas production function, linear *learning-by-doing* and risk-premium functions, and values of the parameters for the Philippines, the extended model's equilibrium is locally stable in the neighborhood of the steady state.[26]

6.3   Application to the Philippines

Developments in fiscal policies and in access to external sources of capital in East Asia (as elsewhere) often raise important external debt issues. This section presents an illustrative numerical example[27] using representative parameters for the Philippines: $\alpha = 0.4$, $\delta = 0.04$, $\tau = 0.07$, $n = 0.025$, $\lambda = 0.02$, $r^f = 0.03$, $\phi = 0.41$, and $\theta = 0.005$.[28] Using Microsoft Excel's "Goal Seek" tool, the solution values are $d^* = 0.07$ and $k^* = 6.8$. Note that d^* and k^* are functions of s in the reduced model (equations 16, 17, and

24. For derivation, see Villanueva (1994, 7–17).

25. In the calibration of the model to Philippine data in the next subsection, the optimal s estimated for the open-economy and closed-economy versions are 0.34 and 0.30, respectively. Both values are less than the share of income going to capital, equal to 0.40, consistent with the result first shown by Villanueva (1994) in an endogenous growth model.

26. Outside the neighborhood of the steady state, multiple equilibria, jumps, and the like are theoretically possible.

27. The next section discusses the linkages between fiscal policy and the management of external debt in the Philippines. The discussion in this section is specific to the Philippine case and, in particular, does not cover a situation in which the state is part of a federal currency union.

28. $\phi = \phi^* k^{*(1-\alpha)}$ where $\phi^* = 0.13$ was estimated using averages of the ratio of changes in the risk spread to changes in the ratio of external debt to GDP. See appendix B.

18), while the (optimal) s is a function of d^* and k^* (equation 23). Therefore, iterations were performed to obtain a unique value for s that satisfies equations (16), (17), (18), and (23). The resulting optimal value of the domestic saving rate $s = 0.3429$.

Steady-state per capita GDP growth is 5.4 percent per year, of which the endogenous component is 3.4 percent per year.[29] The steady-state risk premium is 288 basis points, steady-state gross external debt is 43.5 percent of GDP, and steady-state net external debt/GDP ratio is 22.1 percent of GDP.[30] Steady-state interest payments are 2.6 percent of GDP. Using the relation,

$$\left(\frac{\dot{D}}{D}\right)^* = \left(\frac{\dot{K}}{K}\right)^* = \left(\frac{\dot{L}}{L}\right)^* = g^* = \left(\frac{\dot{Y}}{Y}\right)^* \text{ (in the steady state),}$$

or,

(24)
$$\left(\frac{\dot{D}}{Y}\right)^* = \left(\frac{\dot{Y}}{Y}\right)^* \left(\frac{D}{Y}\right)^*$$

$$= \frac{g^* d^*}{k^{*(\alpha-1)}}$$

$$= \frac{(0.079)(0.07)}{(6.8)^{-0.6}} = 0.017;$$

the steady-state external current account deficit is 1.7 percent of GDP.[31]

The previous calculations are based on a 0.13 average ratio of changes in spread to changes in the external debt/GDP ratio estimated over the period 2000 to 2003. Table 6.1 shows the sensitivity of the results to alternative values of this ratio.

The estimated optimal domestic saving rate, steady-state per capita GDP growth rate, and the number of years it would take for per capita GDP to double are robust to alternative values of the ratio of changes in spread to changes in the external debt/GDP ratio of 0.10 to 0.15. However, as expected, the steady-state gross external debt/GDP ratio declines from 53 percent to 39 percent, and the steady-state net external debt/GDP ratio from 31 percent to 17 percent, as the sensitivity of the spread to the debt ratio rises from 0.10 to 0.15.[32]

In the Philippines, optimal long-run growth requires raising the domes-

---

29. It would take about thirteen years for per capita GDP to double.
30. $(D/Y)^* = d^*/k^{*(\alpha-1)}$.
31. Recall that $-1 < d^* < 1$. When $-1 < d^* < 0$, equation (24) solves for the external current account surplus (e.g., Singapore). When $d^* = 0$, the long-run current account is in balance.
32. If the sensitivity parameter is 0.15, it means that a 1 percent increase in the net external debt/GDP ratio is associated with an increase of 15 basis points in the spread.

Table 6.1   Sensitivity calculations

$\phi^* = \Delta$ Spread/Δ (Debt/GDP)	0.10	0.13	0.15
Optimal domestic saving rate	0.3519	0.3429	0.3372
Gross external debt/GDP	0.5274	0.4353	0.3883
Net external debt/GDP	0.3134	0.2213	0.1743
Per capita GDP growth	0.0558	0.0540	0.0532
Years to double per capita income	12.54	12.96	13.13

tic saving rate from the historical average of 18.8 percent of GNP (IMF 1999, table 5) during 1993 to 1998 to a steady state 34 percent over the long term. This is necessary to achieve external viability while maximizing long-run consumption per effective labor. The savings effort should center on fiscal consolidation and adoption of incentives to encourage private saving, including market-determined real interest rates. From the national income identity (3), the external current account deficit CAD is equal to the excess of aggregate investment I over domestic saving S (= GNDI – C), or CAD = I – S. Decomposing I and S into their government and private components, CAD = $(I_g - S_g) + (I_p - S_p)$, where the subscripts g and p denote government and private, respectively. The first term is the fiscal balance, and the second term is the private-sector balance. Fiscal adjustment is measured in terms of policy changes in S_g (government revenue less consumption) and in I_g (government investment). Given estimates of the private sector saving-investment balance and its components, the optimal government saving-investment balance may be derived as a residual; from this, the required government-saving ratio can be calculated because the optimal growth model implies a government-investment ratio.

Assume, however, the following *hypothetical* worst-case scenario for the Philippines. For whatever reason (political, social, etc.), owing to the initial high level of the external debt, market perceptions reach a very high adverse level. Despite a high-expected marginal product of capital, the risk premium is prohibitively high at any level of the debt ratio and the risk-free interest rate, such that the Philippine public sector faces credit rationing.[33] In such circumstances, as Agénor (op. cit., 595–96) suggests, increased foreign aid targeted at investment broadly defined to include physical and human capital may benefit the Philippines, provided that economic policies are sound.

---

33. The credit risk is included in the risk premium. The higher is the credit risk assigned by international creditors/investors, the higher is the risk premium and, consequently, the higher is the effective real interest rate.

6.4   Implications for Fiscal Policy and External Debt Management

The implications for fiscal policy and external debt management are clear for the Philippines. The first step is to launch an effective external debt-management strategy that will articulate the short- and long-run objectives of fiscal policy and debt management and ensure effective centralized approval and monitoring of primary debt issues to global financial markets, aided by (a) detailed electronic data on external debt, both outstanding and new debt, by borrowing institution, maturity, terms, and so on, and by (b) an interagency desk exclusively responsible for top quantitative and analytic work on external debt for the benefit of policy makers.

The level of external debt can be reduced only by cutting the fiscal deficit immediately and at a sustained pace over the medium term. In this context, the privatization of the National Power Corporation (NAPOCOR) is essential, since a big chunk of sovereign debt issues is on behalf of NAPOCOR.

Interest payments on total government debt currently eat up a significant share of government revenues, leaving revenue shortfalls to cover expenditures on the physical infrastructure and on the social sectors (health, education, and the like). With a successful and steady reduction of the stock of debt and the enhancement of domestic savings led by the government sector (via increases in S_g), the sensitivity of the risk spread to the external debt would decrease, resulting in interest savings that would provide additional financing for the infrastructure and social sectors. Furthermore, there are clear implications for both revenue-raising and expenditure-cutting measures. On the revenue side, although the recently enacted and signed VAT bill is welcome, there remains low compliance on the VAT, resulting in very low collections. There is evidence of VAT sales being substantially underdeclared on a regular basis. Our concrete proposal would be to set up a computerized system of VAT sales wherein an electronic copy of the sales receipt is transmitted in real time by merchants, producers, and service providers to the Bureau of Internal Revenue (BIR). In this manner, total sales subject to the VAT submitted come tax time can be compared by the BIR against its own electronic receipts. It is estimated that if only 50 percent of total sales were collected from VAT, the current budget deficit (some P200+ billion) could be wiped out. This proposal easily beats current proposals to raise taxes because as they stand, marginal tax rates are already very high (resulting in tax evasion and briberies). The imposition of *sin* taxes (on cigarettes and liquor sales) would provide little relief. Individual and corporate tax reforms are also necessary—different tax brackets should be consolidated into a few, with significant reductions in marginal income tax rates; at the same time, the number of exemptions should be drastically reduced to widen the tax base. The whole customs tariffs structure should be reviewed with the aim of reducing average tariff rates further, while eliminating many exemptions. The role of the customs assessor and collector should be severely restricted, with computerized assessment and collection being put in place, similar to our VAT proposal.

6.5 Conclusion

This paper has explored the joint dynamics of external debt, capital accumulation, and growth. In developing countries in East Asia and elsewhere, external debt issues are often associated with public policy decisions about fiscal policy. This has been especially relevant since the Asian financial crisis in the late 1990s. The relative simplicity of our model makes it convenient to analyze the links between domestic adjustment policies, foreign borrowing, and growth. We estimate the optimal domestic saving rate for the Philippines that is consistent with maximum real consumption per unit of effective labor in the long run. As a by-product, we estimate the steady-state ratio of net external debt to GDP that is associated with this optimal outcome. The framework is an extension of the standard neo-classical growth model that incorporates endogenous technical change and global capital markets. Utilizing this framework, the linkages between fiscal policy and external debt management are discussed in the context of a calibrated model for the Philippines. The major policy implications are that, in the long run, fiscal adjustment and the promotion of private saving are critical; reliance on foreign saving in a globalized financial world has limits; and when risk spreads are highly and positively correlated with rising external debt levels, unabated foreign borrowing depresses long-run welfare.

The obvious policy conclusions of the extended model are:

1. Fiscal consolidation and strong incentives for private saving are essential to achieving maximum per capita GDP growth;

2. The domestic saving rate should be set below the share of capital in total output, owing to positive externalities arising from learning by doing associated with capital accumulation. Equivalently put, income going to capital as a share of total output should be a multiple of the amount saved and invested in order to compensate capital for the additional output generated by endogenous growth and induced learning;

3. Reliance on foreign savings (external borrowing) has limits, particularly in a global environment of high interest rates and risk spreads;

4. When real borrowing costs are positively correlated with rising external indebtedness, the use of foreign savings is even more circumscribed; and

5. When risk spreads are prohibitively high despite high-expected marginal product of capital, there is a role for increased foreign aid earmarked for education and health, provided that economic policies are sound.

Appendix A

Stability Analysis

Partially differentiating text equations (16), (17), and (18) with respect to k and d and evaluating in the neighborhood of the steady state yield

(1) $a_{11} = H_k = [s(1 + \tau) - \varepsilon\phi d^*]\left[\dfrac{1}{(1 - d^*)}\right](\alpha - 1)k^{*\alpha-2}$

$\qquad + (\alpha - \varepsilon\phi)[(\alpha - 1)d^*k^{*\alpha-2}]\left[\dfrac{1}{(1 - d^*)}\right] - \theta$

$\qquad = ?$

(2) $a_{12} = H_d = -[s(1 - d^*)^{-2}][(1 + \tau)(k^{*\alpha-1}) - r^*d^*]$

$\qquad - s(r^* + \phi d^*)(1 - d^*)^{-1} - \phi d^*(1 - d^*)^{-1} + \delta(1 - d^*)^{-2}$

$\qquad = ?$

(3) $a_{21} = J_k = (\alpha - \varepsilon\phi)(\alpha - 1)k^{*\alpha-2} = ?$

(4) $a_{22} = J_d = -\phi < 0$

In the steady state, text equations (19) and (20) are equated to zero:

(5) $$H(k, d) = 0$$

(6) $$J(k, d) = 0$$

Totally differentiating (5) and (6) with respect to k and d yields,

(7) $$\frac{H_k dk}{dd} + H_d = 0$$

(8) $$\frac{J_k dk}{dd} + J_d = 0$$

The slope of the $\dot{k}/k = 0$ curve is given by:

(9) $$\frac{dk}{dd}\bigg|\frac{\dot{k}}{k} = 0 = -\frac{H_d}{H_k} = -\frac{a_{12}}{a_{11}} = ?$$

The slope of the $\dot{d}/d = 0$ curve is given by:

(10) $$\frac{dk}{dd}\bigg|\frac{\dot{d}}{d} = 0 = -\frac{J_d}{J_k} = -\frac{a_{22}}{a_{21}} = ?$$

Let A be the matrix of partial derivatives defined by equations (1) through (4). For stability, a necessary and sufficient condition is that the eigenvalues of A have negative real parts, and a necessary and sufficient condition for this is that:

(11) $\text{tr}(A) < 0,$

and

(12) $|A| > 0.$

Since the signs of equations (1) through (3) are ambiguous, both trace (11) and determinant (12) conditions are indeterminate. The trace condition is:

$$a_{11} + a_{22} < 0.$$

The determinant condition is:

$$a_{11}a_{22} - a_{12}a_{21} > 0.$$

Assuming values of parameters estimated for the Philippines and evaluating the matrix of partial derivatives in the neighborhood of the steady state, $a_{11} = -0.4226$, $a_{12} = -0.2516$, $a_{21} = -0.0112$, and $a_{22} = -0.4107$. Thus, the trace condition (11) $a_{11} + a_{22} < 0$ is met. The determinant condition (12) is also met. The extended model's phase diagram shown in text figure 6.1 reflects these considerations.

The second-order condition for maximum consumption per unit of L is:

$$(13) \quad \partial^2\left(\frac{C}{L}\right)*\partial s = (1 + \tau)\alpha(\alpha - 1)k^{*(\alpha-2)} - r^*\left(\frac{dd^*}{dk^*}\right)$$

$$- d^*\left[\left(\frac{\partial r^*}{\partial k^*}\right) + \left(\frac{\partial r^*}{\partial d^*}\right)\left(\frac{dd^*}{dk^*}\right)\right] - \left(\frac{1}{\phi}\right)[(r^* + \phi d^*)(\alpha - \phi\varepsilon)]$$

$$\cdot [(\alpha - 1)k^{*(\alpha-2)}] - \left(\frac{1}{\phi}\right)(r^* + \phi d^*)(\alpha - \varepsilon\phi)(\alpha - 1)(\alpha - 1)k^{*(\alpha-2)}$$

$$- \left(\frac{1}{\phi}\right)(\alpha - 1)k^{*(\alpha-1)}\left[(\alpha - \varepsilon\phi)\left(\frac{\partial r^*}{\partial k^*} + \frac{dd^*}{dk^*}\right)\right] - (1 - d^*)\theta$$

$$+ \theta k^*\left(\frac{dd^*}{dk^*}\right) - [2(\alpha - \varepsilon\phi) + \varepsilon]\left[d^*(\alpha - 1)k^{*(\alpha-2)} + k^{*(\alpha-1)}\left(\frac{dd^*}{dk^*}\right)\right]$$

$$- \left[1 - d^* - (\alpha - \varepsilon\phi)(\alpha - 1)\left(\frac{1}{\phi}\right)k^{*(\alpha-1)}\right]\theta$$

$$+ g^*\left[\frac{dd^*}{dk^*} + (\alpha - \varepsilon\phi)(\alpha - 1)\left(\frac{1}{\phi}\right)(\alpha - 1)k^{*(\alpha-2)}\right] < 0$$

where

$$\frac{dd^*}{dk^*} = (\alpha - \varepsilon\phi)(\alpha - 1)k^{*(\alpha-2)}\left(\frac{1}{\phi}\right)$$

$$\frac{\partial r^*}{\partial k^*} = \phi\varepsilon(\alpha - 1)k^{*(\alpha-2)}$$

$$\frac{\partial r^*}{\partial d^*} = \phi\left(\frac{\partial d^*}{\partial k^*}\right)$$

$$g^* = \theta k^* + \lambda + n$$

When evaluated at the steady state, $\partial^2(C/L)^*\partial s = -0.01847 < 0$ and, thus, satisfies the second-order condition (13) for a maximum.

Appendix B

Data

Definitions

1. C: Deflated Consumption Expenditures
2. GNP: Deflated Gross National Product
3. GNDI: Deflated Gross National Disposable Income
4. CAB: Deflated Current Account Balance
5. JACI: JPMorgan Asia Credit Index on Asian U.S. dollar denominated bonds, containing more than 110 bonds, using their dirty prices and weights according to respective market capitalization. It includes sovereign bonds, quasi-sovereign bonds, and corporate bonds from those countries.

Data Sources

1. JACI Spread: JP Morgan Markets
2. U.S. GDP Deflator: International Financial Statistics (IFS)
3. U.S. CPI for all urban consumers: U.S. Bureau of Labor Statistics (USBLS)
4. Philippine External Debt: Bangko Sentral ng Pilipinas (BSP)
5. External Assets: Bangko Sentral ng Pilipinas (BSP)
6. Nominal GDP: IFS
7. Average Exchange Rates: BSP
8. Consumption, GNP, GNDI, CAB, Current Transfers, GDP Deflator: (IFS)

Sample Period

Philippine JACI Spreads: 2000–2003

Software Used

1. Philippine JACI Spreads: Microsoft Excel
2. Philippine Optimal Domestic Saving Rate: Microsoft Excel, "Goal Seek"

References

Agénor, Pierre-Richard. 2000. *The economics of adjustment and growth.* San Diego, CA: Academic Press.

Arrow, Kenneth. 1962. The economic implications of learning-by-doing. *Review of Economic Studies* 29:155–73.

Becker, Gary, Kevin Murphy, and Robert Tamura. 1990. Human capital, fertility, and economic growth. *Journal of Political Economy* 98:S127.

Chen, Si. 2006. *External debt and growth dynamics.* Unpublished M.A. thesis, School of Economics and Social Sciences, Singapore Management University.

Conlisk, John. 1967. A modified neo-classical growth model with endogenous technical change. *The Southern Economic Journal* 34:199–208.

Grossman, Gene, and Elhanan Helpman. 1990. Comparative advantage and long-run growth. *American Economic Review* 80:796–815.

Inada, Ken-Ichi. 1963. On a two-sector model of economic growth: Comments and generalization. *Review of Economic Studies* 30:119–27.

International Monetary Fund. 1999. *Philippine statistical index.* IMF Staff Country Report 99/93, August.

Kraay, Aart, and Vikram Nehru. 2004. When is external debt sustainable? World Bank Policy Research Working Paper no. 3200, February.

Lucas, Robert. 1988. On the mechanics of economic development. *Journal of Monetary Economics* 22:3–42.

Manasse, Paolo, and Nouriel Roubini. 2005. Rules of thumb for sovereign debt crises. IMF working paper no. WP/05/42, International Monetary Fund.

Manasse, Paolo, Nouriel Roubini, and Axel Schimmelpfenning. 2004. Predicting sovereign debt crises. Unpublished manuscript, University of Bologna, IMF, and New York University.

Mariano, Roberto, and Delano Villanueva. 2005. Sustainable external debt levels: Estimates for selected Asian countries. SMU Economics and Statistics Working Paper no. 07-2005. Singapore Management University.

Otani, Ichiro, and Delano Villanueva. 1989. Theoretical aspects of growth in developing countries: External debt dynamics and the role of human capital. *IMF Staff Papers* 36:307–42.

Patillo, Catherine, Helene Poirson, and Luca Ricci. 2004. What are the channels through which external debt affects growth? IMF working paper no. WP/04/15, International Monetary Fund.

Phelps, Edmund. 1966. *Golden rules of economic growth.* New York: W. W. Norton.

Reinhart, Carmen, Kenneth Rogoff, and Miguel Savastano. 2003. Debt intolerance. *Brookings Papers on Economic Activity,* v2003 (1), 1–74.

Rivera-Batiz, Luis, and Paul Romer. 1991. International trade with endogenous technical change. Working Paper no. 3594. Washington, DC: National Bureau of Economic Research.

Romer, Paul. 1986. Increasing returns and long-run growth. *Journal of Political Economy* 94:1002–37.

Roubini, Nouriel. 2001. Debt sustainability: How to assess whether a country is insolvent. Unpublished manuscript, Stern School of Business, New York University, December.

Solow, Robert. 1956. A contribution to the theory of economic growth. *The Quarterly Journal of Economics* 70:65–94.

Swan, Trevor. 1956. Economic growth and capital accumulation. *Economic Record* 32:334–62.

Villanueva, Delano. 1994. Openness, human development, and fiscal policies: Effects on economic growth and speed of adjustment. *IMF Staff Papers* 41:1–29.

Comment   Francis T. Lui

Villanueva and Mariano's paper provides us with a useful framework for identifying the conditions under which the external debt level is sustainable. The latter is defined as the existence of a steady state to which the external debt/GDP level converges, and at the same time the economy is on a balanced growth path. To achieve this objective, prudent fiscal policy and promotion of private saving are recommended. These policy implications make a lot of sense. The actual application of the model to the Philippines is also credible. Countries with governments that are overspending or with people who do not save enough should take the paper seriously. Philippine policymakers may also find estimate of the Golden-Rule saving rate interesting.

The model, built on earlier papers by Villanueva (1994, 2003), consists of 15 equations, which include identities, laws of motion, a production function, and an equation governing the rate of change of technology. There is also an equation, the consumption function, that is behavioral. A major improvement of this model over its earlier version and Villanueva (2003) is that an explicit optimization problem has been incorporated. By solving for the steady state and maximizing per capita consumption, the model can generate Golden-Rule consumption and saving paths. This exercise is important because it provides the calibrated results with a more solid microfoundation. Without the maximization, one may easily cast doubt on whether coefficients in the model are robust to policy changes.

The objective function of the maximization problem in the paper is per capita consumption. While this has the advantage of making the model simple and easily interpretable, it is not the same as the more conventional utility function. Concavity in the latter can allow us to take into account

Francis T. Lui is a professor of economics and director of the Center for Economic Development at the Hong Kong University of Science and Technology.

risk aversion in a more satisfactory manner. Because of this shortcoming, the authors have to resort to introducing some risk premium in the interest rate. Although the risk premium is not entirely exogenous in the model, it is nevertheless independent of consumers' preferences or attitudes toward risks. It is not clear how significant it would be in affecting the quantitative calibrations.

A nice feature of the paper is that it has reduced the system of 15 equations into two first-order differential equations. This allows the authors to use simple phase diagrams to present their arguments. This is a convenient approach that helps the readers substantially in seeing through the possibly complicated dynamics involved. Although the paper has focused on the case that the equilibrium path is locally stable, this is not a necessary property of the model. Divergence is also possible when the slopes of the two curves in figure 6.1 change. It would be interesting or perhaps important for the authors to analyze situations of nonconvergence. The latter could lead to economic crises. Given the calibrated values of the parameters for the Philippine economy, as shown in the paper, there is local stability. However, the same model may also shed light on how certain parametric changes could result in divergence, and therefore possibly economic crises. While policymakers should know what is good for the economy, it may be even more important for them to avoid making major mistakes.

The Golden-Rule saving rate for the Philippines has been estimated to be 34 percent. Steady-state per capita GDP growth along the Golden-Rule path is 5.4 percent. These estimates seem to be consistent with each other, since we do see some Asian countries that save at similar rates can grow at around 5 percent or more per year. Although not unusual in Asian countries, a 34 percent saving rate would nevertheless be one of the highest in the world and would clearly be much higher than the Philippine historical average of around 19 percent. As such, one may ask how it is possible to raise the saving rate by such a substantial margin. Reducing government spending, as suggested in the paper, is clearly a possibility. However, the quantitative effect depends on whether government consumption and private consumption are substitutes or complements. If they are substitutes, reduction in government spending may not necessarily help to reduce overall consumption in society. Yum Kwan's paper on estimating the elasticity of substitution between government and private consumptions may shed light on this issue.

References

Villanueva, Delano. 1994. Openness, human development, and fiscal policies: Effects on economic growth and speed of adjustment. *IMF Staff Papers* 41:1–29.
———. 2003. External debt, capital accumulation and growth. SMU-SESS Discussion paper Series in Economics and Statistics.

IV

Sustainability
Country Issues

7
Australian Government Balance Sheet Management

Wilson Au-Yeung, Jason McDonald, and
Amanda Sayegh

7.1 Introduction

The Australian government has taken steps over the past decade to improve the sustainability of government finances. In particular, the government has significantly reduced its debt liabilities, avoiding many of the risks associated with high debt levels. In April 2006, the Australian government announced that it had eliminated general government net debt.

Having reduced net debt, the government's attention has turned to the financing of broader balance sheet liabilities, such as superannuation obligations to its employees. The government has announced that it will establish a "Future Fund" to finance public-sector superannuation liabilities.[1] This will assist in relieving future generations of some of the financing burden associated with other intergenerational fiscal pressures that are expected to emerge over the medium term.

The creation of the Future Fund raises the significant policy question of how best to structure the government's balance sheet to reduce overall finan-

Wilson Au-Yeung is an analyst in the Domestic Economy Division of the Treasury of the Australian Government. Jason McDonald is the manager of the Budget Policy Division of the Treasury of the Australian Government. Amanda Sayegh is an analyst in the Budget Policy Division of the Treasury of the Australian Government.

The authors are from the Fiscal Group, Australian Treasury. We are grateful for technical assistance from Jim Thomson and comments/suggestions by Michael Anthonisz, Michael Bath, Graeme Davis, Ben Dolman, Matt Flavel, David Gruen, Rob Heferen, David Martine, Adam McKissack, Louise Lennard, Robb Preston, and David Tune. The authors also wish to thank participants at the 16th East Asian Seminar on Economics in the Philippines for their comments, particularly Roger Gordon, Roberto Mariano, Takatoshi Ito, and Andrew Rose. The views in this paper are those of the authors and are not necessarily those of the Australian Treasury or the government.

1. These liabilities relate to public sector employees only, not broader social insurance obligations found in many OECD countries.

cial risk. This paper sets out a framework for optimal government balance sheet management and presents some preliminary estimates of the types of financial assets and liabilities that would reduce overall financial risk.[2]

7.2   The Australian Government Balance Sheet

The Australian government's *Charter of Budget Honesty Act 1998* (the Charter) highlights the need for governments to manage balance sheet risks. The purpose of the Charter is to improve fiscal policy outcomes by requiring the fiscal strategy to be based on principles of sound fiscal management and by facilitating public scrutiny of fiscal policy and performance.

The Charter facilitates optimal balance sheet management in two ways. First, the Charter requires governments to make regular financial reports that comply with external reporting standards, including the Australian Bureau of Statistics (ABS), Government Finance Statistics (GFS), and Australian Accounting Standards (AAS). This means the government balance sheet is comparable across entities and jurisdictions. Second, the Charter requires the *prudent* management of financial risks, including those relating to the broader government balance sheet (such as risks relating to the tax base). By requiring transparent presentation of the balance sheet and effective management of financial risks, the Charter allows the community to hold the government accountable for its financial performance.

7.2.1   The Balance Sheet

The Australian government's general government sector has published a balance sheet in the budget papers since the 1999 to 2000 period, consistent with international reporting standards.[3] The balance sheet reported in the 2004–2005 Final Budget Outlook is reproduced in table 7.1.

The major assets on the government's balance sheet are: financial equity, mainly reflecting the government's remaining share in Australia's major telecommunication company Telstra ($50 billion); nonequity assets, mainly taxes owed but not yet received by the government ($17 billion); and investments, loans, and placements, largely deposits at the Reserve Bank ($35 billion). The major liabilities are superannuation liabilities ($91 billion) and gross debt issuance ($62 billion).

2. The paper does not discuss the appropriate size of government expenditure, the level or composition of taxation necessary to fund it, or the optimal size of a net asset portfolio (Future Fund) through time.
3. The Charter requires a balance sheet to be published as part of the budget papers (usually produced in May), the mid-year economic and fiscal outlook (by the end of January in each year, or within six months after the last budget, whichever is later), and at the final budget outcome (up to three months after the end of the financial year). The Charter requires the balance sheet to be on the ABS, GFS, and AAS basis. However, the primary budget statements (and therefore all references in this paper) are on a GFS basis.

Table 7.1   **Australian government balance sheet, 2004–05 ($ millions)**

	2004–05 estimate at 2005–06 budget	2004–05 outcome
Assets		
Financial assets		
Cash and deposits	927	1,808
Advances paid	19,314	20,199
Investments, loans, and placements	31,066	35,022
Other nonequity assets	17,147	16,772
Equity[a]	50,895	50,183
Total financial assets	119,351	123,984
Nonfinancial assets		
Land	4,863	6,140
Buildings	13,894	14,195
Plant, equipment, and infrastructure	8,411	8,209
Inventories	5,299	4,524
Heritage and cultural assets	6,698	7,275
Other nonfinancial assets	2,085	2,032
Total nonfinancial assets	41,250	42,374
Total assets	160,601	166,358
Liabilities		
Deposits held	365	403
Advances received	0	0
Government securities	61,452	62,331
Loans	5,595	5,648
Other borrowing	224	182
Superannuation liability	91,071	91,172
Other employee entitlements and provisions	7,605	8,178
Other nonequity liabilities	28,416	30,423
Total liabilities	194,727	198,337
Net worth[b]	–34,126	–31,979
Net debt[c]	16,328	11,534

Source: Final Budget Outcome 2004–05, Australian Government.

[a]The 2004–05 equity and net worth outcomes include the Telstra shareholding valued at the closing share price on 30 June 2005.

[b]Net worth is calculated as total assets minus total liabilities.

[c]Net debt equals the sum of deposits held, advances received, government securities, loans, and other borrowing, minus the sum of cash and deposits, advances paid, and investments, loans, and placements.

There are two notable aspects to the Australian Government balance sheet. First, the government has reduced net debt to very low levels—net debt has fallen from $96 billion (18.5 percent of GDP) in 1995 to 1996 to $11.5 billion (1.3 percent of GDP) in 2004 to 2005. Having achieved further reductions in net debt the government announced, in April 2006, that it had eliminated general government net debt. This is in stark contrast with the net debt positions in nearly all other OECD countries (figure 7.1).

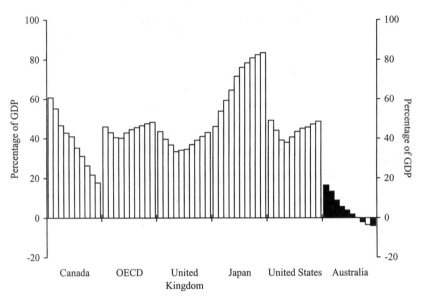

Fig. 7.1   General government net debt in selected countries (1998–2007)
Source: Budget Strategy and Outlook, 2006–07, Budget Paper No. 1, Australian Treasury.

The reduction in net debt reflects fiscal surpluses and asset sales over a number of years. It also reflects that these surpluses have been invested in debt assets. Following the *Review of the Commonwealth Government Securities Market 2002,* the government decided to maintain the domestic bond market to facilitate interest rate risk management by the private sector. The government therefore maintains a stock of around $50 billion of mainly long-dated securities, while investing the proceeds of debt issuance in term deposits at the Reserve Bank of Australia.

The other notable feature about the balance sheet is that the government's most significant financial liability is public-sector superannuation, estimated at $91 billion (10.2 percent of GDP) as of June 30, 2005. While this liability is expected to increase further in the future, a significant portion reflects liabilities to past government employees. The Australian government closed the main public-sector superannuation fund to new members from July 1, 2005. This means the government will pay the superannuation liability for new public servants employed after this date as they accrue, rather than growing the superannuation liability further. Also, in 2004 to 2005 the government paid $4.6 billion to Telstra and Australia Post to extinguish remnant superannuation liabilities from the corporatization of these firms a decade or so ago.

Despite these policies, the existing superannuation liability is expected to remain sizable, reaching $140 billion in 2020 (7.1 percent of GDP),

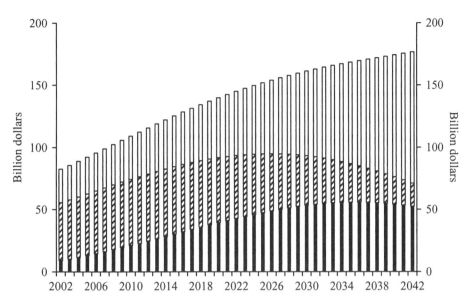

■ Public sector Superannuation Scheme   ☑ Commonwealth Superannuation Scheme
☐ Military superannuation schemes(a)

Fig. 7.2   Public sector superannuation liability (2002–42)
aIncludes the Military Superannuation and Benefits Scheme and the Defence Force Retirement and Death Benefits Scheme.
Source: Australian Treasury.

largely due to growth in the superannuation schemes for military and defense employees (see figure 7.2).[4]

In response to these financial management challenges, the government has announced the creation of a "Future Fund" with the aim of offsetting the government's unfunded superannuation liabilities by 2020. The fund will assist in increasing the government's net worth and increasing national savings. Contributions will be made to the fund whenever the budget is in surplus. That is, rather than realized budget surpluses being used to retire debt or build up term deposits at the Reserve Bank as currently occurs, they will be invested in the fund.

The fund will be established using accumulated cash reserves currently on term deposit with the Reserve Bank. Additional contributions from realized surpluses and the reinvestment of returns on the fund's assets will be needed to meet the government's target.

4. Since the liability depends on the final salaries of public-sector employees, there are risks around this estimate. Revaluations of the liability are regularly reported in the budget papers.

7.2.2   Contingent Risks

The government balance sheet provides important information on the financial performance of the government from period to period. An increasing net worth means that a government is reducing rather than increasing net liabilities on future generations. However, there are many rights and obligations of government that are excluded from the balance sheet, mainly because of valuation problems. The most significant item missing from the balance sheet is the *primary asset* of the government—the power to tax.[5] While this power is limited by such factors as the constitution, international tax competition, the size and growth of the economy, the effects of tax rate and base changes on economic efficiency and equity—the taxing power provides strong assurance of the government's ability to meet its liabilities.

On the other side of the ledger, certain explicit government obligations that do not meet accounting standards tests for the recognition of liabilities are also not recorded.[6] Under the international IMF GFS framework, only obligations payable *in any event* are on the balance sheet, whereas those that occur only on *uncertain events* (even if they are probable) are not (International Monetary Fund 2001:34). Unless presented carefully, this can lead to misunderstanding of the underlying economic value of specific assets and liabilities on a government's balance sheet. For example, the Australian government departs from the GFS framework by recording provisions against expected defaults on student loans in the balance sheet.[7]

Probably the largest contingent liabilities not recorded on the balance sheet relate to future pensions and public health costs. However, these obligations to fund future expenses have an impact on the economy today, as well as on fiscal sustainability. So the Charter also requires the government to produce an intergenerational report every five years, which essentially captures those obligations not recorded on the balance sheet. The last report from 2002 to 2003 projected spending associated with an aging population to require a fiscal adjustment of 5.0 percent of GDP by 2041 to 2042, or $87 billion in 2002 to 2003 dollars (Commonwealth of Australia, 1:2002a).

These conceptual and measurement problems mean the government

5. Problems also exist in valuing substantial heritage assets on the balance sheet, such as Parliament House and the Australian War Memorial.

6. This paper is concerned only with explicit financial risks, defined as rights or obligations on government established by law or contract. Implicit financial risks provide a different set of policy problems, such as policy issues, which are beyond the scope of this paper.

7. The Swedish government budgets by appropriating the anticipated loss from guarantees for individual risks, ensuring equivalence between traditional outlays and financial instruments that transfer risk to the government (Hagelin and Thor 2003). Similarly, the governments of the United States and the Netherlands explicitly appropriate the subsidy component of concessional loans and loan guarantees (Schick 2002:90). The Australian National Audit Office has valued the potential exposure from other selected financial instruments containing contingent risks—such as financial guarantees—at $115 billion (ANAO 2003).

balance sheet is not directly comparable with similar private-sector financial statements.[8] Government balance sheet management therefore requires a different framework for determining whether investment strategies are optimal. In particular, contingent assets and liabilities are likely to have a significant influence on how best to structure the government balance sheet to reduce risk and improve fiscal sustainability.

7.3   Government Balance Sheet Management

The government balance sheet is a measure of the government's financial position at a point in time. Government balance sheet management is concerned with how the balance sheet may move through time. Managing the risks affecting the government balance sheet can assist in avoiding, or at least ameliorating, sharp changes in the financial position flowing from macroeconomic shocks. In particular, a government's balance sheet can be significantly affected by contingent risks affecting the tax base. This paper argues that a government financial portfolio—including financial assets, superannuation liabilities, and government securities—can be structured to reduce the financial impact of these risks.

Despite reportedly sound monetary and fiscal policies, as well as high domestic savings rates, many Asian economies suffered serious recessions in the late 1990s (for example World Bank 1993). These recessions were compounded, if not caused, by the crystallization of contingent liabilities, particularly around commitments to support exchange rates and banking systems. Public injections into the banking system after the Asian crisis more than doubled the size of government debt to GDP in Korea and Thailand (Wheeler 2004:105).[9] In emerging countries more generally over the 1990s, bail outs to public enterprises and banking systems have contributed more to the build up of government debt than recurrent deficits (Kharas and Mishra 2001). Indeed, the deterioration in the debt positions of emerging countries since the 1990s has been largely attributed to interest rate and exchange rate movements and the recognition of off-balance sheet and contingent liabilities (International Monetary Fund 2003:117).

For developed nations, managing balance sheet risks may not be as important in averting crises. However, balance sheet management can be used to improve the fiscal sustainability of government through time (and ultimately, avoid financial crises).[10] Since governments can rely on taxation to

8. Indeed, the *National Commission of Audit* (Commonwealth of Australia 1996) recommended that the term *balance sheet* be replaced with *Statement of Assets and Liabilities* to avoid misleading comparisons with the private sector.

9. Korea's government debt to GDP ratio went from 10.5 percent to 26.5 percent after the costs of bank recapitalization, while Thailand went from 14.6 percent to 46.6 percent.

10. There are other potential objectives of debt management policy, such as attempting to ameliorate the effects of incomplete or imperfect markets (e.g., improving market efficiency through improved risk sharing). However, alternative objectives have a less secure conceptual basis and some implementation problems (see Missale 1997).

finance themselves, the concept of fiscal sustainability must relate in some way to the expected path of taxation. Fiscal sustainability not only requires that governments are likely to remain solvent—in the sense that the anticipated path of taxation is reasonable—but that the volatility (or risks) around that path are not significant. The International Monetary Fund is incorporating country risk analyses into their fiscal sustainability assessments for some countries (for example, Barnhill and Kopits 2003). Indeed, the relationship between taxation and balance sheet assets and liabilities is central to the economics literature on balance sheet management.

7.3.1   A Framework for Analysis

Intertemporal Budget Constraint

An important conceptual tool for analyzing government balance sheet management is the intertemporal budget constraint. This budget constraint requires that at any date the sum of net worth and the net present value of taxation be equal to the net present value of government spending.

In this way, the intertemporal budget constraint relates the government balance sheet in any period to the contingent asset and liabilities that can affect the balance sheet.[11] If current period government spending is higher than current period taxation, the government can issue debt (or some other liability). However, this simply means taxes need to be higher sometime in the future. In this framework, debt (and other liabilities) passed onto the future are effectively *congealed taxation*. The intertemporal budget constraint requires taxes to rise from their current levels to finance future anticipated expenses.

Tax Smoothing

Once the limit to future taxation and spending is identified, the optimal path of taxation needs to be found. Barro (1979) uses the standard public finance assumption that the excess burden of taxation rises by more than any rise in the tax rate—a doubling of tax rates has more than twice as many costs. These costs are the loss in overall welfare caused by tax rates distorting individuals' and firms' consumption choices.

Given anticipated government expenditure, these costs are minimized through time if tax (defined as a proportion of GDP) is constant, with temporary macroeconomic shocks leading to deficit financing and surpluses. That is, for a given financing requirement, a constant tax rate through time will impose a smaller cost on the economy than would a low tax rate in one year and a high tax rate in the next. An important implication of tax

---

11. In a series of excellent papers (from Bradbury, et al. 1999 and Grimes 2001, onward) the New Zealand Treasury has used the intertemporal budget constraint to derive the concept of *comprehensive net worth* for balance sheet management purposes.

smoothing is that it is *anticipated* future tax rises, rather than simply current tax rates, which distort economic behavior. For example, if tax rates are expected to rise significantly in the future, investment (and therefore growth) is likely to be discouraged. This standard result on optimal long-run fiscal policy accords with the Australian government's commitment of no increase in the overall tax burden from 1996–97 levels.

This result depends critically on assumptions of the excess burden of taxation.[12] In the absence of these costs, there may be no role for government to smooth taxes through time, since individuals could adjust their own portfolios to account for the uncertainty in future tax liabilities. It is the presence of such costs that gives government balance sheet management its power.

Balance Sheet Risk

For a macroeconomic shock that temporarily reduces economic growth, the government could resort to deficit financing by selling financial assets or issuing debt. However, if an unanticipated shock led to a permanent change in the resources available to government (for example, a fall in the present value of taxation revenue), the government would need to adjust fiscal policy because deficit financing would not be sustainable. Alternatively, governments could attempt to structure their financial portfolios to hedge against such risks.

Bohn (1990) extends the tax smoothing result to incorporate such uncertainty by imposing a budget constraint across all anticipated states of the world, as well as across time. Bohn shows that the government can reduce the expectation that tax rates will change by holding and issuing specific financial instruments.[13] In particular, an effective budget hedge would see the government's financial returns vary negatively with tax revenue during a macroeconomic shock. For example, the government's balance sheet is protected somewhat if it issues debt where repayments fall with economic growth and tax revenue.

This framework suggests that the optimal portfolio for a country depends on the structure of the economy. If an economy is susceptible to supply-side shocks, where inflation and growth move in opposite directions, then nominal debt issuance performs such a role. For example, the real value of government debt falls if an oil shock causes recession and inflation. Alternatively, if an economy is subject to demand-side shocks, where inflation and growth are positively correlated, then inflation-indexed and variable inter-

---

12. If the loss function is linear, then there is no need to minimize the variance in tax rates (Hansen 2003:9).

13. Bohn (1990) assumes risk-neutral individuals, so the costs relate to the expectation that taxes will change. For risk-averse individuals, the uncertainty that the government will raise taxes at times of low financial returns (i.e., high marginal utility of consumption) is an additional cost (see the Appendix in Hansen 2003).

est rate debt are better hedges. Of course, ex ante, it is extremely difficult to form an assessment of the types of shocks an economy will be subjected to in the future.

7.3.2   Formal Presentation of the Model

Using the model developed by Bohn (1990) we can express more formally the intuition previously outlined.

Individuals are assumed to be infinitely lived and risk neutral, and maximize the expected utility derived from all future consumption:

$$(1) \qquad U_t = E_t \sum_{j \geq 0} \rho^j c_{t+j}$$

where ρ is a discount factor, and c_{t+j} is consumption in period $t + j$.

Individuals receive a stream of endowments Y_{t+j} and pay taxes on endowments at a rate τ_t. As taxes are distortionary there is an excess burden of taxation denoted by a convex loss function $h(\tau_t)$. Individuals are also able to trade a given set of assets, so that the individual budget constraint is given by

$$(2) \qquad c_t + \sum_k p_{t,k} A_{t,k} = Y_t[1 - \tau_t - h(\tau_t)] + \sum_k (p_{t,k} + f_{t,k}) A_{t-1,k}$$

where $A_{t,k}$ is the quantity of asset k held at the end of period t; $p_{t,k}$ is the price of asset k (denoted in terms of consumption goods); and $f_{t+j,k}$ is the stream of cash flows derived from holding asset k. Individual optimization implies that expected returns across assets are equal, that is: $E_t(1 + r_{t+1,k}) = 1/\rho$ for all k, where $r_{t+1,k} = (p_{t+1,k} + f_{t+1,k})/p_{t,k} - 1$. This assumption is nontrivial, particularly so when we introduce equities into our analysis.

The government can use tax revenues $\tau_t Y_t$ and issue debt, $B_{t,k}$, to finance government expenditure, G_t (which we treat as exogenous in this model), and to meet outstanding debt obligations. The government budget constraint is given by:

$$(3) \qquad \tau_t Y_t + \sum_k p_{t,k} B_{t,k} = G_t + \sum_k (p_{t,k} + f_{t,k}) B_{t-1,k}$$

The government can choose the type of debt instrument, k, and may be a net lender or net borrower in any security, as such B_t should be interpreted as the government's net liabilities. Following Bohn, we recast the objective function in terms of government policy by substituting equations (2) and (3) into equation (1), which gives[14]

$$(4) \qquad U_t = E_t \sum_{j \geq 0} \rho^j \{ Y_{t+j}[1 - h(\tau_{t+j})]\}$$

---

14. As in Bohn (1990) we drop exogenous terms for simplicity, as they are irrelevant for deriving the first-order conditions for optimality.

The government chooses an optimal tax rate and debt portfolio to maximize individual utility, equation (4), subject to its own budget constraint, equation (3). In effect, the government's objective is to choose the structure of taxes and debt that minimize the expected present value of the excess burden of $h(\tau_t)$. The first-order conditions are[15]

(5)
$$E_t[h'(\tau_{t+1})] = h'(\tau_t) \text{ for } k = 0 \ \Big\}$$
$$\rho E_t[h'(\tau_{t+1})(1 + r_{t+1,k})] = h'(\tau_t) \text{ for } k > 0 \ \Big\}$$

where $k = 0$ is the risk-free asset. That is, optimality requires that the expected marginal excess burden of taxation is constant through time.

As in Bohn, we assume a quadratic excess burden, so that the deadweight loss of a tax rate, τ_t, is $h(\tau_t) = (h/2)\tau_t^2$. It follows then from the first-order conditions that an optimal policy requires

(6)
$$\text{Cov}_t(\hat{\tau}_{t+1}, \hat{r}_{t+1,k}) = 0$$

where $\hat{\tau}_{t+1} = \tau_{t+1} - E\tau_{t+1}$ is the innovation in the tax rate, and $\hat{r}_{t+1,k}$ is the innovation in the return to asset k. These innovations reflect the unanticipated components of changes in tax rates or returns.

Equation (6) implies zero conditional covariance between taxes and returns on available securities. That is, if the covariance between innovations in the tax rate and returns, for a specific debt, is negative then the government could improve tax smoothing by issuing more of this form of debt. The converse is also true: if the covariance is positive then the government could improve tax smoothing by purchasing more of this form of debt. This is the principal conclusion of Bohn—the government should smooth tax rates across different states of the world, as well as over time.

7.3.3   The Optimal Structure of the Government's Balance Sheet

To estimate the government's optimal portfolio an expression for the innovation in tax rates is required. The innovation in the tax rate determined by the government's budget constraint is:

(7)
$$\hat{\tau}_{t+1} = (1 - \psi)e^{-\bar{y}}\left(\sum_k \hat{r}_{t+1,k}d_{t,k} + \sum_{j\geq0} \rho^j\hat{g}_{t+1+j}\right) - \tau_t\sum_{j\geq0} \psi^j\hat{y}_{t+1+j}$$

where y_t is the growth rate of real output and $\bar{y}$ is its mean. The term $\sum_{j\geq0}\psi^j\hat{y}_{t+1+j}$ is the present value of innovations in future growth rates of real output, where ψ is the discount factor and $\hat{y}_{t+1+j} = E_{t+1}y_{t+1+j}$. That is, it captures unexpected permanent changes in output and therefore in the government's ability to raise tax revenues at a constant tax rate. Similarly, $\sum_{j\geq0}\rho^j\hat{g}_{t+1+j}$ is the present value of innovations in government spending relative to output, where $\hat{g}_{t+1+j} = (E_{t+1}G_{t+1+j} - E_tG_{t+1+j})/Y_t$. The ratio of security k debt to output is denoted by $d_{t,k}$.

---

15. See Appendix 7.A for derivation of the first-order conditions.

The intuition behind equation (7) is that the present value of tax revenues must cover initial debt plus the present value of government spending. That is, tax rates will need to adjust whenever there are *unexpected* changes in the value of government debt, government spending, or output growth. For a government that is already optimally managing the balance sheet, the current tax rate already incorporates anticipated obligations.

Substituting the previous into equation (6) gives the optimality condition for each government security:

$$(8) \qquad \sum_l cov_t(\hat{r}_{t+1,k}, \hat{r}_{t+1,l})d_{t,l} + cov_t(\hat{r}_{t+1,k}, \sum_{j \geq 0} \rho^j \hat{g}_{t+1+j})$$

$$- w_t cov_t(\hat{r}_{t+1,k}, \sum_{j \geq 0} \psi^j \hat{y}_{t+1+j}) = 0$$

where $w_t = [e^{\bar{y}}/(1 - \psi)]\tau_t$ is a weighting factor.[16]

That is, the government can smooth taxes to offset unexpected shocks in the present value of government spending and output through the issuance or purchase of state-contingent securities.

As the paper focuses on shocks that affect the present value of output growth, we assume that the covariance between innovations in the present value of government spending and returns on assets (the second term in equation [8]), is zero. The following equation provides us with a solution to the government's optimal portfolio:[17]

$$(9) \qquad \mathbf{d}_t = w_t \sum_r^{-1} \cdot \sum_{y,r}$$

where Σ_r is the variance-covariance matrix of returns (assumed to be nonsingular) and $\Sigma_{y,r}$ is the covariance vector matrix between returns and the present value of unexpected innovations in real output growth.

Methodology

In order to solve equation (9) and evaluate the optimality of various portfolios of government assets, we need to calculate innovations in returns and the present value of future rates of growth in real output.

We limit our analysis to a bivariate comparison. For our first analysis we are interested in the optimal share of long-term domestic debt and long-term foreign debt. We then extend this analysis to consider alternative asset classes, such as equities.

The real return on long-term domestic debt, $r_{t+1,d}$, is influenced by the domestic nominal long-term interest rate l_{t+1}, changes in the current long-

16. For the purposes of the empirical analysis, we assume a discount factor of 0.98 (which equates to a 2 percent per quarter discount), an average tax rate of 24 percent, and an average real growth rate of 0.75 percent per quarter. The value of the weighting factor does not affect any of the qualitative conclusions.

17. For derivation of equation (9) see Appendix 7.B.

term market interest rate (which is used as an approximation of the capital gain component), and domestic inflation, π_{t+1}.[18] Foreign long-term debt returns, $r_{t+1,f}$, will in addition be influenced by the change in the exchange rate Δs_{t+1}. Innovations in returns are therefore given by:

$$\hat{r}_{t+1,d} = -(\ell_{t+1,d} - E_t\ell_{t+1,d}) - (\pi_{t+1} - E_t\pi_{t+1})$$

$$\hat{r}_{t+1,f} = -(\ell_{t+1,f} - E_t\ell_{t+1,f}) - (\pi_{t+1} - E_t\pi_{t+1}) + (\Delta s_{t+1} - E_t\Delta s_{t+1})$$

To calculate these innovations in real returns, vector autoregressions (VARs) are used to formulate expectations for the inflation rate, the percentage change in the exchange rate, the long-term domestic interest rate, and the long-term foreign interest rate. Following Hawkesby and Wright (1997), expectations are formed for each variable (y_{t+1}, π_{t+1}, $l_{t+1,d}$, Δs_{t+1}, $l_{t+1,f}$) by regressing that variable on a constant and one lag of the variable, together with long lag of all other variables.[19] As expectations at time t depend only on information available up to time t, we must run a new VAR for each time period.[20]

The same method is used to calculate innovations in the growth of real output: $\hat{y}_{t+1+j} = E_{t+1}y_{t+1+j} - E_t y_{t+1+j}$. Expectations for real output growth need to be formed at each time period for rates of growth in all future time periods. That is an expectation that is formed at time t, for ($y_{t+1}, y_{t+2}, \ldots$ y_{t+n}) and at time $t + 1$ for ($y_{t+1}, y_{t+2}, \ldots y_{t+n}$) given the additional information. The differences in expectations are then discounted at a rate, ψ (assumed to be 0.98).[21] This process is repeated for each time period to derive a time series for innovations in the present value of output.

The methodology used to derive innovations in equity returns and output is the same as that outlined previously, with innovations in equity returns given by:

$$\hat{r}_{t+1,e} = (p_{t+1,f} - E_t p_{t+1,f}) - (\pi_{t+1} - E_t\pi_{t+1}) + (\Delta s_{t+1} - E_t\Delta s_{t+1})$$

where $\hat{p}_{t+1} = (p^*_{t+1} - E_t p^*_{t+1})$ is the unanticipated component of capital gains. Capital gains are calculated using accumulation share indices for each country, which incorporate both share price growth and dividend growth.

18. The proxy used for capital gains may lead to an understatement of this component in the innovation of real returns since it does not take into account the time to maturity. The longer the time to maturity the larger will be the capital gain (or loss) associated with changes in interest rates.

19. The lag specification was chosen based on the lag length that minimized the Akaike and Schwarz information criteria. The estimated model does not capture the full range of variables that could be expected to determine output and inflation. For a more complete model of the Australian economy see Dungey and pagan (2000).

20. This essentially involves growing the sample size with each estimation. We also investigated an alternative approach of rolling the sample, thereby keeping the sample size constant. However, this did not have a material impact on the results.

21. We also estimated the results using a lower discount factor, which did not change our broad conclusions. However, the case for investing abroad was slightly weaker under this scenario.

Data

All data are quarterly data for the post-float period 1983:4 to 2004:3. Long-term interest rates are the long-term government bond yields converted into quarterly returns. We take the first difference in bond yields, as we cannot reject nonstationarity over the sample period (based on the Augmented Dickey-Fuller and Phillips-Perron tests). Expectations for bond yields are then derived from summing the expectations of the first difference. Equity returns are derived using accumulation indices when these are available and for the periods when they are not, capital weighted share indices are used (this effectively assumes that dividend growth is constant over this period). The exchange-rate data are the log difference of the spot exchange rate expressed as the Australian dollar price of foreign currency. Inflation is estimated by taking the log difference of the GDP deflator. Growth rates in output are the log differences of real GDP.

Results

Table 7.2 shows the variance-covariance matrix for innovations series using domestic and foreign debt. The results show that innovations in domestic returns and foreign returns vary negatively with innovations in output. This suggests that it is optimal for the Australian government to purchase securities denominated in both domestic and foreign currency. These results are consistent with the findings of Hawkesby and Wright (1997) and Missale (1999).

We also report the optimal portfolio of domestic and foreign debt as a ratio to quarterly GDP, calculated by solving equation (9). These shares should be interpreted with some caution, as the magnitudes are sensitive to the estimation methodology. We discuss some of the key qualifications in detail in the following. With this in mind, the results show that it is optimal for the government to invest a relatively larger amount in domestic rather than foreign debt. This is largely driven by the volatility in the exchange rate, which acts as a *penalty* on foreign investment. Volatility in the exchange rate (and therefore in foreign returns) is not necessarily bad, provided innovations in the exchange vary negatively with innovations in output. While this is the case for Japan and Germany, our results show a positive covariance between innovations in the exchange rate and output for the United States.[22]

The previous results can be disaggregated into the various elements that make up innovations (or unexpected changes) in returns (see Appendix 7.C). Doing so reveals that there is a positive covariance between innova-

---

22. The volatility in the exchange may be partly driven by the method used to derive exchange rate innovations. Meese and Rogoff (1983) have shown that models used to explain exchange rate movements over short intervals generally perform worse than a simple random walk.

Table 7.2   Variance-covariance matrix for innovations series: Debt securities

	U.S.	Japan	Germany
Variance-covariance matrix			
$\mathrm{Var}(r_d)$	0.32	0.37	0.37
$\mathrm{Var}(r_f)$	10.11	41.81	36.95
$\mathrm{Cov}(r_d, r_f)$	−0.21	0.28	0.11
$\mathrm{Cov}(r_d, y)$	−0.12	−0.10	−0.04
$\mathrm{Cov}(r_f, y)$	−0.02	−0.38	−0.26
Optimal portfolios			
Domestic	−4.59	−3.17	−1.22
Foreign	−0.12	−0.09	−0.08

Notes: The results are for pair-wise comparisons between Australia and the reported country. This means that a separate VAR is calculated for each country including five variables: output, inflation, nominal domestic bond yield, nominal foreign bond yield, and the percentage change in the exchange rate.

tions in output and inflation, which is a key driver of our results. This implies that periods of unexpectedly low inflation (and therefore high returns) have tended to occur during periods of unexpectedly low output. This may largely result from the early 1990s recession, when inflation and domestic interest rates fell substantially.

Turning now to equities, a priori, we might expect that it would be unlikely that domestic equity investment would provide an effective hedge against macroeconomic shocks, given the high correlation between company profits and output. This is confirmed by our results, which show that the covariance between innovations in domestic equities and output is positive (table 7.3).

In contrast, the covariance between innovations in foreign equities and output is negative, suggesting that an optimal portfolio would include some investment in foreign equities for the countries considered.

7.3.4   Qualifications

There are some significant qualifications to our results that require further investigative effort. First, the paper focuses on unconstrained portfolios for only a select number of countries. Further work to determine the optimal constrained portfolio involving multivariate financial assets needs to be undertaken before using the model for policy purposes. For example, the optimal portfolio suggests that 2 percent of quarterly GDP should be invested in German shares. This is clearly unrealistic. However, in the absence of obvious constraints on the portfolio at the time of writing this paper, we decided to report the unconstrained case only. Similarly, Japan, Germany, and the United States were chosen since they represent the largest economies in their respective geographical regions of Asia, Europe, and the Americas.

Table 7.3   Variance-covariance matrix for innovations series: Equities

	Australia	U.S.	Japan	Germany
Variance-covariance matrix				
$\mathrm{Var}(r_d)$	0.31	0.32	0.34	0.33
$\mathrm{Var}(r_e)$	206.98	60.30	91.40	204.61
$\mathrm{Cov}(r_d, r_e)$	0.56	0.35	0.50	−0.10
$\mathrm{Cov}(r_d, y)$	−0.04	−0.07	−0.08	−0.05
$\mathrm{Cov}(r_e, y)$	0.21	−0.10	−0.18	−0.25
Optimal portfolios				
Domestic debt	−1.52	−2.49	−2.85	−1.75
Equities	0.02	−0.01	−0.01	−0.02

Notes: The results are for pair-wise comparisons between domestic debt securities and equities in the reported country. This means that a separate VAR is calculated for each country including five variables: output, inflation, nominal domestic bond yield, equity prices (to proxy capital gains), and the percentage change in the exchange rate.

Second, we have ignored the relationship between innovations in output and government spending. That is, government expenditure is also likely to be linked to macroeconomic shocks and potentially able to be offset by government financial investment policy. It is likely that the effects of a macroeconomic shock on spending reinforce the impact on taxation. However, Bohn (1990) suggests that this impact is likely to be small and insignificant. In theory it should be possible to determine the present value risk characteristics associated with major expense obligations (such as health care) and invest in assets to offset these risks.

Third, the results are based on agents forming expectations on future financial risks based on past financial events. This expectations formulation defies the rational expectations (Lucas) critique that economic agents should use all available information when forming expectations—past returns (or risks) are no guide to future returns (or risks) in the presence of significant policy change (Lucas 1976). In particular, Australia has been subject to significant economic reforms over the past two decades, which may make relying on certain systematic relationships to form expectations difficult. However, nearly all financial models in regular use rely on past data to measure risks (for example, the capital asset pricing model). Further, our results use data from 1983, after the floating of the Australian dollar, which was perhaps the largest structural change in the financial sector.

Finally, the model does not explicitly incorporate the existing stock of assets and liabilities held by other levels of government and by the private sector. In Australia, the state governments are in net asset positions (2 percent of GDP in 2004 to 2005), however the private sector has significant net external debt (48 percent of GDP in 2004 to 2005). The current model assumes that the obligations of the private sector and other governments are independent of the fiscal position of the Australian government. By focusing only on the *explicit* assets and liabilities of the central government (i.e., rights or obligations established by law or contract), the paper ignores those that may be *implicit* (i.e., rights or obligations dependent on moral suasion). For example, the community may expect the government to take over some of the financial obligations of large financial institutions that would otherwise be subject to failure. These expectations make the distinction between private- and public-sector debt in the paper (and by investors) less clear.

One potential way around this caveat is to include the net external obligations of the private sector when determining the optimal government portfolio.[23] For example, roughly half of net Australian private-sector debt is held in U.S. dollars, implying that an optimal portfolio would hold less of these liabilities if the government were also considering implicit risks on the government balance sheet. Of course, there may be significant moral hazard type problems for any government that makes this an explicit portfolio objective (see the discussion on policy endogeneity in section 7.4).

7.4   Discussion

7.4.1   Policy Implications

The key conclusion from the debt management literature is that the optimal financial investment strategy depends on the types of shocks affecting the macroeconomy. That is, the optimal way to structure debt (short or long, nominal or price-indexed, domestic or foreign currency) or invest in financial assets is an empirical question. Hansen (2003; following Missale 1997) summarized the main results from this literature:

1. Buy (short-sell) assets whose returns have a positive (negative) correlation to public spending and negative (positive) correlation to the tax base; and
2. Issue
   - nominal debt for government spending and productivity shocks;
   - price-indexed debt for monetary and real demand shocks causing inflation;
   - foreign currency debt when output and inflation shocks are correlated internationally;
   - maturity structure of debt to match structure of planned fiscal surpluses; and
   - short maturity debt when positive correlation between output and real interest rates.

---

23. The model incorporates implicit liabilities to the extent they are incorporated in G_t. Managing the government balance sheet against implicit obligations is problematic for the moral hazard reasons discussed in section 7.4.2.1.

Our results suggest that the Australian economy has been subject to more demand shocks than supply-side shocks over the sample period. If this were to continue to be the case going forward, then the tax-smoothing framework adopted in this paper suggests that the government should purchase domestic nominal bonds. During high-output periods in Australia, inflation and tax revenues would increase offset by lower real returns on domestic nominal bonds, such as government (including state government debt) or high-grade corporate debt. However, during low-output periods, inflation and tax revenues will fall and be offset by higher real returns to domestic nominal bonds. These results support the government's policy of reducing net debt—both by reducing the size of gross debt issuance and investing in debt assets. The results also suggest that balance sheet risk could be further reduced by issuing price-indexed bonds (such as treasury indexed bonds), rather than nominal bonds.

Our results also suggest that investing in foreign equities is likely to reduce overall balance sheet risk. In effect, the government already has a significant stake in Australian equities because of the tax revenue earned from domestic capital income (not to mention the presumably highly correlated flow on effects through taxation of domestic labor income). Auerbach (2004) notes that, even though the U.S. government does not hold much equity directly, it has significant exposure to variations in stock prices through its claims to future tax revenues. Indeed, Auerbach argues that the U.S. government's implicit equity position is larger than the stock market itself, consistent with the fact that revenues from all sources are responsive to stock market returns.

7.4.2   Potential Criticisms

Policy Endogeneity

There are some important criticisms of the tax-smoothing approach that can affect our policy conclusions. First, there is the potential problem of *policy endogeneity.* If the government's improved financial asset performance encourages greater government spending then the independence between government spending and taxing is violated. Similarly, there may be risks that if the government takes a controlling interest in a domestic company, some sections of the community may expect increased assistance for that company. In such circumstances, the optimal balance sheet strategy for government might be to avoid accruing a financial asset portfolio altogether and simply eliminate all risk, balancing the budget through the cycle (see Pinfield 1998). Another potential solution is to restrict the degree of controlling interest a government investment fund can maintain in specific domestic companies. Further, it is unlikely that the Future Fund will increase the incentive of future governments to spend more on public-sector superannuation expenses. The bulk of the super liability relates to previously accrued entitlements that are reasonably well defined. Finally, the government reports its underlying cash surplus exclusive of fund earnings so that they cannot be used for recurrent expenditure.

Moral hazard is a particularly severe form of policy endogeneity that appears to have limited the use of some financial instruments to manage government balance sheets. Traditionally, the economics literature on optimal debt management has focused on *state-contingent* debt. As early as 1941, inflation-indexed bonds were seen as a means for removing the incentive of governments to inflate the economy and reduce the real value of their obligations (Bach and Musgrave 1941). However, in the real world there is little evidence of state-contingent debt instruments being issued by governments.[24] This may primarily be due to some state-contingent debt instruments being subject to moral hazard problems (sometimes referred to as *time inconsistency*) if governments can affect the states (Calvo and Guidotti 1990; Bohn 1990). For example, bond returns that fall when an index of government expenditure rises would hedge the balance sheet against economic downturns. However, governments would also have an incentive to increase expenditure. This risk would then be priced in the value of such bonds, making them unattractive even for well-intentioned governments to issue.

More recently, the literature has focused on hedging the balance sheet by optimal design of the maturity and denomination of conventional debt securities. For example, a shorter average debt maturity increases the exposure to short-term interest rate rises. Long maturities can avoid exposure to *roll-over* (Barro 1995). It is not necessary, as our results show, to issue state-contingent debt to offset specific balance sheet risks. Investing in a broad and diverse range of financial assets effectively eliminates moral hazard type problems.

Agency Costs

Second, there are significant *agency costs* associated with government management of financial assets. In the tax-smoothing model, the government is assumed to maximize the welfare of all individuals in the community. However, in practice the incentives of government and the agents used by government may not be so aligned. This can lead to poor investment decisions. The solution to the agency cost problem is to ensure that the governance of the Future Fund is clear and transparent and investments are made on a commercial basis within the investment guidelines set by gov-

---

24. Real-world examples include Mexico issuing bonds tied to oil prices and Costa Rica, Bulgaria, and Bosnia issuing bonds containing an element of indexation to GDP (Borensztein and Mauro 2002). Even in Australia, the pool of inflation-indexed bonds is relatively small, with outstanding Treasury Indexed Bonds around 10 percent (or $6.4 billion) of total Commonwealth debt (Commonwealth of Australia 2002b).

ernment. Indeed, applying best corporate practice would allow individual government financial entities to set their own strategic asset allocation, after taking into account the nature of their liabilities (Grimes 2001). This is likely to improve governance, accountability, and entity performance. In the case of the Future Fund, this would involve directing the Fund to invest in assets of a similar risk to the government's superannuation liabilities.

In dealing with agency costs, the government imposes constraints on the optimal portfolio. The significance of these constraints has been highlighted by the results of Fowlie and Wright (1997) for New Zealand. They found that the optimal financial portfolio incorporated foreign-currency denominated debt when taxes are included, but only domestic debt when taxes are excluded. This means that a narrow focus only on balance sheet assets can lead to financial investments that increase the chances of volatile tax changes.

However, this does not mean that financial investment decisions should not be decentralized (down to an agency level) or linked to narrow portfolio benchmarks (such as matching financial assets to future superannuation liabilities). Rather, a single central agency needs to be aware of how individual elements of the balance sheet interact with each other during macroeconomic shocks. Some commentators see the centralization of broader balance sheet risk management with debt management as a *logical step* (Currie and Velandia-Rubiano 2002). For example, the Swedish Debt Management Office advises government on the costs of contingent liabilities and the government debt portfolio (Hörngren 2003).[25] Such a structure allows natural hedges in the balance sheet to be identified, reducing the need (and costs) from individual agencies hedging. Alternatively, such a balance sheet perspective allows for large cumulative risks to be identified and brought to the attention of government (Wheeler 2004:67).

Imperfect Capital Markets

The model discussed in this paper assumes that capital markets are not perfect; or at least that certain restrictions exist that stop governments from using financial instruments to perfectly hedge balance sheet risk. While governments can use some existing financial instruments to reduce balance sheet risk, certain types of risks are still likely to remain unhedged. In particular, incomplete capital markets may mean governments are unable to hedge against certain types of risks (such as catastrophic risk). There may be no private sector substitutes for government bonds (Arrow and Lind 1970, Stiglitz 1983). If capital markets are incomplete, there may be gains from governments issuing standardized products that can outweigh benefits from state-contingent products (Missale 1997). Alternatively, governments may have other policy objectives, such as maintaining some debt to allow the development of important financial products (Comley and Turvey 2005). There may also be other reasons for investing domestically. For example, informational, governance, or tax advantages may lead to a home country bias for equities (for a review, see Karolyi and Stulz 2002). Such constraints can limit the ability of government's movement toward the optimal portfolio outlined in this paper.

Even if capital markets are imperfect, governments can still invest in financial assets to the fullest extent possible using available securities. For the remnant unhedged risks, the government should consider building and maintaining a positive balance of net worth as self-insurance against large rare events.[26]

7.5   Conclusion

The economics literature relating to balance sheet management suggests that the government's financial portfolio should be structured to reduce the budget impacts of macroeconomic shocks. More specifically, an optimally structured balance sheet can reduce the risk that a major macroeconomic shock will see large changes in tax rates. This not only reduces the distortions caused by volatile tax rates, but increases the flexibility of governments to respond to unexpected fiscal pressures. A government that invests well has less need to significantly raise taxes or cut spending to finance itself. In most countries, this has meant structuring the debt portfolio so that liabilities do not become overly burdensome during recessions. However, Australia is amongst a small number of countries determining how best to structure a financial portfolio that includes positive net financial assets.[27]

This paper has shown that it is not only the budget position that is important for sustainability, but how the financial assets and liabilities of government are allocated. Our results support the Future Fund investing in a broad range of financial assets that includes nominal domestic debt and equities from selected countries. Indeed, by investing optimally the government is likely to reduce risks on the budget and improve growth prospects.

26. Hansen (2003:11) notes that building a *precautionary balance* is worthwhile if and only if the unhedged risks would otherwise result in a negative correlation between tax rates and consumption.

27. Other OECD countries with significant financial asset funds (including pension funds) are New Zealand, Norway, Ireland, Finland, and Denmark (see Comley and McKissack 2005).

Appendix A

Derivation of First-Order Conditions

The government chooses taxes and debt to maximize the individual objective function (A1) subject to its budget constraint (A2).

$$(7.A1) \qquad U_t = E_t \sum_{j \geq 0} \rho^j \{ Y_{t+j} [1 - h(\tau_{t+j})] \}$$

$$= E_t Y_t [1 - h(\tau_t)] + \rho E_t \{ Y_{t+1} [1 - h(\tau_{t+1})] \} + \ldots$$

$$(7.A2) \quad \tau_t Y_t + \sum_k p_{t,k} B_{t,k} = G_t + \sum_k (p_{t,k} + f_{t,k}) B_{t-1,k}$$

From the budget constraint, we can solve for τ_t, τ_{t+1}, and so on, and substitute into the objective function, U_t, which can then be maximized with respect to $B_{t,k}$, $B_{t+1,k}$, and so on.

The first-order condition with respect to $B_{t,k}$ is:

$$(7.A3) \quad \frac{\partial U_t}{\partial B_{t,k}} = E_t \left\{ Y_t \left[-h'(\tau_t) \frac{\partial \tau_t}{\partial B_{t,k}} \right] \right\} + \rho E_t \left\{ Y_{t+1} \left[h'(\tau_{t+1}) \frac{\partial \tau_{t+1}}{\partial B_{t,k}} \right] \right\} = 0$$

Now, from the constraints:

$$(7.A4) \qquad \frac{\partial \tau_t}{\partial B_{t,k}} = -\frac{p_{t,k}}{Y_t} \text{ and, } \frac{\partial \tau_{t+1}}{\partial B_{t,k}} = \frac{(p_{t+1,k} + f_{t+1,k})}{Y_{t+1}}$$

Substituting into equation (A3) gives:

$$E_t [-h'(\tau_t) p_{t,k}] + \rho E_t [h'(\tau_{t+1}) (p_{t+1,k} + f_{t+1,k})] = 0$$

Since $p_{t,k}$ is known at time t, and τ_t is chosen at time t, equation (A4) can be written as:

$$h'(\tau_t) = \rho E_t \left[\frac{h'(\tau_{t+1})(p_{t+1,k} + f_{t+1,k})}{p_{t,k}} \right]$$

Recalling that $r_{t+1,k} = (p_{t+1,k} + f_{t+1,k})/p_{t,k} - 1$, and noting also that the condition that expected returns must be equal implies that for the risk-free asset (defined as $k = 0$), $r \equiv 1/\rho - 1$, then the previous expression will yield the first-order condition obtained in equation (5) of section 7.3.

Appendix B

Derivation of Equation (9)

The optimality condition for each government security k ($k = 1, \ldots, K$) given in equation (8) is:

$$(7.\text{B}1) \quad \sum_l cov_t(\hat{r}_{t+1,k}, \hat{r}_{t+1,l})d_{t,l} + cov_t\left(\hat{r}_{t+1,k}, \sum_{j\geq0} p^j \hat{g}_{t+1+j}\right)$$
$$- w_t cov_t\left(\hat{r}_{t+1,k}, \sum_{j\geq0} \psi^j \hat{y}_{t+1+j}\right) = 0$$

As discussed in section 7.3 we assume that the second term is equal to zero and so the previous equation can be reduced to:

$$(7.\text{B}2) \quad \sum_l cov_t(\hat{r}_{t+1,k}, \hat{r}_{t+1,l})d_{t,l} - w_t cov_t\left(\hat{r}_{t+1,k}, \sum_{j\geq0} \psi^j \hat{y}_{t+1+j}\right) = 0$$

$$(7.\text{B}3) \quad \begin{bmatrix} cov_t(\hat{r}_{t+1,l}, \hat{r}_{t+1,l}) \cdots cov_t(\hat{r}_{t+1,l}, \hat{r}_{t+1,l}) \\ \vdots \qquad \ddots \qquad \vdots \\ cov_t(\hat{r}_{t+1,k}, \hat{r}_{t+1,l}) \cdots cov_t(\hat{r}_{t+1,K}, \hat{r}_{t+1,l}) \end{bmatrix} \begin{pmatrix} d_{t,1} \\ \vdots \\ d_{t,l} \end{pmatrix}$$

$$= w_t \begin{bmatrix} cov_t\left(\hat{r}_{t+1,l}, \sum_{j\geq0} \psi^j \hat{y}_{t+1+j}\right) \\ \vdots \\ cov_t\left(\hat{r}_{t+1,K}, \sum_{j\geq0} \psi^j \hat{y}_{t+1+j}\right) \end{bmatrix}$$

Rearranging this gives:

$$(7.\text{B}4) \quad \begin{pmatrix} d_{t,1} \\ \vdots \\ d_{t,l} \end{pmatrix} = w_t \begin{bmatrix} cov_t(\hat{r}_{t+1,l}, \hat{r}_{t+1,l}) \cdots cov_t(\hat{r}_{t+1,l}, \hat{r}_{t+1,l}) \\ \vdots \qquad \ddots \qquad \vdots \\ cov_t(\hat{r}_{t+1,K}, \hat{r}_{t+1,l}) \cdots cov_t(\hat{r}_{t+1,K}, \hat{r}_{t+1,l}) \end{bmatrix}^{-1}$$

$$\cdot \begin{bmatrix} cov_t\left(\hat{r}_{t+1,l}, \sum_{j\geq0} \psi^j \hat{y}_{t+1+j}\right) \\ \vdots \\ cov_t\left(\hat{r}_{t+1,K}, \sum_{j\geq0} \psi^j \hat{y}_{t+1+j}\right) \end{bmatrix}$$

This can be simplified with the following notation:

(7.B5)
$$\mathbf{d} = w_t \sum_r^{-1} \cdot \sum_{y,r}$$

In our first estimations, we restrict ourselves to the analysis of domestic and foreign currency debt.

(7.B6)
$$\begin{pmatrix} d_d \\ d_f \end{pmatrix} = \frac{w_t}{\Delta} \begin{bmatrix} \mathrm{cov}(\hat{r}_{t+1,2}, \hat{r}_{t+1,2}) & -\mathrm{cov}(\hat{r}_{t+1,2}, \hat{r}_{t+1,1}) \\ -\mathrm{cov}(\hat{r}_{t+1,1}, \hat{r}_{t+1,2}) & \mathrm{cov}(\hat{r}_{t+1,1}, \hat{r}_{t+1,1}) \end{bmatrix}$$

$$\begin{bmatrix} \mathrm{cov}\left(\hat{r}_{t+1,1}, \sum_{j\geq0} \psi^j \hat{y}_{t+1+j} \right) \\ \mathrm{cov}\left(\hat{r}_{t+1,2}, \sum_{j\geq0} \psi^j \hat{y}_{t+1+j} \right) \end{bmatrix}$$

where

$$\Delta = \begin{vmatrix} \mathrm{cov}(\hat{r}_{t+1,1}, \hat{r}_{t+1,1}) & \mathrm{cov}(\hat{r}_{t+1,2}, \hat{r}_{t+1,1}) \\ \mathrm{cov}(\hat{r}_{t+1,1}, \hat{r}_{t+1,2}) & \mathrm{cov}(\hat{r}_{t+1,2}, \hat{r}_{t+1,2}) \end{vmatrix}$$

We recall that the domestic and foreign innovation of returns is given by the following equations

$$\hat{r}_{t+1,d} = -(\ell_{t+1} - E_t\ell_{t+1}) - (\pi_{t+1} - E_t\pi_{t+1})$$

$$\hat{r}_{t+1,f} = -(\ell^*_{t+1} - E_t\ell^*_{t+1}) - (\pi_{t+1} - E_t\pi_{t+1}) + (\Delta s_{t+1} - E_t\Delta s_{t+1})$$

and define $\Delta s = \Delta s_{t+1} - E_t\Delta s_{t+1}$, $\pi = \pi_{t+1} - E_t\pi_{t+1}$, $l = l_{t+1} - E_t l_{t+1}$, $y = \sum_{j\geq0}\psi^j\hat{y}_{t+1+j}$ and denote $Cov(x, y) = c(x, y)$ and $Var(x) = v(x)$. Expanding equation (B6) we get:

$$\begin{pmatrix} d_d \\ d_f \end{pmatrix} = \frac{w_t}{\Delta}$$

$$\begin{bmatrix} v(\Delta s - l^* - \pi)c(-l - \pi, y) - c(\Delta s - l^* - \pi, -l - \pi)c(\Delta s - l^* - \pi, y) \\ v(-l - \pi)c(\Delta s - l^* - \pi, y) - c(-l - \pi, \Delta s - l^* - \pi)c(-l - \pi, y) \end{bmatrix}$$

Appendix C

Disaggregated Variance-Covariance Matrix of Innovations

Table 7C.1   Variance-covariance matrix: U.S. and domestic currency debt securities

	Y	π	l_d	Δs	l_e	r_e	r_d
Y	0.873						
π	0.108	0.330					
l_d	0.013	−0.014	0.020				
Δs	0.089	0.635	−0.106	10.895			
l_e	0.004	−0.006	0.010	−0.078	0.008		
r_e	−0.022	0.311	−0.101	10.338	−0.080	10.106	
r_d	−0.120	−0.317	−0.006	−0.529	−0.003	−0.210	0.322

Table 7C.2   Variance-covariance matrix: Japan and domestic currency debt securities

	Y	π	l_d	Δs	l_e	r_e	r_d
Y	0.510						
π	0.072	0.362					
l_d	0.028	−0.006	0.022				
Δs	−0.326	0.181	−0.109	41.692			
l_e	−0.016	−0.010	0.004	−0.063	0.006		
r_e	−0.381	−0.171	−0.107	41.574	−0.060	41.805	
r_d	−0.100	−0.356	−0.017	−0.072	0.006	0.279	0.373

Table 7C.3   Variance-covariance matrix: Germany and domestic currency debt securities

	Y	π	l_d	Δs	l_e	r_e	r_d
Y	0.298						
π	0.009	0.365					
l_d	0.029	−0.010	0.022				
Δs	−0.259	0.529	−0.258	37.293			
l_e	−0.003	0.014	0.007	−0.155	0.008		
r_e	−0.264	0.150	−0.255	36.918	−0.177	36.946	
r_d	−0.038	−0.355	−0.012	−0.271	−0.021	0.106	0.367

Table 7C.4   Variance-covariance matrix: Domestic debt and domestic equities

	Y	π	l_d	Δs	l_e	r_e	r_d
Y	0.873						
π	0.108	0.309					
l_d	0.013	−0.014	0.021				
Δs	0.089	0.635	−0.106	10.895			
l_e	0.004	−0.006	0.010	−0.078	0.008		
r_e	−0.022	0.311	−0.101	10.338	−0.080	10.320	
r_d	−0.120	−0.317	−0.006	−0.529	−0.003	−0.210	0.314

Table 7C.5   Variance-covariance matrix: Domestic debt and U.S. equities

	Y	π	l_d	Δs	l_e	r_e	r_d
Y	0.298						
π	0.046	0.329					
l_d	0.019	−0.016	0.020				
Δs	−0.104	0.750	−0.103	10.882			
l_e	0.052	−0.680	−0.006	−4.939	59.111		
r_e	−0.098	−0.259	−0.093	5.193	54.851	60.304	
r_d	−0.065	−0.313	−0.004	−0.647	0.686	0.352	0.317

Table 7C.6   Variance-covariance matrix: Domestic debt and Japanese equities

	Y	π	l_d	Δs	l_e	r_e	r_d
Y	0.319						
π	0.057	0.337					
l_d	0.023	−0.011	0.022				
Δs	−0.410	−0.113	−0.136	40.406			
l_e	0.290	−0.160	0.231	−8.798	67.711		
r_e	−0.178	−0.609	0.106	31.720	59.072	91.402	
r_d	−0.080	−0.326	−0.011	0.250	−0.072	0.504	0.337

Table 7C.7   Variance-covariance matrix: Domestic debt and German equities

	Y	π	l_d	Δs	l_e	r_e	r_d
Y	0.328						
π	0.014	0.323					
l_d	0.033	−0.010	0.022				
Δs	−0.540	0.809	−0.235	31.201			
l_e	0.303	−0.074	−0.087	−37.678	249.916		
r_e	−0.252	0.413	−0.312	−7.286	212.312	204.613	
r_d	−0.047	−0.313	−0.013	−0.574	0.160	−0.101	0.326

References

Arrow, K., and R. Lind. 1970. Uncertainty and the evaluation of public investment decisions. *American Economic Review* 60 (2): 364–78.

Auerbach, A. J. 2004. *How much equity does the government hold?* NBER Working Paper no. 10291. Cambridge, MA: National Bureau of Economic Research.

Australian National Audit Office. 2003. Management of Commonwealth guarantees, warranties and letters of comfort. Audit Report No. 27, 2002-03, Performance Audit.

Barnhill, T., and G. Kopits. 2003. *Assessing fiscal sustainability under uncertainty.* IMF Working Paper no. WP/03/79.

Bach, G. L., and R. A. Musgrave. 1941. A stable purchasing power bond. *American Economic Review* 31:823–25.

Barro, R. J. 1979. On the determination of the public debt. *Journal of Political Economy* 87 (5): 940–71.

———. 1995. *Optimal debt management.* NBER Working Paper no. 5327 Cambridge, MA: National Bureau of Economic Research, October.

Bohn, H. 1990. Tax smoothing with financial instruments. *The American Economic Review* 80 (5): 1217–30.

Borensztein, E., and P. Mauro. 2002. *Reviving the case for GDP-indexed bonds.* IMF Policy discussion paper No. 02/10. Washington, DC: International Monetary Fund, September.

Bradbury, S., J. Brumby, and D. Skilling. 1999. *Sovereign net worth: An analytical framework.* New Zealand Treasury Working Paper 99/3.

Calvo, G. A., and P. E. Guidotti. 1990. *Credibility and nominal debt.* IMF Staff papers 37 (September).

Comley, B., and A. McKissack. 2005. *Expenditure growth, fiscal sustainability and pre-funding strategies in OECD countries.* Paper prepared for the Bank D'Italia Conference on Public Finance, Perugia, forthcoming.

Comley, B., and D. Turvey. 2005. *Debt management in a low debt environment.* Australian Treasury, Treasury Working Paper 2005–2002. Retrieved from http://www.treasury.gov.au/contentitem.asp?NavId=049&ContentID=957.

Commonwealth of Australia. 1996. *National commission of audit: Report to the commonwealth government.* Canberra: AGPS. Retrieved from http://www.finance.gov.au/pubs/ncoa/coaintro.htm.

———. 2002a. *Intergenerational report 2002–03.* Canberra: AGPS. Retrieved from www.budget.gov.au.

———. 2002b. *Review of the commonwealth government securities market: Discussion paper.* Canberra: AGPS. Retrieved from http://debtreview.treasury.gov.au/content/discussion/html/CCSMReview.asp.

Currie, E., and A. Velandia-Rubiano. 2002. *Risk management of contingent liabilities within a sovereign asset-liability framework.* Retrieved from http://treasury.worldbank.org/web/pdf/currie_velandia_cl.pdf.

Davis, N. 2001. *Does crown financial portfolio composition matter?* New Zealand Treasury, Treasury Working Paper 01/34.

Dungey, M., and A. Pagan. 2000. A structural VAR model of the Australian economy. *Economic Record* 76 (235): 321–42.

Fowlie, K., and J. Wright. 1997. Optimal currency denomination of public debt in New Zealand. *New Zealand Economic Papers* 31(2): 137–51.

Grimes, A. 2001. *Crown financial asset management: Objectives and practice.* New Zealand Treasury Working paper 01/12.

Hagelin, N., and M. Thor. 2003. Pricing of state guarantees in practice. In *Central government borrowing: Forecast and analysis.* Stockholm: Swedish National Debt Office.

Hansen, E. 2003. *Objectives, targets and instruments for crown financial policy.* New Zealand Treasury working paper 2003/21.

Hawkesby, C., and J. Wright. 1997. The optimal public debt portfolios for nine OECD countries: A tax smoothing approach. Mimeo. New Zealand: University of Canterbury.

Hörngren, L. 2003. *Contingent liabilities in debt management.* Paper for the Working Party on Government Debt Management, Ministère de l'Economie, des Finances et de l'Industrie, 139 rue de Bercy, Paris 75012 (23-24 October).

International Monetary Fund. 2001. *Government finance statistics manual 2001.* Retrieved from http://www.imf.org/external/pubs/ft/gfs/manual/pdf/all.pdf.

———. 2003. *Public debt in emerging markets.* World Economic Outlook September 2003. Washington, D.C.: International Monetary Fund.

Karolyi, A., and R. Stulz. 2002. *Are financial assets priced locally or globally?* NBER Working Paper 8994. Cambridge, MA: National Bureau of Economic Research.

Kharas, H., and D. Mishra. 2001. Fiscal policy, hidden deficits, and currency crises. In *World Bank Economists' Forum,* ed. S. Devarajan, F. H. Rogers, and L. Squire, 31–48. Washington, DC: World Bank.

Lucas, R. E. 1976. Econometric policy evaluation: A critique. *Journal of Monetary Economics* Supplementary Series 1(2): 19–46.

Meese, R., and K. Rogoff. 1983. Empirical exchange rate models of the seventies: Do they fit out of sample? *Journal of Monetary Economics* 14:3–24.

Missale, A. 1997. Managing the public debt: The optimal taxation approach. *Journal of Economic Surveys* 11 (3): 235–65.

———. 1999. *Public debt management.* Oxford and New York: Oxford University Press.

Pinfield, C. 1998. *Tax smoothing and expenditure creep.* Treasury Working Paper 98/9. New Zealand.

Schick, A. 2002. Budgeting for fiscal risk. In *Government at risk,* ed. H. Polackova Brixi and A. Schick, 79–98. The International Bank for Reconstruction and Development/The World Bank.

Stiglitz, J. 1983. On the relevance or irrelevance of public financial policy. NBER Working Paper No. 1057. Cambridge, MA: National Bureau of Economic Research.

World Bank. 1993. *East Asian miracle: Economic growth and public policy.* Washington, DC: World Bank.

Wheeler, G. 2004. *Sound practice in government debt management.* Washington, DC: The International Bank for Reconstruction and Development/The World Bank.

Comment   Youngsun Koh

This paper discusses a framework for optimal balance sheet management from the tax-smoothing perspective and concludes that the Future Fund

Youngsun Koh is senior research fellow, director of Macroeconomic and Financial Policies, and head of Programs Evaluation Division at the Korea Development Institute.

of the Australian government should be invested in a broad range of financial assets that includes nominal domestic debts and foreign equities. The optimal portfolios derived through numerical exercises are not sufficiently credible in quantitative terms, but they give strong qualitative implications that are based on a sound economic reasoning and match our intuitions.

Korea is another country that is accumulating a large amount of government assets. The National Pension Scheme (NPS) that was introduced in 1988 requires a minimum 10 years of contribution for full old-age pension benefits. For now, there exists a far larger number of contributors than beneficiaries, and the annual surplus amounts to 3 to 4 percent of GDP. At its peak, the stock of assets is expected to exceed 100 percent of GDP, and then fall as benefit payments increase rapidly.

The NPS fund is invested mostly in domestic fixed-income assets, and none in foreign assets. There are talks of increasing the share of equities, and also of investing in foreign assets. Without such diversification, NPS is likely to have distortionary effects on domestic financial markets. The framework suggested in the paper provides a good starting point for the diversification of NPS assets. It would be interesting to check whether a similar numerical exercise leads to a similar optimal portfolio including nominal domestic debts and foreign equities.

Still, this approach will entail several problems when applied to the Korean NPS. Most serious is the rapidly changing economic environment in Korea. The annual growth rate, recorded at over 8 percent in past decades, declined to around 5 percent after the recent economic crisis, and further deceleration is expected in the future with the rapid population aging and the technological catch-up with advanced countries. It would be very naïve to believe that the variance-covariance matrix remains unchanged in this changing environment.

An equally important question concerns the parameter endogeneity (not policy endogeneity as discussed in the paper). Due to its very large volume, the portfolio selection of NPS can affect the market returns and the variance-covariance matrix; NPS may not be a price-taker but a price-setter. Similarly, its foreign investment can affect the exchange rate and the rate of return in terms of domestic currencies.

Despite these limitations, however, the framework suggested in the paper provides a very useful benchmark on which modifications can be made to reflect the realities more closely. Future works in this direction are called for.

Comment   Corrinne Ho

This paper deals with the question of how best to structure the government's balance sheet (i.e., the mix of assets and liabilities) in order to safeguard against contingent risks. The paper approaches this timely question for the case of Australia by applying the Bohn (1990) model to data from the floating exchange rate regime period (1983 Q4 to 2004 Q3).

Bohn's model is basically an optimization problem in which the government chooses the tax rate and portfolio mix to maximize the utility of the individual, subject to the usual intertemporal budget constraints. A key feature here is the assumption that changes in the tax rate are distortionary, thus resulting in the preference for tax smoothing. Accordingly, the model suggests that the optimal government portfolio depends on the covariances between the innovations in returns and those in output (and, in principle, government spending). The main empirical findings are:

- There are more demand shocks than supply shocks in the sample period, suggesting it is optimal for the government portfolio to be net long on domestic nominal bonds.
- When given a choice of both domestic and foreign debt securities, there is some scope to be net long in foreign securities.
- When given a choice of debt securities (domestic) and equities (domestic and foreign), domestic equities are found to provide no hedge against output shocks, as expected, and there is some scope to be net long in foreign equities.

In short, there is evidence to support portfolio diversification across currencies and asset classes, at least based on past macro data and returns of the set of assets included.

As with most policy-oriented research work, this paper faces some usual—though not insurmountable—challenges. For instance, the validity of some technical details or assumptions (e.g., tax smoothing) of Bohn's model may be subject to debate. I shall not hold the authors responsible for Bohn's model, but I would suggest that they could preempt such criticisms by clearly stating up front that their paper is only a straight application of Bohn (1990). As it stands, the paper seems to sound like it is developing its own framework that is *drawn on* Bohn (1990). But anyone who has read the original Bohn article would have noticed that the model is actually the same. Perhaps it is only a matter of drafting, but *truth in advertising* could help limit the authors' liability.

That said, however, I do want to hold the authors accountable for their choice of this particular model to address Australia's particular problem

Corrinne Ho is an economist at the Bank for International Settlements.

and their presentation thereof. On choice, it is not immediately clear from the text why the Bohn (1990) model straight out of the box is the best tool for analysis. Perhaps the rationale is obvious for people who are familiar with the literature, but not necessarily so for others. It would be useful if the authors could briefly explain and defend their choice in section 7.3.1, at least for the benefit of those readers who are not experts in this field. And, not to mention, it could make the paper more authoritative and convincing.

On presentation, I sense a kind of *mismatch* or *disconnect* between the rich institutional background in section 7.2 and the more abstract analytics in section 7.3. Bohn's article, which features exactly the same analytical framework, does not have this *disconnect* because its introductory section is relatively brief. This allows the paper to get to the *main feature* (the model) quickly. The reader can thus focus squarely on the theoretical and empirical analyses and take them for their own worth. So, while Bohn's article may not be as rich in institutional background, it has a cleaner presentation that ultimately makes for more satisfying reading. For the present paper, I would suggest tightening up the connection between sections 7.2 and 7.3 by cutting down on (or moving to footnotes) those details and diversions that slow down the flow from background to analytics, and by making more cross references throughout the text to link Australia's situation to the model and vice versa. This should help to keep the reader's train of thought on track from the first page to the last.

Finally, beyond the immediate confines of the present paper, I see potential for extensions and further research. Perhaps one can ask if there are any modifications one can make to Bohn (1990), which deals with a (U.S. case-inspired) generic government debt structure problem, to make it more specific to the current Australian situation. For instance, the authors mention the government's conscious effort to maintain a certain stock of government bonds—can this and other potential portfolio choice constraints be built into the model to make it more Australia-specific? Alternatively, can Australia's government balance sheet management problem be addressed by other models or approaches? Further afield, perhaps one can investigate the political economy of government asset and liability management, or the implications of reform for fiscal policy, monetary policy, and the financial markets. It could also be interesting to consider what similarities and difference there are between the government's portfolio choice problem and the central bank's reserve management problem. The possibilities are vast, and this paper is a good start.

Reference

Bohn, H. 1990. Tax smoothing with financial instruments. *The American Economic Review* 80 (5): 1217–30.

8

Dealing with Contingent Liabilities
The Philippines

Gilberto M. Llanto

8.1 Introduction

In recognition of the significant role the private sector can play in the provision, financing, and implementation of infrastructure projects, the Philippine government has adopted specific measures to encourage private-sector participation in infrastructure. The acute budgetary constraints facing the Philippine government motivated the entry of the private sector in the provision of certain infrastructure services, which can be priced accordingly, thus making it possible to exclude nonpayers from the service. Through user charges, the private investors can recover their investments and generate profits.

The passage of Republic Act 6957 or the Build-Operate-Transfer (BOT) Law in 1990, as amended by Republic Act 7718, provides the avenue for tapping private-sector expertise and resources in infrastructure.[1] The BOT law provides the legal framework governing financing, construction, and operation of an infrastructure project that the government delegates to a private proponent. The amended BOT law has increased the scope of private-sector participation, providing for direct negotiation of contracts and investment incentives in certain cases, and addressing the problem of unsolicited proposals.[2] Executive Order No. 215, issued in 1987, allowed the private sector to invest in power generation. The Electric Power Indus-

Gilberto M. Llanto is a senior research fellow at the Philippine Institute for Development Studies.

1. The amended BOT law allows for various modes of private participation: build-operate-transfer, build-run-and-operate, build-transfer, build-lease-and-transfer, contract-add-operate, develop-operate-transfer, rehabilitate-operate-transfer, and rehabilitate-own-operate.

2. The local government units have also entered into BOT-type arrangements with private proponents for providing infrastructure in the local areas.

try Reform Act (EPIRA) enacted in 2002, paved the way for greater private-sector participation in the electric power industry. It laid down the basis for competition in power generation and supply segments of the industry. Distribution and transmission of electricity have continued to be monopolies. A newly created Energy Regulatory Commission was created to regulate the price of transmission and distribution of electricity. The law also created a National Transmission Company that will be initially set up as a state monopoly but that will eventually be privatized.

Thus, the creation of a new infrastructure policy environment has been rewarded by a surge in private investor interest and investments in various infrastructure projects. In 1998 President Ramos reported that the BOT law enabled government to enforce power projects on scale and speed that was unprecedented worldwide. In one year alone (1996), the government added 1,000 megawatts of capacity through BOT power plants. By the end of 1993, the ten-hour power outage affecting many metropolitan areas and manufacturing establishments in 1990 to 1992 was eliminated.

To encourage private-sector participation in infrastructure, the Philippine government has invariably provided state guarantees. This chapter draws the attention of policymakers and legislators to the fiscal risk brought by contingent liabilities arising from government guarantees given to privately driven infrastructure projects. The unmitigated provision of government guarantees has given rise to large amounts of contingent liabilities that has created a serious fiscal risk for the government. The chapter discusses the current attempt of the Philippine government to address this outstanding issue. Drawing from existing literature (Lewis and Mody 1997, Mody and Patro 1996, Irwin et al. 1997, Mody 2000) the chapter sketches how the Philippine government may organize a management framework for contingent liabilities. It concludes by pointing out the need for the government to develop credible regulatory and competition policy frameworks to minimize the demand for guarantees in the future.

8.2   Demand for State Guarantees

Private proponents faced the daunting problem of entering highly regulated and distorted markets for infrastructure, where political patronage and intervention present grave constraints to efficient operation. Confronted with the problem of providing services in a highly politically charged environment, private providers seek state guarantees on a wide variety of perceived risks. Economic and political uncertainties increase the cost of investing in a country. Mody (2000) explains the provision of government guarantees as a necessary step in view of the fact that the transition from government infrastructure monopoly to multiple private infrastructure providers would require significant investments in regulatory capacity and since such capacity cannot be built overnight, contractually specified public-private partnerships are necessary intermediate steps in a rapid infrastructure development strategy. Government guarantees serve as second-best instruments in the absence of a stable political environment, effective regulatory bodies, independent judicial systems, and an overall competitive climate.[3] Thus, a crucial condition of an effective public-private partnership in infrastructure projects is the provision of state guarantees.

The fiscally challenged Philippine government realizes it has a duty to provide its citizens adequate and better infrastructure services. It has turned to the private sector to fill the huge gap in infrastructure services that the government felt impossible to address given a debilitating fiscal deficit. To encourage private investments in infrastructure services, private proponents or investors should be able to recover costs and generate normal profits from the endeavor. It would be critical to allow the private investor the freedom to set tariffs or user charges that would adequately cover costs as well as generate profits. Since they were bringing risk capital to the project, the private investors wanted an assurance of adequate return to their investments and recovery of invested capital. Awareness of the difficulty of charging cost-recovering tariffs or user charges in heavily politicized environments, unfamiliarity with the Philippines and weaknesses in the regulatory framework only whetted their appetite for government guarantees.

Government guarantees create contingent liabilities that could spell financial trouble for the government if not properly managed. In the drive to motivate private-sector participation in infrastructure, especially in the energy sector, the Philippine government provided guarantees that covered a wide variety of project-specific and general risks (Llanto and Soriano 1997). The expectation was that high Philippine economic growth could be sustained in the future, which would somehow avert guarantee calls.

8.3   Experience with Government Guarantees to BOT Projects

The BOT scheme is a contractual arrangement between the government and the private proponent that obligates the latter to finance and construct an infrastructure project for the government, and operate and maintain the facility during the cooperation period established in a contract. During the cooperation period, the proponent can charge rent, user charges, and toll fees to recover his or her investment outlay and generate a reasonable return to investment. The private sector brings not only financing for the project but also cost efficiencies together with operating know-how and

3. See Ashoka Mody 2000.

technical advantage.[4] Thus, the government used the BOT schemes to address the power crisis and, more recently, to move other infrastructure, such as the Manila Skyway Project, the light railway system along Metro Manila's main highway (EDSA MRT III), and others, from the drawing tables to the project-implementation stage.

8.3.1   Private Power Generation

The government has privatized power generation in a bid to provide greater efficiency in the power sector after the government realized the inadequacies of state provision of power and the regulatory and clearance procedures in that sector. The first successful project was the 200 megawatt (MW) Hopewell Navotas I, which began operation and was synchronized with the National Power Corporation (NPC) grid in 1991. The Ramos government extensively used BOT arrangements to lick the power crisis, believing that private-sector participation was the best way to increase power generation capacity in the shortest possible time. The government and NPC launched a *fast track* program with some 10 suppliers for additional power-generation capacity of about 1,000 MW within 18 months. By the end of 1993, the power crisis was history after the private sector responded positively to its new-found role. Between 1992 and mid-1994, the government and NPC had about 24 more BOT contracts. Initially, the arrangements were done on a transaction by transaction basis with individual project sponsors because of the urgency of the situation and the lack of experience with BOT schemes in the country. The resultant contractual agreements called for the implementation of those projects on a cost plus or a minimum rate of return basis. As the economy recovered and private capital regained confidence in the country, the government awarded more recent contracts on a competitive basis.

As of 1994, more than 35 power plants accounting for some 5,000 MW were either already in production or under active development/construction with a total cost of U.S. $5 billion. According to the Department of Energy, except for hydro and geothermal power, all future power-generation capacity will be with the private sector.

Because the power crisis was the single most important constraint to economic recovery and growth in the early 1990s, the government accepted the installation of *peak-load* power plants that provided the much needed power but at a relatively higher cost to the consumer. After the power crisis eased up, the government sought less expensive power projects.

During the *fast track* period of installing more power capacity through

---

4. Private power projects were completed at lower costs and used 25 percent to 30 percent less time than public projects. In Argentina, Chile, Malaysia, and Macau, private concessionaires of water supply projects have reduced unaccounted water from 50 percent to 60 percent of the total to 15 percent to 25 percent and staffing costs by 30 percent to 50 percent (Kohli 1995).

the BOT schemes, independent power producers (Ipps) required comprehensive government guarantees to cover sovereign, foreign exchange convertibility, market, and credit risks. The private proponents required comprehensive guarantee coverage in exchange for a commitment to install in the shortest possible time much-needed generation capability. In view of its inability to finance and install the required generation capability because of severe budgetary constraints and very limited access to the capital markets, the government had no choice but to grant guarantees sought by private proponents, including guarantees for National Power Corporation's (NPC) obligations, *take or pay* undertakings. The government through NPC and the private proponents agreed to have Purchased Power Agreements (PPAs), which required the government to pay for the building of capacity or power plants needed to ensure there is adequate supply of electricity, and reserve electricity in case a few power plants bog down.

Ideally, the government should have provided guarantees only to *fundamental* risks, such as sovereign and political risks. Subsequent BOT projects seemed to indicate the country's progress in attaining an improved credit standing in the international capital markets, which enabled government to provide less comprehensive risk coverage. This is seen in BOT arrangements in toll road construction and in urban mass transit system.

8.3.2 Tollways Construction

The project was the construction of a 25.5 kilometer toll road costing U.S. $500 million connecting Metro Manila to Cavite province.[5] The government awarded a 35-year BOT concession to a joint venture between a private-sector consortium and the government's Public Estates Authority. The government's guarantee cover was limited to political and sovereign risks, including right of way, force majeure during construction and operation, and cost escalation arising from variations in design. A guarantee on the adjustment of toll rates assured the proponents compensation for any shortfall in toll revenues arising from the nonimplementation of an agreed-upon parametric adjustment of toll rates. While the government took the tariff risks, all other commercial and market risks (e.g., the volume of traffic that will actually use the toll road) were absorbed by the private investors and lenders.

8.3.3 Light Railway System

This involved the construction of a 17-kilometer light railway system traversing Epifanio de los Santos Avenue (EDSA). The U.S. $650 million project was awarded to the private sector on a 25-year build-lease-transfer

---

5. Drawn from the speech of Secretary of Finance, Roberto de Ocampo, in the High Level Conference on Frontiers of the Public-Private Interface in East Asia's Infrastructure, Jakarta, Indonesia, September 3, 1996.

arrangement. The original plan was to finance the project from commercial borrowing from foreign capital markets with the government providing only fundamental guarantees. However, government, through the Department of Transportation and Communication (DOTC) and the Department of Finance (DOF), took the initiative of helping the private-sector consortium negotiate for lower financing costs with the senior lenders of the projects. The government guaranteed the lease payments of DOTC to the proponents with confirmation from DOF that the obligations carry the full faith and credit of the Republic of the Philippines. With this performance undertaking, the interest rate to investors was brought down from 20 percent to 15 percent. The project was also made more commercially attractive to the private-sector consortium by awarding them the right to commercial development in the depot and stations. The private-sector consortium would have to pay lease to the government. Thus, the fare revenues will be supplemented by revenues from commercial developments.

8.4   Contingent Liabilities in Infrastructure Projects

In the Philippines, Llanto and Soriano (1997) first raised the problem of the fiscal risk of contingent liabilities arising from the provision of government guarantees to infrastructure projects. The provision of comprehensive guarantees to infrastructure projects has generated huge contingent liabilities that must be managed well; otherwise the government will be exposed to substantial payment burdens once a guarantee call is triggered. Subsequent studies (Llanto et al. 1999; Bernardo et al. 2004) confirmed this as a potentially very serious fiscal problem if not properly managed by the government. Table 8.1 shows project-specific risks in certain sectors that impelled private proponents to ask for government guarantees.

8.5   Risks Most Commonly Shouldered by Government

The most often shouldered risks by the national government in BOT-type projects are the following:

- *Site availability.* The government guarantees right-of-way for the project. This involves purchasing the site for the project as well as relocating people who will be affected by the project;
- *Market risk.* If the buyer of the service is a government entity, the government typically agrees to minimum off-take contract purchases and prices (take or pay arrangements). These have the effect of guaranteeing a market for the output of the proponent (e.g., power, water);
- *Payment risk.* If the buyer of the service is a government entity, the government guarantees contractual performance;

Table 8.1   Selected project-specific risks and sectoral examples

Type of project-specific risks	Sectoral examples
Project-performance risks 　High cost of service 　Bad/inefficient service	Power—Power purchase agreements refer to minimum power plan performance criteria that the proponent has to satisfy. Water—MWSS concession agreement states the minimum criteria for project performance to be satisfied by the proponent. The concessionaires would bear the risk of poor project performance if they are penalized by the MWSS Regulatory Office. Transport—Most toll road concession agreements state the minimum criteria for project performance to be satisfied by the proponent.
Project-completion risks 　Delays 　Cost overruns 　Site availability	Power—NPC normally guarantees right-of-way and site availability for power projects. Water—The MWSS concession agreement stipulates that cost overruns in projects may be passed onto consumers provided they are covered in grounds for extraordinary price adjustments (EPAs). Otherwise, such costs are borne by the concessionaires. Transport—Responsibility for constructing access and feeder roads necessary for ensuring the viability of many toll roads are assumed by the government.
Fuel and other inputs risk 　Fuel availability 　Skilled labor	Power—In many instances, power purchase agreements include commitments by National Power Corporation (also the off-taker) to guarantee the supply of fuel inputs for independent power producers. Water—The MWSS concession agreement transfers input risk to the concessionaire, unless there are grounds for extraordinary price adjustments. Transport—Inputs for road and bridge construction are usually carried by the contractor.
Market risk 　User demand for services	Power—At the height of the power crisis, the government agreed to bear significant market risks by adopting minimum off-take contracts with independent power producers. Water—The MWSS concession agreement transfers market risk to the concessionaire. However, a number of bulk water service contracts with pending approvals have minimum off-take provisions with government-owned off-takers. Transport—The MRT-3 contract includes a stipulation of minimum ridership levels, below which government must compensate the contractor.
Payment risk 　Creditworthiness of 　buyers of output	Power—All power purchase agreements stipulate that NPC's commitments carry a full government guarantee for minimum off-take amounts. Thus, the relevant credit risk is that of NPC and government. All PPAs carry a buyout clause the IPP may invoke in case NPC commits a breach of contract or fails to make required payments to IPPs. Water—Many proposed service contracts between bulk water providers and off-takers, usually municipal water districts, carry \ guarantees of payment from the latter. Thus, the relevant credit risk is of the municipal water districts or the municipal government. Transport—There is no off-taker in most transport projects.

(continued)

Table 8.1 (continued)

Type of project-specific risks	Sectoral examples

Financial risk
  Debt service coverage
  Security
  On-going compliance
	Power—All PPAs carry a buyout clause the IPP may invoke in case there is a change in circumstance that materially reduces or prejudices the IPP return and the parties are unable to agree to a change in the contract after a defined period (guaranteed rate of return risk). In addition, most capacity payments are tailored to cover the project sponsor's debt services plus a fair rate of return.
	Water—In the MWSS Concession Agreement, the government does not assume financial risk. This is instead passed onto the concessionaires.
	Transport—Debt service coverage is a risk assumed by private operators in the case of toll roads.

Country environment risk
  Expropriation
  Regulatory interference
  Concession revoked
  Legal framework
  Environmental approval
  Foreign exchange
	Power—All PPAs carry a buyout clause the IPP may invoke in case there is a change in law or regulations, and if compliance with such laws results in:
	1. The power station being unable to operate; or
	2. The interest of the operator in the project and the operator's expectation of its return on investment being materially and adversely affected,
	and the parties are unable to agree to an amendment of the PPA after the defined period of negotiation (legal framework risk).
	All PPAs carry a buyout clause the IPP may invoke in case there is a force majeure event that is within the reasonable control of the government or NPC that lasts for a defined period and the parties are unable to agree to a contract revision. In a few cases, this applies to all force majeure events (force majeure risk).
	Many PPAs carry a buyout clause the IPP may invoke in case the NPC is privatized and this effectively results in a real or purported assignment of rights or assumption of obligations under this agreement or materially and adversely changes its net assets, projected profits, projected net cash flow from operations, or otherwise would prompt a reasonable person to conclude that the ability of NPC or its successor entity to duly perform its obligations under the PPA on a timely basis has been materially and adversely affected.
	Water—In setting the concession fee equivalent to the annual debt amortization payments of MWSS, the MWSS concession agreement effectively transfers the responsibility for paying MWSS loans to the concessionaires. Since these loans have been contracted in foreign currency, the concessionaires bear the risk. However, the concessionaires have cited the devaluation of the peso in their latest petition for EPA before the MWSS Appeals Board. There are no automatic adjustment mechanisms for passing these risks to consumers.
	Transport—In toll road agreements, most of the country environment risks are assumed by the government.

Source: Llanto et al. (1999).

Note: The Philippines no longer guarantees foreign exchange rates at the time of conversion. What is more prevalent is a guarantee of convertibility of domestic currency into foreign exchange.

- *Change in law risk.* The government assures proponents that changes in the legal framework will not affect contractual agreements;
- *Foreign exchange risk.* The government/central bank agrees to provide forward cover for the proponent. This will entail either: (a) ensuring that foreign exchange is made available for the project; or that (b) foreign exchange may be purchased through a forward contract for delivery at a later date. A common problem is the currency mismatch where project revenues are peso-denominated while debt repayments are in foreign currency. The failure to have cost-recovering tariffs will prevent raising the necessary peso amounts to cover a foreign-currency denominated debt; and
- *Regulatory and political risk.* Regulatory risk concerns the implementation of regulation that would have adverse impact on the financial viability of the project. For example, in toll road projects, the government through the Toll Regulatory Board guarantees that toll adjustment shall be in accordance with a parametric formula determined for the project. Political risks may include changes in law, war, hostilities, belligerence, revolution, insurrection, riot, public disorders, or terrorist acts.

Of the previous risks mentioned, the provision of guarantees to cover market risks and buyouts in the event of project termination contribute the greatest share to increases in the contingent liabilities of government (table 8.2). The amount of uncertainty inherent in the transition period—from a state of direct government provision to a state of privatization and the long gestation period of infrastructure projects—implies that when such guarantees are provided, the government shoulders a larger proportion of the

Item guaranteed	Cost
Table 8.2	Largest sources of contingent liabilities
Power sector	
1. Buyout clause or termination	Buyout or termination price
2. Force Majeure	Buyout or termination price
Transport sector	
1. Toll changes; automatic toll adjustment formula	Costs of inability to implement toll adjustments
Water sector (MWSS)	
1. MWSS to assume loans being paid by concessionaire	Cost of principal and interest on old MWSS loans
2. MWSS to pay early termination fee	Early termination amount
3. Lower of appeal to pay total cost of appeal process for both parties	Cost of appeals process
4. Force Majeure	Early termination amount

risk of insufficient market demand, adverse exchange rate fluctuations, and other negative shocks.

8.6   Contingent Liabilities of the Philippine Government

Total estimated contingent liabilities as of 2003 was P1,672 billion (U.S. $30.4 billion; see table 8.3).[6] Accounting for liabilities that have become actual, total liabilities amount to P1,455 billion. The total estimated value, however, does not include exposures from unfunded liabilities of the social security institutions and implicit contingent liabilities that may arise from defaults on nonguaranteed debts and collapse due to capital outflows. A 2003 report of the Commission on Audit on the Government Service Insurance System (GSIS) reported the institution's actuarial reserve deficiency at P5.24 billion. On the other hand, the Social Security System (SSS) valuation report in 1999 revealed that a portion of its assets would be used for benefit payments by 2008 and the fund would last until 2015 assuming there would be no across-the-board increases in benefits. If there would be annual across-the-board increases, assets would be used starting 2004 and the fund would last till 2012. SSS is currently updating its actuarial valuations.

The contingent liabilities of the infrastructure sector comprised 54 percent of total contingent liabilities estimated by the Department of Finance. BOT projects had a share of 18.5 percent while buy-out costs of independent power producers (IPPs) made up 35 percent. Guarantees on projects and activities of government-owned-and-controlled corporations (GOCCs) and government financial institutions (GFI) loans were 43 percent of the total estimate. Guarantee institutions had 3 percent of the total estimate.

Table 8.4 lists the government corporations and financial institutions that have provided government guarantees. The charters of some of those government corporations allow them to issue sovereign guarantee. Once the guarantee is called upon by the private investor, the national government becomes liable for payment. The table also rates the likelihood of these guarantees to be called, with the Light Rail Transit Authority, National Food Authority, and Philippine National Railways having the highest likelihood of being called. Guarantees on the National Power Corporation (NPC) and Technology Livelihood Resource Center equivalent to P200 billion and P0.32 billion, respectively, are already to be assumed by the national government. Among the GOCCs, NPC presents the highest

6. The estimates for contingent liabilities were based on reports of several key government agencies and external consultants. The report was compiled from the monitoring activities of the Department of Finance (DOF) on the cash flows of GOCCs as well as IPP reports from the National Power Corporation (NPC). Consultants were contracted in 2003 to quantify the contingent liabilities in BOT projects. As the central finance management office, DOF maintains information and annually updates the financial positions of GOCCs.

Table 8.3   **Estimated contingent liabilities as of December 31, 2003**

Types of contingent liabilities	Amount Php billion	Amount U.S.$ billion
Guarantee on GOCC/GFI loans[a]	723.90	13.16
Guarantee Institutions[b]	51.50	0.94
Guarantee on PSP (BOT) projects	308.85	5.62
Buyout of IPPs[c]	587.140	10.68
Total	1,671.65	30.40

Source: DOF.

[a]Excludes NG loans relent to GOCCs amounting to U.S.$2,05 billion or Php112.77 billion. Pertains to outstanding principal balance only.

[b]Guarantees on deposit insurance was not included because there are no provisions in the PDIC Charter that provides for NG guarantee on its obligations.

[c]Beginning January 2005.

[d]Excludes potential NG exposure for the social security institutions.

[e]Exchange rate Php55 = U.S.$1.

risk both in likelihood and cost. The government should review the contracts entered upon by those GOCCs and monitor the guarantees and the concomitant contingent liabilities arising from those contracts. Off-budget obligations such as guarantees provided by GOCC may give rise to a fiscal shock unless monitored and budgeted by the national government.

Republic Act 4860 sets a ceiling of U.S. $7.5 million on outstanding guarantees of foreign loans of GOCCs. However, some corporations have been exempted from the guarantee ceiling: Light Rail Transit Authority, Metropolitan Waterworks and Sewerage System, National Development Corporation, National Electrification Administration, National Irrigation Administration, Philippine National Oil Company, and Philippine National Railways. The national government charges a fixed annual guarantee fee of 1 percent regardless of the risk profile of the guaranteed loan or the institution. However, because the accounting system is still cash based, the fees collected are treated as part of the general revenues and are not kept in separate accounts to fund potential guarantee calls.[7]

Table 8.5 shows the maximum estimated exposure from independent power producers (IPPs). Liability exposures from private-sector participation in infrastructure projects are itemized in table 8.6. As of year-end 2003, the national government has made payments of P11,572 million and P5,258 million on behalf of MRT3 Project and Casecnan, respectively, for a total of P16,831 million. In this case, the contingent liabilities have become actual liabilities.

7. See Bernardo and Tang 2001.

Table 8.4 Total guarantees and relent loans of GOCCs and GFIs (principal only) as of December 31, 2003

Particular	Legal basis	NG guaranteed foreign borrowings		NG guaranteed domestic borrowings		Total guaranteed loans		Relent loans		Total guaranteed and relent loans		Likelihood of guarantee being called	Real in U.S.$ M
		In Php M	In US$ M	In Php M	In US$ M	In Php M	In US$ M	In Php M	In US$ M	In Php M	In US$ M		
Development Bank of the Philippines	RA 4860	118,708.66	2,158.34			118,708.66	2,158.34	2,125.54	38.65	120,834.20	2,196.99	LL	
Home Development Mutual Fund	Charter			10,581.74	192.40	10,581.74	192.40			10,581.74	192.40[a]	LL	
Home Guaranty Corp.	Charter			10,487.12	190.67	10,487.12	190.67			10,487.12	190.67[b]	LL	
Land Bank of the Philippines[m]	RA 4860	37,831.86	687.85			37,831.86	687.85	1,891.10	34.38	39,722.96	722.24	LL	
Light Rail Transit Authority	RA 4860	9,227.71	167.78			9,227.71	167.78	24,370.64	443.10	33,598.35	610.88	AC	
Local Water Utilities Administration	RA 4860	3,520.12	64.00			3,520.12	64.00	4,637.31	84.31	8,157.43	148.32	LL	
Manila International Airport Authority	RA 4860	496.34	9.02			496.34	9.02	9,024.29	164.08	9,520.63	173.10	LL	
Metropolitan Waterworks Sewerage System	Charter	13,341.08	242.57			13,341.08	242.57	419.93	7.64	13,761.01	250.20	LL	
National Development Company	Charter			8,132.30	147.86	8,132.30	147.86	1,662.08	30.22	9,794.38	178.08[c]	LL	
National Electrification Administration	RA 4860	3,592.68	65.32			3,592.68	65.32	8,348.80	151.80	11,941.48	217.12[d]	ML	
National Food Authority	Charter	687.42	12.50	24,046.31	437.21	24,733.73	449.70	277.97	5.05	25,011.70	454.76[e]	AC	
National Home Mortgage Finance Corp.	Charter			7,800.00	141.82	7,800.00	141.82			7,800.00	141.82[f]	ML	
National Housing Authority	Charter							312.58	5.68	312.58	5.68[g]	ML	
National Power Corp.	Charter	421,279.26	7,659.62			421,279.26	7,659.62	36,718.31	667.61	457,997.57	8,327.23[h]	AC	3,636.36[i]
Partido Development Authority	Charter	948.83	17.25			948.83	17.25			948.83	17.25	NB	
Phividec Industrial Authority								3,119.98	56.73	3,119.98	56.73	NB	
Public Estates Authority	RA 4860	3,578.57	65.06			3,578.57	65.06			3,578.57	65.06[j]	ML	

Agency	Legal Basis											Likelihood	
Philippine Export Zone Authority	RA 4860	102.27	1.86			102.27	1.86	2,229.07	40.53	2,331.34	42.39	LL	
Philippine Fisheries Development Authority								91.19	1.66	91.19	1.66	LL	
Philippine National Oil Company w/ECD[n]	Charter	34,381.10	625.11			34,381.10	625.11	3,988.48	72.52	38,369.58	697.63	LL	
Philippine National Railways	RA 4860	2,069.62	37.63			2,069.62	37.63	3,952.00	71.85	6,021.62	109.48[k]	AC	
Philippine Ports Authority	RA 4860	3,597.13	65.40			3,597.13	65.40	3,724.06	67.71	7,321.19	133.11	LL	
Philippine Tourism Authority	RA 4860	693.45	12.61			693.45	12.61			693.45	12.61	LL	
Subic Bay Metropolitan Authority	RA 4860	3,732.30	67.86			3,732.30	67.86			3,732.30	67.86	LL	
Technology & Livelihood Research Center	RA 4860							2,155.42	39.19	2,155.42	39.19[l]	AC	5.91
Trade & Investment Development Corp.	Charter	5,063.85	92.07			5,063.85	92.07			5,063.85	92.07	LL	
Total		662,852.25	12,051.85	61,047.47	1,109.96	723,899.72	13,161.81	109,048.75	1,982.70	832,948.47	15,144.52		3,642.27

Source: DOF.

Note: LL = least likely; ML = most likely; AC = almost certain; NB = no basis.

[a] Total bond flotation as of end-December 2003 is P5.58 B, the rest is the P5.0 B DBP yen loan.

[b] Includes debentures and zero coupon bonds used as payment for calls on its guaranty.

[c] NDC includes exposure in FCCC.

[d] Represents projected advances of NG for 2003 considering that PSALM has cashflow difficulties for 2003. Starting 2004, PSALM shall shoulder repayment of NEA loans.

[e] Because of the negative performance of NFA, a call on the NG guarantee would be forthcoming.

[f] NG guarantees 22% of the drawdowns of NHMFC from funders (SSS, GSIS, and HDMF) under the Unified Home Lending Program.

[g] Paying directly to creditors.

[h] Assumed that NPC repays all advances made by NG with the exception of the US$40 M paid to Sa Roque which will be repaid upon drawdown from JBIC loan.

[i] Equivalent to P200 B of NPC loans to be assumed by NG under the EPIRA law.

[j] Represents ROW of Manila-Cavite Toll Expressway project. Under MOA between PEA and TRB/DPWH, latter will reimburse PEA expenses paid for ROW and include the same in TRB annual budget for years 1999–2004. TRB has not remitted any amount to PEA. Total loans shall be paid on October 3, 2003.

[k] Not paying because of cashflow difficulties.

[l] To be proposed for conversion into subsidy.

[m] NG relent to LBP which the latter lent to its subsidiary the PCFC.

[n] PNOC figures represents Citibank US$175 M and a portion of IBRD 2181 PH Coal Exploration.

Table 8.5   **Estimated contingent liabilities on IPPs beginning January 2005**

Project name	Amount in US$ M	Buyout price at 4% CIRR — Basis other than buyout price	Cooperation period	Remaining project life
2 × 350 Pagbilao Coal Fired Plant (Units I and II)	2,927.15		Oct. 1995–Oct. 2025	19 yrs 9 mos
2 × 100 Mindanao Diesel Power Barge	13.30	2 yrs capacity fees + value of all equipment	July 1994–July 2009	5 yrs 6 mos
300 MW Limay Bataan CC, Block A	6.43	6 months worth of capacity fees	Oct. 1994–Oct. 2009	4 yrs 9 mos
100 MW Navotas Gas Turbine 4 Power Station 2	2.01		Apr. 1993–Apr. 2005	4 mos
300 MW Limay Bataan CC, Block B	6.83	6 months worth of capacity fees	Mar. 1993–Mar. 2007	2 yrs 3 mos
Ilijan City Diesel Plant II (Mindanao NMPC Unit 2)	5.53		Sept. 1993–Sept. 2005	9 mos
108 MW Subic Zambales Diesel Plant/I Enron I	104.04		Feb. 1994–Feb. 2009	4 yrs 1 mo
215 MW Bauang Diesel Power Plant	171.36		Feb. 1995–Feb. 2010	5 yrs 2 mos
63 MW Cavite EPZA Diesel Plant	6.07		Dec. 1995–Dec. 2005	12 mos
203 MW Naga Thermal Power Complex	83.20		May 1994–Feb. 2012	7 yrs 4 mos
2 × 500 Sual Coal Fired Thermal Power Plant	2,327.80		Oct. 1999–Sept. 2024	19 yrs 9 mos
650 MW Malaya Thermal Power Plant (Unit 1)	164.69		Sept. 1995–Sept. 2010	5 yrs 8 mos
100 MW Zamboanga Diesel Plant Project	53.04		Dec. 1997–Dec. 2015	10 yrs 11 mos
50 MW General Santos Diesel Power	27.67		Mar. 1998–Mar. 2016	11 yrs 2 mos

Project	Amount	Notes	Period	Duration
70 MW Bakun A/B & C Hydro Power	181.40		Feb. 2001–Feb. 2026	21 yrs 1 mo
304 MW San Pascual Cogeneration Power Plant	8.00	assignment fee w/c also serve as termination fee for SPCC development costs	25 years	preconstruction stage
200 MW Mindanao Coal Fired Thermal Power Plant Project I	35.00	total contractor's disbursement as of Oct. 2004	25 years	construction stage
345 MW San Roque Multi-Purpose Hydro Project	1,664.22		May 2003–May 2028	23 yrs 4 mos
1200 MW Natural Gas Fired Combined Cycle Power/Ilijan	1,314.00	at 4% CIRR—1,314; at WACC—1,049	June 2002–June 2022	17 yrs 5 mos
379.4 MW Caliraya-Botocan-Kalayaan HEP	1,573.98	at 4% CIRR—1,573.98; atWACC per contract—1,210.39	Kalayaan I Unit 1 & 2 Mar. 2002–Mar. 2027	21 yrs 2 mos
			Kalayaan II Unit 3 Nov. 2003–Nov. 2028	22 yrs 10 mos
			Unit 4 Jan. 2004–Jan. 2029	23 yrs
			Botocan June 2003–June 2028	22 yrs 5 mos
			Caliraya Unit 1 Oct. 2002–Oct. 2027	21 yrs 9 mos
			Unit 2 Dec. 2002–Dec. 2027	22 yrs
Total	10,675.72			

Source: DOF.

Note: CIRR = Commercial interest reference rate; WACC = Weighted average cost of capital.

Table 8.6 Estimated potential liability exposure of NG in BOT projects (based on various parameters depending upon availability of information) as of December 31, 2003

Projects	Implementing agency	Status	Maximum potential liability exposure		Actual payments by NG	
			In Php million equivalent[a]	In US$ million[b]	In Php million	In US$ million
Transport sector						
LRTA Extension 1	Light Rail Transit Authority	Not yet operational	1,794.31	32.62[c]		
NAIA International Passenger Terminal 3	DOTC/MIAA—NG	Completed, not yet operational	94,246.79	1,713.58[d]		
South Luzon Expressway Extension Project	Toll Regulatory Board—NG	Completed	470.65	8.56[e]		
Manila Cavite Expressway Project	Toll Regulatory Board—NG	Operational	51.23	0.93[f]		
North Luzon Expressway Project	Philippine National Construction Co.	Not yet completed	13.37	0.24[g]		
Southern tagalog Arterial Road	DPWH	Partly completed	3,303.36	60.06[h]		
Metro Rail Transit 3	DOTC	Operational	31,265.09	568.46[i]	11,572.39	210.41
Metro Manila Skyway	Toll Regulatory Board—NG	Operational	43,874.54	797.72[j]		
Information technology-related						
Civil Registry System	National Statistics Office—NG	Operational	0.65	0.01[k]		
Database Infrastructure & IT System	Land Transportation Office	Operational	1,219.90	22.18[l]		
Machine Readable Passport and Visa	Department of Foreign Affairs	Not yet operational	560.00	10.18[m]		
Land Titling Computerization Project	Land Registration Authority	Not yet operational	1,120.95	20.38[n]		

Water sector						
Casecnan	National Irrigation Administration	Operational	63,805.96	1,160.11[o]	5,258.25	95.60
MWSS East Zone Concession	Metropolitan Waterworks & Sewerage System	Operational	9,291.00	168.93[p]		
MWSS West Zone Concession	Metropolitan Waterworks & Sewerage System	Operational	17,729.00	322.35[p]		
Subic Water	SBMA & Olongapo City Water District	Operational	529.73	9.63[q]		
Power sector						
Leyte Geothermal Project	PNOC-EDC	Operational	34,392.05	625.31[r]		
Mindanao Geothermal Project	PNOC-EDC	Operational	5,182.10	94.22[r]		
Total			308,850.68	5,615.47	16,830.64	306.01

Source: DOF.

[a]Exchange rate Php55 = US$1.
[b]Mostly U.S. dollar denominated.
[c]Termination payment prior to Financial Closing.
[d]Total liquidated damages payable to concessionaire.
[e]Financial obligation pertains to compensation.
[f]Total financial obligation of TRB in the event the project is terminated.
[g]Financial obligation in the event the project is terminated.
[h]Financial obligation in the event of termination after the completion of construction.
[i]Buyout price if agency is in default. Market/revenue risk is based on deficiency in fee collections vis-à-vis rental payments to proponent. Actual payment by NG pertains to principal and interest payments of MRTC loans to its creditors.
[j]Buyout price in the event the project is terminated.
[k]Financial obligations in the event NSO defaults.
[l]Termination amount plus attendant liabilities if agency is in default.
[m]Liabilities assumed in the event of termination by DFA due to proponent's default.
[n]Termination amount plus attendant liabilities if agency is in default.
[o]Potential payment obligation for the post completion buyout price. Real liability includes water delivery fee and taxes.
[p]Early termination amount due to MWSS in the event of termination.
[q]Termination due to SBMA default.

8.7   Attempts to Manage Contingent Liabilities

The Department of Finance (DOF) is in charge of overall monitoring of contingent liabilities. Two interagency committees (namely, [a] the Development Budget Coordinating Committee (DBCC) composed of the Department of Finance, National Economic and Development Authority, the Department of Budget and Management, and other agencies; and [b] the NEDA Investment Coordinating Committee [ICC]) both work with DOF at monitoring contingent liabilities. The DBCC regularly deliberates on possible claims arising from contingent liabilities and factors these in the budget program. The national government has required all government agencies and GOCCs to seek the approval of the DOF prior to entering into negotiations for foreign loans through Administrative Order 19 in October 2002. A more recent effort was the setting up of a taskforce on Debt and Risk Management within DOF in December 2004, which will be the primary unit responsible for monitoring and managing contingent liabilities.

A contingent liability becomes an assumed liability of the national government only after getting the recommendation of DBCC to absorb the liability. When this happens, the Department of Budget and Management prepares to service the liability, using as legal basis the automatic appropriations provision under the General Appropriations Act. A recent development is the preparation by the Department of Budget and Management of a draft bill entitled the Fiscal Responsibility Act, which has been submitted and is currently being studied by the Senate. One of the salient points of the draft bill is the repeal of the automatic guarantees that certain government-owned and -controlled corporations can provide under their respective charters. This will free the national government of an obligatory financial burden arising from calls on guarantees provided by GOCCs, thus, mitigating fiscal risk. The draft also calls for greater transparency and accountability in the public sector.

The Philippines is still in the process of defining an effective strategy for managing contingent liabilities. Apart from setting a debt cap, charging a uniform 1 percent annual guarantee fee, and the automatic appropriations once the guarantee is called, the government has yet to come up with a more efficient system of budgeting for the contingent liabilities. A direction for reform suggested by Brixi and Mody (2002) is accrual-based budgeting that is built upon an accrual-based accounting platform. Under this system of budgeting, the net present fiscal cost of contingent liabilities will be included in budget documents. The government may be able to analyze the fiscal impact of contingent liabilities sooner than when they become actual liabilities. Thus, this helps the government to more effectively manage them. This would include proper accounting of all contingent liabilities in their net present values. The government will be able to include anticipated contingent liabilities in the regular budget that is submitted for congressional appropriation.

There is now an urgent need to set up a management framework that would take into account the screening, accounting, budgeting, and provisioning of contingent liabilities.

8.8   Toward a Management Framework

This leads to several issues that the Philippine government must work on:[8] (a) an improved framework for the grant of guarantees; (b) accounting, budgeting, monitoring, and management of contingent liabilities; (c) policies that reduce risks including the promotion of competition and developing efficient regulatory frameworks; and (d) maintaining a sound macroeconomic environment.

8.8.1   Framework for Providing Guarantees

The government should recognize that a guarantee cover is not a free resource that government can grant at will. It represents actual claims on government's fiscal resources once certain future events trigger a guarantee call. Without an efficient allocation of this resource, the government could find itself in a fiscal shock once private investors call on guarantees that have been given without regard for efficient allocation principles.

Correct pricing of the guarantee may help ensure an efficient allocation. This means that pricing the guarantee should consider market conditions and relative project risks. A first approximation may relate the guarantee fee to the market price of a long-term government security or bond in the absence of a history or pattern of guarantee calls. The guarantee cover could be seen as a form of insurance made available by the government to the project proponent, which will be paid once a guarantee trigger brings about the call. Since the insurance cover constitutes an allocation of government resources to the project, the premium or fee should be based on the opportunity cost of the allocated resource. There is also a great advantage in calibrating the guarantee fee according to the relative risks in infrastructure projects. Thus, government should identify all the possible risks that can affect the project, rank them according to their weight and likelihood of occurrence, and determine what specific risks the government is willing to cover. Risk-adjusted and market-based guarantee fee will create the proper incentives for private demand for that cover, thereby ensuring allocation efficiency.

---

8. The discussion on the principles and approach behind guarantee provision and management of contingent liabilities draws on Mody, Lewis, Irwin, and others. This section also draws on Gilberto M. Llanto 2004.

A nonprice-allocation mechanism for guarantee cover is the government's ranking of infrastructure projects that would be given such cover. This will require a thorough evaluation of the projects' relative social benefits and costs and of the different projects' contribution to the attainment of desired development outcomes. Reference to the Medium-Term Public Investment Program as well as the budgetary deliberations of the Development Budget Coordinating Committee could provide guidance on the relative ranking of projects. On the other hand, it is not inconceivable that political interests may influence the ranking of infrastructure projects. The reality is that decisions by policymakers are influenced by technical, economic, and political considerations. It will be very important to ensure transparency of the policy debates, the arguments given, and the ultimate choices made by policymakers.

The government should determine the amount of guarantee cover it can prudently provide in any given year. This amount should include not only those granted to infrastructure projects but also to other guarantee programs implemented by various government agencies, especially those that have the nature of sovereign guarantees. In some instances, the national government gives only an indirect guarantee, since the first recourse of the private investor is the balance sheet of the sponsoring government agency. However, this also exposes the government to contingent liabilities and thus indirect guarantees should be considered in the overall appreciation of how much guarantee the government can provide at any given time.

Contingent liabilities should compete on equal footing (e.g., in budgetary terms) with other forms of financial support, such as direct subsidies, tax exemptions, loans, and so on, so that the choice for more contingent liabilities does not lessen public finance efficiency.[9]

A vital principle is to unbundle and assign risks to the party most capable of managing them, or whose actions have a direct bearing on their outcome. Thus, a risk-sharing arrangement with private parties shall reduce demand for government guarantee and minimize government's exposure to contingent liabilities. The sharing of risks has to be reflected in the contracts to be executed between the contracting parties. One advantage of a risk-sharing arrangement is the minimization of moral hazard in implementing projects.

The provision only of a set of core guarantees to BOT projects, which should also be extended to concession arrangements, merits serious consideration. The core guarantees should cover only (a) fundamental risks, for example, uninsurable political risks; (b) fundamental rights, for example, repatriation of profits; and (c) foreign exchange convertibility. Fundamental rights bind the BOT proponent to undertake the project in full accordance with the terms of the contract. These require government to grant

9. See Currie and Velandia.

the exclusive right to the project to the BOT proponent and to guarantee against direct or indirect government takeover unless agreed upon based on a termination or buyout provision of the project contract. Foreign exchange convertibility guarantees the BOT proponent's right to (a) purchase foreign exchange in the open market; (b) transfer its foreign currency funds abroad; and (c) maintain foreign currency bank accounts in the Philippines or abroad. To be neutral, the core guarantees will be applicable to all sectors and are impartial to all types of projects.[10]

Related to this is the recommendation for government to adopt a selective and reasonable set of performance undertakings that are subject to a fall-away clause. More specifically, there should be no guarantee cover for commercial and market risks that appropriately belong to the private sector. The introduction of fall-away clauses in certain performance undertakings will enable the national government to minimize its contingent liability exposure. Fall-away clauses were included in the 1200-MW Ilijan Natural Gas Power Plant and San Pascual Cogeneration Power Plant project agreements. For the Ilijan plant, the performance undertaking for the availability fees shall fall away when the Philippines achieves consecutively for two years an investment grade rating for its Philippine peso debt from Standard and Poor, Moody's, or other internationally recognized rating agency of comparable standing.

The framework for giving guarantees should include an explicit exit strategy for government guarantee. This will minimize government's risk exposure and potential burden on its fiscal position. The exit strategy will prevent perverse incentives and moral hazard in project management and implementation. For example, the government could design a contract that provides for a fall-away of government guarantee for foreign exchange convertibility once the country attains investment-grade rating in international capital markets.[11]

The duration of the guarantee cover or the period of cooperation between the sponsoring agency/national government and the project proponent is another crucial factor in providing guarantees. IPPs' experience in the power sector seems to show that the lengthier the time period within which the guarantee call can be exercised, the more likely it will be exercised by the project proponent. Thus, a higher guarantee fee or premium could be required. The guarantee fee should also be reviewed annually by DOF, the sponsoring agency, and the project proponent to account for changes in business circumstances and, more generally, to give the department the flexibility to determine guarantee fees. The market is very dynamic and circumstances affecting the infrastructure project change. Thus,

10. Drawn from NEDA-ICC Policy Workshop on BOT and Related Policies, May 14, 1999, Tektite Building, Pasig City.
11. See Llanto and Soriano 1997.

there is a need for a regular review of project performance and a reassessment of the guarantee cover provided to the project.

In summary, the suggested framework for government guarantee has the following components:

- treatment of guarantee cover as a scarce resource that should be efficiently allocated
- determination of the annual amount of guarantee cover that government can provide
- pricing of a guarantee according to market conditions and relative risks
- risk sharing between project proponent and government
- core guarantees for selected risks
- core guarantees to be applicable to all sectors and all projects
- exit strategy or fall-away clause in guarantee contracts
- guarantee fee based on cooperation period
- annual review of project performance and required guarantee cover

8.8.2   Programming and Allocation of Guarantees

Together with monitoring, the programming and allocation of government guarantee will provide government useful information on the value of contingent liabilities and the amount of guarantee ex ante that can be reasonably provided without unduly exposing the government to unmanageable fiscal risk. In this respect, there is a need for a system of ranking or prioritizing access to the government's guarantee. At the moment, there are no internally consistent programming and allocation rules, much less provisioning for potential guarantee calls. An unanticipated call will produce a fiscal shock, forcing government to tap the debt market at a high cost in order to pay the claims of the affected party.

8.8.3   Accounting, Budgeting, Monitoring, and Management of Contingent Liabilities

The governments do not usually account for contingent liabilities because they follow cash-based budgeting. Thus, a government loan is actually recorded as an outflow but the government guarantee is not recorded because nothing has been spent during the accounting period. The cost of the guarantee is accounted for only when a guarantee call and the ensuing guarantee payment occur. This is myopic. For fiscal prudence, there is thus a need for an accounting and budgeting system that will take into consideration contingent liabilities. Lewis and Mody (1997) note that cash-based budgeting misrepresents and masks the aggregate exposure associated with loan guarantees and government insurance programs and creates perverse incentives for selecting one form of financing assistance over another. The failure to account for the true cost of guarantees leads to the expansion of guarantee cover for various activities and infrastructure projects without requiring the government to reserve for future claims or losses.

The Philippine government has to introduce reforms into its budgetary system and processes and, in this case, scrutinize the budgetary impact of direct and indirect guarantees. Monitoring the cost of the guarantee claims and appropriating funds to service those claims only when those claims are submitted encourage the extension of guarantees without having to consider the costs, leaving future administrations vulnerable to huge claims. Lewis and Mody (1997) emphasize that only by enforcing budgetary control at the time the financial assistance (that is, in this case, the guarantee) is committed can the appropriate budgetary incentives be realigned to eliminate this moral hazard. A useful example of dealing with this situation is the Federal Credit Reform Act of 1990 in the United States (see table 8.7).

The contingent liabilities generated by the provision of guarantees should be carefully managed to minimize the costs of actual calls on the government. An appropriate contingent liabilities management framework could inform government's decision on providing guarantees, expectation of guarantee calls in the future, and the setting of reserves for the contingent event. The underlying rule is, first, to identify the different types of risks and, second, to determine the best way to improve their management, whether by insuring, transferring, mitigating, or retaining the risk. This approach, when adopted by the public sector, should take into account the government's budgetary processes, the legal environment, and the type of risks being evaluated.

The Philippine government has recognized the seriousness of the fiscal risk created by contingent liabilities. Thus, the Department of Budget and Management has included in the budget submitted to congress for appro-

Table 8.7   The Federal Credit Reform Act of 1990

A systematic accounting, monitoring, budgeting, and reporting of contingent liabilities are important to serve as early warning to the government of potential guarantee calls and the amount of government exposure. A good example of this practice is the requirement under the U.S. Federal Credit Reform Act of 1990 for the budget to reflect the outlays required to cover loan guarantees. Direct loans, guarantees, and grants are valued using a financially equivalent metric—the expected present value of future costs.

Each federal agency that administers credit programs has five accounts: a credit program account, a financing account, a liquidating account, a noncredit account, and a receipts account. There are separate financing accounts for loans and guarantees. In their annual requests for budgets, agencies have to include estimates of the subsidy costs for new loans and guarantees. If an agency exhausts its subsidy appropriations in a given year, it cannot provide further credit assistance in that year. Funding to cover the expected present value of future costs is charged against the appropriation for an agency when the direct loan or loan guarantee is issued and the government's commitment is extended. These costs or subsidies must compete for budgetary resources on the same basis as other government spending.

Source: Lewis and Mody (1997).

priation a line-item budget that is allocated for payment of contingent liabilities that have turned to be actual liabilities following certain triggering events. The Philippine government is also considering the establishment of a debt and risk management office at the Department of Finance, which shall monitor contingent liabilities and advise government on appropriate action, among other responsibilities. However, the attempt to budget and monitor is still in a rudimentary stage and the government still has to develop its capacity for management of contingent liabilities.

8.8.4 Developing Efficient Regulatory Frameworks and Promoting Competition

There is a need for policies that reduce risks and raise expected returns and can help attract private investments that do not depend on government guarantees (Irwin et al. 1997).[12] An important component of those policies is a credible regulatory and legal framework for the provision of infrastructure services. Private investors have repeatedly indicated the weak regulatory framework of the Philippines as a major factor deterring foreign investments. For instance, in the water sector, certain consumer groups such as NGOs have accused the lack of independence of the Regulatory Office as responsible for the high water tariffs. On the other hand, private business has rued their inability to charge cost-recovering tariffs because of political intervention and, thus, the tendency of private proponents is to ask for guarantees that cover this risk.

It is important to note that government risk-bearing is not necessarily required by private investments in infrastructure. Irwin and others (1997) call attention to the experience of the United Kingdom in attracting large amounts of private investments despite its policy of not bearing even regulatory risks except where they relate specifically to a project. In Chile, private investments in telecommunications, gas, and power were made without government guarantees. In Argentina, reforms in the power industry made it possible to get private investment without the government assuming major risks (Klein 1996).[13]

The most important policy measure is to expose infrastructure service to competition whenever possible. When monopolies are unavoidable, it is important for government to establish laws and regulations that protect property rights and to enforce them fairly and consistently (Irwin et al. 1997). Table 8.8 provides policies that reduce risks and increase expected returns.

Privatization, deregulation, and liberalization in the infrastructure sector do not necessarily lead to unadulterated economic benefits to the consumer. As Joskow (1998) points out, there could still be segments of the in-

12. See Irwin et al. 1997.
13. See Klein 1996.

Table 8.8   Economy-wide options to reduce risks

• Establish expert and independent regulatory agencies
• Reform the constitution to impose limits on the power of the executive to act arbitrarily
• Strengthen the independence and quality of the judiciary
• Sign international treaties
• Agree to be bound by international arbitration

Source: Irwin et al. (1997).

frastructure sector that are natural monopolies for which continuing regulation would be needed to safeguard consumer welfare. At the same time, an effective regulatory presence is needed to ensure that potential competitors are not barred from entry into the competitive segment of infrastructure sectors. The Philippine government should recognize this as a crucial component of its overall infrastructure policy and strategy for private participation in infrastructure.

Effective regulation would be necessary to ensure consumer welfare, especially where there are segments of the infrastructure sector that are natural monopolies.[14] In the case of the electric power industry, the EPIRA (RA 9136) created the Energy Regulatory Commission to promote competition; safeguard consumer welfare; ensure performance and compliance with health, safety, and environmental standards; and punish abuse of market power. Prohibition against cross-ownership between subindustries, concentration of ownership, and sourcing of power from bilateral supply contracts is provided for under the EPIRA and its Implementing Rules and Regulations.

Regulatory agencies should be independent and accountable. One of the dangers of not having an independent and accountable agency is to have pricing policies that can become highly politicized. This will prevent private investors from recovering their costs and generating profits, creating uncertainty about future income streams and magnifying the risks perceived by private investors. Accountability is another hallmark of a good regulatory agency. This will discourage arbitrariness in decision making and potential abuse of regulatory power. Campos (1998) cites the need for a judiciary environment that must be trusted by private investors and an effective and credible arrangement for appealing agency decisions to ensure accountability in a regulatory agency.[15]

All these point to the need to install a regulatory framework for the infrastructure sector that is clear, predictable, competent, and independent. Such a regulatory framework will help minimize uncertainty and risks faced by private investors and consumers alike and, thus, the need for gov-

14. See Joskow 1998.
15. See Campos 1998.

ernment guarantees against certain risks. Clarity of procedures for bid and award and dealing with disputes and unforeseen events in an infrastructure sector are indispensable to private participation in the infrastructure sector. Certainty about government's role in implementing commitments (e.g., tariff adjustment) gives private investors a measure of comfort and, finally, a competitive environment assures the private proponent that it will be able to charge tariffs or user charges that will enable it to recover costs and generate profits. This will also help minimize the need for guarantees against market-related risks.

8.8.5   Sharing the Risks with the Private Sector

Public infrastructure projects carry various risks that may discourage private sector financing, construction, or operation. Unless the government assumes some or all of the risks associated with the project, the economy will tend to underprovide it. The underlying rationale of the government's absorption of risks in public infrastructure projects is that the project's social return exceeds its private returns and that society will be better off having the project than doing without it. Thus, a government guarantee is given to project lenders and/or sponsors to minimize the attendant risks of an infrastructure project and thereby, encourage private-sector participation.

A practical approach in dealing with this problem of underprovision is to identify and break down the risks associated with the infrastructure project into several components and assign the component risks to the parties that should absorb them. The key activities are:

- the optimal assignment of risks to the parties that should absorb them
- the minimization of the component risks through efficient risk management

To encourage private-sector participation and performance in public infrastructure projects, the government and the private sector may agree on the assignment of the component risks and the determination of the extent of risk sharing. For instance, the government can guarantee the debt exposure of private sector investors for a limited period of time.

The critical action to take then is to determine which risks are transferable to the private sector and encourage greater private-sector share of those risks. The delineation and sharing of component risks are necessary to prevent perverse incentives that lead to project mismanagement, and to avoid moral hazard problems such as relaxing on project monitoring and concentrating on fund diversion. By taking on the full extent of the risk of defaults, the government may end up holding the proverbial empty bag as private lenders and sponsors take strategic action to capture rents at the expense of the government. The satisfactory allocation of risks between the government and the private sector is essential to the successful implementation of infrastructure projects.

8.8.6 Maintaining a Sound Macroeconomic Environment

Macroeconomic stability characterized by low inflation and low interest rates will enable projects to have more certain cash streams and a positive rate of return on investments. This will minimize the risks of guarantee calls, especially in those instances when the government has been exposed to buy-out clauses.

To build the confidence of private investors in infrastructure, the Philippine government needs to maintain a stable macroeconomic environment and continue with economic and financial reforms that will deepen the financial and capital markets. Infrastructure projects are vulnerable to currency and maturity risks, a source of uneasiness to the private investor. The maturity structure of bank liabilities cannot simply match the long gestation of infrastructure projects. Hence there is a need to develop long-term peso debt finance. This will also take care of currency risks that arise because the infrastructure project generates revenues in pesos while the loan exposure is denominated in foreign currency.

References

Bernardo, R., G. M. Llanto, and M. C. Tang. 2004. Philippine government at risk: The threat of contingent liabilities. Presented at 2004 Annual Meeting of the Philippine Economic Society, De La Salle University, Manila.

Bernardo, R., and M. C. Tang. 2001. *A note on Philippine government contingent liabilities.* Unpublished paper.

Brixi, Hana Polackova, and Ashok Mody. 2002. Dealing with government fiscal risk: An overview. In *Government at risk: Contingent liabilities and fiscal risk,* ed. H. P. Brixi and A. Mody, 21–58. Washington, DC: The World Bank.

Campos, E. 1998. The role of governance. In *Investment infrastructure in Asia,* ed. F. Macaranas and L. Clavecilla, 23–23. Sycip Policy Forum (October). Makati City: Asian Institute of Management.

Currie, E., and A. Velandia. 2002. Risk management of contingent liabilities within a sovereign asset liability framework. Retrieved from http://www.treasury.world bank.org/web/pdf/currie_velandia_cl.pdf.

Irwin, T., M. Klein, G. E. Perry, and M. Thobani. 1998. Dealing with public risks in private infrastructure: An overview. In *Dealing with public risk in private infrastructure,* ed. T. Irwin, M. Klein, G. E. Perry, and M. Thobani, 1–20. Washington, DC: The World Bank.

Joskow, P. 1998. Competition and regulation policy in developing countries. Annual World Bank Conference on Development Economics, Washington, DC.

Kohli, H. 1995. *Infrastructure development in East Asia and Pacific.* Washington, DC: World Bank.

Klein, M. 1996. *Managing guarantee programs in support of infrastructure invest-ments.* Washington, DC: The World Bank, Private Sector Development Department.

Lewis, C., and A. Mody. 1998. *Contingent liabilities for infrastructure projects: Implementing a risk management framework for governments.* Washington, DC: World Bank.

Llanto, G. M. 2004. *Infrastructure development: Experience and policy options for the future.* Makati City: Philippine Institution for Development Studies.

Llanto, G., J. Abrenica, P. Reside, and L. Rufo. 1999. Government policy, regulatory and institutional framework for private participation in infrastructure. Study prepared for the Department of Finance. Unpublished paper.

Llanto, G. M., and M. C. Soriano. 1997. Government guarantees in infrastructure projects: A second, third look at the policy. Philippine Institution for Development Studies *Policy Notes* No. 97-11 (October).

Mody, A. 2000. Contingent liabilities in infrastructure: Lessons of the East Asian Crisis. May 28. Unpublished paper

Mody, A., and D. Patro. 1996. Valuing and accounting for loan guarantees. *The World Bank Research Observer* II (1): 119–42.

Comment   Jason McDonald

The issue of how governments should manage their contingent liabilities is receiving increasing attention internationally (see Polackova-Brixi and Schick 2002). Dr. Llanto's chapter contributes to this burgeoning literature with a valuable examination of government-contingent liabilities in the Philippines. The chapter analyzes the fiscal risks associated with contingent liabilities, many of which are associated with private financing arrangements of public infrastructure, and proposes some possible management solutions.

This increasing attention appears to be driven by two fiscal problems associated with governments using contingent liabilities. The first is the possibility of increasing the adverse implications of macroeconomic risks. Where such risks are not transparent, investors face increased uncertainty as to the true extent of a government's fiscal liabilities. Further, the fiscal risks inherent in contingent liabilities may be systematically related—for example, guarantees over exchange rate values in different contracts can easily crystallize at the same time. Finally, contingent liabilities have no overt budgetary constraint (unlike traditional spending) that can hinder macroeconomic control.

The second fiscal problem is the potential microeconomic distortions from government's using contingent liabilities where no market failures exist. In such cases, contingent liabilities contain an implicit subsidy (equal

Jason McDonald is the Manager of the Budget Policy Division of the Treasury of the Australian Government.

to the market value of the contingent liability less the present value of any expected cash flows to government). This subsidy occurs regardless of whether the contingent liability is called upon and becomes an outlay. The subsidy is also substitutable with other forms of government assistance— such as tax concessions or direct outlays. Governments could, for example, pay other financial institutions to take on many fiscal risks contained in contingent liabilities rather than retaining the risk themselves. All risk has its price.

However, contingent liabilities tend to be more costly policy instruments for meeting government objectives compared to traditional spending, particularly because they are less transparent. Neither of the international financial reporting standards—the International Monetary Fund's Government Finance Statistics or the Generally Accepted Accounting Principles—provide users of government financial reports with much assistance in properly valuing contingent liabilities. Since they are less transparent, governments have an incentive to provide them over traditional expenditures. Contingent liabilities are also very often difficult to measure, making them hard to rank for budgetary purposes. Sometimes they require highly specialized and costly skills to evaluate—resources likely to be scarce in the public sector of even highly developed economies. Contingent liabilities should be seen as a form of financing for government activities, like traditional debt. However, they are significantly less liquid and subject to information problems compared to debt. Contingent liabilities are worth more to a more risky recipient, leading to a severe adverse selection problem. They also have clear moral hazard problems since recipients are absolved from the responsibility of managing the risks covered by the contingent liability.

What is to be done about contingent liabilities? The chapter outlines some best-practice management practices that can be usefully adopted. Integration of debt and contingent liability management—effectively increasing central agency control of expenditure—has been persuasively suggested in other papers (for example, Currie and Velandia-Rubiano 2002). Debt managers are more likely to have the financial skills for assessing and pricing contingent liabilities (see, for example, Hagelin and Thor 2003). Improved budgetary reforms—such as provisioning and charging agencies for supplying contingent liabilities—can also change the incentives facing government agencies. Such steps can improve the information provided to government for decision making.

However, it is questionable whether many governments face sufficient incentive to reduce the use of contingent liabilities, even if they were provided with the correct financial information. Therefore a key to improved management of contingent liabilities by governments must include increased disclosure. While the chapter tends to focus on improving competition and regulation in order to reduce *demand* by businesses for contingent liabilities, increased transparency has the potential to reduce their *supply* by government.

Finally, the chapter raises an interesting question about the efficient extent of contingent liabilities provided by government. For efficiency, risks need to be distributed to those best able to manage them. Governments may be better at managing risks when they have better information. As noted in the chapter, this implies that governments should at least bear *sovereign risks*, such as those associated with governments changing policy to reap rents from large infrastructure projects. However, there is an interesting question about how much sovereign risk the government should be expected to bear if private investors choose to invest in countries with *generally* risky regulatory environments. In such cases, general regulation failure acts like a general tariff—and it is by no means certain that selective tariff exemptions (or regulatory guarantees) for specific projects will improve economic efficiency.

Overall the chapter provides an excellent benchmark for similar studies of other countries—although, while reading the chapter I wondered why so much of the information it contained was not routinely issued by all governments.

References

Currie, E., and A. Velandia-Rubiano. 2002. *Risk management of contingent liabilities within a sovereign asset-liability framework.* retrieved from http://treasury.world bank.org/Services/Public+Debt+Management/Resources/References.html
Hagelin, N., and M. Thor. 2003. Pricing of state guarantees in practice. In *Central government borrowing: Forecast and analysis*, 18–22. Stockholm: Swedish National Debt Office.
Polackova-Brixi, H., and A. Schick, eds. 2002. *Government at risk.* Washington, DC: The International Bank for Reconstruction and Development/The World Bank.

Comment   Shigeki Kunieda

Contingent liability is recognized as one of the important causes of fiscal instability in developing countries. Various measures to manage contingent liability and fiscal risk are actively discussed by international financial institutions and academic researchers (Brixi and Schick 2002).

The Llanto chapter provides a valuable survey on the Philippine contingent-liability problem (especially its depth and seriousness). The policy proposals discussed in the chapter are comprehensive and consistent

Shigeki Kunieda is an associate professor of economics at Hitotsubashi University.

with the recommendations of the recent research. I agree with the general directions of the proposals of this chapter. Here I would like to point out two issues that might be relevant in future discussions of the Philippine contingent-liability problem.

Limits of Risk Sharing by Governments

The previous argument of government's guarantee provision implicitly assumes that the government can share very large risk even if private markets cannot share the same risk. (We can call it a *deep pockets* view of the government.) However, as Bulow and Summers (1984) stress in the case of risk sharing through capital gains tax, the risk shared by the government will be ultimately shared by its taxpayers. Then, the limits of guarantee provision by government should be determined based on the taxpayers' capability of risk sharing. For example, while idiosyncratic risks can be spread efficiently among current taxpayers, economy-wide risks are difficult to be shared among current taxpayers, since every taxpayer suffers the same shocks. In some cases, temporary risks can be spread over generations by the government, since the government has special ability to impose tax on future generations. However, permanent risks are difficult to be shared even with different generations, since every generation suffers the same shocks. While the limits of risk sharing by governments are not so deeply discussed in this chapter and the other research, I would like to stress that we should take not only markets' capability of accepting risks but also the taxpayers' capability of accepting risks into consideration when we discuss the government guarantee in the Philippines or other countries.

More Active Use of Global Market Solutions

With the recent rapid development of global capital, insurance, and commodity markets, even very large risk can be shared through private markets now. For example, the risk surrounding the price volatility and availability of fuel can be shared relatively easily in international markets. With these alternative private ways for efficient risk sharing, as the *core guarantee* proposal in the chapter suggests, the Philippine government should not newly guarantee fuel and other input risk. Further, while the chapter focuses on the restrictions on new provisions of the government guarantee, the government itself can transfer the already existing risks guaranteed by it to private markets through some derivative and insurance products. In order to reduce the total risk guaranteed by the Philippine government, the transfer of the exiting risks to private markets should be considered seriously.

However, for shifting the risk of projects themselves to global investors directly, appropriate governance structure of the projects and sufficient legal protection of investors are necessary. Without these conditions, private investors prefer debt or debtlike investment supported by sufficient guarantee or collateral. Thus, the importance of the establishment of the legal and other environment providing good governance structure of projects and sufficient legal protection of investors should be stressed more in the discussion of the contingent liability in the Philippines or other developing countries.

References

Brixi, H. P., and A. Schick, eds. 2002. *Government at risk: Contingent liabilities and fiscal risk.* Washington, DC: The World Bank.
Bulow, J. I., and L. H. Summers. 1984. The taxation of risky assets. *Journal of Political Economy* 92 (1): 20–39.

9

Reforming the Fiscal Management System in Korea

Youngsun Koh

9.1 Introduction

The Korean government has maintained a strong fiscal discipline since the early 1980s, keeping its budget more or less in balance and its debt at low levels. The fiscal balance showed large deficits after the economic crisis of 1997, but returned to surplus in 2000 thanks to the buoyant economy and the resumed consolidation efforts. The surplus has continued since then.

Fiscal soundness is a characteristic common to many East-Asian countries. Little has been known, however, about the working mechanism of fiscal policies in these countries. Korea is an interesting case in this regard because there is an indication that its fiscal discipline, which was firmly established under the authoritarian government of the early 1980s, is weakening these days with the democratization of Korean politics.

In addition, the Korean government is faced with various risks that can adversely affect its financial position. The aging population and the technological catch-up with the advanced economies imply a much slower economic growth in the decades ahead. While the revenue growth slows down, the demand for public expenditure is increasing rapidly. The financial sector restructuring in the wake of economic crisis has left irretrievable debts of 69 trillion won (9 percent of 2004 GDP) in the public sector, and the burden is expected to fall mostly on taxpayers. All public pension schemes have structural problems due to the imbalance between contributions and benefits. Some of them (those for civil servants and military personnel) are already in serious trouble. The economic cooperation with North Korea

Youngsun Koh is senior research fellow, director of Macroeconomic and Financial Policies, and head of Programs Evaluation Division at the Korea Development Institute.

will demand more and more government support in the future. The spending on social welfare programs has increased substantially after the crisis, and is set to increase further.

The government expenditure has stabilized since 2001 at around 25 percent of GDP after rising rapidly in the 1990s, but it may resume its growth and result in worsening fiscal balances when these risk factors materialize. The Korean government embarked on an ambitious reform agenda to cope with these challenges and to modernize its system of financial management. Its efforts have been concentrated on (a) introducing a medium-term expenditure framework as embodied in the yearly *National Fiscal Management Plans* that cover five years on a rolling basis; (b) moving away from a bottom-up to a top-down approach in budgeting; (c) strengthening performance management; and (d) introducing *program budgeting,* that is, reorganizing budget accounts around a program structure.

This chapter aims to (a) overview the development of public finance in Korea since the 1970s and analyze its current status; (b) explain the Korean fiscal management system and outline the recent reform efforts; and (c) propose ways to improve on these reforms. It is too early to tell to what extent the newly introduced systems are contributing toward stronger aggregate fiscal discipline and greater allocative and operational efficiency. At a more fundamental level, fiscal outcomes depend on the political, social, and economic context of a nation as well as its fiscal management system. In particular, the democratization of Korean politics and the rapid population aging will play a dominant role in shaping fiscal outcomes in the future. The discussions in this chapter will hopefully help readers understand the challenges we are facing and gauge the probability of successful implementation of reforms.

9.2   Korean Public Finance in the Last Three Decades

9.2.1   Large Deficits in the 1970s

In the 1970s and into the early 1980s, the Korean government ran a persistent budget deficit (see figure 9.1). The deficit of the consolidated central government averaged about 3 percent of GDP in this period. Income transfer to the agricultural sector, heavy investment in social infrastructure, and various subsidies to promote heavy and chemical industries required large amounts of public money. But rapid economic growth helped contain the spending at around 20 percent of GDP (see figure 9.2).

9.2.2   Fiscal Tightening in the 1980s

A major change in policy stance took place in the early 1980s. The second oil shock together with political instability left Korea with spiraling inflation and negative income growth in 1980. The new government that

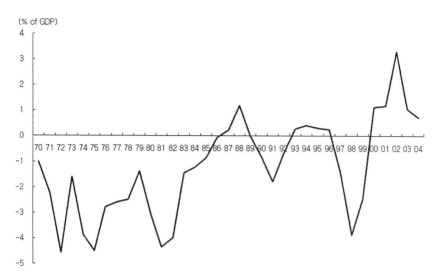

Fig. 9.1   Budget surplus/deficit of the central government
Source: Ministry of Finance and Economy.

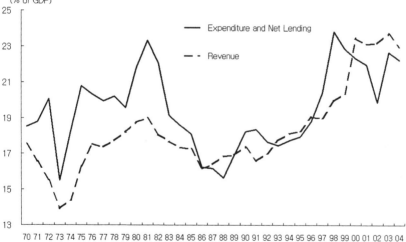

Fig. 9.2   Central government spending
Source: Ministry of Finance and Economy.

came into office in 1981 tightened monetary and fiscal policies rather drastically.[1]

1. The new government recognized the intrinsic problems of the government-led growth strategy, especially those coming from the promotion of capital-intensive industries. This strategy distorted the efficient allocation of resources, helped the formation of large business

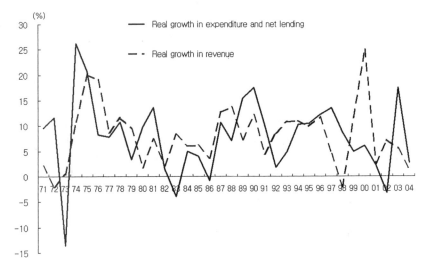

Fig. 9.3   Growth of real spending and revenue of the central government
Note: Real values were obtained by deflating nominal values with GDP deflator.
Source: Ministry of Finance and Economy.

On the monetary front, the annual growth rate of M2 was halved by the middle of the 1980s. On the fiscal front, consolidation took the form of reduced expenditure. The growth of real government spending was –3 percent in 1983, and remained at low levels until 1987 (see figure 9.3). These changes coincided with a substantial reduction in inflation. Overall, the economy grew at a healthy pace up until the recent economic crisis (see figure 9.4).

One important principle in fiscal management was established in this period. It was the principle of *Expenditure within Revenue* or the balanced budget principle. While not formalized in a law or a regulation, it acted as self-discipline imposed on the budget authorities against imprudent management of the tax money.[2]

In fact, the strong economic growth and the moderate-to-high inflation

conglomerates (the so-called *chaebol*), aggravated income inequalities, and produced macroeconomic instability. Consequently, the new government adopted "liberalization and stabilization" as its slogan for economic policy. While the stabilization policy was carried out successfully as explained in the text, the liberalization policy did not induce sufficient structural reforms in the economy. Many people think that this sowed the seed for the economic crisis of 1997.

2. One innovation during this period is worthy of note. The Budget Review Committee (BRC) was set up within the budget office in 1982 (Bahn 2003). BRC is composed of senior management of the budget office. The recommendations of budget examiners regarding the ministerial budget requests are reviewed by the BRC and then final decisions are made in sessions closed to outsiders. When faced with lobbies from line ministries and other interested parties, budget examiners find it convenient to pass the burden of budget cuts to the BRC. The BRC has been very effective in containing the spending increase and establishing fiscal discipline.

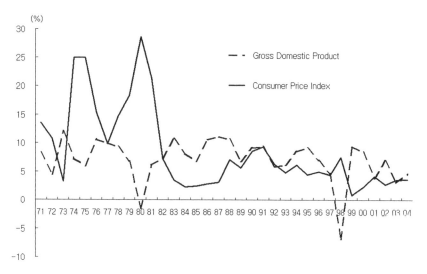

Fig. 9.4   Output growth and inflation
Source: Bank of Korea (2001).

produced larger-than-expected tax revenues in most years. This in turn made it relatively easy to keep the budget in balance. The National Pension Scheme (NPS) that was introduced in 1988 also contributed to the total revenue by 1 to 3 percent of GDP each year.[3]

The balanced budget principle kept the public debt to a minimal level. In 1996, the year before the crisis, the gross debt of the central government was less than 10 percent of GDP, and the net debt was negative; that is, the central government was a net creditor to the other sectors in the economy.[4] The local governments were generally in good shape as well.

Of course, there were costs as well as benefits associated with the balanced budget principle. Some argue that the counter-cyclical role of fiscal policy was constrained, and essential investment in social infrastructure was often postponed to contain the overall spending growth. But the Korean economy was able to achieve strong growth without much cyclical fluctuation in the decades following the adoption of the balanced budget principle.[5]

---

3. But the long-term prospect of the NPS is quite bleak. To finance the system, the contribution rate that stands currently at 9 percent will have to rise substantially in the future.
4. There are doubts, however, about the quality of government assets, which are mostly loans to private entities and local governments.
5. Specifically, the average growth rate was 7.2 percent (with a standard deviation of 3.5 percent) during 1971 to 1982 and 7.0 percent (with a standard deviation of 3.9 percent) during 1983 to 2004. The growth performance does not appear fundamentally different in these two periods. In addition, following the estimation method suggested by Bayoumi and Eichengreen (1995), a formal test can be carried out to see whether the cyclical response of the fiscal policy was weakened in the latter period. I could find no evidence for such claims.

Most importantly, strict application of the principle enabled the Korean government to keep the size of government debt at a manageable level, and provided it with room for maneuver when the crisis hit the economy. Without too much worry about the rapid explosion of the budget deficit and public debt, the Korean government could plan massive fiscal supports to troubled financial institutions. It also expanded the welfare programs for the poor and the unemployed substantially.

9.2.3   Economic Crisis and Ballooning Budget Deficit

The fiscal support to financial sector restructuring primarily took the form of loans to two public corporations—the Korean Deposit Insurance Corporation (KDIC) and the Korea Asset Management Corporation (KAMCO).[6] The loans were spent on repaying the interest on the restructuring bonds issued by these corporations. The total outstanding stock of restructuring bonds stood at 102 trillion won (21 percent of 1998 GDP).

Social welfare expenditure also increased significantly after the crisis. The unemployment rate surged from less than 3 percent in 1997 to 7 percent in 1998, with an accompanying deterioration in income distribution and an increase in poverty (see figures 9.5, 9.6, and 9.7). In response to these developments, public assistance to the poor was almost doubled.[7] The unemployment insurance scheme, which had been introduced in 1995, rapidly enlarged its coverage and increased its benefit level.

These developments left an unmistakable mark on the government finance. The consolidated budget, which remained more or less in balance before the crisis, dipped into deficit in 1998 of 4 percent of GDP. The ratio of government debt to GDP rose from 8 percent in 1996 to 15 percent in 1998 (see figure 9.8). When government debt-guarantees were included, the total public burden climbed to 30 percent of GDP. The bonds issued by the KAMCO and KDIC constitute most of these government guarantees.

Beginning in 1999, the Korean government resumed its efforts to contain the expenditure growth (see figures 9.1, 9.2, and 9.3). Aided by the dramatic rebound of the economy (see figure 9.4) and the rapid growth in revenues, the budget recorded a surplus of 1.1 percent of GDP in 2000. It remained in surplus in following years.

On the other hand, the debt-to-GDP ratio kept rising despite surpluses since 2000. This anomaly is due to the fact that these surpluses came mostly from the National Pension Fund (NPF). The surplus in NPF was 2.6 percent

---

6. The KDIC was responsible for recapitalizing underfunded institutions and paying out the deposits in closed institutions. The KAMCO sold the assets purchased from troubled financial institutions in return for the KAMCO bonds.

7. But these expenditures still take up only a small portion of the total budget compared to western countries, as the social welfare system in Korea is in its early stage of development. In the future, however, public pension benefits and other welfare spending are certain to drive up the social welfare expenditures to a level that is comparable to those in western countries.

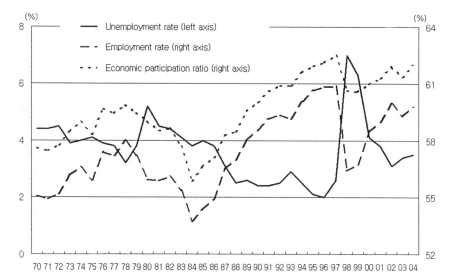

Fig. 9.5   Labor market indicators

Note: The employment rate refers to persons aged 15 and over who are employed divided by the working age population.

Source: National Statistical Office.

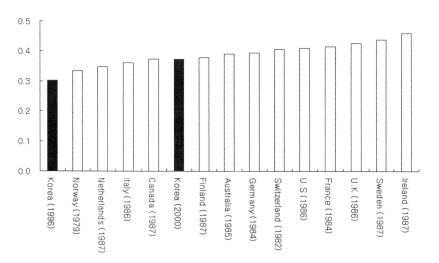

Fig. 9.6   Gini coefficient

Source: Yoo (2003).

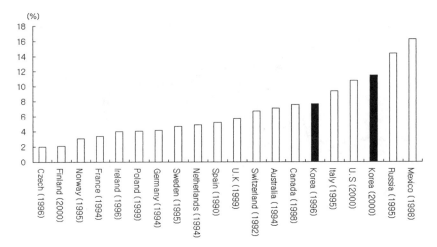

Fig. 9.7   Relative poverty

Note: The relative poverty refers to the households with incomes below 40 percent of the median household income divided by the total households.

Source: Yoo (2003).

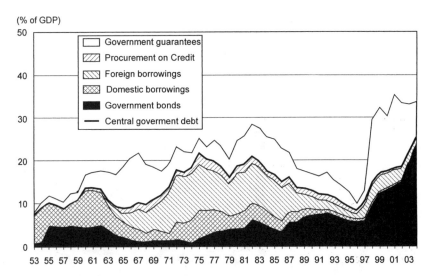

Fig. 9.8   Debt/GDP ratio

Source: 1953–90, Korea Development Institute (1991); 1991–2004, Ministry of Finance and Economy.

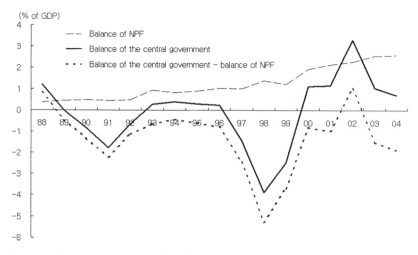

Fig. 9.9   Budget balance excluding the national pension fund
Source: Ministry of Finance and Economy.

of GDP in 2004. Most of the surpluses are used to buy assets in the financial market. These assets will be liquidated later to pay pension benefits to eligible retirees. When we exclude NPF from the consolidated budget, the government has consistently run budget deficits since 1989, except in 2002 (see figure 9.9).

9.3   Current State of Public Finance

9.3.1   Financial Balance

As shown in figure 9.9, the consolidated central government budget balance is overstated due to the surpluses in the NPF. To better assess the financial soundness of the government, we need to exclude the NPF from the consolidated balance. There are two more factors to consider in addition to the NPF in this regard. One is the net lending and the other is the repayment of restructuring bonds by the government.

The large amount of net lending has been a major factor behind large deficits in 1998 and 1999. In fact, the government lending activity has been quite extensive since the early days of government-led economic growth (see figure 9.10). The official statistics show that the default rate on government loans is close to 0 percent.[8] If this is true, loans do not reflect any

8. But it should be noted that the actual deficit rate may be higher. After all, the government has frequently introduced rescheduling programs for agricultural loans.

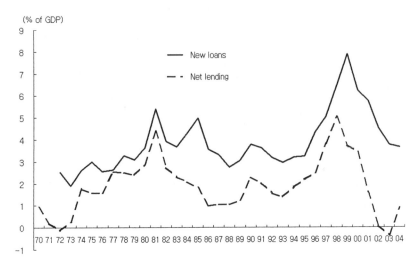

Fig. 9.10   Central government loans
Source: Ministry of Finance and Economy.
Note: Net lending equals new loans minus repayments.

deterioration of the government asset position, and we should disregard the net lending when assessing the financial health of the government.[9]

One exception is the government loans made to the KDIC and KAMCO. In 2002, the government announced a plan to exempt the KDIC and KAMCO from repaying the loans to the government. This decision essentially converted the loans into direct spending in the years they were made. The total amount exempted was 22 trillion won. We include these loans in the consolidated budget balance in the following discussion.

In addition to the loan cancellation, the government is sharing with the KDIC and KAMCO the obligation on restructuring bonds. According to the government estimates, the irretrievable loss incurred during financial sector restructuring would amount to 69 trillion won. The government announced that it would take up a total of 49 trillion won of restructuring bonds, repaying their interest and principal. In 2003, 13 trillion won was spent on transforming part of these bonds into government bonds. The figure for 2004 to 2006 is 12 trillion won each year. As these expenditures mirror the results of past restructuring activities, we exclude them from the consolidated balance in 2003 to 2006 and include them in 1997 to 2002.

Table 9.1 shows the results of these adjustments. The adjusted balance is

9. To be precise, the subsidy cost of loans emerging from the disparity between market interest rates and concessional lending rates should be included in government expenditures. With no reliable estimates on the subsidy cost, however, I decided to simply ignore it.

Table 9.1   Consolidated budget balance and its adjustment

	1998	1999	2000	2001	2002	2003	2004	2005ᵃ
Consolidated balance	–18.8	–13.1	6.5	7.3	22.7	7.6	5.6	5.6
	(–3.9)	(–2.5)	(1.1)	(1.2)	(3.3)	(1.1)	(0.7)	(0.7)
NPF balance	6.7	6.5	11.2	13.3	15.6	18.5	20.2	24.4
	(1.4)	(1.2)	(1.9)	(2.1)	(2.3)	(2.6)	(2.6)	(2.9)
Net lending	24.4	19.8	19.8	10.1	0.4	–2.5	1.4	6.4
Loans to KDIC and KAMCO	1.3	4.0	5.6	6.0	6.9			
Issuance of restructuring bondsᵇ	15.8	9.8	4.6	16.0	1.9			
Assumption of restructuring bonds						13.0	12.0	12.0
Adjusted balanceᶜ	–18.2	–13.6	5.0	18.0	–1.3	–0.4	–1.1	0.3
	(–3.8)	(–2.6)	(0.9)	(–2.9)	(–0.2)	(–0.1)	(–0.2)	(0.0)

Note: Numbers in parentheses are a percentage of GDP. All other numbers are in trillions of won.
ᵃThe figures for 2005 are based on budget.
ᵇIssuance of restructuring bonds is based on the assumption that out of 49 trillion won, 2.1 percent was issued in 1997, 32.2 in 1998, 19.9 in 1999, 9.4 in 2000, 32.6 in 2001, and 3.8 in 2002, which are the shares of total restructuring bonds issued in 1997 to 2002.
ᶜAdjusted balance = consolidated balance – NPF balance + net lending – loans to KDIC and KAMCO – issuance of restructuring bonds + assumption of restructuring bonds.

close to the consolidated balance in 1998 to 2000 but much lower than in 2001 to 2005. For example, in 2004, the balance declines from 5.6 trillion (0.7 percent of GDP) to –1.1 trillion won (–0.2 percent of GDP) after the adjustment. But they have been within ±0.5 percent of GDP since 2001, and we can still say that the financial soundness of the government is not a very serious problem at this stage.

9.3.2   Government Liabilities

Another indicator for the soundness of public finance is government liabilities. The debt-to-GDP ratio amounted to 25 percent at the end of 2004 (see figure 9.5). When government guarantees are included, it rises to 34 percent. The transformation of restructuring bonds is reducing the amount of guarantees at the expense of direct liabilities. But with the *adjusted balance* remaining close to zero, the total public burden including direct liabilities and guarantees is stabilizing at 33 to 34 percent of GDP. If an appropriate amount of control is exercised on the spending growth, the total burden will remain at the current level in the years ahead.

9.3.3   The Size of Government Expenditure

Of course, it is not certain at all whether we would be able to contain the spending growth successfully in the future. Figure 9.11 shows the consoli-

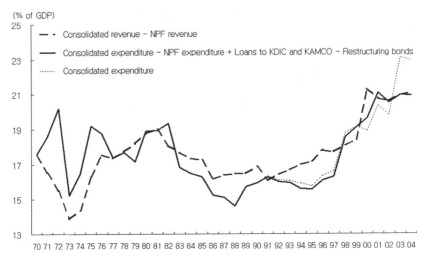

Fig. 9.11   Adjusted revenue and expenditure
Source: Ministry of Finance and Economy.

dated central government expenditure and the adjusted expenditure. Here the adjustment was made in the same way as in table 9.1 (subtracting the NPF expenditure, moving forward the repayment of restructuring bonds to earlier years, and adding the loans to the KDIC and KAMCO). The consolidated expenditure has been increasing rapidly since the mid-1990s. Unless conscious efforts are made to contain it, the spending growth is likely to produce persistent deficits and rising government liabilities in the future.

Of particular importance are the public pension schemes such as the National Pension Scheme (NPS), the Government Employees' Pension Scheme (GPES), the Private School Teachers' Pension Scheme (PSTPS), and the Military Personnel Pension Scheme (MPPS). These pension schemes share one common feature—too generous benefits in relation to contributions. With rapidly aging population (see figure 9.12), this imbalance has produced and will continue to produce devastating effects on their finance.[10]

In addition to pensions, health spending will increase rapidly with the aging population. All in all, the age-related spending will rise from 5 percent of GDP in 2004 to 25 to 30 percent in 2070 according to a projection by the Korean Institute of Public Finance (see figure 9.13).

Increased spending on pensions and other age-related spending will

---

10. MPPS has been in deficits over 10 years and requires government supports of about 1 trillion won each year. GPES entered into deficit in 2001, and the deficit is expected to grow exponentially in coming years. PSTPS has basically the same problem but will experience difficulties in later years. NPS, with its huge coverage, can become a major drain on government budget.

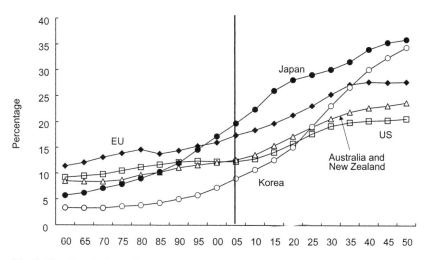

Fig. 9.12   Population aging
Source: United Nations.

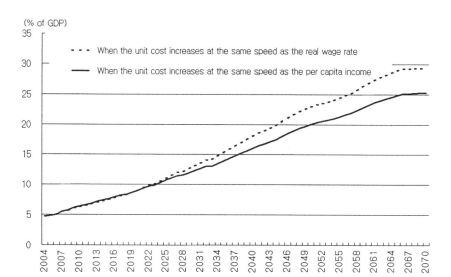

Fig. 9.13   Projected age-related spending
Source: Korea Institute of Public Finance (2005).

drive up the total size of government expenditure. Table 9.2 compares the general government spending across six countries including Korea. In 2000, the spending-to-GDP ratio was 23.0 percent in Korea and ranged between 30 and 50 percent in other countries. But when income transfers are excluded, the ratio declines to 19.4 percent in Korean and 20 to 30 percent in other countries. In particular, the United States has a lower ratio than

Table 9.2   General government expenditures (% of GDP)

	U.S.	Japan	Germany	France	U.K.	Korea
Consumption	15.1	16.8	19.0	23.3	19.4	10.1
Net capital outlays	0.9	6.0	3.0	3.3	2.2	8.3
Income transfers	13.7	10.0	18.9	17.8	13.7	3.6
Subsidies	0.5	0.9	1.6	1.2	0.5	0.3
Interest payments	3.4	3.3	3.3	3.2	2.4	0.7
Total	31.2	37.0	45.7	48.8	38.2	23.0
Excluding income transfers	(17.5)	(27.0)	(26.8)	(31.0)	(24.5)	(19.4)

Source: OECD (2003).
Note: The data for Japan and Korea refer to year 2000. Others refer to year 2001.

Korea. With the increase in age-related expenditures in Korea, the gap between Korea and other countries will diminish in the future.[11]

Containing the spending growth is critical in attaining fiscal sustainability. It will gain greater importance in the future as the growth potential of the Korean economy declines. Han and others (2002) forecast the potential income to grow at a much slower rate in coming years (see table 9.3). Its growth rate already declined from 7.7 percent in the 1970s to 5.6 percent in the 1990s, and will decline further to 5.1 percent in 2000 to 2005 and to 4.2 percent in 2005 to 2010, primarily due to the slower growth of labor force. In fact, the total population is expected to shrink in absolute numbers beginning in around 2030.

The slower economic growth will imply a slower growth in tax revenue. Expanding government expenditures at the same rate as in previous years is likely to produce widening deficits, accelerate the decline in national saving, hamper the fixed capital formation, and further reduce the growth potential.

9.3.4 Functional Classification of Expenditures

Government expenditures can be classified in various ways. Table 9.4 shows the functional classification of the central government expenditure and net lending in Korea. Defense spending declined rapidly in the 1980s and 1990s and now corresponds to 11.4 percent of total spending. Education has traditionally taken up a large share (15 to 17 percent) of total spending, but an even larger share has been allocated to economic affairs (20 to 28 percent). Among the economic affairs, agriculture and transportation have been the major items of spending. On the other hand, social

11. It is interesting to note in table 9.2 the relatively small size of government consumption in Korea. It stands at 10.1 percent of GDP. This seems mainly due to the small size of public employment in Korea. On the other hand, government investment as a percentage of GDP is larger in Korea than in other countries except Japan.

Table 9.3   Forecasts of national income (%)

	1963–70	1970–79	1979–90	1990–2000	2000–05	2005–10
Growth in national income	8.94	7.67	7.29	5.61	5.14	4.17
Contributions from:						
Inputs	4.35	4.23	4.80	3.00	2.85	2.06
Labor	3.67	3.06	2.90	1.60	1.28	0.89
Workers	3.44	2.90	2.39	1.28	1.21	0.82
Capital	0.68	1.17	1.90	1.40	1.57	1.17
Total factor productivity	4.59	3.44	2.49	2.61	2.29	2.11

Source: Han et al. (2002).

protection has received relatively little attention in budgetary spending though its share is growing rapidly in recent years.

The concentration of spending on economic affairs may reflect the less-developed-country status of Korea. Perhaps we still need large investment in roads, ports, and railways. Perhaps we still need to provide large government loans to the agricultural, manufacturing, and construction sectors because the financial market is not yet fully developed. But there are strong doubts about these assumptions.

First, the rapid increase in spending on social infrastructure during the 1990s need not be sustained in the future. Many (but certainly not all) experts in this area agree that, with the ever-stringent budget constraint and the completion of major road-building programs, it is time to reorganize the overall investment strategy. In particular, we should pay more attention to the demand-management (e.g., through an increased use of user-charging) and the proper maintenance of existing stocks of infrastructure.

Second, the Korean financial market has undergone a rapid change since the 1980s and especially after the economic crisis. Banks are rapidly expanding their lending to households and small- and medium-sized enterprises, and large corporations are turning ever more to capital (stock and bond) markets. The government appears to be playing a substitutive, rather than complementary, role to commercial banks in many cases. It is now generally believed that the government should reduce its role as a provider of financial resources for businesses. The reduced government role in this area will not only help restrain the growth of public spending but also promote the development of private financial markets and reduce the distortion in resource allocation.

On the other hand, the government should increase its effort in the provision of basic public service such as security and safety, fire-fighting, judicial services, promotion of competitive business practices, prudential regulation of financial institutions, statistical services, environmental protection, and so on. These services are vital for the long-term economic growth and social development. Unfortunately, their importance has been

Table 9.4   Central government expenditure and net lending

	Percentage of GDP					Percentage of total spending				
	1970	1980	1990	2000	2003	1970	1980	1990	2000	2003
General public services	3.9	0.8	0.7	1.1	1.4	23.1	4.0	4.2	5.2	6.7
Defense	3.8	6.1	3.6	2.5	2.5	22.7	30.6	20.0	11.4	11.4
Public order and safety	0.0	0.9	0.8	1.0	1.1	0.0	4.6	4.3	4.6	5.3
Education	2.8	2.9	3.0	3.3	3.3	16.7	14.6	17.0	15.3	15.0
Health	0.2	0.2	0.3	0.2	0.1	1.3	1.0	1.7	0.7	0.4
Social protection	0.8	1.1	1.4	3.3	2.9	4.9	5.7	8.1	15.3	13.5
Housing and community amenities	0.0	0.5	1.8	1.2	1.1	0.3	2.5	10.1	5.3	5.0
Recreation, culture, and religion	0.2	0.1	0.1	0.2	0.3	1.4	0.7	0.5	0.8	1.2
Economic affairs	4.6	5.1	3.6	5.5	6.2	27.4	26.0	20.4	25.2	28.7
Fuel and energy	0.6	0.4	0.1	0.1	0.4	3.8	2.1	0.6	0.7	1.8
Agriculture, forestry, fishing, and hunting	1.9	1.2	1.8	1.4	1.4	11.2	5.9	10.2	6.2	6.7
Mining, manufacturing, and construction	−0.5	1.5	0.4	0.6	1.0	−3.0	7.4	2.0	2.6	4.5
Transportation and communication	1.3	1.3	1.1	2.2	2.0	7.9	6.7	6.1	9.9	9.3
Other economic affairs	1.3	0.8	0.2	1.3	1.4	7.5	3.9	1.4	5.8	6.5
Other expenditures	0.4	2.1	2.4	3.5	2.8	2.2	10.4	13.7	16.2	12.8
Total	17.0	19.8	17.8	21.9	21.7	100.0	100.0	100.0	100.0	100.0

Source: Ministry of Finance and Economy.

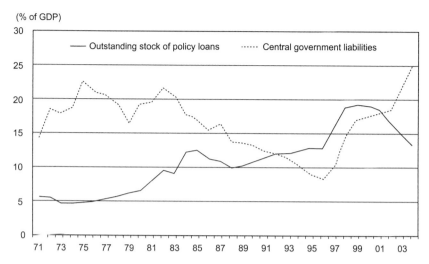

Fig. 9.14   Government assets and liabilities
Source: Ministry of Finance and Economy.

generally understated to this day in Korea. For example, competition policy is still at its early stage of development. Statistical services also have large room for improvement, as illustrated by the lack of reliable data on gross regional product even though the government has historically emphasized the importance of mitigating regional disparities.

At the same time, more efforts are needed to reduce the outstanding stock of government loans. Figure 9.14 shows that in 1997 to 1999, government loans grew by about the same amount as government liabilities. That is, the government issued bonds and other debt instruments and used the proceeds to extend loans to the private sector. The trend was reversed in recent years, but the outstanding stock of loans still stood at 13 percent of GDP at the end of 2004.

Government loans typically have maturity of 5 to 10 years while most of government bonds have maturity of less than 5 years. The interest rates on loans are lower than those on government bonds. Such differences in maturities and interest rates impose a financial burden on the government over longer terms.

9.4   Institutional Setup and Reform Efforts in Korea

9.4.1   The Structure of the Budget

General Accounts, Special Accounts, and Funds

The budget of the central government as voted on in the National Assembly is comprised of one general account and various special accounts.

There were a total of 23 special accounts in the fiscal year 2005 budget (see table 9.5). Revenue sources for the general account include general-purpose (not ear-marked) taxes and nontax revenues. On the other hand, many special accounts have their own special ear-marked taxes or quasi-taxes (i.e., fees, charges, and other mandatory contributions). Transfers from the general account also make up a large portion of resources for special accounts.

On a consolidated basis, the central government budget includes, in addition to the general and special accounts, numerous funds. There were 57 funds in 2005 including the National Pension Fund, the Employment Insurance Fund, and the Foreign Exchange Stabilization Fund. These funds were established much like special accounts to achieve specific policy objectives, and many of them have their own revenue sources including quasi-taxes.[12]

The difference between the funds and the general and special accounts lies in the managerial flexibility allowed for the former. Ministries can freely change fund expenditures within 30 percent of the planned amount without notice to the budget authorities and the National Assembly (see table 9.6). The line items in the operational plans of funds are much less detailed than those in the general and special accounts. Their cash flows are managed independently by line ministries and do not pass through the treasury single account held in the Bank of Korea.

The general account, special accounts, and funds form the consolidated central government budget (see figure 9.15). The share of general account in the total consolidated expenditure and net lending stood at 55 percent in 2004, and those for special accounts and funds at 16 percent and 29 percent, respectively.[13]

Drawbacks

The highly complex structure of the budget has been criticized in many aspects.[14] First, it limits the ability of the budget authorities to centralize all national resources and then allocate them based on national priority. As mentioned previously, special accounts and various funds have their own sources of revenue, which are not easily transferable to the general account or any other special accounts and funds in response to changing circum-

---

12. There were 101 quasi-taxes for special accounts and funds at the end of 2001 and their total revenue was estimated to be around 1 percent of GDP (OECD 2003).

13. The U.S. federal government also has a large number of trust funds, special funds, and public enterprise funds in addition to the general fund (U.S. GAO 2001). In 1999, the spending of the funds other than the general fund corresponded to around 55 percent of total federal spending. But most of them (33 out of 55 percent) represented *long-term commitments* such as social security. In the case of Korea, *long-term commitments* occupy only about 10 percent of total spending.

14. There is much similarity between the Korean and the Japanese budget system. See Bayoumi (1998) for the Japanese system.

Table 9.5   Special accounts

Fiscal financing	Environmental reconstruction
National property management	National medical center management
Agriculture and fisheries structural	Land management and balanced regional
adjustment	development
Rural development tax management	Postal insurance service
Transportation facilities	Automobile traffic management
Registration	Patent management
Management of funds transferred to	Balanced national development
local governments	Grain management
Prison operation	Agency
Military personnel pension	National railroad
Management of funds transferred to local	Communication service
educational agencies	Government procurement
Energy and resources	

Table 9.6   Characteristics of the general account, special accounts, and funds

	General account	Special accounts	Funds
Objective	Supporting general fiscal activities.	Supporting specific programs.	Supporting specific programs.
Revenues	General-purpose taxes and nontax revenues.	Ear-marked taxes, mandatory contributions, transfers from other accounts and funds, etc.	Mandatory contributions, transfers from other accounts and funds, etc.
Expenditures	Unrequited expenditures.	Unrequited expenditures and loans.	Unrequited expenditures and loans.
Linkages between revenues and expenditures	None.	Clear linkages.	Clear linkages.
Authorization and execution of expenditure plans	Voted on in the National Assembly. Controlled and monitored during execution as mandated by the Constitution.	Same as general account.	Same as general account but larger flexibility guaranteed in implementation.[a]

Ministries can change fund expenditures within 30 percent of the planned amount without notice to the budget authorities and the National Assembly. Cash flows are managed independently by the ministries in charge and do not go through the treasury single account held in the Bank of Korea. Unlimited carry-overs of unused cash are allowed.

stances. This compartmentalization and fragmentation of resources reduces the allocative efficiency of the budget.

Second, fiscal transparency and program efficiency are also undermined by the complicated budget structure. Various accounts and funds are intricately interrelated through complicated flow of grants and loans. It is difficult to see how much funding is being allocated to various spending areas. The functional classification of spending is not reported for the consolidated budget, and it is reported only for the previous year's outturns with

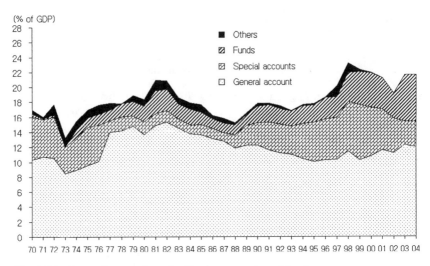

(% of GDP)

- Others
- Funds
- Special accounts
- General account

70 71 72 73 74 75 76 77 78 79 80 81 82 83 84 85 86 87 88 89 90 91 92 93 94 95 96 97 98 99 00 01 02 03 04

Fig. 9.15   Expenditure and net lending by accounts and funds
Source: Ministry of Finance and Economy.

a considerable time-lag of more than a year. We can find many programs with similar policy objectives and tools but under different accounts and funds. Consolidating similar programs would contribute to greater allocative and technical efficiency with increased transparency.

Government Efforts

The government is making efforts to simplify the budget structure and strengthen transparency and accountability. The most important change occurred with the revision of the Fund Management Act and the National Assembly Act in 2001. Previously, there were two types of funds—"public funds" and "other funds." The operational plans of "public funds" were prepared by responsible ministries and reported to the National Assembly but did not require the latter's approval. Those of "other funds" were not even reported to the National Assembly. In this sense, public and other funds were off-budget accounts.

In 2001, they were regrouped into "funds" and "financial funds." "Funds" include all of the previous "public funds" and some of "other funds." "Funds" were moved from off-budget to on-budget: the operational plans of "funds" now require the approval by the National Assembly and their financial reports are submitted to the latter, just like the general account and special accounts.[15] In 2004, further changes were made to move "financial

15. This change in typology produced discontinuity in the time series of fiscal data. Before 2001, the consolidated spending and revenue data included "public funds" and excluded "other funds." After 2001, they include "funds" and exclude "financial funds." As a result, several important funds such as the Teachers' Pension Fund are now included in the consol-

funds" from off-budget to on-budget and subject them to the same degree of control by the National Assembly.

The government also introduced a review process in the Fund Management Act to abolish obsolete funds and consolidate those with similar objectives. The first such review was conducted in 2004 and subsequent reviews are scheduled every three years in the future.[16] In addition, a separate, ad hoc review was conducted on special accounts in 2004. The results of these two reviews were presented to the president in May 2005 in a combined report and received his approval. The government is in the process of revising various laws that provide legal bases for individual special accounts and funds. It remains to be seen how many of the recommendations will survive the opposition from diverse interest groups and succeed in the revision of relevant laws.

The past experience does not offer a very good prospect. The number of funds declined from 114 in 1994 to 53 in 2002 but since then has stayed at around 55 (see table 9.7) despite the government's effort to reduce it further. A few special accounts were to be closed down in past years (the Transportation and the Registration Special Accounts in 2003 and the Rural Development Tax Management Special Account in 2004). But the pressure from interest groups saved their lives and none were closed down.

On the other hand, a series of new initiatives that are recently being introduced—the medium-term expenditure framework, top-down budgeting, performance management, and program budgeting—are expected to reduce the line ministries' incentives to secure funding through special accounts and funds and to help MPB in improving the allocative and operational efficiency of spending. More will be discussed in the following on these initiatives.

9.4.2   Major Players and the Fiscal Discipline

Major Players

Major players in the budget process include the Ministry of Planning and Budget (MPB), the Ministry of Finance and Economy (MOFE), and the Board of Audit and Inspection (BAI, see table 9.8). MPB is responsible for preparing the draft budget with the help of the Tax and Customs Office in MOFE that provides revenue forecasts. When the budget is authorized by the National Assembly, MPB prepares the quarterly budget implementation plans usually within a month and allocates funds to line ministries.

---

idated financial statistics. But no attempt has been made to revise previous data to eliminate discontinuity.

16. These reviews are called *Retention Reviews.* Apart from the Retention Review, the government has also been conducting annual *Management Reviews* since 1999. Management Reviews look at the operational efficiency of funds, including the adequacy of their asset management practices.

Table 9.7   **Number of funds**

	1994	1995	1996	1997	1998	1999	2000	2001	2002	2003	2004	2005
At the start of the year	114	106	99	76	75	76	75	62	53	58	59	
Established during the year	6	4	4	3	3	2	2	1	8	3	2	57
Closed during the year	−14	−11	−27	−4	−2	−3	−16	−8	−4	−2	−4	
At the end of the year	106	99	76	75	76	75	61	53	58	59	57	

Source: Ministry of Planning and Budget (2005).
Note: Includes public and other funds before 2002 and funds and financial funds since then.

Table 9.8   **Major players in Korea's budget process**

Players	Roles
Ministry of Planning and Budget (MPB)	• Compiles budget bids and prepares the draft budget. • Allocates funds to spending ministries (apportionment). • Approves the transfers of funds between line items (virements).
Treasury Bureau of the Ministry of Finance and Economy (MOFE)	• Releases cash to spending ministries. • Manages the treasury single account held in the Bank of Korea. • Issues treasury bonds and manages assets and liabilities. • Collects ministerial financial reports, prepares the whole-of-government financial reports, and sends them to the BAI. • Produces the government financial statistics.
Tax and Customs Office of MOFE	• In charge of tax policy. • Prepares revenue forecasts. • Oversees the National Tax Service and the Customs Service.
Ministry of Government Administration and Home Affairs (MOGAHA)	• In charge of local government tax and spending policies. • Allocates the Local Shared Taxes (a formula-based block grant) to local governments. • Coordinates the central government subsidies to local governments. • Approves the borrowing by individual local governments.
Board of Audit and Inspection (BAI)	• The supreme audit institution in Korea, whose head is nominated by and reports to the president. The National Assembly can also request audits on specific issues to the BAI. • Checks the regularity of ministerial activities. • Prepares and tables the financial report to the National Assembly.
National Assembly	• Deliberates and votes on the budget. • Approves the transfers of funds between programs. • Reviews and approves audit reports.
Spending ministries	• Execute the budget and prepare financial reports.

The Treasury Bureau of MOFE then prepares the monthly cash plans and releases cash to line ministries. The Treasury Bureau keeps track of cash flows into and from the treasury single account held in the Bank of Korea. It is also responsible for issuing government bonds and managing government assets and liabilities.

An important issue concerning the interplay among various players is that of fiscal discipline. The budget process in Korea has generally taken a highly centralized, strategic dominance-based approach in the terminology of von Hagen and Harden (1996). These authors distinguish between two approaches in budgeting. Under *a target-based approach,* the government collectively negotiates a set of binding, numerical targets for the budget. The budget process starts with negotiations among concerned parties over binding limits on the spending total or budget deficits. Once these limits have been agreed upon, they must be observed during the remainder of the budget process. On the other hand, under *a strategic dominance-based approach,* the budget process vests the budget authorities with special strategic powers. Often the main budgeting decisions are made in bilateral negotiations between the budget authorities and spending ministries.

The 1970s and 1980s

In the 1970s and 1980s, the Economic Planning Board (EPB) played a central role in budgeting as well as in preparing and implementing economic development plans. EPB was the leading ministry within government, as reflected in the title of the head of EPB as deputy prime minister. Negotiations over spending bids were conducted bilaterally between the deputy prime minister and spending ministers. Little reconciliation occurred in the cabinet regarding the draft budget prepared by the deputy prime minister.

The authoritarian nature of previous governments also limited the role of the National Assembly in the deliberation of draft budget. The National Assembly has been traditionally dominated by the party of the president. Insofar as the government had already consulted the ruling party before presenting the draft budget to the National Assembly, amendments typically entailed minor changes in the budget (see figure 9.16). In addition, the constitution prohibits the National Assembly from increasing the total spending or introducing new spending items unless agreed on by the government.

EPB also exercised tight control on expenditures in the implementation stage. Ministries were required to spend within the limits set in the quarterly budget implementation plan. EPB could postpone or block part of the expenditures (those classified as *discretionary allocation items*) when deemed necessary. All limits on expenditures were imposed in cash terms. Transfers across appropriation accounts (*virements*) were prohibited un-

(% of draft budget)

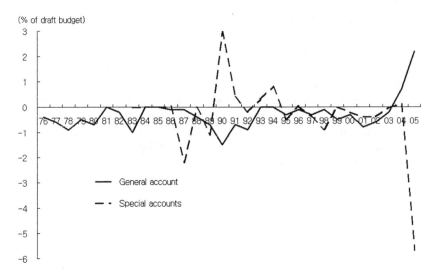

Fig. 9.16   Budget amendments
Source: Ministry of Planning and Budget (2005).

less authorized by the National Assembly or by EPB. In addition, supplementary budgets were normally introduced only once a year.

The Treasury Bureau of MOFE also had a tight grip on cash outflow. All cash disbursements were made strictly within the limits set in the monthly cash plans. Before the crisis of 1997, it was not uncommon for the Treasury Bureau to delay disbursements to line ministries when there was not enough cash left in the treasury account due to the seasonality in tax collection. This was in spite of the fact that they could issue short-term debt instruments within the limit set by the National Assembly to bridge the gap between tax collection and cash needs. In addition, the revenue forecasts prepared by the Tax and Customs Office were often very conservative with the actual tax collection overshooting the forecast by substantial margins.

The 1990s and After

Most of these characteristics carried over until recently. In the early 1990s, EPB and the Ministry of Finance were merged into the Ministry of Finance and Economy (MOFE), and the deputy prime minister-ship was handed over to the head of the MOFE.[17] The latter exercised the same degree of centralizing power in budgeting as the head of the EPB (see figure 9.17).

But the recent reorganization in government resulted in a subtle change

17. This merger signaled the official closing of the *planning-based development era.* At the same time, the newly established Korea Fair Trade Commission took charge of competition policies in place of EPB, and the evaluation function of EPB was moved to the prime minister's office.

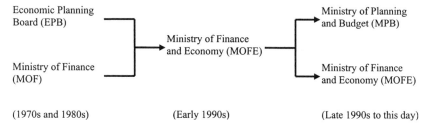

Fig. 9.17   Organizational change in the budgeting function

in the budget process. After the economic crisis, the budgeting function was separated from MOFE and moved to the newly created MPB.[18] Previously, the EPB and then the MOFE had the formal role in setting the overall policy agenda and coordinating activities across the government. After the reorganization, the coordination role together with the prime ministership was kept in the MOFE, and the MPB was devoid of such functions.[19] All these factors can act to reduce the centralizing power of MPB. In addition, the balance of power between the executive branch and the legislature is tipping toward the latter with the democratization of Korean politics.

Assessment

There is not yet a visible sign that these changes have weakened the centralizing power of MPB and the fiscal discipline substantially. But the risk is increasing, as illustrated for example in the increasing number of annual supplementary budgets after the crisis (see figure 9.18). In most cases, the supplementary budgets were introduced to stimulate the economy.

We also observe some changes in the cash management and revenue forecast practices in the post-crisis period. To bridge the gap between tax collection and cash needs, and to finance the front-loading[20] of annual spending that has been popular since 1999, MOFE is resorting more and more to short-term debt issues. The downward bias in revenue forecasts is

18. Before the separation, MOFE was a super-ministry in charge of general economic policy coordination, macroeconomic policies, budget preparation, tax policies, financial market policies, external economic relations, and treasury function. Many believed that the lack of check-and-balance as seen in the previous periods between EPB and MOF, together with the unmanageably large span of control of the Minister for Finance and Economy, veered economic policy-making off the right track, and contributed to the outbreak of financial crisis. The focus of criticism was laid on the bureau of financial market policies within MOFE, which was subsequently reduced in size and whose regulatory function was transferred to the newly created Financial Supervisory Commission. In addition, the Bank of Korea was granted instrumental independence from MOFE.

19. Compared to EPB's responsibilities, MPB's exclude economic policy coordination, external economic relations, and competition policies.

20. In front-loading exercises, MPB would allocate more funds than usual to the first half of the year, and urge line ministries to spend the allocated funds as early as possible. When necessary, that is when the growth is slower than expected despite front-loading, MPB would consider introducing a supplementary budget in the latter half of the year.

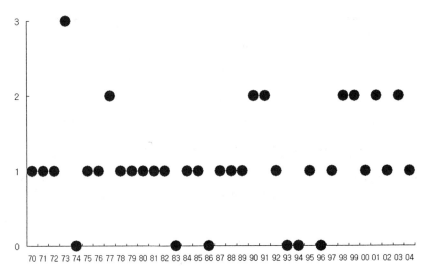

Fig. 9.18   Number of supplementary budgets introduced
Source: Ministry of Planning and Budget (2005).

also being reduced. In 2004, we actually had a large shortfall in tax collection, which was partly blamed on an overly optimistic assumption on the economic growth, which was in turn claimed by some to have been politically motivated.

Part of these changes look inevitable. The democratization of the Korean politics and the devolution of budgetary power to line ministries are an unavoidable trend. The separation of budgeting function from policy coordination function was intended to reduce the concentration of powers in one large *dinosaur* ministry (Ministry of Finance and Economy) that is believed to have contributed to the outbreak of the financial crisis. Utilizing short-term debt instruments to neutralize the impact of seasonality in tax collection is in itself a desirable practice.

But it is also true that there is an increasing risk of overspending and weakened fiscal discipline. We are in need of a new system of expenditure management that can cope with such a risk, for example by gradually moving away from strategic-dominance approach toward target-based approach. The medium-term expenditure framework (MTEF) is one such option. Under MTEF, the budget authorities prepare annual budgets with a medium-term perspective in a top-down way. More will be discussed in the following on the MTEF.

9.4.3   The Budget Process

Before the Introduction of the MTEF

The budget process in the Korean central government has undergone a significant change in recent years. The government introduced the MTEF together with a top-down budgeting in 2004 for fiscal year 2005.[21] The budget process before the change is summarized in table 9.9.

The recent reform was intended to address several defects found in the previous budgeting practice. First, prior to the introduction of the MTEF, budgeting was centered on the next single budget year, lacking a medium-term perspective. MPB and the National Assembly gave little consideration to the out-years beyond the budget year. Line ministries had little information on how much resource would be available to them in the future, and their medium- to long-term planning function was severely limited. Limited planning function in turn reduced the effectiveness and efficiency of overall public spending.

It was also difficult for MPB to identify and cope with the trend increase in spending. Without a long-term view on the appropriate level of tax burden, MPB would simply allow an ever-increasing public spending to accommodate rising demands from various sectors. The focus on a single budget year also fostered incrementalism in budgeting and hindered a strategic reprioritization of spending.

In addition, the counter-cyclical role of fiscal policy could be constrained when the attention was focused on a single year. The principle of *balanced budget in each year* had the potential to produce a procyclical fluctuation in spending as illustrated in panel (a) of figure 9.19. If, on the other hand, spending increases at a constant rate as in panel (b) and the balanced budget is pursued on average over the business cycle, the so-called *automatic stabilizer* can be given a full force.

Second, before the introduction of the top-down process, budgeting relied excessively on a bottom-up approach. At the initial stage of budget preparation, MPB made rough estimates of the total size and the sectoral allocation of the next year's budget. But the estimates were not transmitted to line ministries and therefore could not guide line ministries in preparing their budget requests. When reviewing their budget requests, MPB focused on the microscopic spending control of individual programs. The sectoral allocation and the total size of the budget were determined at the last stage of budget preparation by aggregating the expenditures on individual programs.

As a result, the control of inputs assumed a major significance in budget discussions and little attention was paid to outputs or outcomes. Absorbed

---

21. Potter and Diamond (1999), Schiavo-Campo and Tommasi (1999), and World Bank (1998) provide a useful guide on the reform in this direction.

Table 9.9   Key steps of the budget process before the introduction of the MTEF

	Action
January	• The fiscal year starts on January 1st.
March	• The Ministry of Planning and Budget (MPB) sends the Guide to Budget Compilation to spending ministries.
May	• Ministries send budget bids to MPB by the end of May.
June–July	• MPB compiles the budget bids and prepares a preliminary budget proposal.
August–September	• MPB goes through bilateral negotiations with spending ministries between mid-August and mid-September.
	• MPB discusses the budget proposal with the ruling party.
October	• Authorized by the cabinet and the president, the draft budget is sent to the National Assembly by October 2nd.
	• In mid-October, the Committee on Budget and Accounts begins deliberation on the draft budget. Ministries are typically requested to testify at committee meetings. Meetings are normally open to the public.
December	• The draft budget is modified and approved by the Committee on Budget and Accounts and finally by the National Assembly by December 2nd.

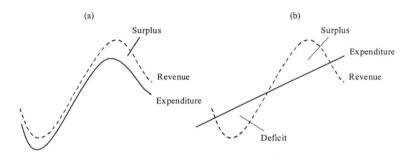

Fig. 9.19   Management of spending over the business cycles

in details, MPB had little time to review and analyze important policy issues, and the linkage between budgeting and policy making was very weak. The budget negotiation between MPB and line ministries was a very time-consuming process for both parties. The accountability and autonomy of line ministries in preparing and managing their budget were also severely limited. Line ministries usually requested an unrealistically large amount of budget, and massive cuts by MPB were inevitable.

A third characteristic of the previous budgeting practice was the central stage accorded to the general account. MPB spent most of its efforts on reviewing and preparing the budget of the general account and paid less attention to special accounts and funds.

The previous approach had certain merits. The budget authorities had large discretion over the annual spending and used their power to contain the spending growth and adjust it to changing revenue conditions. To some degree, such short-termism was inevitable in Korea where the socioeconomic environment changes quite rapidly and unexpectedly. In addition, by emphasizing the input control and the regularity of budget execution, the abuse or misuse of tax money could be minimized. But the growing size and complexity of budget is making it necessary for MPB to deregulate the budgeting process, enhance autonomy and accountability of line ministries, and focus on the strategic management of public finance.

After the Introduction of the MTEF

With the introduction of the MTEF and the top-down budgeting, all these practices are changing. Now the annual budgeting exercise starts with a discussion on fiscal policy over a five-year period including the current year, the budget year, and three out-years. Following this discussion, MPB transmits spending ceilings for sectors and programs to line ministries.[22] These ceilings encompass the general and special accounts and funds. Line ministries are asked to prepare their budget requests within these ceilings. When reviewing the ministerial budget requests, MPB places less emphasis on the microscopic control of line items and more on the strategic alignment of budget requests with overall policy directions.

Key steps of the new budget process are explained in table 9.10. The budget cycle starts in January, earlier than in previous years. The workload of budget examiners are accordingly spread out over a year rather than concentrated in July and August. This is deemed another merit of the new system.

The new system is already producing tangible results. In fiscal year 2005, the budget requests by line ministries represented an increase of 11.7 percent over the previous year's budget. This was much smaller than the 30.8 percent increase in fiscal year 2004. Line ministries also voluntarily shuffled a larger portion of their spending across programs, cutting back 2.7 trillion won on existing ones and introducing new ones worth 3.0 trillion won. The corresponding figures for fiscal year 2004 were 1.6 and 1.5 trillion won, respectively.

Room to Improve

There is of course room to improve. The first three points explained in the following concern the behavioral changes that are needed in MPB and line ministries over the medium term. The next seven points concern the changes in the budgetary system and MTEF that need immediate attention.

22. Ceilings are set for 14 spending areas such as social infrastructure, agriculture, education, and environment and then disaggregated into 56 programs. For example, social infrastructure has 7 programs, including roads, railways, subways, seaports, airports, housing, and water resources. Separate ceilings are also set within each program for the general account and various special accounts and funds.

Table 9.10   Key steps of the budget process after the introduction of the MTEF

	Action
December	• The Ministry of Planning and Budget (MPB) sends to line ministries standard assumptions on macro-variables such as inflation, interest rates, exchange rates, etc. • Sectoral task forces are organized. They are composed of private-sector experts and government officials from MPB and relevant ministries.
January–April	• Line ministries submit to MPB their estimates of spending needs over the next 5 years by the end of January. • Sectoral task forces discuss major policy issues and present their recommendations in a series of public hearings held in March and April. • By the end of April, MPB prepares a draft National Fiscal Management Plan (NFMP) through discussions with line ministries. The draft NFMP contains major policy directions and fiscal aggregates (total spending, deficits, debts, etc.) for the next 5 years and tentative spending ceilings on sectors and programs for the budget year.
Cabinet meeting	• At the end of April, a cabinet meeting, chaired by the president, is held in a secluded place to discuss and finalize the ceilings. • Following the meeting, the ceilings are transmitted to line ministries in the Guide to Budget Preparation.
May–June	• Line ministries prepare their budget requests and send them to MPB.
July–August	• MPB prepares the draft budget. Less emphasis is placed on the microscopic control of line items and more on the strategic alignment of budget requests with overall policy directions.
August–December	• Goes through the same process as before the introduction of MTEF.

First, performance management in line ministries should be strengthened. In the discussion on policy directions and resource allocation, performance information can provide a valuable guide. There have been efforts in this direction, but none of them have yet succeeded in instilling performance orientation in line ministries. Details on the current reform efforts will be given in the next subsection.

Second, the planning and priority-setting capacity in line ministries should be enhanced. For example, line ministries should be required to publish long-term strategic plans, annual business plans, and annual performance reports. The planning and budget divisions of individual line ministries should play a greater role in the coordination of ministerial policies and budget requests unlike in previous years when they would simply compile budget requests from program divisions and send them to MPB with little modification.

Third, the role of MPB should also be changed. As a central coordinator of government policies, MPB should strengthen its capacity for policy analysis and long-term forecasts. It should stress less on input control and pay more attention to outputs and outcomes. It should act as a consultant for line ministries to enhance their program performance and strive to build mutual trust in a collective action game.

Fourth, the medium-term targets in the MTEF should be clarified. Presently, it is not clear which variable the government is targeting at in the medium term—the budget balance, the total spending, or the debt-to-GDP ratio. They are presented in NFMP merely as "projections" rather than as "targets." An ideal strategy would be targeting at a balanced budget over the business cycle.[23] Deficits are allowed in a period of slow growths but they are subsequently offset by surpluses in a period of high growths, and the accumulation of debt is held down over the cycle. The debt-to-GDP ratio declines slowly as the GDP expands. Examples of this strategy can be found in the Growth and Stability Pact (GSP) of the European Economic and Monetary Union (EMU), the *golden rule* of the British government, and the 2-percent structural surplus rule of the Swedish government.[24]

Fifth, it is necessary to set out the annual operational targets that can guarantee the achievement of the medium-term targets. There are two types of operational targets commonly employed, namely *budget balance* and *total spending*. A prime example of the former is the 3-percent deficit rule of the EMU. In contrast, the Swedish government imposes an expenditure ceiling on each of the three years ahead. The United Kingdom has adopted similar practices for expenditure control. The U.S. federal government experimented with both types of targets in the 1980s and 1990s (see box).

Between these types of targets, total spending is a superior choice because (a) it is less influenced by the cyclical position of the economy and therefore easier to control; and (b) it assists in a counter-cyclical management of fiscal policy by leaving the balance to fluctuate flexibly over the cycle. Presently, the Korean government intends to keep the annual spending totals unchanged in successive NFMPs, and thus appears to have the total spending as annual targets. But this point needs to be clearly communicated to the public.[25]

Sixth, it is desirable to introduce various risk analyses in the National Fiscal Management Plan. Such analyses would address such issues as (a)

---

23. Given the low level of debt-to-GDP ratio in Korea, it seems unnecessary to target at surpluses over the cycles.

24. The GSP commits the member countries to achieve and maintain a budget position of close to balance or in surplus over the cycle. The golden rule allows the British government to borrow only to invest and not to fund current spending over the cycle. The current Swedish government is targeting at an average surplus of 2 percent of GDP over the cycle (Gustafsson 2004).

25. With a fixed total spending, it may be difficult to cope with an unexpected surge of spending needs, for example in times of economic hardship. An escape clause may be needed that is not too lax to undermine fiscal discipline or too stringent to accommodate reasonable demands for increased spending.

Experience of the U.S. Federal Government on Deficit Control

The United States experimented with both types of annual operational targets explained in the text. In the 1980s, targets were set up for budget deficits. The Gramm-Rudman-Hollings Act of 1985 (GRH I) prescribed deficit ceilings in nominal dollars for the next five years. The strategy, however, did not work. The actual deficits exceeded the stipulated ceilings in all years covered by GRH I. In 1987, GRH II was enacted and the deficit ceilings were adjusted upward to accommodate this reality. But it did not take long before GRH II also proved to be a failure.

In 1990, a new strategy was adopted with the enactment of the Budget Enforcement Act (BEA). Instead of setting limits on deficits, the congress introduced separate rules for discretionary spending and mandatory spending. On discretionary spending, cash limits were imposed for the next five years. Except in special circumstances, these limits were not to be breached. For mandatory spending (interest payments, social security benefits, etc.), which depend on exogenous variables such as interest rates and the number of the elderly, the so-called "pay-as-you-go (PAYGO)" principle was introduced. In PAYGO, any increase in deficits resulting from policy changes should be offset by corresponding changes in revenues or mandatory spending.

The new strategy worked well. It was renewed in 1993 and 1997. Actual spending on discretionary programs turned out to be larger than stipulated in the law every year except in 1996 (see table 9.11). But the excess was always less than 1 percent of the stipulated amounts, and was mostly due to exception events such as the Gulf war and natural disasters.

Helped by the strong economy, the United States could attain budget surplus in 1999 for the first time since the mankind set foot on the moon. The unusually long period of boom in the 1990s boosted revenues above and contained the mandatory spending below the levels expected at the beginning. But it would be unfair to say that all surpluses were due to the strong economy. The rules introduced by BEA appear to have been quite effective in controlling expenditures and thereby reducing budget deficits.

First of all, these rules were aimed at controlling what could actually be controlled. Discretionary spending is by definition amenable to annual controls by the congress. Mandatory spending can also be controlled through the PAYGO rule by changing relevant laws. On the other hand, budget deficits are difficult to control because they are affected by business cycles as well as by government policies. When a target cannot be directly controlled by the authorities in charge, it is difficult to hold them responsible for the results, and we cannot be sure that they will make their best effort to achieve the target.

---

the deviation of medium-term growth rates and other macroeconomic variables from their projected levels; (b) explicit and implicit contingent liabilities of the government coming from loan guarantees, public corporations, local governments, and others; and (c) population aging.

Seventh, a mechanism for *baseline* projections should be established. MPB currently provides line ministries with standard assumptions on key macrovariables such as wage and price inflation. Based on these assumptions, line ministries project their spending needs for the next five years. But they should go further and distinguish between spending on existing programs (*baselines*), costs of new policy initiatives, and *savings options*. MPB would check the validity of ministerial projections and aggregate

Table 9.11   **Expenditures and revenues of the U.S. federal government (in billions of dollars)**

		1994	1995	1996	1997	1998
Total spending	BEA estimates	1,523	1,578	1,645	1,745	1,843
	Actuals	1,462	1,516	1,561	1,601	1,653
Discretionary	BEA limits	537	539	547	547	548
spending	Actuals	544	545	534	549	555
Mandatory	BEA estimates	765	795	843	920	996
spending	Actuals	715	738	785	809	855
Revenues	BEA estimates	1,230	1,306	1,379	1,440	1,523
	Actuals	1,259	1,352	1,453	1,579	1,723
Deficits/surpluses	BEA estimates	−270	−230	−266	−305	−320
	Actuals	−203	−164	−107	−22	70

Source: OECD (1999).

them to arrive at the government-wide baselines, costs of new policy initiatives, and savings options. Only then can the annual budgeting be closely linked with the National Fiscal Management Plan.

Eighth, a reconciliation process should be put in place to analyze the difference between projected levels of revenue, spending, balance, and debt and their outturns. This is a critical step to secure accountability and transparency of macrofiscal management. In case of the U.S. federal government, the deviation is decomposed into economic, policy, and technical factors.

Ninth, the internal auditing within line ministries and government agencies should be strengthened. An increased autonomy in financial management should be accompanied by an increased awareness of the possibility of fraud, waste, and abuse. In this regard, we can refer to the case of the U.S. federal government, where the independence of internal auditors is guaranteed by the inspector general system, and consider introducing a similar system.[26]

Tenth, *program budgeting* needs to be introduced. The Korean government is currently redesigning the structure of its budget accounts around functions, administrations, and programs. The effort is spearheaded by the

26. Under the Inspector General Act of 1978, the president appoints inspectors general (IGs) for certain specified federal establishments, by and with the consent of the Senate, without regard to political affiliation and solely on each individual's experience in specified areas. Under the Inspector General Amendments of 1988, the heads of designated federal entities appoint IGs, without the necessity of Senate confirmation. The IG Act identifies 26 federal establishments that are to have an IG appointed by the president with Senate confirmation and 30 designated federal entities that are to have an IG appointed by their agency heads. The IGs perform audits in accordance with generally accepted government auditing standards and report suspected violation of criminal law to the Attorney General. Each IG must prepare semiannual reports that summarize the IG's activities. The head of each agency transmits these reports unaltered to Congress and subsequently makes them available to the public (U.S. GAO 1998).

Budget and Accounting Reinvention Office (BARO).[27] The resulting program structure will make it easier to allocate resources according to the national priorities and set ceilings on sectoral spending. *Programs* will also act as the basic units of performance management in the future. More will be discussed on program budgeting shortly.

9.4.4   Performance Management

Overview

As noted previously, budgeting in Korea has traditionally been focused on the ex ante control of inputs. The authorities have little experience in performance management by such tools as performance monitoring and program evaluation. There is no established feedback mechanism that supplies performance information to those in charge of budget preparation and execution, which partly explains the continuation of some ineffective and inefficient programs.

Performance management becomes more important with the introduction of the MTEF and top-down budgeting. These changes will allow greater autonomy to line ministries and can lead to greater inefficiency unless complemented by a new mechanism to secure accountability on the part of line ministries.

Figure 9.20 describes the basic framework of performance management. Starting from the mission of an organization, we set up strategic goals, performance goals, and performance indicators (see table 9.12). Actual performance is assessed through performance monitoring, program evaluation, or program review. These works are documented in strategic plans, annual performance plans, and annual performance reports. Table 9.13 compares the three tools for performance assessment—monitoring, evaluation, and review. Key differences between evaluation and monitoring are listed in table 9.14.

In recent years, diverse efforts have been made to strengthen performance management in government. Some of them are listed in table 9.15. In the following, detailed explanation will be given on Performance Management of Budgetary Programs (PMBP), Self-Assessment of Budgetary Programs (SABP), and Evaluation of Budgetary Programs (EBP).

Performance Management of Budgetary Programs (PMBP)

Performance Management of Budgetary Programs corresponds to performance monitoring in the previous discussion. It is led by MPB, and its

---

27. BARO is a special task force organized in 2004 to lead reforms in the area of program budgeting, financial reporting, government financial statistics, and the IT system. It is officially part of MPB but composed of secondees from various organizations including MPB, MOFE, MOGAHA, and BAI.

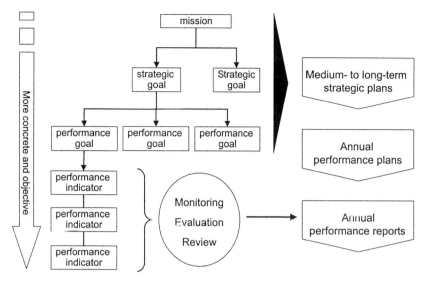

Fig. 9.20   Framework of performance management

Table 9.12   Meanings and requirements

Term	Meanings and requirements
Mission	Means . . . • Major results sought by the program or the organization as a whole. • Starting point for identifying the specific outcomes to be measured and the specific performance indicators that are needed. Should . . . • Focus on the program effect on customers and the public.
Strategic goals	Means . . . • Major policy goals that the organization pursues to complete its mission. Should . . . • Be value-free and avoid general or aspirational expressions. • Be stated clearly and succinctly. • Be minimal in number. • Be focused on the final results that the organization pursues.
Performance goals	Means . . . • Concrete goals that the organization pursues to attain its strategic goals Should . . . • Be specific enough to ascertain, with the help of performance indicators, whether the performance objectives have been achieved.

Table 9.13   **Tools of performance assessment**

Tool	Main characteristics
Performance monitoring	• Measures the program performance with a predetermined set of indicators. • Can produce information on outputs and outcomes in a frequent and timely manner at relatively low costs. • By itself, can rarely explain the causality between inputs and outputs or outcomes.
Program evaluation	• Addresses the question of why and how the program produced certain outputs and outcomes. • Employs analytical tools with varying degrees of sophistication. • Usually requires large amounts of money and time, and cannot be performed on all programs.
Program review	• Assesses the performance and other aspects of a given program with an explicit aim of helping budgetary decision-making. • Relies on information from various sources including monitoring and evaluation. • Is usually led by the central budget office (e.g., Ministry of Finance). • Requires a medium level of effort (in between monitoring and evaluation).

design follows the framework of the Government Performance and Results Act (GPRA) of the U.S. federal government. It is based on the pilot project on performance budgeting carried out in 1999 to 2002, which was not very successful in instilling performance orientation either in line ministries or in MPB.[28] Performance Management of Budgetary Programs requires line ministries to (a) set up performance goals and indicators, (b) prepare annual performance plans and reports, and (c) submit them to MPB at the start of the annual budget cycle (see figure 9.21).

A major drawback of PMBP lies in the fact that it covers only part of ministerial activities. Those activities not involving large sums of expenditure (such as pure policy making) are excluded from performance monitoring. Also, activities for which the benefits of performance monitoring are expected to be small (such as wages and salaries, *basic program* expenditures, and general administrative expenses) are excluded as well. This has the potential to lead line ministries to disregard those activities that are critical in achieving their overall mission but involve small expenditures or

---

28. In 2001, 39 organizations participated in the pilot. A survey of the pilot (Jun and Park 2002) found that over half of the indicators proposed in the performance reports were based on outputs and only one-fifth on outcomes. The rest were input indicators, and about two-thirds of all indicators were nonquantitative ones. The survey also found that many indicators changed from one year to another, making it difficult to trace program performance over time consistently. It subsequently proposed the government to applying performance indicators only to major large-sized expenditure programs for which quantitative indicators are easy to construct.

Table 9.14   Key differences between evaluation and monitoring

Monitoring	Evaluation
• Periodic • Assumes appropriateness of program, activities, and indicators • Tracks progress against small number of indicators • Usually quantitative • Use data routinely gathered or readily available • Cannot indicate causality • Difficult to use for impact assessment • Usually internal	• Usually episodic • Can address a wide range of potential questions about a policy, program, or project • Can identify what has happened as a result of an intervention and provide guidance for future directions • Can address "how" and "why" questions • Wide range of quantitative and qualitative research methods possible • Can use data from different sources • Can identify unintended as well as planned impacts and effects • Can involve internal, external, or self evaluation

Source: Perrin (2002).

Table 9.15   Diverse initiatives for performance management

Performance management initiatives	Organizations in charge
Performance Management of Budgetary Programs (PMBP)	Ministry of Planning and Budget (MPB)
Self-Assessment of Budgetary Programs (SABP)	MPB
Evaluation of Budgetary Programs (EBP)	MPB
Government Operations Assessment System (GOAS)	Office of Government Policy Coordination (OGPC)
Management by Objectives (MBO)	MOGAHA
Performance Audit	BAI

Fig. 9.21   Structure of PMBP

only wages and salaries, and to lose sight of the linkage between the overall mission, strategies, and performance goals.

Unlike GPRA, PMBP does not require strategic planning on the part of line ministries. This is understandable given the position of MPB within the government. MPB is only one of many ministries under the prime minister's office and cannot impose such a broad requirement as strategic planning on line ministries. But the lack of strategic planning renders it difficult to focus performance management exercises on the core values of the ministries and to derive performance indicators from ministerial missions in a systematic fashion.

Performance Management of Budgetary Programs, like its pilot project, has not been very successful. There appears to exist only a lukewarm support from the top management in MPB. Line ministries are also showing little enthusiasm for the PMBP. Most importantly, performance reports are not open to the public, giving little incentive for line ministries to think seriously about the exercise.

The general failure of PMBP can be explained in several ways. First, it has been and will be very difficult to set up quantitative indicators for many government activities, especially when the activity has diverse (and sometimes conflicting) objectives, takes many years to attain the desired objectives, is only one of many factors affecting the outcome, or does not lend its performance to quantitative measurement by its own nature. Second, and more importantly, PMBP is not attracting sufficient attention from major stakeholders such as the budget examiners in MPB, managers in line ministries, parliamentarians, and the general public. Performance information provided by PMBP is not detailed enough for budget examiners in MPB and parliamentarians involved in funding decisions on individual programs. Managers in line ministries do not find the information useful in managing their programs. And the general public cannot even access the information because the reports are not open to them. In short, it is hard to find real demands for PMBP.

Fortunately, efforts are being made to repair PMBP. According to MPB, from this year on, all activities (budgetary and nonbudgetary) will be covered by PMBP, and reports will be open to the public. Real demands for performance information are being created through SABP and EBP as will be explained in the following. But still there is no requirement for strategic planning. So long as strategic plans provide an overarching framework for results-oriented management, including PMBP, SABP, and EBP, the Korean government (to be specific, MPB in coordination with the prime minister's office) should seriously consider introducing strategic planning in ministries.

In the United States, federal agencies should prepare strategic plans, performance plans, and performance reports under the GPRA. Following these examples, prescribing more detailed requirements in Korea would help enrich the performance plans and reports prepared by line ministries. MPB or any other central agency[29] can also review them periodically, rate their quality, and propose best practices.

Self-Assessment of Budgetary Programs (SABP)

Self-Assessment of Budgetary Programs, a form of budget review, is also led by MPB. It was designed after the Program Assessment Rating Tool (PART) of the U.S. federal government. It requires line ministries to assess their own programs with spending levels above a certain threshold in a cycle of three years. The assessment is based on 16 questions common to all types of programs and a few additional questions specific to different types of programs.[30] Table 9.16 lists the common questions asked.

Answers to the questions take the form of "yes (1)" or "no (0)." In case of the questions regarding the achievement of program objectives and the customer satisfaction, 4-scale answers (1.00, 0.67, 0.33, 0.00) are given. A weight is assigned to each question and the overall assessment is based on the weighted sum of the answers. Programs are then classified as "effective (85–100)," "moderately effective (70–84)," "adequate (50–69)," and "not effective (0–50)." MPB reviews the results of ministerial self-assessments, and makes the final assessment.

In 2005, 555 programs were assessed (table 9.17). Among them, 87 (15.7 percent) were classified as *not effective,* and their funding was cut by 10 percent with some modifications. Such practice of directly linking performance to budgeting has been held as taboo by many experts mainly because decision making should be based not solely on a limited set of performance information but on broad considerations on, for example, the social needs for the programs. But MPB felt that without a direct linkage, it would be very difficult to invoke serious interest in SABP from line ministries. Certainly their strategy worked, and they plan to continue this exercise annually.

Even though SABP succeeded in creating *real demands* for performance information within MPB and also in line ministries, improvements are needed in several aspects. Just like PART, SABP increased the workload of budget examiners substantially. It will increase further in coming years as the assessed programs accumulate and the examiners need to reassess the old cases when necessary. To alleviate this problem, an arrangement was made this year with the small division in charge of coordinating SABP

29. The National Assembly Budget Office and the Evaluation Research Institute of the Board of Audit and Inspection can play the role of GAO in this respect.

30. Types of programs are infrastructure investment, procurement of large-scale facilities and equipment, provision of direct services, capital injection, subsidies to private entities, grants to local governments, and R&D.

Table 9.16   Common questions for the SABP

Section	Common questions
Program design	• Does the program have clear purposes and legal or other bases? • Can the government intervention be justified? • Is government spending necessary to achieve the objectives? • Is the program duplicative of other program? • Has the program been subjected to an objective feasibility study? • Is the proposed program design most cost-effective? • Are performance goals and indicators in place? • Do performance goals and indicators fully reflect program objectives? • Are the targets set at reasonable levels?
Program management	• Is the implementation being monitored regularly? • Is the program being implemented as planned? • Are efforts being made to reduce costs or increase efficiency?
Performance assessment and feedback	• Has an objective and comprehensive program evaluation been conducted? • Did the program achieve the intended objectives? • Are customers and stakeholders satisfied with the program performance? • Is the agency utilizing the assessment results for program improvement and budget planning?

Table 9.17   Results of 2005 SABP

Total	Effective	Moderately effective	Adequate	Not effective
555	28	99	341	87
100.0 (%)	5.0	17.9	61.4	15.7

efforts within MPB making a preliminary assessment of the documents prepared by line ministries, and then passing their opinions to budget examiners who make the final assessment. This arrangement is not necessarily optimal given the limited capacity of that division and the possible lack of ownership in SABP results by budget examiners. Greater resource for SABP is being called for.

In addition, efforts are needed to go beyond scoring the programs. The U.S. Office of Management and Budget (OMB) makes recommendations for line ministries to improve their program performance (figure 9.22). This year, MPB plans to start producing recommendations for line ministries. It remains to be seen how effective these recommendations will be to improve the program efficiency and effectiveness. In the United States, difficulties were encountered in communicating OMB's intentions to line ministries, prioritizing among many different recommendations, and securing adequate resources within OMB for the follow-up of recommendations. MPB should prepare themselves for similar difficulties.

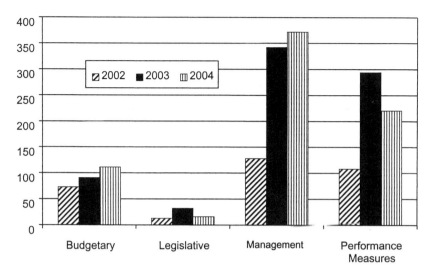

Fig. 9.22   Number of recommendations
Source: U.S. Office of Management and Budget.

Evaluation of Budgetary Programs

The last addition to the armory of performance management is Evaluation of Budgetary Programs (EBP), which is an effort led by MPB to set up a systematic approach to program evaluation in line ministries.

Each year, MPB would commission evaluation studies on programs that it considers need critical assessment. Korea Development Institute (KDI) organizes evaluation teams and oversees the studies. For this purpose, KDI has published a manual for program evaluation, which details the process and standards to be followed by evaluation teams.

Three programs were evaluated from late 2005 to early 2006 on a pilot basis. From 2006 on, around 10 programs will be evaluated each year. Pilot studies uncovered various difficulties in carrying out the evaluation. Most programs lacked clearly specified goals and necessary data to assess the achievement of goals. Evaluators found it difficult to understand the structure and context of individual programs and official documents were not of much help in this regard. MPB and line ministries often had different expectations on evaluation, with the former focusing on funding decisions and the latter on program management, which cannot be easily reconciled with each other.

To overcome these difficulties, KDI's evaluation manual stresses the importance of, at the start of evaluation studies, asking line ministries to provide sufficient details of the program, identifying the program structure and context, redefining the program objectives, describing the intervention logic of the program, setting up performance indicators and benchmarks for program success, and deciding on the purpose and scope of the evaluation. These steps should be taken in a transparent way and in full cooperation with relevant stakeholders including the ministries in charge of the program and MPB.

Perhaps the most difficult part would be describing the intervention logic and setting up performance indicators. The manual recommends the use of logic models for this purpose. Figure 9.23 gives an example of a logic model in the case of a road-safety campaign.

EBP is expected to provide information on program performance that can be used for SABP. In fact, the first question of the last section in table 9.16 asks whether an objective and comprehensive program evaluation has been conducted for a program. On the other hand, the information gathered through SABP can be used in the selection of candidate programs for EBP. In this sense, PMBP and SABP are complementary to each other. A similar relationship exists between EBP and PMBP. EBP can propose new and refined performance indicators for PMBP, as explained previously. At the same time, EBP can utilize the performance data collected through PMBP in conducting evaluation.

EBP has many challenges to overcome in the coming years. The ultimate aim is to set up a standard and provide examples for program evaluation, and to instill *evaluation culture* in line ministries, which, we hope, will conduct evaluation voluntarily on their own programs as part of their daily business.

9.4.5   Program Budgeting

Presently, the budget is classified first by the general and special accounts and funds. Then within these accounts and funds, it is further divided up by five levels of classification—chapters, sections, subsections, items, and subitems.[31] MPB usually examines the budget requests by line ministries at the level of subitems, which totaled 8,038 in fiscal year 2006. Such a detailed control of inputs by the central budget office produced many problems mentioned previously—weak linkages between budgeting and policy making, tiresome budget negotiation between MPB and line ministries, and limited accountability and autonomy of line ministries.

The present classification system has other drawbacks as well. Funding for a program is often scattered across various accounts and funds. For example, the development of fishing villages and ports is simultaneously funded by the general account, three special accounts (fiscal financing, agricultural and fisheries structural adjustment, balanced national devel-

---

31. The first three of these are controlled by the parliament, while the last two by MPB. For example, when a ministry wants to shift appropriation from a subsection to another, it needs an approval from MPB *and* the parliament. But when it wants to shift appropriation from an item to another, it needs an approval only from MPB.

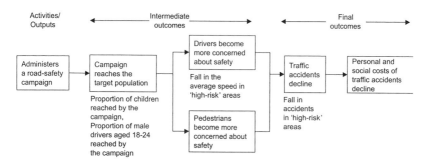

Fig. 9.23   Intervention logic of a road-safety campaign

opment), and one fund (fisheries development). This makes it difficult to identify the total amount of funding provided for a program, and manage its performance.

Inconsistency is another problem; some items or subitems cover a wide range of activities and involve a large amount of funding, while others are associated with very specific activities and a small amount of funding.

To remedy these problems and support other reform initiatives—medium-term expenditure framework and performance management—MPB set out to introduce *program budgeting*. In essence, four instead of five levels of classification are brought in, the input controls are drastically reduced, and the classification by accounts and funds is abolished. The new classification is shown in figure 9.24. The present 26 chapters, 79 sections, and 718 subsections are regrouped into 16 areas and 68 sectors; 718 subsections and 2,411 items into 1,043 programs; and 8,038 subitems into 3,594 projects. The control by MPB will be exercised at the level of projects, and that by the parliament at the level of programs. Line ministries will have full discretion on activities within each project.

9.4.6   Government Financial Statistics

The limited scope of the government financial statistics has been pointed out as one of the major drawbacks of the Korean fiscal management system. As explained previously, the consolidated central government covers the general and special accounts and funds. But it excludes some important fiscal activities of the government. For example, the National Health Insurance is excluded from the consolidated government even though it is a social insurance program that covers over 90 percent of the population. Also excluded are various quasi-government organizations and research institutions (such as KDI), which are mainly financed and whose activities are closely supervised by the government.

Even within the central government, the revenue and expenditure statistics on one hand and the government asset and liability statistics on the other hand have different coverage. The latter excludes some funds that are

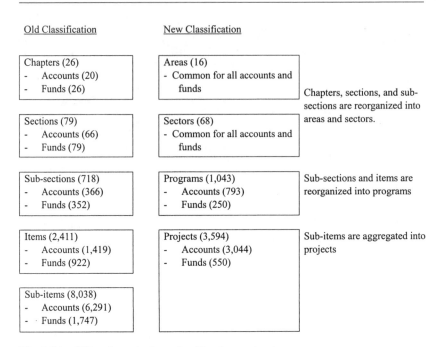

Old Classification   New Classification

Fig. 9.24   Old and new budget classification systems

included in the former, with possible underreporting of the true size of government assets and liabilities. In addition, government assets are reported separately for credits (e.g., government loans), properties (e.g., securities and premises), cash holdings (e.g., deposits at the central bank), and supplies, making it impossible to get the overall picture of financial and nonfinancial assets.

Logical consistency is compromised also in the treatment of treasury bonds held by the National Pension Fund and other funds. These bond holdings are recorded simultaneously as government assets (as they are held by funds) and liabilities (as they are issued by the government). Ideally, such bond holdings should be netted out, and the asset and liability statistics should only reflect the transactions between the government and the private sector.

The consolidated central government also shows large discrepancies with the National Accounts in its coverage. The latter includes the National Health Insurance in the government sector but excludes some activities such as the credit programs of the National Housing Fund (NHF). As a result, the amount of government liabilities differs significantly between two statistical systems.

We have similar problems in the data for public financial and nonfinancial corporations. Together with the general government (the central and local governments and social security funds), public corporations constitute the public sector. In Korea, however, there does not exist a consistent definition of public corporations. For example, various financial funds such as the credit guarantee funds are not included in the public sector even though they have every aspect of public financial corporations. The government does not publish a comprehensive review on the financial status of individual public corporations, let alone consolidated financial statements.

This practice makes it difficult to assess the financial health of the public sector in general, and the implicit fiscal burden incurred through quasi-fiscal activities of financial funds in particular. Of particular concern are credit guarantee funds[32] that significantly expanded their activities after the recent economic crisis. At the end of 2003, the outstanding stock of guarantees amounted to 11 percent of GDP, far higher than in other countries where the public guarantees are usually less than 1 percent of GDP. Yet no reports exist that explain the future risks these funds may impose on government finance.

As a first step to address this problem, BARO is redefining the scope of the public sector. The starting point is the revised 2001 Government Finance Statistics Manual of IMF. BARO is also searching for ways to produce comprehensive, accurate, and timely information on the government financial position by introducing accrual accounting and building a new IT system. The IT system is expected to centralize an array of financial information from all organizations within the government sector. When BARO's work is completed by 2007, big improvements will have been made in financial reporting and government financial statistics.

9.5   Roads Ahead

The primary responsibilities of any fiscal management system lie in supporting aggregate fiscal discipline, allocative efficiency, and operational efficiency (Schiavo-Campo and Tommasi 1999). The Korean government had maintained aggregate fiscal discipline since the 1980s in a strategic dominance-based approach and pursued allocative and operational efficiency through a detailed input control on annual budgets. However, the changing environment after the financial crisis of 1997 necessitated a transition toward a target-based approach and a stronger emphasis on outputs and outcomes.

In response to these challenges, the government introduced the National Fiscal Management Plan, various performance management tools, program budgeting, and a new statistical system. These reforms are all in line with the *global standard* in fiscal management as espoused by international

---

32. These are the Infrastructure Credit Guarantee Funds; the Korea Technology Credit Guarantee Fund; the Credit Guarantee Fund for Agriculture, Forestry, and Fishery; the Korea Credit Guarantee Fund; and the Housing Finance Credit Guarantee Fund.

organizations. It is interesting to note that, unlike other developing countries where fiscal reforms are often imposed by these organizations as a string attached to the aids provided, the Korean government began the reform process on their own initiatives. Accordingly, the *ownership* of reform could be secured and genuine efforts guaranteed. The reforms could also be tailored to the specific needs of the Korean government because they were designed by *insiders* who had better knowledge on the institutional and historical context.

Even after the reform, there remain many improvements to be made in our fiscal management system as explained in the text. Consolidating the reforms will be the main challenge for the Korean government in coming years.

References

Bahn, Jahng Shick. 2003. *A study on the determinants of Korea's fiscal soundness.* [In Korean with an English summary]. Korea University, Seoul, Department of Public Administration Graduate School.

Bank of Korea. 2001. National accounts. Seoul: Bank of Korea.

Bayoumi, Tamim. 1998. The Japanese fiscal system and fiscal transparency. In *Structural change in Japan: Macroeconomic impact and policy challenges,* ed. Bijan B. Aghevli, Tamim Bayoumi, and Guy Meredith, 171–212. Washington, DC: International Monetary Fund.

Bayoumi, Tamim, and Barry Eichengreen. 1995. Restraining yourself: The implications of fiscal rules for economic stabilization. *IMF Staff Papers* 42 (1): 32–48.

Gustafsson, Allan. 2004. MTEF in Sweden. In *Reforming the public expenditure management system: Medium-term expenditure framework, performance management, and fiscal transparency,* ed. Youngsun Koh, 241–56. Seoul: Korea Development Institution.

Han, Jin-hee, Kyung-soo Choi, Dong-seok Kim, and Kyung-mook Lim. 2002. *The potential growth rate of the Korean economy: 2003–2012.* [in Korean]. Seoul: Korea Development Institution.

Jun, Taek-seung, and Ki-paik Park. 2002. *Review of pilot studies on performance-based budgeting.* [in Korean]. Seoul: Korea Institute of Public Finance.

Korea Development Institute. 1991. *Forty years of Korean fiscal policy.* [in Korean]. Seoul: Korea Development Institute.

Ministry of Finance and Economy. n.d. *Government finance statistics in Korea,* various issues. Seoul: Ministry of Finance and Economy.

Ministry of Planning and Budget. 2005. *Annex to summary of 2005 budget.* Seoul: Ministry of Planning and Budget.

Organisation for Economic Co-operation and Development (OECD). 1999. *Budgeting in a surplus environment.* PUMA/SBO(99)3/FINAL. Paris: OECD.

———. 2003. *Economic surveys: Korea.*

Perrin, Burt. 2002. *Implementing the vision: Addressing challenges to results-focused management and budgeting.* Paris: OECD.

Potter, Barry H., and Jack Diamond. 1999. *Guidelines for public expenditure management.* Washington, DC: International Monetary Fund.

Schiavo-Campo, Salvatore, and Daniel Tommasi. 1999. *Managing government expenditure.* Tokyo: Asia Development Bank.

U.S. General Accounting Office (GAO). 2001. *Federal trust and other earmarked funds: Answers to frequently asked questions.* GAO-01-199SP. Washington, DC: GAO.

———. 1998. *Managing for results: The statutory framework for performance-based management and accountability.* GAO/GGD/AIMD-98-52. Washington, DC: GAO.

Von Hagen, Jürgen, and Ian Harden. 1996. *Budget processes and commitment to fiscal discipline.* IMF Working Paper WP/96/78. Washington, DC: IMF.

World Bank. 1998. *Public expenditure management handbook.* Washington, DC: The World Bank.

Yoo, Gyeongjoon. 2003. International comparison of the income distribution. *KDI Journal of Economic Policy.* [in Korean] II: 55–88.

Comment   Gilberto M. Llanto

An observer like me can only look with envy at how the Korean government showed tight discipline in solving the persistent fiscal deficits of the 70s and 80s. Fiscal tightening in the 1980s was a delicate balancing act, but the principle of *expenditure within revenue*—or the balanced budget principle—produced wonderful results in terms of keeping the public debt at a minimal level and taming the fiscal deficit. The notable achievement of observing a balanced budget was that it was not formalized in either *law or a regulation.* It was the determined effort of the government that made the big difference. The self-discipline paid off because the Korean government could plan massive fiscal supports to troubled financial institutions when the Asian financial crisis hit the economy.

The amazing phenomenon was that the Korean government was able to reduce the ratio of government debt to GDP a few years after the financial crisis. The total public debt burden was 30 percent of GDP around 1998 to 1999 but the budget recorded a surplus of 1.1 percent of GDP in 2000. The surplus has remained in the following years. Strong economic growth and rapid increases in revenues no doubt made this possible.

Mr. Young-Sun Koh was, however, quick to point out that excluding the National Pension Fund from the consolidated balance indicates that there were "budget deficits since 1989, except in 2002."

Another indicator of fiscal health is the status of government liabilities.

Gilberto M. Llanto is a senior research fellow at the Philippine Institute for Development Studies.

I would like to thank Mr. Young-Sun Koh of the Korea Development Institute for sharing with us the very instructive experience of South Korea in addressing that country's fiscal problem and the future path of fiscal management from which developing countries such as the Philippines can draw lessons.

The total public burden including direct liabilities and guarantees was around 33 to 34 percent of GDP. On the other hand, the author notes a worrisome feature of Korean public finance: the pension schemes have too generous benefits in relation to contributions. A rapidly aging population creates an imbalance between the expected benefits and the contributions with the former outgrowing the latter. The aging population also implies an increase in health expenditure, projected to rise to as much as 25 to 30 percent in 2070. Age-related expenditures, that is, the pension and health expenditures, create pressure on fiscal sustainability.

The weak side of Korean fiscal management is the budget. The complex structure of the budget reduces allocative efficiency and transparency. However, the government has to be lauded for serious efforts to strengthen transparency and accountability by reviewing various funds with the objective of abolishing obsolete funds and consolidating those with similar objectives. The problem of reducing the number of special accounts has remained an outstanding issue and will certainly merit greater action by the authorities in the near future.

An important reform is the introduction of the MTEF, which moves the budgeting process away from *microscopic control of line items* to the *strategic alignment of budget requests with overall policy directions*. The focus should be on outputs and outcomes rather than the traditional control of inputs. The author has several suggestions to improve the MTEF and one item stands out as a crucial area needing government attention: risk analysis and management, more specifically, the explicit and implicit contingent liabilities of the government arising from loan guarantees, public corporations, local governments, and others.

Another critical reform objective is the introduction of performance monitoring and evaluation. If adopted, this will improve the transparency of the budget process and effectiveness of various government interventions.

This interesting chapter encourages one to await the author's next report on the progress made by the government in pursuing the fiscal reforms highlighted therein.

Comment   Chong-Hyun Nam

This is a very interesting and highly informative chapter. It consists of, largely, two parts. The first part presents an excellent survey on the development of the public sector in the Korean economy, and the second part evaluates institutional reforms that have been taking place in Korea in re-

Chong-Hyun Nam is professor of economics at Korea University.

cent years, suggesting almost an exhaustive list of recommendations as to how the reform can be shaped better for now and in the future.

The chapter is by and large self-explaining, and I have little in disagreement with whatever Koh writes. I have only a couple of quick comments on each part of the chapter.

First of all, I would have liked to see it more focused. The focus may be placed on the role of public finance that has played in the process of Korea's economic development. It is well known that a single most important goal that the Korean government has pursued, all along over the past forty years or so, is rapid economic growth. Almost every means that is available for policymakers has been mobilized to achieve this goal in one way or another. I believe fiscal policy has been no exception.

I think table 9.2 in the chapter provides some useful clues in that regard. The table shows that, as of 2000/2001, the share of capital outlays in total government's expenditure in Korea amounts to 8.3 percent of GDP, which is conspicuously higher than those for other countries compared in the table. This contrasts sharply to the share of transfers, which is substantially lower at only 3 percent of GDP in the corresponding year. Table 9.4 also provides a good indicator on this score. The table shows that the share of government expenditure on economic affairs has not only been large, but has also been increasing over time. The share of spending on economic affairs, for instance, shows a slightly declining trend over the 1970 to 1990 period to 3.6 percent from 4.6 percent of GDP, but it climbs back to an even higher level of 6.2 percent of GDP by 2003.

What does all this mean? This may mean that Korea's public sector has been heavily used, or abused for that matter, as a means of domestic capital formation, possibly replacing private sectors. This kind of fiscal policy may have continued to be in use, even long after Korea joined the OECD in 1996. A natural question to be asked is, then, to what extent and at the cost of what has the public sector been used as an instrument to achieve rapid growth in Korea? The author may be interested in exploring this issue further.

Another minor point that I want to mention is that nowhere in the chapter has the role of local governments as a player in the public sector been discussed. I believe local governments have also been an integral part of the public sector in a broader sense, and may be worthy of mention.

Let me now turn to the second part of the chapter to make a couple of comments. One is concerned with the structure of the budget, and the other with budget process.

I think the author correctly argues that special accounts and various funds are more prone to abuse than general accounts, since they are more likely to suffer from lack of transparency, accountability, and efficiency. Among special accounts and funds, the latter can be more problematic because they tend to remain unattended by the National Assembly, and, therefore, may fall exclusively in the hands of government's bureaucrats, which represents another interest group by itself.

This is not too surprising to me because funds are often managed like a protection scheme in international trade. Though they are often being introduced with very good reasons or causes, once installed, they become extremely difficult to get rid of. This is because interest groups benefiting from the funds, and influence-seeking government's bureaucrats, may work together to make the funds outlive their needs.

Figure 9.15 in the chapter seems interesting in this regard. The figure shows that during the past 34 years, the share of special accounts and funds in the consolidated budget keeps decreasing for the first half of the period, but increasing for the second half of the period. What does it mean? It means that government's budget structure has been drifting toward more inefficient structure lately. I hope it is not true, but one can hardly deny that the Korean government has become more a populist regime in recent years than ever before.

Considering that the share of special accounts and of funds in the total consolidated budget has grown to as high as 16 and 29 percent, respectively, as of 2004, it seems worthy to investigate further into the causes and consequences of that.

My final comment is about the medium-term expenditure framework (MTEF), which was introduced in 2004, as a new budget process in Korea. I recall vividly that the issue of the MTEF was hotly discussed among the government and academic circle as early as in the early 1980s. I wonder why it took so long before such a useful scheme as the MTEF was introduced only in 2004?

10

Population Aging, Fiscal Policies, and National Saving Predictions for the Korean Economy

Young Jun Chun

10.1 Introduction

While the current proportion of old-age population of Korea is lower than other OECD countries, the speed of population aging is very high. Even though the proportion of the population aged 65 and older was 7.2 percent as of 2000, much lower than the developed countries, the proportion is projected to increase to 23.1 percent in 2030, almost the same as their projected average (see table 10.1). More old-age dependents relative to workers resulting from population aging suggests the likelihood of more consumption relative to income and, therefore, less national saving. Increase in the old-age dependency ratio substantially affects the fiscal policies. The government expenditures such as public pension benefits and medical insurance benefits will increase rapidly as the population is aging. Public assistance programs for the low-income classes are also expected to increase since the poverty rate for the old-age population is higher than that for working age groups in Korea. On the other hand, the decrease in working population will restrict the tax base of the future. As a result, the population aging will increase the fiscal burden of future generations and, therefore, decrease resources available for them, which suggests less saving in the future.

The long-term budgetary imbalance in Korea will also contribute to the future savings reduction through the increase in fiscal burden of future generations. Even though the consolidated budget balance at present

Young Jun Chun is a professor of economics at the University of Incheon.

The author would like to thank Laurence Kotlikoff, Shigeki Kunieda, and other seminar participants at the 16th NBER East Asia Seminar on Economics (Manila, June 23–25, 2005), for their valuable comments and suggestions.

Table 10.1   Demographic structure and dependency ratios of selected countries (%)

Country	Demographic structure						Total dependency ratio	
	2000			2030				
	0–14	15–64	65+	0–14	15–64	65+	2000	2030
World	29.7	63.4	6.9	22.4	65.8	11.8	57.7	52.0
Developed countries	18.2	67.4	14.4	15.4	62.0	22.6	48.4	61.3
Developing countries	32.5	62.4	5.1	23.6	66.5	9.9	60.3	50.4
Japan	14.7	68.1	17.2	12.7	59.3	28.0	46.8	68.6
United States	21.5	66.0	12.5	17.8	61.6	20.6	51.5	62.3
Italy	14.3	67.5	18.2	11.6	59.3	29.1	48.1	68.6
France	18.7	65.4	15.9	16.9	59.9	23.2	52.9	66.9
China	24.9	68.3	6.8	17.3	67.0	15.7	46.4	49.3
India	33.3	61.7	5.0	22.3	68.0	9.7	62.1	47.1
Korea	21.1	71.7	7.2	12.4	64.6	23.1	39.5	54.9

Source: United Nations, *World Population Projections,* 1998.

maintains surplus, the budget balance will turn deficit in the near future and the magnitude of the deficit will rapidly rise in the future if Korean government maintains the current fiscal policies. In particular, long-term budgetary imbalance of public pensions due to too generous promised level of pension benefits compared with pension contributions, and prospective increase in Medical Insurance benefits, and the resistance to increase in social insurance contributions, will deteriorate the long-term budgetary imbalance. Therefore, the current fiscal stance of Korean government will shift the fiscal burden to the future generations, which will lower the national savings rate in the future.

The purpose of this chapter is to evaluate the effects of population aging and fiscal policies on national savings in the Korean situation. For the prediction of the national savings rate of Korea for the next several decades, we employ a life-cycle model, which incorporates the generational accounting approach needed to assess the distribution of fiscal burden across generations. Even though our main focus is on the effects of population aging and fiscal stance, we also study the effects of change in asset composition, such as annuitization of asset resulting from maturing of public pensions and introduction of reverse annuity mortgages through the estimation of consumption functions, which enables comparison of elasticity of consumption with respect to various kinds of wealth. We found that the rapid population aging and long-term budgetary imbalance will substantially lower the national savings rate in Korea. A sensitivity analysis based on an alternative model, an altruistic family model, shows that the prediction is robust to the specification of altruism among generations. In addition, the estimation results of consumption functions with respect to various kinds of wealth suggest that the annuitization of wealth due to maturing of public pensions and introduction of reverse annuity mortgages is likely to further decrease the savings rate in the future.

The remainder of this chapter is organized as follows. Section 10.2 briefly describes the demographic transition in Korea for the next several decades, based on our population projection. Section 10.3 explains our basic framework for the prediction of savings rate of the future, a life-cycle model in which the agents' consumption and savings is determined by the propensity to consume and the magnitude of resources available for the remaining lifetime, including human wealth, current asset holdings, and the value of net transfer income from the government. Section 10.4 explains the data source used to estimate the propensity to consume, which is used in the projection of consumption and savings, the method of imputation of human wealth, and net transfer income from government. Section 10.5 presents our findings, and Section 10.6 summarizes and concludes the chapter.

10.2   Demographic Transition in Korea

Figures 10.1 through 10.3 summarize the population projection based on the 2001 population projection model of the National Statistics Office (NSO) of Korea. The 2001 NSO projection covers the period of 2001 to 2050. We extend the population projection up to 2110 by using the NSO's assumptions about fertility rates,[1] mortality rates,[2] and international mobility rates.[3] Baseline calculations are conducted under the assumption that the total fertility rate and age-sex mortality rates will remain constant at their 2050 levels until 2110.

The figures indicate that Korea will experience drastic change in demographic structure as well as total population. The total population is projected to reach its maximum level around 2025 and decrease rapidly thereafter. The proportion of those aged 65 and older will increase from 9 percent (as of 2005) up to 38 percent and that of the economically active population, aged 15 to 64, will decrease from 71 percent to 53 percent, which implies that while the current proportion of old-age population is smaller than other OECD countries (see table 10.2), the speed of population aging is very high, because of a low fertility rate and prolonged life expectancy. In particular, the fertility rate of Korea is much lower than many

---

1. We made three alternative fertility rate assumptions: high, medium, and low fertility rate assumption. Our base case result is based on the medium fertility assumption (see table 10.3).
2. The average life expectancy is projected to rise from 76 years currently to 83 years in 2050.
3. International movement of population is limited in Korea. For example, net immigration in 2000 was 11,000 (emigration 43,000 immigration 54,000). We assume that the international movement rates remain constant at their 2050 levels until 2110.

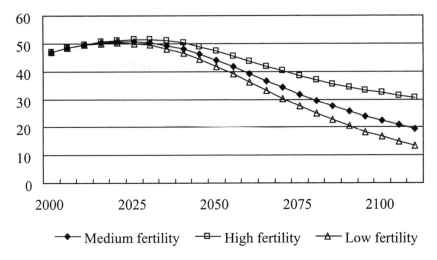

Fig. 10.1   Total population (1 million persons)

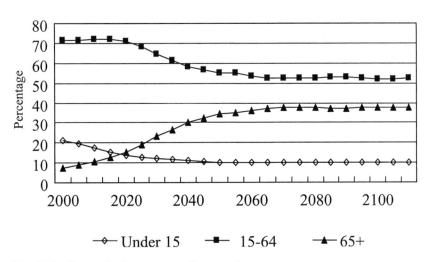

Fig. 10.2   Proportion by age group (base case)

other OECD countries.[4] Moreover, the NSO projects that the total fertility rate will decrease from 1.47 in 2000 to 1.40 in 2040, which will accelerate the process of population aging (see table 10.3).[5]

4. The fertility rate of Korea as of 2000 was 1.47. The rates for other OECD countries are 1.36 (Germany), 1.88 (France), 1.41 (Japan), 2.06 (United States), 1.64 (United Kingdom).
5. The fertility rate has fallen up to 1.13 (as of 2003), lower than its assumed level in 2030 under the base case assumption. However, we do not reflect this drastic change in fertility of recent years in the fertility assumption, since the change might be a temporary one resulting from economic crisis since 1997 triggered by foreign currency deficiency, which is followed by economic recession.

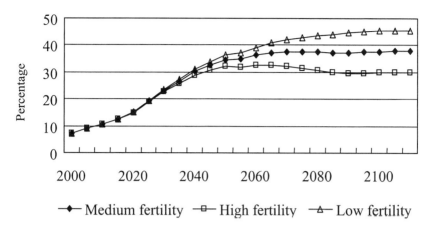

Fig. 10.3   Proportion of the aged 65 and older under alternative fertility rate assumptions

Table 10.2   Speed of population aging of selected countries

	Year attained			Number of years required for transition	
Proportion of old-age population (%)[a]	7	14	20	7→14	14→20
Japan	1970	1994	2006	24	12
France	1864	1979	2020	115	41
Germany	1932	1972	2012	40	40
United Kingdom	1929	1976	2021	47	45
Italy	1927	1988	2007	61	19
United States	1942	2013	2028	71	15
Korea	2000	2019	2026	19	7

Source: United Nations, *The Sex and Age distribution of World Population,* each year.
[a]Proportion of the population aged 65 and older.

Table 10.3   Fertility assumptions (total fertility rate)

Year	Low fertility	Medium fertility (base case)	High fertility
2000	1.47	1.47	1.47
2005	1.35	1.38	1.43
2010	1.32	1.37	1.45
2015	1.31	1.37	1.50
2020	1.27	1.37	1.54
2025	1.21	1.38	1.61
2030	1.15	1.39	1.69
2040	1.10	1.40	1.80

A United Nations (1998) projection also shows that the proportion of the population aged 65 and older will increase from 7.2 percent (as of 2000), much lower than the average of developed countries (14.4 percent), to 23.1 percent (2030), almost the same as their projected average (22.6 percent). The time required for the old-age population proportion to increase from 7 percent (14 percent) to 14 percent (20 percent) is 19 years (7 years), which is much shorter than in other developed countries: France (115 years [41 years]), United States (71 years [15 years]), and Japan (24 years [12 years]). Thus, Korea will age much faster than any other OECD countries.

10.3   Basic Framework

We adopt a life-cycle framework for the prediction of savings rates of the next several decades. The economy is populated with a large number of individuals who belong to different cohorts indexed by the year of their birth. The individuals do not face mortality risks and live for D years. We assume that each agent in the economy makes decisions on consumption flow and the magnitude of bequest to maximize the lifetime expected utility. The objective function and the budget constraint of the agent aged a at year t are as follows:

$$(1) \quad U_{a,t} = \sum_{i=a}^{D} \beta^{i-a} u(C_{i,t+i-a}, i) + \beta^{D+1-a} v(b_{D+1,t+D+1-a})$$

$$(2) \quad \sum_{i=a}^{D} \left(\prod_{s=t}^{t+i-a} \frac{1}{1+r_s} \right) C_{i,t+i-a} + \left(\prod_{s=t}^{t+D+1-a} \frac{1}{1+r_s} \right) b_{D+1,t+D+1-a}$$

$$\leq A_{a,t} + \sum_{i=a}^{D} \left(\prod_{s=t}^{t+i-a} \frac{1}{1+r_s} \right) (W_{a,t+i-a} + B_{a,t+i-a} - T_{a,t+i-a})$$

$$\equiv A_{a,t} + \sum_{i=a}^{D} \left(\prod_{s=t}^{t+i-a} \frac{1}{1+r_s} \right) W_{i,t+i-a} + \sum_{i=a}^{D} \left(\prod_{s=t}^{t+i-a} \frac{1}{1+r_s} \right) (B_{a,t+i-a} - T_{a,t+i-a})$$

$$\equiv A_{a,t} + HW_{a,t} + NB_{a,t}$$

where C, b, $u(\cdot)$, $v(\cdot)$ represent consumption and magnitude of bequest, differentiable strictly concave utility functions of consumption[6] and bequest, respectively. And, β, A, W, B, and T are discount rate, current asset holdings, noncapital income, transfer payment from the government, and tax payment to the government.

The lifetime budget constraint implies that the present value of con-

---

6. We define the utility as function of age as well as consumption amount to reflect the difference in preference across ages.

sumption and bequest is not more than the total wealth available for the remaining lifetime, which is composed of asset holdings at present ($A_{a,t}$); human wealth ($HW_{a,t}$), which is the present value of noncapital income earned for the remaining lifetime; and the net government transfer wealth ($NB_{a,t}$), which is defined as the present value of transfer income from the government minus tax payment.

The optimization of the agent aged a at period t yields the following path of consumption and bequest.

$$(3) \quad \frac{C_{i+1,t+i+1-a}}{C_{i,t+i-a}} = f^{-1}[\beta(1 + r_{t+i+1-a}); i] = s_{i,t+i-a},$$

$$f\left(\frac{c'}{c}; i\right) = \frac{u_{c'}(c', i+1)}{u_c(c, i)}, i = a, \dots, D - 1.$$

$$(4) \quad \frac{b_{D+1,t+D+1-a}}{C_{D,t+D-a}} = g^{-1}[\beta(1 + r_{t+D+1-a}); D] = s_{D,t+D-a}, \quad g\left(\frac{b}{c}; D\right) = \frac{v'(b)}{u_c(c, D)}$$

where f and g are the marginal rate of substitution functions for the homothetic utility.

Using equations (3) and (4) together with the lifetime budget constraint, we solve for the consumption of the aged a.

$$(5) \quad C_{a,t} = \left[\sum_{i=a}^{D+1}\left(\prod_{s=a}^{i} s_{i,t+i-a}\right)\right]^{-1}(A_{a,t} + HW_{a,t} + NB_{a,t})$$

$$= PC_{a,t}(A_{a,t} + HW_{a,t} + NB_{a,t})$$

Equation (5) shows that an individual's consumption at the age of a is the product of total assets available for the remaining lifetime and this age's average propensity to consumption out of the total asset ($PC_{a,t}$). Equation (5) is our basic framework to project the consumption rate for the next several decades.

We follow several steps for the projection. We first estimate the average propensity to consume, by age and sex, out of total assets using a microdata set. Then, we project the magnitude of total assets by age and sex, including current asset holdings, human wealth, and the net government transfer wealth, for the next several decades. Finally, we compute the consumption amount by age and sex for each year and savings rate.

The national savings are composed of the private savings and the government savings. The private savings are the difference of the total income, the sum of wage income, capital income and net transfer from government, and consumption (see equation [6]). The current asset holdings evolve following equation (7).

(6) $S_{a,t} = W_{a,t} + r_t A_{a,t} + B_{a,t} - T_{a,t} - C_{a,t}$

(7) $A_{a+1,t+1} = A_{a,t} + S_{a,t}$

The government saving is defined as the (primary) budget surplus of the government: in other words, tax revenue – transfer payment – government consumption (GC_t; see equation [8]), and the national income (Y_t) is the sum of labor income and capital income (see equation [9]).

(8) $$GS_t = \sum_{a=0}^{D}(T_{a,t} - B_{a,t})\mu_{a,t} - GC_t$$

(9) $$Y_t = \sum_{a=0}^{D}(W_{a,t} + r_t A_{a,t})\mu_{a,t}$$

where $\mu_{a,t}$ is the population of the aged a at period t.

10.4   Data and Imputations

To predict future savings rates, we need to estimate the average propensity to consume, and predict the magnitude of human wealth, and the net government transfer wealth by age for the future, in addition to each year's Gross National Product (GNP) and government consumption, which we discuss in section 10.3. In this section we discuss the procedures of estimating the average propensity to consume, and projection of the magnitude of human wealth, and the net government transfer wealth for the future period.

10.4.1   Estimating the Average Propensity to Consume

We use the Korea Labor and Income Panel Study (KLIPS)[7] to estimate the average propensity to consume. KLIPS consists of a household survey and an individual survey. The household survey contains information about the income, consumption, and asset holdings, including real estate and financial assets, of households. The individual survey contains information about the current employment status, current level of wage and income of the self-employed, job experience of the past, public pension participation status, and current pension benefits amount (see table 10.4).

As mentioned in section 10.3, total asset consists of current asset holdings, human wealth, and net government transfer wealth. We assume that total asset holdings of each household are equally distributed between the household head and his/her spouse.

We compute individuals' human wealth, the present value of noncapital income for the remaining lifetime, $\sum_{i=a}^{D}\{\Pi_{s=t}^{t+i-a}[1/(1 + r_s)]\} W_{i,t+i-a}$, using the

7. The KLIPS started to survey from 1998 and its most recent survey is 2004. We use the 1999 to 2002 surveys for the estimation of the average propensity to consume.

Table 10.4   **Characteristics of KLIPS sample (2002 KLIPS sample)**

Age	Population distribution		Employment rate		Average annual income (1,000 won)	
	Male	Female	Male	Female	Male	Female
15–19	380	358	0.047	0.078	6,687	7,423
20–24	293	415	0.314	0.482	10,143	12,076
25–29	418	403	0.687	0.526	15,963	13,536
30–34	454	376	0.874	0.436	20,942	14,737
35–39	419	379	0.902	0.475	24,807	13,075
40–44	445	381	0.892	0.528	24,491	13,876
45–49	374	332	0.874	0.482	25,756	11,843
50–54	299	266	0.866	0.474	26,436	11,927
55–59	219	208	0.772	0.288	19,336	8,354
60–64	142	227	0.754	0.233	13,203	7,617
65–69	100	178	0.640	0.135	13,013	6,940
70–74	53	130	0.472	0.100	8,981	2,714
75–79	24	105	0.250	0.019	4,260	4,800
80–84	12	50	0.333	0.200	12,060	2,400
85–90	5	26	0.000	0.000	0	0
90+	0	8	0.000	0.000	0	0

age-sex profile of average income and employment rate.[8] We assume that the average wage growth rate and the discount rate are 1.5 percent and 3.5 percent[9] per annum in real term.

To compute the government transfer wealth, we first compute the net public pension wealth from the KLIPS sample. For the retired people, we use the reported public pension benefit amount. For the people currently working, we use the pension benefit formula and contribution rules of public pensions. In that process, we explicitly take into account the value of each individual's already acquired pension benefit wealth, which is reflected in his or her job experience of the past, as well as the expected value of net pension wealth, which will be acquired by the contributions in the future. The value of the latter is dependent upon the expectations about the future employment status and government policy change. We assume that each individual's employment status of the future follows the same path of the employment rate by age and sex. We assume that the individuals in the sample maintain myopic expectations about the future government fiscal policies, since we do not have any consensus about the public pension reform. As for the other components of the government transfer wealth, related with social insurance, means-test public aid programs, and taxes, the

8. Table 10.4 shows the population distribution, employment rate, and the average income by age and sex in fifth year (2002) sample of KLIPS as an example.
9. This value is based on the real interest rate of government bonds in recent years.

KLIPS does not contain enough information to impute their value. Therefore, we take an alternative approach, which uses the generational accounts (GA) separated across the components of fiscal policies. We compute the ratio of the negative value of the whole generational accounts (i.e., the value of the net government transfer wealth[10]) to that of public pensions, reported in table 10.10, and multiply this ratio with net public pension wealth computed using the KLIPS sample to get the value of the net government transfer wealth. Table 10.5 reports the value of net public pension wealth and the net government transfer wealth by age and sex. The value of the net public pension wealth shows an irregular age profile, since Korean public pension consists of two different plans: occupational pensions (OCP), which covers government employees, private school employees, and military personnel; and national pension (NPS), which covers the rest of Korean residents. Since the NPS, which covers most of Korean residents, was introduced in 1998, most of NPS participants have not acquired entitlement of pension benefits. The OCP was first introduced in 1960 to cover the government employees and military personnel, and expanded the coverage to private school employees in 1975. Since the OCPs are relatively mature plans, they have produced many pension benefit recipients. However, the net pension wealth reported in table 10.5 shows that pension wealth of the aged 75 and older is 0, since the KLIPS sample does not cover many occupational pension recipients. The imputed value of the net government transfer wealth shows negative for most of the cohorts, because the value does not reflect the value of government consumption. It is also because the transfer payment from government is not large at present due to immature public pension systems and small magnitude of expenditure of public aid programs.[11]

To impute the individual's consumption, we need assumption on the distribution of consumption within family. We use Besanger, Guest, and McDonald's (2000) estimate of age-profile of consumption within families in Australia.[12] The average propensity to consumption is defined as ratio of consumption level to total wealth (for the composition of wealth in the sample, see table 10.7). We compute the average propensity to consume, using 1999 to 2002 KLIPS samples, and use the average level for the period in the projection of the savings rate for the several decades (see tables 10.8 and 10.9).

10. Section 10.4.3 explains the procedure of GA calculations and the GA values for the components of fiscal policies. The GA is defined as the present value of the net tax payment to government (taxes minus transfer income), of the representative agent of each generation for the remaining lifetime. Therefore, the net government transfer wealth defined in section 10.3 is equivalent to the negative value of the GA.

11. Table 10.10 shows that the generational accounts for most of the cohorts are positive, which implies that most taxpayers pay more taxes than they receive from the government.

12. Besanger, Guest, and McDonald (2000) also estimated the distribution of consumption among family members for the case of the United States.

Table 10.5   **Net government transfer wealth**

Age	Net public pension wealth (1,000 won)		Ratio of net government transfer to net pension wealth		Net government transfer wealth (1,000 won)	
	Male	Female	Male	Female	Male	Female
15–19	12,278	8,903	−5.90	−4.80	−72,443	−42,736
20–24	13,594	10,249	−6.18	−4.08	−84,009	−41,816
25–29	18,699	12,639	−5.49	−3.02	−102,658	−38,169
30–34	27,886	15,228	−2.77	−1.89	−77,243	−28,781
35–39	38,279	19,555	−1.32	−1.17	−50,528	−22,880
40–44	44,533	20,217	−1.32	−1.25	−58,783	−25,271
45–49	49,602	17,115	−1.28	−1.03	−63,491	−17,629
50–54	53,641	13,360	−0.81	−0.29	−43,449	−3,874
55 59	28,077	3,752	−0.37	−0.19	−10,388	−713
60–64	6,514	2,262	−1.15	−1.49	−7,491	−3,370
65–69	10,088	1,671	−1.37	−2.17	−13,820	−3,626
70–74	2,090	934	−2.47	−5.89	−5,161	−5,499
75–79	0	348	−2.70	−6.90	0	−2,403
80–84	0	0	−1.39	−4.18	0	0
85–89	0	0	0.46	1.19	0	0
90–94	0	0	2.80	13.94	0	0
95+	0	0	5.80	27.18	0	0

Table 10.6   **Composition of wealth: 2002 KLIPS sample (1,000 won)**

Age	Current asset holdings		Human wealth		Net government transfer wealth	
	Male	Female	Male	Female	Male	Female
15–19	101	149	464,594	167,397	−72,443	−42,736
20–24	7,621	2,889	527,751	177,062	−84,009	−41,816
25–29	13,694	22,580	557,049	162,465	−102,658	−38,169
30–34	30,600	32,602	547,875	142,664	−77,243	−28,781
35–39	50,813	57,365	493,474	116,059	−50,528	−22,880
40–44	54,826	57,409	409,820	97,866	−58,873	−25,271
45–49	62,701	69,142	339,778	67,157	−63,491	−17,629
50–54	77,351	62,850	255,087	45,279	−43,449	−3,874
55–59	80,646	70,791	148,242	21,792	−10,388	−713
60–64	75,828	66,876	92,097	12,672	−7,491	−3,370
65–69	78,817	61,860	62,572	5,887	−13,820	−3,626
70–74	92,685	49,102	21,315	1,415	−5,161	−5,499
75–79	47,469	26,347	4,208	278	0	−2,403
80–84	42,306	29,215	1,515	0	0	0
85–89	62,100	18,300	0	0	0	0
90–94	0	7,500	0	0	0	0
95+	0	0	0	0	0	0

Table 10.7   Age profile of consumption within family

	0–15	16–24	25–39	40–49	50–59	60–64	65–69	70–74	75+
Australia	0.68	0.89	1.00	0.98	1.00	1.05	0.87	0.95	1.19
United States	0.72	0.72	1.00	1.00	1.00	1.00	1.27	1.27	1.27

Source: Besanger, Guest, and McDonald (2000).

Table 10.8   Average propensity to consume (2002 KLIPS sample)

	Average wealth (A)		Average consumption (B)		Average propensity to consume (A/B)	
Age	Male	Female	Male	Female	Male	Female
15–19	392,253	124,810	4,915	4,956	0.013	0.040
20–24	451,363	138,135	4,578	4,937	0.010	0.036
25–29	468,085	146,876	6,101	5,715	0.013	0.039
30–34	501,231	146,486	8,779	7,104	0.018	0.048
35–39	493,759	150,544	10,769	7,245	0.022	0.048
40–44	405,863	130,004	10,628	6,908	0.026	0.053
45–49	338,989	118,670	9,379	6,061	0.028	0.051
50–54	288,988	104,255	9,031	5,699	0.031	0.055
55–59	218,500	91,870	7,960	5,329	0.036	0.058
60–64	160,435	76,178	6,737	6,073	0.042	0.080
65–69	127,569	64,121	6,139	4,912	0.048	0.077
70–74	108,839	45,017	5,062	4,774	0.047	0.106
75–79	51,677	24,222	3,897	4,879	0.076[a]	0.214[a]
80–84	43,821	29,215	3,480	5,331	0.076[a]	0.214[a]
85–89	62,100	18,300	4,354	6,076	0.076[a]	0.214[a]
90–94	0	7,500	0	4,294	0.076[a]	0.214[a]
95+	0	0	0	4,460	0.076[a]	0.214[a]

[a]We assume that the average propensity to consume is same for the cohorts aged 75 and older.

10.4.2   Projecting Human Wealth and Current Asset Holdings

The magnitude of human wealth and current asset holdings of the future are computed based on the assumption that the productivity growth rate and interest rate remain constant (i.e., we adopt a partial equilibrium approach). The productivity growth rate and interest rate are assumed 1.5 percent and 3.5 percent per annum in real term. The projection begins with imputation of aggregate value of asset and human capital stock at the benchmark year. The aggregate labor income is assumed 60 percent of GDP based on the record of labor income share for the period 1990 to 2003. We compute the distribution of wage income by age and sex, by allocating the aggregate value based on the age-sex profile of wage income estimated by the Ministry of Labor (2001). Then we use the definition of human capital

Table 10.9   **Average propensity to consume (1999–2002 KLIPS sample)**

	1999		2000		2001		2002		Average (1999–2002)	
Age	Male	Female	Male	Female	Male	Female	Male	Female	Male	Female
15–19	0.013	0.044	0.012	0.042	0.012	0.041	0.013	0.040	0.012	0.042
20–24	0.011	0.039	0.010	0.040	0.010	0.036	0.010	0.036	0.010	0.038
25–29	0.014	0.041	0.013	0.046	0.013	0.043	0.013	0.039	0.013	0.042
30–34	0.018	0.049	0.018	0.050	0.016	0.045	0.018	0.048	0.017	0.048
35–39	0.024	0.054	0.024	0.057	0.021	0.049	0.022	0.048	0.023	0.052
40–44	0.028	0.048	0.028	0.052	0.027	0.046	0.026	0.053	0.027	0.050
45–49	0.029	0.041	0.030	0.048	0.025	0.045	0.028	0.051	0.028	0.046
50–54	0.032	0.042	0.033	0.047	0.030	0.045	0.031	0.055	0.031	0.047
55–59	0.036	0.056	0.037	0.058	0.030	0.050	0.036	0.058	0.035	0.056
60–64	0.041	0.060	0.043	0.061	0.040	0.058	0.042	0.080	0.041	0.065
65–69	0.048	0.072	0.053	0.074	0.039	0.084	0.048	0.077	0.047	0.077
70–74	0.057	0.088	0.046	0.085	0.033	0.083	0.047	0.106	0.046	0.091
75+	0.092	0.235	0.137	0.242	0.093	0.207	0.076	0.214	0.099	0.225
									(0.05)[a]	(0.123)[a]

[a]Adjusted value used in predictions of savings rate.

(see equation [2]), to compute the stock value of human capital for the next several decades.

The aggregate value of asset holdings is assumed to be aggregate capital income, 40 percent of GDP, divided by the interest rate. We impute the age-sex distribution of asset holdings in the benchmark year using the asset-holding profile by age and sex using the 1999 to 2002 KLIPS survey. The distribution following the benchmark year is computed using equations (6) and (7).

10.4.3   Projecting Net Government Transfer Wealth

The net government transfer wealth is the present value of the transfer income from the government minus tax payment to the government for the remaining lifetime, which is the negative value of generational accounts.

Computing generational accounts is based on the government's intertemporal budget constraint. This constraint, written as equation (10), requires that the future net tax payments of current and future generations be sufficient, in present value, to cover the present value of future government consumption as well as service the government's initial net debt.

(10)
$$\sum_{s=0}^{D} N_{t,t-s} + \sum_{s=t}^{\infty} N_{t,t+s} = \sum_{s=t}^{\infty} G_s (1 + r)^{-(s-t)} - W_t^g$$

The first summation on the left-hand side of equation (10) adds together the generational accounts of existing generations. The term $N_{t,t-s}$ stands for the account of the generation born in year $t - s$. The index s in this summation runs from age 0 to age D, the maximum length of life. The second summation on the left-hand side of equation (10) adds together the present value of remaining net payments of future generations, with s representing the number of years after year t that each future generation is born. The first term on the right-hand side of equation (10) is the present value of government consumption. In this summation the values of government consumption, G_s in year s, are discounted by the pretax real interest rate, r. The remaining term on the right-hand side, W_t^g, denotes the government's net wealth in year t—its assets minus its explicit debt.

Equation (10) indicates the zero sum nature of intergenerational fiscal policy. Holding the present value of government consumption fixed, a reduction in the present value of net taxes extracted from current generations (a decline in the first summation on the left size of equation [10]) necessitates an increase in the present value of net tax payment of future generations.

The term $N_{t,t}$ in equation (10) is defined by:

$$(11) \qquad N_{t,k} = \sum_{s=\max(t,k)}^{k+D} T_{s,k} P_{s,k} (1 + r)^{-(s-t)}$$

In expression (11), $T_{s,k}$ stands for the projected average net tax payments to the government made in year s by the generation born in year k. The term $P_{s,k}$ stands for the number of surviving members of the cohort in year s who were born in year k. For the generations who are born in year k, where $k > t$, the summation begins in year k. Regardless of the generation's year of birth, the discounting is always back to year t. A set of generational accounts is simply a set of values of $N_{t,k}$, one for each existing and future generation, with the property that the combined present value adds up to the right-hand side of equation (10).

The traditional Generational Accounts are calculated in two steps. The first step involves calculation of the net tax payments of current generations (the first term on the left-hand side of equation [10]). This is done on the basis of current fiscal rules without being constrained by the intertemporal budget constraint of the government. In the second step, given on the right-hand side of equation (10) and the first term on the left-hand side of equation (10), we determine, as a residual, the value of the second term on the left-hand side of equation (10), which is the collective payment, measured as a time-t present value, required of future generations. Accordingly, whereas the fiscal burdens for current generations are based entirely on current fiscal rules, the government budget constraint fully determines the fiscal burdens for future generations.

Based on the collective amount required of future generations, we determine the average present value of lifetime net tax payments for each member of each future generation under the assumption that the average lifetime tax payments of successive generations rise at the economy's rate of productivity growth. Leaving out this growth adjustment, the lifetime net tax payments of future generations are directly comparable with those of current newborns, since the generational accounts of both newborns and future generations take into account net tax payments over these generations' entire lifetimes. Measuring the generational imbalance as the difference between two lifetime tax burdens provides a measure for the sustainability of the public finances. If future generations bear a heavier tax burden than the newly born do, current fiscal rules will have to be adjusted in the future to meet the budget constraint.

We modify the presentation of generational accounts to make the generational accounts appropriate for calculation of consumption level of generations who will survive for the next several decades. We compute the generational accounts by age and sex at every year for the next several decades, because the consumption by age and sex at each year is dependent upon the net government transfer wealth, the negative value of generational accounts, at the year. The standard approach estimates the fiscal gap between current and future generations, assuming existing policy for current generations. It is also customary to express this fiscal gap using other measures, such as the required changes in taxes and/or transfer payments for current and future generations together. Because it is likely that some of the burden will be placed on current generations and there are differing effects of required changes in taxes and transfer payments across future generations, we take this latter approach one step further and actually present alternative estimates of the accounts for current generations and future generations, taking such projected increases in their fiscal burden into account, in addition we also renew the generational accounts for nonzero age groups. For example, we renew the accounts of the cohort aged a every year, who were $a - 1$ years old in the previous year, and this process continues until this cohort reaches the age D, the maximum length of life. The renewal of the accounts is necessary, because the consumption of the aged a is dependent upon the renewed accounts. We denote as GA1 the accounts as conventionally presented, and refer to the modified accounts incorporating the adjustment to restore fiscal balance as GA2.[13]

Table 10.10 reports standard generational accounts (GA1) for Korea,[14] under the base case assumptions for the productivity growth rate (1.5 percent) and the real discount rate (3.5 percent).[15] The table shows positive values of net payments for most cohorts alive in our benchmark year 2000 for GA calculation, except for cohorts aged 90 or older, indicating that

---

13. A similar presentation method to this one has been used by others in the past, including Auerbach and Oreopoulos (2000) and Bovenberg and ter Rele (2000).
14. The data source and calculation procedure is explained in detail in Auerbach and Chun (2006) and Auerbach, Chun, and Yoo (2005).
15. The accounts are expressed in thousands of won, the domestic currency of Korea. As of July 2005, 1,025 won were worth about U.S.$1.

Table 10.10 **Generational accounts (GA1; 1,000 won)**

Age	Net payment	Public pensions	Medical insurance	Employment insurance	IACI	MLSS	OSTP
0	56,025	−9,349	−5,100	−684	186	−2,544	−3,344
5	62,689	−8,914	−4,164	−765	220	−2,501	−3,349
10	67,649	−9,174	−3,793	−844	244	−2,431	−3,231
15	67,707	−14,596	−3,687	−933	260	−2,364	−3,162
20	77,218	−11,430	−3,746	−958	261	−2,281	−3,136
25	73,675	−15,271	−4,433	−819	238	−2,183	−3,106
30	64,700	−18,117	−5,248	−706	166	−2,145	−3,056
35	39,226	−35,332	−5,936	−625	143	−2,104	−2,927
40	36,720	−27,882	−6,834	−590	15	−2,098	−2,832
45	32,425	−23,520	−7,514	−512	−9	−2,076	−2,716
50	22,226	−22,910	−8,034	−450	−16	−1,995	−2,593
55	12,788	−21,396	−8,219	−411	95	−1,958	−2,475
60	14,370	−8,371	−7,764	−324	17	−1,894	−2,381
65	8,448	−6,317	−6,864	−245	19	−1,742	−2,287
70	6,407	−3,756	−5,476	−233	−54	−1,468	−1,889
75	5,837	−1,366	−4,185	−181	−43	−979	−1,491
80	2,818	−990	−3,243	−136	−33	−665	−1,144
85	541	−626	−2,376	−98	−25	−340	−864
90	−2,543	−324	−1,635	−67	−18	−260	−612
95	−1,508	−223	−1,022	−42	−11	0	−392
99	−485	−10	−384	−16	−4	0	−149
Future generations	122,341	41,676	14,316	1,478	−487		

Age	Labor income tax	Capital income tax	Consumption tax	Tax on asset holding	Asset transactions tax	Other taxes	Seigniorage
0	7,265	12,769	37,745	3,935	8,745	6,227	172
5	8,174	14,788	38,513	4,404	9,540	6,549	194
10	8,982	16,849	38,963	4,856	10,199	6,813	217
15	9,815	19,160	39,601	5,368	10,889	7,113	244
20	10,624	22,412	40,150	5,952	11,680	7,417	275
25	10,788	23,492	39,102	6,207	11,901	7,495	264
30	9,951	23,057	36,440	6,186	10,837	7,077	258
35	9,535	21,978	33,071	5,939	8,902	6,344	239
40	7,761	20,860	29,603	5,569	7,275	5,638	236
45	6,169	20,016	26,144	5,318	5,925	4,989	211
50	4,033	17,238	22,862	4,689	4,895	4,299	198
55	1,985	15,181	19,278	3,830	3,243	3,459	175
60	588	11,291	15,834	2,957	1,601	2,655	163
65	54	8,582	12,681	2,082	393	1,963	130
70	0	6,323	9,893	1,517	38	1,404	108
75	0	4,101	7,975	908	0	1,023	74
80	0	2,239	5,453	566	0	708	63
85	0	974	3,198	233	0	422	42
90	0	131	52	31	0	125	33
95	0	49	33	3	0	76	19
99	0	28	13	1	0	29	6

Notes: LACI represents Labor's Accident Compensation Insurance, which is the Korean version of Worker's Compensation. MLSS represents Minimum Living Standards Security System, which is a public aid program to low income classes. OSTP represents the other social transfer programs.

most generations will, on balance, pay more in present value than they receive. One reason for positive burdens even among the elderly is the high taxes on consumption, capital income, and assets, relative to taxes on labor income.[16] The age profile of the average tax burden on capital is more skewed to older age groups than that of labor income taxes, and the consumption tax burden for older age groups is quite high.

The more important reason that even older generations have positive net payments is that social welfare benefits such as public pension benefits, medical insurance (MI) benefits, minimum living standards security (MLSS) benefits, and other social welfare services (OSTP) were quite small in the aggregate as of 2000. Aggregate public pension and MI benefits were 1.1 percent and 1.7 percent of GDP respectively as of 2000, and those for the MLSS and the OSTP were 0.5 percent and 0.6 percent of GDP, respectively. However, maturation of the public pension system and the projected increase in social welfare expenditures will increase transfer payments to old-age groups. This maturation is shown in figure 10.4, which displays the relative (to age-40 males) benefit profile in 2000 along with the corresponding profiles projected at other dates through 2080. As a result, the accounts for a wider range of old-age groups will turn negative in the future, given current policy.

The row labeled "Future Generation" in table 10.10 indicates the present value of amounts that those born in 2001 will, on average, pay, assuming that subsequent generations pay this same amount except for the adjustment for growth. The account for future generations is about 118 percent larger than those for those aged 0, which implies that the current fiscal policies are not sustainable and that a substantial fiscal burden is shifted to future generations.

Table 10.10 also reports the present value, rest-of-life transfer benefits and tax burdens by category. The substantial negative entries for public pensions and medical insurance play a key role in the large overall generational imbalance. On the tax side, three important characteristics of the Korean tax system are: (a) the large share of consumption taxes; (b) the relative unimportance of labor income taxes; and (c) the large proportion accounted for by taxes on asset transactions. The largest present value (for ages 0 and age 30) is the consumption tax, followed by the capital income tax, the tax on asset transactions, labor income tax, other taxes, and taxes on asset holdings. The present value of the tax burden on older age groups, relative to that on younger age groups, is heaviest for consumption taxes, followed by capital income taxes, taxes on asset holdings, taxes on asset transactions, and labor income taxes.

---

16. Revenues from consumption tax, capital income tax, taxes on asset holding, and labor income tax in South Korea as of 2000 were 9.1 percent, 5.1 percent, 1.3 percent, and 2.2 percent of GDP, respectively.

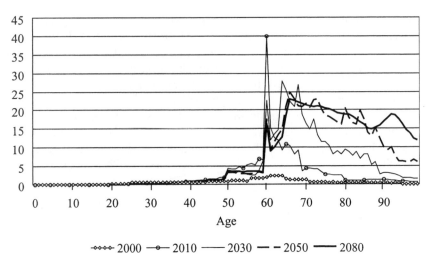

-◇◇◇- 2000   -●- 2010   —— 2030   — - 2050   —— 2080

Fig. 10.4   Public pension benefit profile

Figure 10.5 reports the GA2,[17] omitting the accounts for the nonzero aged in the future, under alternative scenarios to attainment long-term fiscal balance of government budget: (a) no change in fiscal policies; (b) increasing tax burden of the cohorts alive in 2010 and thereafter by 23.1 percent of tax burden under current policies; and (c) maintaining budget balance every year (pay-as-you-go scheme). The case (a) is a hypothetical situation in which the government does not intend to attain long-term budgetary balance, thus, this should be treated as a benchmark case to evaluate the effects of policy changes to attain long-term budgetary balance. The case (b) is a scheme of prefunding, since under this scheme the government (primary) budget balance maintains surplus until around 2025 and thereafter the budget turns deficit. Comparison of case (a) with case (b) or case (c) shows that the current fiscal policies are not sustainable and to maintain the current policies related with government consumption and transfer payments the net tax burden for future generations as well as current generations should be substantially raised. The profile of fiscal burden across generations is crucially dependent upon the method to attain the long-term budgetary balance. The pay-as-you-go scheme (case [c]) further shifts the fiscal burden to the future generations than the prefunding scheme (case [b]).

17. The index for the generations specified in the x-axis is according to the year of birth of each cohort, with the 2000 newborns being generation 0. The generations indexed below zero are current generations and those indexed higher than 0 are future generations. The accounts for the future generations are evaluated at the productivity value as of 2000 to make the accounts for future generations comparable with those of current generations.

10.5   Findings

10.5.1   Projected Savings Rates, 2002–2090

We predict the savings rates for the period 2002 to 2090, based on the life-cycle framework described in section 10.3, and using the imputed value of current asset holdings, the projected value of human wealth, net government transfer wealth explained in section 10.4. Before our prediction, we adjust the average propensity to consume to reproduce the level of aggregate consumption in our benchmark year 2002. We adjust the average propensity in two steps. First, we reduce the propensity to consume for the aged 75 and older by 50 percent, since their estimated value is extremely high, more than 200 percent of the value for the aged 70 to 74. It is also due to the fact that the number of observations of the aged 75 and older is very small, thus, the estimated value of the average propensity to consume is not reliable. The predicted value of aggregate consumption in our benchmark year, using the adjusted propensity to consume, is 413 trillion won, 6.2 percent higher than its actual value. Therefore, we reduce the overall level of the average propensity to consume by 6.2 percent, maintaining its profile by age and sex.

Tables 10.11 to 10.14 summarize the prediction results. Table 10.11 shows the predicted value, evaluated at the fixed price as of 2002, of the wealth and annual values related with the wealth and government budget balance. The noncapital income grows faster than the productivity growth rate (1.5 percent per annum) until the late 2010s despite the population aging, since the total population will increase until it reaches a peak around 2025. The growth rate of noncapital income falls rapidly, which induces the decrease in growth rate of human wealth, which is defined as the present value of noncapital income earned for the remaining lifetime. The growth rate of the human wealth is lower than that of noncapital income, because the former reflects the decrease in the growth rate of the latter in the future. The human wealth has the largest proportion of total wealth.

The transfer wealth, which is defined as the present value of the net transfer income from the government for the remaining lifetime, is negative for the next several decades under the current policies. However, its value becomes positive around 2055, which reflects the fact that the government transfer payments will increase much faster than the tax revenue due to the population aging, maturing of public pensions, and increasing demand for social welfare expenditure. Table 10.10, which summarizes generational accounts for Korea (GA1), shows that the accounts for most of the current generations are positive, reflecting the fact that the current level of government transfer payment is low due to the short history of public pensions and low level of social welfare expenditure at present. Despite the positive accounts for most of the current generations, the generational imbalance

Table 10.11   Predicted values (current policy, medium fertility; 1 trillion won; 2002-fixed price)

| | Wealth | | | | | Annual values | | | | | | |
| | | | | | | Taxes and government transfer | | | | | | |
Year	Total	Asset-holdings	Human wealth	Transfer wealth	Noncapital income	Net transfer	Transfer payment	Taxes	Government consumption	Budget deficit	Private consumption	GDP
2002	15,408	4,213	13,564	−2,369	411	−122	29	153	109	−13	389	685
2005	16,084	4,262	14,148	−2,326	444	−131	34	167	115	−16	415	720
2010	17,134	4,320	15,001	−2,187	500	−141	45	187	126	−14	463	780
2015	18,063	4,336	15,695	−1,967	550	−147	57	206	136	−12	507	831
2020	18,849	4,301	16,228	−1,679	594	−147	74	223	145	−2	548	873
2025	19,531	4,222	16,677	−1,367	635	−139	96	237	155	16	587	910
2030	20,064	4,105	17,017	−1,058	670	−127	120	250	165	38	621	938
2035	20,410	3,936	17,232	−759	697	−113	144	260	174	61	645	953
2040	20,574	3,699	17,353	−479	712	−98	167	268	183	86	661	952
2045	20,584	3,395	17,420	−230	721	−82	190	275	190	108	665	942
2050	20,497	3,061	17,450	−13	726	−68	211	281	196	128	660	925
2055	20,398	2,717	17,506	175	726	−58	225	287	199	141	651	902
2060	20,342	2,395	17,602	345	728	−48	238	290	202	155	642	884
2065	20,369	2,141	17,739	489	728	−37	251	292	205	169	635	867
2070	20,495	1,985	17,897	613	735	−29	261	294	208	179	632	864
2075	20,724	1,910	18,087	728	734	−24	268	297	210	186	633	858
2080	21,054	1,846	18,366	842	733	−22	272	299	211	189	637	853
2085	21,487	1,767	18,757	963	735	−21	275	301	212	192	644	850
2090	22,026	1,658	19,277	1,091	738	−18	279	302	214	196	654	846

Table 10.12 — Annual growth rate of predicted values (Current policy, medium fertility; %)

	Wealth					Taxes and government transfer			Annual values			
Year	Total	Asset-holdings	Human wealth	Transfer wealth	Noncapital income	Net transfer	Transfer payment	Taxes	Government consumption	Budget deficit	Private consumption	GDP
2002	1.5	0.4	1.5	a	2.7	a	5.4	3.1	1.9	a	2.3	1.8
2005	1.4	0.3	1.3	a	2.6	a	6.1	2.6	1.9	a	2.3	1.8
2010	1.2	0.2	1.1	a	2.2	a	5.0	2.3	1.6	a	2.1	1.5
2015	1.0	-0.1	0.8	a	1.7	a	5.9	1.8	1.4	a	1.8	1.1
2020	0.8	-0.3	0.6	a	1.4	a	5.7	1.4	1.3	a	1.5	0.9
2025	0.6	-0.5	0.5	a	1.3	a	5.2	1.1	1.3	28.1	1.3	0.8
2030	0.4	-0.7	0.3	a	1.0	a	4.2	0.9	1.2	12.7	1.0	0.5
2035	0.2	-1.1	0.2	a	0.5	a	3.3	0.7	1.1	8.3	0.6	0.1
2040	0.1	-1.6	0.1	a	0.3	a	2.9	0.6	0.9	5.8	0.3	-0.2
2045	-0.1	-2.0	0.0	a	0.3	a	2.3	0.5	0.6	4.0	0.0	-0.3
2050	-0.1	-2.3	0.0	a	0.0	a	1.7	0.4	0.5	2.5	-0.3	-0.5
2055	-0.1	-2.6	0.1	20.9	0.1	a	1.2	0.3	0.3	1.8	-0.3	-0.4
2060	0.0	-2.4	0.1	9.3	-0.1	a	1.2	0.2	0.3	2.0	-0.3	-0.5
2065	0.1	-1.9	0.2	5.5	0.2	a	0.9	0.2	0.3	1.4	-0.1	-0.1
2070	0.2	-1.0	0.2	3.9	0.1	a	0.7	0.2	0.2	1.0	0.0	-0.1
2075	0.3	-0.7	0.3	3.2	-0.1	a	0.3	0.1	0.1	0.5	0.1	-0.2
2080	0.4	-0.7	0.4	2.9	0.0	a	0.2	0.1	0.1	0.2	0.2	-0.1
2085	0.5	-1.1	0.5	2.7	0.1	a	0.2	0.1	0.1	0.3	0.3	-0.1
2090	0.6	-1.5	0.7	2.4	0.1	a	0.3	0.1	0.2	0.6	0.3	-0.1

[a]The growth rates of these components are not reported because their absolute level is negative.

Table 10.13   Predicted national savings rates (% of GDP)

Year	Low fertility			Medium fertility			High fertility		
	Current policy	Prefunding	Balanced budget	Current policy	Prefunding	Balanced budget	Current policy	Prefunding	Balanced budget
2002	27.1	29.4	27.5	27.2	29.4	27.5	27.2	29.5	27.6
2005	26.3	29.0	27.0	26.3	29.1	27.0	26.3	29.2	27.1
2010	24.5	28.3	26.2	24.5	28.4	26.2	24.6	28.4	26.3
2015	22.8	26.4	25.5	22.8	26.3	25.5	22.7	26.4	25.6
2020	20.7	24.2	24.7	20.6	24.1	24.7	20.5	24.0	24.6
2025	18.7	21.9	24.0	18.5	21.8	23.8	18.2	21.6	23.6
2030	16.6	19.7	23.1	16.2	19.5	22.8	15.7	19.0	22.4
2035	14.3	17.5	22.1	13.9	17.0	21.6	13.3	16.4	20.9
2040	12.0	14.9	20.8	11.4	14.3	20.0	10.5	13.5	19.0
2045	10.0	12.9	19.8	9.2	12.1	18.7	8.0	11.0	17.3
2050	8.5	11.2	19.0	7.5	10.3	17.6	6.3	9.2	15.9
2055	6.6	9.2	17.9	5.7	8.5	16.3	4.6	7.5	14.4
2060	5.0	7.6	17.0	4.4	7.0	15.4	3.6	6.4	13.4
2065	3.3	5.6	15.8	3.0	5.6	14.2	2.8	5.5	12.3
2070	2.5	4.8	15.3	2.8	5.2	13.7	2.9	5.7	12.1
2075	0.5	2.7	13.5	1.6	4.1	12.4	2.5	5.2	11.2
2080	-1.9	0.0	11.3	0.4	2.8	11.0	2.3	5.1	10.6
2085	-5.0	-3.1	8.6	-1.0	1.4	9.5	2.4	5.1	10.3
2090	-8.8	-7.1	5.3	-2.7	-0.4	7.8	2.3	5.1	9.9

Note: The fertility assumption is shown in table 10.3.

Table 10.14 Composition of national savings rates (% of GDP)

| | Low fertility | | | | | | Medium fertility | | | | | | High fertility | | | | | |
| | Current policy | | Prefunding | | Balanced budget | | Current policy | | Prefunding | | Balanced budget | | Current policy | | Prefunding | | Balanced budget | |
Year	Private	Government	Private	Government	Private	Government	Private	Government	Private	Government	Private	Government	Private	Government	Private	Government	Private	Government
2002	25.3	1.8	27.6	1.8	27.5	0	25.4	1.8	27.6	1.8	27.5	0	25.4	1.8	27.7	1.8	27.6	0
2005	24.2	2.1	26.9	2.1	27.0	0	24.2	2.1	27.0	2.1	27.0	0	24.2	2.1	27.1	2.1	27.1	0
2010	22.7	1.8	21.0	7.3	26.2	0	22.7	1.8	21.1	7.3	26.2	0	22.8	1.8	21.1	7.3	26.3	0
2015	21.4	1.4	19.3	7.1	25.5	0	21.4	1.4	19.3	7.0	25.5	0	21.4	1.3	19.4	7.0	25.6	0
2020	20.4	0.3	18.0	6.2	24.7	0	20.4	0.2	18.0	6.1	24.7	0	20.4	0.1	18.0	6.0	24.6	0
2025	20.3	-1.6	17.5	4.4	24.0	0	20.2	-1.7	17.5	4.3	23.8	0	20.1	-1.9	17.4	4.2	23.6	0
2030	20.4	-3.8	17.4	2.3	23.1	0	20.2	-4.0	17.3	2.2	22.8	0	20.0	-4.3	17.0	2.0	22.4	0
2035	20.5	-6.2	17.4	0.1	22.1	0	20.3	-6.4	17.1	-0.1	21.6	0	20.0	-6.7	16.7	-0.3	20.9	0
2040	20.7	-8.7	17.3	-2.4	20.8	0	20.4	-9.0	16.9	-2.6	20.0	0	19.9	-9.4	16.3	-2.8	19.0	0
2045	21.2	-11.2	17.6	-4.7	19.8	0	20.7	-11.5	17.0	-4.9	18.7	0	19.9	-11.9	16.1	-5.1	17.3	0
2050	22.1	-13.6	18.2	-7.0	19.0	0	21.3	-13.8	17.4	-7.1	17.6	0	20.4	-14.1	16.3	-7.1	15.9	0
2055	22.3	-15.7	18.2	-9.0	17.9	0	21.4	-15.7	17.2	-8.7	16.3	0	20.2	-15.6	15.9	-8.4	14.4	0
2060	23.0	-18.0	18.7	-11.1	17.0	0	21.9	-17.5	17.5	-10.5	15.4	0	20.6	-17.0	16.1	-9.7	13.4	0
2065	23.7	-20.4	19.2	-13.6	15.8	0	22.5	-19.5	18.0	-12.4	14.2	0	21.1	-18.3	16.4	-10.9	12.3	0
2070	24.7	-22.2	20.2	-15.4	15.3	0	23.5	-20.7	18.9	-13.7	13.7	0	21.9	-19.0	17.3	-11.6	12.1	0
2075	24.3	-23.8	19.6	-16.9	13.5	0	23.3	-21.7	18.7	-14.6	12.4	0	21.8	-19.3	17.1	-11.9	11.2	0
2080	23.3	-25.2	18.4	-18.4	11.3	0	22.6	-22.2	17.9	-15.1	11.0	0	21.6	-19.3	16.9	-11.8	10.6	0
2085	21.7	-26.7	16.7	-19.8	8.6	0	21.6	-22.6	16.8	-15.4	9.5	0	21.4	-19.0	16.6	-11.5	10.3	0
2090	19.9	-28.7	14.6	-21.7	5.3	0	20.5	-23.2	15.6	-16.0	7.8	0	21.0	-18.7	16.3	-11.2	9.9	0

Note: The fertility assumption is shown in table 10.3.

of the net payment is very high (118 percent), since the forward-looking property of the generational accounting reflects the rapid increase in government transfer payments in the future due to maturing of public pensions, and prospective increase in social welfare expenditure resulting from population aging and increasing demand for social welfare expenditure.[18] The negative accounts of public pensions and medical insurance and social welfare expenditure (MLSS, OSTP) explains a substantial part of the generational imbalance. While the growth rate of tax revenue is lower than that of government transfer payment because of the reduction in the economically active population due to population aging, the government consumption grows faster than tax revenues, which further deteriorates the government budget balance.

The growth rate of aggregate consumption is higher than the GDP growth rate, due to the population aging and increasing age profile of the average propensity to consume, which raises the ratio of private consumption to GDP.[19] The increasing ratio of consumption to GDP results in decrease in the value of asset holdings. The absolute level of the asset holdings falls after the early 2010s, which decreases capital income and the GDP growth rate.[20]

Tables 10.13 and 10.14 show the predicted savings rates under the alternative assumptions about the fiscal policies and fertility rates. We simulate 3 cases: (a) a hypothetical situation in which current fiscal policies are maintains disregarding the long-term budget imbalance; (b) an economy in which the government proportionally adjusts the tax burden of cohorts alive in 2010 and thereafter to match the present value of tax revenue of the present and the future to that of government transfer payment and government consumption (prefunding); and (c) an economy in which the government maintains the budget balance every year (balanced budget or pay-as-you-go scheme).

The private savings, and government savings, defined as the government primary budget surplus, depend crucially upon the method to restore the long-term budgetary balance. Compared with case (a), the national savings rates, the sum of private and government savings rates, in the case of prefunding is higher, since higher level of transfer wealth in case (a) induces higher level of consumption and the government budget in case (a) is more

18. Auerbach and Chun (2006) projected that aggregate public pension benefits will increase from 1.1 percent of GDP as of 2000 to 16 percent in 2080. Benefits of medical insurance and public aid programs are projected to increase from 1.7 percent and 1.1 percent of GDP, respectively, to 5.1 percent and 2.1 percent during the same period. The projected level of the medical insurance benefits and public aid to low-income families is based on very conservative income elasticity (1.2). Therefore, the projected levels should be interpreted as their minimum level under current policies.

19. The ratio rises from 56.8 percent as of 2002 to 72.5 percent in 2050.

20. The effects on the asset holdings might be exaggerated, since our approach is a partial equilibrium approach. Under a general equilibrium approach the effects will be mitigated, since the increase in the rate of return to capital will be a buffer to mitigate the reduction in asset holdings.

imbalanced, which implies that delay in the policy revisions to restore the long-term government budgetary balance will induce lower savings rates. Comparison of case (b) and case (c) shows the effects of intergenerational redistribution of net tax burden. Figure 10.5 shows that transition from the prefunding scheme to the balanced budget scheme redistributes the fiscal burden, defined as net payment to the government, from current generations to future generations. This redistribution of resource from the future generations to the current generations raises the savings rates of current generations. Therefore, the private savings rates of the near future are higher in case (c).[21] However, the private savings rates after 2050 are higher in case (b), because under the prefunding scheme, the resource for the future generations is much larger than that under the pay-as-you-go scheme. The government savings rate of the period after 2020 is lower in case (b), since case (b) allows the budget deficit in the far-away future while the prefunding accumulates the budget surplus in the government fund in preparation for the budget deficit in the future.

Even though there are some variations in the projected savings rate depending on the method to restore the long-term budgetary balance, the overall results imply that the drastic decrease in the savings rate will be inevitable because of the population aging and its magnitude will be substantial. In particular, the decrease in the government savings rate resulting from the increase in government's transfer payments and government consumption contributes substantially to the decrease in national savings rate and the absolute magnitude of the fall in government savings rate is much larger than that in private savings rate.

We try a sensitivity analysis on the fertility rates. Changing the fertility rates substantially affects the savings rate in the long run. However, the national savings rates of the next several decades are not affected much, because we assume gradual change in fertility rates (see table 10.3). It is also because it takes time for the change in the fertility rates, which changes the number of newborns, to affect the age structure of the population, which affects the aggregate value of consumption and savings.

It is remarkable that in the transition period, increase (decrease) in fertility rate decreases (increases) the private and government savings rate, even though the magnitude of the decrease (increase) is not very large. Figure 10.6 shows that even though the increase in fertility rates increases private savings (pri sav), the speed of increase in private savings is lower than that of GDP for a considerable time, because the increase in the proportion of young population reduces the net transfer payments (gov net trf), which makes the speed of increase in disposable income in aggregate lower than that of GDP. Figure 10.6 also shows that the speed of increase in gov-

---

21. The redistribution of resources to the current generations increases the consumption level of current generations. However, the private savings rates also rise since the marginal (also average) propensity to consume is lower than 1.

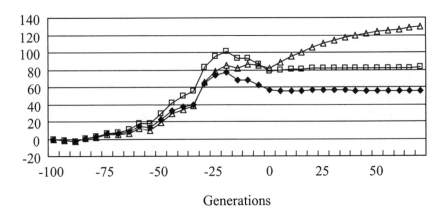

Fig. 10.5   Generational accounts (GA2; 1 million won)

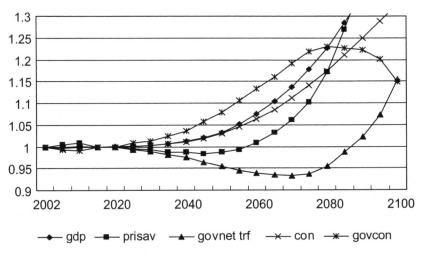

Fig. 10.6   Ratio of variables under high fertility to those under medium fertility (under current policy)

ernment consumption (gov con) is higher than that of GDP in the transition period. It is due to the fact that the increase in the young population dependency ratio resulting from the increase in fertility rate increases the government consumption for the young population, such as educational expenditure, for the transition period, while the rise in the fertility rate will reduce the speed of government consumption increase eventually because it will reduce the proportion of old-age population, which will reduce the old-age-population-specific government consumption.

10.5.2   Further Consideration

Effects of Altruism

The life-cycle framework used for the prediction in this chapter precludes the possibility of consumption smoothing among generations through intergenerational redistribution. We investigate its effects, based on an altruistic family model, in which the family planner maximizes the expected utility over consumption of each surviving member at different dates (see equation 12) subject to household budget constraint (see equation 13):

$$(12) \qquad U = \sum_{t=0}^{\infty} \sum_{a=1}^{D} \theta_a P_{at} U(C_{at})(1 + \delta)^{-t}$$

$$(13) \qquad \sum_{t=0}^{\infty} \sum_{a=1}^{D} \frac{P_{at} C_{at}}{(1 + r)^t} \le R_0$$

where θ_a is the weight in the family utility function given to an age a individual, P_{at} is the surviving population of age a in year t, δ is a pure rate of time preference, and R_0 is full family resources, which is composed of current asset holdings, human wealth, and net government transfer wealth.

The solution of the maximization problem has the distinctive property that the cross-section age-consumption profile is constant over time, and that consumption at each age grows over time at a rate determined by the after-tax interest rate and the rate of time preference:

$$(14) \qquad \frac{C_{jt+1}}{C_{jt}} = h^{-1}\left(\frac{1 + \delta}{1 + r_n}\right) = \eta, \, h\left(\frac{C'}{C}\right) = \frac{U'(C')}{U'(C)}$$

$$(15) \qquad \frac{C_{it}}{C_{jt}} = h^{-1}\left(\frac{\theta_j}{\theta_i}\right)$$

where r_n is the after-tax interest rate, and h is the marginal rate of substitution function of homothetic utility.

We solve the equations (13) through (15) for the consumption level over time for each generation, using the estimated age-consumption profile (see table 10.8), under the assumption that the growth rate of consumption (η) for each age group is the same as the wage growth rate.[22]

Figure 10.7 reports the predicted savings rates over time under the situation in which the current fiscal policies are maintained. The altruistic family model produces similar predictions to those based on the life-cycle model. The national savings rate declines to 4 percent around 2065, and the government savings rate turns to negative value. The difference in the pre-

22. We assume that the nominal interest rate is 5 percent. We adjust the interest rate to this value in order to prevent the labor income share from diverging from the range of 60 to 73 percent.

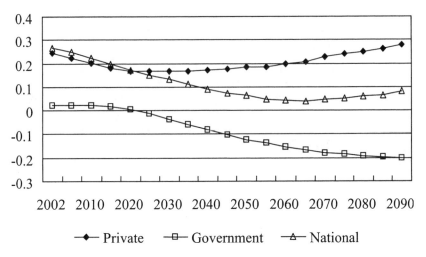

Fig. 10.7   Projected savings rate (altruistic family model)

dicted savings rates between the two frameworks is in the trend of private savings rate. The consumption smoothing across generations due to the altruism between generations produces different trends of private savings rate from that under the life-cycle framework: the private savings rate predicted under the altruistic family model is lower in the transition period when the population rapidly ages than that under the life-cycle model, while the private savings rate in the long-run is higher under the former.

Effects of Annuitization of Wealth

The prediction of the savings rate under the life-cycle framework, described in sections 10.3 and 10.4, is based on the assumption that the propensity to consume does not change over time and is the same regardless of the kind of wealth. However, the previous researches, such as Auerbach and Kotlikoff (1992) and Kotlikoff, Gokhale, and Sabelhaus (1996), suggested the possibility of rise in the propensity to consume resulting from the annuitization of wealth. The investigation of the effect of the annuitization of wealth in the Korean context is very suggestive, since the proportion of the current asset holdings including housing and real estate is projected to decrease (see table 10.11). In addition, the increase in the old-age population and maturing of public pensions and introduction of reverse annuity mortgages imply that the household wealth will be substantially annuitized.

In order to investigate the effects of the annuitization of household wealth, we estimate the consumption functions at the individual level, which include current asset holdings, human wealth, and net pension wealth as explanatory variables. For the estimation, we use 1999 to 2002

KLIPS sample, which is used to estimate the average propensity to consume (see section 10.4.1). For the estimation of consumption functions, we include the individuals who belong to the age group 15 to 64 and who have positive noncapital income. We use log values of consumption and those of explanatory variables as well as their absolute levels for the estimation. We include the age and the age squared as explanatory variables to control the differing preferences across age groups.

Table 10.15 shows mixed implication of the annuitization of wealth. When we use the 1999 to 2002 samples separately or the pooled sample, the elasticity of consumption with respect to the net pension wealth is smaller than that with respect to the current asset holdings.[23] Moreover, the coefficient for the current asset holdings in the estimation using the level variables is larger than that for the net pension wealth in most cases, which implies that the marginal propensity to consume with respect to the former is larger than that with respect to the latter. This suggests that the annuitization of wealth will not lower the savings rate. However, using fixed-effect panel equations produces larger elasticity of consumption and marginal propensity to consume with respect to the net pension wealth than those with respect to the current asset holdings. Considering the fact that the fixed-effect panel equation approach reflects the characteristics of the individuals in the sample better than the pooled sample approach or the estimation using a single-year sample, the result suggests that the annuitization of wealth in the future in Korea, due to the population aging, maturing of public pensions, and introduction of reverse annuity mortgages, will further reduce the savings rate in the future.

We also estimate the consumption function at the household level, since the individual's consumption used as the dependent variable in the estimation of consumption function at the individual level is constructed by allocating the household consumption based on Australia's age profile of consumption (see table 10.7). We use household consumption (and its log value), which is reported in KLIPS, as the dependent variable, and include the number of household members, primary income earner's age, the age squared, and each household's total values of current asset holdings, human wealth, and net pension wealth, as explanatory variables. Table 10.16 shows that change of analysis unit from the individual level to the household level does not change the structure of consumption functions estimated using the fixed-effect models and moreover it reinforces our prediction that the annuitization of wealth is likely to further lower the savings rate, because the marginal propensity to consume with respect to the net pension wealth estimated using single-year samples or the pooled sample is larger than that with respect to the current asset holdings in most cases.

---

23. This result may be partly due to the measurement error incurred in computing the value of the net pension wealth.

Table 10.15   **Individual consumption functions**

	1999 sample	2000 sample	2001 sample	2002 sample	Pooled sample	Fixed effect
	Dependent variable: consumption					
Constant	−652.3	−623.7	−543.7	−726.6	−562.2	−641.4
	(54.4)	(61.4)	(69.8)	(80.1)	(34.62)	(77.1)
Age	42.48	42.93	50.23	53.17	44.04	46.316
	(2.80)	(3.12)	(3.55)	(4.036)	(7.762)	(3.910)
Age^2	−0.442	−0.443	−0.571	−0.552	−0.470	−0.458
	(0.034)	(0.037)	(0.042)	(0.047)	(0.021)	(0.046)
Asset holdings (x_1)	0.011	0.012	0.017	0.018	0.016	0.011
	(0.0008)	(0.0009)	(0.0009)	(0.0009)	(0.0004)	(0.007)
	<0.071>	<0.069>	<0.101>	<0.102>	<0.095>	<0.065>
Human wealth (x_2)	0.006	0.006	0.002	0.005	0.004	0.003
	(0.0002)	(0.0002)	(0.001)	(0.002)	(0.0009)	(0.0001)
	<0.364>	<0.344>	<0.120>	<0.267>	<0.23>	<0.17>
Net pension wealth (x_3)	0.012	0.012	0.013	0.013	0.016	0.029
	(0.002)	(0.002)	(0.002)	(0.002)	(0.001)	(0.0019)
	<0.053>	<0.055>	<0.062>	<0.057>	<0.073>	<0.132>
	Dependent variable: log(consumption)					
Constant	−5.641	−5.365	−4.937	−5.214	−6.146	−7.354
	(0.442)	(0.422)	(0.360)	(0.322)	(0.188)	(0.358)
Age	0.090	0.075	0.080	0.064	0.071	0.063
	(0.0048)	(0.0049)	(0.0046)	(0.0043)	(0.002)	(0.0052)
Age^2	−0.0008	−0.0007	−0.0007	−0.0005	−0.0006	−0.0004
	(0.00006)	(0.0006)	(0.00005)	(0.0005)	(0.00002)	(0.00006)
$log(x_1)^a$	0.224	0.312	0.2310	0.327	0.268	0.1601
	(0.021)	(0.025)	(0.017)	(0.019)	(0.010)	(0.016)
$log(x_2)^a$	0.596	0.529	0.548	0.533	0.577	0.524
	(0.020)	(0.021)	(0.017)	(0.016)	(0.009)	(0.014)
$log(x_3)^a$	0.148	0.150	0.151	0.153	0.231	0.540
	(0.049)	(0.045)	(0.038)	(0.034)	(0.020)	(0.0404)

Notes: Numbers in parentheses represent standard errors. Numbers in angle brackets represent the elasticity evaluated at the mean of the explanatory variable.
[a]We use $log(-min(x_i) + 1 + x_i)$ ($i = 1, 2, 3$) to avoid negative value for the argument of log function.

It is remarkable that maturing of the NPS is likely to further increase consumption levels. Table 10.16 shows the coefficient for the product of dummy variables, for the NPS participation as opposed to the OCP, and the value of net pension wealth, is negative and significantly different from 0 in most of cases,[24] which implies that the elasticity of consumption with respect to net pension wealth is smaller for the NPS participants than that for the OCP participants. It is probably due to the fact that the history of

24. The coefficient is significantly different from 0 at 5 percent significance level in the case of pooled sample II level and log equation. The P-value of the coefficient is 5.4 percent in the fixed-effect panel estimation (fixed-effect II) using log variables. In the case of the fixed-effect panel equation using level variables, the coefficient is not significantly different from 0.

Table 10.16   Household consumption functions

	1999 sample	2000 sample	2001 sample	2002 sample	Pooled sample I	Pooled sample II	Fixed effect I	Fixed effectII
			Dependent variable: consumption					
Constant	−450.6 (170.8)	−663.0 (199.6)	−605.3 (198.1)	−598.4 (218.5)	−351.9 (103.6)	−366.5 (112.9)	268.8 (204.2)	107.5 (214.6)
No. of household members	123.8 (11.3)	157.9 (13.9)	151.5 (13.4)	426.1 (13.4)	218.7 (6.78)	221.0 (6.81)	290.0 (12.32)	288.4 (12.33)
Age	53.9 (7.76)	63.0 (8.93)	66.9 (8.75)	49.3 (9.58)	44.4 (4.60)	45.8 (4.62)	11.8 (8.58)	10.2 (8.59)
Age^2	−0.63 (0.08)	−0.73 (0.09)	−0.81 (0.08)	−0.64 (0.09)	−0.57 (0.04)	−0.58 (0.05)	−0.23 (0.08)	−0.21 (0.08)
Asset holdings (X_1)	0.020 (0.0009) <0.122>	0.019 (0.0011) <0.116>	0.025 (0.0010) <0.152>	0.023 (0.0011) <0.140>	0.023 (0.0005) <0.140>	0.023 (0.0005) <0.140>	0.015 (0.0009) <0.091>	0.015 (0.0009) <0.091>
Human wealth (X_2)	0.0010 (0.0002) <0.035>	0.0021 (0.0002) <0.074>	0.0021 (0.0002) <0.074>	0.0024 (0.0002) <0.085>	0.0024 (0.0001) <0.085>	0.0025 (0.0001) <0.089>	0.0021 (0.0001) <0.074>	0.0020 (0.0001) <0.071>
Net pension wealth (X_3)	0.025 (0.0038) <0.071>	0.029 (0.0036) <0.082>	0.026 (0.0030) <0.074>	0.015 (0.0033) <0.042>	0.034 (0.0017) <0.097>	0.037 (0.0033) <0.105>	0.038 (0.0025) <0.108>	0.044 (0.0045) <0.125>
Dum_NPS[a]						−10.48 (51.24)		211.2 (80.41)
Dum_NPS × X_3						−0.085 (0.0039)		−0.0027 (0.0052)

(continued)

Table 10.16 (continued)

	1999 sample	2000 sample	2001 sample	2002 sample	Pooled sample I	Pooled sample II	Fixed effect I	Fixed effect II
				Dependent variable: log(consumption)				
Constant	-1.158	-2.253	-1.884	0.125	-2.624	-3.358	-1.082	-2.529
	(0.449)	(0.430)	(0.373)	(0.320)	(0.194)	(0.483)	(0.287)	(0.686)
No. of household members	0.101	0.104	0.092	0.174	0.109	0.111	0.119	0.119
	(0.0085)	(0.0096)	(0.0086)	(0.0066)	(0.0042)	(0.0042)	(0.0075)	(0.0075)
Age	0.065	0.073	0.068	0.045	0.059	0.061	0.035	0.034
	(0.0058)	(0.0060)	(0.0055)	(0.0046)	(0.0028)	(0.0028)	(0.0052)	(0.0052)
Age^2	-0.0007	-0.0008	-0.0007	-0.0005	-0.0006	-0.0006	-0.0003	-0.0003
	(0.0006)	(0.0006)	(0.00005)	(0.00004)	(0.00003)	(0.00003)	(0.00005)	(0.00005)
$\log(X_1)$[b]	0.368	0.302	0.348	0.321	0.355	0.351	0.233	0.233
	(0.0192)	(0.0190)	(0.0171)	(0.0165)	(0.0093)	(0.0093)	(0.0148)	(0.0148)
$\log(X_2)$[b]	0.211	0.275	0.253	0.160	0.244	0.253	0.186	0.184
	(0.015)	(0.0164)	(0.0141)	(0.0133)	(0.0076)	(0.0078)	(0.0103)	(0.0106)
$\log(X_3)$[b]	0.073	0.169	0.131	0.097	0.225	0.294	0.300	0.444
	(0.049)	(0.045)	(0.038)	(0.033)	(0.0209)	(0.0484)	(0.0307)	(0.0682)
Dum_NPS						1.451		1.470
						(0.525)		(0.729)
Dum_NPS $\times \log(X_3)$						-0.156		-0.140
						(0.053)		(0.073)

Notes: Numbers in parentheses represent standard errors. Numbers in angle brackets represent the elasticity evaluated at the mean of the explanatory variable.

[a] Dummy variable for National Pension Participant's household.

[b] We use $\log(-\min(x_1) + 1 + x_i)$ $(i = 1, 2, 3)$ to avoid negative value for the argument of log function.

the NPS is very short and most of the NPS participants have not acquired the entitlement to pension benefits. Therefore, it is highly likely that the maturing of the NPS will raise the elasticity of consumption with respect to the net NPS wealth at least to the level with respect to the net OCP wealth in the future, which will further reduce the savings rate.

10.6   Conclusion

This chapter has investigated the effects of population aging and fiscal policies on the national savings rate of the future. For the prediction of the national savings rate of Korea for the next several decades, we employed a life-cycle model, which incorporated the generational accounting approach needed to assess the distribution of fiscal burden across generations, and we tried a sensitivity analysis by using an altruistic family model to investigate the effects of altruism among generations on the savings rates. We also studied the effects of change in asset composition, such as annuitization of assets resulting from maturing of public pensions and introduction of reverse annuity mortgages by estimating consumption functions, which enables comparison of elasticity of consumption with respect to the magnitude of various kinds of wealth. We found that the rapid population aging and long-term budgetary imbalance will substantially lower the national savings rate in Korea, and that the existence of the altruism among generations does not produce qualitatively different results. In addition, the estimation results of consumption functions with respect to various kinds of wealth suggest that the annuitization of wealth due to maturing of public pensions and introduction of reverse annuity mortgage is likely to further decrease the savings rate in the future.

In addition to the population aging and the generational imbalance of fiscal burden, premature reunification of South and North Korea will be a large burden of South Korean taxpayers. Auerbach, Chun, and Yoo (2005) showed that to finance the reunification cost, the tax burden of cohorts alive in 2010 and thereafter should be raised by about 30 percent of tax burden under current fiscal policies, which will further reduce national savings of the future. In order to restore the sustainability of fiscal policies as well as to prevent a drastic decrease in the savings rate, fundamental reforms of fiscal policies, such as public pension reform, medical insurance reform, and restructuring of government consumption policies, are necessary.

For the analysis in this chapter, we adopted a life-cycle framework, under which we implicitly assumed that the propensity to consume is the same across various kinds of wealth. However, the estimated consumption functions suggest that change in the composition of wealth will induce drifts of the propensity to consume. Construction of the model, which enables the analysis of the effects of asset composition changes, such as the annuitization of wealth, will be an important agenda for our future research.

Our projection suggests a drastic decrease in asset holdings due to population aging and fiscal policies. The prediction may exaggerate the decreasing trend of asset holdings and savings rate, since our approach is a partial equilibrium approach. A general equilibrium approach needs to be considered for the future research, because the general equilibrium change in factor prices (i.e., rise in rate of return to capital) resulting from decrease in capital stock, mitigates the drastic downward trend of asset holdings.

References

Auerbach, Alan J., and Young Jun Chun. 2006. Generational accounting in Korea. *Journal of Japanese and International Economies* 20 (2): 234–68.
Auerbach, Alan J., Young Jun Chun, and Ilho Yoo. 2005. The fiscal burden of Korean reunification: A generational accounting approach. *FinanzArchiv* 61 (1): 62–97.
Auerbach, Alan J., and Laurence J. Kotlikoff. 1992. The impact of the demographic transition on capital formation. *Scandinavian Journal of Economics* 84 (2): 281–95.
Auerbach, Alan J., and Philip Oreopoulos. 2000. The fiscal impacts of U.S. immigration: A generational-accounting perspective. *Tax Policy and the Economy* 14:123–56.
Besanger, Serge, Ross S. Guest, and Ian McDonald. 2000. *Demographic changes in Asia: The impact on optimal national saving, investment, and the current account.* IMF Working Paper no. 00/115.
Bovenberg, A. Lans, and Harry ter Rele. 2000. Generational accounts for the Netherlands: An update. *International Tax and Public Finance* 7 (4): 411–30.
Kotlikoff, Laurence, Jagdeesh Gokhale, and John Sabelhaus. 1996. *Understanding the postwar decline in U.S. saving: A cohort analysis.* NBER Working Paper no. 5571. Cambridge, MA: National Bureau of Economic Research.
Ministry of Labor, Republic of Korea. 2001. *Survey report on wage structure.* Seoul: Ministry of Labor.
United Nations. 1998. *World population projections.* New York: United Nations.
United Nations. n.d. *The sex and age distribution of world population.* New York: United Nations.

Comment   Laurence J. Kotlikoff

This chapter by Young Jun Chun is a very impressive study. It shows that one can readily apply the life-cycle theory of saving to make aggregate saving forecasts for countries, to understand the saving impacts of alternative fiscal policy changes, and to consider the saving effects of factors such as the degree of annuitization and the extent of altruism. The paper projects

Laurence J. Kotlikoff is a professor of economics at Boston University and a resea4rch associate of the National Bureau of Economic Research.

Korea's saving by properly treating the country as a small open economy. It considers each cohort's remaining lifetime resources in each future year and multiplies those resources by the cohort's propensity to consume. Since older cohorts have higher consumption propensities, a shift toward an older population leads to more aggregate consumption and lower national saving, other things equal. Korea is slated to age very dramatically. Indeed, by the end of this century, Korea could be the oldest country in the world. The authors suggest a very dramatic decline, indeed a true collapse, in the country's national saving rate, albeit one that can be mitigated to some degree with more generationally responsible fiscal policy. This is a very carefully done study and should serve as a model for future analyses of national saving.

Comment   Shigeki Kunieda

The Chun chapter analyzes the effects of aging and fiscal policy on the national savings in Korea using a life-cycle model. Despite the seemingly sound current Korean fiscal situation, this chapter and another paper by the author and Auerbach (Auerbach and Chun 2006) show that rapid aging will have significant effects on national savings and intergenerational equity in Korea in the near future. Especially, the maturation of PAYGO public pension system and the expansion of medical expense will reduce the national savings significantly. In addition, the chapter points out possible negative effects of annuitization of wealth. I would like to raise three issues that might be relevant for the future analysis and the Korean fiscal policy reform.

Desirability of Dynamic General Equilibrium Analysis

As Chun admits in the chapter, the analysis in it is partial equilibrium analysis, since wage rate and discount rate are exogenously determined. In order to include possible effects of factor price changes, dynamic general equilibrium analysis such as Auerbach-Kotlikoff's model is desirable for further research.

Bequest Motives and the Effects of Annuitization

Chun argues that the annuitization of wealth will reduce national savings further in Korea. However, the claim that annuitization of wealth, especially introduction of reverse mortgage, will reduce savings crucially de-

Shigeki Kunieda is an associate professor of economics at Hitotsubashi University.

pends on the assumption of no or weak bequest motives. For example, if pure altruistic bequest motive is the most important bequest motive, reverse mortgage business cannot attract a large number of customers since the real estate under reverse mortgage contract cannot be left to children. In fact, the recent Annual Report on Japanese Economy and Public Finance (2005) points out that the most important reason why Japanese people do not have reverse mortgages is their desire to leave their real estate as bequest. Thus, I believe that a more detailed study about the most important bequest motives in Korea is desired in order to discuss the possible effects of annuitization of wealth in Korea in a more realistic setting.

Constitutional Rule of Intergenerational Equity

According to the results in this chapter, immediate drastic policy reforms such as tax increase and pension benefit cut are urgent in order to prevent the negative effects of aging in Korea. However, politicians in most democratic countries tend to postpone necessary reforms even when coming "intergenerational exploitation" is clearly predicted. Thus, after realizing the necessity of drastic policy reforms, we should also discuss how to make politicians take necessary policy actions to avoid "intergenerational exploitation" in the real world. One repeatedly proposed remedy is the constitutional constraint on budget deficit such as the balanced budget rule. However, this chapter's result, that the current Korean fiscal situation seems apparently sound even when coming intergenerational inequity is expected, implies that the constitutional constraint on budget deficit may be ineffective for securing intergenerational equity.

In the case of Japan, who is facing the similar political difficulty, I (Kunieda 2004) propose the constitutional rule of intergenerational equity instead of balanced budget rule. If securing intergenerational equity is defined as the constitutional responsibility, politicians cannot postpone politically unpopular, but necessary policy reforms for securing intergenerational equity. However, in political reality, it may be very difficult to amend the existing constitution in order to add a new constitutional article of intergenerational equity rule. Still, if we can establish a new constitutional interpretation claiming that serious intergenerational fiscal inequity is not allowed even under the currently existing constitution, then we can force politicians to take necessary actions to recover intergenerational equity. I believe that it is possible to establish such constitutional interpretation under the current Constitution of Japan. If the constitutional interpretation is widely accepted, we should clarify the government responsibility of securing intergenerational equity by introducing the new "Fundamental Law of Securing Intergenerational Equity," and establish an independent government agency for securing intergenerational equity. The agency calculates and submits the generational accounts annually, and recommends necessary reforms to avoid constitutionally unaccepted intergenerational inequity. While my proposal is based on the current Japanese fiscal and political situation, it may also contribute to prevent "intergenerational exploitation" in Korea.

In conclusion, after reading the Chun chapter, Korean policymakers are strongly expected to start serious discussions of policy alternatives for preventing intergeneration inequity immediately.

References

Auerbach, A. J., and Y. J. Chun. 2006. Generational accounting in Korea. *Journal of Japanese and International Economy* 20 (2): 234–68.

Cabinet Office of Government of Japan. 2005. *Annual report on Japanese economy and public finance.* [in Japanese]. Tokyo: Cabinet Office Government of Japan.

Kunieda, S. 2004. Fukouhei Zesei he Kihonhou Seitei (New Fundamental Law for Securing Intergenerational Equity). *Nihon Keizai Shinbun.* [in Japanese]. October 8, 2004.

11

Sustainability, Debt Management, and Public Debt Policy in Japan

Takero Doi, Toshihiro Ihori, and Kiyoshi Mitsui

11.1 Introduction

Currently it is crucial for the Japanese government to implement tight public debt policy, because the Japanese government has issued a very huge amount of government debts. Japan's fiscal situation has deteriorated rapidly with the collapse of the *bubble economy* in the early 1990s and the deep and prolonged period of economic recession that ensued, and from which recovery has been slow and modest despite the implementation of countercyclical Keynesian policy. Since national income did not grow much, tax revenue did not increase either. On the contrary, government spending has been gradually raised due to political pressures of interest groups, resulting in large budget deficits.

In 1997, the Japanese government tried to implement the Fiscal Structural Reform so as to reduce budget deficits. However, in 1998, it stopped the reform and reduced taxes and increased public investment based on the traditional Keynesian policy because of the severe economic and financial situation, and the defeat of the governing party (the Liberal Democratic Party) in the Upper House election.

Takero Doi is an associate professor of economics at Keio University. Toshihiro Ihori is a professor of economics at the University of Tokyo. Kiyoshi Mitsui is a professor of economics at Gakushuin University.

An earlier version of the paper was presented at the 16th Annual East Asian Seminar on Economics held on June 23–25, 2005, and the Conference on New Perspective of Fiscal Sustainability, Goethe University Frankfurt Campus Westend, October 13 and 14, 2005. The authors thank Professors Dante Canlas, Takatoshi Ito, Anne O. Krueger, Eli Remolona, Andrew Rose, and Jürgen von Hagen, as well as the participants for helpful comments. Any remaining errors are our own.

The concern for sustainability of fiscal deficits is a background for the fiscal reconstruction and structural reform movement by the current Koizumi Administration. The "Structural Reform of the Japanese Economy: Basic Policies for Macroeconomic Development" was decided upon after acceptance of the report compiled by the Council on Economic and Fiscal Policy, an advisory council to the prime minister. In this report the core of policies for the structural reform of the economic society was made clear. In part of the policies shown, a goal to limit the amount of government bond issues to less than 30 trillion yen in the fiscal 2002 budget, and afterward to achieve a primary surplus, was set to show that there exists a necessity to take on full-scale measures toward fiscal consolidation or fiscal reconstruction. However, in order to cope with the bad situation of macroeconomy, 1.8 trillion yen of the advance tax cuts were employed with a view to strengthening the competitiveness of industry, facilitating a smooth transference of assets to the next generation, promoting a shift from *saving to investment,* advancing effective land use, and so on. The goal to limit the amount of government bond issues to less than 30 trillion yen in the fiscal 2002 budget was finally abandoned. In the fiscal 2005, new government bond issues are 34.4 trillion yen and the bond dependency ratio rises to 41.8 percent.

If creditors fear that the government is going to be in a debt trap, the long-term interest rate begins to rise, reflecting an enlarged credit risk. It is noted that although the Japanese Government Bonds (JGBs) have been issued too much, their yields are the lowest among G7 countries in the bond market. In this regard, despite its weakening credit ratings, the ten-year JGB nominal yield of about 1.5 percent in 2005 remains lower than the U.S. bond yield of about 1.8 percent registered during the Great Depression. However, we also have to pay attention to persistent deflation. Also, the performance in the yield of the JGBs may not accurately reflect its credit risk. The Japanese banking sector continues to purchase the JGBs simply because short-term capital gains from the JGBs have been an easy option to offset the existing stock losses.

The purpose of this chapter is to analyze sustainability issues of Japan's fiscal policy and then to discuss the debt management policy using theoretical models and numerical studies. We also investigate the desirable coordination of fiscal and monetary authorities toward fiscal reconstruction.

This chapter consists of five sections. In section 11.2 we survey previous studies on sustainability issues. In section 11.3, we evaluate Japan's debt management policy by providing a theoretical model to analyze public debt policy in a second-best case as a benchmark. We then implement a simple numerical analysis based on the smoothing rule derived by the theoretical model. In section 11.4, we discuss the desirable coordination of monetary and fiscal authorities toward fiscal reconstruction by explicitly investigating confidence crisis of government debt and spontaneous default of fiscal authority. Finally, concluding remarks follow in section 11.5.

11.2 Sustainability Issues and Emergency Reform

11.2.1 Concerns about Sustainability

The events of the 1980s and 1990s in Japan suggest that when a government becomes strapped for funds, it will tend to borrow from the world credit market rather than raise taxes to finance additional public spending. Indeed, many governments did either not raise broadly based taxes (e.g., the Thatcher government in Great Britain, the Reagan and Bush Administrations in the United States) or simply could not raise taxes to prevent causing riots (e.g., countries in Latin American and Eastern Europe, arguably, France in the reign of Louis XVI). There are long-term concerns about the accumulated fiscal deficit. An important one is whether such a large deficit can be sustained. The system will be paralyzed if public finance collapses under the weight of massive deficit. As a result, the financial system and the economy as a whole will be seriously affected. An extreme case of hyperinflation or default could develop.

The so-called chain-letter mechanism (or a Ponzi debt game) involves a situation in which the future time path of taxes is fixed and debt finance is used to pay for any additional public spending; debt issuance is thus endogenously determined by the government's budget constraint. If the mechanism is sustainable, increased taxation need not necessarily be required in order to finance increased government spending as the economy converges to the steady state equilibrium. If the mechanism is unsustainable, the government will eventually go bankrupt in the sense that it will be unable to raise enough revenue to finance public spending and debt repayment. As debt crowds out private capital formation, the economy will also eventually go bankrupt if the mechanism fails. This suggests that studying the chain-letter mechanism and associated sustainability issues is quite important in terms of understanding the effects of government austerity (fiscal reconstruction) measures on the macroeconomy.

A simple way to evaluate the fiscal sustainability problem is to focus on the government bond market. In this regard for Japan, despite its weakening credit ratings, the ten-year JGB nominal yield of about 1.5 percent in 2005 remains. So far the myth that the JGBs are risk-free has been somehow propagated. This episode may imply that Japan's government solvency is not a serious issue right now. However, Japan has experienced deep deflation, so the real rate of interest is about 2 percent, which is not so low. We also have to pay attention to the possibility that the performance in the yield of the JGB may not accurately reflect its credit risk.

Ihori, Nakazato, and Kawade (2002) attempt a standard approach to test the fiscal sustainability condition, using the methodology of Hamilton and Flavin (1986). Hamilton and Flavin (1986) define the sustainability of government debt as follows. Government budget constraint in period t is expressed as

$$G_t + (1 + r_t)D_t = R_t + D_{t+1},$$

where G_t, R_t, r_t, and D_t denote aggregate real government expenditure (excluding interest payment), aggregate real tax revenue, real interest rate, and aggregate real bonds outstanding (at the beginning of period), respectively. We can rewrite this as

$$B_{t+1} = E_t\left\{\sum_{i=1}^{n}\left[\prod_{j=1}^{i}\left(\frac{1}{1+r_{t+j}}\right)\right]S_{t+i}\right\} + E_t\left[\prod_{j=1}^{n}\left(\frac{1}{1+r_{t+j}}\right)B_{t+n+1}\right]$$

where primary surplus $S_t \equiv R_t - G_t$.

Hamilton and Flavin (1986) define the government budget satisfies

$$\lim_{n\to\infty} E_t\left[\prod_{j=1}^{n}\left(\frac{1}{1+r_{t+j}}\right)D_{t+n+1}\right] = 0$$

as the condition of sustainability of government bond. The previous equation means no Ponzi game condition in dynamic macroeconomic models. Therefore we can confirm the sustainability of government bond by testing the following, A is significantly equal to 0;

$$\lim_{n\to\infty} E_t\left[\prod_{j=1}^{n}\left(\frac{1}{1+r_{t+j}}\right)D_{t+n+1}\right] = A \quad A: \text{constant}$$

Hamilton and Flavin (1986) estimate the following regression to test the sustainability:

$$D_t = c_0 + A(1 + r)^t + c_1 D_{t-1} + \cdots + c_p D_{t-p} + d_1 S_{t-1} + d_2 S_{t-2}$$
$$+ \cdots + d_p S_{t-p} + \varepsilon_t$$

where ε_t denotes an error term. They assume that (expected) real interest rate is constant over time, and expectations and error terms of the regression satisfy the relation that the term of $E_t[\sum_{i=1}^{\infty}(1/1 + r)^i S_{t+i}]$ depends on $S_{t-1}, S_{t-2}, \ldots, S_{t-p}$, serial correlation of error terms is eliminated by using the variables, $D_{t-1}, D_{t-2}, \ldots, D_{t-p}$. If the estimator of A in the previous equation is significantly equal to 0, they conclude the government bond is sustainable.

Ihori, Nakazato, and Kawade (2002) conduct the empirical analysis for the Japanese fiscal data from 1957 to 1999. To conduct the test, the values for the nominal growth rate, n, and the nominal interest rate, r, must be specified. Their strategy is to set various values for $r - n$ and to check whether the results are sensitive to the values chosen. The estimated results imply that the null hypothesis cannot be rejected at a 5 percent significance level, suggesting that government solvency was not a serious problem until fiscal 1996. On the contrary, the result for the period 1957 to 1997 rejects the null hypothesis when $r - n$ is above 0.05, and the results for the period 1957 to 1998 and the period 1957 to 1999 also reject the null hypothesis when $r - n$ is above 0.04.

Bohn (1998) proposes a new method different from existing tests for sustainability of government debt. According to Bohn (1998), the test has better properties than the tests based on estimating a transversality condition and on cointegration tests. The condition that fiscal policy satisfies the intertemporal budget constraint (i.e., the condition on sustainability of government debt) is that the primary surplus to GDP (s_t) increases with the ratio of (start-of-period) debt to GDP (d_t).[1] Strictly speaking, when we can express a relation between the two as

$$s_t = f(d_t) + \mu_t$$

Suppose other determinants, μ_t, is bounded and the present value of future GDP is finite. Then, government debt satisfies a transversality condition if there is a debt-GDP ratio d^* such that $f'(d_t) \geq \beta > 0$ for all $d_t \geq d^*$, where β is a positive constant. We draw a scatter plot of s_t against d_t in figure 11.1 (only the general account of the central government) and figure 11.2 (the consolidated account of the central and local governments). Until the early 1990s, the Japanese fiscal policy held the quadratic relation between the two. Recently, the Japanese fiscal policy deviates from the relation excessively. Doi and Ihori (2004) show that Japanese government debt does not satisfy a transversality condition for fiscal 1965 to 2000 by estimating β.

These observations indicate that fiscal sustainability may become a serious issue. The longer the sample period, the more likely we face the fiscal crisis. It follows that the chain-letter mechanism will cause the public debt crisis to occur in the near future. Japan has two serious difficulties in terms of sustainability. First, the Japanese primary surplus is apparently a de-

1. Broda and Weinstein (2005) point out that using gross debt levels to assess Japan's fiscal sustainability is equivalent to treating Japan's financial assets as worthless. They assert, therefore, that net debt levels are more appropriate to assess the fiscal sustainability than gross debt. However, the following aspects need to be considered.

First, Broda and Weinstein (2005) calculate the value of net debt of the Japanese public sector by summing together the net debts of the Japanese government, postal savings, and government financial institutions. Though this net debt of the Japanese public sector includes net debt of social security, the assets of social security accounts are earmarked for the future pension benefit payouts. Therefore, it is better, from this aspect, to exclude net debt of social security to assess the fiscal sustainability.

Second, if fiscal authority and monetary authority act noncooperatively, fiscal authority has to take into account the possibility that the monetary authority sell government bonds independently. Therefore, it is important for the independent fiscal authority to assess the fiscal sustainability without taking account of the government bonds held by the monetary authority. Our analysis mainly deals with a noncooperative case so that we focus our attention on gross debt levels.

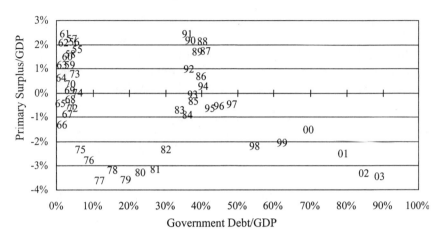

Fig. 11.1   Primary surplus and government debt (the general account of the central government)

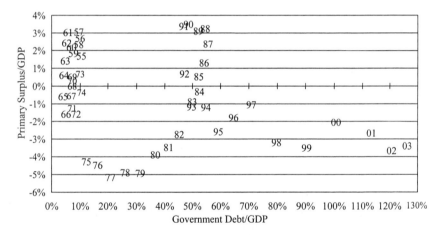

Fig. 11.2   Primary surplus and government debt (central and local governments)

creasing function of the debt-GDP ratio since 1990 and hence it does not satisfy Bohn's test. Second, the rate of interest is greater than the growth rate in Japan in the 1990s. Hence, it is important to reduce the government deficit in the near future.

11.2.2   Non-Keynesian Effect

Many governments prefer to rely on the issuance of debt rather than explicit taxation in financing expenditures. Recent experience suggests that a number of countries are facing potential bankruptcy as a result of issuing too much debt. As shown in Ihori (1988), the chain-letter mechanism would most likely be sustainable when the initial interest rate and stock of government debt are smaller or when the propensity to save and the growth rate are higher.

When the government goes eventually bankrupt, austerity measures as fiscal reconstruction will be required. This will depend critically on the response of the private sector to the specific austerity policy and more specifically the response of capital accumulation. Serious mistakes, which will possibly exacerbate the bankruptcy problem, may occur if the wrong action is taken. The conventional wisdom suggests that either the government must raise taxes or dramatically reduce spending. This is contingent on an increase in capital accumulation taking place in response to the change in policy. However, whether these contractions will be affected through cuts in spending or increases in explicit tax collections and when these actions will be taken are in general unknown. Expectations of future policy changes are crucial in understanding seemingly counterintuitive macroeconomic dynamics. Bertola and Drazen (1993) argue that expectations about the discrete character of future fiscal adjustments can help explain the effects of current fiscal policy. They showed that if government spending follows an upward-trending stochastic process that the public believes may fall sharply when it reaches specific *trigger* points, then optimizing consumption behavior and simple budget-constraint arithmetic imply a nonlinear relationship between private consumption and government spending.

The so-called *non-Keynesian* effect means that cuts in public expenditures and/or tax increases contribute to stimulate private demand under some fiscal situations or macroeconomic environments: that is, when government spending is inefficient and/or the budget deficit is so large, this paradoxical effect may occur. If this is the case, it becomes possible to attain simultaneously two policy objectives of fiscal reconstruction and macroeconomic recovery. This possibility of so-called non-Keynesian effect is consistent with the experience of several countries.

Such a situation might be relevant for the recent Japanese economy. A recent line of economic research suggests that private agents realize that current bond-financed deficits carry with them future tax obligations. Anticipating higher future taxes, private agents change current spending behavior to smooth consumption intertemporally. Although the econometric study of this issue is still in its infancy, some recent research indicates that private Japanese behavior has partially offset recent changes in fiscal policy (see Ihori and Sato [2002] among others).

11.2.3 Emergency Reform for Debt Repudiation

In reality, however, it may be difficult to employ the standard austerity measures in a proper time. For example, Japan's fiscal policy in the 1990s created a problem of a tendency to postpone fiscal reconstruction reforms. The consensus at the time was that there was no immediate need for such painful measures as long as government policy prevented the economy from slipping into recession. There was, indeed, a widespread feeling in the private sector that the government would come to its aid if the economic situation worsened. That feeling fostered certain complacency in the business world, making many corporate managers liable to *moral hazards*—risks stemming from lack of self-discipline. The continuation of the short-term stimulus policy, at a time when the economy needed long-term structural changes, discouraged self-help efforts in the private sector. Lobbying activities of local interest groups were exaggerated in the 1990s, as shown in Ihori, Doi, and Kondo (2001) and Doi and Ihori's (2002) empirical evidence. This is also one of the main reasons why Japan's fiscal reconstruction did not perform very well in the 1990s.

It is thus argued that if the current deficits seem not sustainable, governments in such countries will be forced to in effect repudiate their debt, either explicitly through an introduction of partial default or through inflation depreciation (inflationary taxes). We may call such a policy change the emergency reform for debt repudiation. The consequent fiscal reconstruction postponement is not free from credibility problems: Will the additional debt be paid off in full, or will the government find it optimal to resort to higher inflation or partial default to diminish the burden of the debt, and so on? It should be stressed that if the private sector recognizes such possibilities of future emergency reforms for debt repudiation, government bonds and real capital may no longer be regarded as perfect substitutes. The more likely the current deficits seem not sustainable, the higher the subjective probability of the future emergency reform.

11.2.4   Literature on Debt Ponzi Games Under Uncertainty

Several important papers investigated debt Ponzi games under uncertainty. The average riskless rate may be a poor guide as to whether permanent rollover of debt is feasible when economies are stochastic. Tirole (1985) and Weil (1989) examine in the overlapping-generations framework deterministic and speculative bubbles that are, like government debt, intergenerational schemes based on trust. Weil considered a two-state model with real capital and a bubble. The bubble has probability θ of bursting every period. The main result in Weil is that the highest sustainable bubble (the equivalent of the highest sustainable debt in the present chapter) decreases with the probability of bursting (debt repudiation). Calvo (1988) studies models in which debt repudiation is possible and shows that expectations may play a crucial role in the determination of equilibrium. See also Chari and Kehoe (1993), and Bulow and Rogoff (1989).

Blanchard and Weil (2001) show that whether or not governments can rollover debt in dynamically efficient economies depends on whether the issuance of public debt can partially substitute missing markets. Bohn (1991) shows that the sustainability even of simple policy rules like balanced budgets or tax rate smoothing should not be taken for granted in a stochastic economy and that sustainability is often sensitive to assumptions about debt management. Alesina, Prati, and Tabellini (1990) show that the maturity structure of public debt may influence the likelihood of a confidence crisis on the debt. The shorter and more concentrated is the maturity, the more likely is a confidence crisis. See also Giavazzi and Pagano (1990).

11.2.5   Remarks

Economic theory has begun to catch up with political reality. It has done this by not only studying the optimality of fiscal policy in a context where explicit account is taken of the government's budget constraint, but it has also gone a step further by examining the time consistency of optimal policy. Here, it is the issue of whether it is optimal to keep promises that were optimal to make in the past. The latter lies at the heart of the credibility dilemma faced by any serious politician.

Fiscal regimes differ across countries and change over time. At each point in time there is uncertainty about the regime that will prevail from then on. A high government deficit financed by debt can be regarded as unsustainable and therefore may be taken to signal future contractions in the deficits. The fiscal regime prevailing in an economy, as well as the type of fiscal relationships expected to arise from such a regime, is an important factor in determining the response of private agents to fiscal signals.

The sustainability question in stochastic models is an aspect of fiscal policy that deserves more attention in future research and in policy making.

11.3   Debt Management Policy of the Japanese Government

11.3.1   Japan's Government Bonds

The Japanese government currently issues government bonds, which can be classified into six categories: short-term (6-month and 1-year Treasury bills); medium-term (2-year and 5-year bonds); long-term (10-year bonds); super-long-term (15-year, 20-year, and 30-year bonds); government bonds for individual investors; and inflation-indexed bonds. The short-term government bonds are all discount bonds. On the other hand, all medium-, long-, and super-long-term government bonds, except for the 15-year floating-rate bonds, are the bonds with fixed-rate coupons. The 15-year floating-rate bonds and the government bonds for individual investors feature a coupon rate that varies according to certain rules. The inflation-indexed bonds are issued as the 10-year bonds to finance funds for the Fiscal Investment and Loan Program.[2]

2. The Fiscal Investment and Loan Program (FILP) has been called *the second budget* because the government initially used FILP to undertake projects it was unable to include in the general account budget. Doi and Hoshi (2003) have a good summary of the structure, components, and history of FILP and PSS, and provide estimates of the costs FILP has and might impose on Japanese taxpayers; its appendix provides a further review of the literature. Also see Cargill and Yoshino (2000, 2003).

Table 11.1   Planned issuance of Japanese government bonds (JGBs) classification by issuance methods and maturity (in billions of yen)

	FY2005 initial budget (1)	FY2006 initial budget (2)	(2) – (1)
30-year bonds	2,000.0	2,000.0	0.0
20-year bonds	9,000.0	10,300.0	1,300.0
15-year floating-rate bonds	9,600.0	9,100.0	–500.0
10-year bonds	22,800.0	24,000.0	1,200.0
10-year inflation-indexed bonds	2,000.0	2,000.0	0.0
5-year bonds	24,000.0	25,200.0	1,200.0
2-year bonds	20,400.0	21,600.0	1,200.0
Treasury bills	29,961.5	28,719.7	–1,241.8
Auction for enhanced-liquidity		600.0	600.0
Subtotal	119,761.5	123,519.7	3,758.2
Nonprice competitive auction II		2,658.0	2,658.0
Amount to the market	119,761.5	126,177.7	6,416.2
JGBs for individual investors	3,600.0	4,400.0	800.0
Amount to private sector (x)	123,361.5	130,577.7	7,216.2
Bank of Japan	23,043.6	16,557.4	–6,486.2
Fiscal loan fund	1,000.0		–1,000.0
Fiscal loan bonds (transitional measures)	19,300.0	15,200.0	–4,100.0
OTC sales at post offices	2,800.0	3,100.0	300.0
Amount to public sector (y)	46,143.6	34,857.4	–11,286.2
Total (x) + (y)	169,505.1	165,435.1	–4,070.0

Source: Ministry of Finance (2006).
Notes: Figures may not sum up to the total because of rounding. The amount of buy-backs will be 12,800 billion yen in FY2006 (5,500 billion yen from the Bank of Japan, 5,500 billion yen from the Fiscal Loan Fund, and 1,800 billion yen from the market). The limit of interest-rate swap transactions will be 300 billion yen on the basis of notional principal for FY2005, and will be 1,200 billion yen for FY2006. Nonprice Competitive Auction II is estimated at 3 percent of the primary auction.

The planned issue amount of each JGB for fiscal 2006 is shown in table 11.1. In the past, there used to be some other types of government bonds. But after the August 1988 three-year fixed-rate bonds, the September 2000 five-year discount bonds, the February 2001 four-year fixed-rate bonds, the March 2001 six-year fixed-rate bonds, and the November 2002 three-year discount bonds, these bonds have never been issued. The current maturity structure of the government bonds (outstanding basis) is shown in figure 11.3.

11.3.2   Theoretical Analysis of Debt Management Policy

We construct a theoretical model based on Beetsma and Bovenberg (1997a, 1997b). We include potential possibilities of the government bonds in the model in section 11.4. There are households, firms, the fiscal authority (government), and the monetary authority (central bank). The households live for two periods. The firms produce a private good by using

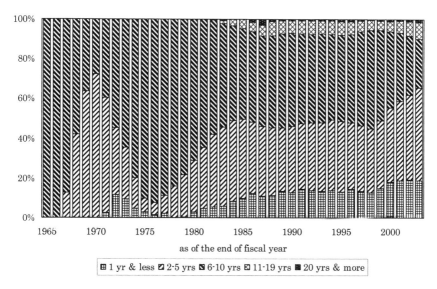

Fig. 11.3   Maturity structure of government bonds (outstanding basis)

labor, at given price level, $P_t (t = 1, 2)$. Their production functions are $Y_t = L_t^{\eta} (0 < \eta < 1)$, where Y_t denotes output, L_t denotes input of labor. Their profits are described as $(1 - \tau_t) P_t L_t^{\eta} - W_t L_t$, where W_t denotes nominal wage rate. The firms' output is taxed at a rate τ_t, as will be described later.

The households organize labor unions, the objective of which is to obtain a target real wage rate. They are assumed to make an expectation to inflation rationally. We also assume that the unions have monopoly power in the labor market. We can normalize the logarithm of real wage rate to zero. Therefore, the (log of the) nominal wage rate is set equal to the (rationally) expected price level.

Under such a situation, the logarithm of output $y_t \equiv \ln Y_t$ is written as

$$y_t = \frac{\eta}{1 - \eta} (\pi_t - \pi_t^e - \tau_t + \ln \eta),$$

where $\pi_t \equiv (P_t - P_{t-1})/P_t$, π_t^e denotes the inflation rate expected by the private sector. Since $\eta/(1 - \eta) \ln \eta$ is a constant, we set $v \equiv \eta/(1 - \eta)$, and normalize y_t as follows

(1) $x_t \equiv y_t - v \ln \eta = v(\pi_t - \pi_t^e - \tau_t)$

Equation (1) is the Lucas supply function.

In a rational expectations equilibrium $(\pi_t - \pi_t^e)$, if there exists no tax distortion $(\tau_t = 0)$, the normalized output is given as $x_t = 0$. This normalized output level corresponds to the natural rate of employment, as mentioned in Fujiki, Osano, and Uchida (1998). Moreover, the socially desirable output, $\tilde{x}_t$, without any distortion of resource allocation is positive, because the socially desirable employment is allowed to exceed the natural rate of employment, as pointed out in Beetsma and Bovenberg (1997a, 1997b). Hereafter, $\tilde{x}_t$ is assumed to be given as a positive constant exogenously.

Next, we describe behavior of the monetary authority. The monetary authority decides level of money supply in each period. We presume that the quantity theory of money is held;[3]

$$\frac{M_t}{P_t} = \kappa \tilde{X}_t$$

where κ is a constant, M_t denotes nominal money supply, and $\tilde{X}_t \equiv \exp(\tilde{x}_t)$. Since $\tilde{X}_t$ is given exogenously, the monetary authority determines the inflation rate directly through controlling money supply. Therefore, $(M_t - M_{t-1})/M_t = \pi_t$ in this model.

Finally, we consider the government's behavior. The government (or fiscal authority) collects revenues from taxes, bond issuing, and seigniorage. Its revenues are used for fiscal expenditures and repayment of government bonds. The government can issue (inflation-indexed) bonds. We assume that the government can issue only one-period bond and the pure expectation hypothesis of interest rate is held. In such a situation, the fiscal authority faces the following budget constraint in each period;

$$P_1 G_1 + (1 + r_{B1}) P_1 B_0 = \tau_1 P_1 X_1 + (M_1 - M_0) + P_1 B_1$$

$$P_2 G_2 + (1 + r_{B2}) P_2 B_1 = \tau_2 P_2 X_2 + (M_2 - M_1)$$

where G_t denotes real government expenditures, r_{Bt} denotes interest rate of bonds in period t, and B_t denotes the outstanding bonds at the end of period t. B_0, outstanding bond at the end of period 0, is exogenously given for the government. The government chooses G_t, τ_t, and B_t.

Dividing both sides of the previous budget constraints by $P_t \tilde{X}_t$ gives the following budget constraints in share of nondistortionary (normalized) output:

(2.1) $g_1 + (1 + r_{B1}) b_0 = \tau_1 + \kappa \pi_1 + b_1$

(2.2) $g_2 + (1 + r_{B2}) b_1 = \tau_2 + \kappa \pi_2$

where $g_t \equiv G_t/\tilde{X}$, $b_t \equiv B_t/\tilde{X}$. We presume that $X_t \approx \tilde{X}_t \approx \tilde{X}$ (a constant).

For simplicity, the real interest rate is assumed to be equal to the world interest rate ρ, which is constant over time. Hence $r_{Bt} = \rho$. From equations 2.1 and 2.2 we can obtain the integrated government budget constraint as follows

---

3. An economy in Japan is now mired in a liquidity trap. We would like to focus on the situation in which an economy in Japan escapes from a liquidity trap.

$$(3) \qquad g_1 + \frac{g_2}{1 + \rho} + (1 + \rho)b_0 = \tau_1 + \kappa\pi_1 + \frac{\tau_2 + \kappa\pi_2}{1 + \rho}$$

11.3.3   Second Best Solution

In this subsection, we analyze the most desirable case with distortionary taxes, in which the two policymakers are integrated and are committed to their policy announcements. We deal with the situation in which the government and the central bank are integrated and are credibly committed to their policy announcements. The credible commitment particularly implies that the policymakers announce an inflation rate and commit themselves to the announced rate at the beginning of each period before nominal wages are concluded.

The society has the social loss function V^S, which is represented by

$$(4) \qquad V^S = \frac{1}{2} \sum_{t=1}^{2} \beta_S^{t-1} [\alpha_{\pi S}\pi_t^2 + (x_t - \tilde{x})^2 + \alpha_{gS}(g_t - \tilde{g}_t)^2]$$

where $\alpha_{\pi S} > 0$, $\alpha_{gS} > 0$, and β_S denotes the discount factor, $0 < \beta_S \leq 1$. We define $\tilde{g}_t$ as the government spending target as the optimal share of the output realized without tax distortions or inflation surprises in period t. Now, for simplicity of the analysis, $\tilde{g}_t$ is assumed to be constant over time: $\tilde{g}_t = \tilde{g}$.

The policymakers minimize the previous loss function. The constraints of each period consist of the Lucas supply function (1), the government budget constraint (3), and the restriction generated by the rational expectations formation of the private sector ($\pi_t^e = \pi_t$). The optimality conditions are given as follows:

$$(5.1) \qquad v^2\left(\tau_t + \frac{\tilde{x}}{v}\right) = \alpha_{gS}(\tilde{g} - g_t) = \frac{\alpha_{\pi S}}{\kappa}\pi_t, \quad (t = 1, 2)$$

$$(5.2) \qquad \pi_1 = \beta_S(1 + \rho)\pi_2$$

$$(5.3) \qquad \tau_1 + \frac{\tilde{x}}{v} = \beta_S(1 + \rho)\left(\tau_2 + \frac{\tilde{x}}{v}\right)$$

$$(5.4) \qquad \tilde{g} - g_1 = \beta_S(1 + \rho)(\tilde{g} - g_2)$$

Equation (5.1) is the static optimization condition in each period. Equations (5.2), (5.3), and (5.4) are the intertemporal optimization conditions for inflation, tax rate, and government spending, respectively. For example, if $\beta_S(1 + \rho) = 1$ (the discount rate is equal to the rate of interest), it is desirable to have the same levels of inflation, tax rate, and government spending over time, respectively. This is a well-known smoothing condition over time a la Barro (1979). See also Barro (1995, 2003).

Several remarks are useful. First, as Beetsma and Bovenberg (1997a, 1997b) mention, the social loss is affected by the initial level of government debt outstanding. In the equilibrium, optimal value of V^S is represented as

$$V^S = \frac{\beta_S + \beta_S(1 + \rho) + (1 + \rho)/[1 + \beta_S(1 + \rho)^2]}{\kappa^2/\alpha_{\pi S} + 1/v^2 + 1/\alpha_{gS}} \left[(1 + \rho)b_0 + \tilde{K} + \frac{\tilde{K}}{1 + \rho} \right],$$

from equations (4) and (5). It means that the larger the initial debt b_0, the larger the social loss.

Second, the income tax and individual preferences of leisure and labor affect the production level of the nation.

Intuition is as follows. To maintain the neutrality of bonds toward social welfare (social loss), it is necessary to issue bonds to cover the part of fiscal expenditures and redemption that cannot be covered from tax revenues and recoinage profits while maintaining budget constraints and not distorting the inflation rate, tax rate, and fiscal expenditures. Issuing bonds should act as a buffer in the budget.

These results are the same as Beetsma and Bovenberg's (1997a).

11.3.4   Numerical Analysis

In this subsection, we numerically examine the second-best debt management policy under commitment, which is theoretically analyzed in the previous subsection. We can easily extend the analytical framework to a more general multiperiod model. For the present numerical analysis, we use a 200-period model and incorporate nominal bonds as well.[4]

In doing the numerical analysis, it is necessary to specify values of some exogenous parameters in the theoretical model. Based on the data of Japanese economy, we set $\eta = 0.7$, $\rho = 0.04$, $\beta_S = 0.964$, $\alpha_{\pi S} = 2$, $\alpha_{gS} = 3$, $\tilde{x} = 0.01$, and $\tilde{g} = 0.1$. We also adapt $\kappa = 0.36$, as mentioned in Fujiki, Osano, and Uchida (1998).

We set the initial outstanding debt to (normalized) output ratio as 100 percent. Under such values of parameters, we derive numerical results by expanding the model to 200 periods. Figure 11.4 shows transitions of government debt outstanding (to the desirable output ratio) in the upper figure, and inflation rate (π), government expenditure (to the desirable output ratio: g), and tax rate (τ) in the lower figure. The upper figure suggests that it is desirable to reduce the bond dependence ratio gradually to redeem fully in the 200th period. The lower figure indicates the smoothing effects of these flow variables a la Barro (1979). These figures reflect the smoothing effect.

---

4. The reason why we set a 200-period model is to weaken effects of the terminal conditions that all stock variables are zero, on this numerical analysis.

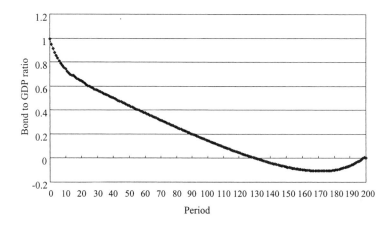

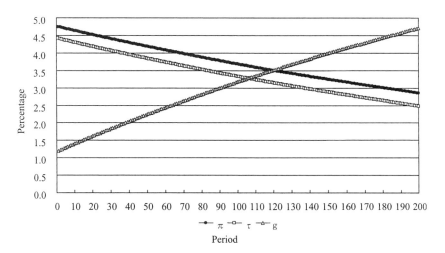

Fig. 11.4   Result of numerical analysis in the second-best case (outstanding bonds, tax rate, government spending, and inflation rate)

11.4   Debt Management and Fiscal Sustainability

11.4.1   Default of the Government Bonds

As analyzed in Beetsma and Bovenberg (1997a, 1997b), among others, when monetary and fiscal authorities are not cooperative and not able to commit their policy announcements, an optimally designed conservative, independent central bank is necessary to establish the second best. The central bank must be made more conservative than society. They showed that correcting monetary policy preferences is a direct way to eliminate the distortions due to the inability to commit. Drudi and Giordano (2000) showed that since default risk increases as the maturity structure of the debt shortens, optimal maturity under bankruptcy risk is in general longer than in the case in which debt repudiation policies can be precommitted or are very much unlikely. See also Persson, Persson, and Svensson (1987, 2005).

If we allow for political distortions, the preferences of the fiscal authority may depart from the preferences of society. In the presence of political distortions a debt target is also needed. For example, if the government discounts the future too heavily, the optimal debt target would de facto act as a ceiling on public debt.

In Japan, the central bank now acts as an independent policymaker and its concern on inflationary targeting is more conservative than the government. In this sense, we could say that the central bank behaves in a good manner to attain the second best.

Let us explain this by including confidence crisis of government debt and spontaneous default of fiscal authority in the model introduced in section 11.3. Investors of government bonds decide whether they buy bonds or not in prospect of behaviors of the government. If they can perfectly expect the government's default, they do not purchase bonds at all. Hence we should investigate such a situation using backward induction. It means that a subgame perfect Nash equilibrium is adopted as a solution concept in this section.

The fiscal authority and the monetary authority have individual loss functions. Loss function of the fiscal authority is written as

$$(6) \qquad V^F = \frac{1}{2} \sum_{t=1}^{2} \beta_S^{t-1} [\alpha_{\pi F} \pi_t^2 + (x_t - \tilde{x})^2 + \alpha_{gS}(g_t - \tilde{g})^2]$$

where $\alpha_{\pi F} > 0$, $\alpha_{gS} > 0$, and β_S denotes the discount factor, $0 < \beta_S \leq 1$. Also the loss function of the monetary authority is written as

$$(7) \qquad V^M = \frac{1}{2} \sum_{t=1}^{2} \beta_S^{t-1} [\alpha_{\pi M} \pi_t^2 + (x_t - \tilde{x})^2 + \alpha_{gS}(g_t - \tilde{g})^2]$$

where $\alpha_{\pi M} > \alpha_{\pi F} > 0$. It implies that the monetary authority is more conservative in inflation than the fiscal authority. Each policymaker minimizes the previous loss function, taking policies selected by the other authority as given. In this section, we set that both policymakers decide policies simultaneously in each period. Investors of the government bonds have the loss function (4).

Now, we describe a situation that the government triggers a debt default. The government can declare the default before policies are chosen in this period. When the default occurs, the government does not pay at all.[5] How-

---

5. The real interest rate is assumed to be equal to the world interest rate. In addition, we exclude the possibility of partial default by assumption. If, therefore, investors expect the default, the interest rate on the government bonds becomes infinity.

ever, the production in this economy is deteriorated due to the default. In this situation, the Lucas supply function is assumed to include default costs.

(1') $x_t = zv(\pi_t - \pi_t^e - \tau_t) \quad 0 < z < 1$

where z is constant over time. It means that the production in default on the government bond is z times as large as that in the normal situation, regardless of the amount of the debt.

The constraints of each period consist of the Lucas supply function (1) or (1'), the government budget constraints (2). We also rewrite the government budget constraints as follows,

$$(8.1) \quad \tilde{K} + \frac{(1 - z)\tilde{x}}{vz} + (1 + \rho)b_0 = \left(\tau_1 + \frac{\tilde{x}}{vz}\right) + \kappa\pi_1 + (\tilde{g} - g_1) + b_1$$

$$(8.2) \quad \tilde{K} + \frac{(1 - z)\tilde{x}}{vz} + (1 + \rho)b_1 = \left(\tau_2 + \frac{\tilde{x}}{vz}\right) + \kappa\pi_2 + (\tilde{g} - g_2)$$

where $\tilde{K} \equiv \tilde{g} + \tilde{x}/v$. Note $(x_t - \tilde{x})^2 = z^2 v^2 [\pi_t^e - \pi_t + \tau_t + (\tilde{x}/vz)]^2$ from equation (1'), $z = 1$ in the normal situation, and $0 < z < 1$ in default of payment.

We assume that, in each period, the monetary authority cannot commit the inflation rate announced at the beginning of each period before nominal wages are set. Under this situation, the policy authorities take inflation expectations as predetermined. Such situation is represented in figure 11.5 as a game tree.

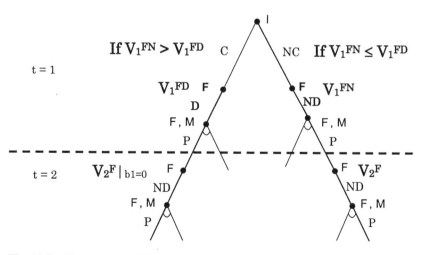

Fig. 11.5   The structure of the policy game
Notes: NC: nonconfidence crisis; C: confidence crisis; D: default; ND: nondefault; P: policy choice; F: fiscal authority; M: monetary authority; I: investors.

11.4.2   Policy Choice in the Second Period

To solve for the two-period decision problem, we use the backward induction method. Thus, we begin with solving for the solution in the second period and then proceed to solve for the solution in the first period. It implies that such a policy is a time-consistent policy, which is analyzed in Lucas and Stokey (1983), Persson, Persson, and Svensson (1987, 2005), Calvo and Guidotti (1990a, 1990b), and so on. In the second period, the fiscal authority chooses $\{\tau_2, g_2\}$ to minimize its loss function, subject to the budget constraint (8.2). Also, the monetary authority chooses $\{\pi_2\}$ to minimize its loss function, taking as given the expected inflation rate (π_2^e), without any regard for the budget constraint (8.2).

The Normal Case

If the government does not trigger a debt default in the second period, we obtain the following conditions from the first-order conditions for the choice of $\{\pi_2, \tau_2, g_2\}$, taking policies decided by the other authority and inflation expectation and b_1 as given,

(9) $$v(\tilde{x} - x_2) = \alpha_{gS}(\tilde{g} - g_2) = \alpha_{\pi M}\pi_2$$

Moreover, from the previous conditions and the government budget constraint and the restriction generated by the rational expectations formation of the private sector ($\pi_t^e = \pi_2$), the following relations are held

$$\pi_2 = \frac{1}{N\alpha_{\pi S}}[\tilde{K} + (1 + \rho)b_1]$$

(10) $$\tau_2 + \frac{\tilde{x}}{v} = \frac{1}{Nv^2}[\tilde{K} + (1 + \rho)b_1]$$

$$\tilde{g} - g_2 = \frac{1}{N\alpha_{gS}}[\tilde{K} + (1 + \rho)b_1]$$

where $N \equiv \kappa/\alpha_{\pi M} + 1/v^2 + 1/\alpha_{gS}$.
Hence, the value of the loss function of the fiscal authority is

(11) $$V_2^F \equiv \frac{1}{2}\frac{N_F^*}{N^2}[\tilde{K} + (1 + \rho)b_1]^2$$

where $N_F^* \equiv \alpha_{\pi F}/\alpha_{\pi M}^2 + 1/v^2 + 1/\alpha_{gS}$.

The Case of Default

If the government *does* declare a debt default in the second period, the government may decrease its values of the loss function. Then, investors would not buy the government bond in the first period if they could predict the debt default in the second period. In this situation, the government cannot issue the bonds in the first period, and does not have any bonds to default in the second period. Therefore, the government cannot trigger a default in the second period.

11.4.3 Policy Choice in the First Period

In the first period, investors of the government bonds expect the possibility that the government may trigger a debt default.[6] If they believe the default occurs, they do not buy the bonds at all. This situation is confidence crisis. Under this situation, the government cannot newly issue bonds (b_1). If investors expect the default does not occur, the government bonds are freely traded.

After that, the fiscal authority chooses $\{\tau_1, g_2, b_1\}$ to minimize its loss function, subject to the budget constraint, equation (8.1). Also the monetary authority chooses $\{\pi_1\}$ to minimize its loss function, without any regard for the budget constraint (8.1).

The Normal Case Under No Confidence Crisis (Case N)

First, we consider a situation that confidence crisis does not occur. Under this situation, the government can newly issue a one-period bond (b_1). The fiscal and monetary authorities minimize their loss functions in consideration of situation in the second period. Thus the authorities in the first period have the following loss functions,

$$(12) \qquad V_1^{aN} = \frac{1}{2}[\alpha_{\pi a}\pi_1^2 + (x_1 - \tilde{x})^2 + \alpha_{gS}(g_1 - \tilde{g})^2] + \beta_S V_2^a$$

where $a = F, M$. V_2^a denotes the value of loss function in the second period. V_2^F is defined as (11), and V_2^M is obtained by assigning equation (10) to (7).

The monetary authority minimizes equation (12) regardless of the government budget constraint, taking policies selected by the fiscal authority and inflation expectation and b_0 as given. From the first-order condition for the choice of $\{\pi_1\}$, we obtain the following condition

$$(13.1) \qquad v(\tilde{x} - x_1) = \alpha_{\pi M}\pi_1$$

The fiscal authority minimizes its loss function.

$$(13.2) \qquad v(\tilde{x} - x_1) = \alpha_{gS}(\tilde{g} - g_1) = \beta_N^*[\tilde{K} + (1 + \rho)b_1]$$

where $\beta_N^* \equiv \beta_S(1 + \rho)N_F^*/N$. From the previous conditions (13.1, 13.2) and the government budget constraint, the following relations are held under the rational expectations formation of the private sector ($\pi_t^e = \pi_1$)

$$\tau_1 + \frac{\tilde{x}}{v} = \frac{1}{Nv^2}[\tilde{K} + (1 + \rho)b_0 - b_1]$$

---

6. As we mentioned previously, the government may default only in the first period, not in the second period.

$$\pi_1 = \frac{1}{N\alpha_{\pi M}}[\tilde{K} + (1 + \rho)b_0 - b_1]$$

(14)
$$\tilde{g} - g_1 = \frac{1}{N\alpha_{gS}}[\tilde{K} + (1 + \rho)b_0 - b_1]$$

$$b_1 = \frac{\delta_2}{1 + \rho}[(1 + \rho)b_0 + \tilde{K} - \beta_N^*\tilde{K}]$$

where $\delta_2 \equiv (1 + \rho)/[1 + \beta_S(1 + \rho)^2N_F^*/N]$

Therefore, we obtain the value of the loss function as follows

(15) $$V_1^{FN} \equiv \frac{1}{2}\frac{N_F^*}{N^2}[\tilde{K} + (1 + \rho)b_0 - b_1]^2 + \frac{1}{2}\beta_S\frac{N_F^*}{N^2}[\tilde{K} + (1 + \rho)b_1]^2$$

$$= \frac{1}{2}\frac{N_F^*}{N^2}\delta_2^2[(\beta_N^*)^2 + \beta_S]\left[\tilde{K} + \frac{1}{1 + \rho}\tilde{K} + (1 + \rho)b_0\right]^2$$

The Case of Default Under Confidence Crisis (Case D)

Next, we consider a situation that confidence crisis occurs. Under this situation, the government cannot newly issue any bond ($b_1 = 0$), and trigger a debt default in the first period.

The fiscal and monetary authorities minimize their loss functions. If once the government defaults on payments in the first period, however, the government has no debt in the second period, that is, there is no default in the second period. Thus the authorities in the first period have the following loss functions

(12') $$V_1^{aD} = \frac{1}{2}[\alpha_{\pi a}\pi_1^2 + (x_1 - \tilde{x})^2 + \alpha_{gS}(g_1 - \tilde{g})^2] + \beta_S V_2^a|_{b_1=0}$$

where $a = F, M$, and $V_2^a|_{b_1=0}$: V_2^a with $b_1 = 0$.

Also the production in this situation is determined by equation (1'). The government budget constraint in the first period becomes as follows

(8.1') $$\tilde{K} + \frac{(1 - z)\tilde{x}}{vz} = \left(\tau_1 + \frac{\tilde{x}}{vz}\right) + \kappa\pi_1 + (\tilde{g} - g_1) \quad 0 < z < 1$$

The monetary authority minimizes equation (12') regardless of the government budget constraint, taking policies selected by the fiscal authority and inflation expectation as given. From the first-order condition for the choice of $\{\pi_1\}$, we obtain the following condition

(16.1) $$vz(\tilde{x} - x_1) = \alpha_{\pi M}\pi_1$$

The fiscal authority minimizes its loss function (12'), subject to equation (8.2). The authority sets policies to satisfy the following condition:

(16.2) $vz(\tilde{x} - x_1) = \alpha_{gS}(\tilde{g} - g_1)$

From the previous conditions (1'), (16.1, 16.2), and the government budget constraint (8.1'), the following relations are held under the rational expectations formation of the private sector ($\pi_t^e = \pi_1$)

$$\pi_1 = \frac{1}{H\alpha_{\pi S}}\left[\tilde{K} + \frac{(1-z)\tilde{x}}{vz}\right]$$

$$\tau_1 + \frac{\tilde{x}}{vz} = \frac{1}{Hv^2z^2}\left[\tilde{K} + \frac{(1-z)\tilde{x}}{vz}\right]$$

(17) $\tilde{g} - g_1 = \dfrac{1}{H\alpha_{gS}}\left[\tilde{K} + \dfrac{(1-z)\tilde{x}}{vz}\right]$

where $H = \kappa/\alpha_{\pi M} + 1/v^2z^2 + 1/\alpha_{gS}$.
Therefore, we obtain the value of the loss function in this case as follows

(18) $V_1^{FD} \equiv \dfrac{1}{2}\dfrac{H_F^*}{H^2}\left[\tilde{K} + \dfrac{(1-z)\tilde{x}}{vz}\right]^2 + \dfrac{1}{2}\beta_S\dfrac{N_F^*}{N^2}\tilde{K}^2$

where $H_F^* \equiv \alpha_{\pi F}/\alpha_{\pi M}^2 + 1/v^2z^2 + 1/\alpha_{gS}$.

Welfare Comparison between Case N and Case D

Whether the confidence crisis occurs or not in the first period depends on welfare loss of the fiscal authority in each case. If the government defaults on payments, investors of the government bonds face losses. Thus, they do not buy the bonds at all when they expect that the government will trigger a debt default in the first period.

If $V_1^{FN} \leq V_1^{FD}$, the fiscal authority does not have any incentives to default in the first period. Hence, investors can purchase the government bonds. We further analyze this situation.

$V_1^{FN} \leq V_1^{FD}$ is satisfied under the following conditions

(19) $0 \leq b_0 \leq -\dfrac{2+\rho}{(1+\rho)^2}\tilde{K} + \dfrac{1}{(1+\rho)\delta_2}\sqrt{\dfrac{\dfrac{H_F^*N^2}{N_F^*H^2}\left[\tilde{K} + \dfrac{(1-z)\tilde{x}}{vz}\right]^2 + \beta_S\tilde{K}^2}{(\beta_N^*)^2 + \beta_S}}$

When $V_1^{FN} \leq V_1^{FD}$, that is, condition (19) is held, investors buy the government bonds in the first period. It means that there is no confidence crisis in the first period under this situation. Otherwise, investors do not buy bonds at all in the first period. Thus confidence crisis occurs in the first period.

11.4.4   Numerical Analysis

In this subsection, we also numerically examine the previous situation, which is theoretically analyzed in the previous subsection. We can easily extend the analytical framework to a more general T-period model. We will describe the detail setting of this numerical analysis in the appendix at the end of this chapter.

In this numerical analysis we introduce the maturity structure of the government bonds to make it more realistic. We adopt this structure in fiscal 2003 (settlement basis) in Japan. The maturity structure of the outstanding debt is assumed to be given in table 11.2. These ratios mean composition ratios to total amount of debt by remaining years to maturity. For example, the ratio of the government bonds that has the remaining years to maturity at less than one year is about 36 percent.

We also calculate the transition of policy variables in the realistic case described in the previous sections. As we mentioned, in the realistic case,

Table 11.2   **Maturity structure of JGBs in fiscal 2003 (%)**

Maturity (years)	Composition ratio	
	Outstanding basis	Issuance basis
1	18.78	36.25
2	13.53	15.86
3	9.94	
4	11.22	
5	12.03	16.23
6	5.09	
7	4.79	
8	4.67	
9	5.03	
10	5.01	22.00
11	0.35	
12	0.91	
13	1.39	
14	1.64	
15	1.73	4.81
16	0.41	
17	0.64	
18	0.48	
19	0.75	
20	0.83	3.78
21		
22		
23		
24		
25		
26	0.11	
27	0.16	
28	0.07	
29	0.20	
30	0.20	1.07

the government may trigger a debt default. Thus can the fiscal authority avoid a default? Or does the authority have an incentive to default? We consider whether the government defaults on payment under our calibration setting.

We set the value of parameters used in this model as the same in the second-best case in section 11.3.4. Also we set $z = 0.9$.

In the numerical analysis, we calculate the value of loss function of the fiscal authority in case of default (V_t^{FD}) and the value of loss function in case of no-default (V_t^{FN}) in each period, and then compare both values. If $V_t^{FD} \geq V_t^{FN}$, the government in period t does not default. If $V_t^{FN} > V_t^{FD}$, the government triggers a default.

In conclusion, under our setting in the 200-period model, we find that the fiscal authority could still avoid a default, fortunately. First, the upper figure of figure 11.6 shows the transition of outstanding debts. In this case, the fiscal authority takes such a policy that the outstanding debt of government bonds first increases and then decreases sharply near the last period . This phenomenon seems to reflect the fact that the fiscal authority issues government bonds strategically. And it suggests that the outstanding debt in this situation does not exceed about 120 percent. It is consistent with no default.

The lower figure of figure 11.6 shows inflation rate (π), government expenditure (to the desirable output ratio: g), and tax rate (τ). When the outstanding debt of government bonds is large, the issuance of new bonds results in the debt default. Therefore, the large amount of outstanding debt limits the fiscal authority to issue new government bonds. As a result, issuance of government bonds leads the fiscal authority to an advantageous position against the monetary authority. In other words, the issuance of bonds works as a credible threat to the monetary authority. This mechanism leads the inflation rate to be higher, comparing to the second-best case. Inflation rate becomes over 6 percent. In contrast, the tax rate is kept low about 3 percent.

11.4.5   Intuitions of the Analysis and Policy Implications

According to conditions (19), the fiscal authority has an incentive to default when the amount of debt outstanding is more than a certain level. Expecting the debt default, the investors do not buy the public bonds at all. The public bonds, therefore, cannot be sold when the issuance leads the amount of debt outstanding to be more than the certain level. In this respect, the fiscal authority has to take into account the upper limit of stocks of public debt.

This possibility of debt default provides the fiscal authority to issue public bonds strategically in the first period. Suppose that the fiscal authority, in the first period, issues public bonds to be paid in subsequent periods in a multiperiod setting. The amount of issuance is, in addition,

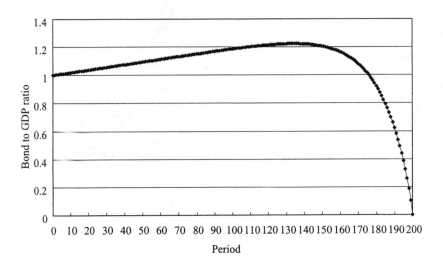

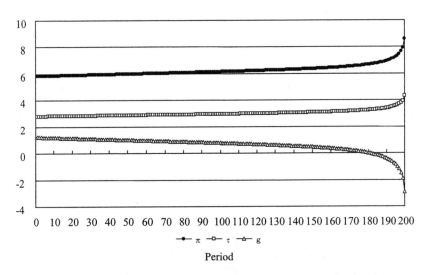

Fig. 11.6   Result of numerical analysis in a realistic case (outstanding bonds, tax rate, government spending, and inflation rate)

supposed to set to the extent that the fiscal authority has to raise the tax rate to finance the government spending and/or cut the government spending itself in the second period because the additional debt issuance is limited due to the possibility of the default in subsequent periods.

This strategic behavior of the fiscal authority induces the monetary authority, in a later period, to boost output and raise seigniorage revenues to eliminate the distortion of resource allocation due to the limitation on debt issuance. Therefore, the monetary policy in a later period suffers from an inflation bias from the ex ante point of view. Expecting such future monetary policy, the fiscal authority has an incentive to issue more public bonds strategically in an earlier period because it will lead the fiscal authority to the advantageous position in the game played in a later period. This strategic bias of the fiscal authority results in the distortion of the resource allocation.[7]

There are two ways to eliminate this distortion toward successful fiscal reconstruction. One of them is to make the monetary authority more conservative than society in the sense that the price stability weight of monetary authority is higher than that of society. If the monetary authority is conservative enough not to raise inflation depending passively on the strategic accumulation of public bonds, the fiscal authority does not engage in the strategic accumulation of debt in an earlier period. Consequently the central bank should be more conservative to eliminate the distortion due to the strategic behavior of fiscal authority.

The other way of eliminating the distortion of the resource allocation is to design an institutional ceiling on the debt issuance. This institutional framework eliminates directly the distortion stemmed from the strategic behavior of the fiscal authority. Needless to say, this direct ceiling does not work effectively if the fiscal authority has not issued public bonds to the extent that the amount of debt outstanding is close to the critical level of debt default. It is therefore natural that the direct ceiling might not be necessary for many countries, but it can provide a binding constraint of the public bond issuance for the fiscal authority of Japan because it has accumulated the debt outstanding much more than other countries.[8]

11.5   Conclusion

If the expansionary trend in Japan's government spending continues at this pace, the fiscal deficit will inflate further and the ability to raise taxes in the future will be politically limited. Investors will lose confidence in Japan's public bonds if they believe that the nation's public finance is bound for long-term crisis. The result is that interest rates will rise and fiscal failure will become a more tangible reality.

This chapter has analyzed sustainability issues of Japan's fiscal policy and then discussed the debt management policy using theoretical models

---

7. Since this strategic issuance of government bonds distorts the resource allocation form the ex ante point of view, it is considered to be one of the time inconsistency problems.

8. One of the reasons why Japan has accumulated the debt drastically is related to the political situation of Japan in the 1990s. Especially after 1993, several parties formed a coalition government. This instability of government party in the diet resulted in the delay of fiscal structural reform toward fiscal reconstruction because the politicians have to take into account the possibility of dropping power when carrying out such policies.

and numerical studies. We also investigated the desirable coordination of fiscal and monetary authorities toward fiscal reconstruction.

We have also investigated confidence crisis of government debt and spontaneous default of fiscal authority. The fiscal authority has an incentive to default when the amount of debt outstanding is more than a certain level. Expecting the debt default, the investors do not buy the public bonds at all. The public bonds, therefore, cannot be sold when the issuance leads the amount of debt outstanding to be more than the certain level. In this respect, the fiscal authority has to take into account the upper limit of stocks of public debt. Our numerical study suggests that the fiscal authority could still avoid a default in Japan.

We have also showed that for a country with large stocks of public debt like Japan, the fiscal authority has an incentive to issue public bonds strategically. This strategic bias distorts the monetary authority to increase inflation too much. To eliminate this distortion bias and to attain fiscal reconstruction, an institutional ceiling on the debt issuance is one of the effective policy tools.

Appendix

Numerical Analysis in a Realistic Case

In section 11.4.4, we also numerically examine a realistic case, which is theoretically analyzed in sections 11.4.1 through 11.4.3. We can easily extend the analytical framework to a more general T-period model. Now we introduce maturity structure of the government bond. The government can issue (inflation-indexed) bonds, and choose their maturity. The pure expectation hypothesis of interest rates is assumed to be held. In such a situation, the fiscal authority faces the following budget constraint in period t;

$$g_t + \sum_{s=0}^{t-1}(1 + \rho)^{t-s}b_{s,t} = \tau_t + \kappa\pi_t + \sum_{v=t+1}^{T} b_{t,v}$$

or

$$(A.1) \quad \tilde{K} + \frac{(1 - z)\tilde{x}}{vz} + \sum_{s=0}^{t-1}(1 + \rho)^{t-s}b_{s,t}$$

$$= \left(\tau_t + \frac{\tilde{x}}{vz}\right) + \kappa\pi_t + (\tilde{g} - g_t) + \sum_{v=t+1}^{T} b_{t,v}$$

where $B_{s,t}$ denotes the amount of bonds issued in period s with a prescribed payout in period t and $b_{st} \equiv B_{st}/\tilde{X}$. Note $z = 1$ in the normal situation, and $0 < z < 1$ in default of payment. The initial maturity structure of the government bond $(B_{0v} \mid v \geq 1)$ is exogenously given for the government in each period. The government in period t chooses $g_t, \tau_t, b_{tv}(t + 1 \leq v \leq T)$.

The Normal Case in the Final Period

If the government does not trigger a debt default in the final period (period T), we obtain the following conditions from the first-order conditions for the choice of (π_T, τ_T, g_T), taking policies decided by the other authority and inflation expectation as given,

$$v(\tilde{x} - x_T) = \alpha_{gS}(\tilde{g} - g_T) = \alpha_{\pi M}\pi_T$$

Moreover, from the previous conditions and the government budget constraint and the restriction generated by the rational expectations formation of the private sector ($\pi_T^e = \pi_t$), the following relations are held

(A.2)
$$\pi_T = \frac{1}{N\alpha_{\pi S}}(\tilde{K} + b_T)$$

$$\tau_T + \frac{\tilde{x}}{v} = \frac{1}{Nv^2}(\tilde{K} + b_T)$$

$$\tilde{g} - g_T = \frac{1}{N\alpha_{gS}}(\tilde{K} + b_T)$$

where $b_T \equiv \Sigma_{s=0}^{T-1}(1 + \rho)^{T-s}b_{sT}$. Hence, the value of the loss function of the fiscal authority is

(A3)
$$V_T^{FN} \equiv \frac{1}{2}\frac{N_F^*}{N^2}(\tilde{K} + b_T)^2$$

Policy Choice in Period T – 1

In period T – 1, investors of the government bonds first expect whether the government will trigger a debt default (in period T – 1 or the period T). If they believe the default occurs, they do not buy the bonds at all. This situation is confidence crisis. Under this situation, the government cannot newly issue bonds ($b_{T-1,T}$). If investors expect the default does not occur, the government bonds are freely treaded.

After that, the fiscal authority chooses $\{\tau_{T-1}, g_{T-1}, b_{T-1,T}\}$ to minimize its loss function, subject to the budget constraint (A.1). Also the monetary authority chooses $\{\pi_{T-1}\}$ to minimize its loss function, without any regard for the budget constraint (A.1).

The Normal Case (Case N)

First, we consider a situation that confidence crisis does not occur. Under this situation, the government can newly issue a one-period bond

($b_{T-1,T}$). The fiscal and monetary authorities minimize their loss functions. Thus the authorities in period $T - 1$ have the following loss functions

(A4) $V^a_{T-1} = \dfrac{1}{2}[\alpha_{\pi a}\pi^2_{T-1} + (x_{T-1} - \tilde{x})^2 + \alpha_{gS}(g_{T-1} - \tilde{g})^2] + \beta_S V^{aN}_T$

where $a = F, M$. V^{aN}_T denotes the value of loss function in the normal case in the final period. V^{FN}_T is defined as (A.3), and V^{MN}_T is obtained by assigning equation (A.2) to equation (7).

The monetary authority minimizes equation (A.4) regardless of the government budget constraint, taking policies selected by the fiscal authority and inflation expectation as given. From the first-order condition for the choice of $\{\pi_{T-1}\}$, we obtain the following condition

(A.5.1) $v(\tilde{x} - x_{T-1}) = \alpha_{\pi M}\pi_{T-1}$

The fiscal authority minimizes its loss function and sets policies to satisfy the following conditions:

(A.5.2) $v(\tilde{x} - x_{T-1}) = \alpha_{gS}(\tilde{g} - g_{T-1}) = \beta^*_N[\tilde{K} + b_T]$

From the previous conditions (A.5.1, A.5.2) and the government budget constraint, the following relations are held under the rational expectations formation of the private sector ($\pi^e_{T-1} = \pi_{T-1}$)

(A.6) $b_{T-1,T} = \delta_{T-1}\left\{\tilde{K} + b_{T-1} - \beta^*_N\left[\tilde{K} + \sum_{s=0}^{T-2}(1 + \rho)^{T-s}b_{s,T}\right]\right\}$

$\tau_{T-1} + \dfrac{\tilde{x}}{v} = \dfrac{1}{Nv^2}(\tilde{K} + b_{T-1} - b_{T-1,T})$

$= \dfrac{1}{Nv^2}\delta_{T-1}\beta^*_N\left\{\tilde{K} + b_{T-1} + \dfrac{1}{1 + \rho}[\tilde{K} + (1 + \rho)^3 b_{03} + (1 + \rho)^2 b_{13}]\right\}$

$\pi_{T-1} = \dfrac{1}{N\alpha_{\pi M}}\delta_{T-1}\beta^*_N$

$\cdot\left\{\tilde{K} + b_{T-1} + \dfrac{1}{1 + \rho}[\tilde{K} + (1 + \rho)^3 b_{03} + (1 + \rho)^2 b_{13}]\right\}$

$\tilde{g} - g_{T-1} = \dfrac{1}{N\alpha_{gS}}\delta_{T-1}\beta^*_N$

$\cdot\left\{\tilde{K} + b_{T-1} + \dfrac{1}{1 + \rho}[\tilde{K} + (1 + \rho)^3 b_{03} + (1 + \rho)^2 b_{13}]\right\}$

where $b_{T-1} \equiv \sum_{s=0}^{T-2}(1 + \rho)^{T-1-s}b_{s,T-1}$, $\delta_{T-1} \equiv (1 + \rho)/[1 + \beta_S(1 + \rho)^2 N_F^*/N]$. Therefore, we obtain the value of the loss function as follows

$$(A.7) \quad V_{T-1}^{FN} \equiv \frac{1}{2}\frac{N_F^*}{N^2}(\tilde{K} + b_{T-1} - b_{T-1,T})^2 + \frac{1}{2}\beta_S\frac{N_F^*}{N^2}(\tilde{K} + b_T)^2$$

$$= \frac{1}{2}\frac{N_F^*}{N^2}\delta_{T-1}^2[(\beta_N^*)^2 + \beta_S]\left\{\tilde{K} + b_{T-1} + \frac{1}{1 + \rho}\left[\tilde{K} + \sum_{s=0}^{T-2}(1 + \rho)^{T-s}b_{s,T}\right]\right\}^2$$

The Case of Default in the Final Period
Under Confidence Crisis (Case C)

Next, we consider a situation that confidence crisis occurs. Under this situation, the government cannot newly issue any bond ($b_{T-1,T} = 0$). The fiscal and monetary authorities minimize their loss functions in consideration of the situation in the final period; whether the government faces a debt default or not in the final period.

At first, we consider the case that default occurs in the final period. When the government *does* declare a debt default in the final period, the government budget constraint in the final period becomes equation (A.1) with $z \neq 0$. Under this situation, we obtain the following conditions from the first-order conditions for the choice of $\{\pi_T, \tau_T, g_T\}$, taking policies decided by the other authority and inflation expectation as given

$$(A.8) \quad vz(\tilde{x} - x_T) = \alpha_{gS}(\tilde{g} - g_T) = \alpha_{\pi M}\pi_T$$

Moreover, from the previous conditions (1′) and (12), and the government budget constraint (A.8) and the restriction generated by the rational expectations formation of the private sector ($\pi_T^e = \pi_T$), the following relations are held

$$(A.9) \quad \pi_T = \frac{1}{H\alpha_{\pi S}}\left[\tilde{K} + \frac{(1 - z)\tilde{x}}{vz}\right]$$

$$\tau_T + \frac{\tilde{x}}{vz} = \frac{1}{Hv^2z^2}\left[\tilde{K} + \frac{(1 - z)\tilde{x}}{vz}\right]$$

$$\tilde{g} - g_T = \frac{1}{H\alpha_{gS}}\left[\tilde{K} + \frac{(1 - z)\tilde{x}}{vz}\right]$$

Hence, the value of the loss function of the fiscal authority is

$$(A.10) \quad V_T^{FD} \equiv \frac{1}{2}\frac{H_F^*}{H^2}\left[\tilde{K} + \frac{(1 - z)\tilde{x}}{vz}\right]^2$$

Next we investigate policy choice in period $T - 1$. The authorities in period $T - 1$ are written as

$$(A.11)\ V_{T-1}^{aC} = \frac{1}{2}[\alpha_{\pi a}\pi_{T-1}^2 + (x_{T-1} - \tilde{x})^2 + \alpha_{gS}(g_{T-1} - \tilde{g})^2] + \beta_S V_{T-1}^{aD}$$

where $a = F, M$. The monetary authority minimizes (A.11) regardless of the government budget constraint, taking policies selected by the fiscal authority and inflation expectation as given. Since this situation is the same as Case C condition with respect to $\{\pi_{-1}\}$ in this case is (A.5.1).

The fiscal authority minimizes its loss functions in consideration of situation in the final period. The government decides policies to satisfy the condition,

$$(A.5.2')\qquad v(\tilde{x} - x_{T-1}) = \alpha_{gS}(\tilde{g} - g_{T-1})$$

Therefore, we obtain the value of the loss function in this case as follows

$$(A.12)\qquad V_{T-1}^{FC} \equiv \frac{1}{2}\frac{N_F^*}{N^2}(\tilde{K} + b_{T-1})^2 + \frac{1}{2}\beta_S\frac{H_F^*}{H^2}\left[\tilde{K} + \frac{(1-z)\tilde{x}}{vz}\right]^2$$

The Case of Default in Period T – 1 Under Confidence Crisis (Case D)

Also, we discuss the situation that the government in period T – 1 triggers a debt default under confidence crisis. Under this situation, the government cannot newly issue a one-period bond ($b_{T-1,T} = 0$).

The fiscal and monetary authorities minimize their loss functions in consideration of situation in the final period. If once the government defaults on payments in period T – 1, however, the government has no debt in the final period—that is, there is no default in the final period. Thus the authorities in period T –1 have the following loss functions

$$(A.13)\qquad V_{T-1}^\alpha = \frac{1}{2}[\alpha_{\pi a}\pi_{T-1}^2 + (x_{T-1} - \tilde{x})^2 + \alpha_{gS}(g_{T-1} - \tilde{g})^2] + \beta_S V_T^{aN}\big|_{b_T=0}$$

where $a = F, M$. The government budget constraint in this period is (A.1) with $z \neq 1$.

The monetary authority minimizes (A.13) regardless of the government budget constraint, taking policies selected by the fiscal authority and inflation expectation as given. From the first order condition for the choice of $\{\pi_{T-1}\}$, we obtain the following condition

$$(A.14.1)\qquad vz(\tilde{x} - x_{T-1}) = \alpha_{\pi M}\pi_{T-1}$$

The fiscal authority minimizes its loss function (A.13), subject to (A.1). The authority sets policies to satisfy the following condition:

$$(A.14.2)\qquad vz(\tilde{x} - x_{T-1}) = \alpha_{gS}(\tilde{g} - g_{T-1})$$

From the previous conditions (1'), (A.14.1, A.14.2), and the government budget constraint (A.1), the following relations are held under the rational expectations formation of the private sector ($\pi_{T-1}^e = \pi_{T-1}$)

(A.15)
$$\pi_{T-1} = \frac{1}{H\alpha_{\pi S}} \left[\tilde{K} + \frac{(1-z)\tilde{x}}{vz} \right]$$

$$\tau_{T-1} + \frac{\tilde{x}}{vz} = \frac{1}{Hv^2z^2} \left[\tilde{K} + \frac{(1-z)\tilde{x}}{vz} \right]$$

$$\tilde{g} - g_{T-1} = \frac{1}{H\alpha_{gS}} \left[\tilde{K} + \frac{(1-z)\tilde{x}}{vz} \right]$$

Therefore, we obtain the value of the loss function in this case as follows

(A.16)
$$V_{T-1}^{FD} \equiv \frac{1}{2} \frac{H_F^*}{H^2} \left[\tilde{K} + \frac{(1-z)\tilde{x}}{vz} \right]^2 + \frac{1}{2} \beta_S \frac{N_F^*}{N^2} \tilde{K}^2$$

Welfare Comparison Between Case C and Case D

Does the fiscal authority trigger a debt default under no confidence crisis? It depends on the value of the loss function of the fiscal authority in each case.

If $V_{T-1}^{FD} \geq V_{T-1}^{FC}$, the government does not trigger a default in period $T-1$. On the other hand, in the case of $V_2^{FD} < V_2^{FC}$, the fiscal authority has incentives to default on payments in period $T-1$.

The details are as follows. In the case of $\tilde{K} > N\tilde{x}vz/1 + z$ and $D > \tilde{K}^2$, $V_{T-1}^{FD} > V_{T-1}^{FC}$ is satisfied under the following conditions

(A.17)
$$b_{T-1} > \sqrt{\beta_S \tilde{K}^2 + (1-\beta_S)D} - \tilde{K},$$

These conditions suggest that the government has an incentive to default when the amount of debt outstanding is more than a certain level.

Welfare Comparison Between Case N and Case C or Case D

Whether the confidence crisis occurs or not in period $T-1$ depends on welfare loss of the fiscal authority in each case. If the government defaults on payments, investors of the government bonds face losses. Thus, they do not buy the bonds at all when they expect that the government will trigger a debt default in period $T-1$ or the final period.

If $V_{T-1}^{FN} \leq \min\{V_{T-1}^{FC}, V_{T-1}^{FD}\}$, the fiscal authority does not have any incentives to default in each period. Hence, investors can purchase the government bonds. We further analyze this situation.

$V_{T-1}^{FN} < V_{T-1}^{FC} < V_{T-1}^{FD}$ is satisfied, under the following conditions

(A.18)
$$0 < b_{N,T-1} < \beta_S D - \tilde{K}^2 \left[\gamma_{T-1} \left(1 + \frac{1}{1+\rho} \right)^2 - 1 \right],$$

where

$$\gamma_{T-1} \equiv \delta_{T-1}^2 [(\beta_N^*)^2 + \beta_S], \, b_{N,T-1} \equiv (\gamma_{T-1} - 1)b_{T-1}^2$$

$$+ \gamma_{T-1} \left[\sum_{s=0}^{T-2} (1 + \rho)^{T-s} b_{s,t} \right]^2 + 2\gamma_{T-1} b_{T-1} \sum_{s=0}^{T-2} (1 + \rho)^{T-s} b_{s,T} - 2\tilde{K} b_{T-1}$$

$$+ 2\tilde{K}\gamma_{T-1} \left(1 + \frac{1}{1 + \rho} \right) \left[b_{T-1} + \sum_{s=0}^{T-2} (1 + \rho)^{T-s} b_{s,T} \right],$$

$$b_{T-1} \leq \sqrt{\beta_S \tilde{K}^2 + (1 - \beta_S)D} - \tilde{K},$$

and

(A.17)
$$\gamma_{T-1} < \dfrac{1 + \beta_S D}{\left(1 + \dfrac{1}{1 + \rho} \right)^2}$$

On the other hand, $V_{T-1}^{FN} < V_{T-1}^{FD} < V_{T-1}^{FC}$ is satisfied under (A.17) and the following conditions

(A.19) $0 < b_{T-1} + \displaystyle\sum_{s=0}^{T-2} (1 + \rho)^{T-s} b_{s,T} < \sqrt{\dfrac{D + \beta \tilde{K}}{\gamma_{T-1}}} - \left(1 + \dfrac{1}{1 + \rho} \right) \tilde{K}$

and

$$\gamma_{T-1} < \dfrac{D + \beta_S \tilde{K}^2}{\left(1 + \dfrac{1}{1 + \rho} \right)^2 \tilde{K}^2}$$

When $V_{T-1}^{FN} \leq \min\{V_{T-1}^{FC}, V_{T-1}^{FD}\}$, that is, conditions (A.17') and (A.18) or (A.17) and (A.19) are held, investors buy the government bonds in period $T - 1$. It means that there is no confidence crisis in period $T - 1$ under this situation. Otherwise, investors do not buy bonds at all in period $T - 1$. Thus confidence crisis occurs in period $T - 1$.

Policy Choice in Period t

In general, in period t, investors of the government bonds first expect whether the government triggers a debt default in subsequent periods. If they believe the default occurs, they do not buy the bonds at all. This situation is confidence crisis. Under this situation, the government cannot newly issue bonds. If investors expect the default does not occur, the government bonds are freely treaded.

After that, the fiscal authority chooses $\{\tau_t, g_t, b_{ts}\}$ to minimize its loss function, subject to the budget constraint (A.1). Also the monetary authority chooses $\{\pi_t\}$ to minimize its loss function, without any regard for the budget constraint (A.1). The structure of this policy game from period $T - 2$ to period T, for example, is shown in figure 11A.1.

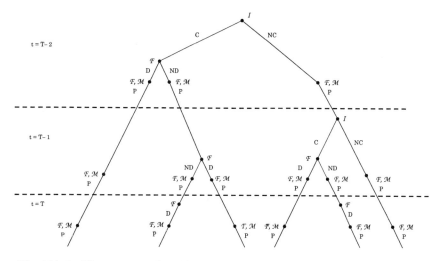

Fig. 11A.1   The structure of a policy game between fiscal and monetary policy authorities

Notes: NC: nonconfidence crisis; C: confidence crisis; D: default, ND: nondefault; P: policy choice; F: fiscal authority; M: monetary authority; I: investors.

The Normal Case (Case N)

First, we consider a situation that confidence crisis does not occur. Under this situation, the government can newly issue bonds. The fiscal and monetary authorities minimize their loss functions. Thus the authorities in period $T - 1$ have the following loss functions

$$(A.4')   \quad V_t^{aN} = \frac{1}{2}[\alpha_{\pi a}\pi_t^2 + (x_t - \tilde{x})^2 + \alpha_{gs}(g_t - \tilde{g})^2] + \beta_S V_{t+1}^{aN}$$

where $a = F, M$. V_{t+1}^{aN} denotes the value of loss function in the normal case in the final period. From the first-order conditions like (A.6), the value of the loss function of the fiscal authority in period t in the normal case becomes

$$V_t^{FN} = \frac{N_F^*}{2N^2}\gamma_t\left\{\tilde{K}\sum_{s=t}^{T}(1 + \rho)^{t-s} + \sum_{s=0}^{t-1}\left[(1 + \rho)^{t-s}\sum_{v=t}^{T}b_{s,v}\right]\right\}^2$$

where

$$\gamma_t \equiv [(\beta_N^*\gamma_{t+1})^2 + \beta_S\gamma_{t+1}]\delta_t^2, \quad \gamma_T = 1, \quad \delta_2 \equiv \frac{1 + \rho}{1 + \gamma_{t+1}(1 + \rho)\beta_N^*},$$

and the (optimizing) newly issued bond in period t is

$$\sum_{v=t+1}^{T}b_{t,v} = \frac{\delta_t}{1 + \rho}$$

$$\cdot\left(\tilde{K} + \sum_{s=0}^{t-1}(1 + \rho)^{t-s}b_{s,t} - \gamma_{t+1}\beta_N^*\left\{\tilde{K}\sum_{s=t+1}^{T}(1 + \rho)^{t+1-s} + \sum_{s=0}^{t-1}\left[(1 + \rho)^{t+1-s}\sum_{v=t+1}^{T}b_{s,v}\right]\right\}\right)$$

The Case of Default Under Confidence Crisis

Next, we consider a situation that confidence crisis occurs in period t. Under this situation, the government cannot newly issue any bond in this and subsequent periods. If the government triggers debt default in period t, we also obtain the value of the loss function of the fiscal authority in period t in default case as follows

$$V_{t,0}^{FD} \equiv \frac{H_F^*}{2H^2}\left[\tilde{K} + \frac{(1-z)\tilde{x}}{vz}\right]^2 + \frac{N_F^*}{2N^2}\gamma_{t+1}\left[\tilde{K}\sum_{s=t+1}^{T}(1+\rho)^{t+1-s}\right]^2,$$

from the first-order conditions like (A.14.1, A.14.2). Likewise, if the government defaults in period $t + j$ ($0 \leq j \leq T - t$), from the first-order conditions like (A.5.1), (A.5.2') and (A.9), the value of the loss function of the fiscal authority in period t becomes

$$V_{t,j}^{FD} \equiv \beta_S^j \frac{H_F^*}{2H^2}\left[\tilde{K} + \frac{(1-z)\tilde{x}}{vz}\right]^2 + \frac{N_F^*}{2N^2}$$

$$\cdot \left\{\beta_S^{j+1}\gamma_{t+j+1}\left[\tilde{K}\sum_{s=t+j+1}^{T}(1+\rho)^{t+j+1-s}\right]^2 + \sum_{h=t}^{t+j-1}\beta_S^{h-t}\left[\tilde{K} + \sum_{v=0}^{t-1}(1+\rho)^{h-v}b_{v,h}\right]^2\right\}$$

We define $V_t^{FD} \equiv \min\{V_{t,j}^{FD}|0 \leq j \leq T - t\}$.

Hence, if $V_t^{FN} \leq V_t^{FD}$, the fiscal authority does not have any incentives to default in period t. We numerically examine a realistic case based on the above setting in section 11.4.4.

References

Alesina, A., A. Prati, and G. Tabellini. 1990. Public confidence and debt management: A model and a case study of Italy. In *Public debt management: Theory and history*, ed. M. Draghi and R. Dornbusch, 94–124. New York: Cambridge University Press.

Barro, R. J. 1979. On the determination of the public debt. *Journal of Political Economy* 87:940–71.

———. 1995. Optimal debt management. NBER Working Paper no. 5327. Cambridge, MA: National Bureau of Economic Research.

———. 2003. Optimal management of indexed and nominal debt. *Annals of Economics and Finance* 4:1–15.

Beetsma, R. M. W. J., and A. L. Bovenberg. 1997a. Central bank independence and public debt policy. *Journal of Economic Dynamics and Control* 21:873–94.

———. 1997b. Designing fiscal and monetary institutions in a second-best world. *European Journal of Political Economy* 13:53–79.

Bertola, G., and A. Drazen. 1993. Trigger points and budget cuts: Explaining the effect of fiscal austerity. *American Economic Review* 83:11–26.

Blanchard, O. J., and P. Weil. 2001. Dynamic efficiency, the riskless rate, and debt Ponzi games under uncertainty. *Advances in Macroeconomics* 1:5–27.

Bohn, H. 1991. The sustainability of budget deficits with lump-sum and with income-based taxation. *Journal of Money, Credit, and Banking* 23:580–604.

Broda, C., and D. Weinstein. 2005. Happy news from the dismal science: Reassessing Japanese fiscal policy and sustainability. In *Reviving Japan's Economy*, ed. Takatoshi Ito, Hugh Patrick, and David E. Weinstein, 40–78. Cambridge, MA: The MIT Press.

Bulow, J., and K. Rogoff. 1989. Sovereign debt: Is to forgive to forget? *American Economic Review* 79:43–50.

Calvo, G. A. 1988. Serving the public debt: The role of expectations. *American Economic Review* 78:647–61.

Calvo, G. A., and P. E. Guidotti. 1990a. Credibility and nominal debt. *IMF Staff Papers* 37:612–35.

———. 1990b. Indexation and maturity of government bonds: An exploratory model. In *Public debt management: Theory and history*, ed. M. Draghi and R. Dornbusch, 53–82. New York: Cambridge University Press.

Cargill, Thomas, and Naoyuki Yoshino. 2000. The Postal Savings System, Fiscal Investment and Loan Program, and modernization of Japan's financial system. In *Crisis and change in the Japanese financial system*, ed. Takeo Hoshi and Hugh Patrick, 201–30. Norwell, MA: Kluwer Academic.

———. 2003. *Postal savings and fiscal investment in Japan*. New York: Oxford University Press.

Chari, V. V., and P. J. Kehoe. 1993. Sustainable plans and mutual default. *Review of Economic Studies* 60:175–95.

Doi, T., and T. Hoshi. 2003. Paying for the FILP. In *Structural impediments to growth in Japan*, ed. Magnus Blomström, Jennifer Corbett, Fumio Hayashi, and Anil Kashyap, 37–69. Chicago: University of Chicago Press.

Doi, T., and T. Ihori. 2002. Fiscal reconstruction and local interest groups in Japan. *Journal of the Japanese and International Economies* 16 (4): 492–511.

———. 2004. Sustainability of government deficits in Japan: Including trends in local government finance. In *Enhancing Market Functions in Japan*, ed. N. Yoshino, S. Inukai, and N. Tamaki, 3–29. Tokyo: Keio University Press.

Drudi, F., and R. Giordano. 2000. Default risk and optimal debt management. *Journal of Banking and Finance* 24:861–91.

Fujiki, H., H. Osano, and H. Uchida. 1998. Optimal contracts for central banker and public debt policy. Institute of Economic Research, Kyoto University Discussion Paper No. 478.

Giavazzi, F., and M. Pagano. 1990. Confidence crises and public debt management. In *Public debt management: Theory and history*, ed. M. Draghi and R. Dornbusch, 125–43. New York: Cambridge University Press.

Hamilton, J., and M. Flavin. 1986. On the limitations of government borrowing: A framework for empirical testing. *American Economic Review* 76:808–16.

Ihori, T. 1988. Debt burden and intergeneration equity. In *The economics of public debt*, ed. K. J. Arrow and M. J. Boskin. Proceedings of a conference held by the International Economic Association at Stanford, Macmillan.

Ihori, T., T. Doi, and H. Kondo. 2001. Japanese fiscal reform: Fiscal reconstruction and fiscal policy. *Japan and the World Economy* 13:351–70.

Ihori, T., T. Nakazato, and M. Kawade. 2002. Japan's fiscal policies in the 1990s. *The World Economy* 26:325–38.

Ihori, T., and M. Sato. (Eds.). 2002. *Government deficit and fiscal reform in Japan*. Norwell, MA: Kluwer Academic.

Lucas, R. E., and N. L. Stokey. 1983. Optimal fiscal and monetary policy in an economy without capital. *Journal of Monetary Economics* 12:55–94.

Ministry of Finance. 2006. Planned bond issuance for FY 2006. Tokyo: Ministry of Finance.

Persson, M., T. Persson, and L. E. O. Svensson. 1987. Time consistency of fiscal and monetary policy. *Econometrica* 55:1419–31.
———. 2005. Time consistency of fiscal and monetary policy: A solution. NBER Working Paper no. 11088. Cambridge, MA: National Bureau of Economic Research.
Samuelson, P. A. 1958. An exact consumption-loan model of interest with or without the social contrivance of money. *Journal of Political Economy* 66:467–82.
Tirole, J. 1985. Asset bubbles and overlapping generations. *Econometrica* 53:1071–100.
Weil, P. 1989. Overlapping families of infinitely-lived agents. *Journal of Public Economics* 38:183–98.

Comment   Dante B. Canlas

The Doi, Ihori, and Mitsui chapter (DIM henceforth) takes off from some down-to-earth facts about the Japanese government's budget deficits and the existing maturity structure of its bonds and other government debt papers. The backdrop is the collapse of the so-called bubble economy in the early 1990s, the aftermath of which has been a prolonged economic slump marked by modest and spotty episodes of recoveries.

The authors attempt to assess the sustainability of Japan's debt policy by using the theory of optimal fiscal and monetary policy to assess the story behind the government's actual fiscal policy choices. From the perspective of a class of models that shares this theoretical platform, the writers try to extract a consistent set of efficiency and welfare principles that could offer guidelines about the future conduct of fiscal and monetary policy.

The usual starting point for the theory that is put to work in the DIM chapter is a government that consumes fixed amounts of goods and services. Prices and quantities are determined competitively. At some point in time, the fiscal authority may decide to increase the existing pattern of government spending to be financed not by a tax increase but by issuance of government debt. This debt may be in the form of interest-bearing bonds or noninterest bearing money. In this setting, the fiscal authority determines the level of the public debt while the monetary authority, the composition of that debt. The degree of independence enjoyed by the monetary authority from the fiscal authority largely determines whether an income tax at some future date or an inflation tax finances the budget deficit.

Theoretically, one can assume, following Frank Ramsey's (1928) canonical growth model, the presence of a central planner, with the fiscal and monetary authorities viewed as acting in a cooperative way. Both authorities take their cue from the central planner who maximizes a social welfare

Dante B. Canlas is a professor in the School of Economics, University of the Philippines.

function with discounted future utilities, and who recognizes the constraints posed by the existing production technology and the government budget. The constrained maximization yields the efficiency and optimality principles that in principle could also be delivered by a system of competitive markets with rational firms and consumers guided by a decentralized price system. The equilibrium situation may be described, using Robert Lucas's words (1986, 117–34), as an "evenly rotating system" through time, where price ratios adjusted for the given tax rates equal the ratios of the marginal rates of substitution for all the commodities taken pairwise. In case the fiscal and monetary authorities do not cooperate, then the situation may be modeled as a game wherein the players behave strategically; multiple equilibria may result, some of which are not Pareto optimal.

Today, there is a large body of aggregative theoretical models that may be regarded as extensions or modifications of the theory of optimal fiscal and monetary policy that I have just roughly described. I would regard the DIM chapter, which presents a number of interrelated models, as belonging to this genre. For example, let me draw attention to the first model of debt management that the authors present in section 11.3.2. The model imagines a world with households, firms, a fiscal authority, and a monetary authority. Households supply labor and form labor unions that possess wage-setting powers. The writers then posit a well-behaved production technology and a short-run aggregate supply function similar to that of Robert Lucas (1973). The two authorities act in a cooperative manner and behave so that a social loss function is minimized subject to the various constraints that the agents in the model confront. Efficiency and optimality conditions, perhaps second-best, governing inflation, tax rates, and government purchases are derived.

I would like to raise two questions in relation to this basic lead-off model of the DIM chapter. One, does it succeed in deriving a unified and consistent set of welfare-theoretic principles? I have some doubts and I hope the authors can help me out of my quandary. While the first-order conditions may be precise enough, I'm not sure about the propositions or intuitions the authors offer. Consider, for instance, their statement on maintaining "the neutrality of bonds toward social welfare (social loss)." It is unclear whether this is a proposition that flows out of their first-order conditions or is merely an expression of opinion.

The concerns that I have about the basic DIM model may be products of my own severe bounded-rationality affliction. The authors have assembled a seemingly hybrid model that combines insights from some celebrated papers, both descriptive and normative, on optimal fiscal (e.g., taxation, public debt management) and monetary policy. But major differences in the analytical frameworks of these papers exist; it would not do to pick one principle here and another there, and still hope to produce a unified and mutually consistent set of principles. For example, if tax smoothing is the preferred fiscal policy choice, then tax rates ought to remain the same across time and across states of nature. But suppose debt financing using money prevails; then the inflation tax may have to be followed by an income tax (or consumption tax) to try to induce a rate of deflation that restores the value of people's cash balances in real terms. Time inconsistency results as the constant tax rate is abandoned at some future date.

My second and final question is this: do the efficiency and optimality conditions offer useful guides for the actual conduct of fiscal and monetary policy in Japan? In the concluding part of the chapter, the authors suggest a smoothing rule. The mechanics of the proposed rule have to be spelled out in detail. Moreover, the authors have to go beyond saying, "it is indispensable to restrain the increasing trend of reliance on government debts." Japanese politicians and bureaucrats have known this all along. Why? Will the Japanese, particularly, the elderly, not willingly hold those bonds anymore? At the most rudimentary level, some quantitative estimates of the effects of alternative modes of debt financing on the consumption and saving behavior of Japanese would be of help in this regard.

References

Lucas, Robert E., Jr. 1973. Some international evidence on output-inflation tradeoffs. *American Economic Review* 63:326–34.
———. 1986. Principles of fiscal and monetary policy. *Journal of Monetary Economics* 17:117–34.
Ramsey, Frank P. 1928. A mathematical theory of saving. *Economic Journal* 88:543–59.

12

Policy Options for Financing Future Health and Long-Term Care Costs in Japan

Tadashi Fukui and Yasushi Iwamoto

12.1 Introduction

The 2003 annual report on the Japanese Economy and Public Finance (released by the Japanese Cabinet Office) stated "the sustainability of the present fiscal and social security systems is uncertain and hence, an early commitment toward bold institutional reforms is required" (p. 1). The annual report listed for the first time social security reforms with regard to the aging population, and presented these reforms not in the form of a problem to be dealt with in the future but as an issue of urgent importance.

In the public pension reforms of 2004, Japan cut future pension benefits substantially. Since the ratio of the aggregate pension benefits to the national income (NI) is designed to be stable in the future, the financial problems associated with public pension have been resolved to some extent. Failure to reduce intergenerational inequality is a persistent problem in the public pension program; this is because the primary aim of the reforms was to reduce the pension benefits and contributions of future generations.

The expenditure incurred on health insurance and long-term care insurance is also expected to increase. It is not easy, however, to reduce these

Tadashi Fukui is an associate professor of economics at Kyoto Sangyo University. Yasushi Iwamoto is a professor of economics at the University of Tokyo.

Earlier versions of this paper were presented at two meetings of the Economic and Social Research Institute (ESRI) International Collaboration Projects, February 15–16, 2005 and February 14–15, 2006 Tokyo; the 16th East Asian Seminar on Economics, June 23–25, 2005, Manila; and the Spring Meeting of the Japanese Economic Association, June 3–4, 2006, Fukushima. We would like to thank Henry Aaron, Raj Chetty, Olivia Mitchell, Epictetus Patalinghug, Motohiro Sato, Wataru Suzuki, and all the participants for their helpful comments at these meetings. Financial Support from the ESRI at the Japanese Cabinet Office is greatly appreciated. Iwamoto's Research is also financially supported by a Grant-in-aid for Scientific Research from the Ministry of Education.

benefits as pension benefits because health care and long-term care services are essential for human welfare. Bradford and Max (1997) and Cutler and Sheiner (2000) have shown that an unfunded health insurance creates considerable intergenerational income redistribution. If these health insurance costs are financed using the current scheme (essentially, a pay-as-you-go system), a large increase in the future burden of these costs will become inevitable, thus creating an intergenerational imbalance of burden. One way to restoring intergenerational equity is for social insurance programs to prefund the expected increase in future costs. In this chapter, we consider the effects of introducing a prefunding scheme on the intergenerational distribution of burdens. Based on the following three points, this chapter gives new insights into the future financial problems of social insurance programs.

First, this chapter examines both health care and long-term care programs. Feldstein (1999) proposed prefunding of the Medicare program, and Suzuki (2000) conducted a simulation study of the prefunding of the Japanese health insurance program. This chapter also explores the concept of prefunding long-term care insurance. Annual spending on long-term care services is smaller than the expenditure incurred on health care services; however, long-term care costs are concentrated heavily on the aged population. Therefore, prefunding the cost associated with long-term care requires a large amount of saving. It is necessary to take into account both health and long-term care insurance in order to be able to comprehend the financial problems faced by social insurance programs in the future.

Our analysis of the intergenerational inequity of burdens is along the lines of the generational accounting pioneered by Auerbach, Gokhale, and Kotlikoff (1991). Since we have focused on the ways in which health and long-term care costs may be financed, the analytical framework adopted is somewhat different from that used in the generational accounting approach. We specify future policy variables and calculate the cost burdens with regard to the specified policy scenario. Our focus is confined only to health and long-term care insurances, while the generational accounting model considers a wider range of governmental programs. We have instead provided a detailed discussion of these programs.

Second, our simulation has a long time horizon until the fiscal year (FY) 2100, while the government has projected social security costs for health care and long-term care until FY 2025. Government projections with regard to social security costs were only until FY 2025 since the aging process was expected to reach its peak at this point with most baby boomers approaching the end of their lifetime. Due to a decline in fertility rates after the late 1970s, aging is now expected to continue beyond FY 2025; a much longer time horizon is required in order to examine the effects of a demographic change on social security costs.

Third, the validity of future projections is examined. The main alternative scenario here assumes that, with the exception of population structure, all the present factors will be sustained in the future. This projection procedure is applied mechanically to the labor force, health care expenditure, and long-term care costs instead of constructing a sophisticated forecasting model. A virtue of the mechanical projection model is that relationships between the variables under consideration can be easily established. Comparing the projected values with the government's forecasts can clarify the manner in which projections are influenced by the government assumptions.

The organization of this chapter is as follows. Section 12.2 describes the current problems in the budget of the Japanese social security programs. We point out that the growth of health and long-term care costs is the most serious problem for the sustainability of the government budget.

Section 12.3 focuses on the projections of labor force participation. The government projection is optimistic because it assumes that a greater number of women and the elderly will participate in the labor market. We provide an alternative projection in which increasing labor force participation is not expected. Although the estimated labor force depends on the assumptions of labor supply behavior, the trend decline in the total labor force will be significant in any scenario.

Section 12.4 focuses on health care expenditure and long-term care service costs. We project these costs until FY 2100 with regard to three scenarios. Even under the most optimistic scenario that assumes stagnation in the growth of per capita cost, the previously mentioned costs to income will steadily increase until the 2060s.

Section 12.5 explains some policy simulations that deal with the financing of future health and long-term care costs until FY 2100. It is shown that the balanced budget operation of health and long-term care insurances will create a large inequity of burden across generations. Raising the premium immediately and prefunding rising future costs will help to equate the burden across generations. However, with regard to our baseline scenario, the total burden must be raised immediately by approximately 60 percent.

We present some concluding remarks in section 12.6.

12.2   Long-Term Projection of Social Security Benefits

The Ministry of Health, Labor and Welfare (MHLW) occasionally publishes "Perspectives on the Benefits and Burdens of the Social Security System" (*Shakai-hoshou no Kyufu to Futan no Mitooshi*), which projects the benefits and burdens associated with public pension, health care, and social work, including long-term care. According to the projections

Table 12.1   Projection of Social Security benefits and burdens (% of NI at factor cost)

	Fiscal year			
	2004	2010	2015	2025
Social Security benefits	23.5	25.4	27.0	29.0
Public pension	12.6	12.8	12.9	12.2
Health care	7.1	8.2	9.2	11.2
Welfare, etc.	3.8	4.3	4.7	5.7
Long-term care	1.4	2.2	2.7	3.6
Social Security burdens	21.3	24.2	26.6	29.5
Social insurance premium	14.2	15.5	16.7	18.3
Government subsidies	7.1	8.7	9.6	11.2

Source: Ministry of Health, Labor and Welfare (2004).

made in May 2004 (we refer to it as MHLW 2004 projection hereafter), total social security benefits are expected to increase from 23.5 percent of the total NI at factor cost to 29 percent between FY 2004 and FY 2025 (see table 12.1).[1]

However, future trends in these benefits vary with social security programs. Public pension benefits will not increase and will actually become slightly lower in FY 2025 as compared to their current levels. This stabilization of future pension benefits was achieved by the pension reform of 2004. Prior to this reform, the contribution rate for private employees toward the pension program was planned to increase gradually from 13.58 percent of total earnings to 23.1 percent of the same in FY 2020. Since this figure appeared to be unacceptable, controlling the contribution rate became the primary focus of this reform. The final contribution rate was reduced to 18.3 percent of total earnings, and a significant reduction in benefits for the future was implemented. However, this reform does not resolve all of the major problems. As explained by Maekawa (2004), since benefits are gradually reduced, the reform fails to correct the inequity in net benefits among generations. An immediate reduction in benefits accompanied by an increase in the contribution rate is necessary to reduce the intergenerational inequity.

An emerging component of social costs is the benefits of health insurance and long-term care insurance. Health care benefit as a fraction of NI will increase by 4.1 percentage points until FY 2025, whereas the long-term care benefit will grow by 2.2 percentage points during the same pe-

---

1. The ratio of total security benefits to IN at factor cost indicates an unnecessary fluctuation when the VAT tax rate changes. The Japanese government had begun to use the ratio of total security benefits to IN at factor cost long before the introduction of VAT. In this chapter, however, we shall focus on the ratio of these benefits to GDP instead.

riod. The big question that needs to be answered by the policymakers is: how to finance these costs?

If health and long-term care insurances are operated by the pay-as-you-go system, the cost burden on workers will steadily increase, thus creating an intergenerational imbalance of burdens. Prefunding future social security costs will help to reduce this imbalance by forcing the present generations to pay more, thereby reducing the extra burden on future generations. The financial condition of a prefunding system relies on future economic variables such as the interest rate, wage growth rate, and technological change in medicine. Since the reliability of a future projection is a crucial factor in determining the success of prefunding schemes, we shall examine how a prefunding system is affected by the future conditions of the Japanese economy.

12.3   Economic Growth and the Labor Force

In this section and the succeeding one, we shall discuss the properties of governmental projections and provide our alternative projections on the labor force, economic growth, health care costs, and long-term care costs. This section focuses on variables that determine income.

The publication "Perspectives on the Benefits and Burdens of Social Security" does not rely on a general equilibrium model of the economy. It assumes the growth rate of real national income to be the sum of the growth rates of wage and labor force. This framework can be justified in the following situation. A production function is homogeneous of degree one with capital K and labor L. This function witnesses a labor-augmenting technological progress. It is represented as

(1) $$Y = F(K, AL).$$

Here, Y and A represent the output and efficiency, respectively. Differentiating equation (1) with respect to time yields

(2) $$\frac{\dot{Y}}{Y} = \frac{F_K K}{Y}\left(\frac{\dot{K}}{K} - \frac{\dot{A}}{A} - \frac{\dot{L}}{L}\right) + \frac{\dot{A}}{A} + \frac{\dot{L}}{L}.$$

When the growth rates of capital and efficiency unit of labor are the same, the first term in the RHS of equation (2) becomes zero. The economic growth rate then equals the sum of the growth rate of labor-augmenting technological change (the wage growth rate) and the growth rate of labor input.

The MHLW 2004 projection assumes the growth rate of labor input to be 0.1 percent until FY 2008, –0.2 percent in FY 2009 and FY 2010, and –0.5 percent from FY 2011 onward. The labor force in FY 2025 will be 61.58 million, which is 7.24 percent smaller than its level in 2004. This framework is based on a detailed projection of the labor force titled "A

Table 12.2   The projection of the labor force by MHLW, by gender and year

	Male		Female	
	2000	2025	2000	2025
Labor force (thousands)	40,140	36,310	27,520	26,655
Labor force participation rates by age group (%)				
15–19	18.4	20.1	16.6	17.8
20–24	72.7	77.6	72.7	73.7
25–29	95.8	95.9	69.9	75.3
30–34	97.7	97.6	57.1	65.0
35–39	97.8	97.8	61.4	67.4
40–44	97.7	97.8	69.3	75.2
45–49	97.3	97.5	71.8	77.0
50–54	96.7	96.9	68.2	73.5
55–59	94.2	94.4	58.7	67.5
60–64	72.6	85.0	39.5	60.5
65–	34.1	29.5	14.4	13.0

Source: The 2025 labor force: the Perspective on the Labor Force Participation Rate (July 2002, the Employment Security Bureau, Ministry of Health, Labor and Welfare) and the 2000 labor force and labor force participation rate: the Labor Force Survey (Statistics Bureau, Ministry of Internal Affairs and Communication).

Note: The 2025 labor force is calculated by multiplying the projected population (medium variant) reported in the Population Projections for Japan: 2001–50 (January 2002, National Institute of Population and Social Security Research) by the labor force participation rates by age groups.

Forecast of Labor Force Participation Rates" (*Rodoryokuritsu no Mitooshi*), which was compiled by the Employment Security Bureau of MHLW in May 2002 (we shall refer to it as the MHLW 2002 labor force projection). The lower section of table 12.2 indicates that the MHLW 2002 labor force projection forecasts an increase ni the labor force participation rates of the elderly and women. The upper section of table 12.2 however, indicates the labor force calculated by multiplying the labor force participation rates as reported by the Employment Security Bureau and the official population projections (medium variant) for each age group. The calculated labor force in 2025 is 62.97 million, which is slightly greater than those estimated by the MHLW 2004 projection. The initial point of the MHLW 2002 labor force projection was 2000, when the total labor force was 67.66 million. Due to the decline in the labor force to 66.42 million in 2004, the MHLW 2004 projection starts with a smaller initial point and adopts a similar growth rate, thus estimating a smaller labor force in the future.

While the government projection assumes an increase in the labor force participation, we are apprehensive of this increase not being realized. To examine the impact of projecting a future labor supply optimistically, we considered an alternative scenario.[2] We used the labor force participation rates by age from the 2000 Population Census and the future population estimates from "The Population Projections for Japan: 2001–2050" (January 2001, National Institute of Population and Social Security Research). The Population Census records the labor force participation rates of individuals up to 84 years of age (individuals aged 85 years and above are categorized as one age group). We rescaled the labor force participation rates of each group in such a manner that our estimates of the total labor force in 2000 were in concordance with the values reported in 2004 by the Labor Force Survey.[3]

Table 12.3 shows our mechanical projection. From 2004 to 2025, the labor force will decrease by 8 million to a level of 58.39 million people. A decrease in the labor force will continue after 2025 and every decade will witness a labor force loss of more than five million people. In 2050, a total labor force of 44.69 million people will be available. The rate of change in the total labor force with regard to its value in 2004 is 32.7 percent. When a population projection is based on a low variant, the projected number becomes more pessimistic. In 2050, the rate of change in the total labor force with regard to its value in 2004 is 38 percent. Since the effects of a low birth rate appear only after newborn generations begin to work, the labor force in 2025 does not show considerable variations.

The MHLW 2004 projection regarded the labor force as a labor input. Since the efficiency of labor varies with age, the overall values of labor force and labor input may fluctuate differently. However, the procedure followed in the MHLW 2004 projection can be refined. We estimated an efficiency unit of labor implied by the two MHLW projections, assuming that efficiency is directly proportional to wage. The age-wage profile by age group and sex was collected from the published cross-tables of the 2003 Basic Survey on Wage Structure (*Chingin Kozo Kihon Chosa,* MHLW). For each age the efficiency unit of labor input is calculated as the product of the total wage per worker and the projected labor force. We rescaled the aggregated efficiency unit of labor in 2004 so that it equaled the total labor force in that year. We considered three scenarios: our mechanical projection (pessimistic),

2. Iwamoto (1998) analyzed existing studies on labor force and also projected the labor force until 2020. His mechanical projection assumes that the present labor force participation rates by age groups will be sustained in the future and that the structure of future populations will change. His estimates are not very different from preceding estimates made in academic studies that also incorporated behavioral changes. This can be attributed to the fact that there is no scope for drastic changes in the labor force participation rates of working-age populations. In addition, although the trend regarding birth rates in the future is uncertain, future population can be predicted with considerable surety.

3. The Population Census recorded the labor force in 2000 to be 66.1 million. According to the Labor Force Survey, it was 67.66 million.

Table 12.3   Mechanical projection of the labor force (in thousands of persons)

	Labor force							Change from 2004 to 2025	Rate of change (%)	Change from 2004 to 2050	Rate of change (%)
	2004	2010	2020	2025	2030	2040	2050				
	Medium variant (baseline)										
Both sexes	66,390	64,432	60,353	58,393	56,000	50,128	44,687	−7,997	−12.0	−21,703	−32.7
Males	39,040	38,059	35,580	34,449	33,134	29,783	26,550	−4,591	−11.8	−12,490	−32.0
Females	27,350	26,373	24,774	23,945	22,866	20,345	18,138	−3,405	−12.5	−9,212	−33.7
	Low variant										
Both sexes	66,390	64,432	60,331	58,172	55,306	48,080	41,190	−8,218	−12.4	−25,200	−38.0
Males	39,040	38,059	35,568	34,336	32,769	28,626	24,520	−4,704	−12.1	−14,520	−37.2
Females	27,350	26,373	24,763	23,837	22,537	19,454	16,670	−3,513	−12.8	−10,680	−39.0

Sources: Author's calculation. The labor force participation rates by age group are from the 2000 Population Census, Ministry of Internal Affairs and Communications, and the figures for future populations are from the Population Projections for Japan: 2001–2050 (January 2002, National Institute of Population and Social Security Research).

Note: The future labor force is calculated by assuming that the labor force participation rates for 2000 will be sustained.

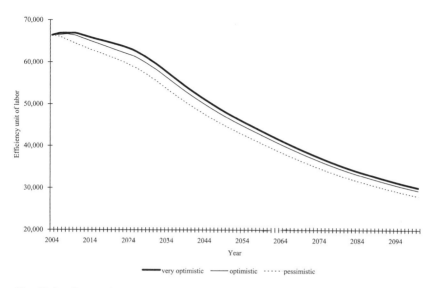

Fig. 12.1   Comparison of three labor input projections

the MHLW 2004 projection (optimistic), and the MHLW 2002 projection (more optimistic).

Figure 12.1 depicts the three scenarios regarding labor input. According to our previously discussed normalization, the MHLW 2002 labor force projection estimated the labor input in 2025 to be 63.02 million. The 2004 counterpart of our mechanical projection is estimated to be 59.03 million. The MHLW 2004 projection underlying the social security cost projection lies between these two values. While the difference between these projections is significant, all of them project a further decline in the value of labor input after 2025. In 2100, the value of labor input is estimated to be 30.08 million in the most optimistic case as against 28.08 million in the most pessimistic one. The bottom line is that even in the most optimistic scenario, the large decline in the availability of labor force will be unavoidable.

12.4   Long-Term Projections of Health and Long-Term Care Benefits

The MHLW projection assumes that the costs incurred by health care and long-term care will grow more rapidly as compared to income. If our mechanical projection procedure is applied to both these costs, the estimates will be smaller than those estimated by official projections. To clarify the meaning of the official projections, this section describes a sensitivity analysis employing alternative settings for the key variables. Combining the two scenarios of health and long-term care costs with the three projection scenarios of labor forces, we apply six cases of projections. The following two subsections describe a procedure used for projecting the two costs. We then present the results obtained for the sensitivity analysis.

12.4.1   Health Care Cost

Table 12.4 compares five recent projections about health care and long-term care costs. Since projections in different years assume different inflation rates, comparing nominal variables is misleading. When we look at the ratios of social security benefits to NI, projected health expenditures differ mildly. The real growth of health care costs appears to be more stable than the nominal growth of the same.

Future health expenditures are projected by extrapolating the most recent actual values of nominal health expenditure; these do not correspond with the values of inflation rate and economic growth rate. For example, the May 2004 projection assumes that the per capita nominal health care cost for the nonelderly (individuals under the age of 69) will grow at 2.1 percent and that for the elderly aged 70 and above will grow at 3.2 percent. These growth rates are based on the historical averages recorded during

Table 12.4   Perspectives on health care and long-term care costs reported by the Ministry of Health, Labor and Welfare (in trillions of yen)

		Projected date					
		November 1996					
Fiscal year	March 1994	(A)	(B)	September 1997	October 2000	May 2002	May 2004
Health care costs							
1993	24						
1995		24	24	24			
2000	38				26		
2010	68					35	34
2025	141	107–108	96	90	71	60	59
	(11–19)	(11.5–18)	(10–16)	(10–15)	(11)	(11)	(11)
Long-term care service costs							
2005						6	
2010						8	9
2015							12
2025			13–20	14–21	21	20	19
			(2)	(2.5)	(3)	(3.5)	(3.5)

Sources: Welfare Vision for the 21st Century (May 1994, Ministry of Health and Welfare) and various issues of Perspectives on the Benefits and Burdens of the Social Security System (Ministry of Health, Labor and Welfare).

Notes: Numbers represent benefits of each type of social insurance. The numbers in parentheses represent the ratio of social insurance benefits to NI at factor cost. The projection in November 1996 contained two scenarios. Case (A) assumed that the long-term care insurance would not be introduced. Case (B) assumed that it would be introduced in FY2000.

1995 and 1999.[4] The extrapolation of nominal health expenditure without taking into account the effects of inflation can be problematic from the viewpoint of economic theory. Economists generally make projections based on real values, and the methodologies adopted by them belong to a family of mechanical projections. Iwamoto (2004) analyzed several projections made in existing studies such as Ogura and Irifune (1990); Ogura (1994); Niki (1995); Iwamoto, Takeshita, and Bessho (1997); Nishimura (1997); and Tokita et al. (1997). He concluded that in the following 30 years, the national health expenditure would increase by about 1.4 times compared to its level in 2000. Our mechanical projection follows a method established by existing studies and assumes that per capita health expenditure by age group reported in the National Medical Expenditure (MHLW, shown in table 12.5) will be sustained in the future. For the future population data, we use the medium variant of the official projection.

Although the previous projection assumes no real growth of health care cost, it can be easily extended to cases in which the health care cost grows. When the economy grows, we focus on the ratio of health care cost to income. When the health care cost and income grow at the same rate, the ratio will not change. In such a scenario, our mechanical projection estimates can be considered as this ratio. In the alternative framework described in the next section, we will concern ourselves only with the difference in growth rates between costs and income and not with the absolute levels of each growth rate.

Since we intend to frame our mechanical projection in such a way that it is comparable with the MHLW 2004 projection, the data with regard to age group were converted so that they were in concordance with the income level of FY 2004. First, per capita health care cost by age group was proportionally adjusted so that the national aggregate of the same matches the figures reported in the Medical Information Analysis System (MEDIAS), which reports the health care costs paid by public health insurance. The national aggregate of health care costs was calculated as the product of population and per capita cost by age group. The rescaled age-cost profile was used to project future health care costs.

Further, we decomposed the total cost toward social insurance payment and out-of-pocket expenses. Unfortunately, MEDIAS does not provide this decomposition. We obtained the figures for social security payment from the National Medical Expenditure survey (*Kokumin Iryohi*).[5] While

---

4. The MHLW provides an estimation of the growth rate in medical expenditure after adjusting for the effects of population aging since 1980. Overall, the per capita medical expenditure had grown less than per capita GDP; however, this correspondence was reversed during the 1990s.

5. The National Medical Expenditure (NME) lags one year behind MEDIAS in the release of data. We first estimated the 2004 NME data by multiplying the growth rate of a comparable MEDIAS variable between 2003 and 2004 with the 2003 NME data. Since out-of-pocket expenses for NME also include payments of medical treatments that are not covered by the social security programs, we estimated the out-of-pocket payments as a residual of the overall payments.

Table 12.5   Expenditures on health care and long-term care per capita, by age group
                    (2004 fiscal year; in yen)

Age group	Health care	Long-term care
0–4	158,900	
5–9	92,100	
10–14	66,700	
15–19	58,100	
20–24	71,200	
25–29	85,600	
30–34	97,500	
35–39	103,000	
40–44	119,100	5,700 (40–64)
45–49	149,900	
50–54	199,200	
55–59	245,000	
60–64	323,100	
65–69	433,400	43,800
70–74	564,800	97,000
75–79	749,400 (75–)	203,200
80–84		429,400
85–89		799,900
90–94		1,236,100
95–		1,786,500

Notes: The values are the sum of benefits from insurers and copayments by patients. Health care expenditure is calculated by proportionally adjusting the FY 2002 value reported in the National Medical Expenditure (Ministry of Health, Labor and Welfare) so that the national aggregate matches the health care expenditure reported by MEDIAS; this system totals the costs of services covered by public health insurance. The National Medical Expenditure categorizes individuals who are 75 years of age and above as one age group. Long-term care expenditure: the values are calculated by multiplying the actual costs of services covered by long-term care insurance in October 2004 as reported in the Monthly Report of Long-Term Care Benefits (Ministry of Health, Labor and Welfare) by 12. Individuals who are 40 years of age and above can be the recipients of long-term care insurance. The report categorizes individuals between 40 and 60 years of age as one age group.

allocating social insurance payment across generations, we used the statutory coinsurance rates of 2004 and assumed that they will be sustained in the future. Since April 2003, the coinsurance rate for the age group 0 to 2 years has been 20 percent, whereas for the age group 3 to 69, it has been 30 percent. For individuals aged 70 years and above, the rate in principle has been 10 percent (a rate of 20 percent is applied to high-income earners). Due to the lack of available data, we assume that a rate of 10 percent is applied to all individuals aged 70 and above. However, the actual out-of-pocket payments are less than the statutory coinsurance rate because of stop-loss rules and other schemes to reduce out-of-pocket expenses. We proportionally scaled the statutory coinsurance rates so that the sum of the estimated social insurance payments matched the aggregate values reported by MEDIAS in 2004.

Since the available data on health expenditure does not separately report the expenditure incurred for the age groups 0 to 2 and 3 to 4, we assumed that the health expenditure per capita will be uniform in these age groups; we then calculated the average coinsurance rate. Since actual costs are concentrated on newborn babies, this procedure may slightly overestimate the true social security payment value. However, at the same time, many municipal governments offer extra benefits toward the health expenditure of infants from their general budget. Since we do not incorporate these subsidies into our estimation process, it results in an underestimation of the social security benefits granted to these age groups. However, the overall impact of these subsidies on our estimation bias is ambiguous.

We then reproduced the MHLW 2004 projection of the future health insurance benefits. The MHLW 2004 projection assumes that the nominal wage growth rate is 2.1 percent per annum. Therefore, per capita health care costs for the nonelderly will grow simultaneously with the growth rate of wage. As against this, the growth rate of per capita costs for the elderly will exceed that for wage by 1.1 percentage points. The projection with regard to the nonelderly is the same as our mechanical projection. For costs beyond 2025, we need to first specify the growth rate of wage for the same. If the growth rate of health care costs continuously exceeds that of wage, it will ultimately exhaust all the resources available to consumers. We thus need to assume that the growth in health care costs will cease sometime in the future. Hence, we consider two cases in which a faster growth in health care costs will eventually stop in FY 2025 or FY 2100. In the former case, the per capita health care cost for the elderly is 5.56 times greater than that for the nonelderly. The counterpart in FY 2004 is 4.3. In the latter case, an extreme increase occurs in the growth of health care cost for the elderly; the ratio in FY 2100 will be 13.09.

As a measure of financial burden, we focus on the ratio of social security benefits to the compensation of employees and the mixed income in terms of national accounts. The denominator of the ratio is assumed to be proportional to the amount of labor input. Changes in future health care costs can be described by the following three scenarios: the per capita health care cost for the elderly will (a) grow at the same rate as that of wage growth (optimistic), (b) will exceed the wage growth rate by 1.1 percentage points until FY 2025 (pessimistic), or (c) will exceed the wage growth rate by 1.1 percentage points until FY 2100 (very pessimistic). Combining these three scenarios with future changes in labor input yields nine different cases of future projection. The upper section of table 12.6 presents these ratios.

The MHLW 2004 projection indicates that the ratio of health expenditure to labor input in FY 2025 will exceed its value in FY 2004 by 1.58. This scenario was reproduced in our social cost pessimistic and labor force optimistic scenarios; this indicates that the ratio will grow by a factor of 1.56 between FY 2004 and FY 2025. On the other hand, the same ratio under

Table 12.6   **Projection of the ratio of health and long-term care costs to labor input, by year**

	2010	2015	2025	2030	2040	2050	2100
			Health care				
Social cost: Optimistic							
Labor force							
Very optimistic	1.08	1.16	1.29	1.35	1.47	1.62	1.55
Optimistic	1.09	1.18	1.32	1.38	1.51	1.66	1.59
Pessimistic[a]	1.12	1.22	1.38	1.44	1.59	1.74	1.66
Social cost: Pessimistic							
Labor force							
Very optimistic	1.12	1.26	1.52	1.59	1.75	1.93	1.84
Optimistic[b]	1.13	1.28	1.56	1.62	1.79	1.98	1.89
Pessimistic	1.16	1.32	1.63	1.70	1.88	2.07	1.98
Social cost: Very pessimistic							
Labor force							
Very optimistic	1.12	1.26	1.52	1.65	1.99	2.41	3.66
Optimistic	1.13	1.28	1.56	1.69	2.04	2.47	3.75
Pessimistic	1.16	1.32	1.63	1.77	2.14	2.59	3.92
			Long-term care				
Social cost: Optimistic							
Labor force							
Very optimistic	1.25	1.52	2.03	2.31	2.81	3.14	3.31
Optimistic	1.26	1.54	2.08	2.36	2.88	3.21	3.39
Pessimistic[a]	1.29	1.59	2.17	2.47	3.02	3.37	3.55
Social cost: Pessimistic							
Labor force							
Very optimistic	1.34	1.73	2.61	2.97	3.61	4.03	4.25
Optimistic[b]	1.35	1.76	2.67	3.03	3.70	4.13	4.35
Pessimistic	1.39	1.81	2.79	3.18	3.88	4.33	4.56
Social cost: Very pessimistic							
Labor force							
Very optimistic	1.34	1.73	2.61	3.15	4.32	5.43	10.41
Optimistic	1.35	1.76	2.67	3.22	4.42	5.56	10.65
Pessimistic	1.39	1.81	2.79	3.37	4.64	5.83	11.15

Source: Author's calculation.

Note: Numbers represent the ratio of health care costs and long-term care costs to labor input (FY 2004 = 1).

[a]Mechanical projection. The future labor force participation rate and per capita social cost by age group will be constant.

[b]A projection that replicates the MHLW 2004 projection, which is reported in table 12.1.

the mechanical projection will grow by a factor of 1.38 during the same period. Therefore, the MHLW 2004 projection is more pessimistic with regard to a future increase in health expenditure as compared to our mechanical projection. However, the most pessimistic scenario is a combination of an extremely pessimistic projection of health care costs coupled with a mechanical projection of the labor force in the future. In this case, the ratio of health expenditure to labor input in FY 2025 will exceed its value in FY 2004 by 1.63.

A noticeable point is that this ratio will keep increasing, and its value in 2050 under the setting employed by the government projection will be 1.98 times greater than its value in FY 2004. In other words, FY 2025 cannot be regarded as the terminal point for examining the sustainability of the health insurance system.[6]

12.4.2   Long-Term Care Costs

The government anticipates that long-term care costs will grow more rapidly as compared to health care costs. According to the MHLW 2004 projection given in table 12.4, the long-term care insurance benefits in FY 2025 (the ratio of long-term care benefits to NI) will be 2.7 times greater than its value in FY 2004. The growth rate of per capita long-term care costs is set to be higher than the wage growth rate although detailed assumptions have not bee explicitly documented.

Municipal governments prepare three-year business plans for long-term care insurance. Prior to the first revision that was made in FY 2003, The Projection of Demand for Long-term Care (*Kaigo Sahbisuryou tou no Mitooshi,* June 2002) was provided by the MHLW; it expected an increased demand for long-term care in the following five years. For example, the provisional nationwide sum of the usage of home-visit services will increase by 39.3 percent from FY 2003 (142,194 visits) to FY 2007 (198,033 visits).[7] The projection however, did not provide the total amount of long-term care costs. We calculated the sum of these provisions weighted by their actual costs in FY 2003 and the resulting growth during FY 2003 to 2007 that amounted to 26.4 percent.

We projected the future long-term care insurance benefits by adopting a methodology similar to that used for the projections of health insurance.[8]

---

6. We should note that our projections may be biased in an upward direction because they do not take into account the effects of aging on terminal care expenses. In Japan, Ohkusa (2002) and Suzuki and Suzuki (2003) provided a modified projection that took into account this aspect. Since terminal care expenses for the more aged tend to decrease, a longer longevity will increase the average age of death; hence, future health expenditure by age group is expected to be lower than its present level. Taking this effect into consideration, the previously mentioned studies pointed out that the MHLW 2004 projection overestimated the future health expenditure. Suzuki and Suzuki (2003) reported this overestimation amounted to approximately 4.4 percent of the total health expenditures for the elderly. On the other hand, Ohkusa (2002) concluded that the overestimation reached a level of approximately 15 to 30 percent of the total health expenditures. The divergence in their estimates is quite large because data limitations made it difficult to separate the medical expenditures of the survivors from the medical expenses incurred by those who died.

7. This projection presumed that the number of individuals certified as requiring care in FY 2003 was 3,279,000; however, the actual number of these certified individuals was 2,983,000 at the end of FY 2003.

8. Mitchell, Pigott, and Shimizutani (2004), Shimizutani and Noguchi (2004), and Suzuki (2002) are involved in projecting the future long-term care costs.

At the time of writing this chapter, the most recent data for annual spending by age group were available for FY 2002; hence, we estimated annual spending on the basis of monthly data. The long-term care expenditure by age group in October 2004 was calculated from the *Monthly Report of Long-Term Care Benefits Survey* (*Kaigo Kyufuhi Jittai Chosa Geppo*) conducted by the MHLW.[9] We then calculated annual spending by multiplying the monthly data with 12 and reported it in the right column of table 12.5. The future long-term care expenditure was then projected under the following three settings. The first one (optimistic) assumed that the age-expenditure profile would not change and that only the population structure would change. We then decomposed the total spending into social security benefits and out-of-pocket expenses by assuming that the ratio of out-of-pocket payments to total costs in FY 2002 (8.99 percent[10]) would be sustained.

We then analyzed the following three scenarios of long-term care costs: (a) the per capita cost of each age group will grow at the wage growth rate (optimistic); (b) until 2025, the rate of growth in per capita cost will exceed the wage growth rate by 1.2 percentage points and, as a result, the total cost per income well approximated the MHLW 2004 projection (pessimistic); and (c) until 2100, the per capita cost will grow at a rate that exceeds the wage growth rate by 1.2 percentage points (very pessimistic). The properties of these settings parallel those applied for health care costs. Combining these settings with three labor force projections yields nine scenarios. The resulting ratios are presented in the lower section of table 12.6.

The rate of growth from FY 2004 to FY 2025 is projected to lie between 2.03 and 2.79. According to the governmental projection, it is estimated to be 2.67, which is relatively pessimistic. If the per capita long-term care cost grows at the existing wage growth rate, the rate of growth is estimated to range between 2.03 and 2.17 depending on the labor force scenario.

12.5   Simulation of Health Care and Long-Term Care Insurance Policies

12.5.1   Procedures of the Simulation

This section deals with the simulation of policies that finance future health and long-term care insurance benefits, the projections of which were described in the previous section. This section focuses on the effect of these policies on fiscal balances and burdens across generations.

---

9. The data source does not directly report cost by age group. The available cross tables indicate (a) the cost by the severity of disability and (b) the total number of beneficiaries by the severity of disability and age group. Assuming that the long-term care cost of each level of disability was the same across all age groups that were considered, we estimated the total cost by age group by using these two cross tables.

10. It is slightly lower than the statutory coinsurance rate (10 percent) because there are some measures that lighten the burden of out-of-pocket payments.

Since we regard the benefits derived from these insurances as necessary services when a person becomes sick or disabled, it is not very meaningful to discuss the intergenerational distribution of these benefits. Hence, our simulation focuses only on the financing of these benefits.

From October 2007, half of the benefits derived from the health insurance of those aged 75 and above will be financed with government subsidies that are in turn financed by general tax revenues. Until October 2002, only 30 percent of these benefits for those aged 70 and above were financed with government subsidies. From 2002 to 2007, a transition process gradually raised the eligible age and the share of government subsidies. Half of the long-term care insurance benefit is financed with government subsidies. The other major subsidies granted by the government are 50 percent of the benefits of National Health Insurance schemes (*Kokuho*) and 13 percent of the Government-Managed Health Insurance for Employees (*Seikan Kenpo*).

We assume that social insurance premiums and taxes for social insurance benefits are paid from the same income base, which is the compensation of employees and the mixed income in terms of national accounts. For simplicity, we further assume that these incomes will grow at the same rate as GDP (and labor input) after FY 2004 and that there are no administrative costs involved in the implementation of such social insurance programs.[11]

The initial and terminal years of the simulation process are set as FY 2004 and FY 2100, respectively, because the population projection carried out by the National Institute of Population and Social Security Research is available only within these periods.

We consider the following two policies:

Policy A: A balanced budget operation in which the benefits during each year are financed by the taxes and insurance premiums of the corresponding year

Policy B: An attempt to reduce the intergenerational inequity of burdens by prefunding future social insurance payments for the elderly (details will be described in section 12.5.3).

12.5.2   Balanced Budget

We define burden rate as the ratio of burdens (the sum of insurance premiums and government subsidies financed by taxes) to 90 percent of the sum of compensation of employees and the mixed income. We aimed to calibrate the statutory premium rate by rescaling the sum of the compensation received by the employees and the mixed income. The health insur-

---

11. For instance, the administrative cost involved with the implementation of Society-Managed Health Insurance for Employees is about 0.4 percent of the total benefits derived from such programs during FY 2001.

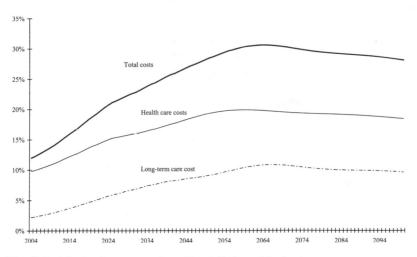

Fig. 12.2   The burden rates under policy A (balanced budget)

ance premium (including government subsidies for the nonelderly and ex-cluding those reserved for the elderly) for the initial year (i.e., FY 2004) is calculated to be 8.21 percent. The actual health insurance premium for the enrollees of the Government-Managed Health Insurance for Employees is calculated to be 8.2 percent. Since the enrollees of the Government-Managed Health Insurance for Employees are employed with small companies, their average salary is lower than that of all the workers. Since government subsidies aim to offset the earnings difference, we tried to calibrate the statutory insurance premium. With regard to long-term care insurance, the simulated premium rate for FY 2004 is 1.11 percent; this matches the actual insurance premium paid by the enrollees of the Government-Managed Health Insurance for Employees. Under the balanced budget, the burden is equal to social insurance benefits (excluding out-of-pocket payment). Therefore, we calculated the ratio of benefits to incomes.

Figure 12.2 presents the burden rates associated with health care, long-term care, and a total of both of them when Policy A is implemented under the governmental projection (social cost–pessimistic and labor force–pessimistic). The burden rate for health care continues to increase until FY 2059 when it touches 19.94 percent. As against this, the burden rate for a long-term care will touch 10.97 percent in FY 2066. Although the paths followed by these two burden rates appear to be parallel to each other in figure 12.2, we must however, note that the absolute level of long-term care costs is low. The burden rate for long-term care grows much more rapidly than that for health care because compared to health care benefits, long-term care benefits are concentrated to a greater extent on the aged population. For the same reason, a peak representing the burden rate for long-

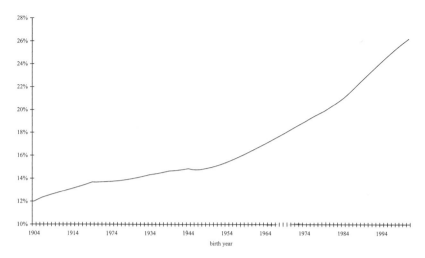

Fig. 12.3   Lifetime burden rates by generation under policy A (balanced budget)

term care will follow a peak of the burden rate for health care. The total burden rate of both the insurances reaches a peak that is 30.65 percent in FY 2064. The ratio of total burden to GDP then amounts to 15.63 percent in the same year.

Figure 12.3 presents the lifetime burden rate of each generation under the governmental projection. It is defined as the ratio of lifetime burden to lifetime income. The lifetime variable is the sum of the present discounted values of the reported annual numbers during the period between the initial and the terminal points of the simulation process. Therefore, the burden rate is the prospective lifetime burden for the generation born in 2001 or earlier. To estimate lifetime income, we adopted the age-wage profile, which was used to calculate the labor input in section 12.3. The interest rate is assumed to be 1 percentage point higher than the wage growth rate.

The horizontal axis of figure 12.3 represents the birth year of each generation. The curve representing the lifetime burden rates are not smooth for early generations, possibly because our prospective calculation covers only a short period for these generations. Figure 12.3 indicates that a balanced budget system will impose heavier burdens on the younger generations. The inequality of burdens is particularly severe for the current working-age generation. The lifetime burden rate for those who were born in 2001 is estimated to be 26.2 percent while the same for those born in 1945 is 14.8 percent.

12.5.3   Equalizing the Burden by Prefunding Policies

The increasing burden on future generations, as depicted in figure 12.3, may be circumvented by implementing a policy that levies a constant burden rate over time. Such a policy aims at charging a high burden rate in advance so that sufficient funds can be accumulated in order to prepare for increasing costs in the future. Feldstein (1999) advocated the idea of prefunding Medicare, which is the U.S. public health insurance for the elderly.

As an example of the prefunding of health and long-term care costs, we consider the following policy. With regard to health insurance, a portion of the prefunding would be channelized in order to finance the insurance payments dealing with health care costs with regard to the elderly (age 65 and over). Workers who are aged 15 and above make payments in the form of premiums. The health care costs for those aged 64 and below and government subsidies in the form of benefits to the elderly are financed by a pay-as-you-go system. Long-term care insurance employs a prefunding scheme, while government subsidies are financed by a pay-as-you-go system. Since the enrollees of the current system are those who are aged 40 and above, we assume that workers falling into this age group pay these premiums.

The setting of the interest rate is a key factor in determining the performance of a prefunding scheme. When we focus on the proportion of burdens to income, it is not the absolute levels but the difference between the interest rate and the wage growth rate that matters. The MHLW projection on public pension finance in May 2004 assumed that the nominal interest rate would be 3.2 percent and that the growth rate of nominal wage would be 2.1 percent. Our baseline case sets a 1 percentage point difference between the interest rate and the growth rate of wage. As an alternative scenario, the difference is set either as 0 percent or 2 percent.[12]

Since the current health and long-term care insurance program is set within a pay-as-you-go framework, a transition to a funded system should be designed. With regard to health care costs, we first calculate the contribution rate that is sufficient for the entire cohort born in FY 2001 to finance the expected value of their lifetime health insurance benefits beyond the age of 65 years. This rate is estimated to be 4.96 percent under the governmental projection and the baseline scenario of the interest rate. If the co-

---

12. Feldstein and Samwick's (1997) simulation of the prefunding of the U.S. social security program assumed that the real rate of return is 9 percent, which is considerably higher as compared to ours. Their following researches (Feldstein and Samwick 1998) used 5.5 percent as the rate of return, which is still higher as compared to ours. We employed lower interest rates due to the following reasons. First, their rates of return are based on risky capital; however, we considered the risk-free rate of return. We think that the investment strategies pertaining to funded health care and long-term care insurance should be conservative because these insurances aim to finance a strictly targeted consumption item that cannot be easily substituted. Second, our simulation process does not incorporate the general equilibrium effect, in which an accumulated social insurance fund tends to lower the interest rate of a large open economy. We therefore attempt to infer the consequences of this effect by looking at a particular case in which the interest rate is maintained at a low level from the beginning. Third, given the recent poor performance of Japanese asset prices, a high rate of return does not appear plausible.

Table 12.7   Contribution rates under the balanced budget and prefunding schemes

	(A) Balanced budget		(B) Prefunding	
	2004	2005–2100	2005–2100	2101–
Total	12.01	12.28–28.12	19.62–26.70	
Health insurance				
Nonelderly	4.32	3.97–4.30		
Elderly	3.89	3.98–9.08	8.52	4.96
Government subsidies	2.69	2.84–10.07		
Long-term care insurance	1.11	1.16–4.83	3.95	2.17

Notes: Numbers represent the percentage of earnings (90 percent of compensation of employees and mixed income). The interest rate is based on the baseline case, and other parameters are based on the governmental projection.

horts born after FY 2001 pay the premium at this rate, the total accumulated funds in FY 2100 would amount to 111.11 percent of the GDP. Hence, the transition process is designed in such a manner that it accumulates this level of funds with a constant premium rate until FY 2100. Since the current generations did not prefund their health care costs, 4.96 percent of the premium rate is not sufficient to meet the target in FY 2100. It is therefore concluded that a contribution rate of 8.52 percent will successfully accumulate the required funds.

The evolution of the funded system will be achieved in the following manner (table 12.7 summarizes the numbers that represent the burdens under Policies A and B). When health care costs (excluding government subsidies) are financed by a pay-as-you-go scheme in FY 2004, the contribution rate with regard to the same for individuals aged 64 and below is 4.32 percent and for those aged 65 and above is 3.89 percent. When a transition toward a prefunding scheme begins in FY 2005, the contribution rate for the elderly increases to 8.52 percent under the governmental projection and maintains this value until FY 2100. Beyond FY 2100, the contribution rate for the elderly will shrink to 4.96 percent. As against this, the contribution rate for the health care costs of the aged below 64 is almost stable. It ranges between 3.97 percent and 4.3 percent.

The transition process of the long-term care insurance program is designed along lines parallel to the health insurance program. The contribution rate that is sufficient for the cohort born in FY 2001 to finance the expected value of their lifetime long-term care insurance benefits is 2.17 percent under the governmental projection. If the cohorts born after FY 2001 pay the premium at this rate, the total accumulated funds in FY 2100 would amount to 68.35 percent of the GDP. This amount of funds will be accumulated by a contribution rate of 3.95 percent during the transition process. When long-term care costs (excluding government subsidies) are financed by a pay-as-you-go scheme in FY 2004, the contribution rate is estimated to be 1.11 percent. When a transition toward a prefunding scheme begins in FY 2005, the contribution rate increases to 3.95 percent, and maintains this value until FY 2100. Beyond FY 2100, the contribution rate will shrink to 2.17 percent.

For the calibrated value in FY 2004, the health insurance payments for the nonelderly is estimated to be 4.32 percent of the total earnings and those for the elderly is estimated to be 3.89 percent of the total earnings, with the long-term care costs being estimated as 1.11 percent. When social insurance premiums and government subsidies are combined, the overall burden rate becomes 12.01 percent. Under the pay-as-you-go system, the social costs for the elderly will grow steadily. The total burden ratio will go up to 28.12 percent of the total earnings. The burden rate of health insurance payments will go up to 9.08 percent. The growth of government subsidies however, is more rapid, the highest level attained by it being 10.07 percent.

Under the prefunding scheme, it is estimated that the burden rate will increase from 12.01 percent in FY 2004 to 19.62 percent in FY 2005. The rate of change in total burdens at the initial point is 63 percent. Since government subsidies are bound to grow, as in the case of the pay-as-you-go system, the highest level attained by the total burden rate will be 26.70 percent in FY 2064.

Figure 12.4 compares the lifetime burden rates between the balanced budget and the prefunding schemes. We should note that the burden rates for those born after 2001 do not cover their whole lifetime because the sim-

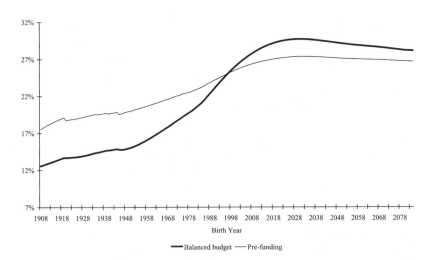

Fig. 12.4   Lifetime burden rates under policy A (balanced budget) and policy B (prefunding)

ulation terminates in FY 2100. When the system is changed from a balanced budget to a prefunding one, generations who are born prior to 1997 will face a higher lifetime burden, and younger generations will benefit from a lower lifetime burden. The curve representing lifetime burden in figure 12.4 becomes flatter. Hence, a prefunding scheme helps to reduce the inequality of burdens. This will be made possible only if the current generation agrees to share burdens with future generations.

Suzuki (2000) conducted a similar study dealing with the calculation of the transition to a fully funded health insurance system. While our calculation unites the whole sector of health insurance, his calculation was based on the decomposition of the same into subsidiary systems of insurance. The transition was assumed to begin in FY 1995 and attain the state of a fully funded scheme by FY 2100. With regard to the Society-Managed Health Insurance for Employees (*Kumiai Kenpo*), the contribution rate is estimated to increase from 7.8 percent to 9.8 percent.

According to Suzuki's specification, a fully funded scheme finances an individual's lifetime health care costs. Before individuals begin to work, their prefunding account has to borrow money. This account needs to borrow money during the early stages of an individual's life. The resulting number of aggregate funds would still be lower than the number involved in our scheme. This is primarily the reason why we reported a much larger hike in the contribution rate during the transition process as compared to that reported in Suzuki (2000).

12.5.4   Sensitivity Analysis

Table 12.8 represents the contribution rates of the prefunding scheme in FY 2005 to 2100 and beyond FY 2100 under 27 diverse scenarios. The assumption of a labor force participation does not affect the contribution rate to a large extent. The difference in the health insurance contribution rate between a pessimistic scenario and the most optimistic scenario is 0.36 to 0.92 percentage points. The gap between the two is large, when the projection of social costs is pessimistic. This reflects the fact that a funding scheme is not influenced by a demographic change. On the other hand, the interest rate affects the contribution rate. Under the optimistic scenario (in which the interest rate is 2 percentage points higher than the wage growth rate), the contribution rate is 1.5 to 4.68 percentage points lower than that under the pessimistic scenario. The setting of social costs has an even larger impact on the contribution rate, as compared to the impact of interest rate on the same. The difference in the contribution rates during a transition period between a pessimistic scenario and an optimistic scenario is 3.13 to 6.33 percentage points.

The previous findings can also be applied to the case of long-term care insurance. The effect of interest rate is relatively large as compared to the size of the benefits. The difference in the contribution rate between the op-

Table 12.8   **Sensitivity analysis of contribution rates in a prefunding social insurance scheme (%)**

	Health care for the elderly		Long-term care	
	2005–2100	2101–	2005–2100	2101–
Interest rate = Growth rate = 2%				
Social cost: Optimistic				
Labor force				
Very optimistic	6.25	2.74	2.66	1.08
Optimistic	6.36	2.81	2.71	1.10
Pessimistic	6.61	2.90	2.82	1.14
Social cost: Pessimistic				
Labor force				
Very optimistic	7.56	3.45	3.31	1.38
Optimistic	7.69	3.53	3.37	1.41
Pessimistic	7.99	3.64	3.51	1.46
Social cost: Very pessimistic				
Labor force				
Very optimistic	9.38	6.06	4.47	2.81
Optimistic	9.55	6.20	4.55	2.88
Pessimistic	9.92	6.40	4.73	2.97
Interest rate = Growth rate = 1%				
Social cost: Optimistic				
Labor force				
Very optimistic	6.84	3.85	3.08	1.65
Optimistic	6.97	3.94	3.14	1.69
Pessimistic	7.26	4.08	3.27	1.75
Social cost: Pessimistic				
Labor force				
Very optimistic	8.36	4.84	3.88	2.12
Optimistic	8.52	4.96	3.95	2.17
Pessimistic	8.88	5.14	4.12	2.25
Social cost: Very pessimistic				
Labor force				
Very optimistic	11.09	8.58	5.69	4.35
Optimistic	11.30	8.78	5.80	4.46
Pessimistic	11.78	9.10	6.04	4.62
Interest rate = Growth rate				
Social cost: Optimistic				
Labor force				
Very optimistic	7.75	5.36	3.74	2.51
Optimistic	7.91	5.48	3.81	2.57
Pessimistic	8.27	5.72	3.99	2.68
Social cost: Pessimistic				
Labor force				
Very optimistic	9.58	6.75	4.74	3.23
Optimistic	9.77	6.90	4.84	3.31
Pessimistic	10.22	7.19	5.06	3.44
Social cost: Very pessimistic				
Labor force				
Very optimistic	13.68	12.05	7.62	6.71
Optimistic	13.96	12.33	7.78	6.86
Pessimistic	14.60	12.84	8.14	7.15

Notes: Numbers represent the percentage of earnings (90 percent of compensation of employees and mixed income). In FY2004, the contribution rate of health insurance for the elderly is 3.89 percent and that for long-term care insurance is 1.11 percent.

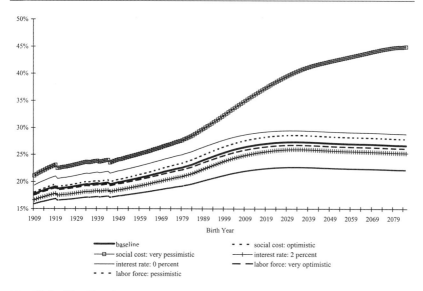

Fig. 12.5   Total burden rates under alternative scenarios

timistic and the pessimistic scenario ranges between 1.08 to 3.41 percentage points.

Even under the most optimistic scenario, the burden rate associated with health care and long-term care costs increases at a rate of 16.05 percentage points from the starting point. The rate of change in the total value of the burden rate is 34 percent, which is smaller than the governmental projection, but is still quite significant. Under the most pessimistic scenario, the rate of change is 85 percent. Although quantitative implications depend on the individual settings associated with each of the programs, a significant increase in the contribution rate is needed to implement a prefunding scheme.

Figure 12.5 maps the total number of burden rates that are associated with the baseline scenario and six alternative scenarios that in turn take an alternative scenario with one variable among the three available. Since the baseline scenario takes into account an intermediate assumption regarding the three variables, it takes the centermost line of all the seven lines. The line at the highest level represents the case of the most pessimistic social cost scenario. Since the growth of social costs is assumed to continue till the end of this century, the burden rate for future generations is far larger in this scenario as compared to that in other scenarios. The lowest line represents the case of the most optimistic social cost scenario. Social costs have the most significant impact on the burden rate. The impact of labor force on the burden rate is the least among the three variables considered so far. Higher interest rates can reduce the burden rates considerably. For the generation born in 2001, the lifetime burden rate is estimated to be

25.62 percent under the baseline scenario and 20.15 percent under the scenario with an interest rate higher by 1 percentage point.

12.6   Conclusion

As the Japanese population structure changes, the current approach of financing (pay-as-you-go) the social costs will create a large increase in the magnitude of future burdens. It will also create an intergenerational inequity of burdens. We analyzed an alternative policy that prefunds the benefits for the elderly aged 65 and above. Prefunding is not very popular in Japan. Our analysis aims at providing real-life scenarios with regard to this policy option and to stimulate policy discussions.

During the transition process until FY 2100, the scheme maintains a higher contribution rate in order to accumulate sufficient funds. With respect to the parameters implied by the governmental projection, the sum of the contribution rates with regard to health insurance and long-term care insurance increases from 5.00 percent of the total earnings to 12.47 percent of the same. The rate of increase in total burdens including taxes for subsidies is 63 percent.

Our sensitivity analysis has indicated that quantitative implications depend on the settings of the social costs, the labor force, and the interest rate. However, labor force scenarios do not have a considerable impact on the rate of burden. As against this, the setting of social costs has a significant impact. Although we cannot predict the exact amount of the necessary contribution rate that would be sufficient to transfer the funded system, it is certain that a significant increase in the contribution rate is inevitable. Even under the most optimistic scenario of the 27 possible scenarios, a necessary increase in the contribution rates of the two social insurances is 3.91 percentage points. The rate of increase in the total amount of burdens is 34 percent.

Implementing a prefunding social cost program may be a challenge because the initial increase in burdens is politically unfavorable. However, the cost of not introducing this scheme implies a heavier burden on future generations. Raising the contribution rate in an aggressive manner will help to reduce the intergenerational imbalance of burdens.

References

Auerbach, Alan J., Jagadeesh Gokhale, and Laurence J. Kotlikoff. 1991. Generational accounts: A meaningful alternative to deficit accounting. In *Tax policy and the economy,* ed. David Bradford, 5:55–110. Cambridge, MA: MIT Press.
Bradford, David F., and Derrick A. Max. 1997. Implicit budget deficits: The case

of a mandated shift to community-rated health insurance. In *Tax policy and the economy,* ed. James M. Poterba, 11:129–67. Cambridge, MA: MIT Press.

Cutler, David M., and Louise Scheiner. 2000. Generational aspects of Medicare. *American Economic Review Papers and Proceedings* 90 (2): 303–7.

Feldstein, Martin. 1999. Prefunding Medicare. *American Economic Review Papers and Proceedings* 89 (2): 222–27.

Feldstein, Martin, and Andrew Samwick. 1997. The economics of prefunding social security and Medicare benefits. In *NBER macroeconomics annual 1997,* ed. Ben S. Bernanke and Julio Rotemberg, 115–48. Cambridge, MA: The MIT Press.

———. 1998. Potential effects of two percent personal retirement accounts. *Tax Notes* 79 (5): 615–20.

Iwamoto, Yasushi. 1998. 2020 Nen no Rodoryoku Jinko. [Japan's labor force in the year 2020]. *Keizai Kenkyu* 49 (4): 297–307.

———. 2004. Jinko Koreika to Shakai Hosho. [Aging population and Social security]. *Financial Review* 72 (August): 58–77.

Iwamoto, Yasushi, Satoshi Takeshita, and Masashi Bessho. 1997. Iryo Hoken Zaisei to Kohi Futan. [Public health insurance and government subsidies]. *Financial Review* 43:174–201.

Japanese Cabinet Office. 2003. Keizai Zaisei Hakusho. *[Annual report on the Japanese economy and public finance].* Tokyo: Japanese Cabinet Office.

Maekawa, Satoko. 2004. Shakai Hosho Kaikaku ni Yoru Sedaibetsu Jueki to Futan no Henka. [Changes in benefits and burdens, by generation, arising from social security reform]. *Financial Review* 72:5–19.

Mitchell, Olivia S., John Pigott, and Satoshi Shimizutani. 2004. Aged-care support in Japan: Perspectives and challenges. NBER Working Paper no. 10882, November. Cambridge, MA: National Bureau of Economic Research.

Niki, Ryu. 1995. Nihon no Iryohi: Kokusai Hikaku no Kanten Kara. *[Medical expenditure in Japan: From a viewpoint of international comparison].* Tokyo: Igaku Syoin.

Nishimura, Syuzo. 1997. Choki Tsumitategata Iryo Hoken Seido no Kanosei ni tsuite. [On the possibility of full-funded social health insurance]. *Iryo Keizai Kenkyu* 4:13–34.

Ogura, Seiritsu. 1994. The cost of aging: Public finance perspectives for Japan. In *Aging in the United States and Japan,* ed. Noguchi, Yukio, and David A. Wise, 139–43. Chicago: The University of Chicago Press.

Ogura, Seiritsu, and Takeshi Irifune. 1990. Waga Kuni no Jinko no Koreika to Kaku Koteki Iryo Hoken no Syushi ni tsuite. [Population aging and fiscal conditions of public health insurance in Japan]. *Financial Review* 17:51–77.

Ohkusa, Yasushi. 2002. Koreika no Iryohi heno Eikyo oyobi Nyuin Kikan no Bunseki [Aging effects on medical expenditure and analysis for duration of hospitalization]. *Kikan Shakai Hosho Kenkyu* 38 (1): 52–66.

Shimizutani, Satoshi, and Haruko Noguchi. 2004. *Kaigo Hoiku Sabisu Shijo no Keizai Bunseki. [Economic analysis of long-term care and child care service markets].* Tokyo: Toyo Keizai Shinposha.

Suzuki, Wataru. 2000. Iryo Hoken ni okeru Sedaikan Fukohei to Tsumitatekin wo Motsu Fea na Zaisei Hosiki heno Iko [A proposal for removing intergenerational inequity from the Japanese health insurance system]. *Nihon Keizai Kenkyu* 40:88–104.

———. 2002. Kaigo Sabisu Juyo Zoka no Yoin Bunseki [Analysis of recent increase of demand for long-term care in Japan]. *Nihon Rodo Kenkyu Zasshi* 502:6–17.

Suzuki, Wataro, and Reiko Suzuki. 2003. Jumyo no Chokika wa Rojin Iryohi Zoka no Youinka? [Does longevity cause a rapid rise in medical costs for the elderly?]. *Kokusai Kokyo Seisaku Kenkyu* 7 (2): 1–13.

Tokita, Tadahiko, Theturo Chino, Hideeaki Kitaki, Izumi Yamamoto, and Mitsuyoshi Miyagi. 1997. The present and future national medical expenditure in Japan. *Economic Analysis* 152 (September): 1–68.

Comment   Epictetus Patalinghug

Introduction

This chapter estimates the quantitative magnitude of implementing a prefunding scheme to finance Japan's future health and long-term care costs. It starts by arguing that Japan's social security benefits will grow at a double-digit rate, and a growing component of these benefits is the benefit due to health insurance and long-term care insurance. The authors argue that the burden of workers will steadily increase and it will create intergenerational imbalance of burdens if the health and long-term care insurances are continued to be financed under the current pay-as-you-go system. In estimating the general magnitude of the prefunding burden, the authors provided an alternative projection of the labor force (assuming less optimistic labor-participation rates), projected health and long-term care benefits, and conducted sensitivity analysis of contribution rates under a prefunding scheme. The chapter concluded that the prefunding scheme will significantly increase the appropriate contribution rate, but it will likewise reduce the intergenerational inequity of burdens. The analysis of the chapter is consistent with the findings of Takayama and Kitamura (1999), which looked at the impact on generational imbalance of fiscal policy. In this study, the authors also suggested the use of the prefunding scheme as a way of restoring equity in the social insurance program in Japan. The chapter is very timely because Japanese policymakers are currently contemplating on economic policy reforms to ensure the sustainability of its fiscal and social security programs.

Analysis and Findings

The efforts of the authors are to be lauded. However, the authors need to address some gaps in their work. Economists argue that political feasibility is a crucial element in the formulation of policy. The authors do not address the issue of how a change to a prefunding scheme that would alter the redistributive burdens can be more palatable to those adversely affected. The chapter does not explicitly take into account the response of individuals and firms to changes in the health and long-term care insurance system.

Epictetus Patalinghug is a professor of economics and finance in the College of Business Administration, University of the Philippines.

The chapter seems to imply that the burdens of financing social security systems in Japan rely solely on private contributions and government subsidies. If taxes are inadequate to finance benefits, the solution is either to increase taxes or to lower benefits. The authors argue that the latter is not politically feasible because health care and long-term care services are considered basic services by Japanese people.

The chapter needs to provide estimates of the deadweight loss of the higher taxes that would be needed to finance the social insurance system under the pay-as-you-go tax system compared to the prefunding scheme (see Feldstein 1999). The chapter likewise argues that higher interest rates can reduce the burden considerably. However, there is no explanation in the chapter on how the trust fund of the prefunding scheme is invested to produce higher returns and improve its financial condition.

The authors suggest that the recent poor performance of Japanese asset prices precluded using interest rates approaching the U.S. level. This is a relevant point but they could have demonstrated if there are advantages in investing some of the health and long-term insurance fund in private securities. Diamond (1997) has demonstrated that investing some of the trust fund in high-yielding equity may lessen tax increases but significant intergenerational redistribution remains.

Though the chapter has analytically and graphically illustrated the intergenerational consequences of shifting from the pay-as-you-go system to the prefunding system, it needs to measure its distributional consequences. What happens to disposable income of low- and middle-income workers under each scheme? Feldstein and Samwick (1997) had estimated the impact of prefunding Medicare in the United States on the growth of capital stock and the level of national income. Doing such kind of analysis on estimating the impact of prefunding the cost of Japanese health and long-term care insurance on its capital stock and its level of national income would have given a broader insight.

Conclusion

I commend the authors for doing a pioneering study that looks at the intergenerational impact of prefunding both the health and long-term care costs in Japan.

References

Diamond, Peter. 1997. Macroeconomic aspects of social security reform. *Brookings Papers on Economic Activity* (2): 1–87.
Feldstein, Martin. 1999. Prefunding Medicare. *American Economic Review* 89 (2): 222–27.
Feldstein, Martin, and Andrew Samwick. 1997. The economics of prefunding social security and Medicare benefits. In *NBER Macroeconomics Annual 1997,*

ed. Ben S. Bernanke and Julio Rotemberg, 115–48. Cambridge, MA: The MIT Press.

Takayama, Noriyuki, and Yukinobu Kitamura. 1999. Lessons from generational accounting in Japan. *American Economic Review* 89 (2): 171–75.

Comment   Raj Chetty

Many governments now provide large-scale social insurance and pension programs as a safety net for the elderly. As populations age, these programs have led to rapidly growing fiscal obligations that governments must meet. However, under current tax policies, most governments will collect far less revenue than the total amount of benefits they have promised to elderly citizens in the future. Generational accounts show that the magnitude of the fiscal imbalance is very large for most developed countries (Auerbach, Kotlikoff, and Leibfritz 1999).

Japan is no exception to this problem. According to calculations by Takayama, Kitamura, and Yoshida (1999), Japan faces one of the largest fiscal imbalances, owing largely to its rapidly aging population and longevity of the elderly. Takayama et al.'s generational accounts imply that future generations will have to bear 2.7 to 4.4 times the fiscal burden that current generations do, meaning that sharp increases in tax rates are needed to sustain fiscal balance.

These generational accounts rely on detailed assumptions about the trajectory of the economy and demographics over a long horizon. The accuracy of the underlying assumptions is thus critical in obtaining reliable projections of fiscal imbalances.

In this chapter, Tadashi Fukui and Yasushi Iwamoto focus on the assumptions underlying one aspect of the generational imbalance problem in Japan: the fiscal burden of health and long-term care costs. Fukui and Iwamoto take issue with the *structural* forecasting methods used by the Japanese government to make projections about economic activity over the next century. Their primary criticism is that these methods are quite opaque and make many implicit assumptions that are hard for the user to decipher. They instead advocate a reduced-form or *mechanical* approach that does not rely on this complex structure. Fukui and Iwamoto's projections are based on transparent statistical extrapolations that do not rely on a specific economic model.

The author's mechanical method yields significantly less pessimistic estimates of the degree of fiscal imbalance due to health care costs. This is

Raj Chetty is an assistant professor of economics at the University of California, Berkeley, and a faculty research fellow of the National Bureau of Economic Research.

primarily because their projections imply a slower rate of growth in health care expenditure than the Japanese government predicts.

While transparency is certainly a virtue, the ultimate measure of the value of a forecasting method is its accuracy. Fukui and Iwamoto describe forecasts of both the structural and reduced-form methods in detail, but do not discuss which of these methods is more likely to be accurate. This issue is at least in principle empirically resolvable using historical data. For example, one could develop both structural and reduced-form forecasts using data available in Japan as of 1990. One could then predict the trajectory of variables such as labor force participation and health care costs, as well as total fiscal imbalance, for the next 15 years using each method. By computing the forecast errors for each method using data from 1990 to 2005, one could determine which method is more accurate.

Such an analysis could be particularly valuable in the context of two assumptions that Fukui and Iwamoto discuss at length in their chapter. First, the authors assume that the growth rate of health care costs will equal the rate of economic growth. In recent years, the fraction of GDP devoted to health care has risen sharply, suggesting that this assumption could be inaccurate. Second, the authors argue that the models used by the Japanese government overstate the rate of labor force entry by women and the elderly. Both of these claims can be tested by comparing the performance of the two forecasting methods in predicting historical trends in labor supply and health care costs.

In summary, Fukui and Iwamoto have raised a number of interesting and important issues regarding the assumptions underlying generational accounts in Japan. However, further research is required to determine whether the methods they propose will indeed outperform those used by the Japanese government.

References

Auerbach, Alan, Laurence Kotlikoff, and Willie Leibfritz, Ed. 1999. *Generational accounting around the world.* Chicago: University of Chicago Press.
Takayama, Noriyuki, Yukinobu Kitamura, and Hiroshi Yoshida. 1999. Generational accounting in Japan. In *Generational accounting around the world,* ed. A. Auerbach, L. Kotlikoff, and W. Leibfritz, 447–69. Chicago: University of Chicago Press.

Contributors

Michael M. Alba
Department of Economics
De La Salle University
Room 123-A La Salle Hall
2401 Taft Avenue
1004 Manila, Philippines

Dante B. Canlas
School of Economics
University of the Philippines
Diliman, Quezon City 1101,
  Philippines

Raj Chetty
Department of Economics
University of California, Berkeley
521 Evans Hall #3880
Berkeley, CA 94720

Young Jun Chun
Department of Economics
University of Incheon
Dowha-Dong 177, Nam-Ku
Incheon, 402-749, Korea

Takero Doi
Faculty of Economics
Keio University
2-15-45 Mita, Minato-ku
Tokyo 108-8345 Japan

Hans Fehr
Lehrstuhl für Finanzwissenschaft
Universität Würzburg
Sanderring 2
D-97070 Würzburg Germany

Tadashi Fukui
Faculty of Economics
Kyoto Sangyo University
Motoyama, Kamigamo
Kita-Ku, Kyoto-City 603-8555, Japan

Roger Gordon
Department of Economics
University of California, San Diego
9500 Gilman Drive Dept. 0508
La Jolla, CA 92093-0508

Cielito F. Habito
Department of Economics and
  Director, Ateneo Center for
  Economic Research and
  Development
Ateneo de Manila University
Loyola Heights, Quezon City 1108,
  Philippines

Corrinne Ho
Bank for International Settlements
78th floor, Two International Finance
  Centre
8 Finance Street, Central
Hong Kong

Seok-Kyun Hur
Fellow, Department of
  Macroeconomic and Financial
  Policies
Korea Development Institute (KDI)
Cheongnyang, Seoul, Korea 130-012

Toshihiro Ihori
Faculty of Economics
The University of Tokyo
7-3-1 Hongo, Bunkyo-ku
Tokyo 113-0033 Japan

Takatoshi Ito
Graduate School of Economics
The University of Tokyo
7-3-1 Hongo, Bunkyo-ku
Tokyo 113-0033 Japan

Yasushi Iwamoto
Faculty of Economics
The University of Tokyo
7-3-1 Hongo, Bunkyo-ku
Tokyo, 113-0033 Japan

Sabine Jokisch
Centre for European Economic
  Research (ZEW)
L 7,1
D-68161 Mannheim Germany

Youngsun Koh
Department of Macroeconomic and
  Financial Policies
Korea Development Institute
207-41 Chongnyangri-Dong
Dongdaemun-Gu, PO Box 113
Chongnyang, Seoul, Korea

Laurence J. Kotlikoff
Department of Economics
Boston University
270 Bay State Road
Boston, MA 02215

Shigeki Kunieda
Graduate School of International and
  Public Policy
Hitotsubashi University
2-1-2 Hitotsubashi, Chiyoda-ku
Tokyo 101-8439 Japan

Yum K. Kwan
Department of Economics & Finance
ACAD-P7306
City University of Hong Kong
83 Tat Chee Avenue
Kowloon Tong, Hong Kong

Mario B. Lamberte
EMERGE
Unit 2003, 139 Corporate Center
Valero St., Salcedo Village
Makati City 1227
Metro Manila, Philippines

Wei Li
Darden Graduate School of Business
  Administration
University of Virginia
PO Box 6550
Charlottesville, VA 22906

Gilberto M. Llanto
Philippine Institute for Development
  Studies
NEDA sa Makati Bujilding
106 Amorsolo St.
Legaspi Village, Makati, Philippines

Adam Looney
Division of Research and Statistics
Board of Governors of the Federal
  Reserve System
20th Street and Constitution Avenue,
  NW
Washington, DC 20551

Francis T. Lui
Center for Economic Development
Hong Kong University of Science and
  Technology
Clear Water Bay
Kowloon, Hong Kong

Roberto S. Mariano
School of Economics & Social Sciences
Singapore Management University
90 Stamford Road
Singapore 178903

Jason McDonald
Budget Policy Division
The Treasury
Australian Government
Langton Crescent
PARKES ACT 2600 Australia

Kiyoshi Mitsui
Faculty of Economics
Gakushuin University
1-5-1 Mejiro Toshima-ku
Tokyo 171-8588 Japan

Chong-Hyun Nam
Department of Economics and
    Director, The BK21 Research Group
Korea University
5-1, Anam-dong, Sungbuk-ku
Seoul, 136-701, Korea

Epictetus Patalinghug
College of Business Administration
University of the Philippines
Diliman, Quezon City, Philippines

Andrew K. Rose
Haas School of Business
    Administration
University of California, Berkeley
Berkeley, CA 94720-1900

Amanda Sayegh
Budget Policy Division
The Treasury
Australian Government
Langton Crescent
PARKES ACT 2600 Australia

Delano P. Villanueva
School of Economics and Social
    Sciences
Singapore Management University
90 Stamford Road
Singapore 178903

Wilson Au-Yeung
Domestic Economy Division
The Treasury
Australian Government
Langton Crescent
PARKES ACT 2600 Australia

Author Index

Subject Index